D1408152

Terrorism, Crime, and Public Policy

Terrorism, Crime, and Public Policy describes the problem of terrorism; compares it to other forms of aggression, particularly crime and war; and discusses policy options for dealing with the problem. It focuses on the causes of terrorism with the aim of understanding its roots and providing insights toward policies that will serve to prevent it. The book serves as a single-source reference on terrorism and as a platform for more in-depth study, with a set of discussion questions at the end of each chapter. Individual chapters focus on the nature of terrorism, theories of aggression and terrorism, the history of terrorism, globalization vs. clash, the role of religion, nonreligious extremism and terrorism, the role of technology, terrorism throughout the modern world, responses to terrorism, fear of terrorism, short-term approaches and long-term strategies for preventing terrorism, balancing security and rights to liberty and privacy, and pathways to a safer and saner twenty-first century.

Brian Forst joined the American University faculty after twenty years in nonprofit research, including positions as research director at the Institute for Law and Social Research and the Police Foundation. He is the author most recently of *After Terror* (with Akbar Ahmed, 2005); *Errors of Justice: Nature, Sources, and Remedies* (Cambridge University Press, 2004); and *The Privatization of Policing: Two Views* (with Peter Manning, 1999). He is a member of the American University Senate and chairs the Department of Justice, Law, and Society's doctoral program. He is also a voting member of the Sentencing Commission for the District of Columbia.

Terrorism, Crime, and Public Policy

Brian Forst
American University

CAMBRIDGE
UNIVERSITY PRESS

CAMBRIDGE UNIVERSITY PRESS
Cambridge, New York, Melbourne, Madrid, Cape Town, Singapore, São Paulo, Delhi

Cambridge University Press
32 Avenue of the Americas, New York, NY 10013-2473, USA

www.cambridge.org
Information on this title: www.cambridge.org/9780521676427

First published 2009

Printed in the United States of America

A catalog record for this publication is available from the British Library.

Library of Congress Cataloging in Publication Data

Forst, Brian.
Terrorism, crime, and public policy / Brian Forst.
    p.   cm.
Includes bibliographical references and index.
ISBN 978-0-521-85924-0 (hardback) – ISBN 978-0-521-67642-7 (pbk.)
1. Terrorism.   2. Terrorism – Prevention.   I. Title.
HV6431.F667   2009
363.325′1561–dc22   2008008301

ISBN   978-0-521-85924-0 hardback
ISBN   978-0-521-67642-7 paperback

For Judith

Contents

Contents

Contents

Contents

Contents

Contents

Credits

Photo Credits

Chapter 1   Page 15: © Kevin Coombs/Reuters

Chapter 3   Page 45: Portrait of Genghis Khan produced by a Chinese artist at the Imperial Court, National Palace Museum, Taipei; Page 46: (top) Maximilien de Robespierre, homme politique (c.1790), Musée Carnavalet; Page 46: (bottom) Black and Batchelder photographers, 1859, Library of Congress; Page 68: U.S. Government

Chapter 4   Page 76: (top) © David Fukuyama; Page 76: (bottom) Jagdish Bhagwati; Page 78: Used by permission of Martin Wolf; Page 79: (top) Joseph Stiglitz; Page 79: (bottom) Walter Russell Mead; Page 80: © Charles Haynes; Page 87: Alan Kolc (2003)/Office of Communications, Princeton University; Page 89: Samuel P. Huntington

Chapter 6   Page 147: © Brandon McWhorter; Page 153: (top) Italian Red Brigades; Page 153: (bottom) Symbionese Liberation Army; Page 154: © Reuters; Page 160: Environmental Protection Agency; Page 161: Released by U.S. Government; Page 162: Federal Bureau of Investigation/U.S. Government

Chapter 8   Page 225: Taken by CCTV and released by Scotland Yard; Page 226: © Reuters; Page 233: © Ayman Bardaweel; Page 239: © Reuters; Page 244: Federal Bureau of Investigation; Page 246: © AP; Page 247: U.S. Government

Chapter 9   Page 273: U.S. Military; Page 288: U.S. Army, taken by Sergeant Curtis G. Hargrave [from DefenseImagery.mil, VIRIN 030722-A-3450H-064]

Credits

Chapter 10 Page 300: U.S. Department of Homeland Security; Page 305: ©
          Brainexplorer
Chapter 11 Page 352: U.S. Customs and Border Protection; Page 354:
          FEMA/Marty Bahamonde
Chapter 12 Page 378: Scene from "Three Faiths, One God: Judaism,
          Christianity, Islam." Courtesy Auteur Productions, Ltd.,
          threefaithsonegod.com; Page 402: U.S. Military
Chapter 13 Page 424: Publicly Released by U.S. Government; Page 425: ©
          Ralf Roletschek

Article Credits

Chapter 1 Pages 6–8 (Box 1.1): © San Francisco Chronicle
Chapter 3 Pages 60–62 (Box 3.1): From USA TODAY, a division of
          Gannett Co., Inc. Reprinted with Permission.
Chapter 4 Page 95–96 (Box 4.2): Roger Sandall is a Sydney writer and
          author of *The Culture Cult*. He comments on social and
          cultural matters at www.rogersandall.com.
Chapter 7 Pages 173–174 (Box 7.1): © MIT Technology Review; Pages
          178–179 (Box 7.3): Norman Ornstein / From *The Washington
          Post*. Reprinted with Permission of Norman Ornstein; Pages
          183–185 (Box 7.4): Reprinted by permission of *The Wall Street
          Journal*, Copyright © 2005 Dow Jones & Company, Inc. All
          Rights Reserved Worldwide. License number 1861680545672;
          Page 186–189 (Box 7.5): Rita Katz and Michael Kern / From
          The Washington Post. Reprinted with Permission of Rita Katz
          and Michael Kern.
Chapter 9 Pages 274–275 (Box 9.2): Reprinted with Permission of
          Geoffrey Nunberg; Pages 279–280 (Box 9.3): Eric Fair / From
          The Washington Post. Reprinted with Permission of Eric Fair.
Chapter 10 Pages 311–312 (Box 10.1): © David Ropeik, a consultant in risk
          communication; Page 313 (Box 10.2): CALVIN AND HOBBES
          © 1995 Watterson. Dist. By UNIVERSAL PRESS SYNDICATE.
          Reprinted with permission. All rights reserved; Pages 314–315
          (Box 10.3): © 2003, The Washington Post. Reprinted with
          Permission; Page 321 (Box 10.4): From THE ELEMENTS OF
          JOURNALISM by Bill Kovach and Tom Rosenstiel, copyright
          © 2001 by Bill Kovach and Tom Rosenstiel. Used by
          permission of Crown Publishers, a division of Random House,
          Inc.; Pages 324–326 (Box 10.5): From "The Media and
          Terrorism: A Reassessment," by Paul Wilkinson, in *Terrorism
          and Political Violence*, 1997, 9 (2). Reproduced by permission
          of Taylor & Francis Group, LLC., www.informaworld.com;

Pages 330–333 (Box 10.6): Copyright © 2003 by The New York Times Co. Reprinted with permission.

Chapter 11   Pages 358–360 (Box 11.1): Baruch Fischhoff / From *The Washington Post*. Reprinted with Permission of Baruch Fischhoff; Pages 371–373 (Box 11.2): Reprinted by permission of *The Wall Street Journal*, Copyright © 2005 Dow Jones & Company, Inc. All Rights Reserved Worldwide. License number 1861700133788.

Chapter 12   Pages 378–380 (Box 12.1): This article appeared originally on www.beliefnet.com, the leading website for faith, spirituality, inspiration & more. Used with permission. All rights reserved; Page 385 (Box 12.2): Reprinted by permission of *The Wall Street Journal*, Copyright © 2005 Dow Jones & Company, Inc. All Rights Reserved Worldwide. License Number 1861700514125; Pages 387–389 (Box 12.3): (c) 2005, James Traub. Reprinted by permission; Pages 398–399 (Box 12.4): Martha Bayles / From *The Washington Post*. Reprinted with Permission of Martha Bayles; Page 407 (Box 12.5): Reprinted with permission from *What Is Enlightenment?* Magazine; August–October 2004. © 2004 EnlightenNext, Inc. All rights reserved. http://www.wie.org

Chapter 13   Pages 427–429 (Box 13.3): Paul Ekman / From *The Washington Post*. Reprinted with Permission of Paul Ekman; Pages 432–433 (Box 13.4): From USA TODAY, a division of Gannett Co., Inc. Reprinted with Permission.

Preface

Terrorism was a fringe subject in the fields of criminal justice, political science, public administration, and public policy prior to the terrorist attacks of September 11, 2001. Suddenly, it emerged as the most critical problem of our time. The 9/11 disaster shocked, mystified, and angered people. It awakened us to the reality of a world becoming more aware of itself and more connected than ever before and, at the same time, much more perilous. Although the shock has subsided – at least, until the next such event – much of the mystery and confusion remains. This textbook aims to demystify the event and its aftermath and provide clarity about the prospects for public interventions and private initiatives and actions that may serve to prevent further acts of terrorism.

The purpose of this text is to serve two primary audiences: undergraduate and graduate students interested in a comprehensive reference source of essential information about the nature of terrorism, its causes, and interventions that respond to terrorism and work to prevent it. For students wanting to understand terrorism and learn how to cope and deal with it, the text should thus serve as a source of useful information. For students wishing to pursue a career in antiterrorism, it should be more than useful, providing an essential foundation on which to build more specialized information about how to understand terrorists and terrorism, protect targets, improve our ability to manage fear and prevent terrorism from occurring in the first place, and minimize the damage when those efforts fail. Students of criminal justice will find it useful as a source that recognizes the relevance of, and limits to, criminology and criminal justice theory and practice to the problem of terrorism. No prior foundational material should be required for a course that uses this text as a primary resource.

Preface

A central idea of this book is to satisfy the interests of both scholarship and public policy. It describes the nature of terrorism; distinctions among terrorism, crime, and war; the sources of terrorism; and interventions aimed at preventing and responding to terrorism, and it attempts to do so in an interesting and occasionally provocative manner. The text is based on a course that proved successful when introduced in the School of Public Affairs at American University in the Spring 2004 semester, a course that has been substantially refined and updated over subsequent semesters.

The approach of the book is multidisciplinary – much like the approaches of criminology and criminal justice; it is not driven by a single theoretical perspective. Terrorism, like crime, simply cannot be dealt with adequately through the lens of a single discipline. Accordingly, the text draws from the literature of criminology, psychology, political science, public administration, economics, and related disciplines to provide the reader with a comprehensive understanding of the nature of the problem and prospective solutions and to avoid the problem of reductionism common to treatment under a single perspective. The intent has been to present the material in a critical, yet clear and balanced, manner.

Students with pet theories about terrorism will find their theories subjected to scrutiny. Each chapter ends with a set of discussion questions, and additional questions are found at various places throughout the text. The overview that opens each chapter aims to get the student thinking about the central issues to be addressed in the chapter. The questions in and at the end of each chapter can serve either for classroom discussion or written homework assignments or both, at the discretion of the instructor. All questions are designed to induce the student to engage actively with the text material. The boxes are designed to reflect on and amplify issues raised in the text, occasionally drawing material from essays appearing in major newspapers, periodicals, and scholarly journals. Tables, photographs, and graphs are used to illustrate and complement material in the text and boxes, give life to abstractions, create substantive variety, and break the monotony of a text-only format.

A few words are in order about what this book is not. It is not a how-to manual on the investigation of acts of terrorism. For that, you should consult textbooks on criminal investigation and forensic science, as well as training manuals of agencies involved in the homeland security network. Nor is it a book that attempts to prove either the superiority or wrong-headedness of any particular point of view or doctrine on terrorism. For that, you should subscribe to any of a vast array of publications of the political left or right.

Rather, the intent of this text is to provide a survey of essential information on the nature and sources of terrorism and interventions that can serve to remove its causes. The driving idea is that we can prevent terrorism and respond to it most effectively when we understand what it means, what are its roots – why people choose to engage in acts of terrorism in the first place – and how we can protect the targets that are susceptible to attack. The text makes use of analytic frameworks designed to give a balanced presentation of critical perspectives on all significant sides of major issues of contention and often sharp contentiousness, including the role of religion, balancing security with rights to privacy and liberty, and the role of terrorism in the U.S. invasion of Iraq and in the Israel-Palestine struggle. The book aims to serve as a single-source reference on terrorism and as a platform for more in-depth study, with each chapter ending with a set of discussion questions and a list of further readings on the topics covered.

One of the great challenges in creating this book has been that of finding a balance between the goals of universality and relevance. We look for principles that are universal and immutable, but the world is not so tidy. We look for real-world events to bring abstractions down to earth, but events change, and as they change, so too do the lessons learned. We try to make sense of important events without appreciating their fluidity and uniqueness and the prospect that reasonable people will often disagree on their significance and the implications for policy. My intention throughout has been to find the most salient aspects of terrorism and bring them to life with the richest examples I could find, recognizing the limitations inherent in both generalizations and particulars.

Acknowledgments

I wish, first, to thank my research and teaching assistant, Kelley Moult, who has been an uncommonly dedicated, intelligent, well-organized, and delightfully good-humored collaborator. Her fine-toothed reviews of early versions of this book, her diligence in getting permissions for copyrighted material, and her many thoughtful suggestions have improved the work beyond measure both substantively and stylistically. I am extremely fortunate to have found such an extraordinary person.

My colleagues and friends Jim Lynch and Jack Greene have helped to validate several key ideas that relate core concepts of criminology to real problems in terrorism, and they have induced me to rethink and reshape others. Their willingness to expand these suggestions with contributions of their own and enlist others in this enterprise in the form of an anthology that complements this textbook has enriched this project substantially and made it all the more useful.

Deirdre Golash, Meg Weekes, and Bill LeoGrande, my good and conscientious colleagues in the School of Public Affairs at American University, have been especially supportive in encouraging me to do this work and ensure that it finds its way to our outstanding students. These three individuals are living proof to the proposition that effective teachers and scholars can be equally effective as administrators.

My good friend Tom Brady has been a most willing and effective sounding board all along the way. He has persuaded me to reconsider and refine many of the ideas in this text while they were still in one stage or another of development, and to find ways of presenting them more clearly and compellingly.

I owe a particular debt of gratitude to Akbar Ahmed for planting some of the book's central ideas on the power of dialogue and the goal of mutual understanding as antidotes to clashes among civilizations, cultures, religions,

Acknowledgments

nations, tribes, and individuals. He is an inspiring friend, an eloquent scholar of remarkable scope and depth, and a tireless warrior in the noble campaign to find lasting alternatives to war and solutions to the sources of alienation that breed terrorism. He has persuaded me that we need not consign ourselves to self-fulfilling prophecies of doom as inevitable, that if we must be in the business of making self-fulfilling prophecies it will be much more sensible to commit ourselves to healthy ones, while remaining vigilant to the reality of living in a world that includes dangerous fanatics.

Each of these generous people has contributed in a unique and palpable way. None is in any way responsible for lapses in this book that may have gone undetected or unattended to.

My publisher, Cambridge University Press, lived up once again to the stellar reputation that drew me to them in the first place, several years ago. Acquisitions editor Ed Parsons exercised the keen judgment, stewardship, and advice, and project manager Mary Cadette at Aptara, Inc., and her copy editor contributed the superior support, for which Cambridge is renowned and respected among criminologists worldwide.

This book is, above all, for the students. I will be forever grateful to those who have taken my courses to learn about terrorism. They have provided the strongest possible motive for me to understand an extremely complicated subject and work to make it understandable to them and others.

I wish, finally and foremost, to express deep gratitude to my wife, Judith, who not only has shown patience with yet another obsession of mine – four years' worth for this project – but has also been an active and interested partner in reviewing drafts and offering valuable suggestions. I dedicate this book to her, and I very much look forward to spending more time enjoying the rest of our lives together.

~ Brian Forst

ONE

The Nature of Terrorism

This chapter introduces the subject of terrorism, considers prevailing def-initions of the term and the manifestations of terrorism, describes basic typologies of terrorism, and distinguishes terrorism from crime and war. Its primary purpose is to clarify fundamental principles, concepts, and terms and thus set a foundation for understanding the material in the rest of the book.

A. Introduction

One of the clichés of our time is that the terrorist attack of September 11, 2001, changed our world. That it is a cliché does not diminish its truth. In a single day, individuals operating in four small teams, outside the authority of any state, revealed themselves able to organize and inflict damage on civilians on a scale and in a manner that shocked the vast majority of both the general public and responsible authorities. They attacked noncombatants, young and old, male and female, and people of all major religious denominations. They exploited the vulnerability of an open, free, and bountiful society. The offenders had been operating under the radar, not closely followed. As suicide murderers, it was impossible to bring them to justice through conventional avenues. The event was unprecedented; it stunned people the world over.

Cliché or not, the event did produce monumental changes in our inter-connected world. Security became much more extensive at airports at home and abroad, imposing time delays and inconvenience costs on millions of people everywhere. Fear of terrorism and enmity toward Muslims grew sub-stantially as the media became preoccupied with stories of terrorist activities

1

and threats of fringe extremists, both real and imagined. Economies and global markets were seriously shaken everywhere by threats of severe disruption to an international economic network reliant on open borders, the free movement of people, and the instantaneous flow of goods under fragile just-in-time inventory distribution systems. The markets were disturbed no less by concerns about the prospect of sharp reductions in the future availability of energy supplies, particularly oil and gas. Major military actions were launched, first in Afghanistan and then in Iraq, both in the name of counterterrorism. The standing of the United States plummeted throughout the world in the years immediately following 9/11.

Prior to the 9/11 attack, scholars and public commentators had been writing that the fall of the Berlin Wall in 1991 and the ending of the Cold War, along with the rise of advanced information and communication technology, were bringing the world closer together. They had witnessed the creation of a global community and a movement away from hostile political ideologies, notions of mutually assured nuclear destruction, and alienation and toward global economic and cultural exchange – the essential elements of a more peaceful world. The events of 9/11 and its aftermath raised serious questions about this bright scenario. In the words of Francis Fukuyama (2002a),

> The September 11 attacks represent a desperate backlash against the modern world, which appears to be a speeding freight train to those unwilling to get onboard. But we need to look seriously at the challenge we face. For a movement that has the power to wreak immense damage on the modern world, even if it represents only a small number of people, raises real questions about the viability of our civilization. The existence of weapons of mass destruction in the hands of virulently anti-American or anti-Western forces and their possible use has become a real threat. The key questions that Americans face as they proceed forward with this "war" on terrorism are how deep this fundamental challenge is, which sorts of allies it can recruit and what we must do to counter it.

These questions and challenges make it essential that ordinary citizens, students, scholars, and others operating in the public and private sectors acquaint themselves with a basic understanding of terrorism: its nature, causes, and consequences. Our actions as prospective voters, consumers, producers, and even bystanders can alter the course of these events. It is extremely important that we understand these matters, so that we can act more thoughtfully, aware of opportunities to remove the sources of terrorism and thus reduce its consequences. Let us begin with the basics.

B. Definitions and Typologies of Terrorism

We need first to understand the relevant basic terms that describe both how terrorism is a unique form of aggression and how it is distinguishable from other forms of aggression – especially, crime, war, and insurgency. It is essential also to consider different types of terrorism and the basic settings within which each type manifests.

1. Definitions

What is "terrorism"? Bruce Hoffman (1998) observes that standard dictionary definitions are unhelpful because they tend to be overly broad and tautological and are often outdated. He notes also a primary difficulty in defining the term: the meaning of terrorism has changed frequently and fairly substantially over the past 200 years.

Edmund Burke (1993) was among the first to use the term, which he invoked to describe Robespierre's "Reign of Terror," a strategy aimed at stifling opponents and controlling the masses after the French Revolution. Robespierre was the radical Jacobin leader of the new French government. He used terrifying means – tens of thousands were executed at the guillotine, and hundreds of thousands of others were shot or left to die in prisons – in the name of virtuous democratic ideals, as an instrument of social control by the state to restore order in a climate of anarchy. This somewhat positive connotation of terrorism remained largely until the 1930s, when the term became used to connote repression of the masses by totalitarian states, including Nazi Germany, Fascist Italy, and Stalinist Russia.

The modern usage of the term, developed in the mid-twentieth century, regards terrorism as a tool of ethnic and religious fanatics to serve political ends, such as liberation from an alien occupying group, or simply to exact righteous vengeance against a group labeled as a threat or enemy. Citing research published by Schmid and Jongman in 1988, Hoffman (1998, p. 40) notes that, of 109 definitions of "terrorism," most include elements of violence or force (84%), psychological impacts (41%), victim-target differentiation (37%), and method of combat, strategy, or tactic (30%). He adds, "On one point, at least, everyone agrees: terrorism is a pejorative term" (p. 31).

Gus Martin (2006) refines these notions by observing that terrorism today is widely understood to involve loose, cell-based networks that wage politically motivated, asymmetric violence against "soft" targets – that is, civilian and administrative targets rather than military ones. He observes that use of the term is typically justified through extremist language – replete with intolerance, moral absolutes, broad conclusions, conspiratorial beliefs, and religious or mystical references – aimed at disturbing or eventually destroying a target group, if not an entire population.

International organizations such as the League of Nations and the United Nations have had considerable difficulty developing a consensus on the definition of terrorism (Saul, 2006). In 2005, UN Secretary-General Kofi Annan proposed a broadening of the official definition of terrorism, so that the UN could have a stronger mandate to intercede where needed. Under his redefinition of the word, terrorism encompasses any act intended "to cause death or serious bodily harm to civilians." Some Arab countries took exception to this proposition. With the Palestinians in mind, they requested exemptions for those "resisting foreign occupation" ("Can Anyone Fix the U.N.?," 2005).

In the face of such difficulties, Jonathan White (2006, p. 4) offers a serviceable and concise definition, which he attributes to Brian Jenkins: "the use or threatened use of force designed to bring about a political change." Others add that terrorism is a premeditated and unlawful act or threat, that it may be employed against human or property targets, that it usually targets noncombatant civilians, and that it involves the following: indiscriminate violence, an intention to achieve a political objective through intimidation, and elements of organization and planning to achieve a tactical objective or strategic goal (Coady, 2004; Crenshaw, 1983; Laqueur, 1987; Primoratz, 2004). Still others question whether terrorism requires a political agenda, arguing that it may be motivated by a compulsion to eradicate an objectionable group of people that is often based on an exclusivist religious rationale (L. Wright, 2006a).

The generic dictionary definition of "terror" is quite similar to that of "fear"; accordingly, we devote an entire chapter to the anatomy of fear (Chapter 10). The central role played by fear of acts of terrorism is significant and largely underappreciated. Understanding the role of fear deepens our understanding of terrorism, for terrorism is largely about the behavior of the at-large target population, of how it acts in the face of threats. This is an important concept because the seeds of solutions to the problem of terrorism may be found in considering that a target population may tend to behave in ways that immobilize itself, weaken its quality of life, and thus support the objectives of terrorists – and such self-destructive inclinations may be manageable. In many circumstances, interventions that aim to manage the public's fear of terrorism may be more effective than those that aim to strike back at the terrorists.

In any case, a precise definition of terrorism with which all authorities would be inclined to agree is elusive. Some definitions ignore threats, some focus on harms to human life and ignore property targets, and definitions vary as to what constitutes a noncombatant. A few definitions regard taxpayers who provide financial support for objectionable government acts as collaborators and legitimate targets. Some include acts of "ethnic cleansing" that are motivated strictly by hatred and lacking in any legitimate political objective; some exclude acts committed by sovereign states against their own people, regarding these as acts of tyranny rather than terrorism; and others add that terrorism requires an element of secrecy to ensure that the act shocks a target population.

A few authorities offer minimalist definitions to avoid these complexities. Sunil Khilnani (1993), for one, asserts that "terrorism is simply a tactic, a method of random violence." Igor Primoratz (2004) gives an even more austere characterization: "Only two things are clear: terrorism is a type of violence, and it is a bad thing, not something to be proud of or support." The problem with such definitions is that they are conceptually limited and offer little help to either policymakers and practitioners working to prevent and respond to the problem or to scholars working to test hypotheses about terrorism and thus understand its causes (Gibbs, 1989). Suicide bombings of subway riders are clearly distinguishable from other types of violence, such as barroom brawls and violent acts of emotionally disturbed people, and we would do well to examine more precisely what they have in common and how they differ.

Khilnani's point that terrorism is a tactic is one that can have profound implications for policy and politics. If terrorism is just a tactic, like an ambush or a sniping, rather than an ideology, as with most other "isms," then a political campaign to wage a "war on terrorism" may be doomed to failure, a rhetorical trick likely first to resonate with the public and then frustrate them over the longer term. As U.S. Marine General Wallace Gregson observes of the war on terrorism, "This is no more a war on terrorism than the Second World War was a war on submarines" (Packer, 2005).

Linguist Geoffrey Nunberg, in a 2001 essay heard on National Public Radio that is reprinted in Box 1.1, reiterates an important related point that has been made often: one person's "terrorist" is another's "freedom fighter." In a similar vein, Robert McNamara observes in the 2003 documentary film, *The Fog of War*, "Curtis LeMay said if we'd lost the war, we'd all be prosecuted as war criminals. . . . What makes it immoral if you lose, but not immoral if you win?" Although Nunberg does not attempt to resolve this question, he does make a critical point that echoes an element of Khilnani's minimalist definition: the distinguishing characteristic of terrorism is that it is an act of *indiscriminate* violence.

Recognizing these important nuances and the associated difficulties in relying on a one-size-fits-all definition of terrorism, the following definition is used in this textbook:

Terrorism is the premeditated and unlawful use or threatened use of violence against a noncombatant population or target having symbolic significance, with the aim of either inducing political change through intimidation and destabilization or destroying a population identified as an enemy.

Box 1.1. "Terrorism": The History of a Very Frightening Word

– Geoffrey Nunberg

A few weeks ago, the *Washington Post* disclosed that the global head of news for Reuters had written an internal memo asking reporters to avoid using the word "terrorist" to describe the airplane hijackers. As he explained, "One man's terrorist is another man's freedom fighter." And Reuters dispatches have since avoided using the word "terrorism" unless quoting someone.

Given the circumstances, Reuters' scruples seem misplaced – there are times when even-handedness can tip over into moral abdication. But its policy actually goes back more than twenty years and reflects the equivocal history of the word itself.

"Terrorism" is one of those terms like "crusade," which began its life at a particular historical moment – in the case of the crusades, in 1095 when Pope Urban II asked Europeans to wrest the Holy Land from the Muslims.

In 1792, the Jacobins came to power in France and initiated what we call the Reign of Terror and what the French call simply La Terreur. The Jacobin leader, Maximilien F.M.I. de Robespierre, known to history by his surname, called terror "an emanation of virtue." In 1793, he said, "Terror is nothing but justice, prompt, severe and inflexible." In the months that followed, the severe and inflexible justice of the guillotine severed 12,000 heads, including Robespierre's.

Of course, not everyone shared Robespierre's enthusiasm for the purifying effects of terror. One of the first writers to use the word "terrorist" in English was Edmund Burke, that implacable enemy of the French Revolution, who wrote in 1795 of "those hell-hounds called terrorists [who] are let loose on the people."

For the next 150 years, the word "terrorism" led a double life – a justifiable political strategy to some, an abomination to others. The Russian revolutionaries who assassinated Czar Alexander II in 1881 used the word proudly. And in 1905, Jack London described terrorism as a powerful weapon in the hands of labor, though he warned against harming innocent people.

But for the press and most of the public, the word "terrorist" connoted bomb-throwing madmen. Politicians weren't above using the word as a brush to tar socialists and radicals of all stripes, whatever their views of violence. When President William McKinley was assassinated by an anarchist in 1901,

Congress promptly passed legislation that barred known anarchists from entering the United States.

By the mid-twentieth century, terrorism was becoming associated more with movements of national liberation than with radical groups, and the word was starting to acquire its universal stigma.

One of the last groups willing to describe itself as terrorist was a Zionist organization called Lehi (Lohamei Herut Israel), known earlier as the Stern Gang. In 1946, when Palestine was still under a British mandate, Lehi terrorists killed ninety-one people, twenty-eight of them Britons, by planting a bomb in the King David Hotel in Jerusalem.

Most of the Third-World movements that resorted to political violence in the 1950s and 1960s preferred terms like "freedom fighters" or "guerrillas" or "mujahedeen."

"Terrorist" became a condemnation by the colonial powers. That's the point when news organizations started to become circumspect about using the word to describe groups like the Irish Republican Army, the Ulster Defense Association, or the African National Congress. It seemed to be picking sides, and perhaps a little imprudent – particularly when you consider that former "terrorists" like Nelson Mandela and Menachem Begin ended their careers as winners of the Nobel Peace Prize.

By the 1980s, "terrorism" was being applied to all manner of political violence. There was a flap over the word in 1989 when *New York Times* editor A. M. Rosenthal attacked Christopher Hitchens for refusing to describe the fatwah against Salmon Rushdie as terrorism. Hitchens had a good point. The fatwah may have been repugnant, but it was far from an act of indiscriminate violence – more like state-sponsored contract killing. But by then the word had acquired a kind of talismanic force – as if refusing to describe something as terrorism was the next thing to apologizing for it.

By the 1990s, people were crying terrorism whenever they discerned an attempt at intimidation or disruption. Hackers who concocted computer viruses were cyberterrorists, cult leaders were psychological terrorists. Software companies accused Microsoft of terrorism in its efforts to maintain its Windows monopoly, and Microsoft accused Apple Computer of "patent terrorism" after the companies got into a dispute over intellectual property. And when photographer Spencer Tunik got thirty people to lie down naked for a picture in front of the United Nations Building in New York, a critic described the piece as "artistic terrorism at its best."

With that kind of freewheeling precedent, it probably shouldn't have been surprising that the antiterrorism bill passed by Congress defined terrorism very broadly, so that a "terrorist offense" could include anything from hijacking an airplane to injuring government property, breaking into a government computer for any reason, or hitting the secretary of agriculture with a pie. Civil libertarians are concerned that the notion of "terrorism" could become an all-purpose pretext, the way "racketeering" did after the passage of the RICO Act in the 1970s.

That would be a linguistic misfortune, too. Granted, it's natural to appropriate the language of violence when we want to dramatize our zeal or outrage – we make war on poverty, we skirmish over policy, and we cry bloody murder when the newspaper is late. But when things happen that merit the full force of our outrage, a legacy of careless usage can leave us at a loss for words.

2. Typologies

Given the virtually infinite variety of circumstances surrounding terrorist events, every group or act that fits any conventional definition of terrorism is unique, usually in several respects. Still, there are a few generic dimensions that distinguish some terrorists, terrorist groups, and terrorist acts from most others. Particular terrorist groups and individual acts of terrorism fall into any of a variety of categories, based on the following dimensions:

- Whether or not politically motivated
- Whether or not operating under state authority
- Degree of association with larger terrorist organizations or networks
- Extent of organization and planning
- Whether justified in religious or ethnic terms
- Whether aimed primarily at people or at symbolic targets
- The types of people targeted

Each case can usually be characterized conveniently and usefully in terms of the particular combination of these and possibly other dimensions that fit. The variation of behaviors among these various categories may in most instances be greater than the variation of behaviors within a particular category. Let us consider each of these dimensions more carefully.

Politically and Nonpolitically Motivated Terrorism

Acts of terrorism are generally carried out with a political agenda: to induce the state or citizens in a state to act in ways that those who carry out the acts perceive are unattainable through legitimate means. Typically, a terrorist act achieves its aim by instilling fear in a target group and thereby pressuring the state to act in accordance with the wishes of the terrorists. It may aim to destabilize the political, economic, or social order. It may attack symbolic targets, such as government buildings, a venerable statues (e.g., those of Buddha in Bamiyan, Afghanistan), or a sacred shrine – a mosque, temple, or church – rather than people.

In some cases, however, the acts of terror are committed out of sheer hatred, strictly with the goal of exterminating a group of people perceived as undesirable – referred to euphemistically as "ethnic cleansing" by the perpetrators and as "genocide" by objective observers – or inducing the targeted group to flee the territory. Gus Martin refers to these acts as cases of "communal terrorism" (2006, p. 171). Such acts are not generally characterized as politically motivated, although principled political motives may be claimed to provide an element of legitimacy to a terrorist cause that is rooted, in fact, primarily in hatred.

Terrorism by the State

We have noted that the term "terrorism" was coined in the nineteenth century to describe acts conducted by the French Republic. More than a century later, some of the most devastating episodes of terrorism continue to be committed by or sponsored under the authority of sovereign nations. Among the most brutal examples are the following:

- The Khmer Rouge killing of nearly two million Cambodians under the dictatorship of Pol Pot in the late 1970s
- The Baathist Army gassing of thousands of Kurds in Northern Iraq by Saddam Hussein in 1988
- The Serbian killing of several thousand Muslims in Bosnia under Slobodan Milosevic in the 1990s

These three are all examples of state-sponsored acts of terrorism that were ordered directly and monitored closely by the leaders who sanctioned them.

In other instances, the acts are carried out more along the lines of patronage or assistance than direct control. Iranian support for Hezbollah, the Popular Front for the Liberation of Palestine, and terrorist activities in Iraq and elsewhere throughout the Middle East and other parts of the world all exemplify the patronage model of state-sponsored terrorism. Cuba is also known to have supported terrorist activities in South America and Spain, and Pakistan is known to have supported such activities in Kashmir. Support of a prolonged insurgency against communists by the United States and Britain during the Cold War also qualifies. The support can range from ideological encouragement and indoctrination to training and assistance in insurgency, intelligence, operational support in the form of providing false documents and safe havens, and financial rewards to the families of suicide bombers.

The Nature of Terrorism

These various forms of support may have any one or a combination of several aims:

- To destabilize a state to gain greater influence in the region
- To create international visibility for a persistent problem, such as that of Palestine
- To retaliate against a target state in the region perceived as an enemy
- To undermine the influence of a larger power operating in the region

Although acts of state-sponsored terrorism are well known – both those involving direct initiation and control and those involving patronage and indirect support – few sovereign nations officially acknowledge involvement in or support of these activities. Today, terrorism is widely thought to originate with groups like al Qaeda, operating outside the official auspices of the state. Constitutional democracies have taken particularly strong stands against terrorist attacks on noncombatants, especially in the post-Cold War era. Leaders of nondemocratic nations generally express opposition to terrorist activities as well, especially when the targets of those activities are people who are friends of the state or when the activities are aimed directly against the state and its resources. Although some nations provide covert support to terrorist groups and activities, typically indirectly through intermediaries to obfuscate their involvement, none officially acknowledge support of terrorism.

Connection to Larger Networks and the Extent of Internal Organization

Terrorist groups and individuals are, at one extreme, operatives of larger terrorist networks, much like business franchises. Some are only loosely affiliated – al Qaeda is the best known of such loosely associated networks. At the other extreme, terrorists act as independent lone-wolf operatives, such as "Unabomber" Ted Kaczynski, Austrian letter bomber Franz Fuchs, and abortion clinic and Atlanta Olympic Park bomber Eric Rudolph. Larger, more connected groups can benefit by taking advantage of teamwork, division of labor, and power in numbers, but they tend to be subject to a greater risk of detection because their exposure is increased with each additional individual involved. Of course, even individuals must plan their attacks if they wish to enhance the prospects for success, but the need for planning and coordinating activities increases as the operations become more complex and the number of individuals needed to carry out the act or acts increases. The effectiveness of the group can be enhanced through practice, preparation, and secrecy, as in the cases of 9/11 and the London subway attack of 2005, but any group is generally only as effective as the competence of its weakest member.

Terrorism by Militant Religious Extremists

Much terrorism is conducted in the name of a religious mission. With the 9/11 attack, Islamic jihadism[1] became the most prominent example of terrorism motivated by religious extremists, but by no means the only example of terrorist acts done in the name of religion. Millions of innocent people were slaughtered as infidels by Christian Crusaders for some 200 years beginning in 1099, as were countless others by militant extremist factions of all the major religions over the years. Examples are discussed in some detail in Chapters 2 and 4.

Ethnic Terrorism

Ethnicity is typically associated with unique combinations of genetics, culture, language, religion, and common heritage, and ethnic terrorism is terrorism involving an ethnic group. It occurs typically following long-standing ethnic or tribal rivalries and is accompanied by slogans, such as the following: you are not one of us, you interfere with our well-being and thus threaten us, and we must defend ourselves against you and your kind. Ethnic terrorism usually follows acts of persecution, with the persecutor and persecuted often switching roles in episodes of mutual retaliation. When a government supports one side in an ethnic dispute, the other side often engages in acts of terrorism against the government.

Ethnic terrorism ranges from the local level of the clan or tribe to the level of the nation and beyond, as when an ethnic group has migrated to various points throughout the world in diaspora. At the smallest level, warring clans and tribes generally share a common ethnic heritage within a region, yet they often feud over territorial or property disputes, acts of disrespect, or petty matters involving unresolved grievances. A prominent example of terrorist acts between clans in the United States is the decades-long feud between the Hatfields and McCoys of Eastern Kentucky. Toward the other end of the scale, the disputes become questions of national identity, such as whether two warring ethnic groups are better as a single nation or as separate ones.

Daniel Byman (2007) observes that ethnic terrorism is often the product of government interventions against ethnic minorities. He identifies several common characteristics of such interventions. When a government acts with force to stifle the dissent of an ethnic minority against government rule, the actions tend to polarize the opposition and induce a stronger-than-anticipated reaction. Such acts of force often induce other countries and institutions that are unfriendly to the government to provide support to the ethnic minority. The government often underestimates the advantages that local insurgents have against an invading army, the principal one being the opportunity to outlast the invaders and wear them down through acts of insurgency, as the American colonialists did to the British military in the late eighteenth century. In the end, overly aggressive government action tends to escalate ethnic terrorism.

Every continent has its history of ethnic rivalries that simmer and then boil over into acts of terrorism, some not involving government intervention. Although each of these histories has its own unique elements, they tend to share many attributes: small differences become greatly magnified while large commonalities and shared values are ignored; intermarriage between individuals of opposing clans or tribes become taboo, and the identities of the children of such marriages become confused; extremists on both sides put moderates under pressure to choose sides and give up conciliatory or neutral positions; and government interventions tend to be alternately inept and needlessly brutal, with both sorts of reactions having the eventual effect of energizing the opposition. In Chapter 3, I discuss several major examples of ethnic terrorism in which there have been decades and sometimes centuries of fighting: between Kurds and Turks in Turkey, Sunnis and Kurds in Iraq, Sunnis and Shi'a in Iraq, Russians and Chechens in the Trans-Caucuses, Basques and Spanish nationalists in Spain, Hutus and Tutsis in Rwanda, English Protestants and Irish Catholics in Northern Ireland, and the Tamils and Sinhalese in Sri Lanka.

C. Critical Distinctions: Terrorism, Aggression, Crime, and War

Terrorism is an extreme form of both crime and aggression. The social costs and consequences of terrorism tend to be vastly greater than are customarily associated even with serious acts of street crime and of violent aggression, because of the scale of both the immediate harms caused by the acts and the widespread fear produced by the acts and the consequences of that fear. That terrorism is extreme, however, does not mean that it is fundamentally different from those other acts: many of the sources of crime and aggression are common to terrorism. Terrorism is in some ways more similar to war than to crime, but it differs from war in important respects as well, despite the use of war metaphors to garner political support for aggressive interventions against terrorism. Box 1.2 highlights distinctions among several overlapping concepts: aggression, crime, guerrilla action, insurgency, terrorism, and war.

Aggression is common to the other five concepts in the box, except for crimes that do not involve force or threats of force.[2] The primary distinctions among the concepts have to do with the targets and motives of the aggression involved. Each manifestation of aggression is similar to the others in several ways, but is distinct in at least one way. Acts of insurgency are similar to guerrilla acts, except that they include targets other than military or law enforcement agents. Insurgents often use the tools of terrorism, and they may

Box 1.2. Critical Distinctions: Terrorism, Aggression, Crime, and War

Aggression: any act or threat of force by an individual or group against another

Crime: the intentional violation of a criminal statute by an individual acting either alone or with others

Guerrilla action: an act of aggression by an individual or group against a state's military or law enforcement authority

Insurgency: the systematic use of subversion and aggression against a constituted government by an organized group of individuals opposed to the government and acting outside of formal sovereign authority; insurgents who succeed become heroic revolutionaries, whereas those who fail are known as criminals

Terrorism: the premeditated and unlawful use or threatened use of violence against a noncombatant population or target having symbolic significance, with the aim of either inducing political change through intimidation or removing a population identified as an enemy

War: the systematic use of aggression or counteraggression by one sovereign nation against another sovereign nation, following a formal declaration by the nation's legitimate rulers or leaders

either be citizens of the country in which they operate or operatives of a larger cross-national terrorist organization, but they generally strike at combatants and noncombatants alike. Terrorism usually involves a crime, but it extends beyond ordinary street crime because of the political or hate motive. War is unlike terrorism because it is, in the strict rather than rhetorical sense, a formal matter between sovereign nations. We examine these distinctions in greater detail below.

A few other points are worth keeping in mind as we proceed. Although the term "terrorism" was first used in the context of acts of a state against its own people in late eighteenth-century France, today terrorism usually refers to acts committed outside of state authority. A state that provides support to terrorists at the expense of another state may be subjected to legitimate formal sanction by the victimized state or its allies. Acts of war are generally characterized by a ruling authority as acts in the name of defense, often as preemptive or preventive acts, and rarely as acts of aggression. The individuals who commit acts that fit the definition of terrorism rarely regard themselves as terrorists. Although this book focuses primarily on terrorism, it makes frequent use of the other terms, so it will be useful to be clear about these distinctions.

The Nature of Terrorism

To fully understand terrorism and its many manifestations, it will help, first, to establish how terrorism differs from other forms of crime and aggression and then to establish what is known about sources of aggression in general and of terrorism in particular.

1. Terrorism and Crime

Acts of terror are almost always criminal acts too, involving the violation of a local or federal criminal statute. This fact has practical implications: state and local justice agencies are responsible for protecting communities against all forms of crime, and federal agencies responsible for homeland and international security can use federal criminal statutes and intervention policies to ensure that the public is protected against terrorism. Federal agents can accomplish this goal not only by protecting the borders and points of entry against hostile invasion but also by enforcing and prosecuting violations of federal laws domestically – from crimes that cross state boundaries, to crimes on the grounds of federal property, to organized crimes and conspiracies.

Terrorists are like other violent criminals in many ways. They inflict harm on people and property. They act with intent, committing their crimes with an instrumental goal in mind. They are predominantly young and male, aware that they are breaking the law, but not dissuaded by the law from committing their acts, and are typically disrespectful of social norms, order, and systems of social control. They often operate in small teams to overwhelm targets of opportunity. In addition, the more effective terrorists, like the more effective criminals, tend to operate outside of predictable patterns to minimize the prospects of detection and prevention by law enforcement officials and private citizens and authorities.

Terrorists are different from criminals, however, in at least three important respects. They tend to do crimes that are more serious than most violent crimes. They aim quite purposefully to inflict fear in a large target population. And they do so typically to serve an extremist political agenda, justifying their acts as supportive of a larger social goal, often with the hope of winning recruits to their cause. These differences are profound, especially to the extent that terrorists succeed in drawing in others to a massive, sustained campaign of violence against a civil population. Accordingly, terrorists are inclined to commit acts designed to achieve maximum media exposure (Hoffman, 1998). According to anthropologist Scott Atran, "The difference between terror and other forms of violence ... is publicity" (quoted in Fidler, 2007). Street criminals, by contrast, ordinarily conduct themselves so as to minimize the amount of attention their acts receive.

Like terrorists, serial killers and mass murderers do crimes that are more serious than other violent offenders, and like terrorists, they may thrive on the attention they receive. But serial killers and mass murderers do not generate

A New York City police officer, wearing a protective mask, stands guard near the Stock Exchange building one day before its reopening on September 16, 2001.

widespread sympathy, for they make no pretense of serving any larger social or political purpose. Terrorists, by contrast, aim both to generate interest in and to enlist others to support and participate in like crimes in order to serve a larger ideological cause.

Although most acts of terrorism can be adjudicated under either federal or state authority, they are usually prosecuted in federal court. Ramzi Ahmed Yousef, mastermind of the World Trade Center bombing of 1993 that killed six people, was convicted and sentenced in federal court, as were "Unabomber" Theodore Kaczynski and Oklahoma City bombers Timothy McVeigh and Terry Nichols. In contrast, John Allen Muhammad and Lee Boyd Malvo, the two men who terrorized the Washington, D.C., area in 2002 with the sniper killings of ten people in Maryland, Virginia, and the District of Columbia, were prosecuted and convicted in courts in Virginia and Maryland. The opportunity to exercise discretion to prosecute terrorist cases in either federal or state court – under *dual jurisdiction* authority – and possibly in more than one state court, without violating the double jeopardy clause of the Fifth Amendment to the Constitution, gives federal prosecutors and county district attorneys a wider range of options to ensure that terrorists will be brought to justice.

In short, when aggression manifests as an act of crime, it can be prosecuted as such, and when it manifests as an act of terrorism, it can be prosecuted also under any of several criminal statutes – federal, state, or local. The existence of such options may offer unique potency for the prevention of subsequent acts of terrorism and thus serve to quell sustained terrorist campaigns.

Because of the infectious and volatile nature of terrorism and the grave social costs it can impose on a population, the sanctions that apply to ordinary criminals are likely to be inadequate for terrorists. Common street criminals may be more readily reintegrated into a neighborhood without grave risk to the community than terrorists who aim to destroy an entire population. Even when terrorists violate the same laws as nonterrorist criminal offenders, it may be appropriate to impose more severe sanctions against them to protect society against the more harmful subsequent attacks that they have expressed a propensity to commit. Terrorism is, after all, a close relative of hate crime, which also receives more severe sanctions than crimes that are otherwise similar to it.

2. Terrorism and War

A Brief History of War

Warfare among tribes is surely as old as the inclination of humans to form tribes. At various points in the early development of the human species, individuals turned from the exclusive use of weapons for hunting to their use in defense of life and property against aggression from other individuals; they began eventually to organize for defense of a clan or tribe's territory or to conquer and occupy (Keegan, 1994; Tzu, 2002). With the rise of the nation-state, this process took place on a larger, more organized scale. Warfare became a formal process to be used following the failure of peaceful persuasion – in the words of von Clausewitz, "the continuation of policy with the admixture of other means" (quoted in Howard, 1983, p. 34). Modern war involves the formal declaration between two or more sovereign nation-states to engage in hostility.

This basic definition of warfare was established in the 1648 Peace of Westphalia, a series of treaties that ended the Thirty Years' War among central European nations, waged between Protestant (principally Lutherans and Calvinists) and Catholic blocs. The treaty was significant in that it put an end to the idea that the Holy Roman Empire had secular dominion over the entire Christian world. It replaced this notion with the principle that the nation-state would henceforth be the highest level of government, subordinate and subservient to no other.

The matter of warfare was a central concern to the framers of the U.S. Constitution. In establishing the separation of powers, they dealt explicitly with the formal initiation and waging of warfare. They were particularly interested in making it difficult for the country to enter into and wage war, so they divided the powers of war between the legislative and executive branches. The Constitution gives Congress the power to declare war, to "make rules concerning captures on land and water," and, through its powers to tax and spend, the ability to "raise and support armies." The framers complemented this formal power of Congress to initiate and support a war with the power of the president to direct the conduct of war as Commander-in-Chief of the armed forces.

Congress has not formally declared war since World War II. However, it did vote to commit troops to Vietnam under the Gulf of Tonkin Resolution in 1964, and it authorized the use of force against Iraq in 1991. Then, in September 2001, Congress authorized President George W. Bush "to use all necessary and appropriate force against those nations, organizations, or persons he determines planned, authorized, committed, or aided the terrorist attacks that occurred on September 11, 2001, or harbored such organizations or persons." The United States has thus waged a Vietnam War, a first Iraq War, a war in Afghanistan, and a second Iraq War, all under officially sanctioned war powers, yet all without formal declarations of war.

Differences between Rules of Military Engagement and Legal Procedure

In warfare, military actions operate under rules that are quite different from the legal procedure that governs the conduct of law enforcement agents in our system of criminal justice. The differences show up at three important stages: *pursuit*, *capture*, and *sanction* (Feldman, 2002). The Constitution limits the behavior of criminal justice agents in each of these three aspects of the justice process, imposing considerably greater restraints than do codes of military conduct.

At the pursuit stage, an enemy combatant is fair game for eradication on a field of battle, whereas crime suspects cannot be killed unless they pose an immediate threat to others, even if they are fleeing from the scene of a felony offense (*Tennessee v. Garner*, 1985). After their capture, prisoners of war are detained at camps that are bound by codes of humane treatment, whereas the criminal justice system typically releases the suspect on bond or recognizance. At the sanction stage, combatants are often killed if they do not surrender, and they can be imprisoned for as long as the war continues, whereas the criminal justice system rarely executes offenders, and the burden is on the prosecutor to prove the guilt of the suspect beyond a reasonable doubt. Criminal justice sanctions are typically announced by the judge at the time of sentencing; prisoners of war are imprisoned for indefinite periods.

At all three stages, the criminal justice agent is obliged to presume that the suspect is innocent. On the field of battle, such a presumption could excessively endanger the safety of the force that makes the presumption.

The War on Terror

What about the "war on terror"? Isn't that a war too? Haven't the wars in Afghanistan and Iraq been essential components of this war on terror? Didn't al Qaeda declare war on the United States? The answers to these questions reside in an important distinction: between war as a formal concept and "war" as a rhetorical device to generate political support for a cause. If war is truly a matter between sovereign states, and a particular group of terrorists do not act as agents of any nation, then Congress has no formal power to wage war against them. It can act against them in many of the same ways as if against a state, but it cannot enact a war against terrorists acting outside of state authority. When the Taliban government of Afghanistan harbored the al Qaeda forces that masterminded the 2001 attacks on New York and Washington, the president and Congress initiated formal action to overthrow that government: a war on *Afghanistan*. References to the "war on terror" and the "war on terrorism" were more rhetorical than formal. As legal philosopher Ronald Dworkin (2003) notes, "We can conquer Kabul and Baghdad, but there is no place called Terror where the terrorists live." Nor is there a President of Terror with whom a formal peace treaty can be signed at the end of the war.

The war on terror is, to be sure, more than mere rhetoric. Several interventions – military, legislative, and administrative – have been associated with it. A major military intervention was launched in Afghanistan in 2001 to overthrow the Taliban regime, and another in Iraq in 2003 to remove weapons of mass destruction and topple Saddam Hussein from power. The 2001 USA Patriot Act expanded the authority of law enforcement agencies to search communication, medical, financial, and other records; ease restrictions on foreign intelligence gathering within the United States; expand the Treasury Department's authority to regulate financial transactions involving foreigners; and expand the discretion of law enforcement and immigration authorities in detaining and deporting immigrants suspected of terrorism-related acts. The Homeland Security Act of 2002 then integrated domestic and international intelligence gathering within the Department of Homeland Security. These actions were all associated with the war on terror.

The war on terror is, nonetheless, largely semantic. Wars run a wide spectrum – from formal declarations of war against real *adversaries* such as Germany, Italy, and Japan in December 1941; to the Cold War from 1945 to 1989 and its explosive and deadly manifestations in Korea and Vietnam; to purely rhetorical wars against *adversities* such as poverty, crime, and drugs starting in the 1960s. The problem with rhetorical wars is that, unlike formal wars against sovereign nations, they are generally unwinnable. There is no clearly defined enemy who can surrender to mark the ending of hostilities in "wars" on poverty, crime, drugs, or terrorism, as in the case of a bona fide war against the ruling government of a sovereign power. (Recall General Gregson's observation, noted earlier, likening wars on terrorism to wars on submarines.) A "war" on a particular terrorist group, such as al Qaeda, which occupies no fixed statutory geographic boundary, could conceivably be won if all the known members of such an organization were to surrender, but even that would provide no guarantee that new members would not emerge as replacements in the same cause. The Allied victory over Hitler's Germany in 1945 involved conquest over a particular sovereign regime, as did the Allied victory over Kaiser Wilhelm II's Germany in 1918, but the treaties that ended those two wars did not signify final victory over fascism or tyranny. Similarly, the eradication of any particular terrorist group in no way guarantees the ending of terrorism, which is, after all, a generic concept like poverty, crime, and drugs.

However much we may dislike poverty, crime, drugs, and terrorism, and however much it may energize us in the short term to take action against them by elevating the cause rhetorically to the level of "warfare," wars against concepts tend generally to frustrate the public over the long term. A nation can wage a successful campaign of defense against terrorists, but not warfare against it, except as political talk designed to win public support in the short term through the expression of passion or deep commitment (Beinart, 2007).

Over the long term, waging an unwinnable war against terrorism may serve to dispirit the public and weaken its sustained resolve for security. It may do even worse: it may strengthen the hand of the terrorists by legitimatizing their cause as one involving "warriors," rather than criminals (Malinowski, 2007). According to former National Security Advisor Zbigniew Brzezinski (2007), "The damage these three words have done – a classic self-inflicted wound – is infinitely greater than any wild dreams entertained by the fanatical perpetrators of the 9/11 attacks."

Ethics and the Survival of Populations

One final distinction between terrorism and war is worth noting. Waged justly, warfare attempts to limit collateral damage: a fundamental principle of military ethics is to minimize harm to noncombatants (Walzer, 1992). This principle has been violated too often, but to the extent that it has been honored, it has meant that conventional wars have tended to wind down as the stock of warriors became depleted, extending the survival of the populations involved (Hanson, 2005a; Keegan, 1994). The killing of noncombatants under terrorism and the increasing availability of weapons of mass destruction are likely to reduce this tendency to minimize harm to noncombatants, making it all the more important to remove the sources of terrorism. The next chapter, and several more to follow, focus on these sources.

3. Legal and Military Interventions

Given these critical distinctions between matters that are military and those that are criminal, are the interests of the United States in protecting itself against the reality of terrorism and the continuing threats it imposes better served through the law or by military means? Fortunately, most terrorist events do not force us to make such a choice. Acts of terrorism are invariably crimes prosecutable by law, and they are often also matters that can be effectively dealt with on foreign soil through military means or international diplomacy. For most matters, the choice is fairly straightforward.

Discussion Questions

1. *Definitions of terrorism.* How might different definitions of terrorism alter responses to questions about how to prevent terrorism and how to respond to it when acts are not prevented?
2. *Policy implications.* Might some federal, state, or local agencies or non-governmental organizations have reason to prefer some definitions of terrorism over others? Can you give an example?
3. *Terrorism and crime.* In what ways is terrorism like crime? In what ways is it different? How might policies for the prevention of crime benefit the prevention of terrorism? How might they be limited or even counterproductive?
4. *Terrorism and war.* In what ways is terrorism like war? In what ways is it different? How might military policies be relevant for intervening against terrorism? How might they be limited or even counterproductive?

TWO

Theories of Aggression and Terrorism

This chapter considers the basic theories of the sources of aggression in general and of terrorism in particular. Its primary purpose is to build on the principles of the first chapter – which explores the definition and nature of terrorism – to understand terrorism's various sources. One of the first principles is that terrorism is a manifestation of aggression, and it will be useful to begin by considering what is known about the general sources of aggression, then how terrorism is a particular kind of aggression, and finally the significance of that distinction.

A. Introduction

Much has been learned over the past several decades about preventing crime by developing a clear understanding of its causes. The application of sophisticated research methods to reliable data has benefited the following areas of criminal justice policy: strategies for the prevention of delinquency in general and of gang crimes and crimes in schools in particular; approaches to the design of defensible community space; and more effective policing, sentencing, and correctional strategies. If we are to prevent terrorism through the design of effective intervention strategies and policies, it will be essential first to understand its causes. Some of the findings on the prevention of crime may have only limited relevance to the problem of terrorism. Even for prevention strategies that are relevant, both for crime and terrorism, it is important to distinguish between long-term ("root") causes – especially the deep alienation and hatred that can provide the foundation for individual acts of terrorism – and short-term causes, which serve to ignite or permit such acts once the alienation has become firmly rooted. These distinctions are useful both for policy purposes and for the coherent social scientific understanding of terrorism.

Terrorism is an extreme form of both crime and aggression, as described in the preceding chapter, and many of the sources of crime and aggression are sources of terrorism as well (LaFree and Dugan, 2004). To understand the causes of terrorism, it will help, first, to establish what is known generally about the sources of aggression and, then, to determine how terrorism is distinct from other forms of crime and aggression. This distinction has practical implications: state and local justice agencies are responsible for protecting communities against all forms of crime, and agencies with responsibilities for homeland and international security are primarily interested in ensuring that their policies and intervention strategies are tailored uniquely to the protection of society against terrorism.

Before we proceed with the dominant theories of aggression and terrorism, it will be useful to understand what we mean by "theory." A theory is an explanation, conjecture, or assertion about a relationship or set of relationships. It is essential for building knowledge systematically about the relationships between two or more factors and to provide a framework for the empirical analysis of data that can confirm, or fail to confirm, those relationships. Theory gives meaning to relationships. Without theory, a correlation between two factors is unexplained and may in fact be just a coincidence or a product of spuriousness, the omission of factors that precede the two factors. For example, drug use and the homicide rate may be correlated because drug use causes crime, because it follows crime, because another factor or set of factors precedes both drug use and crime and thus creates a correlation between the two, or perhaps because all of these relationships may be occurring in varying degrees at the same time. The same may be true of terrorism and its correlates. It will be useful to keep these prospects in mind as we consider theories of aggression and terrorism.

B. Nature and Nurture

Perhaps the oldest and most basic question about aggression is whether it is based primarily in nature or in environmental and social factors, starting with the quality of nurturance, bonding, and social education in the family (Hirschi, 1969). Two factors that are fairly distinctive about terrorists support the innate nature of aggression: age and sex. Like street offenders, terrorists are predominantly male and typically in their late teens or early twenties. There are, of course, important exceptions, as with individual street crimes, but the predominance of young males as both criminals and terrorists – and the strong correlation with aggression generally – is beyond dispute

22

(Mednick et al., 1987; Raine, 2002; Wilson and Herrnstein, 1998). Criminologists generally group the theories that explain relationships between age and aggression under the "life course" theories, aimed at describing various stages of life and pertinent aspects of the relationship among age, aggression, and crime (Laub and Sampson, 2006; Sampson and Laub, 1993; Thornberry, 1997). The life course perspective has shown that people who commit crimes in their teens and early twenties tend to cease such activity as they develop enduring social connections and a stake in society, especially through marriage and work; the few who persist beyond their early twenties tend to be social nomads (Laub and Sampson, 2006).

One of the most exhaustive surveys of suicide terrorists, by Robert Pape (2005), confirms the disproportionality of young males as suicide bombers. Pape and a team of University of Chicago graduate students collected data on as many cases of suicide terrorism for which reliable information was available from international newspapers and other public sources. The Chicago Project on Suicide Terrorism assembled a database of 462 cases of people who committed suicide in terrorist attacks over the period 1980 through 2003. Fifty percent of the cases involved Arab attackers in Lebanon and Palestine who were associated with al Qaeda, and most of the rest were Kurds, Chechens, and Tamils. The Chicago team was able to establish the sex of the offender in 82 percent of the cases, age in 60 percent, education level in 67 percent, and income level in 77 percent.

The researchers found that the average age of suicide terrorists was as low as 21.1 years for Lebanese Hezbollah suicide terrorists, followed by 21.9 years for Tamil Tigers, 22.5 years for Palestinians, 23.6 years for Kurds affiliated with the PKK, 26.7 years for al Qaeda terrorists, and 29.8 years for Chechens, the oldest group in the survey. Some portion of these age differences is attributable to differences across the general populations from which the terrorists come: the median ages of the Lebanese and Palestinian populations are about ten years younger than that of the Chechen population.

Pape and his colleagues found that sex varies more considerably than age across these groups, ranging from no females among the al Qaeda terrorists to more than half females among the Chechens and Kurds. The percentages by group were as follows: al Qaeda 0 percent, Palestinians 5 percent, Hezbollah 16 percent, Tamil Tigers 20 percent, Chechens 60 percent, and PKK 71 percent. Pape attributes the lower percentages for first three groups to the tendency for Islamic fundamentalists to discourage females from participating as warriors.

The 48 women suicide terrorists studied were significantly older than the 213 men in the survey. More than 60 percent of the men were in the 19–23 age group and about 25 percent were at least 24 years of age, whereas only 40 percent of the women were in the 19–23 group and nearly half were at least 24 years old.

Theories of Aggression and Terrorism

As with crime, other biological characteristics may well be associated with terrorist behavior, such as prenatal and neonatal health, brain chemistry, glandular health, and the functioning of the autonomic nervous system, but such links to terrorism have been neither well documented nor empirically validated.

Although there are basic similarities between the characteristics of terrorists and of street criminals, there are also some noteworthy differences, primarily related to nurturance factors. Terrorists tend to be better educated and better off financially in their respective societies than street criminals are in ours (Pape, 2005; Sageman, 2004). In this regard, terrorists roughly resemble a hybrid between street offenders and white-collar offenders. Women who engage in terrorism are also different from those who engage in conventional crime. They are more inclined to act as suicide bombers than as violent street criminals, for a variety of reasons: detonating a bomb does not require the same degree of physical size and strength as, say, a mugging on the street; women can get close to targets often without receiving the same degree of scrutiny as men; and they may be more inclined to see themselves as martyrs willing to sacrifice themselves for a cause than to see themselves merely as self-interested criminals.

Although terrorism is dominated by men, women do play a role as suicide terrorists. Women committed to terrorist acts are particularly dangerous because they tend to be regarded as less serious security threats and hence can often make their way more readily to vulnerable targets. One of the more notorious such cases was the 1991 suicide bombing and assassination of the former Prime Minister of India, Rajiv Gandhi, an act committed by a Tamil woman, Thenmuli Rajaratnam, known simply as "Dhanu." Some of the most puzzling cases of terrorism by women are those involving mothers – suicide bombers who had children when they committed their acts. If there is a fundamental difference between men and women regarding motives for participation in suicide bombing, it is that women are more inclined to sacrifice themselves as an act of personal revenge for the loss of a loved one or to absolve themselves from shame, whereas men are more likely to be motivated by religious or political fanaticism (Bloom, 2005). The next chapter explores these issues more fully.

One final thought about the nature–nurture issue. An ongoing debate among scholars interested in the study of aggression centers on the question, Why fuss over the importance of nature as a source of aggression if nothing can be done about it? The usual answer to this question focuses on *interactions* between nature factors and interventions: it is valuable to know how specific interventions at our disposal vary in their effectiveness for reducing aggressive behaviors across different types of populations. With regard to terrorism, the pertinent question moves up to a higher level: Why fuss over the importance of factors that pertain to the individual if terrorism policy operates at the federal level? One answer to this question is that terrorism can be home-grown – a serious crime and a local matter – and at least to this extent it is as valuable to know how specific interventions at our disposal to prevent domestic terrorism vary in their effectiveness as it is to know about interactions between nature and crime prevention interventions. This information might benefit all nations interested in reducing terrorism and its export.

C. Normlessness and Alienation

One of the first criminological explanations emphasizing the nurture perspective is the idea that aggression is rooted in the absence of norms, a framework established largely by Emile Durkheim. Durkheim's pioneering late nineteenth-century research on suicide concluded that suicide was closely associated with *anomie* or normlessness (1895/1951). Durkheim's research inspired Robert Merton (1938) and others to expand our understanding of the forces that cause alienation, perhaps foremost of which are unrealistic expectations faced by people with limited opportunities for improvement in their condition.[1] One of the primary sources of alienation is *social disorganization*, the absence of coherent regulatory agents in a community or society. Disorganized or noncohesive settings tend to lack informal social control mechanisms; they are common breeding grounds for patterns of widespread misbehavior (Bursik, 1988).

The relevance of this theory to terrorism has been observed by Akbar Ahmed (2003, 2007), Marc Sageman (2004), and Cass Sunstein (2003a), among others. Alienation is almost surely spawned by the accessibility of modern communication technologies that draw attention to the gap between rich and poor, and to offensive aspects of Western culture. There can be little doubt that the rapid expansion of terrorism in recent years derives at least in part from access to media presentations that were previously unavailable to nations with high rates of poverty and illiteracy. Alienation may be no less the product of programs of indoctrination in poor, predominantly illiterate nations in which the support of ideologically driven outsiders has filled the void. A prominent example is the spread of madrassas (religious schools) in Pakistan and Afghanistan in the latter half of the twentieth century, created and financed by wealthy Muslims, especially from Saudi Arabia and neighboring oil-rich countries. There has been no clearly established empirical link between the growth of madrassas and terrorism, but the deep influence of Wahhabi doctrine in these schools appears to have had anything but a peaceful influence on the populations in which they have been introduced (Pape, 2005; L. Wright, 2006a). A similar, if less publicized, influence appears to have occurred in South Asia. Robert Pape documents the support, at least until 2005, that Marxist-Hindu groups gave to Tamil suicide bombers in Sri Lanka.

The problem of alienation is by no means restricted to the Middle East, South Asia, and Indonesia. Millions of Muslims migrated to Europe during the latter half of the twentieth century looking for jobs and an escape from tyranny, persecution, and poverty. Especially large numbers of North African Muslims emigrated to France, South Asians to Britain, and Turks to Germany. Although most Muslims led quiet, pious lives in their new homes, others were drawn to extremist indoctrinations preached in local mosques. Most Muslims in Europe, including second- and third-generation Muslim Europeans, identify first and foremost with their Islamic affiliation, rather than with their nationality as British, French, or German (Kohut and Stokes, 2006; Sullivan and Partlow, 2006). By the end of the century, the extremist factions made themselves quite visible, and in the years following the 9/11 attack, calamitous acts of terrorism and rioting by these factions occurred in Britain, Spain, France, and elsewhere. The violence was clearly a product of disenchantment and alienation that emanated from a toxic brew that combined social isolation, substantially higher unemployment rates for Muslims than for mainstream society, radical indoctrination, and governmental neglect (Bawer, 2005; Kepel, 2005; Leiken, 2005; Roy, 2004; Sullivan and Partlow, 2006).

Viable opportunities to intervene against deep-seated sources of terrorism by reducing alienation may be available, primarily in the form of policies aimed at education, poverty reduction, and the elimination of extremism and intolerance, both cultural and religious (Ahmed and Forst, 2005; Tolson, 2005). Such interventions will be more likely to succeed when the hysteria surrounding these problems and their manifestation as occasional acts of terrorism can be better managed (Walker, 2006). These interventions are generally regarded as public sector responsibilities, but private sector, international and local nongovernmental organizations, and faith-based institutions are often better situated to act to reduce these sources of alienation than are governments. Perhaps a silver lining in the dark cloud of 9/11 and the rise of terrorism is that they may serve to stimulate policies and direct resources to improve the education and economic well-being of people who have long suffered from poverty, illiteracy, and associated factors that diminish the quality of life.

D. Strain and Deprivation Theories

First cousins of Durkheim's theory of anomie and normlessness are theories about the effects of strain and deprivation on behavior. According to the strain-deprivation theories of criminology, people are more inclined to commit crime when they feel poor, socially stigmatized, or otherwise frustrated with their situation. The frustration derives typically from an awareness that they are not as well off as people in higher social and economic classes in the society and that pulling themselves up from poverty to a satisfactory status, if at all possible through legitimate pursuits, would involve considerably more struggle and further frustration than are bearable. Strain theory grows out of the ancient idea that, in the words of Aristotle, "poverty engenders rebellion and crime" (quoted by Quinney, 1970). It emanates more directly from Merton's 1930s theory of anomie and its emphasis on widely shared goals combined with unequal opportunities. This theory was developed more fully in the 1950s and '60s, with the idea that individual hostilities become mutually enforced and stimulated through associations with like-minded peers, especially in areas with limited opportunities for legitimate alternatives to participation in criminal activities (Cloward and Ohlin, 1960; A. Cohen, 1955).

Has poverty, in fact, been found to be associated with terrorism? The evidence is mixed. On the one hand, al Qaeda's well-documented recruitment of poor young men from throughout the Middle East to blow up people in Shi'ite mosques and public places in Iraq in the name of holy war certainly provides ample support to the theory that poverty is behind terrorism. On the other hand, the fact that the nineteen terrorists who participated in the 9/11 attack were predominantly from middle-class families stands as compelling anecdotal counterevidence. More generally, the vast majority of known terrorists are from poor countries, but impoverished, illiterate, and disease-ridden nations have produced relatively few terrorists.

Several studies provide more systematic evidence suggesting that suicide bombers tend to be among the more well off and better educated members of the populations from which they come (Barro, 2002; Krueger, 2007). Pape's (2005) study of more than 450 suicide terrorists indicates that terrorists are significantly more likely to come from middle- and upper-class families. Evidence consistent with Pape's findings has been reported by Alberto Abadie (2004), who finds that terrorism is driven primarily by a country's level of political freedom rather than by its level of poverty. Similarly, Sageman's (2004) study of 172 jihadist terrorists provides support for the idea that alienation is behind terrorism, but that much of the alienation is experienced by educated middle- and upper-class people, predominantly men, deriving from their inability to get the sort of jobs they feel they deserve, and is encouraged primarily by the social bonds created with other middle-class alienated young men. Alan Krueger and Jitka Maleckova's (2003) study of 129 members of Hezbollah who died in action in the Middle East from 1982 to 1994 found that the terrorists were better educated and less impoverished than Lebanese of comparable age and regional origin. Charles Russell and Bowman Miller (1983) studied eighteen non-Muslim revolutionary groups, including the Japanese Red Army, Germany's Baader-Meinhof Gang, and Italy's Red Brigades, and found the vast majority to be well educated, with about two-thirds having some university education and coming from the middle or upper classes in their respective homelands. And Victor Davis Hanson (2005b) notes that oil money from Saudi Arabia has been used to finance Wahhabi mosques and madrassas all over the world, as has oil money from Iran to prop up Hezbollah and from Saddam Hussein's Iraq to support mayhem in Iraq and elsewhere in the region.

French scholar Gilles Kepel concludes that today's militant global jihadis are not so much poor Third Worlders as they are "the privileged children of an unlikely marriage between Wahhabism and Silicon Valley, which al-Zawahiri visited in the 1990s. They were heirs not only to jihad and the *ummah* but also to the electronic revolution and American-style globalization (Kepel, 2005, p. 112)."[2]

The evidence, in short, suggests that the most serious acts of terrorism tend to be committed by people who have access to resources that are not readily available to other terrorists, and they are conducted in places that are inaccessible to others. Terrorist acts carried out in the Middle East and other poor places may be committed predominantly by poor young men, but even in those cases there is little evidence that they are poorer than the mainstream of young people in the region.

This does not mean that poverty cannot be a motivator for the alienation that leads to terrorism. Nor does it mean that strain, regardless of whether it is related to poverty, is not a source of terrorism. Strain theory was originally conceived as an explanation for crime related to frustration arising primarily from poverty, but a *general strain theory* (GST) has evolved that focuses on crime that arises from stressors that may have nothing to do with poverty. Robert Agnew, a leading proponent of GST, argues that people engage in crime and delinquency primarily because of negative treatment by others, and the effect of that negative treatment tends to be cumulative. They become upset and experience a range of emotions from frustration to anger and depression. Criminal acts serve as a coping mechanism that reduces or provides an escape from the strains.

Agnew elaborates by describing three types of strain: strain associated with the loss of something valued (property or a loved one), strain associated with disrespect or physical abuse, and strain associated with the blockage of valued goals or thwarting of intentions (Agnew, 1992, p. 50; 2005, p. 26). Each of these three sources of strain may apply as well to an individual's terrorist acts, and one may be a more common source than the other two in particular circumstances. Many suicide bombings have been accompanied by videotapes of the bombers explaining their acts beforehand, and these explanations often include stories of the loss of a loved one or loved ones at the hands of people associated, however loosely, with those about to be attacked. The bombers often characterize their acts as "revenge killings," but it may be more precise and valid to describe them as the product of a mixture of stress and anger associated with loss, perhaps accompanied by other motives such as martyrdom and loyalty. Agnew goes on to say that, although the strains are typically experienced directly, they may instead be either vicarious or anticipated. The crimes that result are a manifestation of the individual's mechanism for coping with the strain. They provide temporary relief through a medium more accessible than legitimate activity, giving a momentary feeling of power and the opportunity to express rage, release built-up negative emotion, and exact revenge.

Strain theory has been validated empirically as arising from stresses on both the communal and personal levels, such as stressful personal events and events occurring in the community, failures to achieve important personal goals or specific obstacles blocking the attainment of those valued goals, and the presence of despised people, extremely unpleasant circumstances, or conflict (Aseltine, Gore and Gordon, 2000; Mazerolle and Piquero, 1998; Paternoster and Mazerolle, 1994). Although this research has focused on conventional crimes, these stresses can quite clearly be the source of episodes of terrorism.

E. Routine Activities Theory

In addition to interventions designed and implemented to deal with deep-seated sources of terrorism, we should allocate resources and develop policies to track and prevent willing terrorists from doing damage and to protect the targets of terrorism. For these efforts, the routine activities theory is particularly relevant.

According to *routine activities theory*, developed by Lawrence Cohen and Marcus Felson in 1979, crimes are the product of three essential components: motivated offenders, suitable targets, and the absence of capable guardians to protect the targets. Much as heat, oxygen, and fuel are all required to produce fire, crime requires all three essential components of crime. The routine patterns of work and leisure influence the convergence of these three components in time and place, and motivated, rational offenders are inclined to seize opportunities presented by such patterns. (It is no coincidence that the theory is alternately referred to as *"opportunity theory."*) This theory has particular significance for the development of situational controls for the prevention of crime through a more purposeful application of guardianship resources.

Criminologists and crime prevention specialists typically discuss routine activities theory in the context of street crimes – it has obvious implications for the prevention of crimes through the use of bullet-proof shields and other forms of target hardening for convenience stores and banks, burglar alarm and surveillance systems for commercial establishments and homes when occupants are not present, an increase in the intensity of guardianship at peak crime times and places, and so on. But the theory may be no less applicable to homeland security strategies. Federal buildings have been made less accessible to street bomb attacks following Timothy McVeigh's 1995 bombing of the Murrah Federal Building in Oklahoma City, and major monuments, bridges, buildings, and other sites in the United States that are known to have been targeted by jihadist terrorists have been similarly "hardened." Enhanced airport security systems and the surveillance of persons with known militant extremist inclinations are also consistent with prevention strategies that grow logically out of routine activities theory. James Fallows, in a 2005 *Atlantic* article, argues that we could do much better along these lines than we have to secure the homeland against terrorist threats. Routine activities theory could help in the development of a system of weights to assign to the allocation of scarce screening and surveillance resources, so as to maximize their effectiveness.

The theory of routine activities brings good news: as with fire control, the absence of just *any one* of three elements will prevent a harmful event. Diligence in tracking willing offenders, hardening targets, and creating guardianship has made it considerably more difficult to commit terrorist acts in the United States than before 9/11. It may be no coincidence that there has not been a serious terrorist act for several years.

But the news is not all good. First, the gains from diligence in moving aggressively along all three fronts have come at a considerable expense to individual freedoms and economic well-being. Actions against prospective offenders have alienated countless people both at home and abroad, quite possibly creating many more willing offenders in the name of homeland security. And actions to protect vulnerable targets, create guardians, and engage in other aspects of the war on terror have displaced resources from other productive uses in amounts that reach the trillions of dollars (Belasco, 2008; Stiglitz and Bilmes, 2008).

More fundamentally, however, the numbers of attractive targets and motivated offenders are too large, and the availability of guardianship resources too limited, to offer realistic assurance that serious terrorist events will not be committed on U.S. soil. Under the law of large numbers, a 99.9 percent success rate assures that, over many thousands of opportunities, terrorists will eventually succeed now and then. As Richard Posner (2004) observes, "There is no way the government can survey the entire range of possible disasters and act to prevent each and every one of them." We must prepare ourselves, both physically and emotionally, for the inevitability of such events. Failure to do so will add immeasurably to the immediate harm caused by such attacks.

F. Gangs, Territory, and Honor

If a routine activities approach to prevention is to succeed, it must recognize that many, if not most, acts of terrorism are committed by terrorists operating in small cells. In settings in which these cells resemble gangs, gang intervention strategies become increasingly relevant to the prevention of terrorism. One has only to compare photographs of members of Hamas or Hezbollah with those of ethnic urban gangs in the United States to see obvious parallels: young males with menacing glares in hostile poses, holding weapons, invoking ritual symbols, and so on. The similarities extend beyond what is apparent in these photographs to include secrecy, a deep sense of honor and loyalty, severe punishments for violations of group codes, engagement in criminal activities to provide support, flaunting of formal and informal civil authority, alienation from elders, and hostility with rival groups, among others.

The tendency for young men to bond through aggressive activity in order to establish social legitimacy has been well established by anthropologists (Peterson and Wrangham, 1997; Tiger, 1969). One of the seductions offered by both gangs and terrorist cells is the personal validation that often derives from the intense camaraderie generated by such involvements. These bonds tend to be particularly close in the most dangerous and elusive terrorist groups. The most lethal acts of terrorism require unconditional loyalty among the members and tenacious commitment to a cause, if the terrorists are to evade detection and ensure success of the mission. Suicide bombers need associates to receive training and supplies, but it is their zeal, typically fueled by comrades, that induces them to strap on suicide vests or drive cars on suicide missions. Lone-wolf suicide bombers are fairly rare (Pape, 2005; Stern, 2003).

Effective gang intervention strategies vary depending on the nature of the gang. Entrepreneurial gangs tend to be smaller and more hierarchical, calling for intervention strategies that focus on disruption of the markets in which the gangs operate, intensive surveillance, and disruption of the gang hierarchies. Strategies for ending waves of crimes caused by territorial gangs include bridge-building to informal social control agents and networks in the neighborhood, the creation of athletic and recreational opportunities to rechannel youth activity, and community policing interventions that bring the police closer to families and communities to solve problems before they escalate into crimes (Huff, 1996).

Many criminologists who specialize in gangs are loathe to apply what is known about street gangs to terrorists, and for good reason: interventions

Menacing poses: U.S. and Palestinian gangs.

that have been found to be effective for street gangs may have limited relevance to terrorist cells. Street gangs tend to be more materially motivated; they rarely have strong political agendas or are driven by profound religious visions. That said, it would be a serious error to overlook strategies that are relevant to both street gangs and terrorist cells. Intervention strategies that focus on surveillance – through wiretaps, cell phone intercepts, blog monitoring, and e-mail messages – and on the disruption of sources of illicit income that support gang violence could be particularly useful and relevant, especially for terrorist cells that are known to finance their operations through such activities. Network analysis, which can help clarify the relationships among individuals and groups generally, has proven to be an increasingly useful approach to understanding the dynamics of specific gangs and could have relevance as well to the understanding of relationships among members of terrorist cells and groups (Rosenfeld, White and Phillips, 2003). Longer term approaches that remove the sources of alienation that drive young people to commit terrorist acts of the sort perpetrated in London, Madrid, and elsewhere may be even more pertinent.

Marc Sageman (2004) argues that terrorist groups are much like gangs in that they emerge spontaneously from below, rather than through a "top-down" recruiting approach. Terrorist cells – "bunches of guys" – often evolve from friendships and kinships, and the seeds of terrorism germinate as some members of a cell influence the thinking of the others. A former CIA spy recruiter and authority on al Qaeda, Sageman finds that the existence of social bonds among alienated young men who happen to be Muslim has considerably more explanatory power in understanding jihadist violence than do poverty, religious belief, or political frustration. These young men enjoy a sense of clandestine belonging. The cells become effective instruments of terrorism "through mutual emotional and social support, development of a common identity, and encouragement to adopt a new faith." Sageman finds these internal group ties to be more powerful than external factors "such as common hatred for an outside group." Because participation in these associations is more fraternal than deeply ideological, the members are more likely eventually to become more receptive to positive Western influences than their parents and grandparents were (Ignatius, 2006e).

Sageman's analysis has some potentially useful implications for prevention. He argues that secular Arab governments have used peaceful Muslim political movements to undermine the popular support enjoyed by jihadists, much like socialist and democratic communist parties in Europe helped isolate Soviet-supported communists and radical Marxist cells. The United States and other Western nations might do well to consider using similar strategies wherever applicable. Such an approach has in fact been used successfully by European colonial administrations in the Middle East. This approach could be considerably more effective than political displays of toughness in the "war on terror" and aggressively prosecuting – thus alienating – people who might otherwise be persuaded to provide useful information about the sources of support to terrorism, as was done, for example, in the case of the Lackawanna Six in upstate New York in 2002.

Another approach to the problem of terrorist cells is suggested by political scientist Quintan Wiktorowicz. His book, *Radical Islam Rising: Muslim Extremism in the West* (2005), documents a case study in which Wiktorowicz embedded himself with al-Muhajiroun, a London-based extremist Salafist group. The group indoctrinated impressionable, directionless young Muslims, feeding them ideas aimed to transform them from passive bystanders into warriors in the fiery cause of battle against nonbelievers. Wiktorowics observes that successful intervention against such seductive dogma requires the same sort of intense deprogramming that has been used to wean converts away from modern cults in other societies; these young Muslims must be persuaded that Islam is rooted in notions of peace and harmony and is not a fundamentally hostile faith.

Can such deprogramming succeed? To have some chance for success, it is important that those doing the deprogramming understand the group dynamics at work. Members of terrorist cells have been described as driven, fiercely loyal, cohesive, and unyielding – qualities that do not lend themselves readily to rapid transformation (Crenshaw, 1998; Martin, 2006; Post, 1998). Deprogramming is more likely to work when applied to groups of individuals who are still young and malleable, before their indoctrination and experiences have hardened them.

Some go further in drawing parallels between street gangs and terrorist cells, suggesting that urban gangs may yet transform themselves into organized crime and terrorist networks that are hybrids of entrepreneurial gangs and terrorist cells. Tony Corn (2006), for example, characterizes the November 2005 Parisian intifada as a "dress rehearsal" for such a development. John P. Sullivan (2002) and Max Manwaring (2005) see the arrival of "third-generation gangs," following a first generation of turf gangs and English soccer hooligans, and a second generation of entrepreneurial drug gangs. Sullivan regards the Bloods, Crips, and El Rukn gangs in the United States; the Medellin and Cali cartels in Colombia; and Russian "mafiyas" as forerunners of third-generation urban gangs. Manwaring focuses more on the insurgent means and government-overthrow aims of the new groups. Both authorities see these burgeoning organizations trafficking in drugs, weapons, and other contraband items and becoming more organized, politicized, sophisticated, mercenary, and international, operating largely through communication and information network technologies that had not been widely available before the twenty-first century.

Regardless of the precise nature of these new hybrid gangs, how pervasive they are, and the actual threats of violence against innocent people they pose, one aspect of successful gang intervention policy is clearly pertinent to the prevention of terrorism by Sageman's "bunches of guys" doing bad things: there is no magic bullet, no single strategy that can be effective across the board. Finn-Aage Esbensen (2000) observes that the complexity of circumstances that lead to gangs doing violent acts does not lead readily to cookie-cutter solutions. Dealing effectively with these groups is likely to require comprehensive strategies that incorporate a variety of creative approaches targeting individuals and peer groups, as well as forging positive relationships with families and entire communities. Each of these entities typically contributes in varying degrees to the problem, and each can contribute no less to the solution.

To prevent serious acts of terrorism by groups, it will be essential in the short term to use effective means of surveillance – including both human and technological intelligence – together with the protection of known targets. These efforts should include activities to develop and maintain the support of, and coordination with, informal social control institutions and networks in the immediate community and from wherever else these groups receive help. For the long term, the most effective strategy is likely to be one that removes the sources of alienation that drive young people to gangs and terrorist cells in the first place. To succeed, such a strategy is likely to require a concerted program aimed at winning the hearts and minds of the community at large – including parents, teachers, religious leaders, and ordinary citizens – so that the public is more inclined to support the police and other formal institutional mechanisms for controlling illegitimate behavior and less inclined to view official authorities as aliens invading and disrupting the community (Akerlof and Yellin, 1994). Law enforcement officials alone cannot successfully prevent terrorism by small, organized groups. The support of the community is needed too, and it does not come automatically. It must be earned.

G. Strategic and Psychological Motives

The growth of terrorism may be related to the political agendas and strategic views of the leaders and the psychological motives of their followers. Suicide bombers are widely presumed to be psychologically disturbed and their leaders deranged. How, after all, could a well-adjusted person do or direct such an act? Many such terrorists may, indeed, be troubled souls, and all reveal themselves to be fanatical in the extreme, but there is both a logic and a method to the madness.

1. Motives of Leaders and Followers

As noted in Chapter 1, one important feature of terrorism is its use of asymmetric violence against soft targets. Because terrorists typically lack the resources and training required to wage conventional warfare against

35

strong, endowed adversaries, they circumvent superior military and police powers by striking at vulnerable targets, typically using available low- or medium-technology, high-explosive devices. The selection of large concentrations of innocents as primary targets violates conventional rules of military engagement and norms of civil society. However, when no viable short-term alternatives present themselves, it becomes a logical option to achieve one's political goal by targeting ordinary citizens and characterizing them as culpable members of the enemy, disregarding social mores and military conventions; the goal then is to intimidate and confuse a target population, often provoking them to react badly, either ineptly or by overreacting, or both. The challenge of the terrorist leaders is to find ways of attracting people to carry out the attacks. How do the leaders enlist others in such a dangerous and morally corrupt cause?

To provide a justification for the attacks and thus gain the support of followers along the way, it is essential first for terrorist leaders to claim legitimacy for such acts. That the acts are regarded as illegitimate and inhumane by a stronger adversary and its allies becomes irrelevant. The basic rationale of terrorist organizations is that means regarded by some as inhumane or "dirty" are often required to achieve a worthy end: to rid the landscape of an evil enemy, who threatens our "correct" way of life and our very well-being. This requires leaders with enough charisma to attract followers by persuading them that the targets are dangerous and less than human – and then to convince them to persist in the engagement with a strategic sense of the importance of staying the course; leaders must also have enough practical sense to be able to provide tactical guidance on how to carry out the missions. Terrorist organizations also require followers who are sufficiently alienated and malleable to sacrifice themselves in the cause, either through suicide attacks or missions that expose them to grave risks.

2. Rationality and Culture

The 9/11 attacks were possible because the aviation security system that prevailed until 2001 was based on the assumption that rational people would not hijack a jet airplane and be willing to blow themselves up in some cause, however "holy" or politically worthwhile. The assumption was, of course, incorrect, and it was made despite the fact that the idea was not totally without precedent: the United States had, after all, learned nearly sixty years earlier that young Japanese pilots were willing to sacrifice themselves in what they too regarded as a heroic venture in the name of a noble cause.

Yet, terrorists' motives and behaviors are all perfectly logical and rational when considered in the context of accomplishing a mission, even if suicide bombing and other risky ways of killing civilians violate most conventional standards of rational behavior. To fully grasp the rationality of terrorists, it is important first to understand our own perspective on rational thinking and behavior. It has been difficult for the West to accept terrorist acts as rational for a variety of reasons. Perhaps the most significant is an insularity that has been largely invisible to the insulated. During their lifetimes and prior to 9/11, most people in the United States and Europe had not witnessed mayhem on a large scale on their home soil. Terrorism is shocking because it is unfamiliar, something that happened only long ago or in far-away places. The United States, in particular, has been protected by two vast oceans and a system of national defense that had for centuries been virtually impenetrable.

Our own notions of rationality have thus been shielded by both physical and psychic distance from competing notions derived from other value systems. We have come to think of our ideas about rationality as universal rather than unique to our culture, and to a very large extent have succeeded in exporting these ideas to others and persuading people in many corners of the world of the superiority of this value system. Post-Enlightenment notions of rationality have served the West quite well for centuries, but – leaving aside for the moment the prospect that the logic of terrorism, if not the ethics of it, may in fact be consistent with our own notions of rationality – our system is in fact not the only framework of rational thought.

The notion of terrorism as irrational derives further from the widespread perception that suicide bombers and their supporters are lunatics, driven by mad, evil forces and caught up in mindless, fist-shaking rage. Photographic and videotaped images of crowds of enraged men and women and beheadings of hostages serve to deepen this perception of the madness, depravity, and irrationality of a distant other. The West is told again and again that the suicide bombers are young unmarried men driven by promises of seventy-two virgins in paradise, yet Sageman (2004) and others find this account to be misleading: many of the suicide bombers are married, and some are women. Jessica Stern (2003) further undermines the notion that suicide terrorists are irrational. Based on four years's worth of extensive interviews with militant jihadists and non-Muslim religious terrorists alike, she has found that the followers are, by and large, disenfranchised souls caught up in moral fervor, but not psychologically disturbed within the context of their environment. The idea of a high holy calling that gives the disenfranchised an opportunity to achieve martyrdom in a flash of exalted glory, if not limitless sex with virgins, makes some sense, given the limited range of legitimate alternatives and resulting sense of hopelessness these people tend to experience.

Terrorists and their supporters may be seriously uninformed, misguided, and deluded about essential facts, conducting themselves in ways that make them seem crazed by conventional Western standards, but this does not mean that they are irrational. They appear, rather, to be following both an individual and a collective means-ends rationale in a manner that adapts quite well to the means available to them (Benmelech and Berrebi, 2007; Iannaccone,

2006). Western expressions of wishes for freedom and democracy for the subjects of autocratic rule, however well intended, combined with images of extraordinary affluence in the West and lack of respect for non-Western cultures, may offer more frustration than promise, especially when those receiving the messages have no direct personal experience of freedom or democracy and little credible hope of having either. Western military intrusions into Islam lands, in the name of countering and punishing terrorism, can add defiance to the frustration (Crenshaw, 2002; LaFree, 2007). Although the rage that follows often manifests in ways that are indecent, immoral, and unacceptable under Western and non-Western systems of ethics alike, it is not irrational (Lewis, 1990).

The rage underlying terrorism may or may not be regarded as rational by conventional Western systems of psychology and norms of behavior, but most terrorists would not be qualified as clinically psychopathic. It has been discussed above that terrorists are not unusual within the societies from which they come. They are typically neither less educated nor less financially well off than their peers, and they do not appear generally to be psychologically maladjusted. According to Jerrold Post, a renowned political psychologist, research on the psychopathology of terrorists indicates that "the family backgrounds of terrorists do not differ strikingly from the backgrounds of their politically active counterparts" (Post, 1998, p. 9). Engagement in terrorism can thus provide an exciting channel for ordinary alienated youths to experience group cohesion and build self-esteem; it may give the weak an opportunity to feel strong. Terrorist leaders may have megalomaniacal designs, but their followers do not appear to be particularly unusual.

The 9/11 attackers have been likened to the Japanese kamikaze pilots; although they were better educated than most of their contemporaries, they were more like soldiers in a cause designed to give purpose to their lives than brainwashed zombies or psychopaths (Dyson, 2006; Sageman, 2004). They have been likened, similarly, to household members who place the welfare of the family above their own individual welfare (Enders and Sandler, 2006). Clearly, the idea of rational behavior is incomplete if it ignores the individual's willingness to subordinate his or her own personal well-being to that of the community. Although such inclinations may be stronger in some cultures than others, they are found in all societies. The ultimate sacrifice of self for the community or culture is regarded as "heroism" and awarded a position of honor in most societies.

3. Rationality, Passion, and Shame

The 2005 bombing of a wedding party at a hotel in Amman, Jordan, provides a lesson in the logic of winning and losing hearts and minds, and the tension between the passions and rational thinking of terrorists. After the U.S.-led invasion of Iraq in March 2003, Abu Musa al-Zarqawi, who directed the attack in Amman, had experienced strong and growing popularity and increased enlistments of radical Muslims from throughout the region as al Qaeda's supreme commander on the ground in the terrorist operations in the Middle East (see Chapter 6 for a profile of Zarqawi). Zarqawi directed his campaign against U.S. forces and Iraqis trying to rebuild civil society, his recruitments fueled by the growing unpopularity of the United States. Although much of the insurgency against the United States in Iraq was indigenous, originating with native Sunni and Shi'ite Iraqi militia groups opposed to U.S. occupation of their communities and perceiving that the United States favored the wrong Iraqi factions, Zarqawi's ability to import Muslims to engage in "freedom fighting" activities against the United States and Iraqis who supported the U.S. "puppet" government was fed by the popular view that the United States was engaged in a holy war against Islam; this perception gained force following the Abu Ghraib torture exposé, a "recruitment poster" for Zarqawi's mission in Iraq. Zarqawi, a Jordanian, was known to despise the Jordanian government and was hoping to create the same sort of breakdown of order in Jordan as he had in neighboring Iraq. But when he directed the bombing of the wedding party, he seriously miscalculated, creating considerably more backlash than support for his cause. The Jordanian people rose up in large numbers to express their sense of outrage at Zarqawi's latest attack, and Jordan emerged as a closer ally to the United States in the months that followed (Solomon, 2006).

The turnaround in Zarqawi's popularity is consistent with another counterterrorism intervention that has proven successful in dealing with crime: *shaming*. Shaming is an ancient solution to the problem of crime, revived by John Braithwaite in the late 1980s. The concept derives from people's moral sense, their natural inclination to be accepted by people around them (J. Wilson, 1993), and their rational expectation that they are likely to be more well off when they are accepted socially. Braithwaite (1989) maintains that social cohesion is created informally through people's desire to fit in and not be social outcasts. Social stigmatization has deterrent power, and gossip is a basic medium for achieving social cohesion. In addition, Braithwaite holds, consistent with strain theory, that this cohesion reduces crime and that it does so most effectively when offenders feel genuine regret for the harms done to others associated with their acts. Shaming may be useful as well in countering the forces that induce young people to participate in terrorism. It may be used as a tool of public policy, but to be effective it must appeal to people locally and at the smallest and closest levels of social relationship – family and peers – who can serve effectively as shaming forces.

4. Rationality and Deterrence

The rationality of most people also provides the basis for one of the most fundamental of all justifications for imposing sanctions for misbehavior: *deterrence*. The deterrent effect of sanctions, invoked either publicly or privately, derives from the rational expectation that if one misbehaves, authorities may respond in ways that will make one regret the misbehavior. The effect can occur in either or both of two ways. Under *general deterrence*, one is discouraged from misbehaving because of the threat of sanctions that may be imposed, even if one has never experienced the sanction before. Under *individual* or *special deterrence*, one is discouraged from misbehaving because one has previously experienced the sanction and wishes not to repeat the experience. Implicit in both types of deterrence is an understanding that people will gauge their behaviors in accordance with a rational calculus that compares the expected benefit of the misbehavior with the expected cost of the sanction.

Can deterrence be an effective tool against terrorism? Yes, but it can also backfire if not used prudently. The English utilitarian Jeremy Bentham (1830) wrote that punishments can be too small and not achieve the desired effect, but they can also be too large, causing a sense of injustice and a defiant backlash against authority (see also Sherman, 1993). Sanctions used in the name of deterrence can thus create precisely the opposite effect. The key is proportionality: to be effective, the sanction must be widely perceived as proportional to the misbehavior. If it is widely perceived as disproportionate, it can create not only a counter-deterrent effect but also much deeper harms by undermining the legitimacy of the authority imposing the sanction.

The rationality of terrorists has been underestimated, but so too has the intensity of their passion. The West need not abandon its systems of rationality and social control that took so long to develop and that have served both the West and others well over the centuries. At the same time, however, we should be clear that serious problems can follow if the West projects its own notions of rationality on others – following archaic patterns of colonialism and imperialism – without first testing the water to learn about the cultures and deeply held traditions of others. We might, instead, keep our own views of rational behavior in perspective and avoid regarding them as universal and other systems as irrational or foolish, not only out of a sense of humility and respect for others but also in the interest of rational self-protection.

H. Other Theories of Aggression

Other theories of aggression and crime, such as biological defect theory (Wilson and Herrnstein, 2003; Lombroso, 1876; Raine, 2002) and labeling theory (Tannenbaum, 1938), may be applicable to terrorism, but they appear to have greater relevance to crime and aggression generally. With regard to labeling theory, for example, one could assert that some terrorists have been emboldened by the West's inclination to label people as terrorists; however, it appears that more people have been drawn to terrorism against Western targets in response to the actions of the West than by its use of the term "terrorist" (see Tittle, 2000, for a discussion of these theories).

The explanations for terrorism considered above focus largely on individual terrorists and their motives. The following chapters focus more on macro theories of terrorism, explanations that pertain to the environments that shape the behaviors of individuals: religion and culture, intolerance and the role of the state, globalization, technology, and so on.

I. Do Explanations of Terrorism Lend Legitimacy to It?

We have reviewed the standard definitions of terrorism, considered similarities and differences between terrorism and other forms of aggression – particularly, crime – and discussed the sources of and explanations for an individual's participation in terrorist activities. Terrorism manifests in a variety of ways, and it is important to understand the fundamentally distinct types of terrorism – whether or not politically motivated, whether or not state sanctioned, whether or not closely affiliated with larger organizations, whether manifesting individually or in groups, and so on – and how one set of circumstances that might explain a particular individual's participation in terrorism might not apply to another individual.

Does offering explanations for terrorism lend legitimacy to the cause of terrorists bombing innocent people? No. Does it justify their behavior or shift blame from the terrorists to victims? Not at all. How, then, is it helpful to regard terrorism as having elements of rationality or to suggest that it may have something to do with their weaknesses and our own limitations? The answer is that a better understanding of both the terrorists and victims can enable us to respond more effectively to terrorism. We need not relinquish valid concerns about terrorism or abandon our vigilance against it. Nor should our gaining an understanding of the nature and causes of terrorism come at the expense of our core moral values. Such understanding can help us prevent actions that are a product of our own ignorance and can induce us to engage more purposefully in effective interventions to prevent further acts of terrorism.

This should become increasingly clear as we proceed through successive topics in this book, starting with the history of terrorism, the focus of the next chapter. As we review this material, we will do well to consider Santayana's warning that those who ignore history are condemned to repeat it.

Discussion Questions

1. *Causes of terrorism and crime.* What strikes you as the primary cause or causes of terrorism? Which theories of the causes of crime appear to be most relevant to terrorism? Which ones strike you as least relevant? Why? Do you see any useful policy implications growing out of such inquiry? If so, what are they?

2. *The 9/11 Commission Report.* The preface to the 9/11 Report asks: "How did this happen, and how can we avoid such tragedy again?" Does the report's discussion of al Qaeda appear especially consistent with any of the causes of terrorism suggested in #1? Which one(s)? If none, do you think it might be worthwhile to probe more deeply into the sources of al Qaeda's appeal? How might that be done?

3. *Testing theories of terrorism.* Can you think of ways to subject any of the theories and policy questions raised above to empirical testing? What data would be needed? What threats to the validity of such tests appear to be most serious? How might you minimize those threats? How have Pape, Sageman, Stern, and others who have tested theories of terrorism dealt with these questions?

4. *The conservative view of alienation.* Conservatives often regard alienation as a socially constructed concept that is used too easily as an excuse for immoral behavior. In *The Moral Sense*, James Q. Wilson (1993, p. 3) argues that the concept of alienation has no moral significance without a theory of human nature and that Karl Marx and others who write about alienation offer no such theory. He goes on to identify four elements of the moral sense: sympathy, fairness, self-control, and duty. Does Wilson's criticism apply to Durkheim, Merton, Ahmed, Sunstein and others who use alienation as an explanation for aggression or terrorism? Can you outline a moral justification that might serve to answer Wilson's argument?

THREE

A Brief History of Terrorism

This chapter provides a historical context for the book, showing how terrorism has changed over three major periods: from its origins to the mid-twentieth century, the latter half of the twentieth century, and the emerging post-9/11 era. While the essential nature of terrorism has remained unchanged, many of its manifestations have mutated and adapted in response to some of the same circumstances that have induced and discouraged it.

A. Early Forms of Terrorism: Babylon and Rome, Asia, Europe, and America

Much of the world has become preoccupied with terrorism since September 11, 2001, but the terror dragon has in fact been marauding the planet for many centuries. Let us look at some of the more prominent episodes of terrorism over the past three millennia.

Ancient Era. Acts of violence consistent with most definitions of terrorism are about as old as crime and war. Before the creation of sovereign nation-states, battles among men in defense of their tribes and territories, or to conquer others, often crossed the line to inflict damage on noncombatant populations. Among the earliest recorded such acts were those associated with the conquest of the kingdom of Judah and destruction of temples in Jerusalem by Nebuchadnezzar, ruler of Babylon, in the sixth century BCE (before the Common Era, pre-Christ). The assassinations of Roman emperors – Julius Caesar in 44 BCE, Caligula in 41 CE, Galba in 68 CE, Domitian in

96 CE, Commodus in 193 CE, and others – are often cited as other examples of early acts of terrorism.

Middle Ages. One of the more celebrated terrorists was Genghis Khan the early thirteenth-century military leader who was known for his ruthlessness in assaulting and destroying ethnically diverse enemy tribes in the land that is now Mongolia. Named "Temujin" at birth, he assumed the title *Genghis Khan* ("Universal Ruler") in 1206, while still in his early forties, after his rise to vast power in his Mongol homeland. Although he created unprecedented order there, he developed considerable notoriety for ravaging conquered enemies – first in China and then at fronts to the west. By the time of his death in 1227, his empire extended to Persia, Baghdad, Afghanistan, and much of Eastern Europe.

Much of the same Middle Eastern land conquered by Genghis Khan had been under assault for more than a century by marauders from the west, in the name of Jesus Christ. The Crusades created the model for a parallel cause that would follow centuries later: religious fighters destroying infidels, with high honor bestowed on martyrs who died in the just and noble cause of holy war. A series of nine numbered crusades occurred from the eleventh to the thirteenth centuries, the first involving a massacre of the population in Jerusalem in 1099 and the last initiated in 1271 by the man who would later become King Edward I of England.

Terrorism in Eighteenth- and Nineteenth-Century Europe and America. Given this ancient history of acts that would today be regarded as terrorism, it might come as a surprise that the term "terrorism" was coined only slightly more than 200 years ago. As noted in Chapter 1, the term has been widely attributed to Edmund Burke's coining of the expression "reign of terror," which referred to brutal acts committed during the French Revolution, including the beheadings of as many as 40,000 "enemies" by France's radical Jacobin government in 1793–94. Others died of malnutrition, disease, and torture in prison, and still others perished in mass shootings and drownings. For the Jacobin leader, Robespierre, "Terror is nothing but justice, prompt, severe and inflexible."

In much the same way that other terms evolve, sometimes becoming nearly the opposite of their original meaning, the term "terror" is used today by people who see acts of terror as severe and inflexible – about the opposite of Robespierre's usage of terror as a legitimate instrument of justice – and usually as acts done by small groups of individuals rather than by governments.

The shift in Europe from terrorism by the state to terrorism by individuals was stimulated by anarchists, often with socialist agendas, in the mid-nineteenth century. The anarchists started peacefully under the leadership of Pierre Joseph Proudhon (1809–64) in France, but they eventually escalated their activities to attacks on factories and, occasionally, the police and armed forces in France, Germany, and Austria, typically in the name of revolution.

Genghis Khan

In addition to Proudhon in France, underpinnings of the anarchist movement are attributable to Karl Heinzen (1809–80) in Germany, Mikhail Bakunin (1814–76) in Russia, and, perhaps most significantly, Karl Marx (1818–83). Anarchists did not enjoy the widespread support of mainstream European populations; their use of violence made them especially unpopular among the vast majority of the public.

The anarchist movement managed to spill over to the United States with the assassination of President William McKinley in 1901. But acts of terror had in fact occurred on U.S. soil decades earlier. In 1856 John Brown and his men massacred five unarmed citizens at Pottawatomie, Kansas. Brown said the killings had been committed in accordance with "God's will" and that he aimed to "strike terror in the hearts of the proslavery people." His killings provoked fear and reprisals and served to bring the United States closer to civil war (Reynolds, 2005).

Walter Laqueur (2003) identifies two further waves of terrorism in Europe, one in the late nineteenth century in Russia and the other early in the twentieth century in Russia and Ireland. The terrorist attacks in Russia were stimulated by student anarchist unrest during the reign of the czars in the 1870s. The most aggressive of these organizations was the People's Will, led by Nikolai Morozov. The People's Will terrorized all major centers of authority, assassinating government officials, heads of the police and military, and officials of the Orthodox Church. In 1881, they succeeded in assassinating

Maximilien Robespierre

the head of government, Czar Alexander II, in a suicide bombing attack. Alexander's son, Alexander III, responded by arresting and killing leaders of the People's Will, whose remaining members went underground and plotted the unsuccessful 1905 Russian Revolution.

John Brown

Two campaigns of terror followed in Russia a few years later: the "Red Terror" of 1918 and the "White Terror" response that it provoked. The Red Terror was a Bolshevik campaign against counter-revolutionaries during the Russian Civil War. Mass arrests, deportations of suspected enemies of the state, and the deaths of some 10,000 people followed the successful assassination of the Bolshevik head of the secret police, Moisei Uritsky, on August 17, 1918, and the failed attempt thirteen days later to assassinate the top Bolshevik leader, Vladimir Lenin. By 1921, some 70,000 people had been imprisoned by the state, in what would eventually become known as the Gulag system. The White Terror was a failed, but bloody, anti-communist response by supporters of the monarchy that followed the Red Terror. Although the Russian Gulag system continued under Stalin through much of the twentieth century, terrorism by nonstate actors subsided in Russia and elsewhere after World War I.

B. Ethnic and Religious Terrorism in the Twentieth Century

Some of the more prominent examples of ethnic terrorism include the Kurds and Turks in southern and eastern Turkey, the Sunnis and Kurds in Iraq, the Sunnis and Shi'a in Iraq, the Russians and Chechens in the Trans-Caucasus region, the Basques and Spanish nationalists in north central Spain, the Hutus and Tutsis in Rwanda, the English Protestants and Irish Catholics in Northern Ireland, and the Tamils and Sinhalese in Sri Lanka. A very brief description of each of these struggles follows.

1. Turks and Kurds

The Kurdish people reside in a region often referred to as "Kurdistan," an area encompassing southeastern Turkey, northern Iraq, the northeastern tip of Syria, and northwestern parts of Iran. Numbering between 25 and 30 million people, the Kurds share a kinship with ancient Persians and speak a variety of languages that derive from the Farsi, Arabic, Latin, and Cyrillic languages. One distinctive feature of the Kurdish people has given rise to two long-standing struggles with neighboring ethnic people: the Kurds are one of the largest ethnic groups in the world that do not have their own separate identity as a nation. They are by no means a united people – the Kurds in Turkey have had deadly, long-standing disputes with the Kurds of Iraq – but their struggles with ethnic Turks and Iraqis became especially prominent in the latter part of the twentieth century. The Kurdish Workers' Party (PKK) was founded in 1974 to create an independent Kurdistan. Extreme Marxist-leaning factions of the PKK have advocated terrorist attacks to create a break from Turkey, with the goal of eventually creating their own sovereign nation.

However, the PKK has relied heavily on drug smuggling, kidnapping, and thuggery – targeting both Turks and moderate Kurds – and has not won widespread support either from within or outside the Kurdish community.

2. Sunnis and Kurds

The Kurds have had similar problems in Iraq as in Turkey, with much more brutal opposition from Saddam Hussein. In 1988, Saddam destroyed between 3,000 and 5,000 people in the Kurdish village of Halabja with rockets and poison gas. The Iraqi Kurds were emboldened by encouragement from the United States to help overthrow and defeat Saddam's army in the 1991 Gulf War, but a fledgling Kurdish uprising was quickly overwhelmed by Iraqi forces, and the Kurds received no military support from the United States or other coalition forces. Kurdish hopes for sustained independence from Sunni oppressors rose substantially in 2003 with the fall of Saddam.

3. Sunni Arabs and Shi'a

Although Sunnis and Shi'a are primarily religious rather than ethnic groups, significant ethnic, cultural, and political differences have evolved between Sunnis and Shi'a over the centuries. The split began with a disagreement over the question of who should be the proper successor to the Prophet Muhammad. (For a more in-depth discussion of the doctrinal disagreements between Sunnis and Shi'a, see Chapter 5.) This dispute has never been resolved, and Sunnis and Shi'a have grown into separate communities in most of the lands in which they now reside. Today Sunnis make up the vast majority of the world's more than one billion Muslims, outnumbering Shi'a by about four to one. Sunnis are the dominant Muslim population in the world's largest Islamic regions: Indonesia, South Asia, North Africa, and much of the Arabian peninsula. Shi'a live primarily in the countries of Iran, Iraq, Azerbaijan, Bahrain, Lebanon, and Yemen – and Pakistan, much of which was once ancient Persia. Except in Iran and during a few brief interludes elsewhere, the Sunnis have dominated the Shi'a as political rulers, giving the Sunnis a legacy of power and leaving the Shi'a as a marginalized faction, even in places where they were a significant majority of the population, notably Iraq. This has left the Shi'a with a narrative of martyrdom, persecution, and suffering (Nasr, 2005).

The Iranian Revolution in 1979 drove fear into the hearts of many Sunni Muslims in the Middle East. The eight-year war between Iran and Iraq was largely initiated by Iraq's Sunni Ba'athists against Iran's Shi'a to prevent Iran's Grand Ayatollah Khomeini from spreading his influence throughout what was then a more secular, less devoutly Islamic Middle East than exists today. Sunnis had ruled Iraq for generations, despite their constituting less than 25 percent of the Iraqi population. After the fall of Saddam Hussein in 2003, the Sunni minority largely resisted U.S. attempts to create a coalition Iraqi government, in the hopes that somehow they might return to the undiluted power they had experienced since the country's creation in 1920. The February 22, 2006, terrorist bombing of the Al Askari "Golden Shrine" Mosque in Samara, one of Shi'a Islam's holiest sites, set off sectarian violence in and around Baghdad. Thousands of Iraqi Muslims were killed in tit-for-tat terrorist attacks in the following weeks, first involving Shi'ite militias retaliating against Sunni mosques and innocent people, and then Sunni groups launching counterattacks.

Iranian influence has emerged and become stronger throughout the "Shi'ite crescent" – running from Iran through Iraq and down to Lebanon – in the years following the U.S. invasion of Iraq and the fall of Saddam Hussein, as the Shi'a made significant inroads against traditional Sunni rule in much of the Middle East (Nasr, 2005). To the extent that one can make out distinct Sunni and Shi'a blocs across a sea of ethnic and tribal factions that constitute Islam, they are headquartered in Riyadh (Saudi Arabia) and Tehran (Iran), respectively. These centers distribute money accumulated from vast oil resources to support a variety of outreach programs: from fundamentalist Sunni madrassas (religious schools) throughout much of South Asia to welfare programs for families in southern Lebanon and weapons and supplies for Hezbollah. Sunni Arabs are torn today between their distinct identities as Arabs and as members of the traditional ruling majority in struggles against Persians and Shi'a, on the one hand, and as Muslims joined with Shi'a in a more recent struggle against decadent Western influences, on the other. The world watches with great interest to see how these multiple identities and conflicting loyalties will play out, especially as the Iranians continue to advance their development of nuclear technology.

4. Russians and Chechens

Chechnya is a territory about the size of the state of Connecticut, in the Trans-Caucasus region, with a population of just over one million people. The people speak Russian, but are mostly Muslims, having converted to Islam in the fifteenth century when the region was part of the Ottoman Empire. Ethnically, Chechnya is a loosely knit assemblage of more than 100 clans that declared independence from Russia after the fall of the USSR in 1991. Russia rejected the claim, invaded Chechnya in 1994, and then agreed to a ceasefire two years later, after the killing of more than 10,000 Russian soldiers and some 200,000 Chechen citizens. The Russian heavy-handedness had the effect of unifying the previously loose collection of autonomous

Chechen clans. Militant Chechens retaliated by launching suicide bombing strikes against Russian civilians on trains, subways, and elsewhere. The two most serious attacks were against 700 hostages at a theater in Moscow in 2002 and 1,200 at a school in Breslan in 2004, the latter involving the deaths of 330 people, mostly children.

Ethnicity plays a role in the unification of Chechens, but given the history of disconnectedness among the clans that make up Chechen society, their cohesion today is attributable as much to political necessity – aimed at achieving order, increasing defensive effectiveness, and attaining independence from Russia – as to religious or ethnic kinship. The Chechen separatists have been sharply divided over whether their struggle is primarily a secular or Muslim matter. Some militant leaders, such as Shamil Basayev, have sought assistance from al Qaeda and other Islamist organizations, whereas others, such as Aslan Maskhadov (killed by Russian soldiers in 2005), have opposed such help.

5. Basques and Spaniards

Basque separatists are among the oldest groups of ethnic militants who have organized themselves politically to create their own independent state after feeling marginalized and exploited by an alien majority. The Basques are a distinct Roman Catholic ethnic group who make their homeland in the north central part of Spain, near Spain's border with France; they speak their own distinct language – a distant derivative of Latin, with overtones of Spanish, French, and German. The Basque resistance movement organized itself as Euskadi Ta Askatasuna (ETA) – "Basque Fatherland and Liberty" – in 1959, in opposition to the rule of Generalissimo Francisco Franco, who had imposed particularly oppressive rule over the Basques. The Spanish government granted the Basques considerable autonomy in 1979, including their own elected parliament, police force, and school system; the right to tax themselves; and the institution of other social reforms. ETA has nonetheless frequently marginalized itself even among the Basque population by committing desperate acts of terror, including attacks on tourists in Madrid and the bombing of rescue workers.

6. Hutus and Tutsis

Rwanda, a small country in the southern part of central Africa, became one of the fastest growing and most densely populated countries on the continent in the twentieth century. Its cultural roots can be traced back at least to the early fifteenth century, when its several clans were fused into a single kingdom, known as "Abanyiginya." The two dominant clans in twentieth-century Rwanda and neighboring Burundi were the Tutsis, who held political and military superiority, and the Hutus, who were traditionally the spiritual leaders and advisors in the kingdom. Although some ethnic characteristics differentiate the Tutsis from the Hutus, the primary differences are social and economic rather than ethnic: over the centuries, the Tutsis were the feudal overlords, and the Hutus were the subjugated.

The tables turned in 1959, with the emergence of the Hutu nationalist party of the Hutu Emancipation Movement (PARMEHUTU), which killed about 20,000 Tutsis and caused up to 500,000 to flee to neighboring lands. A Tutsi response – the Tutsi Rwandese Patriotic Front (RPF) – was formed in 1985 under the leadership of Paul Kagame. In 1990 RPF forces invaded Rwanda from a base in neighboring Uganda. Then in 1994, two extremist Hutu militia groups carried out a campaign of genocide over a 100-day period, following the assassination of the Rwandan president. More than one million Tutsis and moderate Hutus were slaughtered and raped during this period, the most extensive genocide since the Nazi Holocaust. The RPF eventually restored order, causing the killers to flee to Zaire, now the Democratic Republic of the Congo. Two wars followed in the Congo in the late 1990s.

The absence of an organized response and rescue operation was one of the great failures and controversies that followed this genocide. UN peacekeepers had been stationed in Rwanda, but the United Nations refused to deploy them to confront the militias and to stop the slaughter of innocent, helpless people. President Clinton later called his failure to act "the biggest regret of my administration." In 1998, a UN International Criminal Tribunal for Rwanda (ICTR) indicted several suspected Hutu war criminals and convicted one, an ex-mayor, of war crimes, crimes against humanity, and genocide. No compelling ethical justification has come forth to explain why the West has reacted so much more forcefully to acts of terrorism in Bosnia and the Middle East than to the slaughter of innocents in Rwanda.

7. English Protestants and Irish Catholics

Northern Ireland, located on the northeast tip of the island of Ireland, was constituted by the British Parliament in 1920 under the Government of Ireland Act as one of four components of the United Kingdom. Its population of just under two million is about 45 percent Protestant and 40 percent Catholic, with the other 15 percent mostly undeclared as to religion. Northern Ireland's serious ethnic, religious. and political problems are rooted in the Protestant Reformation and King Henry VIII's split from the Catholic Church in the sixteenth century. Many Irish Catholics with deep ties to the Irish culture rejected the split, and a large minority (the "Greens" or Republicans) prefer to be part of the Republic of Ireland. In contrast, Irish Protestants (the "Orange" Unionists) tend to be more closely related – both genealogically and culturally – to the British and Scots and to feel a kinship with

Great Britain. These cultural differences have created considerable political disharmony over the years.

The ethnic and religious split boiled over into an extended period of sporadic terrorist activities and militia firefights known as the "Troubles" – from 1969 to 1997 – during which time militant Irish Catholics, fighting as paramilitary groups under the umbrella of the Provisional Irish Republican Army (IRA) campaign, aimed to end British rule and make Northern Ireland a part of the Republic of Ireland. The British government responded by professing neutrality and responsibility for maintaining law and order throughout the province of Northern Ireland, while engaging in its own antiterror campaigns involving the British Army, the Royal Ulster Constabulary, and the Ulster Defence Regiment. This official expression of neutrality was betrayed by the events of "Bloody Sunday" – January 30, 1972 – when British paratroopers killed thirteen Irish demonstrators in Londonderry, which served primarily to bolster the recruitment efforts of the IRA. In all, some 3,000 people were killed during the Troubles in Northern Ireland.

In 1993 a formal peace process was launched. The Northern Ireland Act was passed, setting conditions of partial martial law. A joint declaration of peace was made by the end of the year. Four years' worth of negotiations followed among Britain, the Republic of Ireland, and major political factions of Northern Ireland – the most significant of which was Sinn Fein, the political arm of the IRA. The eventual result was a landmark accord: the Good Friday Agreement, signed by the British and Irish Republic on April 10, 1998, and endorsed six weeks later in a referendum by a majority of Northern Irish voters. Except for the typical levels of serious crime that occur in urban areas, the 1998 accords have, remarkably, been followed by several years of relative calm.

There are a number of noteworthy aspects of this episode. Over the course of the ordeal, the civil disturbances both in Belfast, the capital and largest city of Northern Ireland, and elsewhere in the country tended to occur less often in integrated middle-class suburbs and to be more frequent and deadly in the poorest, most highly segregated areas. In Northern Ireland as in other places with histories of ethnic violence, the longer and deeper the hostilities, the more difficult it is to bring political processes to bear to control the attitudes and behaviors of combatants on the ground, especially in poorer, more volatile areas.

8. Tamils and Sinhalese

Sri Lanka, known as Ceylon until 1972, is a large tropical island nation in the Indian Ocean, off the southeast coast of India. It had been a colony of Britain until 1948, when it gained independence. It now has a population of more than 20 million, about 15 million of whom are Sinhalese, 4 million

Tamil, and the rest a mixture of other ethnicities. The two dominant ethnic groups, the Sinhalese and the Tamils, are quite distinct from one another: the Sinhalese are mostly Buddhist and the Tamils are mostly Hindu, they speak different languages, and they have different genealogies.

Although there had been tension between the Sinhalese and Tamils from the time of independence from Britain – when the Sinhalese gained control of the government and tilted the laws in their favor, making Sinhalese the official language of the state and gaining increased access to higher education and good jobs – the two groups nonetheless managed to avoid major hostility. Then, in 1983, a reported gang rape of a Tamil doctor by Sinhalese soldiers sparked a retaliation attack by a group of Tamil militants known as the Liberation Tigers of Tamil Eelam (LTTE), in which the "Tamil Tigers" killed thirteen government soldiers in Jaffna. The government responded, in turn, with two weeks of pogroms (a Russian term that applies to government-induced riots against ethnic minorities), involving the murder and rape of Tamils and looting of their villages; this period came to be known as Black July. The mayhem ended when the Indian government, then headed by Indira Gandhi, issued a stern warning to the Sri Lankan government to stop the violence.

The government's heavy-handedness galvanized support among the Tamils for an independent Tamil state in the northeast corner of the island. During the next twenty years there were a string of suicide bombings, mostly by Tamil teenagers and occasionally by pre-teens, and strong government crackdowns in retaliation. Some of the most serious Tamil attacks include the 1991 assassination of Indian Prime Minister Rajiv Gandhi in a suicide bombing by a Tamil girl; the killing in 1996 of 1,200 soldiers at a government camp; and deadly terrorist attacks on commercial targets in Colombo, the nation's largest city. During these twenty years, Sri Lanka experienced about 65,000 deaths, with disastrous effects on the social and economic stability of the country. A ceasefire was declared in 2002, but new violence erupted in late 2005, leading to a renewed threat of civil war, with no clear end in sight.

C. Emergence of the Suicide Bomber

The terror dragon arose from decades of slumber in the mid-twentieth century, when indigenous groups in Algeria, Egypt, Indonesia, Israel and Palestine, Kenya, and elsewhere rebelled against ruling colonial regimes, often using dramatic, vicious acts of violence to gain attention to their causes.

Algeria. Among the most historically significant of the terrorist groups of the latter half of the twentieth century was Algeria's Front de Libération Nationale (FLN), which introduced the tactic of massive targeting of civilians. When France's government executed two Algerian rebels in 1956, the FLN responded sensationally over a three-day period, slaughtering forty-nine

French citizens vacationing in Algeria. The FLN terrorists launched lethal attacks on beachfront cafes and other targets where tourist families, including children, were concentrated. The terrorists succeeded not only in grabbing headlines that seized the world's attention but also in sending shockwaves across the French countryside that were especially deep and broad: the FLN raised the price of France's continuing colonization of Northern Africa to unaffordable levels. The French had given up Morocco as a protectorate in 1956, and the mayhem in Algeria surely accelerated France's inclination to relinquish its rule there as well, giving Algeria full independence by 1962. In the process, the FLN gave the tactic of attacking vulnerable civilians with brutal, overwhelming aggressive force a new strategic validity that had no recent historical precedent.

Spain. The FLN's crusade for Algerian autonomy inspired like-minded groups elsewhere to use similar tactics, but not always with the same effectiveness. In 1959, Basque separatists in Northern Spain, under the banner of Euskadi Ta Askatasuna (ETA), started a long campaign of car bombings and assassinations that killed more than 800 people over the ensuing years, including President Luis Carrero Blanco in 1973 and other prominent politicians, judges, government officials, officers of the armed forces, journalists, professors, businessmen, and children. Although the attacks by ETA failed to produce full national independence from Spain, they did induce the Spanish government to give the Basques greater political autonomy. By the 1990s, however, Basque terrorists lost both focus and the widespread support of the mainstream Basque population, as noted in Chapter 2 (see the section on ethnic terrorism).

Quebec. In Canada, Marxist-oriented Québécois separatists formed the Front du Liberation de Quebec (FLQ) in 1963, launching a campaign of bombings aimed at achieving independence from Canada. The borrowing of the first two letters of FLN's acronym was no coincidence, but both the intensity and success of the FLQ turned out to be less profound than the FLN's. Through the mid- and late 1960s, the FLQ carried out bombings, bank robberies, and other acts of violence, at least five of which resulted in the deaths of targeted civilians. The FLQ campaign achieved a rhetorical victory in 1967 when Charles de Gaulle offered unusual words of support: "Vive le Quebec Libre" ("Long live free Quebec"). In 1970, the FLQ kidnapped British Trade Commissioner James Cross, and in 1980 it kidnapped and killed the Minister of Labor and Vice-Premier of Quebec, Pierre Laporte. In the latter half of the twentieth century, terrorism by the FLQ became a sensational distraction, serving largely to undermine the legitimate interests of the Québécois separatist movement.

Israel and Palestine. The seeds of Palestinian terrorism were planted on November 29, 1947, with the passage of Resolution 181 by the United Nations General Assembly, partitioning the British Mandate of Palestine into two separate states – one Jewish and one Arab – with Jerusalem part of both and under international control. The Arabs were particularly unhappy with the UN resolution. Hostilities began almost immediately between Jews and Arabs, with hundreds killed on each side from the time of passage of the resolution until May 14, 1948, when David Ben-Gurion declared independence and statehood for Israel. The State of Israel was officially recognized by Britain, the United States, the Soviet Union, and most other non-Arab nations. A formal declaration of war was issued immediately by the Arab League, made up of Egypt, Jordan, Lebanon, and Syria, and supported by volunteers from Libya, Saudia Arabia, and Yemen who joined in the campaign.

After two failed attempts to achieve a truce between the warring factions in the summer and fall of 1948, the Israelis were able to repel the Arab coalition forces and forge separate armistices with Egypt, Jordan, and Syria in 1949. In the war and its aftermath, some 700,000 Arabs and a similar number of Jews living in Palestine were uprooted, with most of the Jews migrating to Israel and Arabs moving to Palestine and elsewhere in the Middle East and Europe.[1] The quick, efficient, and complete defeat of the Arab armies by the Israeli forces left the Arabs generally and Palestinians in particular with a sense of humiliation and loathing.

The years that followed saw the rise of Palestinian nationalism led by the Palestine Liberation Organization (PLO), founded by the Arab League in 1964 and led by Yassir Arafat. The PLO engaged in extensive guerrilla and terrorist operations over the ensuing years. Arafat's PLO pioneered hijacking, hostage-taking, and a long series of school bus bombings to win global recognition. In the pantheon of terrorism, Arafat's distinctive achievements include the following:

- the first major hijacking of an Israeli commercial jet in 1968
- the murder of 11 Israeli athletes at the 1972 Olympics in Munich by a PLO faction calling itself "Black September"
- the hijacking of an Israeli plane en route to Entebbe, Uganda, in 1976, resulting in an Israeli commando raid to liberate the hostages
- the sensational killing of a wheelchair-bound American, Leon Klinghoffer, during the 1985 hijacking of the Italian cruise ship *Achille Lauro*

Arafat gradually pulled back from direct involvement in such activities in order to win political and financial support from the West and gain international legitimacy. He was awarded the Nobel Peace Prize in 1994 after signing the Oslo Accords the previous year, in which Arafat agreed to recognize Israel's right to exist, guarantee Israel's security within its defensible borders, and work through a series of negotiations toward a peaceful resolution of the remaining problems.

In the meantime, a new wave of fundamentalism swept the Middle East, starting with the 1979 Iranian Revolution. More radical organizations then emerged in Palestine, including Hamas in 1987, under the leadership of Shaykh Ahmed Yassin; Hezbollah, created and supported by Iran; and the Islamic Jihad. These organizations all targeted Israel as an oppressor, professed unwavering support for the Palestinian cause of freedom and justice, and rejected pressures from the United Nations, the United States, and European nations to find a peaceful two-state resolution to the conflict with Israel. Acts of terrorism came in waves throughout this period, but they became increasingly deadly over the long arc of the last three decades of the twentieth century, as opposition mounted to the expansion of Jewish settlements the West Bank and Gaza and the tactic of suicide bombing became more popular.

Leftists in Europe, Africa, and the Americas. The idea of poor people rising up against a powerful oppressor is one of the most dominant and enduring themes underlying terrorism. The success of this idea in France in the nineteenth century, in Russia in the early twentieth century, and against colonial rulers in Algeria and elsewhere inspired leftists in much of Europe, Africa, and North and South America throughout the latter half of the twentieth century. These campaigns were typically stimulated by mixtures of idealistic Marxist and nihilistic anarchist notions, as well as by romantic martyr icons such as Che Guevara or Malcolm X. Most prominent among these terrorist groups are the following:

- Baader-Meinhof Gang, which kidnapped and murdered people and robbed banks and stores in West Germany
- Red Brigades, which committed kidnappings, murders, and bombings in Italy in the 1970s and '80s, including the notorious kidnapping and assassination of former prime minister Aldo Moro in 1978
- Weather Underground (or "Weathermen"), a dissident splinter group of the Students for Democratic Society, which set off bombs in Chicago, Berkeley and San Francisco, New York, Washington, and elsewhere in 1969 and the early '70s, inspired largely by opposition to the Vietnam War

Leftist revolutionary movements in Africa (including the Movement for the Liberation of Angola [MPLA] and the Ethiopian Peoples' Revolutionary Democratic Front) and South America (most notably, the Revolutionary Armed Forces of Colombia [FARC] and the Shining Path in Peru) also engaged in terrorist activities throughout much of the latter half of the twentieth century. These groups might, however, be described more accurately as guerrilla revolutionary groups rather than conventional terrorist groups, because the targets they attacked were primarily military and governmental rather than civilian.

The Emergence of the Suicide Bomber. Perhaps the most devastating legacy of the latter half of the twentieth century is the legitimation of suicide bombing as a popular tactic for achieving political objectives. When people see themselves as rendered collectively helpless, humiliated, or otherwise aggrieved by overwhelming military or police power, asymmetric attack in the name of martyrdom and collective justice can become a compelling alternative to remaining in a state of hopelessness. Suicide bombing offers to such people what the French president called "strength of the weak" (*la force du faible*; Hoagland, 2006a).

But the gains for the society from which the attackers come may be illusory – there is little evidence that suicide terrorism diminishes the sense of hopelessness among the people of those societies much beyond the time of the attacks. Nonetheless, increased frustration and dreams of change have been the essential justifications used in the escalation from rock-throwing by young Palestinians to suicide bombings of Israeli buses, restaurants, and marketplaces in the 1990s; by the Tamil Tigers in Sri Lanka; and by al Qaeda in Sudan during the same decade.

Although suicide attacks are an ancient practice, traceable at least to Samson's biblical era attack on the Philistine temple, the practice was not widely used until the kamikaze raids on U.S. military targets in the Pacific, which proved effective during World War II. The tactic was revived in 1983 by Hezbollah's landmark suicide bombing of the U.S. embassy in Beirut, Lebanon, an attack that killed 63 people, including 17 Americans, and injured more than 100 others. Among the dead were the Central Intelligence Agency's director of Middle East operations. The weapon was a van carrying some 400 pounds of explosives, deployed by a suicide driver. Six months later, a delivery truck filled with TNT rammed its way into the Marine barracks in Beirut and exploded, killing 241 U.S. servicemen. About twenty seconds later, another truck exploded at the French military compound, killing another fifty-eight paratroopers there. Within six months, all multinational forces had withdrawn from Lebanon, signaling a victory for those behind the attacks.

Sharp increases in the number of suicide bombings internationally are undeniable. Scott Atran reported fewer than 5 suicide bombings throughout the world annually in the 1980s, about 16 annually in the 1990s, and 180 annually from 2001 to 2005 – with a more than fivefold increase from 2001 to 2005, from 81 attacks in 2001 to 460 in 2005. By 2007, Nordland and Dehghanpisheh reported a higher number of suicide bombings in Iraq alone. Similar increases have been reported by Pape (2005), by Benmelech and Berrebi (2007), and others. Rand terrorist researcher Bruce Hoffman (2005) reported that 80 percent of suicide bombings that have occurred since 1968 took place after 9/11. That percentage had increased to 95 percent by 2007.

A Brief History of Terrorism

As a tactic, suicide bombing can be extremely efficient and effective. The explosives are aimed precisely at a target by means of the most direct form of human guidance possible, with both the physical location and timing of the explosive device under full human control. Target selection plans can be modified at the discretion of the bomber as circumstances warrant. Because of the ability to exercise such discretion on the ground, the amount of damage to a target can be more devastating than that achieved by conventional guided weapons, which are, in any event, unavailable and unaffordable to those who plan such attacks. Suicide bombings tend to be especially destructive when directed by more capable attackers at more carefully selected targets (Benmelech and Berrebi, 2007). The acts are difficult to prevent without imposing sharp restrictions on normal freedoms of assembly and movement. The psychological damage – the extent of terror – and its destructive impact on the economic and social vibrancy of the larger target population can be immense. In Iraq, the tactic made it very difficult for the U.S. military to achieve its objective of winning hearts and minds by getting close to the people because it had to protect itself against strangers with bombs: military convoys routinely warned Iraqis to stay 100 meters away or risk getting shot (Nordland and Dehghanpisheh, 2007).

And there is no shortage of suicide bombers. The supply of willing bombers in areas with high concentrations of alienated people can be seemingly inexhaustible. They are attracted not only because they view their alternatives as somewhat limited, if not bleak, but also because they perceive distinct benefits from engaging in the attacks: martyrdom, revenge against enemies for prior wrongs, fame in death, honor to the family, virgins in paradise, and so on.

Suicide bombing became a particularly common occurrence in Israel in the 1990s. The Palestinian groups Hamas, the Islamic Jihad, and the al-Aqsa Martyrs Brigade developed and refined the use of suicide belts containing shrapnel, worn under loosely fitting clothes, and designed to inflict maximum damage on targets with large concentrations of people, such as crowded buses, cafes, and open-air markets. It became common practice afterward for the offending group to declare responsibility for the act and release a tape of the suicide bomber explaining him- or herself before the attack. The Israelis often responded by bombing the home of the parents of the attacker or the headquarters of the group claiming credit for the act.

Suicide bombings spiked internationally after 2001 and were heavily concentrated in Iraq and Afghanistan. Statistics compiled by the National Counterterrorism Center, under its Worldwide Incidents Tracking System, reveal that during the 25-year period 1983 through 2008, over 1,840 suicide bombings killed about 22,000 people (Robin Wright, 2008). The rate of suicide bombings jumped from 12.9 annually throughout the world from 1983 through 2002, to over 316 annually for the five years afterward, a 25-fold increase in the annual rate of suicide bombing attacks. Nearly 1,200 – 64 percent of all suicide bombings accounted for internationally from 1983 through 2007 – occurred since 2001 in the two countries with a significant U.S. presence: 920 in Iraq and 260 in Afghanistan.

What about the moral dimension of suicide bombing? Suicide bombers often leave tape-recorded justifications that make various claims of martyrdom, personal or family revenge, social justice, a holy cause, assertions that the people targeted are not truly innocent, the desire to end one's feeling of despair, and so on. Suicide bombers may be able to offer a coherent moral justification for attacking military targets, but there can be no moral justification for killing noncombatants (Walzer, 1992). To do so violates all conventional codes of ethics, including the holy scriptures of all the major religions. One can stretch to find interpretations of the Bible, the Qur'an, and other religious texts that appear to condone such acts, but serious religious scholars invariably find such interpretations to be taken out of context or to be otherwise invalid.

We may not be able to find a coherent justification for killing noncombatants, but a wealth of data have been accumulating from these attacks, and they are now being studied (Benmelech and Berrebi, 2007; Hoffman, 1999; LaFree and Dugan, 2004; Mickolus, 1982; Pape, 2005; Sabasteanski, 2006). It will surely be worthwhile to continue to learn systematically about the several hundreds of suicide bombings about which we have useful data. As Ralph Peters (2005) says in Box 3.1, "It's much harder to defeat an enemy you don't understand."

Suicide attacks are not likely to end in our lifetime, but we may be able to substantially reduce such attacks by understanding why and how they occur. The key will be to remove both the desire and opportunity for future such attacks.

Terrorism on U.S. Soil. In addition to its Weather Underground experience during the early 1970s, the United States saw its own fair share of homegrown terrorists acting alone or in pairs during the latter half of the twentieth century, including Unabomber Ted Kaczynski and Oklahoma City bombers Timothy McVeigh and Terry Nichols. A precursor to the 9/11 attack on the World Trade Center (WTC) occurred in 1993, when a car bomb linked to al Qaeda exploded in the parking garage of the WTC, killing six people and injuring 1,000 others. All of these episodes fit the basic definition of terrorism – violent crimes against noncombatants that induce widespread fear and panic, typically involving a political agenda. (They are discussed in more detail in Chapters 6 and 8.)

In short, terrorism became considerably more visible and more sophisticated in the latter half of the twentieth century. Both the frequency and

Box 3.1. Living, and Dying, with Suicide Bombers

– Ralph Peters

After spending trillions of dollars on high-tech armaments, the United States finds itself confounded by a dirt-cheap weapon of genius: the suicide bomber. The ultimate precision weapon and genuine "smart bomb," the suicide bomber is hard to deter and exasperatingly difficult to defeat.

This is the "poor man's nuke." For a few hundred dollars (or less) and a human life, a suicide bomber can achieve strategic effects the U.S. Air Force can only envy.

For all of the claims that technology would dominate the twenty-first century – and not only in the realm of warfare – we find that impassioned faith still trumps microchips. Armed with a fervent belief in his god's appetite for blood, the suicide bomber can dominate headlines around the world with a few pounds of explosives.

A paradox of the Information Age is that it's simultaneously the new age of superstition. As calcified social orders collapse under the pressures of global change, those who feel most threatened flee into debased, occult religion. Increasingly, fanaticism finds outlet in shedding the blood not only of unbelievers but also of co-religionists whose beliefs are seen as imperfect.

The suicide bomber views himself (more rarely, herself) as fulfilling a divine mission whose execution will be rewarded in paradise. How do we discourage an enemy who regards death as a promotion? How do we identify the religious madman among the masses in time to stop him from killing? On a practical level, defeating the increasing numbers of suicide bombers is our most difficult security mission.

Homeland Vulnerable

The suicide bomber is so powerful a weapon that not even the terrorists have realized its full potential. Today, we see intermittent, localized attacks. The suicide bomber is at the same stage of development as the tank was in World War I: used in small numbers, armored vehicles did not achieve and sustain critical mass.

The obvious forerunners of today's Islamist fanatics were the Assassins, the notorious cult that operated from Persia through Syria in the eleventh and twelfth centuries. Armed only with sacramental knives and patience, the Assassins terrorized governments by killing sultans and grand viziers. It took the invading Mongols – the all-time masters of counter-insurgency warfare – to destroy the Assassins in their mountain strongholds.

To be fair to the Assassins, they attacked only the mighty, not the masses. And, as Bernard Lewis, a respected authority on the Middle East and Islam, has pointed out, Islam's prohibition against suicide meant that yesteryear's murderers allowed themselves to be caught and suffer torture rather than kill themselves.

But the new age of faith is also an era of the perversion of religion, from the primitive blood-cult evident in ritual beheadings to the rationalization of a suicide bomber's death – not as self-murder but the consequence of a brave attack in the conduct of holy war.

Nor should it be as difficult as we assume for Westerners to grasp the psychology at work in the suicide bomber. Our own history is full of martyrs and religious warriors who went boldly and knowingly to their deaths. In every culture, the really good haters die well.

Who Are They?

Deplore his act though we rightly do, the suicide bomber who imagines himself a defender of his threatened faith and humiliated people is the extremist equivalent of the soldier we revere for throwing himself on a grenade to save his comrades' lives. Our rules for self-sacrifice are different, but the psychology is uncomfortably familiar. The results may differ terribly, but the motivation has filial roots.

We see only the indiscriminate carnage, the apparent madness. Until we recognize his crazed valor, we cannot understand the suicide bomber. And it's much harder to defeat an enemy you don't understand.

Suicide bombers are recruited from the ranks of troubled souls, from those who find mundane reality overwhelming and terrifying. The suicide bomber longs for release from the insecurities of his daily experience. He is fleeing from life every bit as much as he's rushing toward paradise.

We have faced enemies more dangerous, but none so implacable.

The world's great strategic struggle of this century is between those who believe in a generous, loving god – in any religion – and those who serve a punitive, merciless deity.

The suicide bomber has chosen his side.

Shattering Warfare's Rules

The U.S. military faced suicide bombers in the past: in the closing months of World War II, Japanese kamikaze pilots flew bomb-laden planes into U.S. Navy ships. The kamikazes generated casualties but could not change the outcome of the war. Strapped into their aircraft, those who volunteered to die for the "divine emperor" were the closest thing we ever faced to today's Islamist fanatics.

But there were key differences: The kamikaze pilots were disciplined military men attacking military targets. Their goal wasn't to slaughter civilians but to stave off defeat. They were fighting for an imperial idea, not for a global religious crusade.

Driven by a nihilistic desire to achieve salvation through slaughter, today's suicide bombers are a genuinely new phenomenon. With their twin goals of self-annihilation and creating mass carnage, they've fundamentally shifted the battlefield's rules – and its location. We've heard a great deal about our high-tech "revolution in military affairs."

Welcome to the counter-revolution.

[Excerpted from *USA Today* (January 4, 2006).]

lethality of terrorist attacks were largely the product of emerging information-processing and communication technologies, which facilitated the coordination of terrorist activities and gave terrorism a stage on which it could be publicized. Terrorism also developed a new face, one distinctly less political and rooted more apparently in agendas related to religious fundamentalism and alienation against modernity. As we proceed, we shall visit and revisit the question of whether this association is real or largely illusory and whether religion has been appropriated to lend legitimacy to interests that are more deeply rooted in political agendas than spiritual callings.

D. Women in Terrorism

It was noted in Chapter 2 that due to factors pertaining to both nature and nurture, the preaching and practice of terrorism are dominated by men, but that women play a role nonetheless. The factor relating to nurture that facilitates that role is opportunity: because women are known to be generally less dangerous, they tend to be given less scrutiny in security screening processes, which provides openings for them to commit acts of terrorism not available to men.

Women were involved in dangerous revolutionary activities long before the advent of suicide bombing. They made up as many as one-fourth of reported Russian terrorists in the nineteenth century, and some, such as Vera Zasulich, were prominent as leaders of the movement and participants in acts of aggression (Siljak, 2008; Townshend, 2002). Women were among the leaders of the extremist groups behind the 1917 Bolshevik revolution in Russia and among the anarchist leaders in Europe and the United States during the same period (Martin, 2006). The founder of the Japanese Red Army, Fusako Shigenobu, in 1971, was a woman. Nearly one-third of the Italian Red Brigades in the 1970s were women (Siljak, 2008; Townshend, 2002). Two of the first recorded suicide terrorist attacks involving women were car bombings against Israeli soldiers in South Lebanon in March 1985 – the first involved an 18-year-old who killed twelve soldiers and wounded fourteen others; the second, two weeks later, involved a 16-year-old who killed two soldiers and injured two others (Stern, 2003; Taheri, 1987). The suicide assassin of Indian Prime Minister Rajiv Gandhi in 1991 was a young Tamil woman.

The Chechnyan insurgency movement has made especially significant use of women as terrorists. Nearly half of the forty-one Chechnyan terrorists who killed more than 300 captives in a Moscow theater in 2002 were women. Two of the attackers in the 2004 Beslan school hostage crisis – which resulted in 334 deaths of civilians, mostly children – were women. The Chechnyans refer to women suicide bombers as *Shahidkas* or the "Black Widows," despite the fact that most are teenage girls and young women who have never been married (Jusik, 2005).

Suicide terrorism has increased among women in other Muslim extremist groups as well. The first Women have been responsible for more than two-thirds of the suicide bombings by the Kurdish Workers Party in Turkey (Stern, 2003). In 2003, an influential Islamic scholar from Egypt issued a fatwa sanctioning female suicide bombings: "When the enemy assaults a given Muslim territory, it becomes incumbent upon all its residents to fight against them to the extent that a woman should go out even without the consent of her husband" (Bergen and Cruickshank, 2007). After years of al Qaeda's not giving prominent roles for women in jihad, a 2004 posting on its Saudi web site began to encourage women to participate actively in acts of aggression. In addition to the examples cited above in Lebanon, Ossetia-Alania (the Beslan crisis), and Russia, suicide bombing attacks by women have been documented in Afghanistan, Chechnya, Egypt, Iraq, Israel, Jordan, Kashmir, Pakistan, Palestine, Somalia, Sri Lanka (non-Muslim), Turkey, Uzbekistan, and elsewhere (Bergen and Cruickshank, 2007; Dickey, 2005; Zedalis, 2004).

Do women participate in terrorism for the same reasons as men? Partly yes, but they do so for other reasons perhaps to a greater degree. Mia Bloom (2005) attributes the participation of women in terrorism since the latter part of the twentieth century largely to more personal justifications – typically related either to family honor, such as to avenge killings of family members, or to absolve themselves from shame, sometimes following an extramarital affair. Neuburger and Valentini add that women participate in terrorism largely "because sacrifice is rooted in their being" (1996, p. 94).

Tim McGirk (2007) reports that Palestinian women made eighty-eight attempts to commit suicide bombings from 2002 through early 2007, of which eight were completed. After analyzing these cases, he echoes the personal redemption explanation, citing counterterrorism authorities who observe that women's acts of terrorism are motivated largely by personal despair and a desire for absolution from sin, often after having broken taboos of strict Palestinian tradition. He notes also that many of these acts are not fully voluntary, that women often fall prey to male recruiters who seek out women – on campuses and Internet chat rooms – because women can insinuate themselves into places that are inaccessible to men. McGirk adds that some women regard an act of suicide terrorism as preferable to an arranged marriage, which is common in the Arab world.

Some women who commit acts of terrorism out of a sense of honor are mothers, but they evidently regard their acts as fulfilling a higher purpose than serving as caregivers for their children. For men, acts of terrorism are more likely to be driven by religious or political fanaticism than by family honor, and in some cases, men are lured by the ninth-century Islamic scholar al-Tirmidhi's promise, written in a hadith, that every man will have six dozen virgins in paradise.[2]

Clearly, we have much more to learn about the involvement of women in terrorist activities, both as leaders and as foot soldiers. The study of women in terrorism has been ignored by many and treated with awe by others; it is a topic shrouded in mystery.[3] Just as the study of the involvement of women in crime should be of considerable interest to criminologists – to learn why women engage in crime in the first place, why some of those persist in criminal activities for long periods while others do not, and why even women criminals eventually stop – the study of women involved in terrorism should be of no less concern to scholars interested in terrorism. Women may be the strongest counter to terrorism available – a point to which we return in the concluding chapter – but they have shown themselves to be willing and able contributors to terrorism as well.

E. Post-9/11 Terrorism: Alienation Meets Advanced Technology

The September 11 attack. In the hundred years following the Declaration of Independence, three episodes of war or war-like hostility each produced many thousands of deaths on American soil: the Revolutionary War, the wars against Native Americans, and the Civil War. Hundreds of thousands of U.S. citizens have been killed in wars abroad – in Europe, the South Pacific, Korea, and Southeast Asia – but except for the 1941 attack on Pearl Harbor, virtually none had been killed at home. The fifty years following the Pearl Harbor attack saw the ending of World War II, and then some forty years of

64

Cold War between the West, led by the superpower United States, and the communist bloc of nations, led by the other superpower, the Soviet Union. Then, after the fall of the Berlin Wall in 1989 and the ending of the Cold War soon after, Francis Fukuyama (1992) wrote as follows: "What we may be witnessing is not just the end of the Cold War, or the passing of a particular period of post-war history, but the end of history as such: that is, the end point of mankind's ideological evolution and the universalization of Western liberal democracy as the final form of human government."

Then, in 2001, a new chapter was opened in history. The idea of a new millennium beginning with massive violence against noncombatants, committed by individuals acting outside state authority and with no interest in improving themselves materially was bizarre enough, perhaps a plot concept for a novel or motion picture thriller. But the killing of some 3,000 people and destruction of buildings that had been international symbols of vast power – making dust of the 110-floor World Trade Center Twin Towers and destroying a major sector of the Pentagon – made the September 11 attack an event of unprecedented scale and huge symbolic importance. Osama bin Laden's videotaped gleeful reaction to the attack suggests that the prospect of such a shocking, unprecedented strike against the world's sole superpower was a strong motivating factor behind the plan to attack New York and Washington in such a spectacular way.

Other factors contributed to the incomprehensibility of the event and the public shock that followed: it was a suicide attack, committed by a large team of aliens, who managed to orchestrate and successfully carry out a complicated scheme, on U.S. soil, involving the training of pilots, the simultaneous hijacking of four large passenger jets, the evasion of federal antiterrorist surveillance systems, slipping through airport security, and overpowering the pilots and crews of each and every one of the planes.

The attack involved nineteen men from four Middle Eastern countries – fifteen from Saudi Arabia and the others from Egypt, Lebanon, and the United Arab Emirates. It had been thoroughly planned in Hamburg and rehearsed in the United States, and it benefited from financial support and loose guidance from al Qaeda, which at the time was headquartered in Afghanistan. The plan had called for four teams of five men, each team consisting of a trained pilot and four strongmen who were prepared to commandeer the jets after takeoff and then crash them into major targets. The four jetliners departed within minutes of one another on a brilliant, cloudless morning – two from Boston's Logan International Airport, one from the Newark International Airport, and the fourth from Washington Dulles International Airport. The terrorists carried out the plan with a 75 percent success rate: three of the four jets struck their intended targets, and the fourth – apparently set to strike the U.S. Capitol building, or possibly the White House – crashed into a field near Shanksville, Pennsylvania, a rural area in Somerset County, in the southwestern portion of the state. The hijackers used box cutters and well-prepared commando techniques to overwhelm the pilots, crew, and passengers. Each aircraft was thus transformed from a passenger jet into a giant incendiary bomb, the fuel tanks of each filled to near capacity with 24,000 gallons of highly combustible jet fuel.

The fatalities included 265 in the four planes and 2,595 more on the ground, including 343 New York City firefighters, 23 officers from the New York Police Department, 37 Port Authority police officers, and 125 civilians and military personnel at the Pentagon. Five buildings in addition to the Twin Towers were destroyed or badly damaged at the site of the World Trade Center in New York, as well as four subway stations and major radio and television communications equipment.

The Aftermath of 9/11. The immediate shock from the attack of 9/11 was heightened by the extended period of calm and optimism that preceded it. The event came more than a decade after the fall of the Berlin Wall and following years of unusual economic growth and relative peace on most of the planet. People the world over were now suddenly overcome with horror and bewilderment: Why would anyone want to do such a thing? How could such a large group successfully orchestrate such an attack? The immediate outpouring of sympathy and support was both moving and reassuring. The day after the attack, the headline of the Paris *Le Monde* newspaper read, "Nous sommes tous Américains" (We Are All Americans").

The sense of siege was deepened further in the United States by an anthrax attack launched days later, with a series of letter envelopes postmarked as early as September 18, 2001. The envelopes contained highly refined anthrax spore powder sent from Trenton, New Jersey, to government officials in Washington, D.C. – including Senators Tom Daschle of South Dakota and Patrick Leahy of Vermont – and to prominent media people in New York City and Boca Raton, Florida. This attack produced twenty-two cases of anthrax poisoning by inhalation and five deaths. Although it was concluded that the attack was probably launched by a disgruntled U.S. scientist thinly veiled as a Muslim, it served to confound and add to the horror of the 9/11 attack. Stores throughout the United States experienced a run on gas masks, duct tape, and emergency provisions as people prepared for more such attacks.

Response to the Attack: The War on Terror. In the weeks that followed, numerous narratives came forth attempting to make sense of the attack of 9/11: what it meant, why it happened, and what should be done about it. From the White House came an "Axis of Evil" narrative, delivered in President Bush's January 2002 State of the Union speech, about menacing tyrants and barbarians with dark intentions in Iraq, Iran, and North Korea.[4] From the left both at home and abroad came strident messages about American imperialism, corporate greed, and globalism as the primary sources of the problem.[5]

Such divergent rhetoric notwithstanding, the United States responded expeditiously and assertively to the 9/11 attack. It began by assembling substantive support from a large coalition of nations and appealing to Afghanistan's Taliban government to turn over the al Qaeda leaders to whom they had been granting safe harbor. After those appeals were rejected, the United States launched "Operation Enduring Freedom" on October 7, 2001, the centerpiece of which was a decisive assault that destroyed al Qaeda facilities in Afghanistan and overthrew the ruling Taliban government. Thus began the U.S. "war on terror."

The Invasion of Iraq. The next phase of the War on Terror was considerably more controversial: the March 2003 invasion of Iraq, under the banner, "Operation Iraqi Freedom." The principal initial justification for the invasion was the clear and widespread perception – by international teams of inspectors and others – that Iraq possessed weapons of mass destruction, including chemical, biological, and possibly radioactive weapons. That Iraq was providing financial and moral support to suicide bombings in Israel provided further justification for the invasion. A more controversial justification was the characterization of the invasion as an integral part of the war on terror, including the claim that Iraq had significant links to al Qaeda.

In October 2002, the U.S. Congress passed a resolution giving President George W. Bush the authority to attack Iraq if Saddam Hussein did not give up his weapons of mass destruction. Then, in March 2003, following Hussein's failure to comply, more than 200,000 U.S. military personnel, including 100,000 soldiers and marines; some 45,000 British military personnel, including 25,000 British soldiers and marines; and an additional 2,000 Australians and 2,400 Polish military personnel were deployed to staging areas in Kuwait. The bombing of Baghdad commenced on March 20. Plans to invade from the north had to be aborted when the Turkish Parliament refused to permit its land to be used to support such an operation.

Although the invasion of Iraq succeeded in ending the brutal twenty-four-year rule of Saddam Hussein, it also gave rise to an insurgency that had not been widely anticipated. The insurgents were predominantly Sunnis and former Ba'athist members, but over the next several months they began to include as well a growing number of jihadists from neighboring countries, led by Abu Musa al-Zarqawi, the Jordanian associate of Osama bin Laden. The link between Saddam Hussein's Iraq and al Qaeda may have been tenuous, but it did not take long for the new Iraq to become tied strongly to a seemingly endless stream of al Qaeda-inspired insurgents.

Many of the same Iraqis who celebrated the overthrow of the harsh tyrant Saddam Hussein, especially among the Shi'a population, soon became equally animated over their displeasure with the U.S. occupation of their country and the conduct of the U.S. effort in the years following Saddam's overthrow. As the number of casualties on both sides mounted seemingly without end, it

The overthrow of Saddam Hussein in 2003 opened an historic wave of terrorist attacks throughout Iraq.

became clear that the effort to bring democracy and order to Iraq would not be as clean, quick, and easy as many had believed. The April 2004 release of vivid photographs revealing the serious abuse of Iraqi prisoners by Americans at the Abu Ghraib prison – American soldiers cast as villains – served grievously to undermine the claims of legitimacy and moral authority of the U.S. effort and to generate opposition in Iraq, the United States, and the rest of the world. Even though the vast majority of servicemen and women had been serving bravely and honorably in Iraq, the perception of abuse and brutality by a few U.S. military personnel became considerably more significant to people in many parts of the world than the nobility of the service of many others.

The campaign in Iraq may yet, in years to come, make the country more democratic and generally better off than it had been under Saddam Hussein, and it could even serve, eventually, to stabilize the region and stimulate democracy, freedom, and the rule of law. Many observers, however, see the U.S. effort in Iraq increasingly resembling the disastrous campaign in Vietnam waged several decades earlier. The debate over the wisdom of invading Iraq, over the manner in which it was done, and over its ultimate effect on terrorism is likely to continue for years to come without a clear resolution.

Making Sense of 9/11 and the War on Terror. What then are the distinctive characteristics of the post-9/11 era concerning both terrorists and the way the world responds to them? Let us consider the terrorists first. Has the number of terrorists increased since September 11? Coming up with hard figures of the number of terrorists either before or after September 11 is even more difficult than attempts to achieve agreement on the definition of "terrorism." However, the National Counterterrorism Center (2007) reports a considerable increase in the number of lethal and nonlethal terrorist attacks since its creation in 2003, with some 14,000 attacks and more than 20,000 deaths in 2006 – and 13,000 in Iraq alone.

One fact is undeniable: the coverage of terrorism in the media is many times greater than it was before the 9/11 attack. In much the same way that increased coverage of crime in the United States during the 1990s created an impression that there was more crime during that decade – despite the fact that crime actually declined substantially – it might be that increased coverage of terrorism has created a false impression of increases in the number of terrorists. In fact, estimates by the U.S. Department of State (2006) suggest that the number of terrorist attacks worldwide declined from the 1980s to 2003, but that it rose sharply from 2003 to 2005, due largely to the spike in terrorist attacks in Iraq during this period (DeYoung, 2006; Glasser, 2005; Sabasteanski, 2006).

More clearly documented than the number of terrorists is the plummeting popularity – among people in both Muslim and non-Muslim countries – of both the United States and the terrorists since September 11, 2001. Surveys by the Pew Research Center of more than 90,000 people in fifty nations reveal that a primary source of the growing unpopularity of the United States is a clear sense that it prosecuted its war on terror in a manner that was excessively unilateralist and nationalistic (Pew Global Attitudes Project, 2004). U.S. policies and actions against terrorism altered its image from that of champion of freedom and land of opportunity to world bully and exploiter (Kohut and Stokes, 2006).

What about the nature of terrorism? Research on terrorists and their attacks has uncovered the emergence of what has been referred to as the "new terrorism," which is characterized by small, diffused networks with dubious sponsorship and unclear, nihilistic goals (Lesser et al., 1999; G. Martin, 2006; Robb, 2007). Much of this new terrorism is informed by revolutionary approaches to the conduct of guerrilla operations, especially in densely populated areas, where terrorists can inflict damage and spread fear on a much grander scale.

Perhaps the single, most important development in the conduct of terrorism, especially in urban areas, is the validation of tactics developed decades ago by Carlos Marighella, a Brazilian revolutionary who wrote the *Minimanual of the Urban Guerrilla*. Marighella's manual is an accessible guide

Policy Box 3.2. Countering the New Global Guerrillas

John Robb, a former planner and commander of U.S. counterterrorism operations, characterizes the terrorism of the new millennium as one consisting of networks of small groups of "global guerrillas." These groups operate with greater lethality within the crevices of sovereign nations and focus on "systems disruption." Robb observes that many of the same technologies that fuel globalization also allow terrorists to attack much larger adversaries by targeting infrastructure such as energy supply lines, power grids, and financial markets. They can thus weaken the cumbersome bureaucratic nation-state with remarkable ease and relatively little expense. These nimble groups can then thrive in the lawless spaces they create.

The effectiveness of this approach has been clearly revealed in Iraq, which has proven to be a rich training ground for the development of tactics of "open source warfare." In 2004, for example, an attack in southern Iraq that cost about $2,000 to execute – with no attackers since apprehended – produced an explosion resulting in some $500 million in lost oil exports. This is a rate of return of about 250,000 times the cost of the attack.

Robb's solution to the problem? Decentralize counterterrorist operations and convert tightly coupled systems, which have been effective in peaceful settings but vulnerable to terrorist attacks, to systems with greater redundancy and self-sustainability:

> Because we are unable to decapitate, outsmart, or defend ourselves against global guerrillas, naturally occurring events, and residual nationalism from causing cascades of failure throughout the global system, we need to learn to live with the threat they present.... (T)his doesn't mean an activist foreign policy that seeks to rework the world in our image, police state measures to ensure state security or spending all of our resources on protecting everything. It does mean the adoption of a philosophy of resilience that ensures that when these events to occur (and they will), we can more easily survive their impact (Robb, 2007, p. 182).

to the effective waging of asymmetric warfare. Written in 1969, his manual describes techniques that have now been well tested and refined over several decades. They involve the principles of demoralizing and winning against a larger military or police force with stealth and surprise, flexibility and speed, planning, and knowledge of the physical area. The core idea is to shock the government forces and in the process win over the public using ingenuity and skill in small teams fighting against numerically and financially superior forces that are less flexible and burdened with heavy equipment, rules, and rigid hierarchies. When a population is won over to the cause of the insurgents, it becomes more difficult for the government forces to distinguish friend from foe. This leverages the small numbers of the insurgents, consistent with the asymmetric "smoke-and-mirrors" approach of terrorism.

Such techniques have been put to use by al Qaeda and other terrorist and insurgent forces, which had to decentralize because their own hierarchy was crippled by effective counterterrorist strikes and activities that killed many of their key operatives, driving their organizations and remaining leaders more deeply underground and forcing them to shift emphasis from operations to inspiration. Terrorism has also become more lethal, as information about how to acquire and use weapons of mass destruction is now more widely accessible than ever to multitudes (see Box 3.2, "Countering the New Global Guerrillas").

Countering this new brand of terrorism is not likely to succeed if it focuses exclusively on the prosecution of a war against terrorists and the protection of targets. Terrorism is produced by terrorists, but it has a "demand" side too. Of course, few targets of terrorism *wish* to be victims, as might be suggested by use of the term "demand." But to the extent that the targets make themselves more attractive by calling attention to the acts of terrorism and overreacting to them, they contribute actively to the expansion of terrorism. We look more closely at an important aspect of this phenomenon – the fear that gives life to terrorism – in Chapter 10.

Discussion Questions

1. *Terrorism before 1950.* How do the terrorist events that typified the ancient era differ from those of the Middle Ages? How do those of the Middle Ages differ from those of the eighteenth and nineteenth centuries? Do any of these qualify only marginally as terrorist events? Which ones? Why? Does the United States killing of American Indians in the nineteenth and twentieth centuries qualify as state-sponsored terrorism? Explain your answer.

2. *Significance of terrorist events.* The terrorist attacks of Algeria's Front de Libération Nationale (FLN) have been described as "historically significant." What makes them significant? What does it mean, more generally, for a terrorist event to have "historical significance"? Identify a terrorist event that had historical significance of a fundamentally different type than the FLN attacks.

3. *Success and failure in terrorism.* Terrorism aimed at change in political rule sometimes succeeds and sometimes fails. Giving examples, what are the

elements that make for successful and unsuccessful acts and campaigns of terrorism?

4. *The morality of suicide attacks.* Would anything make a suicide attack morally justifiable? What? What would make it unjustifiable?

5. *Confronting the new terrorism.* John Robb characterizes the new global guerrillas as particularly dangerous and argues that nations are ill equipped to deal with them. What is it that makes them so dangerous? How should nations respond to the threats posed by this new brand of terrorism?

FOUR

Two Trajectories of Humankind: Globalization or Clash?

This chapter focuses on the global stage on which terrorism has come to play a prominent role. It identifies two long trajectories of humankind: first the smiling muse of globalization – a world of economic and cultural exchange – and second, the frowning mask of conflict between vast cultural blocs. The globalist trajectory is described in the perspectives of Fukuyama, Bhagwati, Friedman, and others. The clash of civilizations model was first put forth by Princeton scholar Bernard Lewis and then embellished and adapted by Harvard political scientist Samuel P. Huntington. The fundamental positions of the proponents and critics of the two models are described. The chapter asks how these two models can inform our understanding of terrorism and policies for preventing it in both the near and the long term.

A. From Alexander the Great to Twenty-First-Century Globalization

1. A Short History of Globalization

Globalization is the process of economic, technological, and cultural exchange linking people in different parts of the world. It involves the creation and use of pathways that connect people both physically and electronically

73

across continents. Most people think of globalization as having to do with cell phones and the Internet – fostering interconnections through modern communication and computerization technologies. The roots of globalization, however, bear little resemblance to modern technology. They begin with the most primitive of forces: the migration of species. Humans originated in Africa, along with so many other species of life, and over many millennia they diverged and migrated to the other continents. As people moved, they differentiated themselves from one another, but they also brought with them remnants of the cultures and traditions from which they came, and some eventually returned to their homelands.

Over several hundreds of thousands of years, cultural differentiation became generally more pronounced. In time, however, the divergences reached a natural limit as the physical boundaries of migration on a finite planet became increasingly apparent. At that point the processes of exchange and convergence – the hallmarks of globalization – began. The seeds of a long trajectory of convergence were planted well over 2,000 years ago, dating back to at least 325 BCE, when Alexander the Great made peace with and opened paths to trade with Chandragupta, a dominant South Asian ruler. In time, this system of pathways of discovery and commerce became fairly well traveled; Marco Polo's landmark adventures from Europe to Asia in the late thirteenth century took place along a course that would later become known as the Silk Road.[1] In the sixteenth, seventeeth, and eighteenth centuries, Europeans traveled to the New World, Africa, and elsewhere to get precious minerals and goods such as furs, moccasins, and ivory from indigenous populations. The goods were sometimes stolen from the natives, but they were more typically obtained in exchange for items not previously available to them, such as steel knives and tools. Either way, the goods could be marketed in Europe for profits that justified the investments in labor, the items given up in trade, and the long travel.

By the nineteenth century, global routes of trade had become well established and traveled. Walter Russell Mead (2004) offers an insightful historical analysis of the evolution of capitalism in the nineteenth and twentieth centuries and the implications of this evolution for globalism and global politics in the twenty-first century. He distinguishes among three forms of capitalism:

1. Nineteenth-century *Victorian capitalism* characterized by unfettered laissez-faire enterprise with a total absence of government regulation
2. The more orderly and managed *Fordist capitalism* (named after industrialist Henry Ford) of the twentieth century, marked by government regulation, mass prosperity with social security, and control of the economy by strong oligopoly and union power

3. The more flexible *millennial capitalism* that emerged during the Reagan-Thatcher years, characterized by government regulation aimed at making markets more efficient rather than protecting special interest groups through elaborate systems of subsidies, quotas, and other forms of market interference

Globalization is largely associated with open markets and free trade. It accelerated especially under Mead's millennial capitalism, which blossomed in the 1980s and in the decades that followed.

Globalization thus derives from the expansion of trade routes, but it derives no less from these developments in science and technology:

- early technologies, such as the wheel, compass, telescope, and printing press
- Industrial Revolution developments, such as the steam engine and ocean-going ships, cotton gin and the industrialization of agriculture, and the typewriter and telephone
- modern and postmodern technologies such as the automobile and airplane, computer hardware and software, and advanced communication technology

These technologies provided both the goods that made possible the expansion of international trade and the means to distribute them worldwide more quickly and inexpensively.

Globalization has, in short, been expanding for at least two millennia, although not at a steady rate. It accelerated considerably with the mid-twentieth-century explosion of the multinational corporation; the creation of vast wealth in Europe, the United States, and the Pacific rim of Asia; and the flow of unprecedented amounts of capital, goods, and services from continent to continent. This trajectory accelerated even more significantly as information and communication technologies advanced at a previously unimaginable rate in the late twentieth century.

Several scholars have written extensively about a convergence of civilizations under this trajectory of globalization, perhaps foremost of whom is Francis Fukuyama, starting with his landmark 1992 book, *The End of History and the Last Man* (see Box 4.1). Others have taken up Fukuyama's basic thesis of a convergence of civilizations in the post-9/11 era, including economists Jagdish Bhagwati, Joseph E. Stiglitz, and Martin Wolf; political scientist Walter Russell Mead; *New York Times* columnist Thomas Friedman; and military scholar Thomas Barnett.

Professor Bhagwati (2004), a renowned authority on international economics, describes globalization – when implemented intelligently – as the most powerful force for social good in the world today, providing especially great opportunities for economic and social uplift in the poorest pockets of the globe. He defines globalization as the "diverse forms of international

Two Trajectories of Humankind: Globalization or Clash?

Francis Fukuyama

integration such as foreign trade, multinational direct foreign investment, movements of 'short-term' portfolio funds, technological diffusion, and cross-border migration."

Bhagwati presents statistics in support of the tendency for open markets to create decent jobs, reduce poverty, and expand the buying power of previously impoverished people, and he gives numerous examples of globalization's positive impact, starting with his native land of India. Using

Jagdish Bhagwati

Box 4.1. The Globalist Perspective of Francis Fukuyama

One of the champions of globalization is Francis Fukuyama, professor of international political economy at the Johns Hopkins School of Advanced International Studies. Fukuyama argues, along with others, that the expansion of globalization occurs most rapidly in lands that nurture the freedom of expression and enterprise, and the economic power that results in turn strengthens liberal democracy itself. In his widely acclaimed book, *The End of History and the Last Man*, Fukuyama wrote that modern liberal democratic societies had grown sufficiently aware and interconnected through modern technology to protect against cataclysmic warfare among superpowers, marking an end to the Cold War, limiting prospects for authoritarian regimes, and substantively altering pre-existing patterns of history. Although some argued that his "end of history" thesis was itself ended by the September 11, 2001 attack on the United States, the attack did not move Fukuyama from his fundamental globalist position.

Acknowledging that the ascendancy of modernization and globalization is a "juggernaut," Fukuyama argued after 9/11 that Osama bin Laden's "desperate backlash against modernism" was unlikely to succeed and that poor people in developing lands, like the Afghans freed of Taliban rule, revealed a strong desire to become a part of the connected world and thereby enjoy the fruits of modern society.[2] Despite 9/11, Fukuyama continues to argue that time and resources are still on the side of modernity,[3] although he has become less optimistic about the likelihood and speed of modernization and democratization throughout the world.[4]

Fukuyama nonetheless remains a strong advocate for public policies that counteract the active social agendas of terrorist organizations like Hamas in Palestine, Hezbollah in Lebanon, and the Muslim Brotherhood in Egypt:

> If true supporters of liberal democracy and free markets are ever to compete successfully with the Islamists and populists of the world, they need to have a social agenda that gives some hope not just to the middle-class and educated, but to those who are isolated and excluded as well. Above all, we need to stop seeing this issue through the old left-right ideological lens of American domestic politics, and recognize that our influence is dependent in large measure on our ability to offer people around the world what they want, and not what we think they should want (2007).

Two Trajectories of Humankind: Globalization or Clash?

Martin Wolf

Asian Development Bank data, he shows that India's opening of economic markets to trade and investment led to higher growth rates and less poverty: from 1980 to 2000, India's poverty rate fell from 55 to 26 percent. Similarly, China's globalist policies reduced the percentage of the population in poverty from 28 percent in 1978 to 9 percent twenty years later.

Martin Wolf, columnist for the *Financial Times*, echoes many of Bhagwati's basic arguments, elaborating on the need for intelligent governance: "The world needs more globalization, not less. But we will only have more and better globalization if we have better states" (Wolf, 2004, p. 320). Wolf observes that poverty tends to increase and economies tend to stagnate when governments interfere excessively, either by implementing policies that restrict trade or regulate it inefficiently; by giving subsidies that distort prices; or by restricting the freedom of choice of consumers, producers, or investors (pp. 173–219). He sees much brighter prospects for the flow of desperately needed capital to developing nations that succeed in protecting property and eliminating barriers that restrict capital flows, barriers that are typically the product of incompetence and corruption (pp. 315–16). Wolf notes that economic fragmentation is the product of political fragmentation and that barriers to trade and capital flow are often justified politically by claims of the need for self-sufficiency. Villages and manorial economies – the antithesis of globalization – are created by "lunatics" who reside largely, but not exclusively, in poor, autocratically ruled nations (p. 317).

Joseph Stiglitz (2003) also emphasizes the importance of more efficient flows of capital to poor nations, seeing them as key to the ability of globalization to reduce world poverty and create stable growth. According to Stiglitz, these capital flows are heavily dependent on an effective international financial network, particularly the International Monetary Fund (IMF), World Bank, and World Trade Organization. Stiglitz concludes that the policies and practices of these organizations, especially those of the IMF, have retarded the success of globalization.

Two Trajectories of Humankind: Globalization or Clash?

Joseph Stiglitz

Walter Russell Mead (2004) offers a cartoon portrait of the power of millennial capitalism to promote globalization through "the glorious triumph of technology and entrepreneurial spirit over a decadent and stagnant era," with "new and more dynamic opportunities to eliminate poverty and transform the human condition" (2004, p. 71). He also offers a countervailing

Walter Russell Mead

Two Trajectories of Humankind: Globalization or Clash?

Thomas Friedman

cartoon – of the dark side of millennial capitalism – which is discussed in the next section.

Essayist Thomas Friedman offers a more popular, metaphor-filled view of globalization in his books and numerous *New York Times* essays on the subject. In *The Lexus and the Olive Tree*, Friedman describes globalization as "The One Big Thing" driving international affairs in the post-Cold War world – a tectonic shift rather than a mere trend, an international system with its own rules and logic that influences the geopolitics and economics of virtually every country in the world (2000, p. xxi). Under his "Golden Arches" theory of conflict, Friedman postulates that trading partnerships reduce the prospect of war: no two countries ever engage in wars with one another after both have opened a McDonald's restaurant (pp. 248–75). He sees leaders of impoverished nations having to choose between the lesser of two evils: "revolution from below" under the status quo of closed markets and corruption, and "revolution from beyond" under "globalution" (p. 169).

Some nations, including India, Indonesia, South Korea, Sri Lanka, and Thailand, have opted to strengthen the middle class by opening markets and attracting foreign capital, despite the disruptive forces of rapid growth, job displacement, economic and social intrusion, and democratization (pp. 167–77). Friedman points to residual benefits in the countries that do make the leap to the global economy: less corruption, a freer press, the emergence of bond and stock markets, and democratization (pp. 179–93).

Two Trajectories of Humankind: Globalization or Clash?

In a sequel, *The World Is Flat* (2005), Friedman expands on his Golden Arches theory of conflict. He describes horizontal collaborations – connectedness across geographical, political, and cultural boundaries – and the flattening of previously hierarchical corporations as products of substantially lowered costs of communication associated with new technologies. These horizontal collaborations can bring about stronger bonds between groups and nations that were previously hostile to one another. Friedman observes, for example, that the 2002 crisis between nuclear powers India and Pakistan subsided when United Technologies threatened to leave India if the country could not provide a safe environment for business. Both sides soon came to realize the devastating economic blow that each country would incur if the tensions continued to mount. Friedman notes, however, that even in the most advanced nations, politicians often appeal to the public's fears of jobs lost through globalization, sending to the doghouse any staff economist who speaks publicly of the advantages of free trade.

Friedman explains that the economic connectedness that comes with globalization is especially important because it provides opportunities for "win-win" transactions around the globe, in sharp contrast to the everyone-loses tradition of political hardball and warfare. This idea is one that Robert Wright focuses on in his 2001 book, *Nonzero: The Logic of Human Destiny*. Wright describes nonzero-sum situations as ones in which the gains of one person or group do not necessarily come at the expense of another person or group. He advances the thesis that moral behavior is "rooted ultimately in the genes" (Wright, 2001, p. 22) and is a key to survival: nonzero-sum cooperation is a more successful social and economic strategy than is a survivalist, go-it-alone strategy. Evolution has thus favored, and will continue to favor, human groups and cultures that are more altruistic and are able to work out effective nonzero-sum cooperative arrangements. Wright sees this as both a prescription for future public policy and as a description of evolutionary forces historically.

Much of the interest in globalization has focused on the advantages of economic and financial exchange, but the social and cultural aspects of globalization are in many ways more double-edged and profound. In his classic *The Descent of Man* (1871, reprinted in 1997), Charles Darwin expressed his awareness of cultural globalism as a social imperative:

> As man advances in civilization, and small tribes are united into larger communities, the simplest reason would tell each individual that he ought to extend his social instincts and sympathies to all the members of the same nation, though personally unknown to him. This point being once reached, there is only an artificial barrier to prevent his sympathies extending to the men of all nations and races (pp. 126–27).

Two Trajectories of Humankind: Globalization or Clash?

Anthony Giddens, while concerned about the out-of-control juggernaut aspects of globalization, points to its having strengthened social relations throughout the world (1990, pp. 151–54). There is, to be sure, no small irony here: although "global" ordinarily means approximately the opposite of "local," globalization has accelerated the transformation of social relations that were once only local into social relationships that are now international. The geographic distances and political boundaries that have for centuries cut people off from one another and created cultural distance have receded under the influence of globalization. On the one hand, this change has facilitated the spread of freedom, democracy, the rule of law, and human rights. Abuses of basic freedoms and rights are subject to exposure and condemnation today as never before, thanks in no small part to globalization. Hence, globalization can to a large extent be regarded as a success. On the other hand, much of the world has become numb to images of gross humanitarian abuses and is resigned to tolerating the intolerable. Moreover, to the extent that globalization has facilitated the spread of the worst aspects of cultures everywhere – greed, depravity, indulgence, instant gratification, and the capacity of nations to wage war and individuals to engage in terrorism – it can be regarded as a failure, if not an instrument of evil.

Thomas Barnett (2004) recognizes both sides of the double-edged sword of globalization and concludes that there is a clear net good. Nations that join the global economy experience not only prosperity, but perhaps more importantly, they experience the benefits that accrue from the rule of law. Thus, globalization is a geopolitical formula for peace in the post-9/11 age. Barnett sees globalization as the primary long-term solution to the problem of terrorism. He draws a long and winding boundary over a map of the world, demarcating two vast areas at odds with each other: the "functioning core" of interconnected countries with rule sets, norms, and ties that bind people together in mutually assured dependence on the one hand, and the "non-integrating gap" of countries in globalization's "ozone hole" on the other (Barnett, 2004, pp. 4–8). He sees globalization as the central and defining element of global security in the post-Cold War era. Barnett describes the implications of this connection between globalization and security for the development of a defense strategy that focuses on U.S. military needs, but he states that there is no less a diplomatic responsibility to work effectively to help countries in the gap move to the core.

Others have written extensively on participation in the global economy, and in legitimate economic enterprise generally, as the most immediate antidote to the toxic brew of poverty, alienation, and terrorism that poisons much of the world. The French economist Guy Sorman (1989) documents, in the case of India, "barefoot capitalism" as the pathway out of this morass. In *The Universal Hunger for Liberty: Why the Clash of Civilizations Is Not*

Inevitable, former U.S. ambassador Michael Novak sees "an alternative to terror": "By whatever name you call it, a dynamic economic sector is the poor's best hope of escaping the prison of poverty" (Novak, 2005, p. xxviii). In *The End of Poverty: Economic Possibilities for Our Time*, economist Jeffrey Sachs (2005) writes of the critical need to raise poor people throughout the world up the first rung of the "ladder of economic development" as a solution both directly to the problem of poverty and indirectly to the problem of instability that so often accompanies poverty. In *The Fortune at the Bottom of the Pyramid: Eradicating Poverty through Profits*, C. K. Prahalad (2004) writes, "If we stop thinking of the poor as victims or as a burden and start recognizing them as resilient and creative entrepreneurs and value-conscious consumers, a whole new world of opportunity will open up." There is, in short, a large body of theoretical and empirical support for engagement in global economic and social exchange as a process for removing the sources of terrorism.

2. Critiques of Globalization and Counter-Critiques

Globalization is not universally appreciated; it never was. Even long before the Industrial Revolution, the expansion of trade routes brought disruptive changes to previously stable communities and cultures, and occasionally worse. For example, the bubonic plague (or "Black Death") – transmitted through rodents – spread from Asia to the Black Sea in 1347; to the Middle East, Africa, and Italy in 1348; and on to the rest of Europe the following year, a harmful side effect of international trade. Globalization has not always produced win-win outcomes.

Today many are strongly opposed to what they see as dangerous disruptions that have spread throughout the world in the name of globalization. They see intrusions that disrupt the social order, harm the environment, exploit children and women, and threaten traditional cultures and associated moral behaviors. They regard these residual effects of globalization as an essential tool in the spread of international terrorism.

One of the best-known critics is political scientist Benjamin R. Barber. Barber argues that globalization is fundamentally at odds with civility and with an effectively functioning democracy, in which people think for themselves while maintaining a sense of duty to, and alignment with, their similarly civic-minded neighbors. He sees this ethic being undermined by the forces of "McWorld," the pervasive and harmful existence of transnational corporations headquartered elsewhere: "Globalism is mandated by profit, not citizenship" (Barber, 1992, p. 24). For Barber, the antidote is to reinvigorate the middle ground between governmental and business spaces everywhere, especially civic spaces, such as the village green, voluntary associations, churches, and community schools – places where genuine citizenship can thrive. Barber opens his famous 1992 essay with this passage on the clash of two trajectories:

> Just beyond the horizon of current events lie two possible political futures – both bleak, neither democratic. The first is a retribalization of large swaths of humankind by war and bloodshed: a threatened Lebanonization of national states in which culture is pitted against culture, people against people, tribe against tribe – a Jihad in the name of a hundred narrowly conceived faiths against every kind of interdependence, every kind of artificial social cooperation and civic mutuality. The second is being borne in on us by the onrush of economic and ecological forces that demand integration and uniformity and that mesmerize the world with fast music, fast computers, and fast food – with MTV, Macintosh, and McDonald's, pressing nations into one commercially homogenous global network: one McWorld tied together by technology, ecology, communications, and commerce. The planet is falling precipitantly apart *AND* coming reluctantly together at the very same moment.

Other critics of globalism take a more traditional Marxist position, arguing that the forces of globalism serve the interests of the rich by exploiting the poor and worsening income and wealth disparities around the world. According to political scientist Manfred Steger (2003), for example, globalization elevates market values over human values by creating sweatshops in poor nations to bring profits to large multinational corporations and by supporting conspicuous consumption by the wealthy, with Americans at the forefront of over-consumption of the world's scarce resources. Steger echoes Benjamin Barber's position that globalization is anti-democratic, adding that it contributes to disruption: "There is no question that interstate rivalries intensified at the outset of the twentieth century as a result of mass migration, urbanization, competition, and the excessive liberalization of world trade."

Michael Ignatieff (1993) introduces the dimension of alienation to this already volatile mix, writing, "The liberal virtues – tolerance, compromise, reason – remain as valuable as ever, but they cannot be preached to those who are mad with fear or vengeance" (p. 190). Ralph Peters (2005) adds that globalization is the messenger of frustrating news by making billions of people throughout the world aware of economic disparities. Images of suffering in faraway places are a more immediate part of our landscape and experience than in earlier times. David Ignatius (2006a) notes that the disparities occur *within* communities too: as local elites become enmeshed in the global culture, they tend to lose touch with local realities, opening a vacuum that gets filled by religious parties and sectarian ideologues.

Jagdish Bhagwati responds to Barber, Steger, and other critics of globalization by arguing that the forces of globalization alleviate the most serious problems that its critics attribute to it. He explains that globalization tends to reduce poverty by putting more money in the hands of parents, thereby expanding educational opportunities, reducing child labor, and increasing literacy. He argues that globalization works similarly to advance the status and improve the condition of women throughout the world. More generally, the expansion of multinational corporations creates jobs and consumption power in the countries where the expansion occurs. Bhagwati acknowledges that economic growth can increase pollution, but not when coupled with the appropriate environmental safeguards, such as retroactive taxes on carbon dioxide emissions, the proceeds of which could go to developing countries to help them reduce their own greenhouse gas emissions. Bhagwati acknowledges also that globalization can lead to cultural hegemony and bland "McWorlds," but that more often it contributes to diversity and cultural hybrids that are richer and more interesting than the original products and services.

Walter Russell Mead sees the millennial capitalism that underlies contemporary global markets as a two-edged sword, with strong mixed implications for global politics. He notes that Middle Easterners are especially inclined to oppose millennial capitalism, largely on the grounds that it attacks traditional values with libertine images such as homosexuality and with women in prominent positions of authority. Peter Berger (2003) generalizes these sentiments by observing that globalization opens the way to pluralism, a profusion of diversity, and a journey from determinism to choice. This journey can threaten deeply held convictions and thus lead to turbulence.

Joseph Stiglitz, a proponent of globalization, argues that many of the evils attributed to globalization are in fact due to government policies that interfere with globalization. In addition to the problems associated with the IMF, noted earlier, he calls attention to the hypocrisy of Western nations urging poor countries to eliminate trade barriers while retaining their own systems of subsidies and trade protections. Fareed Zakaria (2003, 2008) attributes these and other retardants to effective globalization to populist legislation enacted by politicians pandering to special interest groups; one such group is the aging populations of many Western nations that impose extreme pressures to maintain generous but unsustainable welfare benefits that have been in place for generations. He sees institutions that are not subject to the short-term pull of the next election, such as the Federal Reserve and the Supreme Court, as more responsive to the long-term needs of the people and hence more responsible than legislative bodies.

Robert Wright (2004) adds that the most significant problems associated with globalization derive largely from its unidirectional top-down character, its domination by the most powerful economically, and the absence of adequate moral responsibility and reciprocity. He calls for a "parallel transformation of moral sensibility." He sees such transformation as dependent on progress toward a more effective system of global governance, and he fears that even the high-stakes importance of this endeavor does not guarantee the sort of international cooperation that the transformation requires. He predicts that a failure to achieve such fundamental change could result in collapse and chaos.

The criticism that globalization is the essential instrument for the rapid spread of terrorist causes internationally is also difficult to counter. Ralph Peters (2005) puts it this way:

> (T)he Internet, for all its practical utility, has been the greatest tool for spreading hatred since the development of movable type for the printing press.

> Islamist fanatics, neo-Nazis and pedophiles now can find each other with startling ease. Those who hid in dark corners a dozen years ago are all but unionized today. The real global brotherhoods of the Internet age are conspiracies of hatred. This is an age of new possibilities for the most talented humans. Yet it is also an age of bigotries reborn, with digital propaganda as the midwife.

Harold Meyerson raises a related concern: globalization increases the prospect of foreign government ownership of private American companies. He asks, "Upset that Rupert Murdoch, who kowtows to China, will buy the *Wall Street Journal*? What if China itself buys the *Journal*? Would the *Journal's* hypercapitalist editorial board oppose that free-market transaction? Globalization . . . scrambles everything" (2007, p. A25).

One might add defense industries, transportation, utilities, and ports to the list of potentially troublesome prospects of foreign ownership in the world of globalization. Such ownership could conceivably compromise security by increasing foreign access to critical security information. When Dubai Ports World, a holding company based in the United Arab Emirates (UAE), purchased the rights to manage the ports of New York, New Jersey, Baltimore, New Orleans, Miami, and Philadelphia in 2006, it raised concerns about national security: might such a transaction permit sensitive information about port security to fall into the hands of employees more willing than before, motivated either ideologically or financially, to share the information with terrorists? (Blustein and Pincus, 2006; Ervin, 2006; Etter, 2006). The United Arab Emirates, one of the strongest Middle East allies of the United States, had also been a conduit for terrorism. It was one of just three nations (with Saudi Arabia and Pakistan) to officially recognize Taliban rule of Afghanistan while harboring al Qaeda prior to 9/11. The International Atomic Energy Agency identified Dubai as headquarters of a nuclear black market run by the notorious Pakistani, Abdul Qadeer Khan. Two of the 9/11 hijackers were from the UAE, and the UAE opted not to recognize U.S. sanctions against Iran (Etter, 2006).

Bernard Lewis.

In short, many of the same resources and advantages of globalization that have spurred economies and cultural exchange throughout the world have become accessible as well to terrorist organizations with global aspirations, and these organizations have not hesitated to exploit them. Globalization has helped advance the world's economies and cultural exchange substantially, but it has also made the West more dependent on Middle Eastern oil and given terrorists unprecedented opportunities to expand both their geographic horizons and the lethality of their attacks – to play "catch up" with military and law enforcement powers throughout the world, challenging even the world's sole superpower. We examine this global spread of terrorism that is attributable to advances in communication and information technologies in more detail in Chapter 7.

B. The Clash of Civilizations Theory

1. Bernard Lewis

The phrase "clash of civilizations" is widely associated with Samuel P. Huntington, but it did not originate with him. It had been given standing in a prominent 1990 essay in *The Atlantic* by Princeton University Professor Bernard Lewis, the concluding section of which was entitled "A Clash of Civilizations." Lewis attributed the clash, particularly between Islam and the West, to a variety of factors: a sense of Muslim humiliation; two devastating world wars; the corruptive intrusion of an alien, seductive, and decadent

Western culture into pious Muslim communities; and the mounting struggle of fundamentalism against pagan secularist and disruptive modernist forces. These forces caused a long-standing ethic that combined humility with dignity and courtesy to give way to feelings of rage and hatred. Lewis concluded,

> This is no less than a clash of civilizations – the perhaps irrational but surely historic reaction of an ancient rival against our Judeo-Christian heritage, our secular present, and the worldwide expansion of both. It is crucially important that we on our side should not be provoked into an equally historic but also equally irrational reaction against that rival.

Lewis then added these prescient words of warning:

> The movement nowadays called fundamentalism is not the only Islamic tradition. There are others, more tolerant, more open, that helped to inspire the great achievements of Islamic civilization in the past, and we may hope that these other traditions will in time prevail. But before this issue is decided there will be a hard struggle, in which we of the West can do little or nothing. Even the attempt might do harm, for these are issues that Muslims must decide among themselves. And in the meantime we must take great care on all sides to avoid the danger of a new era of religious wars, arising from the exacerbation of differences and the revival of ancient prejudices.

Lewis ended the essay urging people to be less insular, to follow the advice of U.S. President John Tyler for greater religious tolerance and understanding, to "strive to achieve a better appreciation of other religious and political cultures, through the study of their history, their literature, and their achievements."

2. Samuel P. Huntington

In 1993, Harvard University Professor Samuel P. Huntington wrote an essay in *Foreign Affairs* that expanded on Lewis's "clash of civilizations" idea, elevating it to the title of his essay and modifying its thesis. Huntington broadens the focus from Islam to all major civilizations, arguing that global politics is entering a new phase, with deep and increasingly important differences in religion and culture:

> It is my hypothesis that the fundamental source of conflict in this new world will not be primarily ideological or primarily economic. The great divisions among humankind and the dominating source of conflict will be cultural. Nation-states will remain the most powerful actors in world affairs, but the principal conflicts of global politics will occur between nations and groups of different civilizations. The clash of civilizations will be the battle lines of the future (1993a).

Two Trajectories of Humankind: Globalization or Clash?

Samuel P. Huntington

Huntington concludes his landmark essay with both short- and long-term policy recommendations. His short-term advice: prevent the escalation of local inter-civilization conflicts into major inter-civilization wars. His long-term recommendation involves both the arrows of security and the olive wreaths of understanding and tolerance:

> The West will increasingly have to accommodate these non-Western modern civilizations whose power approaches that of the West but whose values and interests differ significantly from those of the West. This will require the West to maintain the economic and military power necessary to protect its interests in relation to these civilizations. It will also, however, require the West to develop a more profound understanding of the basic religious and philosophical assumptions underlying other civilizations and the ways in which people in those civilizations see their interests. It will require an effort to identify elements of commonality between Western and other civilizations. For the relevant future, there will be no universal civilization, but instead a world of different civilizations, each of which will have to learn to coexist with the others.

Huntington substantially refines and updates the ideas expressed in this essay in his 1996 book, *The Clash of Civilizations and the Remaking of World Order*. His expressed purpose is to produce a simplified model of the world that would be useful for analytic purposes. The book posits a multipolar world consisting of seven or eight major civilizations: Western, Confucian ("Sinic"), Japanese, Islamic, Hindu, Slavic-Orthodox, Latin American, and "possibly" African (1996, p. 81). Huntington predicts the decline of the West, the ascent of Asia, and an explosion of Islam.

Huntington's book highlights the shift from a post-Cold War world that featured a clash of ideologies and political and economic systems to a clash of cultures. A central premise of his book is that the creation of enemies is essential to cultural identity (1996, p. 20). Huntington posits that people would shift from the Cold War struggle over the question, "How should we think?" to the more basic question, "Who are we?"(p. 20). He predicts that this shift would cause long-standing conflicts and wars between tribes and ethnic groups to escalate to the level of civilizations (p. 28). He asserts further that the prospects for economic and political development in the Muslim republics are bleak (p. 29).

Huntington goes on to elaborate on the nature of the clash as the transcendence of culture over ideology: "The West won the world not by the superiority of its ideas or values or religion (to which few members of other civilizations were converted) but rather by its superiority in applying organized violence. Westerners often forget this fact; non-Westerners never do" (1996, p. 51). But as the West ran out of prospects for expansion and conquest in the twentieth century and imperialism lost its luster, Western expansion would be transformed to revolt against the West (p. 53).

Huntington observes that the euphoria at the end of the Cold War in the early 1990s was an illusion. Bloody conflicts in many parts of the world had shattered the appearance of harmony by the mid-1990s, and the United Nations proved unable to suppress them (1996, p. 32). Just as Americans did not become "Japanized" by eating sushi or buying Japanese automobiles, Huntington asserts that "only naive arrogance" could lead Westerners to believe that non-Westerners would become Westernized merely by acquiring Western goods: "Somewhere in the Middle East a half-dozen young men could well be dressed in jeans, drinking Coke, listening to rap, and, between their bows to Mecca, putting together a bomb to blow up an American airliner" (p. 58). The terrorist attacks of 9/11 gave his predictions and the larger idea of the inevitability of a clash of civilizations a stamp of real-world validation.

Huntington was prescient in other ways as well. He recognized before 9/11 that terrorism was an essential instrument in the clash of civilizations. Islamist terrorism was already decades old, and international supply networks had become fairly sophisticated: by the early 1990s, North Korea had supplied Syria with Scud missiles by way of Iran (Gertz, 1992; Scioline and Schmitt, 1991). He recognized that the population explosion in Muslim countries was contributing to the expansion of the more terrorist-inclined cohort of 15- to 24-year-olds (Huntington, 1996, p. 103). He saw that terrorism was historically a weapon of the weak, but that at some point terrorists would be able to produce massive violence and massive destruction, that the combination of terrorism and nuclear weapons could make the non-Western weak strong (1996, pp. 187–88). He saw that Western security was threatened by "immigrants from other civilizations who reject assimilation and continue to adhere to and to propagate the values, customs, and cultures of their home societies. This phenomenon is most notable among Muslims in Europe, who are, however, a small minority" (p. 312).

Huntington's overarching prescription is "to recognize that Western intervention in the affairs of other civilizations is probably the single most dangerous source of instability and potential global conflict in a multicivilizational world" (1996, p. 312). He argues that the United States can neither dominate nor escape the world, that it should instead work to find a middle ground of "adopting an Atlanticist policy of close cooperation with its European partners to protect and advance the interests and values of the unique civilization they share."

3. Critiques of the Clash of Civilizations Theory

Huntington's 1993 essay in *Foreign Affairs* received a firestorm of criticism, more comments than any other article published in that journal for nearly fifty years. Criticisms of Huntington's clash of civilizations theory have continued to appear in book reviews and policy journals episodically over the ensuing years. The criticisms fall into two camps. The first is that his theory is biased in several respects: it is tilted against non-Western cultures; it is parochial, insulting, and divisive; and it is a needlessly dark prophecy. The second criticism is that the distinctions he makes are arbitrary and less than useful, that his theory is simplistic and facile, glossing over essential distinctions while making others that have little value and, worse, may be harmful if used as a basis for policy. Let us examine these in order.

The Charge of Bias. Several critics of Huntington's clash of civilizations theory comment that narrow perspectives like his limit understanding and have the potential to do grave harm. They argue further that his theory adopts a distinctly harmful Western-centered perspective. Here is an example of Huntington's writing that concerns these critics:

> The political identity of the United States is rooted in the principles articulated in its founding documents. Will the de-Westernization of the United States, if it occurs, also mean its de-Americanization? If it does and Americans cease to adhere to their liberal democratic and European-rooted political ideology, the United States as we have known it will cease to exist and will follow the other ideologically defined superpower onto the ash heap of history (Huntington, 1993b).

The critics argue that, of course, every sovereign nation must protect its interests, but that there is a line beyond which those interests are harmed by overreaction – excessive, overly aggressive interventions used in the name of security and defense against the barbarians at the gate. Kishore Mahbubani (1993), for example, observes that the West tends to be blind to "the benign nature of Western domination.... Today most Western policymakers, who are children of this era, cannot conceive of the possibility that their own words and deeds could lead to evil, not good." Mahbubani concludes that there is much good that the West stands to learn from the rest.

In his book three years later, Huntington elaborates: "Civilizations are the ultimate human tribes, and the clash of civilizations is tribal conflict on a global scale" (1996, p. 207). He shows little restraint in asserting that Muslims have a "high propensity to resort to violence" in both internal and international crises (p. 258). He concludes, "Islam's borders *are* bloody, and so are its innards." His concern that immigrants are undermining the Western character of Europe and the United States is explicit: "While Muslims pose the immediate problem to Europe, Mexicans pose the problem for the United States." Huntington expands on this theme substantially a few years later in his book, *Who Are We? The Challenges to America's National Identity* (2004).

One of the best-known critics of Huntington's suggestion that the West should protect itself against the barbarians at the gate was the late Edward Said. A professor of English and Comparative Literature at Columbia University, Said (2001) had this to say about Huntington's clash of civilizations model:

> How finally inadequate are the labels, generalizations, and cultural assertions. At some level, for instance, primitive passions and sophisticated know-how converge in ways that give the lie to a fortified boundary not only between "West" and "Islam" but also between past and present, us and them, to say nothing of the very concepts of identity and nationality about which there is unending disagreement and debate.

Professor Said concludes, "'The Clash of Civilizations' thesis is a gimmick like 'The War of the Worlds,' better for reinforcing defensive self-pride than for critical understanding of the bewildering interdependence of our time."

The Charge of Arbitrariness. Professor Said's criticism of Huntington's "inadequate" and biased labels and sweeping generalities gives rise to the second general line of criticism, that the clash of civilizations theory is arbitrary. Political scientist Glenn Perry (2002), for one, says that Huntington's concept of civilizations "suffers from imprecision" and that his notion of "growing civilizational clashes also is slippery." Another political scientist, Jeane Kirkpatrick (1993), says of Huntington's identification of seven or eight civilizations, simply, "This is a strange list." She goes on to explain that many of the struggles *within* civilizations have considerably greater strategic significance than those that exist among the civilizations listed by Huntington. Here is one of her prime examples:

> The most important and explosive differences involving Muslims are found within the Muslim world – between persons, parties, and governments who are reasonably moderate, nonexpansionist, and nonviolent and those who are anti-modern and anti-Western, extremely intolerant, expansionist, and violent. The first target of Islamic fundamentalists is not another civilization, but their own governments.

Albert Weeks (1993) expands on Kirkpatrick's point, arguing that historians have attempted before to describe the world in terms of arbitrary notions of civilizations, with limited success. Weeks argues that conflicts in the world are more politically and situationally determined than based on arbitrary notions of civilizations:

> The world remains fractured along political and possibly geopolitical lines; cultural and historical determinants are a great deal less vital and virulent. Politics, regimes, and ideologies are culturally, historically, and "civilization-ally" determined to an extent. But it is willful, day-to-day, crisis-to-crisis, war-to-war political decision-making by nation-state units that remains the single most identifiable determinant of events in the international arena. How else can we explain repeated nation-state "defections" from their collective "civilizations"? As Huntington himself points out, in the Persian Gulf War "one Arab state invaded another and then fought a coalition of Arab, Western and other states."

Nobel laureate Amartya Sen (2006) criticizes the arbitrariness of Huntington's classification system by noting that other potentially more important distinctions can be made among people throughout the world:

> The people of the world can be classified according to many other partitions, each of which has some – often far-reaching – relevance in our lives: nationalities, locations, classes, occupations, social status, languages, politics, and many others. While religious categories have received much airing in recent years, they cannot be presumed to obliterate other distinctions, and even less can they be seen as the only relevant system of classifying people across the globe. In partitioning the population of the world into those belonging to "the Islamic world," "the Western world," "the Hindu world," "the Buddhist world," the divisive power of classificatory priority is implicitly used to place people firmly inside a unique set of rigid boxes. Other divisions (say, between the rich and the poor, between members of different classes and occupations, between people of different politics, between distinct nationalities and residential locations, between language groups, etc.) are all submerged by this allegedly primal way of seeing the differences between people.[5]

Two Trajectories of Humankind: Globalization or Clash?

Even accepting religion as a valid basis for making distinctions does not resolve a basic question: is it really more useful to focus on clashes between religions than within religions? Numerous scholars have documented the fact that there have been vastly more struggles and killings within Islam than between Muslims and other civilizations over the past several centuries. A 2006 *Wall Street Journal* editorial refers to the problem as a "clash of civilization." In his book, *No god but God: The Origins, Evolution and Future of Islam*, Reza Aslan (2004) sees the reality of this internal struggle as having been buried in widespread misperception following the 9/11 attack:

> For most of the Western world, September 11, 2001, signaled the commence-
> ment of a worldwide struggle between Islam and the West – the ultimate
> manifestation of the clash of civilizations. From the Islamic perspective, how-
> ever, the attacks on New York and Washington were part of a continuing clash
> between those Muslims who strive to reconcile their religious values with the
> realities of the modern world, and those who react to modernism and reform
> by reverting – sometimes fanatically – to the "fundamentals" of their faith
> (2004, p. xx).

Aslan concludes his book by observing that Islam was divided in its early days into conflicting sects and – despite popular belief and incessant media presentations to the contrary – that the reform to a more tolerant Islam is underway and the eventual success of this reform is inevitable:

> The notion that there was once an original, unadulterated Islam that was
> shattered into heretical sects and schisms is a historical fiction. Both Shiism and
> Sufism in all their wonderful manifestations represent trends of thought that
> have existed from the very beginning of Islam, and both find their inspiration
> in the words and deeds of the Prophet. God may be One, but Islam most
> definitely is not. . . . It took many years of violence and devastation to cleanse
> Arabia of its "false idols." It will take many more to cleanse Islam of its new
> false idols – bigotry and fanaticism – worshiped by those who have replaced
> Muhammad's original vision of tolerance and unity with their own ideals of
> hatred and discord. But the cleansing is inevitable, and the tide of reform
> cannot be stopped. The Islamic Reformation is already here. We are all living
> in it (2004, p. 266).

Arbitrariness is a problem on both scholarly and practical grounds. To be arbitrary is to be capricious, lacking in coherence, and coherence is a basic requirement for sound theory. If the clash of civilizations theory is to be both rigorous and useful, it should be coherent. We can see the problem in asking this question: how does Huntington's clash of civilizations theory help explain the 9/11 bombings in New York and Washington? This question and its relevance to the larger issue of the arbitrariness of the clash theory are addressed by Roger Sandall (2003) in Box 4.2.

Box 4.2. The Politics of Oxymoron

– Roger Sandall

One of the stranger things about Samuel Huntington's book *The Clash of Civilizations and the Remaking of World Order* was the debt it owed to anthropology. Throughout much of the past hundred years, anthropologists had been talking about clashes or conflicts among cultures, and at first glance Huntington's formulations seemed like an attempt to raise this mundane phenomenon to the more grandiose level of international affairs. . . .

More than fifty years have passed since Orwell wrote of "the need to recognize that the present political chaos is connected with the decay of language, and that one can probably bring about some improvement by starting at the verbal end . . . " Tendentious political language, he went on, "is designed to make lies sound truthful and murder respectable, and to give an appearance of solidity to pure wind." This was written in 1946 at the height of Stalin's power, and Orwell later developed his thoughts on this issue in his novel *1984*. In the book's appendix on The Principles of Newspeak he wrote that the special function of Oceania's vocabulary "was not so much to express meanings as to destroy them." Words could be destroyed, he said, by wantonly expanding their meanings so that they came completely to replace a whole range of older, more specific, and more definite terms and usages. This all sounds painfully familiar. One sees the term "civilization" being deliberately expanded in order to embrace some very uncivilized behavior indeed. . . .

But one thing is clear. When those planes hit the World Trade Center it wasn't a "clash of civilizations." There can no longer be anything honorable in "giving an appearance of solidity to pure wind" as Orwell said, and now is surely the time to call things by their proper names. A number of sick homicidal malcontents is not a civilization. Nor is a conspiracy of religious fanatics. Nor is a savage Arab chieftain like Saddam Hussein. Such men are the tragic byproducts of a backward, chauvinistic, highly aggressive tribal culture – a culture deeply and mortally at odds with the modern world.

Perhaps we should be grateful to Huntington for being so explicit on page 41.* Few of those who have sown terminological confusion in our time have been so candid. Yet at the same time we must say – thanks, but no thanks. Because whether we are dealing with oxymoron, paradoxymoron, or merely a belief that anything at all can be done with words, the pulling down of high and honorable terms for low purposes is perverse. The plain fact is that in contemporary India and China and Islam not only is there plenty that is "uncivilized in the singular sense" there is a great deal that is downright barbaric as well. Great these ancient historic collectivities once were, and it is appropriate to remember their greatness from time to time. But civilizations in any modern sense they are not. Uncivilizations are what they in many respects are now – to use Huntington's own helpful formulation – and it is the clash of backward uncivilization with the modern world that has given rise to most of our present conflicts.

* [Huntington asserts at p. 41 that "civilizations in the plural are the concern of this book," distinguishing between civilizations as large cultural blocs and "civilization" in the singular sense of subscribing to elite Western values and norms. ~BF]
[*Source: The New Criterion* (Summer 2003).]

The Charge of Self-Prophecy. Both of these lines of criticism of the clash of civilizations theory – that it is biased and that it is arbitrary – contribute to a more fundamental problem with the theory: it can too easily become a self-fulfilling prophecy of Apocalypse. Author and political commentator Robert Wright (2006) puts it this way: "The growing academic fad of thinking in primarily, almost obsessively, tribal terms is...analytically sloppy, it can become a self-fulfilling prophecy"[6] (see also Burke, 2006; Skidmore, 1998) Thomas Friedman, in a similar vein, calls Huntington's theory excessively "black-and-white (mostly black)," asserting that he "vastly underestimated...the lure of global markets, diffusion of technology, rise of networks and the spread of global norms" (2000, pp. xx–xxi).

To prepare adequately for the future it is essential to analyze trends, and responsible analysis must include worst-case scenarios. But responsible analysis also includes an awareness of the danger of *reification* – allowing our models of reality to influence and alter reality. The problem of reification is especially great when the models are excessively narrow, biased, or limited to exclude viable alternative specifications, and the consequences of the problem are great when the stakes associated with these limitations are potentially catastrophic. To the extent that the clash of civilizations theory induces "bunker-mentality" policies in the West, it can in turn induce people in other lands and from other cultures to see the West as a hostile force and prepare themselves for the worst. This perception tends in turn to lead to the further escalation of concerns, anxieties, and preparations for still worse to come. The process of sound policy analysis recognizes the danger of reification – that policies implemented in reaction to mere threats can make threats manifest as realities – and recognizes as well the prospect that reification need not be a negative. Sound policy is also based on facts, and a fact often overlooked by advocates of the clash of civilizations theory is that the world has experienced significant declines in the number of armed conflicts, genocides, human rights abuses, military coups, and battle-related deaths per armed conflict since 1990 (Human Security Centre, 2006).

If we are to be in the business of making self-fulfilling speculations on trends, it might be considerably more sensible and effective to speculate from a set of reasonable assumptions that produce an outcome that improves the course of humankind. Critics of the clash of civilizations model do not think that the model passes this critical test (Ahmed and Forst, 2005).

C. Reconciling the Irresistible Force of Globalization with the Immovable Object of Tradition

In the years following the 9/11 attack and the United States's war on terror, developments on the ground that dominated media coverage of world events served largely to support the clash of civilizations model, clearly more so than they did the model of globalization. After a brief outpouring of sentiment for the United States from people throughout the world in the days after the 9/11 attack, the tide began to swing away from a uniting of nations against terrorism to a world of disunity and disagreement about what to do about the emerging problem of terrorism.

One of the most disturbing developments was an increase in the number of terrorist attacks, attackers, and supporters. Five years after the 9/11 attack, the 2006 National Intelligence Estimate, based on the assessments of sixteen U.S. intelligence agencies, concluded that "activists identifying themselves as jihadists, although a small percentage of Muslims, are increasing in both number and geographic dispersion" ("Trends in Global Terrorism," 2006).

According to essayist David Brooks (2006), a Middle East that was once renowned for the splendor of its bazaars has come to define glory instead largely through acts of anti-Western defiance: "Superseding market entrepreneurs, there are terror entrepreneurs competing to see who can issue the most militant call and perform the most galvanizing act of violence. They are driven by resentment toward the West, but also by the internal competition for prestige and standing."

Brooks sees solutions to this grave threat lying largely in the West, but to a greater extent in the hands of Muslim moderates:

> The blunt fact is that groups of Islamic extremists will continue to compete and grow until mainstream Islamic moderates can establish a more civilized set of criteria for prestige and greatness. Today's extremists are not the product of short-term historical circumstances, but of consciousness and culture. They are not the fault of the United States, but have roots stretching back centuries. They will not suddenly ignore their foe – us – when their hatred of us is the core of their identity.

Two Trajectories of Humankind: Globalization or Clash?

Others view matters a bit more broadly. Late in 2005, Turkey's best-selling novelist, Orhan Pamuk was brought to trial in Istanbul for "publicly denigrating Turkish identity" by saying in an interview with a Swiss journalist that approximately one million Armenians and thirty thousand Kurds had been killed in Turkey. On the eve of his trial, Pamuk (2005) wrote of the real underlying problem:

> The drama we see unfolding is not, I think, a grotesque and inscrutable drama peculiar to Turkey; rather, it is an expression of a new global phenomenon that we are only just coming to acknowledge and that we must now begin, however slowly, to address. In recent years, we have witnessed the astounding economic rise of India and China, and in both these countries we have also seen the rapid expansion of the middle class, though I do not think we shall truly understand the people who have been part of this transformation until we have seen their private lives reflected in novels. Whatever you call these new elites – the non-Western bourgeoisie or the enriched bureaucracy – they, like the Westernizing elites in my own country, feel compelled to follow two separate and seemingly incompatible lines of action in order to legitimatize their newly acquired wealth and power. First, they must justify the rapid rise in their fortunes by assuming the idiom and the attitudes of the West; having created a demand for such knowledge, they then take it upon themselves to tutor their countrymen. When the people berate them for ignoring tradition, they respond by brandishing a virulent and intolerant nationalism. The disputes that a Flaubert-like outside observer might call *bizarreries* may simply be the clashes between these political and economic programs and the cultural aspirations they engender. On the one hand, there is the rush to join the global economy; on the other, the angry nationalism that sees true democracy and freedom of thought as Western inventions.

Pamuk's case raises awareness of the tension between the openness of globalization and centuries of heart-felt honor and tradition – not only in Turkey but throughout the world. The historical evidence of clashes both within and between cultures is beyond dispute, as is the historical record of globalization. The question is not whether there will be a clash of civilizations and what we should do about it. A more useful question is, How can we prepare for more security in the short term while putting much more productive energy and resources into a continuance of the trajectory that achieves the net benefits of globalization for the long term? Globalization has been the more dominant trend, in spite of frequent deadly wars, for centuries. Friedman, Robert Wright (2001, pp. 229–30), Zakaria (2008), and others speculate that this trend can be made to continue, especially with prudent stewardship.

The question we live with now, and are likely to revisit again and again for the rest of our lives, is whether the irresistible forces of economic and cultural exchange will be more powerful than the immovable objects of tradition and clash. One would hope for an even better prospect: that we can find ways to combine the best aspects of economic and cultural exchange with the best aspects of tradition to make for a more attractive force than a toxic brew that combines the worst elements of the two paradigms – made even more volatile by the spread of nuclear and biological technology. It is clear that public and private institutions can work to minimize the risks of clash and promote the best elements of globalization and culture. The challenge is to stimulate people to find and choose those paths and not be sidetracked by depictions of the world that are misleading and dangerous.

Discussion Questions

1. *Appeal of the clash idea.* Many find Samuel P. Huntington's clash of civilizations analysis compelling and many find it maddening. With regard to both the overarching theory and particular aspects of his analysis, why do you suppose it has generated such heat?

2. *Critiques of Huntington.* Are the critiques of Huntington fair? Do they overlook pertinent facts or ideas? Please be as specific as you can in addressing these two questions.

3. *Models of reality.* Huntington discusses alternative ways of distinguishing the world, using distinctions based on wealth, culture, religion, and other factors that constitute "civilizational paradigms." He goes on to argue that such distinctions are useful for understanding the world, for ordering events and evaluating their importance, for predicting trends, for distinguishing among types of chaos and their possibly different causes and consequences, and for developing guidelines for governmental policymakers. How does his identification of seven or eight civilizations serve these interests? Do you see dangers of this system? If so, what are they?

4. *Clash "of" or "within" civilizations?* Bernard Lewis writes, in his 1990 essay, "Roots of Muslim Rage," that there will be a hard struggle within Islam about which the West can do little or nothing, adding, "Even the attempt might do harm, for these are issues that Muslims must decide among themselves. And in the meantime we must take great care on all sides to avoid the danger of a new era of religious wars, arising from the exacerbation of differences and the revival of ancient prejudices." What does Huntington say that echoes the central idea of this quote? What does he say that is inconsistent with it? Lewis subsequently supported the 2003 invasion of Iraq. How might one reconcile such support with the above quote from his 1990 essay?

5. *Appeal of the idea of globalization.* Many find the ideas of Fukuyama's *End of History* and the principles of globalization expressed by its proponents persuasive while others find them seriously misguided. Explain why this is so with regard to both the overarching idea of a trajectory of international

economic and cultural exchange and particular aspects of the idea as expressed by Fukuyama, Bhagwati, Wolf, Mead, Friedman, and Barnett. Explain how you think this trajectory will play out against that of Huntington's trajectory of clash. How does globalization inoculate civilizations against clash, and how does it exacerbate the problem of clash?

6. *9/11 and the globalization and clash models.* How are the events of 9/11 and the policies that have followed likely to influence the trajectories of globalization and clash and the geopolitical landscape for the near and distant futures?

FIVE

Religion, the State, and Terrorism

This chapter describes the major religions of the world in terms of their origins, holy scriptures, geographic centers, and distributions. It then discusses distinctions among religious moderates, fundamentalists, and extremists and describes connections between religion and the state and between religious extremism and terrorism, addressing these questions: Does religion cause violence, or does it serve more as a civilizing agent, by giving people a set of moral standards that deter terrorism? Has mainstream religion been hijacked by fundamentalists and extremists, criminals, and thugs? What role do governments and nongovernmental organizations play in mediating these relationships?

A. The Major Religions: Origins, Scriptures, Followers, and Links to Violence

Both of the trajectories of humankind discussed in the previous chapter – globalization and the clash of civilizations – were influenced by the Age of Enlightenment, which brought with it the flowering of the sciences and a gradual shift away from theological dogma and adherence to liturgies and symbolic rituals. The Enlightenment spawned a trend toward the secularization of politics, private affairs, and daily family life and what Mark Lilla (2007b) refers to as the "Great Separation" of the institutions of religion and state. Several intellectual giants of the nineteenth century – Emile Durkheim, Sigmund Freud, Karl Marx, Friedrich Nietzsche, and Max Weber, among others – saw clear evidence that knowledge from the sciences and ethical principles from secular philosophers were gradually replacing theological superstitions and symbolic rituals of ancient times, and would continue to do so as industrialization and the modern era took further shape (Norris and Inglehart, 2004).

This gradual trend was reversed toward the end of the twentieth century, as attendance at places of worship escalated and religious fundamentalism took hold both in parts of the West and in Muslim societies throughout the world. These developments have led sociologist-theologian Peter Berger (1999) to conclude as follows:

> The assumption that we live in a secularized world is false. The world today, with some exceptions … is as furiously religious as it ever was, and in some places more so than ever. This means that a whole body of literature by historians and social scientists loosely labeled "secularization theory" is essentially mistaken (1999, p. 2).

For most of the past 150 years, terrorism has in fact been associated not so much with religion as with ethnic hatreds and political revolutionary ideologies: radical French Jacobinism, Marxism, environmental extremism, and waves of ethnic cleansing campaigns throughout the world are examples. The rise of terrorism by Islamic extremists in the latter part of the twentieth century – and, especially, the 9/11 attack on the United States – changed both the popular and the official view of terrorism in the United States. According to the 9/11 Commission Report (2004, p. 362), "The enemy is not just 'terrorism,' some generic evil. … The catastrophic threat at this moment in history is more specific. It is the threat posed by *Islamic* terrorism[1] – especially the al Qaeda network, its affiliates, and its ideology" (emphasis in the original).

The 9/11 Commission Report then proceeded quickly to distinguish and distance Islam generally from Islamist terrorism, practiced only by an extreme faction of Muslim believers: "Islam is not the enemy. It is not synonymous with terror. Nor does Islam teach terror. America and its friends oppose a perversion of Islam, not the great faith itself. Lives guided by religious faith, including literal beliefs in holy scriptures, are common to every religion, and represent no threat to us" (p. 363).

Of course, links between religion and terrorism are not limited to Islam. Tensions involving other religions also exploded into acts of terrorism during the twentieth century, including Tamil attacks on the Sinhalese in Sri Lanka, Jewish extremist attacks on the British army in Palestine, and Irish Republican Army (Catholic) attacks on Protestants in Northern Ireland.

Taking a longer historical perspective, acts of terrorism over the past several centuries by Christians and non-Christians alike against people identified as "infidels" raise several critical questions: Does religion cause terrorism? Does religion create a moral sense in people who would otherwise be more aggressive? Does the good of the moralizing force of religion outweigh the bad of the violence that may stem from religious fervor? How can people within religions that are associated with terrorism help put out the fires of terrorism? How can others help them do so?

People throughout the world have experienced religion as a source of inspiration and meaning. Religious people generally view themselves as ethical and see their moral sense as informed by their faith. Religious study is often a primary source of their moral education. Religion gives their lives inspiration and meaning, often replacing emptiness and despair. It provides answers to important questions that elude scientific inquiry, such as "What does it mean to be human?" Religion sanctifies birth, the transition to adulthood, and marriage, and it gives comfort in time of suffering. Continued faith and practice provide a basis for sustaining moral thought and behavior, providing answers to vexing moral dilemmas. For the faithful, to abandon religion would be to abandon the hope for salvation. Many read holy scriptures and attend services in places of worship regularly to restore, maintain, and reinvigorate their moral sense. For them, the very idea of terrorism violates fundamental moral teachings and thinking.

Others see religion as a primary source of terrorism. They cannot easily dismiss the claims of terrorists who commit their acts as "holy warriors" or "servants of God." Many who see religion as a primary force behind terrorism are nonbelievers (e.g., Dawkins, 2006; Harris, 2005; Hitchens, 2007b). But even the religious faithful are typically aware that the extreme religious beliefs of others can be a source of terrorism, even for terrorists who pray to the same deity and read the same scriptures as they do. They tend to regard those who claim to commit acts of terrorism in the name of God as misguided, as tragic exceptions to a following that is decent and moral.

This question is often asked: does religion, on balance, do more good than harm? Although it has no clear answer – and is not as useful as the question of how to minimize the extraordinary harm caused in the name of religion – it nonetheless provides a conceptual basis for reviewing the most essential aspects of each major religion, with an eye toward the connections between religion and moral behavior in general and between religion and terrorism in particular. Let us consider briefly the origins, scriptures, and followers of each of the major religions and how they may be related to terrorism.

We begin with Christianity, Islam, and Judaism, the three religions known as the "Abrahamic" faiths. All three are rooted in the same man: Abraham. All three are monotheistic: they pray to the same god, the God of Abraham. We then turn to three other major religions: Hinduism, Buddhism, and Taoism.

Religion, the State, and Terrorism

1. Christianity

Origins. Christianity began some 2,000 years ago, with Jesus of Nazareth and his leading disciples, Peter and Paul. It began as a Judaic sect that diverged from Judaism as non-Jews embraced the faith and Christ as their savior. Christianity spread across the Mediterranean region despite persecution by Roman emperors. In the early fourth century, the Emperor Constantine legalized Christianity, and by the end of the century it became the official religion of the Roman Empire. Two major schisms produced three branches of Christianity: Roman Catholicism, the Eastern Orthodox Church, and Protestantism. The first schism, in the eleventh century, separated Roman Catholicism from the Eastern Orthodox religion. The second major schism occurred in the sixteenth century, with the creation of Protestantism, led by Martin Luther; it occurred predominantly in Germany and Northern Europe. Not long afterward, King Henry VIII created the Church of England (Anglican Church), which evolved into the Episcopalian church. Subsequent splits within the Protestant wing produced the Lutheran, Presbyterian, Methodist, Baptist, and Mormon denominations.

Scriptures. The primary scriptures of Christianity are the Old and New Testaments of the Bible (also known as the Holy Bible and "The Book"), both of which are collections of sacred writings. The Old Testament has three parts: the Torah (the five books of Moses), Prophets (seven major prophets and twelve minor ones), and Writings (eleven books, starting with the Psalms, Proverbs, and Job). The New Testament, written from about 45 to 140 CE, consists of six books: Gospels, Acts, Pauline Epistles, General Epistles, Prophecy, and Apocrypha.

Leaders and Followers. Christ's immediate followers were his disciples, who in turn became leaders of Christianity after his execution. As word spread of Christ's extraordinary divine powers, Romans, Greeks, and others in Europe joined as believers and followers. Although Christianity began several millennia after Hinduism and Judaism and centuries after Buddhism and Taoism, a few centuries of Christian missionary work to spread the gospel and convert others made it the most widely practiced religion in the world – today with more than two billion followers, about one-third of the world's population.

Each Christian denomination is governed differently. Roman Catholics are led by the Pope, and the Anglican Church is led somewhat less hierarchically by the Archbishop of Canterbury. Presbyterians, by contrast, are loosely governed by a general assembly, the United Methodist Church by a council of bishops, the Church of Latter Day Saints (Mormon Church) by a president and board of trustees, and so on.

Links to Violence. Perez Zagorin's (2005) *How the Idea of Religious Toleration Came to the West* opens with this remarkable sentence: "Of all the great world religions past and present, Christianity has been by far the most intolerant." Violence born of Christian righteousness has been documented also by Juergensmeyer (2003), Stern (2003), and many others. These scholars observe that much of this violence is the product of readings of biblical text that is interpreted as justification for aggression against infidels.

The Bible is often cited as a source of peace and nonviolence, as in passages that urge followers to "love thy neighbor" (Leviticus 19: 17–18; Matthew 5:43), to "do unto others as you would have others do unto you" (Matthew 7:120), and to "turn the other cheek" when attacked (Matthew 5:38:45). But passages can also be found in the Bible that can be interpreted readily as inducements to violence. In Exodus, for example, Moses sings, "The Lord is a man of war" (Exodus 15:3). Then, in Deuteronomy we read that if one should try to entice you to "go out and serve other gods.... You shall stone him to death.... because he sought to draw you away from the Lord" (Deuteronomy 13:6–10). In the first book of Samuel, the Lord orders Saul to "smite Am'alek, and utterly destroy all that they have; do not spare them, but kill both man and woman, infant and suckling" (Samuel I:15:3). And in the New Testament, Christ says, "But as for these enemies of mine, who did not want me to reign over them bring them here and slay them before me" (Luke 19:27).

Such passages from the holy scriptures may be read as parables, but over the centuries they have been interpreted literally to exhort Christians to kill others in the name of God – from as early as 1095, when Pope Urban II launched the first Crusade (see Chapter 1). It took such literary and scholarly giants as John Milton, with his "Areopagitica" (1644/1999), and John Locke, with his "Letter Concerning Toleration" (1689), to create an awareness of the importance of tolerance and the legitimacy necessary for a movement away from religious intolerance and aggression in the name of Christ. Nonetheless, Catholics have in recent times bombed Protestants in Northern Ireland, and extremists have bombed abortion clinics in the United States, using the rhetoric of Christian righteousness. It is no small irony that such episodes of violence have unfolded in the name of the Lord: they present an ongoing challenge to the leaders of various denominations of the vast empire that has evolved from the spirit widely known as "the Prince of Peace."

2. Islam

Origins. The lineage of the Islamic people begins with Abraham and his first son, Ishmael. The Islamic faith arose some 2,700 years later, in seventh-century Saudi Arabia, from the teachings of the Prophet Muhammad, commonly referred to today simply as "the Prophet." The lessons of the Prophet were passed down to followers through his disciples, known as the "caliphate," who were the leaders of the international community of Islam (known as "ummah"). The primary role of the caliphate was to determine who was to succeed Muhammad and what sort of authority he was to exercise (see Box 5.1 for a glossary of basic terms relating to Islam.)

Islam achieved political dominance and considerable military power under the Ottoman Empire during the sixteenth and seventeenth centuries, its

Box 5.1. Glossary of Basic Terms of Islam

Adl: Justice.

Allah: The Arabic name for "God"; the word refers to the same God worshiped by Jews and Christians.

Arab: The ancient and present-day inhabitants of the Arabian Peninsula and often applied to the peoples closely allied to them in ancestry, language, religion, and culture. Bernard Lewis notes that secular Westerners have "great difficulty understanding a culture in which not citizenship, not nationality, not descent, but religion, or more precisely, membership of a religious community, is the ultimate determinant of identity." Under the Islamic caliphate, Arabic became the language of scripture, government, law, literature, and science. Majority Arabic-speaking communities remain in southwest Asia, Egypt, and North Africa. The Arab League includes Algeria, Bahrain, Comoros, Djibouti, Egypt, Iraq, Jordan, Kuwait, Lebanon, Libya, Mauritania, Morocco, Oman, the Palestine Liberation Organization, Qatar, Saudi Arabia, Somalia, Sudan, Syria, Tunisia, the United Arab Emirates, and Yemen. See the entry on Persia.

Asabiyya: Social cohesion, group loyalty, solidarity (from Ibn Kaldun: "binding").

Ayatollah: From the Arabic *ayat Allah*, meaning "sign of God," a high-ranking Shi'ite religious authority. In Iran, it refers to the nation's political and religious leader. Generally not used by Shi'ites in Arab countries or in India.

Caliph: The prophet Muhammad's successors were known as caliphs, and their empire was the caliphate. (Muhammad was a political as well as a religious leader.) The first four caliphs are known as the *rashidun* (the "rightly guided" caliphs). Sunni Muslims consider the rule of the rashidun to be the golden age of Islam. Shi'a Muslims believe that the power of the fourth caliph, Ali, was usurped by the first three caliphs and that his descendants are the proper heirs to the caliphate. (One sect of Shi'ites set up a rival caliphate in Egypt in 983. It lasted nearly 200 years.) Umar, the second caliph, decreed that Jews and Christians should be removed from Arabia. (Such an expulsion was much rarer than the evictions of Jews and Muslims from medieval Christendom.) Since Umar's decree, Islam's holiest sites have been off-limits to non-Muslims.

Emir: Also Amir. Leader or commander. *Amir-ul Momineen* means "commander of the faithful." In the tenth century, the amirs were Turkish army officers who seized power in Iraq, Iran, and central Asia. Emir can also be used as the Arabic equivalent of "prince."

Fatwa: A judgment rendered by a mufti, often issued to settle a question where Islamic jurisprudence (*fiqh*) is unclear.

Hadith: Teachings attributed to Muhammad that are not recorded in the Qur'an.

Hajj: The pilgrimage to Mecca, which Muslims with the physical ability and financial means should perform at least once in their lives. It is one of the five pillars of Islam. The others are *shahada* (profession of faith), *salat* (prayer), *zakat* (alms giving), and *sawm* (fasting). The hajj takes place during the twelfth lunar month of the Islamic calendar and focuses on rituals around the Kaaba (see definition below). A pilgrimage that takes place at another time is called the *umra*. Around two million Muslims carry out the hajj each year.

Ihsan: Compassion, kindness, balance.

Ilm: Knowledge.

Imam: Shi'ite Muslims use the term "imam" for Muhammad's descendants, whom they believe to be the true rulers of Islam. For Sunni Muslims, imam means "prayer leader."

Islam: In Arabic, the word means "surrender" or "submission" to the will of God. Most Westerners think of Islam as one of the three major monotheistic world religions (the others being Judaism and Christianity). Historian Bernard Lewis observes that "Islam" means both a religion (analogous to "Christianity") and the civilization that developed under that religion (analogous to "Christendom").

Islamic calendar: The first year of the Muslim calendar is 622 CE, the year of Muhammad's flight to Medina. The Islamic calendar consists of twelve lunar months. Ordinary years last 354 days, and leap years last 355 days.

Jihad: An Arabic word meaning "to strive" or "to exhaust one's effort." The "effort" can mean preaching Islam and living virtuously in accordance with God's commands, an internal, personal matter. But it can also apply to actual fighting to defend Muslims. Even military jihad, however, is to be fought with respect for rules of war under Shari'a (see Shari'a below).

Kaaba: The most sacred shrine of Islam, it is a cube-shaped stone structure in Mecca. Traditionally, Muslims believe the Kaaba was built by Abraham and his son Ismail. On the outside of one corner is the sacred Black Stone, kissed by pilgrims. The angel Gabriel gave the Black Stone to Abraham, according to one Islamic tradition; according to another, the stone was set in place by Adam.

Koran: See Qur'an.

Mecca: Islam's most sacred city, located in what is now western Saudi Arabia. Mecca is the birthplace of Muhammad and the site of the Kaaba.

Medina: Also located in western Saudi Arabia, Medina is Islam's second holiest place. Muhammad migrated to Medina with 70 Muslim families in 622 CE after being persecuted by the Meccan establishment. It is also the site of Muhammad's tomb.

Mosque: The Arabic word is *masjid*, meaning "place of prostration" before God. Muhammad built the first mosque in Medina. A mosque should be oriented toward Mecca. In many Islamic societies, mosques serve social and political functions in addition to religious ones.

Mufti: A Muslim scholar who interprets Islamic law. Only a mufti can issue a fatwa, a formal ruling on a matter of Islamic law.

Mullah: The definition can vary regionally. In Afghanistan, Ahmed Rashid's Taliban defines it as the traditional prayer leader at a local mosque.

Muslim: In Arabic, "one who surrenders to God"; a follower of Islam. There are one billion Muslims in the world and six million in the United States.

Persia: An historic land in the Middle East adjacent to Arabia, centered in modern-day Iran. Conquered by Arabs in 641 CE, the people of Iran are alone among Middle Easterners in retaining their language, ancestry, religion (Shi'a), and cultural identity. Ethnic Persians make up 60 percent of modern Iran, and Farsi is the official language.

Prophet, The: Muhammad.

Qur'an: The holy book of Islam, recorded by the prophet Muhammad in the year 610 CE. For Muslims, it is the word of God. Islam teaches that the Christian and Hebrew scriptures are also holy books, though they had become distorted over time. The Qur'an is the primary source of Islamic law, followed by *hadith* (teachings of Muhammad not recorded in the Qur'an) and the *sunna* (the habits and practices of Muhammad's life). The word Qur'an means "recitation."

Shah: Formerly the title for Iran's hereditary monarch. A title for the Persian emperor was *shah-en-shah*, or "king of kings."

Shari'a: The Path, consisting of the Qur'an and the Sunna (life of the Prophet).

Sheikh: An elder or religious leader; a wise person.

Shii: The "partisans" of Ali, the fourth caliph, the Shiis eventually became a distinct Muslim sect. The largest Shii Muslim sect is the "Twelver Shii," named after the first 12 leaders (or imams) of Shii Muslims. Twelver Shii believe that the descendants of Ali, Muhammad's cousin and son-in-law, were the legitimate leaders of Islam. Shiis believe the last imam is in hiding, and they await his return. Shiis are the majority in Iran, and many can be found in Iraq, Syria, Lebanon, and Pakistan. There are more than 165 million Shii Muslims in the world. (Also known as Shi'a or Shi'ite Muslims.)

Sunna: The habits and practices of the Prophet Muhammad's life. The Sunna is a documented account of these habits and practices; it is a holy book of Islam. The word "sunna" also connotes "middle of the road."

Sunni: Unlike Shii Muslims, Sunni Muslims believe that Islamic leadership is vested in the consensus of the community, not in religious and political authorities. Their name comes from the word "sunna." The religious scholar Karen Armstrong (2006) emphasizes that, despite their differences, Sunnis and Shiites alike observe the five pillars of Islam. "Like Judaism, Islam is a religion that requires people to live a certain way, rather than to accept certain credal propositions," she writes. "It stresses orthopraxy rather than orthodoxy."

Ummah: The worldwide community of Muslims.

Wahabbism: A puritanical form of Islam that flourishes primarily in Saudi Arabia. It is named after Muhammad ibn al-Wahhab, an eighteenth-century Islamic reformer who wanted to return Islam to its beginnings by emphasizing a fundamentalist approach to the Qur'an.

---

* *Sources:* Akbar Ahmed's *Islam under Siege* (2003); Karen Armstrong's *A History of God* (1994), *The Battle for God* (2001), and *Islam: A Short History* (2002); Bernard Lewis's *The Multiple Identities of the Middle East* (1998); Ahmed Rashid's *Taliban: Militant Islam, Oil and Fundamentalism in Central Asia* (2001); and various online sources.

influence centered in Constantinople, Turkey. The empire extended from Hungary, the Balkans, and Greece in Southeastern Europe, through the Middle East, and to much of North Africa, with a navy that controlled much of the Mediterranean. Although predominantly Muslim, the Ottoman Empire was influenced by other cultures as well, notably the Polish-Lithuanian and Greco-Roman. The empire declined in the late nineteenth and early twentieth centuries and fell eventually in 1923, following the end of World War I.

Scriptures. The Qur'an is the holy book of Islam, regarded as the word of Allah (the Islamic name of God) as passed down to the Prophet in two parts by the angel Gabriel. The first part, received at Mecca, consisted of ethical and spiritual lessons; the second, received at Medina, conveyed social and political principles for organizing the community. The Qur'an consists of 114 chapters ("surahs").

Religion, the State, and Terrorism

Muslims praying at *hajj* in Mecca.

A second major source of Islamic principles can be found in the Sunnah, an account of the deeds and sayings of the Prophet. The writings of the Sunnah can be found in the hadith, which includes also a commentary on the Qur'an (known as the "tafsir") and an account of specifics of Islamic juristic reasoning (the "fiqh"). The fiqh, together with broader principles underlying Islamic law, constitute the "Shari'a," which provides both a framework and rules governing daily life, including matters of criminal law, marriage, financial transactions, food, prayer, and attire. The overarching moral imperatives revealed in both the Qur'an and the hadith are reverence and pious service to Allah, humility, charity, and justice.

Leaders and Followers. In Arabic, the word "Islam" means "surrender." The fundamental religious tenet of Islam is that the follower surrenders to the will of Allah. Followers of the teachings of the Prophet are called "Muslims" (a word derived from the active participle of "Islam"). Muslims traditionally follow Five Pillars of Islam: the profession of faith (known as "shahada" – the idea that there is no god but Allah and that Muhammad is his Prophet), five daily prayers ("salat"), the paying of alms for the needy ("zakat"), self-purification by fasting during the month of Ramadan ("sawm"), and a pilgrimage to Mecca ("hajj") in the western part of Saudi Arabia.

Today there are about 1.3 billion Muslims, mostly in the Middle East, South Asia, and Indonesia. Islam is the second-largest religion in Europe

110

and the third-largest in the United States (Esposito, 2007). Contrary to a widespread impression, Arabs constitute only about 20 percent of all Muslims in the world. Islam is far from monolithic. The vast majority of Muslims – about 85 to 90 percent – are Sunnis, and most of the rest are Shi'a, centered in Iran and the eastern half of Iraq and scattered elsewhere, mostly in the Middle East and Pakistan. Political power in the Middle East has shifted dramatically from Sunni to Shi'a in the new millennium, with the replacement of a Sunni-dominated government in Iraq with a Shi'ite-centered one after the overthrow of Saddam Hussein in 2003, the rise of Hezbollah as both a political and military Shi'ite force in Lebanon in 2006, and most significantly, the emergence of Iran as the dominant political and military power in the region (Nasr, 2005). A third wing of the world of Islam are the Sufis, adherents to an early and once popular form of Islam who today are a relatively small and peaceful group, followers of the Muslim poet and mystic, Rumi (1997).

The key doctrinal differences between Sunnis and Shi'a include sharp disagreement over the question of succession – who should inherit the mantle of authority as leader of Islam after the death of the Prophet in the year 632 – and questions over whether the emphasis in legal rulings should be based on transcendental ideals (the Shi'a position) or on "qiyas," a more pragmatic reasoning-by-analogy approach (the Sunni position). The Prophet left no clear instructions as to who should succeed him as the leader of Islam. The Shi'a minority regarded Ali as the first caliph, the Imam successor to the Prophet, by virtue of family lineage – the Prophet had no sons, and Ali was the husband of Muhammad's eldest daughter – whereas the Sunni majority regarded this appointment as heresy and proceeded to elect instead Muhammad's father-in-law and close friend, Abu Bakr. The Shia's desires were later realized, as Ali became the fourth caliph for all Muslims. However, the split with the Sunnis became irreparable when, in 680, Sunnis killed Ali's son, Hussein, and massacred seventy-two of his Shi'ite followers in the desert of what is now southern Iraq after they had challenged the authority of the sixth caliph, making Hussein a preeminent Shi'ite martyr. The term "Shi'a" derives from their position as "Shiat-Ali" or "partisans of Ali"; the term "Sunni" derives from their position as followers of the Prophet's "Sunna" or "tradition" (see Chapter 1 for a discussion of tensions that have played out between Sunnis and Shi'a over the centuries).

Muslims of all sects remain faithful to Islam through a process known as "jihad," the personal struggle to serve Allah realized in a striving to control one's base instincts and to achieve harmony in the world (Ahmed, 2003, 2007). The term "jihad" has come to be widely understood as something quite different in the era of terrorism – a justification to engage in holy war against infidels – but many regard this connotation to be a political concept rather than a personal, religious one. For mainstream Muslims, nonviolent personal jihad has traditionally been the dominant form of jihad, and violent jihad the lesser form.

Religious leadership is quite important in Islam, but it is less centralized than in the Catholic Church, which is both a strength, in that it allows diversity, and a weakness, in that it makes for factionalism. Leadership in the Sunni arm of Islam is less settled than among the hierarchically structured Shi'ite arm and has a greater variety of leadership styles – from the "Jinnah" model that stresses constitutional democratic principles and social reform, to the autocratic monarchies that have ruled Saudi Arabia for years – with no particular leadership model standing out as the norm. (Muhammad Ali Jinnah was founder of Pakistan in 1947 and its first president, champion of an independent Muslim state separate from India.) This variety may be at least in part the product of greater ethnic and tribal diversity among Sunnis than among Shi'a populations.

It is not unusual for reactionary mullahs to issue hostile fatwas against misbehaving individuals and for moderate mullahs to issue counter-edicts (Khwaja, 2005). This decentralization applies both within and between major sects of Islam. Within the Shi'ite realm, for example, two distinct Shi'ite domains have emerged: the authoritarian style of the Iranian Grand Ayatollah Khomeini and the more quiet, apolitical manner of the Iraqi (originally Iranian) Grand Ayatollah al Sistani, who is more tolerant of secular society (Nasr, 2005).

Muslim spiritual leaders are known as "imams." They lead the prayers at services, and they are religious teachers. In Sunni services, whereas imams lead the prayers, sheikhs often deliver the sermons. Grand muftis rule in important Sunni doctrinal disputes. For the Shi'a, the lines of leadership are more distinct than for the Sunnis, and more hierarchical. A few high priests of Shi'ite Islam are selected as ayatollahs. The highest rank in the Shi'ite hierarchy belongs to the grand ayatollah. These designations are granted by consensus, rather than by vote or ceremony, and are based on the earned respect of teachers and peers. Ayatollahs issue edicts based on their knowledge of Islamic law and their reputations for intellect and wisdom in the community.

Leadership in Islam is also reserved for males. In both Sunni and Shi'a tradition, religious scholars and clerics are all men. Women are assigned roles primarily in the home, are required under the Qur'an (Surah 24:31) to dress modestly, and are urged by the community to avoid succumbing to Western neocolonial excesses (Lalami, 2006). They are not allowed to drive motor vehicles in many Muslim countries. In extreme cases, such as under Taliban rule in Afghanistan, women are barred from education and routinely subjected to domestic violence and gender apartheid, frequently to genital mutilation, and sometimes to severe community sanctions if their dress or conduct is regarded as even slightly provocative and hence out of line. These traditions are bound primarily in culture rather than in scripture.

In response, a few prominent women born in traditional Muslim cultures – notably, Ayaan Hirsi Ali, Shirin Ebadi, and Irshad Manji – have spoken out forcefully against these traditions and, in the face of explicit threats, have expressed moral outrage at the atrocities of Muslim men and written passionately about the hopes and prospects for reforms for Muslim women.

Links to Violence. As with other faiths, it is not difficult to find references to Islam both as a religion of peace (e.g., see Ahmed, 2003, 2007) and as one of violence (e.g., Ahmed, 2007; Harris, 2005; Karsh, 2006). Muslims traditionally assigned a charitable status to Christians and Jews as "people of the Book" ("ahl al-kitab" in Arabic) who are aligned with Muslims in monotheism. They have coexisted peacefully and unremarkably alongside Christians and Jews for more than fourteen centuries, commonly greeting their neighbors with the salutation, "As-Salamu Alaykum" or "peace be upon you" (Karabell, 2007).

It is nonetheless understandable that Muslims would be apprehensive about Christians after centuries of Crusades, aimed at converting Muslims to Christianity. They are upset no less at Jews, who are widely regarded as intruders in a land that had for centuries been the exclusive territory of Arabs and Muslims and who are widely perceived to have humiliated Muslims economically and militarily in that land. In the Qur'an the Jews are alternately characterized as God-loving Abrahamic kin and in other passages placed alongside monkeys and pigs. Muslims have been sharply at odds as well over the years with Hindus, having been discriminated against for centuries in India. In the course of the twentieth century, these religious and ethnic conflicts exploded in a series of wars (in 1947, 1965, 1971, and 1999) between India and Pakistan over Kashmir, a divided territory to the north of India and east of Pakistan.

Many Muslims have come to idolize the *mujahideen*, or holy warriors (derived from *jihad*), for struggling to protect the interests of Islam not only in the wars against India but also against infidels elsewhere. The mujahideen of Afghanistan developed a distinctive aura of heroism for standing up bravely against a vastly larger and more technologically sophisticated Soviet military power in the 1980s, repelling them eventually from Afghan soil, although with considerable help from the CIA and other outsiders. Mujahideen were active against the Soviets as well in Bosnia and Tajikistan and, more recently, against the Russians in Chechnya. Many Muslims regard Muslims who attack U.S. forces in Iraq and elsewhere in the Middle East as members of a larger mujahideen struggle.

The primary links from Islam to violence in general and to terrorism in particular are through individuals who have combined fundamentalism with virulent intolerance and militancy. One common pathway to such a toxic mix is a Sunni school of Islam known as "Salafism," named after the seventh-century ancestors who were closely associated with the Prophet.

113

Salafist ideas were embraced and carried forward in the twentieth century by Sayyid Qutb, leader of the Muslim Brotherhood in Egypt.

Once a narrow sect, Salafism spread substantially during the 1970s and 1980s through the establishment of madrassas in poor Islamic lands, sponsored primarily by oil-rich Saudi patrons (Habeck, 2006). The version of Salafism that was spread by the Saudis is known as "Wahhabism" after its eighteenth-century Arabian founder, Muhammad ibn Abdul Wahhab. Wahhabism was promoted by Saudis in the 1980s and '90s largely as an antidote to the radical Shi'ite Islam that became popular after the 1979 revolution in Iran (Murphy, 2006).

Salafist and Wahhabist schools attract large numbers of vulnerable boys and young men, who typically have no opportunity for secular education. The schools fill them with fiery ideas that give their lives new meaning; then the schools often arrange for them to be sent out into battle against the infidels, despite official Saudi discouragement of violence as a legitimate means to achieve sacred ends (Esposito, 2002). Salafists tend to interpret the Qur'an and hadith selectively, in a way that emphasizes the evils of non-Islamic religions and the decadent lifestyles that often accompany them. These teachings are based on the puritanical belief that the seductions of decadence are ominous, an affront to Allah, and must be defeated at all costs, lest they corrupt the pious following of the principles and life of the Prophet. After 9/11 and the launching of the war on terror, Salafist terrorists began to make extensive use of the Internet and car bombs to carry out acts of violence, often following intensive deprogramming efforts to shed young converts of prior beliefs and align them with pure Salafist doctrine (Wiktorowicz, 2005).

Salafist extremism appears to have influenced the appointment of state judges in the more theocratic Muslim nations. These judges follow Shari'a law closely, and they occasionally rule in support of jihadist defendants. A judge sitting on a special terrorism court in Yemen ruled in 2006 that nineteen defendants – fourteen Yemenis and five Saudis – who had traveled to Iraq to kill American soldiers and fight alongside al Qaeda there had done nothing wrong. The judge acquitted the defendants on the grounds that "Islamic Sharia law permits jihad against occupiers" of Muslim lands (Jaffe, 2006).

If it is ironic that the Christian Crusades were waged on behalf of the Prince of Peace, it is no less ironic that the greatest damage in human lives inflicted by Muslims is against other Muslims. For centuries, verbal rivalries between Sunnis and Shi'a, as well as among sectarian, tribal, and ethnic factions within each of these two major wings of Islam, have escalated to bloodshed. The 1980s war between Shi'ite-dominated Iran and Sunni-ruled Iraq claimed more than one million lives. The insurgency in Iraq following the U.S. overthrow of Saddam Hussein – widely attributable to the unwillingness of Sunnis to cede rule of Iraq to the Shi'a (Ajami, 2006) – has claimed many thousands of Iraqi lives, with no foreseeable end in sight. It has also shifted the monopoly of force in Iraq and elsewhere from governmental authority to that of tribal militias with loose ties within each of two broad camps, Sunni and Shi'a. Muslims in the United States have been particularly peaceful, which many attribute to the fact that they have integrated more successfully into the mainstream economy and culture than in Europe and elsewhere (Cooperman, 2003; Marks, 2006; Pew Research Center, 2007).

The picture is more complex still. Some sects within Islam strongly discourage the use of violence and focus instead on elements of the Qur'an that emphasize the loving and peaceful side of Allah. Perhaps the best known of these is the Sufist sect, noted earlier. The central tenets of Sufism include the importance of cleansing the spirit so that it becomes purified and has the capacity for reflection ("Tazkiya-I-Qalb"), thereby expanding one's ability to absorb Allah's love ("Ishq"), be illuminated ("Tajjali-I-Ruh"), and be fortified with an ongoing awareness of God's attributes ("Dhikr"). These principles are reflected in the poetry of the thirteenth-century Persian theologian and teacher Rumi.

It is impossible to say how these complex forces are likely to play out over the coming years. Historian Diana Muir sees strong parallels to a mix of forces that confronted Christianity centuries ago:

> In some European countries, the Reformation or the Counter-Reformation produced a rigid orthodoxy that stifled development for generations. In other countries the wars of religion were followed by the Enlightenment. Muslims might not follow a European course. They will choose whether they prefer societies shaped by Sayyid Qutb, who advocated closing the Islamic mind to everything but the ancient texts, or Ibn Rushd (also known as Averroes), who preferred the open embrace of all knowledge.
>
> In the near term, though, the Islamic Reformation will divide Muslim society as the Reformation divided Europe. A fervent minority in many countries is already pressing for narrow interpretations on issues such as veiling, whether to listen to music, and replacing secular laws with religious codes. As we have seen in Europe and more recently in Afghanistan, Muslim Puritans are likely to take over communities where they are far from being the majority. Meanwhile, the majority has yet to construct an effective ideological defense of moderation (2007, p. B7).

3. Judaism

Origins. Judaism is the oldest, and the smallest, of the three major monotheistic and Abrahamic religions. (Today, there are about 150 Christians and 100 Muslims for each Jew.) The birth of Judaism is generally agreed to have occurred some 4,000 years ago with Abraham, the patriarch who received blessings directly from God, together with the message that there are no other gods. According to the Bible, the lineage of the Jewish people extends directly from Abraham through his second son Isaac, Isaac's son Jacob, and Jacob's twelve sons, who spawned the Twelve Tribes of Israel. Several generations afterward, Moses led the Jewish people out of slavery under the Egyptian Pharaoh, and later received the Ten Commandments and the messages that constituted the Torah from God on Mount Sinai. Several generations later, the Jewish people were led by King David and then by his son, King Solomon. The distinction is often made between Judaism the religion and the Jewish culture, a broad collection of ethnicities spread throughout the world after two major diasporas – from ancient Judea by the Babylonians in the sixth century BCE and from Jerusalem by the Romans in the second century BCE – yet with a common geneology and culture (Boyarin, 1994; Gartner, 2001).

Scriptures. The Hebrew Bible (for Christians, the "Old Testament") is the primary sacred text of Judaism. Under traditional Jewish doctrine, God revealed His laws and commandments to them in the form of the Torah, the first five books of the Bible, often referred to as "the books of Moses." The Hebrew Bible, which has three major sections, is often referred to as the "Tanakh"; this word is derived from the first letters of each of the three sections: the *Torah* (the Law), *Nebi'im* (the Prophets), and *Ketubim* (the Writings). Jewish law is prescribed in detail in the Talmud, which records rabbinical discussions about Jewish law, ethics, and traditions. The two primary components of the Talmud are the Mishnah, a written compendium of Judaism's oral law, and the Gemara, which discusses the Mishnah and expounds on related writings and issues.

Followers. Approximately 15 million Jews today are divided among three basic doctrinal camps: Orthodox, Conservative, and Progressive. The Orthodox wing (including modern Orthodox and the more traditional Haredi and Hasidic camps) follows the traditions of Judaism most carefully, adhering strictly to the laws of Judaism as set forth in the Torah and the Talmud. The Conservative wing follows a more liberal version of the practice of Judaism, with flexible interpretations of the Torah and Talmud, to accommodate tradition in the modern world. The Progressive wing, including the Reform and Reconstructionist camps, is more distinctly secular than the Orthodox and Conservative wings; its members regard the more traditional interpretations as quaint, if not archaic, needlessly restrictive, and out of touch with the modern world. The Jewish people are often distinguished ethnically between two distinct genealogies: the Ashkenazic or European genealogy and the Sephardic or Mediterranean genealogy.

Links to Violence. As noted earlier, under the discussion of Christianity's links to violence, the Old Testament has numerous passages that can be interpreted as justifications for violence in the name of God. These passages – taken together with the compelling historical precedent of forced exiles; the destruction of temples, slavery, pogroms, and discrimination over the millennia; and the Nazi Holocaust in the past century – provide theological and practical justifications for violence by Jewish extremists, on behalf of both Judaism as a faith and the Jewish people as a persecuted group. A conventional theme is that the Jews must defend themselves with a sufficiently aggressive force to deter future assaults. Such ideas are uncontroversial enough, but when justifiable notions of defense become infused with intolerance and a Zionist, messianic righteousness born of the idea that the Jews are the Chosen People, the result can be extremism and terrorism (Juergensmeyer, 2003; Stern, 2003).

It was in this spirit of extremism that Baruch Goldstein, an American-Israeli physician, saw fit to shoot and kill 29 Muslims and wound 125 others worshiping at the Tomb of the Patriarchs in Hebron, on the West Bank in 1994. It was in a similar vein that Yigal Amir, in the following year, felt justified in assassinating the prime minister of Israel, Yitzhak Rabin, after Rabin signed the Oslo Peace Accords. The Jewish mainstream, like the mainstreams of other faiths, has had only limited success in controlling these fringe radicals.

Many people, particularly Muslims, regard the Israelis as violent and by extension – because Israel is constituted as a Jewish state – they see the Jewish people there as violent. This image is reinforced by the reaction of many Israelis when their military forces inflict excessive harm on civilians in their periodic attempts to root out terrorists in neighboring lands, especially in Palestine and Lebanon. The Israelis respond to these charges typically by saying that they regret all collateral damage, that they do exercise restraint in selecting and attacking targets, and that the responsibility for the death of innocent civilians lies primarily with terrorists who take cover among civilian populations.

4. Hinduism

Origins. Hinduism is the oldest and the third largest religion in the world. It is unlike the other major religions in that it has multiple origins and lacks an iconic figure such as Jesus, Muhammad, or Moses who serves as a single, dominant historical patriarch. Hinduism evolved as a faith in India over the centuries and exists today as a collection of spiritual philosophies, beliefs, and practices of people who chose not to convert to Islam, Christianity, or other major faiths. Schisms similar to those in Christianity and Islam have occurred over the centuries under Hinduism, most notably the split of the Jains and Buddhists from Hindu Vedic traditions and authority, based on their disagreement over the issues of reincarnation and sacrifice, diet, and nonviolence. The somewhat loose and eclectic nature of Hinduism caused these doctrinal splits to be considerably less cataclysmic and hostile than in other major religions, as for example between Catholicism and the Church of England, or between Sunnis and Shi'a.

Scriptures. Hinduism does not have an equivalent to the Bible or Qur'an, a single text that sets forth an orthodoxy, guides doctrinal teaching, and serves as a body of dispute-resolving legal doctrine. Hindu tradition holds instead that people can achieve divine knowledge along many paths. The nearest counterpart to a Bible are the four Vedas – *Rig-Veda, Yajur-Veda, Saama-Veda,* and *Atharva-Veda* – texts written originally in Sanskrit (and commonly referred to collectively simply as "the Veda"). These constitute the most important body of sacred text for Hindus. Each of the Vedas contains four types of texts: *mantra* (the hymns), *braahmana* (words of the high spirits), *aaranyaka* (words of the sages), and *upanishad* (philosophical, somewhat mysterious texts).

Another book widely read as a testament of Hinduism is the *Bhagavad Gita* (commonly referred to as "the Gita"), an ancient Sanskrit text consisting of approximately 700 poetic verses. The verses appear in the form of a conversation between a divine spirit known as "Krishna" and the mortal prince "Arjuna," who is confused about his duty when confronted with moral dilemmas on the battlefield. He receives guidance from Krishna about Yogic and Vedantic philosophies. A fundamental message of the Bhagavad Gita is that true enlightenment comes from awareness of the false self of ego and the ability to choose to identify instead with the immortal self through detachment from material things and transcendence into the realm of the Supreme. In the Yogic tradition, enlightenment comes with the ability to still the mind and overcome selfish desires through self-discipline, which can be achieved through meditation.

Hindu leaders such as Mohandas ("Mahatma") Gandhi have been extremely influential through their writings and actions. Gandhi's thoughts on nonviolent protest and accounts of his experiences are described in his autobiography and in several anthologies of his essays.

Followers. Today there are about 900 million followers of Hinduism, about 20 million of whom live outside of India, principally in Bali, Bangladesh, Bhutan, East and South Africa, Fiji, Nepal, Singapore, Sri Lanka, and the West Indies. Other Hindus are scattered throughout Europe and the United States. Many non-Hindus in the West have also been strongly influenced by Hindu principles and include Ralph Waldo Emerson and Henry David Thoreau in their development of transcendentalism in the nineteenth century; Martin Luther King, Jr., who studied Hindu leader Gandhi's work on nonviolent protest; and millions of Westerners who practice yoga and meditation derived from Hindu teachings and practice.

Common Hindu rituals include the pressing together of the palms of one's hands (symbolizing the meeting of two people), placing the hands over the heart (symbolizing one's meeting the self in another), and bowing one's head with the salutation *"namaste"* when meeting someone, which signifies respect for the other and reverence for the divine in them. Prayer rituals are also common in Hindu temples, at other sacred sites, and in the home. Life-cycle rituals are performed to sanctify birth, the passage to adulthood, weddings, cremation ceremonies, and periodic religious festivals. The red dot worn by many Hindu women on their foreheads – the *bindi* – symbolizes spirituality and good fortune. It is applied deliberately over an energy point (*chakra*) to help focus concentration during meditation.

Links to Violence. As in other major religions, it can be extremely difficult to distinguish religious disputes from political ones, and this is certainly the case with Hinduism and the politics of India. As with the Bible and the Qur'an, justification for violence can be found in Hindu scriptures. The Bhagavad Gita, for example, raises the question of the just war (Chapter 4, Verse 7) and states that it can be a divine act to establish righteousness in the world. It also can be interpreted as trivializing the killing associated with warfare as a matter that is rectified through reincarnation: "he who slays, slays not; he who is slain, is not slain."

These justifications for violence get played out from time to time on the ground. Hostility between Hindus and Muslims has simmered for centuries, occasionally exploding in violence. The partitioning of Pakistan from India in 1947 was justified principally on religious grounds: to give Muslims their own sovereign nation in what had been the western part of India. Tension continues today, with questions over the fate of Kashmir one of the most serious points of contention. The Hindu extremist group Bajrang Dal is the counterpart to extremist Muslim groups in Pakistan. According to Jessica Stern (2003), it serves inadvertently to justify the existence and spread of Muslim extremism in Pakistan. And though relations between Hindus and Sikhs have been mostly civil and often friendly over the years, hostilities have erupted from time to time between the two religions over the status and fate of India's Punjab state. The assassinations of Mohandas Gandhi by a Hindu radical in 1948 and Indira Gandhi in 1984 by a Sikh were based principally on religious grievances (Juergensmeyer, 2003).

Hindu extremism is embodied today in Hindutva, a right-wing movement that originated in the early twentieth century, following the thinking of Vinayak Damodar Savarkar. Hindu nationalism is a core principle of Hindutva advocates. In 1992 an angry Hindutva mob razed the sixteenth-century Muslim mosque, Mughal Babri, in Ayodhya, which led to riots in Bombay and the 1993 Mumbai Bomb Blast. Today the Bharatiya Janata Party of India is closely associated with organizations that advocate Hindutva.

5. Buddhism

Origins. Buddhism is one of the two dominant Far Eastern religions, along with Taoism. Buddhism originated in Northeast India in the sixth century BCE

119

with the teachings of Buddha Sakyamuni (Siddhartha Gautama), originally from Nepal. It migrated eastward to China, Southeast Asia, Japan, and Korea over many centuries and more recently to places throughout the world. Buddhism is generally divided into three traditions: Theravada (a traditional school, literally "the way of the elders"), Mahayana (emphasizing universalism and compassion), and Vajrayana (Tibetan and Japanese forms of Buddhism, similar to Mahayana).

Because of its strong emphasis on meditation and introspection and its focus on the nature of reality, Buddhism is considered by many to be as much a philosophy as a religion. A goal of Buddhist teaching is the achievement of *bodhi*, a transformational awakening or enlightenment – the state of the Buddha. Buddhism emphasizes an awareness of one's attachments to things and ideologies, holding that this attachment generally leads to suffering. Once this awareness is achieved, one begins a process of transformation from the negative energy of desire to a state of enlightenment and, ultimately, *nirvana*, the total extinction of passions, hatreds, and delusions.

Scriptures. Unlike most other major religions, Buddhism has no primary text that is universally read by the various branches of Buddhism. The closest to a "bible" of Buddhism is the Tripitaka, which has three major parts: the *Vinaya Pitaka*, which sets forth disciplinary rules for Buddhist monks and nuns; the *Sutra Pitaka*, which gives the literal discourses of the Buddha; and the *Abhidharma Pitaka*, which interprets those discourses with commentaries on the teaching of the Buddha.

Followers. Estimates of the number of Buddhists today range from between 300 to 700 million people, depending on how the survey is conducted. Questions about whether one is a practicing Buddhist produce smaller numbers than questions about mere belief in the principles of Buddhism.

Links to Violence. Although followers of Buddhism over the centuries have experienced warfare and violence, this religion is not generally associated with the sort of violence common to the other major religions.

A notable exception is the Aum Shinrikyo sect, which has been characterized as an offshoot of Japanese Buddhism, mixed with elements of Hinduism and symbols borrowed from other religions. Founded by Shoko Asahara in 1989, the Aum Shinrikyo cult is responsible for a 1995 sarin (nerve gas) attack that killed twelve people and injured thousands of other commuters on the Tokyo subway (Rosenau, 2001). Asahara was convicted of murder and sentenced to death in 2004 (Cameron, 1999).

6. Taoism

Origins. The roots of Taoism (or Daoism) are in China, around the fourth century BCE; it was founded and inspired by Lao Tsu. Although Buddhism and Confucianism are also historically important as major religions of China,

Taoism remains the most popular. The word "Tao" means, literally, "way" or "path." Like Buddhism, Taoism is regarded both as a religion and a philosophy. A central notion of Taoism is that there is a oneness in all things, a universal foundation from which all life emanates and then returns in a never-ending, cyclical process. Another basic tenet is the concept of *wu wei* (literally, "not doing") – the avoidance of aggression, turbulence, and wasted energy. Wisdom is manifested in one's achieving harmony through quiet contemplation of nature and in gaining an awareness that one can live in much the same way that water flows smoothly and effortlessly over rocks. Thus, people can relate to one another with the humility of nature and with kindness and tolerance.

Scriptures. Taoism, referred to by some as "Chinese folk religion," has two scriptures that are more universally read than those of Buddhism. They are the *Tao Te Ching*, a book of profound poetic verses that describe "the Way" and was written by Lao Tsu, and the *Chuang Tzu*, a book of parables – stories that offer insights on life. These writings describe the path to virtue. The central ideas are as follows: wisdom is achieved by overcoming the ego and understanding others; self-absorption and self-importance are self-destructive; virtue and usefulness begin with uncluttered thinking, in a space of nothingness; true understanding requires a humble acceptance of ambiguity and uncertainty, an awareness that there is much that we do not know; wealth comes from the experience of sufficiency rather than the accumulation of assets, which tend not to enrich the spirit; one achieves more, and with less waste, when one acts in harmony with nature; and force begets force.

Followers. Estimates of the number of Taoists run slightly lower than for Buddhism, generally in the neighborhood of 300 million. Over its long history, Taoism has inspired some of China's great poets and artists to reflect on nature, the human condition, and a world of contradiction.

Links to Violence. As noted above, Taoism is not associated with violence. The *Tao Te Ching* contains specific passages advising forcefully and explicitly against war at virtually all costs. In Chapter 30, Lao Tsu writes, "Thorn bushes spring up wherever the army has passed. . . . Achieve results, but never glory in them. . . . Force is followed by loss of strength; this is not the way of Tao." In Chapter 31, he writes, "Weapons are instruments of fear; they are not a wise man's tools. He uses them only when he has no choice. . . . When many people are killed, they should be mourned in heartfelt sorrow. That is why a victory must be observed like a funeral."

We have noted that within each of the major religions one can find factions that are more or less inclined to violence, that religion is not everywhere and always a cause of terrorism. Taoism serves to demonstrate that an entire religion can be an institution that is first, foremost, and always about spirituality without violence.

B. Moderates, Fundamentalists, and Extremists

There is in every major religion considerable variation in the degree of intensity of its followers' commitment to the faith and to its spiritual leaders, to active participation in the services and ritual practices of the institutions that represent the faith, and to engagement in dialogue on matters of faith with like-minded believers and others. In every major religion, there is also a range in the interpretations of the sacred texts that document the principles of the religion and how those principles should manifest as religious practice. On the right, each of the Abrahamic religions has its traditionalists or *fundamentalists*, who subscribe to the view that the only correct interpretation of the sacred texts is a strictly literal reading of the writings as the word of God; they believe that secular society tends to intrude on this interpretation and undermine the basic principles of the faith. On the left are the *reformers*, who regard the texts as figurative and allegorical, properly interpreted only under the light of hard scientific facts and the stubborn realities of contemporary life. In the middle are the *moderates*, who find a common ground – or, short of that, a compromise – between the two extreme positions, which allows them to enjoy the fruits of both their religion and the secular world and move comfortably within and between the two.[2] It is not uncommon to see much more heated conflict – sometimes leading to violence – among the fundamentalists, and between the fundamentalists and others within a given religion, than between them and members of other religions.

Yet, these tendencies are not constant across religions. As the overview of six major religions in the previous section indicates, fundamentalism is more likely to lead to violence in some religions than in others. A thorough understanding of the relationship between religion and terrorism warrants an awareness of these differences and an understanding of their sources.

One distinction that is useful and pertinent to the problem of terrorism is that between religious fundamentalism and religious extremism. Religious fundamentalists are, by definition, doctrinaire and often rigid in their thinking, but they are not necessarily violent. One can find in every religion fundamentalists who strongly oppose violence. Here is how Middle East scholar Bernard Lewis described Islamic fundamentalism in a landmark 1990 essay:

> Ultimately, the struggle of the fundamentalists is against two enemies, secularism and modernism. The war against secularism is conscious and explicit, and there is by now a whole literature denouncing secularism as an evil neo-pagan force in the modern world and attributing it variously to the Jews, the West, and the United States. The war against modernity is for the most part neither conscious nor explicit, and is directed against the whole process of change that has taken place in the Islamic world in the past century or more and has transformed the political, economic, social, and even cultural structures of

Muslim countries. Islamic fundamentalism has given an aim and a form to the otherwise aimless and formless resentment and anger of the Muslim masses at the forces that have devalued their traditional values and loyalties and, in the final analysis, robbed them of their beliefs, their aspirations, their dignity, and to an increasing extent even their livelihood.

Religious extremists, by contrast, like other extremists (see Chapter 6), are inclined to use violence to rid the land of dissenters. They often see themselves as holy warriors doing work necessary to serve their god. They can be actively hostile to modernity and intolerant of all who disagree with them, including moderates of their own faith. However, religious extremists are not always fundamentalists. Although they rarely acknowledge it, their underlying motives may be more political than religious. Some regard these elements as fascistic (e.g., Hitchens, 2007b).

Two researchers, independently, have explored in considerable depth this phenomenon of religious extremism leading to terrorism committed in the name of God: Mark Juergensmeyer and Jessica Stern. Both used extensive interviews with terrorists and their associates to draw elaborate portraits of terrorism rooted in religious extremism.

Juergensmeyer's research consisted of case studies of religious activists who either used violence or justified its use in the service of religious fervor. He studied Christians involved in abortion clinic bombings and militia actions in the United States, Catholics and Protestants involved in terrorism in Northern Ireland, Muslims associated with the attacks on the World Trade Center and targets in the Middle East, Jews who supported the assassination of Yitzhak Rabin and terrorist attacks in Palestine, Sikhs identified with the killing of India's prime minister Indira Gandhi and Punjab's chief minister Beant Singh, and followers of the Japanese Aum Shinrikyo sect involved in the nerve gas attack on Tokyo's subway system.

Sociologist Juergensmeyer found a variety of common factors underlying terrorism committed by religious extremists. They tended to view their acts of violence as more symbolic than strategic – a sort of "performance violence" – aimed at dramatically humiliating the forces of modernity by destroying its icons, which they felt intruded on and insulted ancient traditions. They saw themselves as heroic agents of social empowerment, giving themselves and the religious groups with which they associated a status that godless institutions had conspired to marginalize, if not destroy. They rejected the compromises that less extreme members of their religion had to endure to survive, and the boundaries within which they were required to operate. They preferred the difficulties of religious sacrifice to the "mind-numbing comforts of secular modernity" (Juergensmeyer, 2003, p. 226).

Does Juergensmeyer see a solution to the problem of religious extremism? He holds that the conventional public response – overreacting to terrorist provocations and thereby lending legitimacy to the cause of religious extremism – only exacerbates matters. He recognizes that makers of public policy may be inclined to ignore the complex constellation of motives associated with religious extremism, but argues nonetheless for a measured, proportionate response as the best antidote – a response that has clear moral grounding, based on a consistent application of the rule of law.

Jessica Stern's (2003) research parallels that of Juergensmeyer in several ways. Her four years of field research, involving in-depth interviews with religious extremists around the world, revealed a similar mix of explanations and motives for their attitudes and behaviors. Stern did this work to discover what motivated religious zealots to become terrorists in the first place and then to remain in terrorist groups, and to learn how they were organized and what might be done to prevent such activities in the future. She interviewed Muslim extremists in refugee camps and prisons in the Middle East, Christian anti-abortion crusaders in the United States, Jewish militants in Israel, and religious extremists of various stripes in Beirut and Gaza, Pakistan and India, and Indonesia.[3] She found that the primary source of religious terrorism was a mix of alienation and humiliation associated with a discomfort with complex, modern life, which led to an apocalyptic fatalism. She opens her book with the following characterization of the mindset of the typical religious terrorist:

> Religious terrorism arises from pain and loss and from impatience with a God who is slow to respond to our plight, who doesn't answer. Its converts often long for a simpler time, when right and wrong were clear, when there were heroes and martyrs, when the story was simple, when the neighborhood was small, when we knew one another. When the outside world, with its vulgar cosmopolitanism, didn't humiliate us or threaten our children. When we did not envy these others or even know about them. It is about finding a clear purpose in a confusing world with too many choices. It is about purifying the world. The way forward is clear: kill or be killed. Kill and be rewarded in heaven. Kill and the Messiah will come.

Stern found that the men and women who lived in the cloud of such thinking were not irrational. She discovered that they derived several benefits from a commitment to violence:

- Spiritual – killing in the service of God, to purify the world of evil
- Emotional – feelings of dignity and honor instead of alienation and humiliation
- Fraternal – camaraderie with like-minded people bound in a common cause
- Educational – schooling in the madrassa system that spawned religious terrorists in large numbers

Stern found that the spiritual, emotional, and educational inducements drew people into terrorist groups in the first place and that a fraternal aspect combined with an addictive state of bliss induced them to stay in the groups, train, provide support, and carry out terrorist missions. She found also that, although some terrorists operated as "lone-wolf avengers" like Unabomber Ted Kaczynski, or as "freelancers" like the al Qaeda-trained shoe-bomber Richard Reid, terrorists more commonly operated in groups requiring financing and logistical support. They were organized along a variety of institutional structures ranging from elaborate franchising systems to leaderless resistance networks. The high-capacity, hierarchical terrorist organization turned out to be a popular entertainment myth, too readily penetrable to be a viable real-world arrangement.

Perhaps the most appealing and effective solution to the problem of extremism in religion – avoiding clashes between religions, if not between civilizations – is for the moderates within the religion to control the extremist factions, so these conflicts can play themselves out internally. As noted in the previous chapter, serious scholars of Islam such as Bernard Lewis have warned that ill-conceived attempts by the West to intervene in these struggles are likely only to serve the extremists and transform internal struggles into clashes between Islam and the West by inflaming ancient enmities.

Although the outrageous acts of extremists can be counted on to make the headlines and show up sensationally as breaking news on television, moderates often do act effectively, typically below the radar, to calm the fires of extremism. Occasionally such efforts do make the news, although rarely on the front page. In 2005 Jordan's King Abdullah, heir to a Hashemite throne that traces its lineage back to the Prophet, convened an Islamic conference of major Sunni and Shi'ite clerics in Amman that produced a communique emphasizing the traditional faith and orthodox interpretations of the Qur'an; it provided a strong alternative to the harsh, narrow themes emphasized by the extremists (Ignatius, 2005a).

C. Religion and the State

What is the relationship between the state and religion? This is a complex question, rooted in the relationship between the individual and the institutions of state and religion, respectively, and in the extent of influence that religion, the state, and secular society hold over the individual in any place and time. For the fundamentalist of any of the major monotheistic religions – Christianity, Islam, and Judaism – the first rule is not to betray God, and the domain of His authority is universal, not to be compromised by rules of government or any secular authority. For many fundamentalists, the very idea of a separation of religion and state is inconceivable, as it raises the prospect of such compromise, which is impossible if everything is subordinate to the word of God.

Religion, the State, and Terrorism

Mark Lilla (2007a, 2007b) observes that Westerners often take the separation of church and state as part of a natural order, dismissing the fundamentalist's perspective. He remarks that Americans, in particular, have little difficulty navigating between devotion to their faith and the conception of themselves as loyal citizens:

> On the one hand, religious Americans believe in the absolute truth of their faiths, even (among fundamentalist Protestants) in the literal truth of scripture. On the other, due to the humanistic turn of modern political thought, they believe that those revealed truths should not affect the rules of the democratic game making it possible for them to practice their faith.... Americans do not argue about the wisdom of federalism by referring to Holy Scripture (Lilla, 2007b).

Lilla adds that many Americans are "astonishingly provincial" and parochial, inclined to believe that this basic principle of the separation of church and state should be the case throughout the world. He warns that failure to appreciate the uniqueness of our views on such matters is bound to create problems.

For most nations, tensions between religion and the state play themselves out in the form of overlapping roles of government and religious institutions. The two domains are viewed largely as complementary, with each providing something that the other does not. The state is considered the domain of the secular. It preserves public order and protects the public against both foreign and domestic threats; it collects taxes, provides public education and other basic services that are not adequately provided by the private sector, and manages the monetary sector to keep the economy strong. Religious institutions, by contrast, provide facilities and leaders to support people's private spiritual needs.

Even in states heavily influenced by theocratic doctrine, the distinction between the affairs of religion and those of the state is typically well understood and respected. Most countries in the world follow the ancient biblical precept, "Render to Caesar the things that are Caesar's, and to God the things that are God's" (Mark 12:17). For example, although it is not clearly spelled out in the U.S. Constitution, a "wall of separation" between the church and the state in the United States serves both to ensure that state rule will be unencumbered by the doctrine of any particular religion and to guarantee religious freedom for all and protect religious minorities against persecution.

Thus, the two domains differ fundamentally, even in theocracies, but their operations often overlap, and that is where tensions arise. State jurisdictional boundaries are geographically determined, whereas religious boundaries are not. People cross national boundaries, literally on the ground, based on a system of official rules of nationality and passport control. Crossing religious boundaries occurs fundamentally outside geography, although the two often

126

coincide. While people who belong to the dominant religions establish permanent residence in countries all over the globe, people of particular faiths are often less welcome in some nations than in others.

North and South American nations and those on the European continent are populated predominantly with Christians, but the nations on these continents generally separate the affairs of government from those of the church and from any particular denomination of Christianity. Asian nations, as well, are similarly constituted along lines that shield the affairs of state from religious influence. However, there was nothing automatic about these developments. Today's religions are, after all, much older than any of the world's nation-states, and allegiance to religion often runs much deeper than allegiance to the state (Sacks, 2002). At the same time, even nontheocratic governments are often constituted and governed in such a way that recognizes God and religion. The name of God is firmly implanted, for example, in the U.S. Constitution, the Pledge of Allegiance, and on the national currency. The relationship between religion and the state, in short, varies from nation to nation and from religion to religion.

The relationship between religion and the state is further complicated by a host of mediating factors. One factor correlates especially strongly with religiosity internationally: fertility rates. After a careful analysis of four waves of data from the World Values Survey, Pippa Norris and Ronald Inglehart (2004) found that countries with higher fertility rates tend to embrace traditional and religious values more strongly, whereas countries with lower fertility rates tend significantly to follow more secular and rational values.[4] They also found, along with numerous other studies, that fertility rates tend to be highest in the poorest countries. It is tempting to draw inferences about the effect of religion on terrorism from these relationships, but other factors may be no less important, including the role of the state. Religiosity may be correlated to terrorism in the twenty-first century, but it is also correlated to fertility rates, education levels, and type of government. It remains an open question precisely how religion, the state, and these other factors combine to produce terrorism.

The complex relationship between religion and terrorism and how this relationship is mediated by the state and other factors are exemplified by the case of the 9/11 terrorists. Here is an account by *New York Times* reporter Dexter Filkins (2006), in his review of a book by Lawrence Wright:

> At the root of Islamic militancy – its anger, its antimodernity, its justifications for murder – lies a feeling of intense humiliation. Islam plays a role in this, with its straitjacketed and all-encompassing worldview. But whether the militant hails from a middle-class family or an impoverished one, is intensely religious or a "theological amateur," as Wright calls bin Laden and his cohort, he springs almost invariably from an ossified society with an autocratic government that

127

is unable to provide any reason to believe in the future. Islam offers dignity,
even in – especially in – death.

Islam is unique among the major religions in its relationship to the state.
Western notions of the separation of church and state have no counterpart in
Islam (Lilla, 2007a, 2007b). Many Muslim nations are theocracies in which
religious law transcends and defines the power of state. Non-Muslim countries, by contrast, generally have constitutions that merely reflect religious
principles. Tendencies toward theocratic rule in Muslim nations derive from
the first of the Five Pillars of Islam, that the follower surrenders first and
foremost to Allah. Islam thus unites the spiritual and temporal aspects of
life, regulating social institutions as well as the individual's relationship to
others and to God. Councils that issue fatwa rulings typically are affiliated
with the government. Accordingly, the separation of church and state, an
underpinning of Western civilization, is impossible in a Muslim theocracy,
as it violates a pillar of Islamic law.

As a result of the unique, deeply embedded doctrinal support for the
supremacy of Islam over secular statehood, Muslims tend to identify first
with Islam rather than primarily as Iraqis, Jordanians or Kuwaitis (Kohut
and Stokes, 2006). To the extent that this follows Islamic doctrine, we might
expect governments in the Middle East to be weaker than those in most
other regions. One should not be surprised to hear Palestinians say that
their sense of nationality has given them only grief, in contrast to their identity as Muslims, which gives them a sense of dignity. Among nations with
Muslim-majority populations, Turkey and Egypt are unique for their dominant secular political entities; Turkey is the only Muslim-majority nation
with a constitution that recognizes an explicit separation between the religious and the secular. A combination of two major factors – setbacks in
attempts of the United States to impose Western notions of freedom and the
protection of individual rights, and failures of secular governments to deliver
basic services efficiently and without corruption – have led to the rise of
Islamism in Iraq, Lebanon, Egypt, and other countries in the Middle East in
the years following the 2003 U.S. invasion of Iraq (Slackman, 2006).

In the West and in other places where the laws of the state conflict with
Islamic law ("Shari'a"), Muslims sometimes organize so as to resolve the
conflicts, operating in the spirit of Islamic community ("ummah"). In 1997,
for example, the Federation of Islamic Organizations created the European
Council for Fatwa and Research, a body comprising more than thirty Islamic
clerics and scholars, to issue rulings ("fatwas") to guide the behavior of
the approximately twenty million Muslims in Europe. Although it operates
primarily to protect the religious rights of Muslims, the body also acts to
ensure that reasonable local civil laws are recognized and respected and that
the Qur'anic principle of respect for non-Muslims is honored. By at least one

account, however, the advice tends to be skewed toward interpretations of Shari'a that make integration with the local secular culture more difficult (Johnson, 2005).

How binding are fatwas? It depends. They are issued in the name of Allah, so they cannot be taken lightly. However, realities on the ground – particularly, conflict with local civil and criminal laws – often make them difficult to enforce, so they are enforced irregularly. One of the most famous fatwas in recent times, issued in 1989 by Iran's supreme spiritual leader, Grand Ayatollah Khomeini, against the British writer Salman Rushdie, was clearly in conflict with British law. Mr. Rushdie, of course, took it seriously and for years afterward took precautions not to make his whereabouts widely known.

D. Does Religion Cause Terrorism?

Religion as a Source of Terrorism. Media sound images of a Muslim terrorist shouting "Allah is the greatest! Allah is the greatest!" as one of the four 9/11 hijacked jets was spiraling toward the ground in Shanksville, Pennsylvania, left an indelible mark of association between Islam jihadists and terrorism. Such a connection is not unique to Islam. Comparable images were etched in people's minds about Christianity by the Crusades and the Inquisition, by John Brown's nineteenth-century killings of slave owners in the name of Christ, and more recently by fundamentalist Christians who killed people at abortion clinics. Similar connections have been established with other religions: Hindu militants slaughtering Muslims, a Jewish extremist spraying machine-gun fire inside a Muslim mosque, and Buddhist extremists poisoning passengers in a train in Japan. It is tempting to conclude from such events, as many have, that religion is a source of conflict in general and an important cause of terrorism in particular.

There can be little doubt that religious extremism and intolerance have contributed to serious acts of terrorism. Still, religious intolerance and violence begin typically, and often most violently, *within* rather than between religions. Sunnis and Shi'a have killed many more Shi'a and Sunnis than they have Christians or Jews, as have Muslim militias in Afghanistan and elsewhere throughout the Muslim world. For many centuries, Christian fundamentalists have killed other Christians who departed from a prevailing orthodoxy, labeling them as "heretics." More than 3,000 Christians were killed by other Christians during the strife between Catholics and Protestants in Northern Ireland in the 1970s and 1980s. Wars have often had strong undercurrents of religious intolerance among different sects within major religions. The killing is often justified by references to sacred text, typically involving literal interpretations of passages that are often invoked out of context, separated from the larger meaning of the surrounding text.

129

Religion, the State, and Terrorism

Killing has become increasingly common as well between major religions. After centuries of relative calm among the religions of the world following the Crusades, battles have raged for decades between Muslims and Hindus in the twentieth century, both within India and, after the creation of Pakistan in 1947, between India and Pakistan. Then, what had been a fairly low-level struggle in the Middle East exploded into a major conflict with the 1967 Six-Day War between Palestinians and Israelis. Subsequent conflict in the Middle East has been fueled largely by Iranian support of Palestinians and Lebanese factions since the Iranian Revolution of 1979; what were once primarily local conflicts have now escalated into a far more dangerous and expansive one between the world of Islam (consisting of more than a billion people) and the West, consisting predominantly of Christians (more than two billion) and Jews (about 15 million).

It is the *extreme militant* factions of any particular religion that are the source of most episodes of religious conflict that lead to violence, both within and between religions. Militant extremists are typically fanatical and fundamentalist, but religious fundamentalism is generally less of a problem than militant extremism. In the domain of comparative religion, *fundamentalism* refers to the strict, literal interpretation of sacred texts – for Christians the Bible, for Muslims the Qur'an. Generally, fundamentalists who read the text literally take strong positions against modernism. But religious fundamentalists may have no interest in resorting to violence to defend their positions, whereas militant extremists typically do – it is, after all, the willingness of some religious fanatics to resort to violence that makes them militant. If the sacred text says that killing is forbidden, many fundamentalists will not kill; militant extremists are more inclined to find passages that can be interpreted as providing a justification for violence.

Some scholars see religion as the major impetus behind today's wave of terrorism. Mark Juergensmeyer, for example, sees religion as "crucial...since it gives moral justifications for killing and provides images of cosmic war that allow activists to believe that they are waging spiritual scenarios" (2003, p. xi). He goes on to say that, although most people feel that religion should provide tranquility rather than terror, "all religions are inherently revolutionary...capable of providing the ideological resources for an alternative view of public order" (p. xii). He argues that religion provides "the motivation, the justification, the organization, and the world view" to facilitate acts of terrorism (p. 7). Juergensmeyer sees the "drama of religion" as "especially appropriate to the theater of terror." Terrorists act out of religious and symbolic images: they play the martyrs, and their targets are the demons (p. 219).

Edward O. Wilson, the Pulitzer-Prize-winning biologist – the father of biodiversity and sociobiology – makes a similar point, contrasting religious thinking to the thinking that emanated from the Enlightenment. Wilson

(2005) sees reason and ethics offering a more direct path toward moral behavior and away from violence than does religion: "Religion divides, science unites. In particular, religious dogma amplifies global conflict, and humanism based on science offers the only sure way to ameliorate this malign effect." Wilson posits that, although the epic of scientific discovery tends to bring people together, the human brain is hard-wired through evolutionary forces in a way that induces humans to engage in myth-making and religious passion.[5] He grants that religion has contributed to culture and to the ideals of altruism and public service, but that these gains are more than offset by the dark side of religion:

> The essentially tribal origin of religions renders them forever and dangerously divisive, a fundamental and intractable flaw that has persisted into our own time. Our gods, the true believer asserts, stand against your false idols; our purity of soul against your corruption; our true knowledge against your error. This discordance, whether expressed as hate or mere humanitarian forbearance, continues in spite of the manifest absurdity of the mythologies that underlie traditional religion (Wilson, 2005, p. 108).

Wilson regards this as a cause for optimism. Arguing that "the more fantastical mythic beliefs are growing harder to swallow by all but the ignorant" and that educated people have a natural evolutionary advantage, he predicts that the naturalistic perspective, based on science, is likely to spread and "will secularize the foundations of moral reasoning: tragic conflicts make it clear that religious dogmas are no longer adequate guides" (Wilson, 2005, p. 110).

In a similar vein, theologian Peter Berger (1999) sees religion tipping the balance toward more violence, not less:

> It would be nice to be able to say that religion is everywhere a force for peace. Unfortunately, it is not. Very probably religion in the modern world more often fosters war, both between and within nations. Religious institutions and movements are fanning wars and civil wars on the Indian subcontinent, in the Balkans, in the Middle East, and in Africa, to mention only the most obvious cases (pp. 15–16).

Sam Harris (2005) takes this view a few steps further. He argues, first, that most of the major religions tacitly encourage violence by diminishing their followers' appreciation for the value of life in the here and now, elevating the status of life in the hereafter and thus discrediting what is ordinarily regarded as rational thinking to preserve life. Preference for heavenly immortality over a mundane mortal life becomes particularly harmful to society when the believer perceives that the path to eternal life is enhanced by righteous intolerance of nonbelievers and the courage to act out against infidels. Harris goes on to argue that this link between religion and violence is exacerbated by taboos, especially in the West, on criticizing either religion generally or the religion of a particular person:

> On this subject, liberals and conservatives have reached a rare consensus: religious beliefs are simply beyond the scope of rational discourse. Criticizing a person's ideas about God and the afterlife is thought to be impolitic in a way that criticizing his ideas about physics or history is not. And so it is that when a Muslim suicide bomber obliterates himself along with a score of innocents on a Jerusalem street, the role that faith played in his actions is invariably discounted. His motives must have been political, economic, or entirely personal. Without faith, desperate people would still do terrible things. Faith itself is always, and everywhere, exonerated (Harris, 2005, p. 13).

Harris concludes: "For anyone with eyes to see, there can be no doubt that religious faith remains a perpetual source of human conflict. Religion persuades otherwise intelligent men and women to not think, or to think badly, about questions of civilizational importance" (2005, pp. 236–37).

As for the relationship between religion and terrorism in particular, a few scholars see the connection as largely illusory. Robert Pape (2005), for one, after a careful analysis of 462 suicide terrorist cases from 1980 to 2004, concludes that more than 95 percent of the cases were motivated by a secular rather than a religious goal: to compel democracies to withdraw their military forces from the land the terrorists regard as their homeland. It is, moreover, all too easy for people with strong political agendas to attempt to legitimize their acts under the cloak of religion. As the lines between the religious and the secular thus remain largely muddled, distinctions among religious, political, and megalomaniacal motives for acts of terror will continue to be difficult to assess.

Religion as a Source of Moral Behavior. Religion is also widely seen as a source – and for many the *ultimate* source – of moral behavior. Devout practitioners of all the major faiths tend to see their beliefs and practices as a source of moral strength. Sacred texts of all the major religions include sets of prescriptions for good behavior: tolerance and restraint, love and charity, forgiveness and redemption, humility and kindness, faithfulness and fidelity, discipline and restraint, reflection and reverence, the ability to listen and attend to human distress, and so on. Accounts of sinners discovering the truth are often stories of people discovering moral lessons in passages from the sacred texts. They discover the value of reforming themselves through faith in a transcendent power – sometimes to go to heaven and avoid an afterlife in hell, sometimes to discover the richness available in the here and now, but always to experience a more profound meaning in their lives than is otherwise apparent or available.

We have noted that eminent scientists such as E. O. Wilson hold dissenting opinions on this point, but other scholars, including some physical scientists, see religion as a net stimulus for morality. Physicist Freeman Dyson (2006), for example, puts it as follows:

> In church or in synagogue, people from different walks of life work together in youth groups or adult education groups, making music or teaching children, collecting money for charitable causes, and taking care of each other when sickness or disaster strikes. Without religion, the life of the country would be greatly impoverished.

Dyson concludes, "My own prejudice, looking at religion from the inside, leads me to conclude that the good vastly outweighs the evil."

Jonathan Sacks (2002) sees this good as long-lasting and indelible. He regards the long-term survival of the great faiths – the fact that they have outlived nation-states for centuries – as indirect evidence that they speak to something enduring in the human character. He observes that it was religion that first taught human beings to look beyond the city-state, the tribe, and the nation to see instead humanity as a whole. Holy texts, including the Bible and the Qur'an, advise followers to treat others as they would wish others to treat them. Rabbi Sacks reports meeting religious leaders from all the major faiths who embrace the tradition of unity worshiped in diversity, a spirit he calls "the dignity of difference." We may be more alike than we are different, and we could use a universal "theology of commonality"; but to the extent that we *are* different, we can acknowledge the dignity of this too and can respect both the commonalities and the differences. For Rabbi Sacks, this is a deeply held religious belief, one that leaves little room for clashing civilizations: "Religion binds." Difference is not to be merely tolerated; it is to be celebrated. It enlarges the sphere of human possibilities. The test is to see the divine presence in the face of a stranger – a capacity that builds trust and civility and may, in the process, inoculate societies against terrorism.

Given this prospect, how can religion possibly be invoked to justify violence? One answer is that it is done typically by people for whom political or genocidal goals underlie avowed spiritual expressions. The Ku Klux Klan's justification of its savage racist acts in the name of Christianity is a case in point. Sacks sees Saddam Hussein as another such case: "Saddam Hussein's Iraq is a good example – religion is invoked by essentially secular leaders as a way of mobilizing and directing popular passions. There are some combinations that are incendiary, and the mixture of religion and power is one" (2002, p. 41). He elaborates as follows:

> The great tragedies of the twentieth century came when politics was turned into a religion, when the nation (in the case of fascism) or system (communism) was absolutized and turned into a god. The single greatest risk of the twenty-first century is that the opposite may occur: not when politics is religionized but when religion is politicized (p. 42).

Religion, the State, and Terrorism

We noted in the previous section a complementary explanation by Sam Harris (2005): in giving people hope for salvation in an eternal hereafter, religion diminishes their appreciation for the value of living fully here on earth. This creates an opportunity for religious moderates and leaders to step up and control their extremist brethren and to distinguish in a public way those who use religion to legitimize political motives from those who are true first to their faith. Moderates are better positioned than others to constrain the most radical members of their own faiths. Therefore, Rabbi Sacks sees that moderates have an essential responsibility to maintain moral integrity and legitimacy: "Religious believers cannot stand aside when people are murdered in the name of God or a sacred cause. . . . *If religion is not part of a solution, it will certainly be part of the problem*" (emphasis in the original).

Along a similar line, Daniel Dennett (2006a) likens religion to a swimming pool: those who derive the benefits of ownership must also be responsible for the harms that result when people are lured into causes that can kill others. Dennett sees it increasingly difficult to exercise this responsibility in an age of information and communication technology in which religious intolerance can spread and mutate like a pandemic virus.[6]

How to exercise this responsibility raises a deep, ancient philosophical dilemma. Under what circumstances, if any, should religious intolerance be met with intolerance? Tolerance does have a downside. Knowledgeable observers attribute the establishment of Britain as a hotbed of radical Islamic violence to its tradition of tolerance, especially during the 1980s and '90s, when it became a major refuge for political outcasts and expelled preachers of hatred from around the world (Sullivan and Partlow, 2006). The large influx of Pakistani and other Muslim immigrants into London over this period resulted eventually in people referring to the city snidely as "Londonistan." Then, after a series of terrorist attacks originating from these populations in the years following the 9/11 attack, Britain began a difficult process of deporting some of the most radical of these immigrants. Under such circumstances, the commonsense interests of self-preservation can outweigh the exercise of tolerance.

Another answer to the moral component of the dilemma – whether it is right to be intolerant of intolerance – may be suggested by a Christian teaching from the book of Matthew: turn the other cheek. One historical anecdote suggests that, when used skillfully, such a strategy can be not only moral but also effective. Walter Isaacson (2005) writes about how Benjamin Franklin dealt with the intolerance of Puritans in New England: he reacted not with intolerance, but with an ingenious mixture of tolerance and humor. Franklin put his capacity for tolerance to good use at the Constitutional Convention, displaying a willingness to compromise some of his core beliefs to help produce a near-perfect document. Isaacson observes, "It could not have been accomplished if the hall had contained only crusaders who stood on unwavering principle."[7] Franklin's idea of confronting violent intolerance with humor was echoed a century later by the journalist Ambrose Bierce: "War is God's way of teaching Americans geography."

In the end, whether religion, on balance, produces more or less moral behavior remains an open question. Freeman Dyson sees "no way to draw up a balance sheet, to weigh the good done by religion against the evil and decide which is greater by some impartial process."[8]

E. The Future of Religion

Religion is unlikely either to find itself in the dustbin of history or to eliminate secular thinking any time soon. Its popularity and influence have grown over some periods of time and in different parts of the world and declined in others – sometimes rapidly, more often gradually – but it is here to stay. The Age of Enlightenment brought with it the ascent of reason and secularism and the decline of faith and religion. But even the great scientists – Galileo, Newton, Darwin, and Einstein – were inspired by faith in God and remained committed to their faith as they advanced scientific knowledge and removed uncertainty from a world of bewildering complexity. As science continues to unravel what was previously unknown and relegated to the domain of faith, it continues to raise new questions about the sources and nature of life and the place of the human species in the universe, yet it is unlikely ever to answer all these questions fully. Science has also produced technologies that disrupt people's lives and induce them to find solutions to losses of dignity and tranquility. It is largely for these reasons that the building of scientific knowledge has been accompanied by the *growth* of religion over recent decades, a trend that some authorities expect to continue for the foreseeable future (Berger, 1999).[9]

Religion has its limitations. While science has little to say about proper moral behavior, religious authorities have been known frequently over the ages to resist valid scientific discoveries that have conflicted with religious dogma. Religious dogma has been invoked perniciously in the causes of extremism and intolerance, even though serious religious scholars of every faith hold that the deeply held tenets of their faith need not be interpreted dogmatically. Their faiths can provide truths and comfort for those who find that reason alone does not make life worth living, and this can be done effectively without coercion. There can be no doubt that for the vast majority of the human species, both faith and reason are certain to continue to play essential roles for the future course of humankind.

One thing is clear: the prospects for harmony among religions, and between the faithful and the skeptics, can only grow as each side chooses tolerance over intolerance; these prospects will decline if the path of intolerance is taken (Vattimo and Rorty, 2006).

Discussion Questions

1. *Religion and moral behavior.* What is it about religion that makes people behave better than they would otherwise? What is it about religion that makes them behave worse?

2. *A religion's emphasis on peace or violence.* Each religion has its factions that are relatively peaceful and others that are more violent, and these change over time. For Islam today, for example, Salafists tend to be more inclined to violence, and Sufists toward peace. What do you think causes violent sects to emerge from time to time from the more peaceful sects? What are the central lessons to be learned from the ending of the Crusades in the thirteenth century and the emergence of secularism that followed? What implications might these lessons have, if any, for religious violence in the twenty-first century?

3. *Interventions by religious authorities.* What can religious authorities do to reduce inclinations for the faithful to behave aggressively toward others?

4. *Interventions by others.* How can people outside a faith that is associated with terrorism act in such a way that does more good than harm? What should be done about religious authorities who preach hatred?

5. *Tolerating intolerance.* Under what circumstances should intolerance be ignored? Under what circumstances should it be confronted? How should it be dealt with? How do the answers to these questions differ for intolerance among members of one's family, one's associates, and strangers? What is the nature of each of these forms of intolerance, and what are the sources of each? What are the nature and sources of your intolerance for others?

Nonreligious Extremism and Terrorism

This chapter focuses on political extremism, on both the left and right, and how it and other forms of nonreligious ideological extremism can spawn terrorist activities. It identifies and describes specific ideologies, factions, and issues that have been associated with terrorism and then looks more closely at specific extremist groups that are like most others in some ways and unusual in others, to exemplify the problem of extremism and its variants and how the common product of extremism – isolation – can have deadly consequences, both for members of extremist groups and for others.

A. Extremist Ideologies

Terrorism grows typically out of a constellation of factors, but it is almost always a product of extremist belief. In the post-9/11 era, discussions about extremism are usually about religious extremism. However, in the more than two centuries since the word "terrorism" was first used, terrorism has been linked predominantly to political, racial, and ethnic extremism, rather than religious extremism (George and Wilcox, 1996; Hewitt, 2003; Pape, 2005).[1] In the case of both political and religious extremism – and recognizing that it is not always a straightforward matter to disentangle the two – one of the great puzzles has been that of figuring out how to reduce or eliminate the tensions that emerge from extremist factions and give rise to acts of aggression. The problem has become far more volatile with the rise of weapons of

137

mass destruction and new technologies for spreading extremism, which give extremist factions far greater reach and the capacity to harm others both nearby and in places far away.

There is much to be gained in understanding extremism: what it is, why it appeals to so many people, which sorts of people are most susceptible to it, when it is dangerous, what are the most basic varieties of extremism, and what can be done about extremism and extremists. In this chapter, we look at each of these issues in turn.

What Is Extremism? Extremism means more than merely being out of the mainstream; it means taking an idea to its limits and sometimes beyond, regardless of repercussions and impracticalities (Scruton, 1982). As a source of terrorism, it encompasses that and more: *intolerance* of the beliefs or opinions of others, or of a class of people who are simply different racially, behaviorally, or in appearance, regardless of their beliefs or opinions. Extremism, whether motivated by religion, politics, or hatred of others, does not ordinarily give rise to terrorism. In the most benign case, a group of people might have extreme ideas and express them by electing to remove themselves from the mainstream by, say, always dressing in black and having their bodies pierced and covered with tattoos. Although such people are likely to be of interest to anthropologists and psychologists, they do not qualify as representatives of the sort of extremism that gives rise to terrorism.[2] Extremism becomes a force to reckon with when it is coupled with a desire to use intrusive means that diminish the well-being of others; the greater the intrusion, the more dangerous the extremism.

Why Is it Appealing? Extremism of the sort that produces terrorism appeals especially to people who see themselves as underdogs or intruded upon and feel inclined to react against those whom they perceive as oppressors or intruders. Martha Crenshaw (1998) refers to terrorism, the hostile reaction of the extremist, as the "weapon of the weak" (p. 11; see also Pape, 2005, pp. 27–37). Of course, most people in such societies may not consider themselves as weak or oppressed; the experience of weakness can be largely a matter of perception. But perceptions are important: they drive behavior. Extremists who see themselves as underdogs generally justify their hostile actions in terms of survival and intolerance, and as noted above, intolerance is the common ingredient of the sort of extremism that spawns terrorism.

Intolerance derives typically from a mixture of paranoia, anger, and righteousness. The *paranoia* results generally from a sense of threat posed by an alien other, often based on one's own sense of inferiority and unsubstantiated or poorly substantiated conspiracy theories (see Box 6.1). The *anger* provides a way of responding to the paranoia by giving the individual a sense of control over the perceived threat and the disruption it causes. And a sense of *righteousness* is usually used to justify the paranoia and anger, based on a belief in the moral superiority of the group's position, often validated by

Box 6.1. Conspiracy Theories, Tragedies, and Extremism

Extremist groups often rely heavily on conspiracy theories to provide the rallying cry to their causes. Conspiracy theories attempt to explain events, often calamities, as secret plots planned by powerful individuals or groups, rather than as isolated acts committed by individuals or simply as random occurrences. Here are four prominent examples of conspiracy theories that have been debunked to the satisfaction of all but a few diehard holdouts: (1) Franklin D. Roosevelt participated in the planning of the 1941 attack on Pearl Harbor; (2) Lyndon B. Johnson was behind the 1963 assassination of President John F. Kennedy (or Fidel Castro or the Soviet Union planned it); (3) Robert F. Kennedy was assassinated by members of the CIA's failed Bay of Pigs operation; and (4) the 9/11 attack was perpetrated by Zionists, and Jews had been warned prior to the attack not to go to the World Trade Center (or it was done by the U.S. government).

Conspiracy theories are especially attractive to the uneducated and to those who are cynical of information presented by conventional authorities. In some cases, of course, conventional authorities turn out to be incorrect, as in the case of the widespread belief – not only held by U.S. authorities, but by United Nations inspectors and many others – that in 2003 Saddam Hussein had vast stockpiles of weapons of mass destruction. Such instances may feed conspiracy theories by increasing public cynicism of official accounts of major events. The cynicism may be deepened by a media industry that has a commercial interest in shocking people with scary stories, rather than presenting the more boring conclusions that may be indicated clearly by the facts.

In those cases in which conspiracy theories gain currency – perhaps in most of them – the theories turn out under scrutiny to be demonstrably false. Often they are contradicted by overwhelming reliable evidence to the contrary. In other instances the conspiracy theories are the product of information that has been fabricated; one such case is *The Protocols of the Elders of Zion*, a book describing a Jewish plot to rule the world, which had been plagiarized from a 1864 fictional pamphlet by the French satirist Maurice Joly, entitled *The Dialogue in Hell between Machiavelli and Montesquieu*. Epistemologist Karl Popper (1966) has observed that even conspiracy theories that cannot be disproven are nonetheless generally dubious because, in the real world, "conspirators rarely consummate their conspiracy."

According to Walter Laqueur (2003), the appeal of conspiracy theories about tragic events is widely underrated, a product of ignorance, and sometimes the source of further tragedy:

The belief in conspiracy theory is much more widespread than generally assumed. It is usually present in paranoia – the assumption that there is a pattern (usually negative or hostile) in random events. Nothing in the world happens by chance; obvious motives of other persons are rejected, and in severe cases this mental attitude leads to vengeful attitudes and violent confrontation. There is a close connection between terrorism (and the interpretation of terrorism) and conspiracy theory. There were and are terrorist groups in history that were more or less free of such symptoms. But they were certainly present in terrorist movements of the extreme right... (p. 155).

How should one assess whether a particular conspiracy theory is true or false? We have several ways of testing the validity of any particular explanation of a phenomenon. One of the most basic is the application of the rule of "Occam's razor": the simplest explanation of a phenomenon, the one requiring the fewest number of unreasonable assumptions, is best. When empirical validation is possible, science has developed a coherent and well-tested system for validating conclusions based on a set of facts: develop plausible theories, collect reliable data to provide a basis for testing the theories, conduct the test using an appropriate set of empirical techniques, see which theories turn out to be most plausible in light of the findings, and replicate the test in other settings. Of course, many events do not lend themselves to this sort of empirical scrutiny, in which case logic, common sense, and thoughtful discussion will play a larger role.

Can the public be inoculated against conspiracy theories? Only to an extent. Education is a key; educated people are less susceptible to believing conspiracy theories. But even educated people are susceptible to conspiracy theories, especially when they know they have been misled by authorities they previously trusted. The best way to weaken the strength of the conspiracy theory may be to build institutions that provide consistently reliable information on issues of importance.

an assortment of half-truths, passages from a holy scripture (typically taken out of context), or quotes from secular authorities (often fabricated and then passed on as authentic), as well as rituals and dogma espousing moral absolutes (such as "we are good; they are evil"). The fears of the extremist groups thus tend to give rise to emotionally loaded thinking, fallacious reasoning, appeals to group loyalty to provide a commitment and camaraderie against the alien others, and sometimes calls for action. The group's bonds are usually created and sustained by a compelling figure, or a pair or trio of people, who provide leadership and coherence to the cause.

What Makes Extremism Dangerous? Extremism is not a bad trait in itself. It is common in most healthy societies. Political scientist Laird Wilcox observes that mere advocacy of a fringe position "gives our society the variety and vitality it needs to function as an open democracy, to discuss and debate all aspects of an issue, and to deal with problems that otherwise have been ignored" (1996, p. 55). He goes on to say that extremism hampers understanding when it "muddies the waters of discourse with invective, defamation, self-righteousness, fanaticism, and hatred, and impairs our ability to make intelligent, well-informed choices."

Extremism is particularly dangerous when it is coupled with intolerance. The late Robert F. Kennedy put it this way: "What is objectionable, what is dangerous about extremists is not that they are extreme, but that they are intolerant. The evil is not what they say about their cause, but what they say about their opponents" (quoted in Lowe, 1964).

Most people learn to manage intolerance when the feeling emerges. Intolerance becomes dangerous when it is not managed, when it becomes habitual, or when it is accompanied by a compulsion to act aggressively. For extremist groups, this compulsion is often justified as a means of demonstrating this sentiment to the alien other: We do not approve of you, and we are a force to be taken seriously. Alternatively, the extremist group may act preemptively out of a sense of defense, to rid the area of the threat before it intrudes excessively on the interests of the group. At the point where such a threat is perceived as real, either the extremist group or the alien others may feel compelled to engage aggressively in the challenge, unless either the others or a third party acts to address and resolve the perceived threats and reduce the tensions that give rise to the conflict. (In Chapter 12, we consider strategies for dealing with intolerance.)

We turn now to the basic varieties of extremism.

1. Political Extremism

The Political Spectrum. The forces of extremism appear to be the most common in the political arena. Political extremists show up in societies throughout the world at both the left and right ends of the spectrum. Consider the primary elements of the political spectrum. Leftist moderates generally tend to be interested in changing the status quo and are concerned about economic and social inequality, corporate power, and the rich, and they favor the rights of minorities and ordinary workers. Advocates on the left tend to emphasize the need for the expansion of rights and entitlements of the poor and disenfranchised and the responsibilities of the rich and powerful, whereas those on the right are more inclined to reverse the emphases, arguing for lower taxes as a means to shrink government and grow the economy. Right-wing moderates generally tend to resist the redistribution of wealth (especially economic conservatives) and emphasize the restoration of moral values (especially social conservatives); they are typically opposed to big government and regulation, except on matters of security and the restriction of particular rights: abortion, gay marriage, stem cell research, and other institutions regarded as immoral.

These differences are real, and they appear to have grown in recent years, opening doors to extremism (Abramowitz and Saunders, 2005). Demographic factors and geography also correlate with liberalism and conservatism. For example, people tend to become less extreme and more moderate as they age. And people in urban areas tend to lean more to the left than people who live in rural or suburban areas (Clark and Lipset, 2001).

How Extremists Differ. Extremists on both the left and right take these basic distinctions as launching pads for positions that depart substantially from the mainstream, based on fervent commitments to deeply held beliefs. Extremists on the left, often referred to as "radicals," range from neo-Marxist utopians who disrupt meetings of world trade organizations, to environmental extremists who sabotage the harvesting of trees or mining operations, to anarchists who disrupt law enforcement operations more generally. Extremists on the right, often referred to as "reactionaries," vary from protestors who prevent staff and patients from entering abortion clinics, to xenophobes who patrol the borders as vigilantes against the instructions of government officials, to members of hate groups. Extremists on both ends tend to receive attention far out of proportion to their numbers, because of their deep commitments to their respective causes – often the product of fear, anger, and righteousness, as noted earlier – but often as well because the media tend to be attracted to the outrageousness of extremists' acts and their occasional resort to violence, which can create incentives for further violence (see Chapter 10). Because both extremes are inclined to isolate themselves ideologically and socially from the mainstream, they often develop misguided perspectives, thinking of their own positions as normal rather than extremist, while characterizing anyone whose views differ from theirs as an "extremist": either an "ultraconservative" or "ultraliberal."

As is the case with religious extremists, political extremist groups often struggle not just with extremists on the other side, but often more frequently and furiously with those in the moderate center. And because they tend to be rabidly committed and aggressive, they commit acts that receive media attention that is disproportionate to their numbers in society. Both of these factors – their inclination to alienate the mainstream and the negative public response to attention they receive from the media – make political extremists generally quite unpopular with the vast majority of the public. According to historian Walter Laqueur, "The history of terrorist movements shows that those motivated by nationalism always had a greater reservoir of sympathy than those of the extreme left or right" (2003, p. 148).

Cross-Cultural Variation. These basic distinctions between left and right apply particularly to the political spectrum in the United States, but similar patterns are found elsewhere throughout the world. Conservatives and liberals elsewhere, however, often place emphases on different issues than do their counterparts in the United States. European right-wing extremists, for example, are less likely to focus on abortion clinics and more likely to advance agendas of hatred against immigrant minorities. Skinheads in Europe are generally more organized and dangerous than in the United States, and Marxist and communist extremists tend to be stronger among the left-wing factions of Europe and South America than in the United States (De Lange, 2005; Minkenberg, 2000; Schafer and Navarro, 2003).

2. Racist and Ethnic Extremism and Hate Groups

Racial and ethnic extremism has been one of the more common sources of terrorism over the past 150 years. Two prominent examples of racial or ethnic extremism that has given rise to terrorist events are the Ku Klux Klan's reign of terror over blacks from the end of the Civil War until the early to mid-twentieth century and Nazi Germany's reign of state terror over Jews throughout Europe from the late 1930s until the end of World War II in 1945.[3] Racial and ethnic extremism qualify clearly as extremism that can give rise to terrorism. Both involve intolerance of others based on perceptions of feeling intruded upon by the races or ethnicities identified as worthy targets of attack. In the case of racial and ethnic extremism, one of the great fears is that the intrusion will take the form of "mongrelization" of one's own race or ethnicity – resulting in the loss of racial or ethnic purity and identity due both to the absorption of cultural mores perceived as inferior and biologically through intermarriage.

As with political extremism, it is useful to understand the differences between moderates and extremists – in this case, the distinction between racism and racial extremism. Racism is bigotry or prejudice against particular races. It may involve mild forms of marginalization and social abuse, such as stereotyping, unconscious rudeness, or insensitive racial or ethnic slurs, or it may involve less benign forms of bigotry, such as policies that encourage segregation in housing or discrimination in lending, employment, education, and other essential services. It becomes racist or ethnic extremism when it promotes the solution of "cleansing" society of any race or ethnic group it labels as undesirable. It becomes terrorism when it acts out on such notions in the form of threats or violent attacks against the group targeted.

Racial and ethnic extremism are expressed as terrorism through *hate groups* in the West and through militias or state-supported groups elsewhere.[4] Much as terrorists regard themselves as "freedom fighters" or "servants of God" rather than as terrorists, members of hate groups tend to regard themselves as "Christians" or "patriots," rather than as criminals, members of hate groups, or terrorists. Hate groups typically target minority races and ethnicities, but they often target immigrant groups as well, especially from non-European countries. Non-Christians, homosexuals, and other "undesirables" are also common targets of hate groups, as is the government that is perceived as having been infiltrated by, and trying to protect, these and other minorities. Some borderline hate groups are more interested in simply being outrageous, as in the case of skinhead counter-culture groups that appeal to rebellious teenagers by producing punk rock music and provocative magazines ("skinzines") and comic books. Others are more inclined to violence. After 9/11, Muslims moved up prominently in the rankings of targets worthy of hate-group attention. Hate groups in the United States generally justify themselves on grounds that the people targeted are dangerous, that they threaten not only the purity of the dominant culture but also the economic well-being, social order, moral norms, and ultimately the existence and continuing survival of a white, Christian America.

Hate groups typically support their claims of superiority and exploit the public's fears and patriotic sentiments using propaganda, pseudoscientific assertions, and fabrication. Prominent examples include the 1915 motion picture, *Birth of a Nation*, which lionized the Ku Klux Klan and demonized blacks, and a book published in the late 1890s that targeted Jews as the enemy: *The Protocols of the Elders of Zion* (Ben-Itto, 2005; Franklin, 1989). The immediate aim of such propaganda is to create a sense of urgency by characterizing the target population as evil and menacing, based on conspiracy theories supported by an assortment of partial truths and clear lies. In the process, hate groups hope to recruit new members and gain financial support while unsettling – if not terrifying – the targeted group, consistent with the behavior of terrorist groups generally. They may then act on these theories by either threatening targeted populations – increasingly using the Internet and e-mail – or by assaulting individuals perceived as warranting such treatment (Bushart, Craig, and Barnes, 2000; George and Wilcox, 1996; Levitas, 2004; Petrosino, 2003; Schafer and Navarro, 2003).

John Schafer and Joseph Navarro identify several ingredients common to hate groups, based on observations and interviews with several hundred skinheads apprehended by the Federal Bureau of Investigation over a seven-year period during the 1990s. They find, first, that the attraction to hate groups usually begins with a relatively uneducated white teenage boy or young man wanting peer validation. The hate group typically provides such validation and does so with a degree of anonymity, giving the members of the group the sense that they can escape responsibility for their actions. The group then develops symbols and rituals, such as Nazi salutes, military boots, tattoos, ornamented jackets, and so on, to distinguish themselves, validate the enterprise, and create a sense of loyalty and camaraderie. The group members then direct their attention to one or more minority groups over which they can feel a sense of superiority. Next comes a process of systematic reinforcement of core hatreds and justifications, often accompanied by verbal abuse of the singled-out group or groups. These taunts may occur either face to face, through any of the channels of computer communications noted earlier, or through various combinations thereof. When worked up to a sufficient call-to-action frenzy, the members commit an act that fills a recreational thrill-seeking purpose: they find a member, or occasionally members, of the despised group and assault them physically, often after a bout of drinking and drug use, and sometimes using crude weapons such as baseball bats or broken bottles. In launching such attacks, they cross a clear line: these acts qualify as crimes and as acts of terrorism too, broadly defined – acts of violence against innocent people motivated by ideology.

Recognizing this line between legal and illegal behavior, some hate groups have learned to operate just beyond the reach of the law. They have developed a degree of sophistication, thanks in part to information gleaned from the Internet, repackaging their message and attaching it to more legitimate sources of authority. The goal is to ensure survival and find ways of appealing to a more mainstream audience, both politically and culturally (Perry, 2000).

In the next section we look more closely at two historically prominent hate groups in the United States: the Ku Klux Klan and the White Aryan Resistance.

3. Other Extremist Ideologies

We hear much about religious extremism, political extremism, and racist and ethnic hate extremism, but there are still other forms of extremism that can and have led to terrorist events. Among the more significant are environmental extremism, anti-globalization extremism, and anarchic groups or cults, usually with an extreme libertarian orientation.

Environmental Extremism. Environmental extremists take concerns about nature and the environment to levels that go well beyond the positions taken by mainstream environmentalists on pollution, the destruction of natural resources for commercial purposes, agribusiness, and related matters. Their position is strongly ideological, regarded by most people as unreasonable, impractical, and counterproductive. Environmental extremists include the following:

• Radical environmentalists, such as Edward Abbey, Ron Huber, Mike Jakubal, and members of Earth First, who have taken aggressive positions against logging companies and dam construction operations

Nonreligious Extremism and Terrorism

- Neo-Luddites and primitive anarchists, such as Theodore Kaczynski, who are opposed to technology generally
- Animal liberation activists, such as Steven Best and Robin Webb, who work to liberate animals from laboratories, farms that treat animals cruelly, and fur farms

Environmental extremists graduate to "ecoterrorists" when they break the law to carry out acts of vandalism or sabotage against commercial establishments or others whom they regard as "enemies of the planet." Later in this chapter we look at one such group, the Earth Liberation Front.

Anti-Globalization Extremism. "Anti-globalization extremism" is an umbrella term that covers extremist ideologies opposed to various aspects of globalism. They range from radicals who demonstrate against the power of large corporations and trade agreements to neo-Marxists opposed to capitalism, social injustice, and the skewed international distributions of wealth and income. The members of this assortment of radicals engage in protests from time to time, usually nonviolent, against world trade organizations and international trade agreements, which they regard as exploitive of the poor and the environment and serving mostly a small, extremely wealthy, and powerful minority. They target organizations they regard as visible symbols of globalization, including the International Monetary Fund, the World Bank, and the World Trade Organization.

Occasionally the actions of anti-globalization extremists cross the lines of civility and legality, as in the case of the 1999 "Battle of Seattle." About 50,000 protesters, loosely organized from hundreds of assorted "affinity groups," came to Seattle to block intersections and engage in street theater in a fifteen-block perimeter downtown, disrupting meetings at the World Trade Organization's Ministerial Conference being held there. Police responded with a force of 400 officers to clear intersections, at first gently and then escalating to shouting orders, using pepper spray, rubber bullets, and tear gas canisters in attempts to reopen the streets and allow WTO delegates to pass through the blockade. The result was chaos – miraculously, without any fatalities – as rioting demonstrators upended police vehicles, set fires in trash dumpsters, smashed windows in buildings, and resisted police arrest. The blockade succeeded in disrupting the meeting, but it also prevented medics – many assigned from the ranks of the protesters – from attending to injured protesters. By the time the dust settled, more than 600 protesters had been arrested, the city suffered about $25 million in property damage and lost sales, and it was forced to spend millions more to clean up the mess and cover unbudgeted police overtime pay (Gillham and Marx, 2000).

Anarchic Extremism. Anarchism is the rejection of all forms of coercive control and authority; the word is derived from the ancient Greek and Latin word, *anarchia* ("without ruler"). Anarchist factions can be found at both the

146

Seattle police lined up against demonstrators at the 1999 Seattle meeting of the World Trade Organization.

extreme left (anti-globalist) and right (anti-government libertarian) ends of the political spectrum. The idea of anarchists organizing themselves in groups might seem contradictory, but it isn't really, since individual members are under no external compulsion to associate with others and are free to leave a group when and as they choose. Anarchists do, in fact, bond in association to be with like-minded people and act on agendas of mutual agreement. Many anarchists are lone wolves, but many others are social creatures.

Anarchism of today is quite different from the anarchism of the nineteenth century, when it emerged as an ideology in reaction to governments that protected the propertied class, especially in Russia and France. Anarchists differed from Marxists in their view of the state: Marxists saw the state as a central instrument of socialism, whereas anarchists were suspicious of state power in any form and toward any purpose. Although anarchism was largely a creation of the nonviolent French political philosopher, Pierre Joseph Proudhon, violent anarchists left a bloody trail of terror throughout much of Europe in the late nineteenth century, assassinating nobility and heads of state in Russia (Czar Alexander II was killed by a bomb in

147

1881), France (President Marie François Sadi Carnot was stabbed to death in Lyon in 1894), Austria (Austro-Hungarian Empress Elizabeth of Bavaria was stabbed to death in Geneva in 1898), and Italy (King Umberto I was fatally shot in 1900). American President William McKinley was also killed by an anarchist (shot by Leon Czolgosz, a Polish American, in Buffalo in 1901).

Today, few anarchists are terrorists. Most anarchists today reject terrorism as authoritarian and a fundamental violation of the rights of others. Notable exceptions do exist, however, as in the case of primitive anarchist Theodore Kaczynski, mentioned earlier, so we include them as extremists and potential terrorists, even if they constitute very low-risk threats.

B. Prominent Extremist Groups

The classification of types of extremists and extremist groups described in the first section is generalized and largely abstract. In this section prominent examples of these various types are presented, with a focus on how they can and have moved from extremist groups to terrorists. It presents three prominent foreign left-wing extremist groups, then three prominent left-wing groups in the United States, and finally prominent right-wing extremist groups and small team operations in the United States. Although terrorism has moved to center stage since 2001, there was in fact substantial terrorist activity in many parts of the world during the thirty years preceding 9/11, as was noted in Chapter 3.

1. The German Red Army Faction

One of the most prominent terrorist groups in Europe since the end of World War II was a left-wing extremist group known as the Red Army Faction (RAF), which evolved from the radical student movement in German universities in the 1960s.[5] Founded in 1970 by Andreas Baader, Ulrike Meinhof, and several like-minded radicals – it was widely known as the "Baader-Meinhof Gang" in its early years – the RAF was made up of romantic activists who believed that their government was hopelessly wedded to the reactionary forces of colonialism and was a major obstacle to their utopian outlook. They set themselves on a mission to destroy that obstacle (Varon, 2004).

The group quickly was transformed from extremists to terrorists,[6] waging a nearly thirty-year wave of major violence starting in the early 1970s. By the time of the group's dissolution in 1998, their crime tally included dozens of murders, as well as bank robberies, kidnappings, bombings, arson, and assaults, all justified as forms of "urban guerrilla warfare" and "armed resistance." The RAF had ties to radical groups elsewhere, including the Marxist Popular Front for the Liberation of Palestine.

German Red Army Faction logotype

What, precisely, did the members of the RAF want? German political philosopher Gunter Rohrmoser, who studied the RAF, describes their goals this way:

> They want The Revolution, a total transformation of all existing conditions, a new form of human existence, an entirely new relationship of people to each other, and also of people to nature. They want the total and radical breach with all that is, and with all historical continuity. Without a doubt they are utopians.... Inside their world, or outside their world, there is no voice that could call them back to reason. For them, there is no connection between the vision that drives them and the existing reality that, they feel, keeps them in chains; therefore destruction is the only form of freedom they can accept. In light of their own utopia, the existing system appears to them as hell, as a system which exploits, suppresses and destroys human beings and in which to dwell means living death (quoted in Kellen, 1998).

The RAF shifted its emphasis over the years from a broad utopian goal of overturning all of West German society to a more focused concern on the destruction of the North Atlantic Treaty Organization (NATO) and disassociation with the military enterprises of the United States. Rohrmoser observes that the world of the RAF was one that expressed concern about humanity, but that viewed most individuals as less than human: "They are driven by their pitiless hatred . . . They pretend to serve 'the people,' but the people exist only in their imagination."

The two principal founders of the RAF committed suicide in German prisons: Ulrike Meinhof in 1976 and Andreas Baader the following year. On April 20, 1998, these words appeared in an eight-page letter faxed to the Reuters news agency: "Almost 28 years ago, on May 14, 1970, the RAF arose in a campaign of liberation. Today we end this project. The urban guerrilla in the shape of the RAF is now history" (Reuters, 1998; translated from the original in German).[7]

2. The Italian Red Brigades

In 1970, the same year that the Red Army Faction was being formed in Germany, a parallel organization was created in Italy: the Italian Red

Italian Red Brigades hostage Aldo Moro

Brigades (it was known as "Brigate Rosse" in Italian). Like the RAF, the Red Brigades was a far left extremist group that set out to bring down a government that it felt had become too closely allied with corrupt capitalist influences generally and with NATO in particular (Alexander and Pluchinsky, 1992).

The Red Brigades was the brainchild of Renato Curcio, a student at the University of Trento, in the Alpine foothills of northern Italy. He enlisted two close friends to found the enterprise: his girlfriend Margherita ("Mara") Cagol and Alberto Franceschini. Other leaders emerged over the years, the most prominent of whom were Corrado Simioni, who led a terrorist cell within the Brigades, and Mario Moretti, who in 1978 directed the kidnapping and murder of former Italian Prime Minister Aldo Moro.

In the group's early days, members of the Red Brigades sabotaged equipment and disrupted offices of factories and trade unions in Milan, Turin, and other industrial centers of northern Italy. Its crimes escalated to homicide in 1974 and spread to other urban centers, including Rome and Venice. In 1974, founders Renato Curcio and Alberto Franceschini were arrested and convicted, their capture largely the work of a former monk who had infiltrated the Brigades for the Italian national police.

Following the incarceration of Curcio and Franceschini, other leaders quickly took over and raised the level of the Red Brigades' violence, carrying out the high-profile kidnappings of Genoan prosecutor Mario Sossi in 1974 and of wealthy wine businessman Vittorio Vallarino Gancia for ransom the following year to provide funding for their operations. A bloody gunfight to free Gancia resulted in the death of two police officers and of Mara Cagol,

Curcio's wife. To intimidate juries, disrupt the legal process, and produce mistrials against captured members of the Brigades, the group launched terrorist activities against federal police, court officials, and even lawyers assigned to represent accused members of the Brigades. By the end of the 1970s, the Red Brigades had committed well over 10,000 violent crimes throughout Italy, mostly in urban areas such as Rome and Venice (Martin, 2006).

In 1978, a cell of Red Brigades members, wearing Alitalia uniforms and led by Mario Moretti, ambushed former Prime Minister Aldo Moro in Rome, killed five of his bodyguards, and took him hostage in an attempt to use Moro as a bargaining chip in exchange for the release of incarcerated Brigades members. They had expected this demand to be taken seriously by the Italian government, but the top officials had a policy of refusing to concede to hostage demands, to avoid encouraging further such attempts. Moretti and his gang held Moro for nearly sixty days and then, realizing that the government would not negotiate and fearful of being discovered, killed him, putting ten bullets in his chest. Moretti, the trigger man, was eventually apprehended and sentenced to serve six life sentences for his crime, but he was paroled in 1998 after serving fifteen years in prison.

The Moro killing deromanticized the Red Brigades, even for the Italian left. Any such positive sentiment that remained was lost in 1979 when the Brigades assassinated Guido Rossa, a popular trade union organizer who, unhappy with the Brigades, reported to the police information about their spreading propaganda material to union members. The group was eventually disbanded by Italian investigators in the 1980s, thanks largely to a police crackdown and to investigators who persuaded captured members of the group to provide information that led to the arrest and conviction of the remaining at-large members. Assassinations continued through much of the 1980s, but the group folded by the end of the decade. New terrorist factions that use the name of the Red Brigades have arisen occasionally in the years since, but they have done so without any formal connection to the original group.

3. The Shining Path of Peru

Communist factions have played a varying role in the politics of South America throughout the twentieth century. In the late 1960s Abimael Guzman Reynoso, a Marxist and a charismatic former professor of philosophy at a small college in the Peruvian Andes, formed the Shining Path ("Sendero Luminoso" in Spanish), based on a Maoist model he had embraced while in China in 1965. After recruiting followers at universities throughout Peru in the early 1970s, Guzman went underground in 1978 to develop a serious revolutionary agenda (Arena and Arrigo, 2006; Palmer, 1994).

In 1980 Guzman's organization, numbering in the hundreds, launched a campaign of violence aimed at undermining and eventually overthrowing what he regarded as the bourgeois government of Peru and replacing it with a communist peasant revolutionary regime. Although it may not have made clear distinctions between terrorist and guerrilla operations, the Shining Path engaged in both types of violence. As guerrillas, Shining Path members targeted the army, the police, and members of the government, including elected officials, as well as police stations and government office buildings. As terrorists, they targeted a vast spectrum of society – from peasants, trade union organizers, and members of other leftist organizations to people in business and random members of the general public – as well as electrical power and telecommunication facilities, rail lines, and bridges. The bulk of the terror was committed in rural areas and in Lima, Peru's capital.

The Shining Path terrorized areas and then created its own governing authorities – "zones of liberation" – where it set up tribunal systems of "people's trials" to punish landowners, lenders, and other targeted individuals, frequently executing officials and anyone labeled as a traitor (McCormick, 1990).

By the early 1990s, the bloody path of dead bodies produced by Shining Path operations grew to the tens of thousands, mostly through shootings and bombings, both in the form of targeted assassinations and indiscriminate violence; its members used dynamite, Molotov cocktails, pipe bombs, grenades, and assorted other homemade and stolen military weapons. At its peak, around 1992, the organization comprised more than 5,000 armed militants and a support network of some 50,000 others (Palmer, 1994).

Guzman was eventually tracked down and arrested in Lima in 1992. He was later tried and given a life sentence under draconian antiterrorism sanctions passed under President Alberto Fujimori, who built his political legacy largely on a reputation for bringing down Guzman and the Shining Path through tough laws and restrictions of rights previously afforded to criminal defendants. Several of Guzman's top lieutenants were arrested in 1995.

Although much smaller and weaker, the Shining Path has remained a viable terrorist organization over the years. In 1997 the organization was put on the State Department's list of Designated Foreign Terrorist Organizations, with an estimated strength level in the neighborhood of 2,000 members. By 2006 the State Department estimated that the Shining Path had declined in size to some 300 members (Department of State, 2006). It continues nonetheless to have a romantic legacy, which inspires occasional outbursts of random terror in parts of Peru (Arena and Arrigo, 2006).

4. Symbionese Liberation Army

The United States experienced its own brand of left-wing urban terrorism in the 1970s, perhaps most famously with the Symbionese Liberation Army's

Symbionese Liberation Army soldier Patty Hearst

(SLA) acts of violence against innocents in the name of lofty ideological causes. The SLA grew out of the New Left movement of the late 1960s, which sponsored mass protest movements at college campuses and radical leftist campaigns and demonstrations. The SLA departed markedly from the peaceful approaches to reform popularized by the civil rights movement of Martin Luther King, Jr. and encouraged by much of the New Left. It derived primary inspiration instead from Maoists who visited the Soledad Prison in California in 1973 and from the model of leftist urban guerrilla activities in South America and elsewhere. Over a three-year period starting in 1973, the SLA committed several bank robberies, two murders, one famous kidnapping, and numerous other acts of violence, mostly in the San Francisco and Los Angeles areas. A particularly heinous murder involved the killing of Oakland school superintendent Marcus Foster, using hollow-point bullets coated with cyanide.

Donald DeFreeze, a founding member of the SLA, described the ends and means of the group in his manifesto, *Symbionese Liberation Army Declaration of Revolutionary War and the Symbionese Program* (1973). DeFreeze noted that the name of the organization derived from the word "symbiosis" – the concept of organisms of different species cooperating with one another, as in the case of a bird feeding itself on the back of a rhinoceros while ridding the large beast of parasitic insects. DeFreeze saw a parallel in dissimilar people living together in harmony as a community, if not a family, while working to serve the disparate interests of the several members of the group.

The famous SLA kidnapping occurred with the abduction of the 19-year-old newspaper heiress, Patricia ("Patty") Hearst, from her residence in Berkeley in 1974. The SLA kidnapped Hearst, then a student at the University of California, for ransom and as a bargaining chip in exchange for the release of the two SLA members imprisoned for the killing of Marcus Foster. The capture of a celebrity heiress was extraordinary enough, but the case grew even stranger when, some two months after her kidnapping, Hearst participated in an SLA bank robbery (she was now referred to by her SLA comrades as "Tanya"). Stranger still, she was convicted and given a seven-year prison sentence for her role in the crime, despite clear indications that she had been brainwashed by the SLA and was really more a victim than a criminal acting with clear intent and exercising free will in the matter.

Key members of the group were killed in a blazing shootout and house fire in Los Angeles in 1974. Several others, including Hearst – now referring to themselves as members of the New World Liberation Front – were arrested, convicted, and incarcerated the following year. In 1978, after serving eighteen months in prison, Hearst's sentence was commuted by President Jimmy Carter and she was freed. Twelve years afterward, she was pardoned by Bill Clinton, on his last day as president (January 20, 2001). Five remaining members of the SLA, who had remained fugitives for nearly twenty years, were arrested in 2002 and convicted in 2003 for murder. The final remaining member, James Kilgore, was convicted in 2004 for violation of federal explosives laws and passport fraud (Varon, 2004).

5. *Earth Liberation Front*

One of the best-known extremist groups that express rage over environmental issues is the Earth Liberation Front (ELF). The ELF was created in 1992 by the British faction of Earth First!, but it chose to depart from its parent group's strategy of drawing attention through media coverage of its activities to gain public support for its cause and recruit new members. The ELF turned instead to sabotage to destroy commercial enterprises it regarded as the enemies of the environment, using stealth to make it more difficult for officials to detect and intervene. Accordingly, the ELF has no official hierarchy, leader, spokespersons, or list of members. It is instead a network of self-funded individuals and small teams who regard themselves as kindred spirits in a noble calling. The ELF has been active in the United Kingdom, the United States, and Canada.

The acts of the ELF – including "monkey-wrenching" of logging equipment, arson, and sabotage of mining, transportation, home building, and other operations that alter the environment – clearly qualify as eco-terrorism. The ELF has broken numerous laws in committing acts of vandalism and property destruction, with the objective of taking the profits out of businesses that harm the environment. The group has generally avoided injury against individuals associated with these businesses, although explosives and incendiary devices have been used occasionally as weapons of choice. The Federal Bureau of Investigation named the ELF as a top domestic terrorism threat in 2002 (Jarboe, 2002). In 2006, two ELF members were convicted on arson charges for causing $20 million in property destruction, the most serious incident involving the 1998 fire bombing of a ski resort in Vail, Colorado.

6. Ku Klux Klan

There can be little question about which terrorist group has been the most destructive over the course of the history of the United States. It is the Ku Klux Klan ("the Klan" or "KKK").[8] The Klan is estimated to have lynched – that is, publicly killed, usually by hanging, sometimes accompanied by a celebration – nearly 5,000 individuals over a period of less than a century following its founding in 1866 (Ginzburg, 1996). It was formed by veterans of the Confederate Army to resist the post-Civil War Reconstruction movement. Its initial acts of terror involved the widespread use of violence to intimidate freed slaves and white Northern sympathizers. These efforts were deterred substantially by President Ulysses S. Grant's aggressive counterterrorist measures mandated under the Civil Rights Act of 1871 (known as the "Ku Klux Klan Act").

The KKK was reincarnated in 1915 after decades of dormancy, this time as a more highly organized fraternal order with a focus not only against blacks and Northerners but also Jews and Catholics, immigrants, communists, native Americans, and other minority groups. Its membership grew to more than a million strong by the 1920s – as before, centered in the South – becoming popular due in part to an inducement system that offered money to people to organize chapters throughout much of the United States (Chalmers, 1987; MacLean, 1995). This second version of the Klan was more distinctly rooted in Protestant fundamentalism, resistance to federal authority, anti-urban intellectualism, and anti-communism. Its violence manifested mostly as beatings and lynchings of blacks. Members of the Klan included the prototypical white trash rednecks, as well as middle-class white business and family men hostile to assaults by civil rights agitators and liberals against the prevailing order and supportive of the symbolic protection of white people (MacLean, 1995). The popularity of the KKK declined during the 1930s and 1940s, due to a combination of factors, most prominently the nation's preoccupation with World War II and the Klan's continuing support of the Nazis, as well as negative publicity associated with crimes committed by the Klan's leaders and members. It remained active nonetheless through the 1950s and 1960s, largely in reaction to the growing influence of the civil rights movement.

Today the Klan continues to draw support from hatemongers and racist extremists, although not nearly at the numbers or levels of violence associated with its heydays in the 1870s and 1920s. The organization was modernized under the leadership of David Duke in the 1970s. After founding the Louisiana Knights of the Ku Klux Klan, he moved up to lead the national organization and broke with tradition by replacing the title "Grand Wizard" with that of "National Director" and abandoning the white robe in favor of business attire. He also softened the image of the Klan by promoting nonviolence and lawful policies and by allowing women and Catholics to join as equal members. Despite these efforts, the Klan has not rid itself of the deep legacy of racism and hatred it championed for well over a century. It continues to be an inspiration for vigilante terrorism, a powerful symbol, and a model for white supremist groups and neo-Nazi organizations, such as the Aryan Nations, Aryan Republican Army, White Aryan Resistance, and the Order (B. Smith, 1994).

7. Home-Grown Extremists: Citizen Militias, Small Team Operations, and Lone Wolves

Each of the extremist groups described earlier has a unique political agenda or motive of hatred that induces its members to commit violence for a cause. Some are on the extreme political left, others on the extreme right. In addition, there are a myriad of other small bands of people, as well as the occasional extremist individual, who are not affiliated with larger movements or established groups, but who operate very much as extremists and sometimes as terrorists. Most terrorist incidents in the United States have in fact been the product of small home-grown groups, two-man terrorist teams, and individuals who became obsessed with ideologies that caused them to think and behave as extremists.

What motivates such thinking and behavior? There are several explanations, most having to do with a mix of psychological and social forces that cause polarized, absolutist, and sometimes apocalyptic thinking and behavior that often reflect paranoia, narcissism, righteousness, anger, and invariably alienation (Post, 1998). In some cases these individuals live in society as ordinary people and are not readily identifiable as extremists. In other cases they isolate themselves, sometimes because they are simply uncomfortable around others and sometimes because they fear that their behaviors and agendas will be disrupted if they are subject to frequent exposure to others. Some are obsessed with an intrusive government that they believe has no business collecting taxes, meddling in the affairs of private citizens, and promoting causes that are no good.

Private Militia Groups. One should not be too surprised that extremist groups have been a common occurrence in the land of the free and the home of the brave. Extremism is sometimes an expression of patriotism on steroids, as in the case of a group known as the Minutemen, founded in 1960 by Robert DePugh, a research chemist from Missouri. The story of the Minutemen and DePugh is an aberration of the refrain, "only in America": a one-man show that attracted a following for a few years, only to fade into oblivion. DePugh has been described as a paranoid individual who promoted a "delusional system" (George and Wilcox, 1996). The literature that DePugh distributed reported on enemies behind every tree: not just the tax collector from the IRS, but your auto mechanic and insurance agent too. He created militia units throughout the United States, each no larger than twenty-five members to reduce each unit's exposure to federal and local authorities. Because members were screened hardly at all, however, he ended up attracting what a former member called "the damnedest collection of blabbermouths, paranoids, ding-a-lings and fuckups you have ever seen" (George and Wilcox, 1996, p. 224).

The Minutemen militia saw itself as a more viable alternative against the forces of communism in the United States than the federal government. Its members prepared for the counter-revolution by stockpiling weapons and infiltrating leftist organizations, occasionally mailing a threat to a targeted group indicating that the recipient was in the Minutemen's line of fire. In 1968 DePugh was arrested and charged in federal court for violation of firearms laws. After jumping bail and hiding out for seventeen months, he was caught, convicted of violating felony warrant and federal firearm laws, and then served three years in federal prison. He was convicted again in 1992 on three counts of federal firearms violations. Although DePugh and his Minutemen were not known to have committed any acts of serious violence, they did cast a crude mold for militia groups to follow over the coming years.

Extremist militia groups have arisen fairly commonly in the United States – the Montana Freemen, founded by Leroy Schweitzer, and the Michigan Militia, created by Norman Olson, are two prominent examples. Most are quite small and function well below the horizon or "off the grid" – avoiding the use of credit cards, driver's licenses, Social Security numbers, and other standard systems of identification. Most militia groups are anti-government, yet they see themselves as patriotic, espousing American liberty and traditional Christian values. Some are weekend warriors dressed in camouflage, who train by playing paintball in the woods (George and Wilcox, 1996). Some are racists and anti-Semites. Many are extreme libertarians, individuals who feel little sense of responsibility to anyone who is not a kindred spirit (Aho, 1995). Few small militia groups are known to commit many crimes of violence, yet mutant strains of the militia group remain a continuing threat to the places where they reside – commonly in rural areas of the West and South – and to the larger society (B. Smith, 1994). Those that do commit acts of violence have been referred to as "vigilante terrorists" (Gurr, 1988).

Small Teams. In Chapter 1 we noted the cases of Oklahoma City bombers Timothy McVeigh and Terry Nichols and Washington, D.C.–area snipers John Allen Muhammad and Lee Boyd Malvo. Although their causes were different, both of these exemplify the reign of terror that can be waged by two-man militia terrorist teams.[9]

McVeigh and Nichols were former Army buddies who met at Fort Riley, Kansas, around 1990. McVeigh was trained in the Army as a sniper and in explosives, and he served as a sniper in Kuwait in Operation Desert Storm, where he was awarded a Bronze Star. McVeigh's extremism was fed in part through his infatuation with a book of racist fiction, *The Turner Diaries*, written by neo-Nazi author and founder of the National Alliance, William Pierce. The book, which tells the story of a violent racial revolution resulting in white global rule, portrays events that parallel aspects of McVeigh's modus operandi in the Oklahoma City bombing. McVeigh and Nichols carefully planned the massive – 4,800 pound – ammonium nitrate truck explosion that destroyed the Murrah Federal building in 1995 and killed 168 people, including 19 children in a day care center located there, and injured 800 others. Federal investigators concluded that McVeigh and Nichols were motivated to plan and commit the crime out of sympathy with an anti-government militia movement and to avenge the government's handling of the 1992 Ruby Ridge and 1993 Waco incidents, involving the deaths of right-wing proponents of apocalypse at the hands of federal law enforcement authorities. McVeigh was convicted in 1997 and, four years later, executed by lethal injection. Nichols was convicted in federal court in 1997 and sentenced to a term of life without parole the following year.

Like McVeigh and Nichols, John Allen Muhammad, the older of the two D.C.–area snipers, also served in the Army. And like McVeigh, Muhammad also dabbled actively in extremist causes. Whereas McVeigh's ideological interests leaned against the government and toward white supremacy, Muhammad's leaned more toward the black Islamic movement – he had served on the security team for Louis Farrakhan's "Million Man March" in 1995 and later joined Jamaat al-Fuqra, another black Islamic organization. He then traveled to the Caribbean, where he met and began to mentor a Jamaican teenage boy, Lee Boyd Malvo. In 2002, Muhammad and Malvo rigged up a car so that Malvo could fire a high-powered Bushmaster rifle from the trunk, through a hole, while Muhammad positioned the car and then drove away from the crime scene, undetected. By the end of their shooting

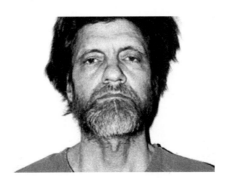

Ted Kaczynski

spree, they had killed one person in Louisiana, one in Alabama, and ten in the Washington, D.C., area, and probably others in Arizona, California, Georgia, Texas, and Washington State. Muhammad was convicted of murder in 2003 and sentenced to the death penalty. Malvo was convicted of murder by a jury in a Virginia court in 2003 and sentenced to a term of life imprisonment without parole.

Lone Wolves. Some extremists turn to violence without collaborators. These "lone-wolf" terrorists can be the most difficult cases to solve, because the offenders neither plan nor communicate with others about their crimes. Because they are loners, they are often more delusional than extremists who work and socialize with collaborators.

Among the most prominent of the lone-wolf extremists is Theodore ("Ted") Kaczynski, known for years only as the "Unabomber." In a series of mail bombings that extended over a seventeen-year period beginning in 1978, Kaczynski killed three people and injured twenty-three others. His journey from eccentric to terrorist was most extraordinary, with stopping points at Harvard University, where he earned a bachelor's degree in mathematics in 1962; the University of Michigan, where he was awarded a PhD in 1967; and the University of California, where he was employed as a math professor for two years and then resigned abruptly. The primary motive for his approximately fifteen-year reign of terror was rebellion against what he saw as an overly technological society. His modus operandi was the letter and package bomb, which he sent to people he regarded as prime culprits in a society that had become corrupted and diminished by technology. Kaczynski's 35,000-word manifesto, *Industrial Society and Its Future* (2005), begins as follows:

> The Industrial Revolution and its consequences have been a disaster for the human race. They have greatly increased the life-expectancy of those of us who live in "advanced" countries, but they have destabilized society, have made life unfulfilling, have subjected human beings to indignities, have led to widespread

159

Nonreligious Extremism and Terrorism

Eric Rudolph

psychological suffering (in the Third World to physical suffering as well) and have inflicted severe damage on the natural world. The continued development of technology will worsen the situation. It will certainly subject human beings to greater indignities and inflict greater damage on the natural world, it will probably lead to greater social disruption and psychological suffering, and it may lead to increased physical suffering – even in "advanced" countries.

After concealing his identity successfully for so long, Kaczynski eventually gave in to his desire to get his message out on a grand stage in 1995, publishing long essays in the *New York Times* and *Washington Post*. Kaczynski's unique syntax enabled his brother, David, to recognize the true identity of the Unabomber, and he turned the information over to the FBI. In 1996, Kaczynski was arrested at his remote cabin in the wilds of Montana. Two years later he pled guilty to murder charges in exchange for a life sentence without the possibility of parole. He is now Prisoner #04475–046 at a maximum security federal prison in Colorado.

A second prominent solo terrorist is Eric Rudolph, known also as the "Olympic Park Bomber" for his having disrupted the 1996 Summer Olympics in Atlanta with a bomb that killed a woman and injured 111 other people. Rudolph was born in Florida and moved to North Carolina at the age of fifteen after the death of his father. His mother was a survivalist, disenchanted with the mainstream community setting. In 1987 he enlisted in the Army and was discharged as a private seventeen months later. An FBI investigation established that Rudolph then developed an association with an extremist group, the Christian Identity movement, and became an anti-abortion and anti-gay terrorist (Cooperman, 2003).

160

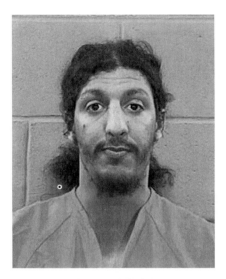

Richard Reid

After the Olympic Park bombing, Rudolph bombed an abortion clinic in an Atlanta suburb, a gay and lesbian bar in the city of Atlanta, and an abortion clinic in Birmingham, Alabama. His bombs, consisting of dynamite wrapped in nails, killed three people and injured more than 150 others. Rudolph then fled to the hills after being identified as a suspect in these cases in 1998 and was caught in 2003 rummaging through a trash bin for food in Murphy, North Carolina. In 2005 he pled guilty to federal and state homicide charges and was given five consecutive life sentences in exchange for the court's assurance that he would not receive the death penalty.

Another well-known lone wolf is Richard Reid, commonly referred to as the "shoe bomber." Reid is a British citizen, born and schooled in London. The son of an English mother and a Jamaican father (who was in prison through most of Reid's childhood), Reid himself got caught up in street crime and prison, where he converted to Islam. He later trained with al Qaeda in Afghanistan. Ten weeks after the 9/11 attack, Reid attempted and failed at what might have been a major terrorist event: the suicide bombing of an airliner flying from Paris to Miami with 198 passengers and crew. He managed to get through security wearing shoes that contained enough plastic explosives to bring down the plane, but due to a combination of his own bungling and the attention and quick action of an airline attendant, Hermis Moutardier, Reid was subdued and arrested on departing the aircraft. He was convicted the following month in a federal court in Boston on terrorism charges and sentenced to a life term in federal prison.

Kaczynski, Rudolph, and Reid are all serving life terms at the federal maximum security ("supermax") prison in Florence, Colorado.

C. Dealing with Extremism

What lessons can be learned from the vast array of differences among extremist groups and from case studies of how some choose the path of violence? In this chapter, we presented information about different types of extremism and focused on cases involving the most violent individuals and extremist groups. A potentially serious problem with the case study method is that, although it can help us know much about the particular cases studied, it does not help us draw valid generalizations about how those cases differ from groups or individuals not studied. The cases studied are typically chosen because they are interesting – they are unique in important ways. As a result, developing policies based on inferences drawn from extreme cases can be not only invalid but also dangerous.

Despite these differences, important commonalities exist across extremist groups. Those that graduate from extremism to violence may do so because the members were more prone to violence to begin with, or because their environments encouraged the choice of violent behavior, or because policies for discouraging violence were ineffective. Worse still, some policies may actually provoke violence, perhaps by isolating the members and making them desperate, or by martyring individuals in the group and raising the stakes for the members, or by elevating the status of the group, romanticizing it so that it is able to recruit new members more easily.

Consistent with the principles discussed earlier in this chapter (see especially Policy Box 6.2), criminologist Franco Ferracuti (1998) urges policymakers to err on the side of caution:

> Because it is impossible to eliminate all terrorists, it is in the interest of every country to make it easy for terrorists to terminate their connection with terrorism – that is, to exit the life of terrorism. In order to encourage dissent within the terrorist group and then defection from it, the state must provide a way out. The best solution to political terrorism is to provide a place, within the country's political system, for persons with dissenting, and even radical views. Thus, in exchange for a renunciation of terrorism, the terrorists find a place, perhaps radical but at least legitimate, in society itself (p. 62).

Policy Box 6.2. What to Do About Extremism?

Extremism can be hazardous; it is the seedbed of terrorism. But the seeds of extremism need not take root and blossom inevitably into terrorist acts.

Extremist behavior is more likely to transform into terrorism when it is either ignored or provoked through ill-conceived action or overreaction.

Extremism can be managed. The prime requisite for the effective management of extremism is the understanding of its causes and manifestations. In addition, the effectiveness of alternative interventions for each of its manifestations – political extremism, religious extremism, racial and ethnic extremism, and other ideological strains of extremism – should be evaluated.

Several lessons can be learned from disasters such as the "Battle of Seattle," which occurred in reaction to anti-globalization extremists protesting meetings of the World Trade Organization there. One lesson is that the police should meet with demonstration organizers in advance of the event to ensure their safety and minimize harm. Secrecy and surprises tend to worsen matters. Another is that designated protest zones should be made available in or adjacent to the targeted area for demonstrators who prefer not to be disruptive, so as to reduce unintended harm to protesters and damage to the community. Yet another is that conferences that are prospective targets of disruption can build more flexibility into the location of their meetings, so that alternative venues can be arranged quickly and on short notice (Gillham and Marx, 2000).

In the case of racial and ethnic extremism, young people who are attracted to hate groups that promote such causes have been found usually to be alienated, often due to an absence of clear pathways to their productive participation in prospects that are socially and financially rewarding. The first, and best, way to prevent extremism is to create and sustain societies and communities that provide healthy alternatives. In countries where such conditions do not exist, communities must rely on a mix of public interventions and informal private control mechanisms to monitor and manage extremists and extremist groups; they should do so as positively and with as little force as possible. When the public sector is weak, help from neighboring provinces and nations may be needed to create conditions for long-term stability.

Nations with stable criminal justice systems can rely on a sensible mix of rules and discretion to manage individual cases of extremism that cross the line of legal behavior. When extremists violate the law, the formal system of justice should begin by classifying the offender on a spectrum from mild, relatively harmless alienation at the low end to fanatical commitment to ideology and terrorism at the high end. If the criminal acts are not serious and the individual is at the mild end of the spectrum, a nonconfrontational approach that combines weak sanctions and stern warnings with inducements to engage in healthy, productive activity is likely to be most successful for integrating

> the individual into the community (Schafer and Navarro, 2003). For people at the other end of the spectrum – the dangerous criminal and incorrigibly committed extremist – aggressive prosecution and long prison sentences are likely to be the safest and most just way of responding to serious acts of violence. In between these two extremes, discretion must be exercised to manage ideological extremism in a manner that provides both justice and effective protection for the community. A prudent mix of rules and discretion – and systems of accountability that induce all who are in positions of authority to act sensibly – is likely to be the most effective approach for defusing the bomb of extremism.

Of course, such an approach could have the opposite effect of enabling terrorists to continue operating as before and, as a consequence, do even more damage to innocent people than the use of sanctions may cause. The question comes down to establishing the blend of carrots and sticks – and the right selection among the various types of carrots and sticks available – that works best to minimize harm to society over both the short and long term for each type of extremist group and individual extremist. Establishing the most appropriate blend requires valid information about what works and, to the extent that such information is limited, the prudent exercise of discretion. Much of the public response to extremism and terrorism has relied too much on impatience, intolerance, and anger and too little on thoughtful and systematic approaches for developing and carrying out public policy in this critical area.

Discussion Questions

1. *The boundaries of extremism.* Senator Barry Goldwater announced in 1964, as the Republican presidential candidate, "Extremism in pursuit of liberty is no vice." Do you agree with this statement? When does extremism in pursuit of a noble goal cross the line?
2. *Extremism and intolerance.* It was noted at several points in this chapter that extremism is a problem especially to the extent that it breeds intolerance. Does this have policy implications? What are they?
3. *Types of extremism.* Case studies of extremist groups include ideologies on both the left and the right and by cause: political, social, economic, ethnic, and so on. What do they have in common? Are the differences significant for policy purposes? If so, how?

4. *Extremist leaders and terrorism.* What distinguishes the extremist leader from a terrorist leader? Might a part of the distinction relate to the validity of the perceived threat to the group? What are the policy implications of the distinction(s) between leaders of extremist groups from leaders of terrorist groups?

SEVEN

Technology and Terrorism

This chapter considers the importance of technology from two fundamentally different perspectives: first, as an instrument of terror, and, then, as a means of preventing and responding to acts of terror. Specific technologies are described in both domains. For terrorists, technology is involved in both the means of terror, including weapons of mass destruction and use of the Internet, and the targets of terror, including technological infrastructure targets. Technology can be a critical tool in counterterrorism too, through smart identification systems, sophisticated technologies for intelligence gathering and analysis, and the use of the Internet as a bridge builder to reduce tensions that can lead to terrorism. The chapter closes with a reflection on the limits of technology both for terrorists and for peace-loving people.

A. Technology as an Instrument of Terror

It was noted in Chapter 4 that some of the same forces of globalization that have facilitated the growth of economies and encouraged cultural exchange throughout the world in the late twentieth and early twenty-first centuries have also become available to terrorists, who have used these technologies to expand their activities and make them more lethal. Political scientist Joseph Nye (2002) refers to this development as the "privatization of war."

Terrorists have traditionally limited their activities to their local areas, targeting people of their own land. Because of the explosion of communication and information technologies used to move goods and financial capital, they have been able to broaden their horizons substantially. Advanced technology

166

does not distinguish between saints and sinners; it is available to all who want it, regardless of the nature of the intended use. Terrorist organizations today can have realistic global aspirations that were previously inconceivable, and the leaders of many of these organizations have not hesitated to take advantage of opportunities to expand both their geographic horizons and the lethality and sophistication of their attacks.

This expansion has happened quite quickly. As the superpowers invaded foreign lands, using massive force to control local populations – first the Soviet Union in Afghanistan and then the United States in Iraq – local insurgents found ways to repel and eventually defeat the technologically superior forces with a combination of cunning and unique ways of using newly available technologies. They succeeded in overcoming overwhelming disadvantages in resources and military technology, steadily improving their ability to bring mayhem to local authorities, to repel alien military forces, and to export the effective uses of technology to terrorists and insurgents elsewhere. Technology has, in short, made terrorism and its central strategy of asymmetric warfare more symmetric.

The 2006 National Intelligence Estimate, a consensus report of sixteen major U.S. intelligence gathering agencies, reached this conclusion:

> The radicalization process is occurring more quickly, more widely, and more anonymously in the Internet age, raising the likelihood of surprise attacks by unknown groups whose members and supporters may be difficult to pinpoint.... We judge that groups of all stripes will increasingly use the Internet to communicate, propagandize, recruit, train and obtain logistical and financial support ("Trends in Global Terrorism," 2006).

Osama bin Laden's al Qaeda network used these technologies to facilitate the 9/11 attack and then spread propaganda throughout the world. These actions called attention to such opportunities for terrorists everywhere to level the playing field to their benefit. But the availability and use of these technologies were well underway prior to the attack. When linked to the prospect of terrorists using weapons of mass destruction (WMD), it became clear that more attention should be paid to their use of technology. We turn now to a review of these linkages between technology and terror.

WMD and technology pose parallel threats. Society is vulnerable to the proliferation of chemical, biological, and nuclear attacks. It is vulnerable also to conventional weapon attacks on complex, "tightly coupled systems" – highly efficient, interconnected systems used for transportation, communications, energy and utilities, information services, and health care delivery. The tight coupling of systems that brings efficiency to an open, contemporary society also makes society more vulnerable to terrorist attacks. These two developments – powerful WMD technologies in the hands of terrorists and the vulnerability of society associated with its openness and tightly coupled

167

Icons for weapons of mass destruction: biological, chemical, and radiological.

systems – give rise to what the National Academy of Sciences refers to as "catastrophic terrorism" (Committee on Science and Technology for Countering Terrorism, 2002).

Let us first consider the weapons of mass destruction.

1. Weapons of Mass Destruction: Chemical, Biological, Radiological, and Nuclear

Terrorists have relied heavily on conventional explosive devices to inflict harm on their victims. Bombs are widely accessible and easily transported by trucks and cars and strapped to suicide terrorists. The September 11 attacks on New York and Washington opened a new chapter in the development of unconventional approaches to calamitous terror. It raised awareness of the prospect that more lethal forms of weaponry can inflict even more horrific harm on people virtually anywhere. Foremost among these lethal forms are WMD: chemical, biological, radiological, and nuclear weapons. These can be vastly more lethal and toxic than conventional explosive devices. They can be delivered in a variety of ways, and each type presents a unique set of challenges both to the terrorist and to societies that must protect themselves against attacks involving such weapons.

Weapons of mass destruction vary in several ways. Some are more lethal than others; they range from mildly toxic agents to a single nuclear weapon capable of killing hundreds of thousands of people. Some WMD are more toxic than others – for example, polonium is extremely toxic, and a very small amount can be lethal to hundreds of people. The toxic agents of WMD are ingested in different ways: through the skin, the lungs, or the digestive system. They cause harm to the body in a variety of ways: from nausea or disorientation to radiation burns, asphyxiation, blindness, or the destruction of organs. They vary as to the length of time between exposure and the manifestation of symptoms and harm and the length of time they remain toxic in the area where deployed (Moodie, 1999; Stern, 1999).

Chemical Weapons. Chemical weapons use toxic, usually lethal chemicals, typically dispensed in a gaseous form through an aerosol delivery system. They are among the easiest types of WMD to deploy. Michael Moodie has identified five categories of chemical weapons:

168

1. **Blister agents** (e.g., mustard gas, lewisite): Delivered in vapor, aerosol, or liquid form, they attack the lungs, eyes, and skin. They remain a hazard for some time after deployment.
2. **Blood agents** (e.g., hydrogen cyanide, cyanogen chloride): Delivered in vapor form, they attack the lungs. They evaporate quickly, posing only a short-term threat.
3. **Choking agents** (e.g., chlorine gas, phosgene): Delivered in vapor form, they attack the lungs, eyes, and skin. They evaporate quickly.
4. **Incapacitants** (e.g., lysergic acid diethylamide [LSD], BZ): Delivered in aerosol or liquid form, they attack the lungs and skin. They evaporate quickly.
5. **Nerve agents** (e.g., sarin, tabun, soman, VX): Delivered in vapor, aerosol, or liquid form, they attack the lungs, eyes, and skin. Some evaporate quickly, whereas others persist.

The deadly chemical weapon sarin, a nerve gas, was used in a lethal terrorist attack in Japan in 1995. It was planned and executed by the Aum Shinrikyo gang, which deployed the gas on a Tokyo subway, killing twelve people and sickening thousands of others. Sarin is appealing as a WMD because it is easy to obtain the ingredients needed to make sarin from supply house catalogues; in fact, two of sarin's main ingredients – rubbing alcohol and methyl alcohol – can be purchased at any drug store (Pearlstein, 2004).

Most sovereign nations have signed the Chemical Weapons Convention, a treaty that went into effect in 1997 prohibiting the development, accumulation, distribution, and use of chemical weapons. Formally known as the Convention on the Prohibition of the Development, Production, Stockpiling and Use of Chemical Weapons and on their Destruction, it was designed to augment the Geneva Protocol of 1925 by providing for extensive on-site inspection and other verification measures and the eventual destruction of chemical warfare devices. In the meantime, stockpiles remain in many countries, including Russia and the United States, and could remain for years to come without action to accelerate and aggressively enforce the terms of the treaty.

Biological Weapons. Biological weapons make use of either natural or artificially engineered bacteria, viruses, or biotoxins. They are potentially more deadly than other WMD because of their capacity to spread naturally after initial contact with a living host organism. Biological weapons can make use of agents that are spread through the air or water or in food (sometimes referred to as "agroterrorism," dispersed through the soil, seeds or crops, feed, or livestock or at food-processing plants or warehouses). They can be difficult to detect and do not cause symptoms or illness for several hours or even days after exposure. Some bioterrorism agents, like the smallpox virus, can be spread from person to person. Others, like anthrax, cannot.

Technology and Terrorism

Biological agents are attractive to terrorists largely because of their capacity to produce widespread panic and mass disruption in a target population. The United States experienced such a panic in 2001, starting just a week after the 9/11 attacks, when letters postmarked in New Jersey and containing anthrax spores were mailed to several news media offices and two U.S. Senators.[1] Five people were killed and seventeen others infected in the bioattack, with direct government costs for the decontamination of buildings and other damages estimated at more than one billion dollars (Lengel, 2005). To date no one has been arrested or convicted for these crimes.

Biological toxins are limited as weapons, however, by their uncontrollable nature. When Japan unleashed fleas infected with bubonic plague on Chinese forces in Manchuria in 1942, many Japanese soldiers became infected with the organism (Stone, 2001). Years later – in 1979 – dozens of people died of poorly managed anthrax in Central Russia. These weapons are capable of doing more damage to the terrorists and their communities than to an affluent foreign target population, especially to the extent that poorer societies tend to be more susceptible to contagion because of weaker public health systems, less sophisticated utility infrastructures, less sanitary environments, and less healthy people living in densely populated areas.

Several biological agents other than anthrax and smallpox, noted above, are potential sources of bioterrorism, including botulism, brucella, cholera, the ebola virus, *Escherichia coli* ("e. coli"), lassa fever, plague, Q fever, recombinant viruses, ricin toxin (from castor beans), salmonella, shigella, tularemia, typhoid fever, and viral encephalitis. Here is a brief description of the most prominent (in terms of the viability of the threat and lethality) of these organisms:

- **Anthrax:** Anthrax is a bacterium that can occur naturally in humans when they eat or are otherwise exposed to dead animals infected by the bacterial spores. The spores can be used as a biological weapon when grown outside the body and inhaled by a victim. Anthrax does not pass from human to human, but people who die of anthrax can be a dangerous source of anthrax spores. Anthrax vaccines require multiple injections and produce dangerous side effects; they are considered unsuitable for the general public.
- **Botulism:** The toxin commonly known as "botulism" is produced by the *Clostridium botulinum* bacterium, one of the deadliest known toxins. Botulism causes death by respiratory failure and paralysis. It is especially dangerous when spread through food, because many people can be poisoned from a single contaminated source. Persons infected with the bacterium may require treatment on a breathing machine for weeks, together with complementary medical care. Induced vomiting can expel much of the toxin when still in the digestive system; after that, patients can be treated with a horse-derived antitoxin that blocks the circulation of the toxin in the blood.

170

- **Ebola:** Ebola is a virus that causes hemorrhagic fever, with fatality rates in the neighborhood of 70 percent. No cure exists, although vaccines are in development. Both the United States and former Soviet Union investigated the use of ebola for biological warfare, and the Aum Shinrikyo group based in Japan had cultures of the virus. Ebola kills its victims through multiple organ failure and hypovolemic shock (a sharp drop in the body's supply of blood plasma).

- **Plague:** The plague is a disease caused by the *Yersinia pestis* bacterium. It has been the source of several pandemics over the centuries, the most serious of which was the Black Plague, which killed about 40 percent of the Eurasian population from 1347 to 1350. Rodents are the usual host of plague, and the disease is transmitted to humans either through flea bites or through the air (a form known as "pneumonic plague"). The disease is dangerous both because it is easy to culture and because it can remain lethal for months – as long as it circulates among local rodents.

- **Recombinant viruses:** Recombinant viruses are artificially engineered combinations of viruses, the "dark side" of genetic engineering. Also referred to as "chimeras" or "designer diseases," these human-made mutants combine the genetic material of two or more organisms, at least one of which is a virus. They are a serious threat for several reasons: their manufacture does not require great scientific sophistication, they can be difficult to detect and trace, and they can be conceivably extremely lethal and communicable (Alibeck, 1999; Block, 1999; Pearlstein, 2004).

- **Smallpox:** Smallpox is a highly contagious virus transmitted through the air, with a mortality rate in the vicinity of 30 percent. The disease occurs only in humans, and it has no external hosts or carriers. Smallpox was eliminated in the 1970s after implementation of an international vaccination program, but samples are still available in Russian and American laboratories, which is a source of concern for many people. In the face of this threat, stockpiles of the vaccine antidote to smallpox have been restored in recent years, reducing much of the risk.

- **Tularemia:** Commonly referred to as "rabbit fever," tularemia is a generally non-lethal but severely incapacitating disease caused by the *Francisella tularensis* bacterium. It has been a popular weapon in biological warfare because it is both highly infectious and easily dispensed in aerosol form.

Bioweapons can be counteracted by boosting the immune systems of prospective targeted victims (Alibek, 1999). DNA technology can also be used to counteract bioterrorism by increasing a target population's ability to analyze and identify unique strains of a biological agent and trace them back to particular sources.

DNA technology has also heightened certain risks of bioterrorism. Genetic engineering that makes use of DNA science raises the troubling prospect that organisms could be made resistant to current medicines or developed to increase their capacity to spread into the environment (Centers for Disease

Control and Prevention). Several authorities point to biological weapons as the most threatening of all WMD because of the large number of people who know how to deploy them and the even larger corps of prospective terrorists inclined to pay for the services of those people. Richard Pearlstein argues that a potentially effective way to prevent biological attacks is to encourage affluent nations to give gainful employment to biologists who might otherwise serve the interests of terrorism.

Perhaps the most effective strategy is for each nation to recognize that bioweapon stockpiles pose a grave threat to any nation that harbors them and therefore it should destroy them, regardless of what other nations do (see Boxes 7.1 and 7.2).

Radiological Weapons ("Dirty Bombs"). Radiological weapons spread deadly radioactive materials such as uranium, plutonium, radium, or cobalt through conventional explosive devices, commonly referred to as "dirty bombs." They differ from nuclear weapons in that they use radioactive material as a poisoning agent, rather than as a medium for setting off a much larger explosion through a chain reaction. They are less dangerous than nuclear weapons, but are much easier and less costly to assemble and detonate. After deployment either in large population centers or to contaminate public food or water networks, they represent a considerable threat to life and health through radiation poisoning, which often leads to leukemia and other cancers. Dirty bombs threaten property damage as well, with potentially huge decontamination costs following the explosion of such devices. The effectiveness of a radiological terrorist attack is likely to depend on several factors: the source and nature of the material, its toxicity and amount, the size of the explosion, the rate of decay of the material used (usually measured as its half-life, the length of time it takes to decline to half of the original amount delivered), the size of the explosion, population density in the vicinity of the explosion, prevailing wind and other weather conditions, and the response of the target population.

The ease with which radioactive material can be obtained makes radiological weapons particularly attractive to terrorists. Two sources of radiological material suitable for terrorism involving such a weapon are military stockpiles and spent fuel from nuclear power plants (Ballard and Mullendore, 2003; Pearlstein, 2004). Former Soviet Union republics such as Kazakhstan, Kyrgyzstan, and Tajikistan are widely believed to be especially rich sources of such material, much of which is unaccounted for (Church, 1991; Collina and Wolfsthal, 2002; Woolf, 2003). Other sources include legitimate commercial and private vendors of new material and radioactive waste, as radioactive material has widespread commercial uses – in medicine, industry, household appliances, wristwatches, and so on. At the shadier end of the market is used radioactive material routinely disposed of by hospitals and other users,

Box 7.1. The Limits of the Bioweapons Threat

– Allison Macfarlane

Could terrorists, intent on causing as much harm and societal disruption as possible, use new biotechnology processes to engineer a virulent pathogen that, when unleashed, would result in massive numbers of dead? Mark Williams, in his *Technology Review* article, "The Knowledge," suggests we should be contemplating this doomsday scenario in the twenty-first century. Williams's article might make you sleep less soundly, but are the threats real? The truth is that we do not really know.

Part of the problem is that even if terrorists could create new pathogens virulent to humans, it's not at all clear that they could "weaponize" them – that is, put the pathogens into a form that is highly infectious to humans and then disperse them in ways that expose large numbers of people.

Past experience suggests that this is not an easy task. During World War II, the Japanese dropped plague-infected materials on Chinese cities, to limited effect. In 1979, the Soviets caused 66 deaths from anthrax by accidentally releasing it from a bioweapons facility in Sverdlovsk. In 1984, the Rajneeshees cult contaminated salad bars in the Dalles, OR, with salmonella, but their actions killed no one. In 1993, the Aum Shinrikyo cult failed to kill anyone after carrying out multiple attacks with anthrax in Japan. The 2001 anthrax letter attacks in the U.S. killed five people. These were all frightening events. They were not, however, grave threats to national security.

Yet estimates of bioweapons dangers tend to be dire, like those in Williams's article. The truth is that the data are too thin to make accurate projections of the effects of bioweapons attacks. I surveyed seven separate estimates of fatalities from a projected anthrax attack. The lowest estimate, by Milton Leitenberg, ranged from zero to 1,440 dead per kilogram of anthrax used, while the highest, by Lawrence Wein and others, put fatalities between 123,400 and 660,000 per kilogram of anthrax. Most of these estimates were made on the basis of little actual data.

To predict accurately the effects of bioweapons, data are needed on the amount of agent required to infect a person, the percentage of people who survive an infection (which depends on the health of the population), the transmission rate if the agent is contagious, the ability to aerosolize and disperse an agent effectively (which depends, in turn, on climatic conditions), the environmental stability of an agent, the population density, and the abilities of the public health system, including when an attack is detected and whether prophylactics, vaccines, or antidotes exist and, if so, in what quantities.

For any one pathogen – even one familiar to us, like smallpox and anthrax – not all of these variables are known, and therefore quantitative predictions are not possible with a high degree of certainty. In the words of the U.S. National Academy of Sciences in a 2002 report, "these factors produce an irreducible uncertainty of several orders of magnitude in the number of people who will be infected in an open-air release."

For example, data on the infectiousness of an agent vary widely, depending on the agent. Because of limited experience with anthrax, susceptibility data have often been extrapolated from animal trials that have little bearing on human response to agents. In the case of smallpox, with which scientists had much experience in the twentieth century, some factors remain uncertain, such as the transmission rate.

In the models of bioweapons attacks, the ability to weaponize an agent and disperse it effectively is estimated in part from open-air trials done by the U.S. Army between the 1940s and 1960s. These trials used live simulants of agents on major U.S. cities, but the behavior of a real bioweapon agent in such a situation remains uncertain. Williams's article doesn't describe in any detail the ability of terrorists to weaponize any of the theorized agents. Yet making effective bioweapons would take a tremendous amount of work.

While a state-sponsored program might have the means to do that work, terrorist groups probably don't. With so much uncertainty surrounding the outcome of a bioweapons attack, it does not make sense to plan extensive biodefense programs when more certain threats, particularly those involving nuclear weapons, require attention.

Allison M. Macfarlane is a research associate in the Science, Technology, and Global Security Working Group in MIT's Program in Science, Technology, and Society.

[Source: Technology Review (March-April 2006)]

which can be bought and sold on the Internet through eBay and other online markets (Collins, 2007).

One type of radiological weapon, polonium, re-emerged in 2006, after having been widely ignored for decades. Discovered in 1898 by Madam Marie Curie and her husband Pierre, polonium is an extremely toxic met-alloid (i.e., a near-metal, like arsenic, boron, and tellurium) that occurs in uranium ore. Polonium gained notoriety in 2006 as the substance used to assassinate Alexander Litvinenko, a former lieutenant colonel of Russia's Federal Security Service, who died of multiple organ failure due to radiation poisoning over an excruciating three-week period. Polonium has a radioactive

Policy Box 7.2. A Treaty to Control Biological Weapons

One way to reduce the prospect of bioweapons finding their way into the hands of terrorists is to eliminate them wherever they are known to exist. In 1975 a multinational agreement – the Convention on the Prohibition of the Development, Production and Stockpiling of Bacteriological (Biological) and Toxin Weapons and on their Destruction, referred to more commonly as the Biological Weapons Convention (BWC) – went into effect to prohibit the development, production, and stockpiling of biological and toxin weapons. Over a period of three years starting in 1972, the agreement was signed by the United States, the former Soviet Union, and twenty other nations. The treaty was extraordinary in that it banned an entire class of weapons. Today more than 150 nations have signed on to the agreement. It is widely considered to be a useful vehicle for condemning biological weapons, as well as a valuable legal and political instrument. The BWC complements the Geneva Protocol, which banned biological warfare methods in 1925.

The primary problem with the BWC is the difficulty in enforcing it. In 1973, the former Soviet Union created a secret agency with more than 25,000 employees, known as "Biopreparat" devoted to the manufacture of bioweapons, in clear violation of the BWC (Alibek, 1999; Stone, 2001). Decades later – because the treaty continues to have no verification mechanism for ensuring that the signatories honor its terms – it remains among the weakest of international arms control agreements. Agreements on other weapons of mass destruction, particularly nuclear and chemical weapons, have established technical systems for monitoring compliance, but the BWC remains an agreement based on trust.

However, even if the treaty has only symbolic value, it may serve nonetheless to complement the unilateral exercise of decency and common sense. A compelling reason for any nation to honor the terms of the BWC – and perhaps every other agreement on weapons of mass destruction – is to preserve its own security and legitimacy. Stockpiles of such weapons have become too inviting a target of opportunity for terrorists, lunatics, and disgruntled people. With the possible exception of nuclear weapons, they are likely to have little deterrent value, and possibly have a stronger counter-deterrent stimulus. If used, they could sooner or later produce an effective blowback response. Bioweapons can scarcely be of value to a nation that regards their use as a violation of the most basic principles of just warfare and self-preservation.

– BF

intensity such that a relatively small amount – 16 curies of polonium 210 – is enough to produce about 5,000 lethal doses.

Nuclear Weapons. Nuclear weapons are bombs that make use of nuclear reactions of fission (the splitting of the nucleus of atoms) or fusion (the process by which atomic particles are joined together to form a much heavier nucleus, accompanied by the release or absorption of vast amounts of energy). The bombs used in Hiroshima and Nagasaki in 1945 were fission devices; uranium was used in the Hiroshima device, plutonium in the bomb detonated over Nagasaki. Modern nuclear weapons, including both hydrogen and thermonuclear weapons, combine thermonuclear fusion with at least one fission stage. They are substantially more lethal than the devices used against Japan in World War II and vastly more powerful than any conventional explosives. A single thermonuclear bomb detonated in a densely populated city is capable of killing hundreds of thousands of people by intense heat, massive projectiles of debris, building collapse in the immediate area, and irradiation in adjacent areas.

Nuclear devices could fall into the hands of terrorists through either of two plausible avenues: state-sponsored terrorism or the black market purchase by wealthy private individuals of either highly enriched uranium (a chemical composed of at least 20% U-235 or U-233) or intact nuclear devices.[2] Under the first scenario, a state that either has nuclear weapons or has access to them makes a device (one or more) available to a terrorist agent or a team of agents, taking care to destroy all evidence linking it to the operation. With the nuclear club of five (France, Britain, Russia, China, and the United States) growing to ten (now including India, Pakistan, Israel, South Africa, and North Korea), and beyond (Iran and others), state-sponsored terrorism is likely to be a continually growing threat.

In the second scenario, the terrorist acquires a "loose nuke" from a black market supplier. Although this would be extremely difficult for several reasons – there would be difficulties in finding a holder who actually has and would sell weapons-grade highly enriched uranium, in moving the material across national borders, in assembling the device, and then in moving it to a target location – one can presume nonetheless that a sufficiently committed effort could conceivably overcome the obstacles. Such a presumption will help also provide a constant reminder that adequately redundant safeguards must be maintained against such threats. Failure to provide such safeguards has led to serious breaches in the past, as evidenced by reports that at least twelve Ukranian cruise missiles, each capable of carrying a 200-kiloton nuclear warhead, were smuggled to China in 2000 and Iran in 2001 (Holley, 2005). The security problem is compounded by the need to move nuclear warhead missiles around frequently both for tactical purposes and for periodic maintenance to repair internal corrosion and prevent decay. This frequent movement increases exposure to sabotage and theft (Blair, 2004).

These problems are compounded each time a new nation joins the "nuclear club."

The worst-case outcome of nuclear proliferation in the era of terrorism is a "decapitating strike," a nuclear attack that would cripple a government by taking out a critical part of one or more of its major branches: executive, legislative, or judicial. This prospect is dealt with in Box 7.3 by public policy analyst Norman Ornstein. Although the best approach is to prevent this scenario from happening in the first place, that approach may be unrealistic over the long term. Ornstein reminds us that it is irresponsible to operate in the meantime as though such an event will not happen – to ignore the unthinkable – rather than develop contingency plans that can prevent a political and social collapse in the event of such a catastrophic event.

One way to reduce the risk of a nuclear catastrophe is to counter the threat of "loose nukes" falling into the hands of terrorists. Toward this end, Senators Sam Nunn and Richard Lugar initiated the Cooperative Threat Reduction (CTR) program in 1992, aimed at securing and dismantling weapons of mass destruction in former Soviet Union states. The CTR provides funding and expertise for republics of the former Soviet Union – Russia, Ukraine, Georgia, Azerbaijan, Uzbekistan, and Kazakhstan – to decommission nuclear, biological, and chemical weapon stockpiles, as agreed by the Soviet Union under disarmament treaties such as the Strategic Arms Limitation Treaties I and II. Under the scrutiny of American contractors, nuclear warheads are to be removed from their delivery vehicles, then decommissioned or stockpiled at designated sites in Russia. The CTR program reports to Congress annually on the status of the initiative as a whole and on the progress made in individual states.

Additional threats associated with Cold War nuclear policies continue even decades after the fall of the Berlin Wall in 1989. The U.S. and former Soviet Union nations possess the vast majority of nuclear devices. Analyst Bruce Blair is concerned about more possibilities than nuclear devices from these spheres getting into the hands of terrorists through black markets, as described earlier. There are other nuclear-related terrorist threats, such as terrorists from Chechnya or elsewhere aiming a non-nuclear missile at nuclear weapon sites in any former Soviet Union country or in the United States in an attempt to set off a Cold War calamity. Blair argues that such terrorist threats loom much larger today than the unlikely risk that either the United States or Russia would deliberately attack the other with nuclear weapons. He concludes, "We need to kick our old habits and stand down our hair-trigger forces."

Related concerns about trafficking in weapons-grade uranium have been raised by Lawrence Sheets. Sheets describes three unrelated incidents of attempts by Russians to sell such material on the black market. He observes that while all three attempts failed, they nonetheless reveal the ease with

Box 7.3. Worst-Case Scenario: The Decapitating Strike

– Norman Ornstein

The recent car-bomb threats in Britain were stark reminders that terrorists continue to probe for ways to attack us – and not every attempt will fail or be repelled.

That this danger extends to the United States was made clearer in May when the White House announced National Security Presidential Directive 51 and Homeland Security Presidential Directive 20 to create a national continuity policy – ensuring that federal agencies could still operate, with clear lines of authority, in the event of a devastating surprise attack on Washington.

These largely sensible directives have received only modest attention. Yet they spotlight the abject failure of our leaders in all three branches to make sure our Constitution remains intact if and when terrorists hit us again.

During the Cold War, elaborate top-secret plans existed, including bunkers for the president, vice president, Supreme Court justices, and members of Congress. If nuclear missiles were launched by the Soviet Union, there would be 30 to 90 minutes' notice to evacuate top officials by plane, train, or automobile.

On Sept. 11, 2001, the era of notice preceding attacks ended. This underscored the fact that none of our branches of government had plans to keep operating if hit in a serious way. An attack on Congress that killed or incapacitated a large number of members would mean no Congress for months. Each house needs half of its members to be present for a quorum to do any official business. The House of Representatives can replace deceased members only by special elections that take, on average, four months. The Senate, under the 17th Amendment, allows states (usually governors) to appoint replacements to fill vacancies, but neither house has a mechanism for replacing incapacitated members.

Presidential succession after the vice president is set by statute; every person in the line is based in Washington. The Supreme Court requires a quorum of six justices to function; if all or most of the justices are killed, there would be no Supreme Court until a president or acting president nominated successors and the Senate confirmed them. If an attack damaged all three branches, replenishing the court could take months or longer.

Consider the worst-case scenario: a suitcase nuclear attack at a presidential inauguration, with the outgoing and incoming president and vice president, most of Congress, and the Supreme Court present; the outgoing

Cabinet scheduled to leave office; and no incoming Cabinet members yet confirmed. There would be chaos – no clear president to take over, probably many Al Haig wannabes announcing that they were in charge, no quorum to reconstitute Congress, no court to sort out the conflicting claims.

This scenario may be unlikely – but the new presidential directives make clear that it is not outlandish. In the aftermath of Sept. 11, I wrote a series of pieces pointing out the vacuum in governance that could be created by another attack. I helped create a Continuity of Government Commission, co-chaired by former senator Alan Simpson and the late Lloyd Cutler, former White House counsel, to consider and recommend reforms to ensure we could quickly constitute legitimate and representative institutions to keep our form of government functioning.

There were, and are, straightforward ways to do so: creating temporary appointments to ensure a representative legislative branch that can function until real and meaningful elections can occur to fill vacancies; revamping presidential succession to ensure that some designated figures are geographically dispersed; creating a temporary Supreme Court, consisting of the chief judges of the federal appeals courts, to adjudicate key constitutional issues until a regular court can be reconstituted.

But my efforts and those of others over the past five-plus years have been met with indifference or hostility. The response of congressional leaders, especially former House speaker Dennis Hastert, was aggressive opposition to serious consideration of any meaningful proposals and slapdash passage of poorly drafted and unworkable stopgap measures to quell the criticism. Former Senate majority leader Bill Frist had no interest. So far, their respective Democratic replacements, Nancy Pelosi and Harry Reid, have shown no greater proclivity to act.

Several times I raised the question of presidential succession directly with Vice President Cheney, to no avail. I discussed Supreme Court succession with Chief Justice John Roberts soon after he took the post. Roberts said, "I just got here, and you want me to deal with the issue of my demise?"

The lack of interest in continuity may stem from the same reasons some smart people refuse to create wills, even though failure to do so leaves behind horrific messes for their loved ones. Yet the threat is real. Our leaders' failure to establish plans to ensure that our Constitution survives is irresponsible. Do we really have to wait until the nightmare scenario becomes a reality to do something?

Norman Ornstein is a resident scholar at the American Enterprise Institute and senior counselor to the Continuity of Government Commission. This essay was published originally as an op-ed article in the *Washington Post*, July 12, 2007.

which extremely dangerous materials can be acquired and sold to interested buyers, including terrorists.

Information about the manufacture and use of all types of weapons of mass destruction – biological, chemical, and radiological – has become widely available through the Internet and other channels. Given the large number of people willing to use these devices and the unlimited array of prospective targets, it is virtually inevitable that someone, somewhere will make use of this information, get their hands on a weapon of mass destruction, and eventually set off a major biological, chemical, radiological, or nuclear attack. To the extent that we understand these weapons and how to protect ourselves against them, we can ward off attacks and, when the defenses against them are overcome, minimize the damage they inflict.

2. Attacks on Technology Infrastructures and Critical Systems

Over the past several decades, economies throughout the world have been fueled by extraordinary growth in technological efficiency and substantial increases in productivity in both the manufacturing and service sectors. These developments have been largely a product of advances in industrial engineering, computerized logistics, and the development of "tightly coupled systems" to reduce redundancies and delays. Sophisticated airport scheduling and "just-in-time inventory systems" are examples of such advances, which have contributed significantly to reductions in the costs of delivering goods and services in economies throughout the world (Barabasi, 2003).

These developments have also made society more vulnerable to terrorist attacks, and they may actually invite terrorist attacks. Systems that are developed to accommodate only normal amounts of demand and occasional shocks due to weather and other random disruptions may be ill equipped to respond to severe shocks not previously encountered, as revealed by Hurricane Katrina in 2005 (see Chapter 11). The world may be no less vulnerable to shocks of terrorism. Of particular concern are critical systems and technology infrastructures: electric power plants, generators, lines, and grids; hydroelectric dams and facilities; telecommunication centers and lines; air and rail traffic control systems; oil and gas pipelines and other energy supply lines; agribusiness supply chains; and the Internet. A basic solution is to protect these systems by building redundancy into them, replacing single-file lines and bottlenecks with adaptive networks, parallel processes, and backups.

Much of this redundancy had already been put in place before the 9/11 attack. Al Qaeda's planners may have anticipated that the attack on the world's financial center would cause more serious disruptions to the U.S. economy than actually occurred. Thanks largely to preparations for an anticipated "Y2K" calamity – computer systems would fail with the arrival of the new millennium – the U.S. financial system turned out to be well prepared to absorb the shock of September 11, 2001. Wall Street operations were hit hard, but not seriously set back by the attack. Essential financial markets, including banks and other financial intermediaries, remained open throughout the day and thereafter. Wholesale and retail payment systems remained operational, and many firms in the World Trade Center resumed business from other offices or from contingency sites within hours of the attack (Ferguson, 2004).

Vulnerabilities remain, however, in many still-fragile systems. Here are three examples:

1. A fallen power line in Ohio in 2003 cascaded into a major power outage throughout the Midwest and Canada, causing a blackout for about fifty million people and producing losses estimated at more than six billion dollars (Anderson Economic Group, 2003).

2. In the deep cold of January 2006, a team of terrorists blew up two major Gazprom pipelines in the southern Russian republic of North Ossetia-Alania, while another team attacked a power transmission pylon carrying electricity from Russia to Georgia. These two attacks effectively closed down both electricity and natural gas supplies to all of Georgia, a country about the size of Maine and home to nearly five million people. Georgian residents experienced great peril during the week of repairs needed to bring the country back to normal energy levels (Robb, 2007).

3. Iraq's oil pipeline system – more than 4,000 miles of it – has been hit repeatedly by terrorists since 2003. These attacks are inexpensive to launch, but they impose huge economic costs on the people of Iraq. The costs of these attacks could be reduced by improved systems of detection and remote control, but these systems are expensive to install and the workers operate under extremely perilous conditions (Robb, 2007).

The National Academy of Sciences devoted a chapter of its 2002 report on the nation's vulnerability to terrorism to the problem of complex and interdependent systems. The report describes how these vulnerabilities can be dealt with through the use of systems analysis and systems engineering. It recommends specifically that governance should be protected through more effective management techniques and the use of decision analysis, which enables better management of the risks. It describes how preparedness can be enhanced by testing different policy responses through the use of simulation models that account for real-world system complexities (Committee on Science and Technology for Countering Terrorism, 2002).

3. Cyberterrorism

One important and rapidly growing type of terrorism involves terrorist attacks on computer networks and systems. Critical government and corporate computer systems are especially vulnerable to these potentially crippling and extremely costly attacks. But so are all other computer users who depend on the Internet and e-mail systems: ordinary and high-profile individuals alike, community and religious groups and other nongovernmental organizations, and others. A nation's information infrastructure qualifies clearly as a prime target for terrorist attacks, as it is vital to the effective functioning of economic and public sector operations.

Cyberterrorist attacks may use any of a variety of devious devices created to overcome even fairly sophisticated identification log-on procedures and firewalls that protect data and software resources. They do so by creating viruses and worms that invade, attach themselves to, and disrupt government, corporate, or individual computers or by launching spam e-mail attacks that shut down entire systems and operations, destroy valuable information along the way, and do so in a matter of seconds. Or they may engage in cyberstalking, whereby attackers intimidate individuals through computer messages with either vague or explicit threats of terrorist attacks. The attacks may involve computer systems that control banking and finance operations, power supplies, communications, transportation, the processing and distribution of food supplies, and other manufacturing, wholesale, retail, or service operations. These attacks may occur alone, or they can be orchestrated to accompany major terrorist events, disrupting efforts to prevent and respond to those more conventional types of terrorist attacks (McQuade, 2006).

An important early cyberterrorist attack was the "Code Red" attack on White House computers in July 2001. Marked with the phrase, "Hacked By Chinese," a generalized computer worm attack on the Internet launched the incident, which also included a denial-of-service attack targeting the White House Web server.

The Federal Bureau of Investigation, Central Intelligence Agency, National Security Agency, and other agencies of federal and local law enforcement have created teams of experts to deal with this growing menace. At the same time, cyberterrorists work largely by attacking critical private sector resources – the very resources that are likely to be an essential weapon in any battle against cyberterrorism. While law enforcement agencies are increasingly acquiring the computerized filters and screens and the human resources needed to prevent such attacks, they must also rely on private agents with unique skills to help counter the attacks. Box 7.4 describes the combination of intelligence and patience that is typically needed to catch this rapidly growing class of cyberterrorists.

One of the most worrisome prospects is the use of methods of cyberterror by militant extremists, especially when orchestrated with other terrorist

Box 7.4. Chasing Internet Villains Privately in Eastern Europe

– Cassell Bryan-Low, with Robert A. Guth

Created in 2002, Microsoft Corp.'s Internet Safety Enforcement Team is part of the U.S. software giant's intensifying efforts to combat cyber crime at a time when consumers and businesses are becoming increasingly frustrated with fraud and virus attacks on their personal computers, most of which use Microsoft's Windows operating system.

As Internet crime proliferates, law enforcement is relying more on the private sector to help counter it. That's because tracking cyber criminals requires a different set of skills than police have traditionally used. Compounding the challenge is the speed at which new online threats are morphing.

Microsoft brings huge resources and technical expertise to the table, ranging from decrypting files to analyzing computer code. Through its security team, the company collaborates with police worldwide. Last month, Microsoft worked with the Federal Bureau of Investigation and authorities in Morocco and Turkey to trace suspects behind the "Mytob" and "Zotob" worms, which recently disrupted computer networks. In less than two weeks, two people were arrested. Microsoft's assistance "was essential," says David Thomas, head of the FBI's computer-intrusion section.

Microsoft's cooperation with law enforcement is unusual. Companies are often reluctant to call in police to solve computer-related crimes, fearing business disruptions and bad publicity if computers are seized. Only about a third of U.S. cyber-crime cases are reported, says the FBI.

Microsoft's efforts haven't stemmed the thousands of new viruses and worms that appear every year, even though arrests of virus writers have increased. In the past 12 months, Microsoft has made about 75 referrals to law enforcement around the world. It has also filed 243 civil actions related to Internet safety threats, such as spam. But Microsoft investigator Peter Fifka acknowledges he is often two steps behind the hackers. "The reality is that people will always try to find new ways to commit crimes," he says.

Microsoft has a lot at stake. It potentially stands to lose its reputation and millions of dollars if customers defect to alternative software suppliers. Security experts have criticized the company's software as particularly vulnerable, and say Microsoft has focused on features at the expense of security.

Viruses caused businesses worldwide $17.8 billion in damages last year including the cost of repairing systems and lost business, estimates Irvine, Calif., research firm Computer Economics. Microsoft's Windows, which dominates PCs with a more-than-95 percent market share, is the company's biggest moneymaker and generated $12.2 billion in revenue for the 12 months ended June 30.

Massive Attacks: Major Computer Virus Attacks through 2004 and Their Global Financial Impact

Virus Name	Year	Impact (billions)
Love Bug	2000	$8.75
MyDoom	2004	$5.25
Sasser	2004	$3.50
NetSky	2004	$2.75
SoBig	2003	$2.75
Code Red	2001	$2.50
Slammer	2003	$2.00
Bagle	2004	$1.50
Blaster	2003	$1.50
Klez	2002	$1.50

Source: Computer Economics

The company created a $5 million bounty fund in 2003 for tips that lead to arrests of virus writers. In July, the company said it would pay its first $250,000 reward to two informants who helped identify the author of a worm known as Sasser, which damaged computer networks worldwide last year. Microsoft is targeting virus writers and others who increasingly use malicious code for financial gain through identity theft, hawking counterfeit goods, and other crimes.

Microsoft's Enforcement Team employs 65 people worldwide, including former policemen, lawyers and paralegals. The group, which gets a seven-figure annual budget, has 25 investigators including Mr. Fifka.

Mr. Fifka, 44 years old, began his career as an analytical chemist in his native Slovakia, researching antibiotic drugs. He joined the Slovak national police's forensic unit as a drug specialist in 1987. In 1995, he took a job with Interpol, the international police group based in Lyon, France, where he investigated drug smuggling and human trafficking.

Microsoft hired him in 2001 to combat software counterfeiting. Mr. Fifka's role soon evolved into fighting hackers and virus writers who work with counterfeiters and spammers in Eastern Europe. The region is a cybercrime hotbed, experts say, because of a large pool of technical talent and a dearth of jobs.

Working from Microsoft's Paris office, Mr. Fifka gathers intelligence on suspects and tries to lure them into the real world where police can nab them. He often trawls the Internet for clues to the identities of digital villains, mining discussion forums in different languages. It helps that he speaks six languages, including Russian and Hungarian. "Many people say it is easy to be anonymous" on the Internet, he says. "It's not true."

Many cybercriminals leave digital trails. E-mails and Web sites typically carry a unique set of numbers, known as an Internet protocol address, which identifies each computer connected to the Internet. Publicly accessible databases can often provide details about the organization the number is assigned to – typically an Internet service provider, university, or company. Police can then subpoena the organization for the name, address, and other details of the person using that computer.

While Mr. Fifka's investigations usually begin in cyberspace, he uses old-school gumshoe tactics to pinpoint a suspect's physical location. He travels around Eastern Europe and Russia, sometimes working with private detectives. Armed with a laptop and a cellphone that rings to the theme tune of the Eddie Murphy movie "Beverly Hills Cop," he says he spends about two-thirds of his time on the road.

Mr. Fifka says he often juggles 15 to 20 cases at a time. Some of his work involves educating authorities on new virus trends. In 2003, for example, he flew to the United Kingdom to teach police about a worm called Randex, which Scotland Yard and Microsoft suspected was being spread from England.

The Randex worm was part of a new family of viruses known as bots. A bot virus allows people to hijack thousands of far-flung computers and marshal them for a specific task, such as overrunning a Web site with traffic to disable it. The Randex worm was being used to send spam from numerous computers at once.

Mr. Fifka briefed U.K. police on how criminals in Russia and elsewhere used bots to make money, such as through hawking counterfeit goods with spam. He explained how bot-controlled networks of computers could be rented online from cybercriminals and what their going price was – between a few cents and $1 per machine.

After the suspected Randex worm writer and his computer were seized around January 2004, Microsoft flew technical experts to London to provide forensic expertise. Scotland Yard credits Microsoft with helping to convict a British and a Canadian teenager for releasing the worm. The Canadian teen received a six-month suspended sentence last November. A month later, the British teen got a nine-month suspended sentence, the equivalent of nine months of probation. British and Canadian police wouldn't release their names because they are minors.

attacks. Box 7.5 gives an account of a young jihadist based in London who committed serious crimes on behalf of al Qaeda through the Internet. He was caught, but the episode illustrated how easy it is for smart, young,

Box 7.5. Catching a Jihadi Cyberterrorist

– Rita Katz and Michael Kern

For almost two years, intelligence services around the world tried to uncover the identity of an Internet hacker who had become a key conduit for al-Qaeda. The savvy, English-speaking, presumably young Webmaster taunted his pursuers, calling himself Irhabi (Terrorist) 007. He hacked into American university computers, propagandized for the Iraq insurgents led by Abu Musab al-Zarqawi, and taught other online jihadists how to wield their computers for the cause.

Suddenly last fall, Irhabi 007 disappeared from the message boards. The postings ended after Scotland Yard arrested a 22-year-old West Londoner, Younis Tsouli, suspected of participating in an alleged bomb plot. In November, British authorities brought a range of charges against him related to that plot. Only later, according to our sources familiar with the British probe, was Tsouli's other suspected identity revealed. British investigators eventually confirmed to us that they believe he is Irhabi 007.

The unwitting end of the hunt comes at a time when al-Qaeda sympathizers like Irhabi 007 are making explosive new use of the Internet. Countless Web sites and password-protected forums – most of which have sprung up in the last several years – now cater to would-be jihadists like Irhabi 007. The terrorists who congregate in those cybercommunities are rapidly becoming skilled in hacking, programming, executing online attacks, and mastering digital and media design – and Irhabi was a master of all those arts.

But the manner of his arrest demonstrates how challenging it is to combat such online activities and to prevent others from following Irhabi's example: After pursuing an investigation into a European terrorism suspect, British investigators raided Tsouli's house, where they found stolen credit card information, according to an American source familiar with the probe. Looking further, they found that the cards were used to pay American Internet providers on whose servers he had posted jihadi propaganda. Only then did investigators come to believe that they had netted the infamous hacker. And that element of luck is a problem. The Internet has presented investigators with an extraordinary challenge. But our future security is going to depend increasingly on identifying and catching the shadowy figures who exist primarily in the elusive online world.

The short career of Irhabi 007 offers a case study in the evolving nature of the threat that we at the SITE Institute track every day by monitoring and then joining the password-protected forums and communicating with the online jihadi community. Celebrated for his computer expertise, Irhabi 007 had propelled the jihadists into a twenty-first-century offensive through his ability to covertly and securely disseminate manuals of weaponry, videos of insurgent feats such as beheadings, and other inflammatory material. It is by analyzing the trail of information left by such postings that we are able to distinguish the patterns of communication used by individual terrorists.

Irhabi's success stemmed from a combination of skill and timing. In early 2004, he joined the password-protected message forum known as Muntada al-Ansar al-Islami (Islam Supporters Forum) and, soon after, al-Ekhlas (Sincerity) – two of the password protected forums with thousands of members that al Qaeda had been using for military instructions, propaganda, and recruitment. (These two forums have since been taken down.) This was around the time that Zarqawi began using the Internet as his primary means of disseminating propaganda for his insurgency in Iraq. Zarqawi needed computer-savvy associates, and Irhabi proved to be a standout among the volunteers, many of whom were based in Europe.

Irhabi's central role became apparent to outsiders in April of that year, when Zarqawi's group, later renamed al Qaeda in Iraq, began releasing its communiqués through its official spokesman, Abu Maysara al-Iraqi, on the Ansar forum. In his first posting, al-Iraqi wrote in Arabic about "the good news" that "a group of proud and brave men" intended to "strike the economic interests of the countries of blasphemy and atheism, that came to raise the banner of the Cross in the country of the Muslims."

At the time, some doubted that posting's authenticity, but Irhabi, who was the first to post a response, offered words of support. Before long, al-Iraqi answered in like fashion, establishing their relationship – and Irhabi's central role.

Over the following year and a half, Irhabi established himself as the top jihadi expert on all things Internet-related. He became a very active member of many jihadi forums in Arabic and English. He worked on both defeating and enhancing online security, linking to multimedia and providing online seminars on the use of the Internet. He seemed to be online night and day, ready to answer questions about how to post a video, for example – and often willing to take over and do the posting himself. Irhabi focused on hacking into Web sites as well as educating Internet surfers in the secrets to anonymous browsing.

In one instance, Irhabi posted a 20-page message titled "Seminar on Hacking Websites," to the Ekhlas forum. It provided detailed information on the art of hacking, listing dozens of vulnerable Web sites to which one could upload shared media. Irhabi used this strategy himself, uploading data to a Web site run by the state of Arkansas, and then to another run by George Washington University. This stunt led many experts to believe – erroneously – that Irhabi was based in the United States.

Irhabi used countless other Web sites as free hosts for material that the jihadists needed to upload and share. In addition to these sites, Irhabi provided techniques for discovering server vulnerabilities, in the event that his suggested sites became secure. In this way, jihadists could use third-party hosts to disseminate propaganda so that they did not have to risk using their own Web space and, more importantly, their own money.

As he provided seemingly limitless space captured from vulnerable servers throughout the Internet, Irhabi was celebrated by his online followers. A mark of that appreciation was the following memorandum of praise offered by a member of Ansar in August 2004:

> To Our Brother Irhabi 007. Our brother Irhabi 007, you have shown very good efforts in serving this message board, as I can see, and in serving jihad for the sake of God. By God, we do not like to hear what hurts you, so we ask God to keep you in his care.
>
> You are one of the top people who care about serving your brothers. May God add all of that on the side of your good work, and may you go careful and successful.
>
> We say carry on with God's blessing.
>
> Carry on, may God protect you.
>
> Carry on serving jihad and its supporters.
>
> And I ask the mighty, gracious and merciful God to keep for us everyone who wants to support his faith.
>
> Amen.

Irhabi's hacking ability was useful not only in the exchange of media but also in the distribution of large scale al Qaeda productions. In one instance, a film produced by Zarqawi's al Qaeda, titled "All Is for Allah's Religion," was distributed from a page at www.alaflam.net/wdkl.

The links, uploaded in June 2005, provided numerous outlets where visitors could find the video. In the event that one of the sites was disabled, many other sources were available as backups. Several were based on domains such as www.irhabi007.ca or www.irhabi007.tv, indicating a strong involvement by Irhabi himself. The film, a major release by al Qaeda in Iraq, showed many of the insurgents' recent exploits compiled with footage of Osama bin Laden, commentary on the Abu Ghraib prison, and political statements about the rule of then-Iraqi Interim Prime Minister Ayad Allawi.

Tsouli has been charged with eight offenses including conspiracy to murder, conspiracy to cause an explosion, conspiracy to cause a public nuisance, conspiracy to obtain money by deception, and offenses relating to the possession of articles for terrorist purposes and fundraising. So far there are no charges directly related to his alleged activities as Irhabi on the Internet, but given the charges already mounted against him, it will probably be a long time before the 22-year-old is able to go online again.

But Irhabi's absence from the Internet may not be as noticeable as many hope. Indeed, the hacker had anticipated his own disappearance. In the months beforehand, Irhabi released his will on the Internet. In it, he provided links to help visitors with their own Internet security and hacking skills in the event of his absence – a rubric for jihadists seeking the means to continue to serve their nefarious ends. Irhabi may have been caught, but his online legacy may be the creation of many thousands of 007s.

[*Source: The Washington Post* (March 26, 2006)]

like-minded people to put modern technology into the service of criminal activity and the support of international terrorist networks.

4. The Internet as a "Rage Enabler"

Technology can be used as an instrument of terror in yet another way, which is perhaps more powerful strategically and more pervasive than any other usage, and that is to spread hatred through the Internet. The Internet was developed largely for productive, commercial, and intellectual purposes: to expand access to and the dissemination of information and thus serve as a marketplace for ideas. The launching of the World Wide Web in the 1990s contributed substantially to the realization of these goals, and the prospects seemed virtually limitless a decade later, with few downside prospects. In time, however, extremists with hostile agendas found and began to exploit this powerful technology with much the same enthusiasm. The Internet thus opened the door to the spread of terrorism by providing extremists with vast access to like-minded people, enabling them to communicate and to enlist others, previously isolated in faraway places, in causes of hatred and violence. The creation of extremist Web sites has fanned these fires of hatred, helping spread local skirmishes into more heated transnational crises.

Technology and Terrorism

Researcher Charles McLean refers to this perverse use of the Internet as its "rage enabling" capacity (Ignatius, 2006a). Daniel Benjamin and Steven Simon (2005) see the Internet as having contributed to a "new breed of self-starting terrorist cells," spewing a brew of quasi-religious doctrine that calls for violence and provides instructions for carrying it out. They report an increase from just 12 Web sites for terrorist groups in 1998 to about 4,400 by 2005.

This perverse use of the Internet by extremists has exploded since the attack of September 11, but it started earlier. The problem had in fact reached a sufficient level of alarm to cause a group of concerned people to launch counter-measures in the 1990s. In the United States, years ago, the Educational Resources Information Center began to create materials and guides for teachers, parents, and others in the community on misuse of the Internet. NetAction, a California nonprofit organization, established a Web site in 1997 to counter hate on the Internet. In Canada, the International Symposium on Hate on the Internet was launched also in 1997. Similar efforts began after 9/11. In the Netherlands, the International Network against CyberHate was created in 2002 to fight hatred and discrimination on the Internet.

What is the appeal of Web sites of hatred? There are several sources of their seductiveness. First, they feed a paranoia common to anxious people everywhere, especially less educated young males (Cogan, 2002; Franklin, 2002; Martin, 1996). They provide superficially appealing conspiracy theories that often blame targeted groups for a variety of sins: religious, cultural, economic, and political. These theories are seductive because they validate the audience's ignorance through fabricated facts and seemingly authoritative writings, such as the *Protocols of the Elders of Zion*, an anti-Semitic hoax forged in Russia in the late nineteenth century using material heavily plagiarized from an earlier non-anti-Semitic political satire about Montesquieu and Machiavelli (Graves). Second, they often invoke references to holy scriptures, historical icons, or pseudo-scientific writings to suggest that their claims have been morally sanctified or authenticated by an ultimate authority (Media Awareness Network, 2008). These claims are typically accentuated by appeals to a need to maintain the survival of the religion or culture, maintain ethnic or ideological purity, or stave off an otherwise inevitable Armageddon. They are often accompanied also by appeals to patriotism and by historical revisionism, such as denial of the Holocaust. They often invoke symbols, such as the swastika or KKK letters, to instill an emblematic sense of loyalty to the cause.

The Internet genie is out of the bottle, and there may be no way of putting it back, but there are ways of controlling the spread of hatred on the Internet. One way is through vigilance: tracking Web sites to see if they cross the line of legality. In the United States, state and federal laws protect people against crimes motivated by animus against race, religion, ethnicity, national origin,

190

gender, sexual orientation or identity, or disability. If such laws have been violated, offenders can be prosecuted. If the violators live outside the country, the offending Web sites can be shut down. Another way is to inoculate children against the virus of hatred on the Internet and elsewhere through education and adult guidance on history and world events, facts about racism, and the false claims of extremists. Such campaigns begin at home and, with the help of the Internet, they can be made available to people abroad.

B. Technology as a Tool Against Terrorism

Technological advances have helped the terrorists, but they help in the cause of counterterrorism too. Soon after the 9/11 attack, the National Academy of Sciences formed a Committee on Science and Technology for Countering Terrorism. The mission of the Committee was threefold: to identify vulnerabilities to subsequent attack, assess critical means by which science and technology could be used to reduce those vulnerabilities and lessen their consequences when they do occur, and develop a strategy by which the strengths of U.S. science could serve the defense of the nation against terrorism. A motivating idea was that – in much the same manner that the scientific community had engaged effectively to meet the challenges of Sputnik and Soviet science during the Cold War and respond to the AIDS epidemic in the 1980s and '90s – it ought to be able to rise as well to meet the challenges posed by the burgeoning threat of terrorism. The Committee set out to do so by generating proposals specific enough to be useful, but taking care not to provide information that could give terrorists new ideas of how to launch attacks.

The Committee – consisting of scientists from universities, industry, government, and professional societies – did its work over a fairly short time span, from December 2001 through May 2002. It focused on nine areas: nuclear and radiological threats, human and agricultural health systems, toxic chemicals and explosive materials, information technology, energy systems, transportation systems, cities and fixed infrastructure, the response of people to terrorism, and complex and interdependent systems.

They recommended fourteen initiatives, seven for immediate implementation and seven to encourage research on specific issues in need of systematic inquiry. The recommendations are itemized in Box 7.6.

The Committee also identified a set of general principles that spanned the specific areas of focus:

- Identify and repair the weakest links in vulnerable systems and infrastructures.
- Use "circuit breakers" to isolate and stabilize failing system elements.
- Build security into basic system designs where possible.
- Build flexibility into systems so that they can be modified to address unforeseen threats.

Box 7.6. Recommendations of the National Academy of Sciences Committee on Science and Technology for Countering Terrorism: Fourteen Important Technical Initiatives

Immediate Applications of Existing Technologies

1. Develop and utilize robust systems for protection, control, and accounting of nuclear weapons and special nuclear materials at their sources.
2. Ensure the production and distribution of known treatments and preventatives for pathogens.
3. Design, test, and install coherent, layered security systems for all transportation modes, particularly shipping containers and vehicles that contain large quantities of toxic or flammable materials.
4. Protect energy distribution services by improving security for supervisory control and data acquisition (SCADA) systems and providing physical protection for key elements of the electric-power grid.
5. Reduce the vulnerability and improve the effectiveness of air filtration in ventilation systems.
6. Deploy known technologies and standards for allowing emergency responders to reliably communicate with each other.
7. Ensure that trusted spokespersons will be able to inform the public promptly and with technical authority whenever the technical aspects of an emergency are dominant in the public's concerns.

Urgent Research Opportunities

1. Develop effective treatments and preventatives for known pathogens for which current responses are unavailable and for potential emerging pathogens.
2. Develop, test, and implement an intelligent, adaptive electric-power grid.
3. Advance the practical utility of data fusion and data mining for intelligence analysis, and enhance information security against cyberattacks.
4. Develop new and better technologies (e.g., protective gear, sensors, communications) for emergency responders.
5. Advance engineering design technologies and fire-rating standards for blast- and fire-resistant buildings.

6. Develop sensor and surveillance systems (for a wide range of targets) that create useful information for emergency officials and decision makers.
7. Develop new methods and standards for filtering air against both chemicals and pathogens as well as better methods and standards for decontamination.

[*Source:* Committee on Science and Technology for Countering Terrorism (2002)]

- Search for technologies that reduce costs or provide ancillary benefits to civil society to ensure a sustainable effort against terrorist threats.

The Committee made several other noteworthy recommendations:

- The United States should accelerate its bilateral materials protection, control, and accounting program in Russia to safeguard small nuclear warheads and special nuclear materials, particularly highly enriched uranium.
- A focused and coordinated near-term effort should be made to evaluate and improve the efficacy of special nuclear material detection systems that could be deployed at strategic choke points for homeland defense, especially for the detection of highly enriched uranium.
- The United States should develop new tools for the surveillance, detection, and diagnosis of bioterrorist threat agents.
- The United States should strengthen its decontamination and bioterrorism forensic programs critical to deterrence, response, and recovery.
- The Food and Drug Administration should develop criteria for quantifying hazards in order to define the level of risk for various kinds of food-processing facilities.
- The Environmental Protection Agency should direct additional research on determining the persistence of pathogens, chemical contaminants, and other toxic materials in public water supplies.
- Scientists and engineers from different settings – universities, companies, and federal agencies – should work together to advance filtering and decontamination techniques by improving existing technologies and developing new methods for removing chemical contaminants from the air and water.
- The National Institute of Standards and Technology, the national laboratories, and other agencies should undertake research and development leading to improved blast- and fire-resistant designs.
- Research and development should be undertaken to produce new, small, reliable, quick-reading sensors of toxic materials for use by first responders.
- The Office of Homeland Security and the Federal Emergency Management Agency (FEMA) should coordinate with state and local officials to develop and deploy threat-based simulation models and training modules for emergency operations centers training of first responders.

- The National Science Foundation, FEMA, and other agencies should support research – basic, comparative, and applied – on the structure and functioning of agencies responsible for dealing with attacks and other disasters.
- All agencies creating technological systems for the support of first responders and other decision makers should base their system designs and user interfaces on the most up-to-date research on human behavior, especially with respect to issues critical to the effectiveness of counterterrorism technologies and systems.
- To reduce the vulnerabilities of complex interconnected systems, threat and infrastructure models should be extended or developed and used in combination with intelligence data.

The Committee concluded its report by strongly urging the U.S. scientific and engineering communities to cooperate with like-minded efforts in other countries, thereby enhancing the prospects for successful counterterrorism efforts both at home and abroad.

Since publication of the 2002 report, three specific technologies have been shown to be particularly well suited for countering the threat of terrorism: for screening people at border crossings, beginning with the ability to verify their identity; for identifying the "dots" of potentially relevant intelligence data, and then for making connections among the relevant dots; and for enhancing the ability of the Internet to serve as a bridge builder among people throughout the world, thereby reducing the alienation that contributes to terrorism.

1. Smart Identification Technologies

Conventional methods for screening people at border crossings and access points to areas vulnerable to terrorist attack, including the use of computerized name recognition systems and unaided human judgment, are notoriously flawed. A host of biometric technologies have been used for many years to identify dangerous people, including fingerprint systems, developed by Henry Faulds, Sir Francis Galton, and Juan Vucetich in the late nineteenth century, and DNA ("genetic fingerprinting") identification technology, developed by Sir Alec Jeffreys in the late twentieth century. Error rates (false matches and missed matches) are fairly low for fingerprint identification, and near zero for DNA identification, but both fingerprint and DNA data are useless without reference prints or DNA samples against which new screening results can be compared.

More sophisticated biometric technologies have emerged to complement these conventional mixes of human judgment, name recognition systems, fingerprints, and DNA used for screening. Some are based on physiological characteristics other than fingerprints and DNA – retinal and iris features; ear distinctions; facial, hand, and finger geometry; and vascular maps – and others are based on behavioral characteristics, such as speech (a mix of physiological and behavioral attributes), handwriting, and computer keystroke patterns (Vacca, 2007). Retinal scans are among the most popular new biometric technologies – commonly used for verification in ATM transactions, in prisons, and to prevent welfare fraud – largely because they are unique even for monozygotic ("identical") twins.

Still other, more controversial, biometric technologies measure stress levels associated with hostile intent at airports and other security checkpoints, based on well-established principles of behavioral psychology and polygraphy, and processed using artificial-intelligence software that makes use of sophisticated algorithms. The rates of both false positives and false negatives for prototypes of this technology are higher than for fingerprint and other biometric methods that require matching data, but the error rates are sufficiently low to make them potentially useful as complements to conventional methods, especially at extremely vulnerable sites; in addition, they do not require matching data (Karp and Meckler, 2006).

The choice of which biometric identification device to use should be based on a variety of relevant considerations:

- **Universality:** Is this biometric feature commonly found in every individual?
- **Uniqueness:** Does this feature differ from each individual to every other?
- **Permanence:** Does this feature remain constant over the life of the person screened?
- **Efficiency or collectability:** How quickly and inexpensively can this biometric feature be measured and processed?
- **Accuracy:** How valid and reliable is the measurement of this biometric feature?
- **Circumvention:** How easy is it to fool the measurement device?
- **Vulnerability:** What are the social costs of a false-negative (failure to detect a real terrorist) result for the target that this screening system is designed to protect?
- **Acceptability:** Do the people screened see this method as intrusive?

These factors can vary substantially from feature to feature, setting to setting, and across measurement devices (Jain, 2004). Retinal scans, for example, are unique even among identical twins, but they cannot be taken for many blind people, and they can change as people develop certain conditions, such as diabetes, cataracts, glaucoma, and retinal degeneration. It is otherwise the most reliable biometric identification instrument. Advanced DNA identification is unique for all except identical twins, but it can be time consuming and relatively expensive to administer. Fingerprints and photographs have the advantage of being available for many more people than retinal scans and DNA information, but they do not score as well on the uniqueness dimension, as they can produce ambiguous results. Setting matters too. Greater care must be taken, for example, in screening people about to meet a head of state than screening those wanting to cross a border.

Technology and Terrorism

One of the many significant success stories with the use of biometric data has been in Iraq, where the U.S. military has taken fingerprints and eye scans from hundreds of thousands of Iraqi men and built a database to track suspected militants. U.S. troops stopped Iraqis at checkpoints, workplaces, and sites where attacks occurred; entered personal data using handheld scanners and laptops; and handed out ID cards to be used at checkpoints. The program met little resistance from Iraqis, who saw it as a way of making their communities safer. The program started in the Anbar province in 2004, a hotbed of insurgency, to root out people who showed up more than once in the vicinity of a bomb site. It was then expanded to the Baghdad area. The data are stored in West Virginia, as part of a much larger database designed to identify known insurgents at and within the borders of the United States (Frank, 2007).

These technologies are being mandated under federal laws to protect against domestic terrorism as well. For example, the Intelligence Reform and Terrorism Prevention Act of 2004 requires the U.S. Department of Transportation to establish federal standards for state driver's licenses to make it more difficult for would-be terrorists to use fake driver's licenses to gain access to resources that might be used in a terror strike. The legislation includes making the cards more secure through advanced technology and a more rigorous issuance process.

2. Technology for Gathering Intelligence Data

Much of the data collected for intelligence purposes aimed at preventing terrorist events are gathered using technology, ranging from simple to extremely sophisticated. Chapter 11, on the prevention of terrorism, describes the role of intelligence, distinguishing three basic sources of intelligence: humans, signals (from telephone, computer, radio, or electromagnetic pulse), and imagery (from high-altitude photography). Technology in the form of agents recording visual or sound images at close range can be an important part of the gathering of *human intelligence*, but technology is not the central aspect of human intelligence. It is a more integral part of both signal and imagery intelligence.

Signal intelligence can involve continuous eavesdropping on an entire radio spectrum in an area, including public broadcasts and military shortwave. It can also involve the interception of radar; microwave telephone, telegraph, and satellite signals; and cables, both land and sea – with real-time computer-assisted interpretation of the data. A modern intelligence arsenal also includes the use of satellites to intercept cell phone and pager traffic. Certain phone numbers or radio frequencies used by terrorists are likely to receive high-priority intercept status, with instantaneous computerized translating. Some traffic will be secret and encrypted, requiring advanced de-encryption software. Technology is, in short, an essential aspect of signal intelligence.

Technology is an important part of *imagery intelligence* too. Sophisticated equipment is needed to position cameras precisely so that they can take detailed, high-resolution photographs or videos of the activities of known or suspected terrorists, typically from a high altitude and often at a precise moment, and while penetrating misinformation and other obstacles in the process. New technologies permit constant real-time satellite and aircraft detection of electromagnetic activity, radioactivity, or traces of chemicals through cloud cover and even buildings and underground bunkers (Warrick, 2007). This technology, together with the expertise needed to use it effectively, can be an indispensable tool in the arsenal of counterterrorism.

3. Technology for "Connecting the Dots"

Once the data are collected, they must be analyzed. Because terrorism is both a crime and military problem, it is useful to draw both from the analysis of crime data and from the analysis of more conventional military intelligence processes, to consider the limits of each approach for dealing with the problem of terrorism, and to see how technology plays a role in both approaches. A more in-depth treatment of the intelligence analysis process is presented in Chapter 11.

Science and technology have made powerful tools available to criminal investigators to help in solving crimes by identifying linkages among people and organizations. These tools have helped solve street crimes and conspiratorial crimes such as narcotics trafficking and corruption, and the technology can be useful as well to the analysis of terrorism and organized hate crimes. Foremost among these are techniques of crime analysis and intelligence analysis that establish *who* is doing or planning to do *what* to *whom*, and *when* and *why* they plan to do it. An integral part of this analysis is the identification and deciphering of historical or recent crime patterns spatially and by type of crime and situation (Ronczkowski, 2003). Crime analysis begins with the collection and validation of crime and victimization data. Statistical tools are then used to describe and explain patterns in these data so that they can be analyzed as to causes and the trends projected forward.

Unfortunately, the most serious terrorist events are not predictable using these methods. They are unpredictable primarily because of a factor that we can applaud: there have been too few terrorist events in the West to form a distinct pattern or provide a basis for statistical prediction. The tools of crime analysis are likely to be more helpful in places where terrorist activities are frequent and committed by fairly unsophisticated people.

Terrorist events are less predictable for another reason as well: ordinary criminals are less inclined to rely on effective methods of deception and concealment than are terrorists. Terrorists do not have the luxury of being frequently caught and released, as is the case with most street offenders. Conventional intelligence techniques can be more helpful for learning about the activities and plans of individual terrorists and terrorist groups.

One example of the use of technology for identifying terrorist networks is through the analysis of patterns in the time and frequency of telephone calls made by known terrorists. The National Security Agency does this "data mining without snooping" routinely. It does not listen to individual calls. Rather, it tracks and records the time each call was placed, the length of the call, and the origin and destination of electronic transmissions. It then analyzes the data for patterns that permit an analysis of networks and of the direction and relative intensity of individual branches within the network. This data mining may be an effective use of the West's comparative advantage in technology. With appropriate constitutional safeguards, it can legitimately enable the collection of information that human intelligence has great difficulty providing, given the formidable barriers to penetrating the cells of radical Islamists, at home and abroad (Harris and Naftali, 2006; Zuckerman, 2006).

Technology can also help overcome one of the greatest obstacles to analyzing data about viable terrorism threats – language barriers. There is, to be sure, a real threat of home-grown terrorism by people born and raised in the same societies they have chosen to terrorize. But at least for the United States, the greater threat that has been identified by the 9/11 Commission and other authorities is that of acts committed by Muslim extremists determined to bring harm to targets in the West. There is a huge backlog of material collected in Arabic, Farsi, and other languages of the Middle East waiting to be translated. The primary bottleneck in the analysis of intelligence data is the lack of analysts with needed language skills, especially in Arabic and its many dialects and unique local colloquialisms, as well as familiarity with cultural nuances of countries and cultures such as those from which the nineteen 9/11 attackers came (9/11 Commission Report, 2004; Pincus, 2006). Technology can help significantly by performing computer translations of foreign languages and flagging items in need of careful scrutiny by people who speak the language (Robb and Silberman, 2005).

4. The Internet as Bridge Builder

The Internet was described as a "rage enabler" in a previous section, but it is also a bridge builder. Well over a billion people use the Internet today.[3] It is, for all users, a technology that allows people to reach others more quickly and inexpensively than any other alternative. Although precise estimates are not available, most of the Internet demand is for commercial, personal, political, and recreational uses. Much Internet traffic also involves extremist, terrorist, and illegal activities, including fraud and crimes such as identity theft, embezzlement, larceny, and human trafficking. Yet, another large component supports individuals and organizations interested in building dialogue with others throughout the world, for service, educational, and philanthropic purposes. Some see this bridge-building component today as a basic feature of global civilization – an international revolution that has transformed civil society mostly for the better, and will continue to do so (Slabbert, 2006).

C. The Limits of Technology

Romantic accounts of technology suggest that there are no limits to the extent to which it is capable of solving our problems. Others suggest that there are no limits to its capacity to destroy us. In the case of terrorism, both of these accounts may be exaggerated. As we have noted, technology is proving to be a critical tool in our effort to minimize the hazards of terrorist attacks – by helping identify threats, gather and analyze intelligence to assist in assessing those threats, and establishing effective strategies for preventing and intervening against terrorism. It is also a useful tool for supporting terrorists' schemes – technology is proving to have an awesome capacity to inflict damage on innocent people. Yet in both cases, the use of technology is now and will always be limited.

Several factors play a role in limiting both the productive and destructive uses of technology. One is the human factor. The more complex the technology, the greater the requirement for capable management and use of the technology, and such skills are in short supply. In the case of intelligence, for example, the United States learned painfully that sophisticated technology surveillance and communication systems were unable to detect and prevent the 9/11 attack, to know whether weapons of mass destruction really existed in Iraq, or to quickly find any of al Qaeda's top three figures: Osama bin Laden, Ayman al-Zawahiri, or Abu Musab al-Zarqawi. These failures were the combined product of limited technology and even more limited human intelligence.

Another factor grows out of a fundamental axiom of economics: resources are scarce. Over a limited time horizon, the resources needed to significantly advance any given technology must be allocated across a vast array of competing prospects. For example, after the transit attacks in Madrid in 2004 and London in 2005, Anne Applebaum (2007) wrote this:

> Here's the truth about mass transit security: There is no technology that can guarantee it. There are no machines that can reliably detect the presence of a backpack filled with homemade explosives in an underground tunnel. There

is no point in putting metal detectors at every single subway entrance or at every single bus stop. There is no amount of money, in other words, that can guarantee that subways and buses will be completely safe from small-time bombers, suicidal or otherwise. It's going to be a temptation, especially for Washingtonians, New Yorkers and others who regularly ride mass transit, to lobby their politicians for more spending. Don't do it.

There are moral objections to technology as well that cannot be ignored. For the German philosopher Martin Heidegger (1954), technology has taken humans from the world in which we were born into one that is purely of our own making. In this contrived, self-referential world, even nature itself becomes primarily an object of research: "man – investigating, observing – ensnares nature as an area of his own conceiving." Similar objections about a tendency for people to become dangerously infatuated with technology have been raised by social commentators Jacques Ellul (1967), Lewis Mumford (1963), and others.

It is easy to dismiss such concerns about technology as quaint, characteristic of Luddite small-mindedness and fear of progress, but many of the concerns that people have about technology are legitimate. Somewhere between irrational fears of technology and inclinations to pray at its altar is a position that recognizes that we can improve the quality of our lives – and possibly our security in the process – by being more conscious of how technology is useful and how it is harmful. As the quality of life improves, so too may our capacity to appreciate our place on earth and how technology can be used against us, not just by terrorists, but by our own laziness – mental, moral, and other.

Discussion Questions

1. Is technology better described as a force of good or of evil? Explain your answer. Would you have answered this question differently before September 11, 2001? If so, explain.
2. Can technology be managed to better serve humans generally? How? How might it be managed to limit its capacity to serve terrorists? How might it be used more effectively to serve the interests of counterterrorism?
3. Are some technologies more in need of control than others? Which ones? Why? Does the need to control technology to minimize the risk of terrorism differ from other needs to control it? If so, how?
4. Which weapons of mass destruction are most in need of tighter control? Why? What sort of controls do you see as most promising? Why? What sort are least promising? Why? How should U.S. policy be used to deal with a rogue nation that is out of line with the community of nations on the control of WMD? How should it deal with an advanced nation that is out

of line on WMD? What should the United States do about its own stockpile of WMD?

5. How should the United States secure its technology, agricultural, and public utility infrastructures to make them less vulnerable to terrorist attack?

6. What, if anything, should be done about Web sites that promote hatred on the Internet? Explain your answer.

EIGHT

Terrorism throughout the World

This chapter applies principles set forth in the preceding chapters to specific historical examples of terrorism in the United States and elsewhere in the Americas, Europe and Russia, the Middle East, and Asia. It identifies the commonalities, differences, and trends in terrorism cross-nationally and concludes with a set of questions as to what might be expected over the coming decades.

A. Terrorism in the United States

Terrorism was not a major issue in the United States before September 11, 2001. There had been two serious attacks in the 1990s – the World Trade Center (WTC) bombing of 1993 and the Oklahoma City bombing in 1995 – but neither had the extraordinary domestic and international impact of 9/11. The 1993 WTC bombing was serious but caused just six deaths, and the Oklahoma City bombing, although killing 168 people, was the product of home-grown terrorists. The 9/11 attack was much deadlier than both of the earlier attacks, it involved extensive planning and years of preparation, and it was an attack by foreigners, which gave it enormous international significance, creating a vast divide between Islam and the West and stoking fires of fear and rage on both sides. This attack revealed in a highly sensational way the vulnerability of the United States to serious terrorist attacks. Terrorism suddenly became the dominant national concern and public policy priority.

Terrorism of domestic origin is quite different in several ways from terrorism produced by foreigners planning primarily from centers abroad. It differs

202

in nature, causes, consequences, and the mix of interventions appropriate for dealing with it. Domestic terrorism falls solidly within the domain of crime, whereas international terrorism, although a crime in most places in which it strikes, is also a matter of foreign affairs, calling for both diplomatic policy and military interventions. These two fundamentally different types of terrorism are considered separately in this chapter.[1]

1. Terrorist Groups and Acts of Domestic Origin

Terrorism in the United States, as in virtually every other country, is for the most part a strictly domestic matter. It was noted in Chapter 3 that the raid in Kansas by John Brown in 1856 involved the killing of five unarmed citizens, committed, according to Brown, to fulfill God's will, with the expressed aim of striking terror in people he viewed as enemies. Since the end of the Civil War, the vast majority of victims of terrorism in the United States, as in other countries, were innocents killed by fellow citizens – in the American case, however, mostly through lynchings (see the Ku Klux Klan, described in Chapter 6). This tradition of terrorism primarily as a domestic matter continued through the last two decades of the twentieth century. The Federal Bureau of Investigation, which categorizes terrorist events and suspected terrorists as either "domestic" or "international," estimates that of the nearly 500 terrorist incidents identified in the United States from 1980 to 2001, about two-thirds were home-grown (Federal Bureau of Investigation, 2004).

Domestic terrorism usually has a political rather than religious or ethnic motive, and the most basic political distinction is between left-wing and right-wing extremists. Brent Smith (1994) makes several useful distinctions between the two in terms of ideology, economic views, geographic sources of support, tactics, and the targets chosen. Left-wing terrorists tend to have a Marxist orientation, oppose the economic status quo, operate predominantly in urban settings and in small cells (often finding sanctuary in safe houses), and often attack symbolic targets of oppression. Right-wing terrorists are, not surprisingly, nearly the opposite. Although they vary in their views of economic matters and tend to be less ideologically committed than their left-wing counterparts, right-wing terrorists tend to be anti-Marxist, usually operate in rural settings, often live in camps or compounds, are often connected to national networks of like-minded extremists, and hit targets that symbolize central government. They tend also to identify strongly with Christian fundamentalism.

Smith has found demographic differences as well between left- and right-wing terrorist groups in the United States. Right-wing group members tend to be about four or five years older, on average, than left-wing members; more predominantly male and white; and much less likely to be college graduates than members of left-wing groups.

Left-Wing Extremism and Terrorism: Working-Class Violence. Most people today associate left-wing violence in America with the extreme radical fringe of the Vietnam protest era. But a legacy of radical violence preceded the Vietnam-era extremism in the United States by nearly a century, with a wave of labor violence following the Civil War. One of the most prominent of these events was a labor riot in Rock Springs, Wyoming, in 1885, which combined labor unrest with racism. Tension had grown between Chinese and European immigrant workers in the Union Pacific Coal mines located in Sweetwater County, Wyoming, due largely to the fact that the Chinese miners were unhappy about receiving lower wage rates than the Caucasians for doing the same work. The problem was exacerbated by racial and ethnic tension – the whites, for example, routinely referred to the Chinese as "coolies." The tension burst eventually into full-blown rioting and acts of terrorism, resulting in the deaths of twenty-eight Chinese miners, injuries to many others, and the burning of seventy-five homes of the Chinese workers. The white offenders were neither arrested nor prosecuted. Instead, coverage of the event, both in Wyoming newspapers and that published elsewhere, was mostly positive about the outcome. Soon after the Rock Springs massacre, a wave of sympathy riots broke out against Chinese laborers in the Washington territory (now Washington State; McLain, 1996; Saxton, 1971).

The following year a working-class riot erupted in downtown Chicago, when police decided to break up what had been a peaceful rally of striking labor activists. The Haymarket rally became the Haymarket riot when a demonstrator hurled a bomb at the advancing police line, killing an officer. The officers responded by opening fire on the demonstrators. When the smoke had cleared, seven policemen and at least four workers were dead, with roughly ten times as many on both sides injured (Avrich, 1986; Green, 2007).

Left-Wing Extremism and Terrorism: The New Left Protest Movement. Far left extremism shifted fairly sharply throughout the world in the late 1960s and early '70s – from labor union interests of the Depression generation to social issues of the generations that followed, particularly war, authoritarianism, and social injustice. Much of this new wave of radicalism was centered in the United States. At the vanguard of this movement was the Students for a Democratic Society (SDS), created in 1962 by Tom Hayden.[2] The SDS was not a primarily terrorist group, as it followed the nonviolent protest approach used effectively by civil rights leader Martin Luther King, Jr., with the expressed aim of expanding "participatory democracy" in the United States. The SDS operated under a large tent as an awkward alliance of peaceful liberals and more militant activists; it was at the forefront of the antiwar movement, which swept college campuses during the Vietnam War. As the war grew ever larger and more deadly, the SDS became increasingly militant, and although its nonviolent emphasis kept it mostly out of terrorist activities, its influence declined as many of its most influential members abandoned the SDS to join groups with more aggressive agendas.

Perhaps the most prominent SDS splinter group was the Weather Underground (or "Weathermen"), a group founded by Mark Rudd in 1969. As noted in Chapter 3, the Weathermen set off bombs in several large cities from the Pacific to the Atlantic coasts in the early 1970s, largely to express opposition not just to the Vietnam War but to what they regarded as an oppressive capitalist government that they aimed to overthrow. The group was predominantly white, upper middle class, educated, and young; but what brought them together was a rejection of nonviolent approaches to dealing with the system. They committed dozens of bombings that targeted military establishments, including the Pentagon, as well as police stations, campus ROTC buildings, and the Gulf Oil corporate headquarters in Pittsburgh, to name a few. They also freed the counterculture LSD hero, Timothy Leary, from prison and arranged his flight to Algeria, and they distributed revolutionary literature to rally support for their cause. They disintegrated, for the most part, by the mid-1970s, although a few diehard Weathermen continued to commit occasional acts of violence into the 1980s.

Another extremist SDS splinter group was the United Freedom Front (UFF), a small but prolifically violent group that focused on the radicalization of prisoners. Led by Vietnam veteran Raymond Luc Levasseur, the UFF was known to have committed about thirty robberies and bombings in the Northeast from 1975 through 1984. All of its eight known members were convicted and imprisoned by the end of the 1980s, following sensational trials highlighted by the histrionics of UFF defense lawyer William Kunstler (B. Smith, 1994).

Another prominent radical group from the New Left was the Black Panther Party, an African American militant group founded by Huey Newton and Bobby Seale in Oakland in 1966. Inspired by Malcolm X (1992) and Chinese Chairman Mao Zedong, the Black Panthers were created out of countercultural ideas that extended well beyond the racial and social justice themes of the mainstream civil rights movement. The Black Panthers called for black nationalism and armed resistance to what they regarded as racial, social, and economic oppression, and they expressed strong disdain for the white-dominated law enforcement establishment and the formal system of justice in the United States.

The Black Panthers reinforced their message with symbols of bravado: the black-gloved fist, paramilitary black beret, shotgun slung over the shoulder, and Malcolm X's notorious slogan, "freedom by any means necessary." But their links to violence went beyond mere symbols. They are reported to have killed more than a dozen police officers (Ayton, 2006). One of the Black Panther leaders, Eldridge Cleaver, with a fellow Panther, wounded three police officers in a 1968 shootout in Oakland. He jumped bail and fled to Mexico City and then to Cuba, Paris, and Algeria, where he was hailed as an international hero. Cleaver's famous book, *Soul on Ice* (1967), asserts at one point that he had regarded rapes he had committed to be "insurrectionary" acts.

The Black Panthers were just two years old when, in 1968, FBI Director J. Edgar Hoover called the group "the greatest threat to the internal security of the country" (Stohl, 1988, p. 249). The group eventually came apart after a few years due to a combination of close federal and local law enforcement attention to their every move and the internal feuding among its leaders – Newton and Seale promoted the racially neutral Maoist slogan, "Power to the people," whereas Eldridge Cleaver and Stokely Carmichael promoted the more incendiary "Black Power" slogan. Some of its members were killed and some went to prison, whereas others joined radical underground movements. Many of those who survived went on to lead peaceful black middle-class lives.

Although the run of the Black Panthers was pretty much over by 1970, the group inspired black liberation movements elsewhere. One such movement was the Black Liberation Army (BLA), an underground organization led by former Panther Assata Shakur (previously known under her given name, JoAnne Chesimard).[3] The BLA had two distinct components: one in San Francisco, across the bay from the Panther's Oakland home base, and the other in New York City. Both cells hit local police departments with gunfire and bombing attacks, and both raised funds by robbing banks. Shakur was convicted as an accessory in the killing of a New Jersey state trooper in 1977, then escaped from prison in 1979, and fled the United States for Cuba, where she was granted political asylum by Fidel Castro in 1984 (K. Cleaver, 2005; Martin, 2006). In 2005 the FBI offered a $1 million reward for information leading to her capture (Williams, 2005).

Another group that rose from the ashes of the Black Panthers was the May 19 Communist Organization (M19CO), named in honor of the same-day birthdays of Malcolm X and Ho Chi Minh, the leader first of the Viet Cong and then of Vietnam. The M19CO was formed in the late 1970s by former members of the Panthers, the BLA, and the Weather Underground. They carried forward the tradition of revolutionary violence of these earlier groups, committing robberies of banks and armored vehicles, bombings of "establishment" targets, and the freeing of comrades in custody, including Assata Shakur's 1979 "rescue" from a New Jersey prison and transport to Cuba. In 1981 the group killed a Brinks security guard and two police officers in the course of a robbery in Nyack, New York, after which key members Kathy Boudin and David Gilbert were arrested and convicted of murder and robbery. The group's violence came to an end in 1985 with the arrest of its last remaining members (Martin, 2006).

One additional African American group is noteworthy: the El Rukn gang. Originally a conventional Chicago street gang known as the Blackstone Rangers, the El Rukns are significant largely for their Muslim connection. The Blackstone Rangers became "El Rukns" after their leader, Jeff Fort, was influenced by the Black Muslim movement while imprisoned in the late 1970s. (Fort borrowed the name "El Rukns" from the cornerstone of the shrine of Kaaba, regarded by many Muslims as Islam's holiest shrine, in Mecca, Saudi Arabia.) Fort and some of his El Rukn associates made contact with Libyan operatives, with the aim of committing terrorist acts in the United States. They never did. Fort and many of his associates ended up in prison. Of special significance is the fact that federal officials, concerned about the prospect of growing bonds between Black Muslims and Islamic terrorists, committed Fort to the maximum security prison at Florence, Colorado, where he was confined under a no-human-contact order.

Right-Wing Extremism and Terrorism. Several right-wing extremist groups were described in Chapter 6, including the Ku Klux Klan and other white supremacist groups, as well as the Minutemen and other private militia groups. These groups fit clearly within Smith's characterizations of right-wing terrorist groups. Although anti-Marxism is not a leading grievance of most hate groups and militia extremists, they do tend to be anti-collectivist and strongly opposed to federal, state, and local governments, which they regard as intrusive of their property and rights. They tend to be particularly protective of their rights to be left alone and to defend themselves with firearms. These groups are based usually outside of urban settings, occasionally barricaded in fortresses. And they often justify their actions based on notions of morality grounded in religious fundamentalism. When they engage in terrorist activities, it is generally against minority individuals and institutions, immigrants, homosexuals, or abortion clinics.

2. Terrorist Groups and Acts of International Origin

Other terrorist groups active in the United States originated outside the fifty states. Because they are driven by forces largely outside the authority of federal and local law enforcement officials, they are more difficult to monitor and control. Previous chapters give several reasons for the growth of the threat of transnational terrorism, including alienation and extremism, historical trajectories and periods of clashing civilizations, accessible and lethal new technologies, attraction to the prospect of successfully striking the world's greatest military and economic power and terrifying its citizens, megalomania, achieving notoriety, and so on.

Several transnational terrorist groups have committed acts of terrorism in the United States. In this section we describe three of the most prominent: Puerto Rican leftists, Cuban nationals, and al Qaeda. Others include the

Irish Republican Army and Libyan, Palestinian, and Syrian groups, which are described elsewhere in this book (see Chapters 3 and 6 and other sections of this chapter).

Puerto Rican Separatists. Puerto Rico is a territory of the United States and Puerto Ricans are officially American citizens, so a strong case can be made for regarding acts of terrorism by Puerto Rican separatists as acts of domestic terrorism. At the same time, however, Puerto Ricans do not have the full rights of American citizens in the fifty states. Puerto Ricans elect a governor, yet their head of state is the president of the United States, for whom they are not allowed to vote. The problem is compounded by another type of disenfranchisement: Puerto Rico's representation in the U.S. Congress is limited to a single nonvoting delegate. Not surprisingly, many Puerto Ricans do not regard themselves as full citizens and have long argued for Puerto Rico to become a sovereign nation with full political independence from the United States. Since the mid-nineteenth century, debates over independence have been stimulated by a legitimate political party for independence, *Lucha por la Independencia Puertorriqueña.*

Occasionally, separatists (*independencistas*) frustrated by the failure of the political process to produce the desired outcome have turned to violence. In 1950, a pair of Puerto Rican separatists attempted to assassinate President Harry Truman while he was residing at the Blair House, across the street from the White House. Although the president was unharmed, the pair killed a White House police officer protecting Truman. About three and a half years later, four Puerto Rican terrorists shot and wounded five members of the U.S. House of Representatives.

The most devastating expression of organized violence for independence has come from a group created in 1974, the *Fuerzas Armadas de Liberación Nacional* (Armed Forces of National Liberation), commonly referred to as the FALN. The FALN has been not only one of the deadliest terrorist groups in the history of Puerto Rico but also one of the more destructive terrorist groups in the Western Hemisphere. From 1974 to 1983, the FALN was responsible for more than 120 bomb attacks on U.S. targets – mostly restaurants, banks, and office buildings in New York and Chicago. No other foreign group has launched as many terrorist attacks on U.S. soil. The deadliest attack, on New York's Fraunces Tavern in 1975, killed four people and injured more than fifty others. In 1980, armed members of the FALN raided the presidential campaign headquarters of both the Carter campaign in Chicago and the Bush campaign in New York.

The FALN's activities came to a virtual end in 1980, when eleven of its members were arrested for attempting to rob an armored truck at Northwestern University in Evanston, Illinois. FALN co-founder, Filiberto Ojeda Ríos, then evaded capture for years. He was finally killed by FBI agents in 2005, after being for several years on the FBI's list of most-wanted fugitives.

One of the most controversial episodes involving the FALN occurred about fifteen years after the group's last attack, when President Bill Clinton offered clemency to sixteen imprisoned members of the FALN. Twelve accepted the terms of the offer and were released (see Box 8.1).

Several groups have carried forward the work of the FALN after its demise, the most prominent of which has been the Macheteros ("machete wielders"). Operating out of Puerto Rico and the Hartford, Connecticut, area, the Macheteros committed numerous bombings and attempted assassinations during the 1980s. Other Puerto Rican separatist groups that have picked up where the FALN left off include the Organization of Volunteers for the Puerto Rican Revolution, the Armed Forces of Popular Resistance, the Guerrilla Forces of Liberation, and the Pedro Albizu Campos Revolutionary Forces (Smith, 1994).

Cuban Nationals. The words etched in bronze at the Statue of Liberty, "Give me your . . . huddled masses, yearning to breathe free," have been a welcoming call for alienated people around the world. The United States has been especially attractive to refugees from Cuba – just ninety miles off the coast of Florida – since the overthrow of the Batiste regime by Fidel Castro's band of guerrillas on January 1, 1959. Castro's revolution set off a major political and social upheaval, including the loss of wealth, power, and status of the Cuban middle class and professionals. An initial wave of Cuban refugees to the United States in 1959 was followed by a second wave in 1961, when Castro nationalized private land and capital assets and cracked down heavily on political opposition, including the execution of some dissidents. The exodus continued for years. In 1980 alone, more than 125,000 refugees came to the United States, despite U.S. Coast Guard attempts to stem the flow, in a wave that came to be known as the "Mariel Boatlift" (named for the harbor from which the refugees departed). The U.S. Census Bureau reported that more than 1.2 million Cubans lived in the United States by 2000, a figure that did not take into account the many others who had fled from Cuba to the United States during the previous forty years who had died since of natural causes. Indeed, about 20 percent of Cuba's 1959 population fled to the United States, with the majority ending up in the Miami area.

It should come as no surprise that a number of extremists and terrorists would eventually emerge from such a huge population of refugees. Many Cuban refugees indeed felt betrayed by Castro, and they dedicated themselves to his overthrow. Some were sufficiently obsessed with this goal to attempt to undermine him even if it meant breaking U.S. laws, including making attacks on pro-Castro individuals and institutions in the United States. A handful of the most extreme counter-revolutionaries formed a terrorist group that called itself Omega 7. Founded by the former Cuban wrestling champion, Eduardo Arocena, in the mid-1970s, Omega 7 engaged in dozens of attacks against Cuban diplomats and businesses, including several shootings and

Box 8.1. Should Convicted Terrorists Ever be Given Clemency?

In 1999, President Bill Clinton offered clemency for sixteen members of the FALN who had been convicted and imprisoned for a variety of serious felony offenses related to terrorist activities committed in New York and Chicago during the 1970s and early '80s. The crimes included bank robbery, bomb making, illegal possession and transport of firearms, explosives violations, interference with interstate commerce by threats or violence, stolen vehicle violations, theft of interstate shipments, and seditious conspiracy.

Ordinarily, public officials are inclined to show little mercy for terrorists. But these were exceptional cases in several respects. None of the sixteen had been convicted of bombing or of any other crimes causing injury to others. All had served terms of at least nineteen years in prison, more time than was ordinarily served for such crimes in the 1990s. The organization the men had belonged to had been dormant for many years.

President Clinton set three conditions for clemency: the FALN members had to (1) agree to renounce violence, (2) admit to the crimes for which they were convicted, and (3) agree not to re-establish associations with one another after release from prison. Twelve accepted the offer and were released or paroled.

The deal was hotly contested. It was strongly supported by ten Nobel Prize laureates and by former President Jimmy Carter, Cardinal O'Connor of New York, Archbishop Nieves of Puerto Rico, politicians and members of the Puerto Rico independence movement, officials of human rights organizations, and others. It was opposed with equal fervor by several others: the U.S. Attorney for the Southern District of New York, officials at the FBI and the Federal Bureau of Prisons, police organizations, and former victims of FALN terrorist activities. Even Hillary Clinton – at the time running for U.S. Senate for the state of New York – was critical of her husband's decision to grant clemency to the twelve who accepted the terms. In her opinion, it had taken too long for the prisoners to renounce violence (Black, 1999).

What do you think of Mr. Clinton's decision? Should convicted terrorists ever have their prison terms shortened? Under what circumstances, if any, might this be worth doing? What strikes you as the most critical factors that should weigh in the decision? Does clemency for terrorists undermine the integrity of the justice system? Should sentencing policies for terrorists differ from those for other criminals? Are these primarily matters of effectiveness or matters of ethics?

bombings in New York and New Jersey. Arocena was arrested in 1983 and sentenced the following year to a life term for the 1980 murder of Felix Garcia Rodriguez, an attache at the Cuban mission to the United Nations.

Al Qaeda. Al Qaeda is, without question, the most notorious and probably the most dangerous of all terrorist groups – due principally to its central role in planning and executing the most sensational terrorist attack in the history of the United States and, arguably, the most significant in recorded history to date.[4] Al Qaeda was created by Osama bin Laden and his associates in 1988 or 1989, following the expulsion of the Soviet military from Afghanistan. Among the mujihadeen entities that defeated the technologically superior Soviet forces was Maktab al-Khadamat, a precursor to al Qaeda, founded by bin Laden.

"Al Qaeda" is Arabic for "the base"; bin Laden saw the organization in its early days as the base of operations against his targets. Then, as now, the central goal of al Qaeda was to expel any and all non-Muslim influences – the "far enemy" – from Muslim lands, and particularly the removal of the Jews from what bin Laden calls "Palestine"; he regards the creation of Israel in 1947 as an artifice of the United Nations, instigated largely by Zionist forces in the United States and Great Britain. Bin Laden's successes, first in Afghanistan and then elsewhere throughout much of world, emboldened him and his al Qaeda organization to work both to expel the far enemy and to overthrow the "near enemy" as well – Muslim regimes that collaborate with the West – replacing them eventually with a pure Sunni-dominated Islamic caliphate (Laden, 2005). One of bin Laden's early targets was the Saudi monarchy, with which his family, ironically, has had long, close ties.

Largely because of U.S. support of the Saudi government – regarded as "veiled colonialism" by al Qaeda strategists (Pape, 2005, pp. 117–19) – bin Laden and his al Qaeda organization began to target the United States, the "far enemy," in the 1990s. There was further irony here, as bin Laden had sided with both the United States and Saudi Arabia in the 1980s, receiving support as a mujahideen leader from the Saudis to fight the Soviets in Afghanistan (Cook, 2005). Equally ironic is the fact that Afghan mujahideen leaders found bin Laden to be "useless" in their struggle against the Soviets, regarding him as a lazy, pathetic figure (L. Wright, 2006a).

Yet, during the 1990s, al Qaeda – headed by bin Laden and his chief associate, Ayman Zawahiri – had become an organization that could effectively recruit, train, finance, and direct terrorist attacks against the United States, as well as against targets in northeastern Africa, the Middle East, Asia, and Europe. In 1993, al Qaeda struck the World Trade Center with a deadly truck bomb; it then killed hundreds of people, mostly Africans, in bombings of U.S. embassies in East Africa in 1998, and it killed seventeen sailors aboard the *USS Cole* in Yemen in 2000.

These incidents were relatively minor, however, when compared to the unprecedented destruction of 9/11 targets in New York and Washington, two of the most powerful cities in the world. One can only wonder, What sort of men did bin Laden attract to al Qaeda who would be willing to commit suicide bombing on such a grand scale? According to Lawrence Wright, they were a strange mixture of idealists and nihilists:

> From the beginning of Al Qaeda, there were reformers and there were nihilists. The dynamic between them was irreconcilable and self-destructive, but events were moving so quickly that it was almost impossible to tell the philosophers from the sociopaths. They were glued together by the charismatic personality of Osama bin Laden, which contained both strands, idealism and nihilism, in a potent mix (2006a, p. 187).

The 9/11 strike on the U.S. was shocking and devastating, but the response was even more devastating. Al Qaeda's training camps in Afghanistan were totally destroyed within a few short weeks of the 9/11 attack, and the Taliban government that had provided sanctuary for those camps was quickly brought down by a crushing air and ground attack led by the United States. With the successful destruction of al Quaeda's base of operations in Afghanistan in the months following 9/11, its leaders retreated to rugged mountain hideaways in eastern Afghanistan and northern Pakistan, largely cut off from its operational cells around the globe. For at least a few years, the organization became less involved in the planning and direction of terrorist attacks; it became more of an inspiration for terrorist activities that were planned and executed by others.

Al Qaeda's cells operate today in various parts of the world with considerable autonomy. Some terrorist groups have neither received al Qaeda training nor met bin Laden or any of his key associates, but nonetheless regard themselves as inspired by the organization. It is therefore impossible to estimate the size of al Qaeda with any reliability.

One can, however, say something about al Qaeda's members based on the most committed of them – those who have killed themselves in suicide bombing attacks. Robert Pape's (2005) analysis of the seventy-one individuals who committed suicide bombings in al Qaeda missions from 1995 to 2003 reveals that they were twice as likely to come from countries with large Islamic fundamentalist populations than from countries with little or no fundamentalist populations; ten times more likely to come from Sunni Muslim countries with an American military presence than from other Sunni Muslim countries; and twenty times more likely to come from Sunni Muslim countries with both an American military presence and large Islamic fundamentalist populations.[5] Pape concludes, "American military policy in the Persian Gulf was most likely the pivotal factor leading to September 11" (2005, pp. 103–04). He adds,

Al-Qaeda is less a transnational network of like-minded ideologues brought together from across the globe via the Internet than a cross-national military alliance of national liberation movements working together against what they see as a common imperial threat.... (T)he pattern of who ultimately decides to die for al-Qaeda's cause is remarkably consistent with the argument that al-Qaeda leaders make (p. 104).

The argument to which Pape alludes has been made most compellingly by one of al Qaeda's most mysterious strategists: Abu Bakr Naji. In 2004 Naji posted a document on the Internet, entitled *The Management of Savagery*. The precise nature and extent of Naji's role in al Qaeda are unclear and, for that matter, just who he (or she) is, if he is a real person,[6] and, if so, where he was raised and educated, where he lives, and so on. It is clear, however, that much of the modus operandi of al Qaeda, as revealed both on the ground and through the al Qaeda Internet propaganda machinery, is consistent with the principles set forth in Naji's widely circulated manuscript. Box 8.2 contrasts the principles described in that document with the logic of the American position, revealed in a collection of interventions that have fallen under the umbrella known as the "war on terror."

B. From Mexico to South America: Narcoterrorism and Leftist Terrorism

Terrorist incidents have been much more frequent and, overall, more deadly in Latin America than in the United States and Canada over the past several decades. Terrorism in Mexico, Central America, and South America is predominantly of two types – drug-related terrorism and terrorism by leftist groups – although there is occasionally some overlap, as groups with political agendas sometimes finance their operations through drug trafficking.

One might reasonably question whether the acts of violence associated with drug trafficking qualify fully as terrorism rather than as street crime. Drug trafficking, per se, is not terrorism, even when used to finance terrorist operations. As BBC correspondent Misha Glenny (2007) observes, "International mobsters, unlike terrorists, don't seek to bring down the West; they just want to make a buck." Terror used as an instrument to protect or expand profits has a limited political agenda: it aims to alter the justice system so that it provides a haven for a particular group, not to overthrow the entire government to achieve an ideological objective. But a limited political agenda is greater than none, and the use of violence by drug cartels against innocents to invoke fear and change the way the government operates is a fact of life. Drug groups that engage extensively in such activities operate at the margin of terrorism and so are worthy of consideration in a comprehensive treatment of terrorism.

Box 8.2. The War on Terror vs. The Management of Savagery

The essential rationale behind the U.S. war on terror is described in Chapter 1. It involves specific military engagements and legislation, yet it is no less political rhetoric designed to win public support for a miscellaneous assortment of interventions and policies, rather than a coherent doctrine or strategy. The interventions and the associated rhetoric were certainly effective for garnering support from a majority of voters throughout the United States from 2001 until the presidential election of 2004. The most significant benefit was the absence of a major terrorist event on U.S. soil for several years after the September 11 attack – likely a product of enhanced airport security, the removal of al Qaeda headquarters and training camps in Afghanistan, and sanctions that induced Libya to abandon its nuclear weapons program. Voter support had dwindled substantially, however, by the mid-term election of 2006.

It is useful to contrast the central elements of the war on terror – military interventions in Afghanistan and Iraq, changes in the law to enhance the ability of domestic and foreign intelligence authorities to detect terrorist activities under the USA Patriot Act, the integration of intelligence operations under the Homeland Security Act of 2002, and a reorganization of executive branch offices within the Department of Homeland Security – with the doctrine and principles set forth in Abu Bakr Naji's 113-page Internet document, *Management of Savagery* (*Idarat al-Tawahhush* in Arabic, alternatively translated into English as "Management of Barbarism" or "Management of Chaos").

In *Management of Savagery*, Naji presents a set of principles and a general strategy for a jihadi victory over the West. He urges fellow jihadists to read up on the principles and practices of Western management, military strategy and tactics, politics, and sociology. The document promotes the purposeful use of asymmetric warfare – disrupting and exhausting the enemy through infiltration and deception and by dispersing attacks on targets where they are weakest and do not have the capacity to respond effectively. It also emphasizes victory in the critical propaganda war over the West through the use of battle approaches that provoke angry military responses and exploit the West's political weaknesses – especially our impatience and bias toward quick results. Naji argues that the media on both sides will report the harsh responses and military errors, and the negative publicity will wear down the will of the West before long, thereby gaining more converts to holy war and martyrdom.

The document will not win Naji a Nobel Peace Prize. It is relentlessly hostile toward non-Muslims and truly advocates savagery. Naji observes, for example, that there can be no forgiveness for an apostate unless he converts to Islam: "Even when he converts, we have the option of either forgiving him or killing him, because he has repented after he had the capacity to do so earlier" (translation, p. 113). It is equally ruthless in enforcing obedience among Muslims and rooting out deviant opinions and "collaborators in our ranks" (p. 152).

Still, for Naji "managing savagery" means finding a balance. When al Qaeda field general Abu Musab al-Zarqawi committed a series of atrocities against Shi'ites in Iraq and a wedding party in Jordan in 2005, chief al Qaeda strategist Ayman al-Zawahiri reprimanded him for his excesses, describing his actions as "unpalatable" at a time when "we are in a media battle in a race for the hearts and minds of our *ummah* (the international Muslim community)."

Managing savagery also requires that the mujahideen win the support of the people by doing the following:

establishing internal security
providing food and medical supplies
providing an armed force to defend the zone of battle from external attack
establishing Shari'a justice and an intelligence service
providing economic sufficiency
defending against hypocrisy and deviant opinions and ensuring obedience
establishing alliances with neighboring groups

The result, according to Naji, will be victory both on the ground and in the minds of the people, as public outrage against the West's occupation of Muslim land and misguided acts of retaliation will exceed the outrage evoked by jihadi savagery.

This strategy worked against the Soviets in Afghanistan, says Naji, and he argues that it should work as effectively against the United States in the Middle East, especially if jihadis can shift from effectiveness in battle to competence in governing civilian populations. The goodwill that Hezbollah created through its social development programs in Southern Lebanon attests to the wisdom of such a strategy.

Many in the West have been extremely critical of the manner in which the United States responded to the immediate threats presented by al Qaeda. Rather than respond to al Qaeda's attack by targeting its military resources principally against al Qaeda and giving more attention to diplomacy and building of infrastructure in countries in need of such aid, the U.S. government elected instead, using the rhetoric of the war on terror, to deploy the majority of its resources to the military effort in Iraq, where al Qaeda had no significant presence at the time of the 2003 invasion. Rather than try to understand our adversary and their culture, as al Qaeda has done with aspects of ours, we acted under the false premise that Iraqis care as much about freedom and democracy as they do about dignity and Islamic concepts of justice. The U.S. response to al Qaeda's attack on New York and Washington thus followed Naji's script in many essential respects.[7]

History will judge whether Naji's thinking was more effective over the long term than the reasoning behind the U.S. war on terror. In the meantime, it is clear that events unfolded in the years following the 9/11 attack – on the streets of Baghdad and Tehran and in the court of public opinion throughout the world – in a manner that suggests the prescience of Naji's strategy and its having served al Qaeda's objectives all too well in the face of our war on terror.

The term "narcoterrorism" is often used to describe terrorism associated with drug trafficking. The Drug Enforcement Administration (DEA) defines this term in such a way as to include both terror as an instrument for increasing profits from drug trafficking – the original definition of narcoterrorism – and, following a DEA amendment to this definition, drug trafficking as a means of financing terrorist activities (Casteel, 2003). The term may be useful as an umbrella that includes different types of associations between drug trafficking and terrorism, although the distinctions are critical. Combining the two raises another risk: drug enforcement officials in particular, and government officials in general, may have strong bureaucratic incentives to err on the side of seeing drug links to terrorism where none exist (Adams, 1986).

One high-ranking official has expressed concern that narcoterrorism in Latin America is even fueling radical Islamic groups in the Middle East.[8] An estimated $6 billion is laundered from the sale of some twelve tons of cocaine annually in the Tri-Border (or "Triple Frontier") region, where the boundaries of Argentina, Brazil, and Paraguay intersect (Adams, 1986). The town of Ciudad del Este (Paraguay), a population center in this region, is home to about 20,000 Muslim Arabs, a great many of whom immigrated from Lebanon in the 1980s. Reports from the intelligence community indicate a significant pool of extremists among this population (Goldberg, 2002b).

The history of terrorist activities from Mexico to Central and South America provides rich examples of both types of narcoterrorism, as well as terrorism by leftist groups that does not involve drug trafficking. We take up narcoterrorist groups first and then turn to leftist terrorists.

1. The Tijuana (Arellano Felix) Drug Cartel

The Arellano Felix cartel, operating out of the far northwest corner of Mexico, exemplifies the first type of narcoterrorism: terror as an instrument of trafficking in drugs. Drug trafficking is a big business in Mexico. More than half of the marijuana and an estimated 90 percent of the cocaine consumed in the United States comes from Mexico (Noriega, 2007). Much of the drugs transported through Mexico are grown in Central and South America. Individual sellers often find that they can maximize profits by organizing as cartels, thereby maintaining high drug prices. Enforcement mechanisms are usually put in place to ensure that individual members do not underprice other members of the cartel, even if they result in a reduction in the amounts sold.

The attractiveness of drug trafficking derives principally from the profits derived from moving cocaine, heroin, and marijuana from the grower to the processor, through the wholesale distribution network, and finally to the retail buyer. The profits at each stage can be enormous. And the more effective the enforcement at each of these levels, the greater the profits needed to compensate sellers for the higher risks of getting caught in the drug trade. More enforcement thus raises drug prices, which in turn creates more incentive to face the risks of getting caught and more incentive to either bribe law enforcement officials or fight them, thus opening the door to terrorism. In Mexico, these pressures are exacerbated by the strong demand for drugs from the United States and strong pressures from the U.S. government to induce Mexico to crack down on traffickers. Because of these pressures, the trafficking of drugs in Mexico frequently manifests as terrorist activity.

The Mexican drug distribution market is partitioned largely along regional lines, with cartels controlling the western, central, and eastern parts of the country. One of the largest drug trafficking organizations in all of Mexico has been the Arellano Felix cartel, operating in the northwest of Mexico and headquartered in Tijuana. This cartel was run by a family of seven brothers and four sisters, led originally by Ramon Eduardo Arellano Felix, who in 1997 was added to the FBI's most-wanted list for the many acts of deadly violence he either directed or committed. Ramon Arellano Felix and his siblings inherited the substantial Tijuana cartel in 1989 from their uncle, Miguel Angel Felix Gallardo ("El Padrino"), when Gallardo was arrested and incarcerated for drug trafficking and violent crimes. The leader of the Guadalajara cartel in the 1980s, Gallardo had been widely regarded as the cocaine czar of Mexico (Ehrenfeld, 1992).

The Arellano Felix cartel was especially violent in the 1990s, when its members assassinated not only police chiefs, prosecutors, and other government officials but also civilians, including journalists and children (the latter mostly when entire families of rival gangs were killed). The cartel was mostly closed down in 2002, when Ramon was killed in a police shootout and his brother Benjamin, Ramon's second-in-command, was arrested and incarcerated in one of Mexico's most secure prisons. The market continued to flourish, however, as rival drug trafficking gangs soon took over the Tijuana cartel territory.

2. Colombian Drug Cartels

Narcoterrorism has been waged on an even grander scale in Colombia, South America. Two drug cartels have been especially violent, operating out of two of the country's three largest cities: Medellin in the north and Cali to the south.

The Medellin cartel. During its twenty years in operation, the Medellin cartel has been the more significant of these two Colombian drug giants, both in drug trafficking and in violence. At its peak, it controlled an estimated 80 percent of the cocaine market, with revenues estimated at $60 million per month and a net worth in the neighborhood of $30 billion. The cartel's primary product was cocaine, most of which it purchased from growers in Peru and Bolivia. On the selling side, the cartel's largest market was the United States, where the demand for cocaine had soared in the 1980s, especially in the form of crack. It trafficked in drugs also in Europe and Asia. Its most lucrative market was to wholesalers in Miami, who then distributed the product to other major urban centers throughout the United States.

Built by Pablo Escobar in the early 1970s, the Medellin cartel eventually became one of the most violent organizations in the world. It began by bribing officials extensively; when bribery failed, it escalated to intimidation and assassination, starting in 1976. This strategy became known as *plata o plomo* – the official was given the choice of silver or lead. Over the next seventeen years, many chose lead: the cartel killed more than 1,000 police officers and military personnel – more than 500 police officers in Medellin alone – and assassinated hundreds of other public officials and more than100 judges, as well as dozens of journalists and other civilians. Members of the Medellin cartel even killed presidential candidates and supreme court judges. In 1989, the cartel declared war against the Colombian government.

Escobar was the driving force behind this machine of greed and destruction. He graduated from car thief to the more lucrative drug trade as a teenager. Both his operation and reputation for ruthlessness soared in 1975, when he killed a leading drug-dealing rival. In 1989 *Forbes* magazine listed him as the world's seventh richest person. Fearing extradition to the United States, Escobar was killed in a shootout with the Colombian police in 1993.

The Cali cartel. The Cali cartel was less violent than Escobar's Medellin cartel – being more prone to bribing government officials than to killing them.

It was also less hierarchical, organized more loosely around independently functioning cells. Created around 1970 by brothers Gilberto and Miguel Rodriguez Orejuela, with an associate, José Santacruz Londoño, the group's first drug trafficking operations were in marijuana. It moved before long into the higher profit market of cocaine trafficking.

The Cali cartel qualifies nonetheless as a terrorist organization both for its extensive use of threats against government officials and its killing of several hundred prostitutes, homosexuals, homeless people, and petty thieves, as well as children, during its social cleansing operations against the *"desechables,"* those it regarded as discardable (Castells, 2000).

The Cali cartel competed fiercely with the Medellin cartel in its operations both in Colombia and elsewhere, but the two cartels occasionally made accommodations to each other. In the United States, Cali focused its operations principally in New York, whereas the Medellin group targeted the Miami area. The Cali cartel took over much of the Medellin's territory and operations after Escobar's death in 1993. Most of the leaders of the Cali cartel were arrested and imprisoned in 1995, but they continued to run the organization from prison. In 2006, the Orejuela brothers were extradited to the United States and convicted on drug conspiracy charges for their extensive operations in cocaine trafficking in the United States. Their plea agreement included the forfeiture of $2.1 billion in assets.

3. The Zapatista National Liberation Front

An important class of terrorism has been characterized by terrorism authority Gus Martin (2006) as "dissident terrorism" or "terror from below": this is terrorism committed by nonstate groups against governments and other institutions with whom they have sufficient grievances to resort to politically motivated violence. Martin puts the Zapatista National Liberation Front (*Ejército Zapatista de Liberación Nacional*, EZLN) squarely in this category.

The EZLN derives its name from Emilio Zapata, an icon in Mexican history, who is widely regarded, with Francisco "Pancho" Villa, as one of the two dominant figures of the Mexican Revolution of 1910–20. Zapata is a hero of the left largely for championing the transfer of land from an unworthy group – the rich, who simply inherited it from their European ancestors – to its rightful owners, the Mayan natives who worked these haciendas for centuries as slaves, after having lived on it in freedom for centuries before that. The EZLN sees itself as an armed revolutionary group fighting for the descendants of the people for whom Zapata fought nearly 100 years ago, and against today's heirs to the colonialists who conquered the indigenous people centuries ago.

The Zapatistas are based in one of the poorest states of Mexico, Chiapas; it is the southernmost state of Mexico, neighboring Guatemala (the country at the northwestern end of Central America). The EZLN regards the regimes operating out of Mexico City as illegitimate pawns of an international system of corrupt capitalism. It works toward the goal of shifting power from the wealthy to the poor and from Mexico City to the Mexican Indians, particularly in Chiapas.

The EZLN was officially formed on January 1, 1994, the very day that the North American Free Trade Agreement (NAFTA) went into effect. Sold as a pathway to jobs for the poor in Mexico, NAFTA, and the larger trend toward globalization, is seen instead by the Zapatistas as a force disrupting the culture and lifestyle of Mexico's indigenous population, particularly in the south; for the Zapatistas, NAFTA tilts the playing field steeply against the simple agrarian economy of Chiapas, which is incapable of competing with the heavily subsidized agribusiness behemoth to the north.

In response to the imposition of NAFTA, the EZLN seized four cities in armed protest, including San Cristobal, a city of about 200,000 residents. The Mexican Army responded, in turn, with considerable force, first removing the EZLN from San Cristobal and the other cities and then bottling them up in rural strongholds. The Mexican Army was soon joined by paramilitaries supported by local landowners, who were overwhelmingly opposed to the Zapatistas. Several massacres ensued, the most serious in the Chiapas town of Acteal, where forty-five people, mostly women and children, were killed in 1997 – after a national peace accord had already been signed by the principals. About 100 people were killed in other towns. The Zapatistas retreated into the wilds of the Lacandon Jungle to regroup. They re-emerged during the following years as a legitimate political force representing Mexico's indigenous populations.

Although the Zapatistas qualified technically as a terrorist group in 1994, they wound up much more on the receiving end of violence during their struggle against the Mexican government and the forces of globalization. They are, in any case, not a terrorist group today.

4. The Sandinistas in Nicaragua

Much as the Zapatistas fashioned their name after a heroic national figure, the Sandinista National Liberation Front (*Frente Sandinista de Liberación Nacional*, FSLN) of Nicaragua chose its name after the charismatic Augusto César Sandino, who led a rebellion against the U.S. military in Nicaragua between 1927 and 1933. But where the Zapatistas failed to overthrow the government in power, the Sandinistas succeeded. Created in 1961 by a group of student activists in Managua, the Sandinistas removed President Anastasio ("Tachito") Somoza Debayle by force in 1979, forcing him to flee to Guatemala, where he was assassinated the following year. The Sandinistas ruled Nicaragua for eleven years after taking power.

In their investigations of Nicaragua after the Sandinista revolution, the Inter-American Commission on Human Rights found clear evidence of acts of terrorism: mass graves (1981) and extensive human rights violations, including imprisonments without trial followed by disappearances (1983). Much of the evidence implicates the counter-revolutionary forces – the "Contras" – that the United States supported through CIA covert operations. Other findings implicate the Sandinistas, although both sides generally regard the evidence as unreliable. Either way, however, it would be a case of state-sponsored terrorism, and killings done by the Contras would be an example of what Martin (2006) calls the "patronage model" of state-sponsored terrorism, involving the use of proxy forces. To the extent that the United States was involved, it serves as a permanent stain on our good reputation throughout the region and the world.

C. Attacks in Europe and Russia

The 2001 terrorist attack on New York and Washington was an attack on the United States, but it was also a symbolic attack on the West generally. Europe had experienced terrorist attacks before 9/11, but the serious attacks that have occurred in Europe and Russia since 2001 are widely regarded as having larger significance, stimulated by the 9/11 attacks and the West's response to the attack – they are perceived as tit-for-tat strikes, as a manifestation of the clash of civilizations frenzy. Or they may simply have been random events that would have occurred anyway. Let us examine three of these events in chronological order: terrorist attacks in Spain, Russia, and England.

1. March 2004 Madrid Commuter Train Attack

On March 11, 2004, exactly two and a half years (eerily, 911 days) after the 9/11 attacks on New York and Washington, a gang of militants who associated themselves with al Qaeda set off bombs, delivered in backpacks, on four commuter trains during the morning rush hour in Madrid, Spain. The attack killed nearly 200 people and seriously injured about 1,500 others, making it the deadliest attack in Europe since the Pan Am jetliner bombing in 1988 over Lockerbie, Scotland. It occurred just days before the Spanish general election, and the government quickly – and erroneously – attributed the act to a Basque separatist group, Euskadi Ta Askatasuna (ETA), the "Basque Fatherland and Liberty." Forensic evidence soon implicated a cell of about a dozen Islamic terrorists from Morocco, four of whom blew themselves up three weeks after the attack when surrounded by police in the town of Leganes, about seven miles south of Madrid.

The commuter rail line that was attacked serves suburbs to the southeast of Madrid, a string of communities that are home to students, blue-collar workers, and others unable to pay for housing in the city, including middle-class immigrants from Latin America and Eastern Europe. About 150 of the dead were middle-class Spaniards. Fifteen of the people killed were Romanians, and most of the others were from Central and South America.

The attack offers a strong morality tale for politicians. The aim of terrorists is typically political, and the most prominent politician in Spain at the time of the attack, Prime Minister José María Aznar, could hardly have handled the Madrid attack worse than he did. He said on the day of the disastrous killings that he believed that ETA was responsible, despite lack of compelling evidence in support of the claim. It became clear within a matter of hours, however, that this was the act of a group loosely associated with al Qaeda. Aznar's standings in the polls plummeted immediately, and he and his party were swept out of power just three days after the bombings. It was of no small consequence that Aznar had made Spain one of the strongest supporters of the U.S. war operations in Iraq, and the new administration quickly withdrew its 1,300 troops and all other Spanish support of the war effort. Although the event itself did little to create sympathy for the causes of the perpetrators, the withdrawal of Spanish forces from Iraq soon after the election made this a clear victory for al Qaeda and the cause of international jihadi terrorism.

2. September 2004 Beslan School Hostage Crisis

The Beslan school hostage crisis ranks as one of the most heinous acts of terrorism in modern times. It targeted hundreds of children, killing 186 of them, and 148 adults as well, without a hint of mercy. It began on September 1, 2004, when a group of thirty-two armed Chechen separatists – thirty men and two women – took 1,200 children and adults hostage at a secondary school in North Ossetia-Alania, a semi-independent republic of the Russian Federation in the North Causasus region about 800 miles southeast of Moscow and 300 miles north of the Iranian border.

Although it is not certain who led the attack on the ground, it is clear that Shamil Salmanovich Basayev, leader of the Chechen separatist radicals, was behind it and probably masterminded it, along with his chief associate, Kamel Rabat Bouralha, an Algerian-born citizen of the United Kingdom. Basayev, who directed the 2002 Moscow theater hostage crisis, took responsibility for the Beslan attack a few days after it ended. As an extreme Chechen separatist and Muslim radical, Basayev had a long-standing grievance against Russia and against Christians, and Beslan's predominantly Christian population provided an opportunity to strike at both.

One aspect of the attack that made it particularly heinous was that it was timed to occur on the first day of the Russian school year, when children are traditionally accompanied by their parents and relatives and first-year students bring flowers to the class of graduating students (Phillips, 2007)

The attackers wore camouflage battle fatigues and black ski masks; several carried machine guns and wore belts with explosives. They corralled the 1,200 hostages into the school gymnasium and ordered them to speak only Russian. When a father tried to calm the hostages and repeat the rules in the local language, a gunman stepped up and killed him with a bullet to the head. Soon afterward, the terrorists took about twenty of the most robust-looking men among the hostages to another room and mowed them down in a hail of machine-gun fire. Other hostages were forced to toss the bodies out of the building and clean the blood from the room.

To deter rescue attempts and escapes, the attackers immediately stripped the hostages of their cell phones. They then mined the gymnasium with explosive devices and surrounded it with trip wires, threatening to blow up the school if the police attacked. They also threatened to kill fifty hostages for every attacker killed by the police and twenty hostages for every attacker injured.

After a day of unsuccessful negotiations with Russian officials, the hostage-takers refused to allow food, water, or medicine to be brought in to the hostages or to allow the removal of the bodies from the school grounds. This, together with the extreme heat in the gym, created unbearable conditions for both the children and adults. Some lost consciousness. As the conditions grew increasingly dire, the hostage-takers became more and more edgy and unreasonable.

Finally, just a few hours into the third day of the crisis, explosions rang out, and there are several conflicting accounts of their cause and the sequence of events that followed. What is clear is that Russian security forces hit the building with heavy weapons – including flamethrowers and three tanks – and the bloody shootout that followed killed 344 civilians, most of them children. Hundreds of others were wounded, many suffering permanent injuries. Few ambulances had been brought to the school to move the injured to hospitals. The vast majority of the children are reported to have suffered profound emotional trauma (Lansford, 2007).

All of the thirty-two hostage-takers were killed in the battle that ended the siege, except for the prime instigator of the operation, Shamil Basayev. Basayev was killed in a truck explosion in 2006 in Ingushetia, a small republic along the northern border of Chechnya.

The Russian government's handling of the episode received sharp criticism from all sides. Three shortcomings of the Russian government's handling of the affair are significant. First, it is likely that a more skillful process of negotiation with the hostage-takers could have saved hundreds of lives. Second, the use of excessive force almost certainly resulted in the deaths of many more hostages. Finally, lack of transparency in reporting the events both during and after the siege produced deep cynicism and further mistrust of the government among the public; when Russian officials initially downplayed the incident and reported about one-third of the actual number of captives, the attackers took out their rage on the hostages (Phillips, 2007). Governments responsible for handling hostage crises everywhere, including those involving U.S. schools, should heed these lessons (Giduck, 2005).

3. July 2005 London Subway and Bus Attack

Most people found the 9/11 attack devastating, but for some young men it represented an exciting challenge, as it opened the door to further sensational acts of terror against the West. London was a particularly ripe target for disaffected, young men of Pakistani heritage who had been stimulated by extremists to participate in what would turn out to be for them the ultimate group adventure in jihadi terror.

During the rush hour on July 7, 2005, three bombs exploded on three different subway trains – within a period of less than a minute – in London's underground system. A fourth bomb went off less than an hour later on a double-decker bus at Tavistock Square; circumstantial evidence suggests that the bus bomber had improvised his attack after being turned away from the subway's Northern Line, which had been temporarily closed due to a mechanical breakdown. The four blasts killed fifty-six in all, including fifty-two commuters. Half of the commuter deaths occurred on a single train near the Russell Square station. The blast also injured about 700 other commuters, and it effectively shut down London for a day.

Although twice as many had been killed in the Madrid subway attack sixteen months earlier, this was the deadliest attack on London since World War II; the deadliest terrorist act in Britain since the 1988 bombing of Pan Am Flight 103 over Lockerbie, Scotland, which killed 270 people; and London's first suicide bombing attack.

The coordinated attack involving deadly suicide attacks on four separate vehicles was eerily reminiscent of the 9/11 attack nearly four years earlier. The London bombing was unique, however (as noted in an earlier footnote in this chapter), because it had elements of both domestic and international terrorism. The act was committed by three second-generation Pakistanis born in Britain and a Jamaican who had converted to Islam five years earlier. All four were radicalized in England; some were trained in Afghanistan and Pakistan. Al Qaeda claimed responsibility for the attack on September 1 in a videotape aired over the al Jazeera network.

The investigation of the four bombing sites and the homes of the bombers was all encompassing, including conventional chemical and blast forensic analyses, analysis of footage of closed-circuit television surveillance videotapes from the train stations, and interviews of survivors and of people who knew the attackers. The bombs were determined to be homemade organic peroxide devices. The coordination of the attackers and the potency of their

From left to right, Hasib Hussain, Germaine Lindsay (carrying bag), Moham-mad Sidique Khan, and Shehzad Tanweer entering the train station at Luton (approximately thirty miles north-northwest of London) on July 7, 2005, about ninety minutes before the three subway bombs exploded. Photo © Crown.

bombs suggested significant planning and probably external support, quite possibly from al Qaeda. The most significant lapse of the British law enforce-ment community occurred two weeks after the attack, when an innocent Brazilian worker erroneously thought to be a terrorist was killed by overly vigilant officers of the London Metropolitan Police Department (see Chap-ter 13, case study box).

The four attackers ranged in age from 18 to 30. Three lived in Leeds, about 160 miles north of London, and the fourth in Aylesbury, about 30 miles northwest of London. Two lived with their wives (both pregnant), one lived with his parents, and the fourth with his brother. None had prior criminal records. At least two were known to have traveled previously to Pakistan. The quartet appears to have been led by Mohammad Sidique Khan, the oldest member of the group.

D. ASIA

1. Japanese Red Army

Asians were not spared the phenomenon of left-wing students acting out as militant extremists in the 1960s and '70s, as they had in Europe, for example,

Japanese Red Army founder Fusako Shigenobu.

in the form of the German Red Army Faction and the Italian Red Brigades (see Chapter 6) and in the United States with the Weather Underground (see the first section of this chapter). Japan, too, experienced its share of rebellious extremism perpetrated by students against the institutions and symbols of capitalist power. The settings and methods were similar to those in the West: demonstrations that became confrontational and then deadly, armed robberies to obtain financing while attacking institutions of capitalism, airplane hijackings, bombings, and assassinations.

The Japanese Red Army was formed in 1971, largely to bring down the Japanese monarchy and stimulate an international revolution – at about the same time its counterparts sprang up in the West. It was founded by Fusako Shigenobu, who was dissatisfied with the nonviolent methods used by the Red Army Faction of the Japanese Communist League – much as counterpart groups in Europe and the United States had splintered off from groups that discouraged the use of violence to achieve their goals.

Unlike its counterparts in the West, however, the Japanese Red Army conducted its most deadly operations outside the country. Most of its actions took place in the Middle East, where Shigenobu led members of her organization to take up the cause of the Palestinians in Lebanon and Palestine, working closely with the Popular Front for the Liberation of Palestine. One of the most sensational events in this collaboration was a 1972 attack that killed twenty-four people and injured about eighty others, described by Gus Martin as "a remarkable example of international terrorism in its purest form: Leftist Japanese terrorists killed Christian pilgrims from Puerto Rico

226

arriving on a U.S. airline at an Israeli airport on behalf of the nationalist Popular Front for the Liberation of Palestine" (2006, p. 288).

The Japanese Red Army also conducted acts of terrorism in India, Indonesia, Malaysia, the Netherlands, and Singapore during the 1970s and '80s. By the 1980s, the Japanese Red Army had, in fact, ended its operations altogether in Japan (Farrell, 1990).

After evading the criminal justice system for 25 years, Shigenobu was eventually arrested during a secret visit to Osaka in 2000. She was convicted in 2006 of kidnapping and attempted murder for a crime committed in the Netherlands in 1974 and received a sentence of twenty years.

2. Aum Shinrikyo

We noted in Chapter 5 that Aum Shinrikyo, a religious sect active in Japan in the early 1990s, was responsible for the sarin gas attack that killed a dozen people and injured thousands of others on a Tokyo subway in 1995. Aum Shinrikyo was formed by Shoko Asahara in 1984, announced its formal status in 1989, and grew to an organization with thousands of members in Japan and tens of thousands in other countries, predominantly Russia. (In a later section of this chapter we describe the organization's founder and leader, Shoko Asahara.) Aum Shinrikyo was, and still is, a classic cult organization, with its own system of beliefs derived from Buddhism, Hinduism, and Christianity, developed and promoted principally by its charismatic leader, Asahara.

Aum Shinrikyo's members have been generally well educated and separated into two distinct classes. The first comprises a corps of monks and nuns who live their lives as ascetics in monastic compounds in various regions of Japan, spending much of their time in meditation (much of it based on traditional yoga). The second is a much larger lay group of practitioners, most of whom lead secular lives. The organization is also divided horizontally according to a system of departments: medical, scientific, martial, and educational.

The ideology of Aum Shinrikyo is a blend of several notions, some spiritual and others more bizarre and dangerous. The spiritual side combines traditional yoga meditation with the idea of a perfect path to enlightenment. The more bizarre side includes a fantastic assortment of beliefs in space missions at the benign end, to international conspiracies, the need to accumulate weapons, and apocalypse at the other. These were not just dark dreams. The police recovered tons of chemicals and other weapons stockpiles at the time of Asahara's arrest, indicating that the organization had planned eventually to overthrow the Japanese government (Lifton, 2000).

The organization officially removed the apocalyptic elements of its ideology following Asahara's prison sentence in 1995, and it changed its name to "Aleph" in 2000. However, the National Police of Japan continue to monitor the organization. In 2005 they estimated its size at about 1,650 members, considerably smaller than before. Aum Shinrikyo remained on the U.S. State Department's list of Foreign Terrorist Organizations for years after he was imprisoned.

The Tokyo attack of 1995 revealed the extreme vulnerability of subway systems in most urban settings to chemical or biological terrorist attacks. In fact, members of Aum Shinrikyo had seriously considered using cyanide, a much more deadly gas than sarin, but chose sarin because it was more accessible in large quantities. Lessons learned: chemical or biological attacks are not difficult to plan and execute; many of the substances capable of inflicting great harm are readily available and inexpensive; and most cities are ill equipped to respond quickly and effectively to such attacks.

3. Jemaah Islamiah and the Bali Bombings of 2002 and 2005

No nation in the world has as large a Muslim population as Indonesia – nearly 90 percent of its 250 million people are Muslims. There are another fifteen million Muslims in Malaysia, just to the north of Indonesia, and four million more in the Philippines to the northeast. Although the vast majority of these people live in peace, extremist factions are present in the area, as in most other parts of the world. The dominant and most deadly of the Islamic extremist groups in Southeast Asia has been Jemaah Islamiah ("community of Islam").

Jemaah Islamiah was founded formally in Malaysia in 1993 by an Indonesian Muslim cleric in exile, Abu Bakar Bashir, and his associate, Abdullah Sungkar, an Islamic extremist from Yemen. They set out to create an organization that would work to consolidate all Muslims across Indonesia, Malaysia, the Philippines, Singapore, and Brunei into a single Islamic state in the region. The organization developed considerable momentum in 1998 with the fall of President Suharto from Indonesia, which allowed its founders to return to Indonesia and establish new headquarters there. Sungkar met with Osama bin Laden not long afterward, thereby aligning Jemaah Islamiah with the al Qaeda organization. This alliance extended al Qaeda's global reach, gave Jemaah Islamiah access to al Qaeda's substantial terrorist training and weaponry resources, and expanded recruitment opportunities for both organizations (Barton, 2003; Ressa, 2003). The organization went on to engage in terrorist activities on a modest scale in Maluku (the "Spice Islands"), Indonesia, and Singapore (Abuza, 2003).

Then, on October 12, 2002, Jemaah Islamiah scored a major terrorist hit on the vacation center of Bali, an Indonesian island in the South Pacific just to the east of Java. Two suicide bombers from Jemaah Islamiyah killed more than 200 people there – 88 of them Australian – and injured many others at the Sari Club, a popular tourist nightspot. The larger of the two bombs was an ammonium nitrate (fertilizer) device, exploded from a car, that left a deep crater. Most of those hospitalized from the bomb suffered severe burns.

Two weeks later, the United Nations put Jemaah Islamiah on its list of terrorist organizations linked to al Qaeda or the Taliban.[9] An Indonesian court convicted Abu Bakar Bashir on charges of conspiracy for his role in planning the 2002 Bali attack, for which he served a prison term of under twenty-six months (released in 2006). Three of Bashir's associates received death sentences, and a fourth a life term, for their more direct involvements in the crime.

Jemaah Islamiah continued its terrorist activities after the Bali event. The organization was implicated in the 2003 Marriott Hotel bombing in Kuningan, Jakarta; the 2004 bombing of the Australian embassy in Jakarta; and a second suicide bombing in Bali, in 2005, involving three suicide bombers who killed twenty people and injured more than one hundred others.

E. The Middle East

The 9/11 attack was committed by nineteen terrorists, all from countries in the Middle East: Saudi Arabia, Egypt, the United Arab Emirates, and Lebanon. We would do well to understand what is unique to the terrorism of this area both to understand terrorism more fully and to respond more effectively to the leading exporters of terrorism

1. Al Qaeda

Al Qaeda is perhaps the most dangerous terrorist threat facing the United States. It is also a threat to the entire Middle East: it was born in the wake of the Soviet flight from Afghanistan, at the far eastern boundary of the Middle East, and its roots are in the center of the Middle East.

Al Qaeda is a Sunni-Arab organization with several distinct enemies in the Middle East: Israel, which it considers a creation of Zionists working through the United Nations, in collaboration with the United States and Great Britain; the Saudi Arabia monarchy, which it regards as a corrupt collaborator with the United States; and Shi'ite Muslims, headquartered in Iran and with strongholds in Iraq, Syria, and Lebanon. It is dedicated to the removal of these and all other regimes that it characterizes as obstacles to al Qaeda's goal of creating a Sunni-Arab caliphate in the Middle East.

Because of the mayhem al Qaeda had caused in the Middle East and elsewhere even before the 9/11 attack, the United Nations formally declared al Qaeda a terrorist organization in 1999, under Resolution 1267. The resolution contains provisions to freeze al Qaeda's assets and those of its leaders, to restrict shipments of the organization's resources, and to limit the travel of its members. After the 9/11 attack several powerful nations – including the

United States, Great Britain, Russia, Australia, and Japan – passed legislation identifying al Qaeda as a terrorist organization, adding further sanctions against the group and its members.

Following U.S. airstrikes and other military intervention in Afghanistan in 2001, al Qaeda's leaders retreated to the mountains along the Afghanistan-Pakistan border. This area is largely in the Waziristan region of Pakistan, but the Pakistan government failed for years to seriously challenge them or to permit foreign military forces to do so. Al Qaeda continues to play an important role both as a supporter and coordinator of operations throughout the Middle East and as a model of inspiration to like-minded terrorists throughout the world.

2. Hezbollah

If al Qaeda is the premier Sunni network of jihadi terrorism, Hezbollah ("Party of God") is its Shi'ite counterpart. There are other large Shi'ite terrorist organizations, such as the Mahdi Army of Muqtada al-Sadr, but none has had the territorial reach, organizational depth, or external support of Hezbollah.

A critical difference between al Qaeda and Hezbollah, apart from their basic Sunni-Shi'ite distinction, is that al Qaeda operates privately by individuals acting outside of, and against, nation-states, whereas Hezbollah has been, since 1985, a creation of Iran. Hezbollah's 1985 manifesto begins as follows:

> We are the sons of the *ummah* (Muslim community) – the party of God (*Hizb Allah*) – the vanguard of which was made victorious by God in Iran. There the vanguard succeeded to lay down the bases of a Muslim state which plays a central role in the world. We obey the orders of one leader, wise and just, that of our tutor and faqih (jurist) who fulfills all the necessary conditions: Ruhollah Musawi Khomeini.

Hezbollah is thus designed to spread the law of Shi'ite Islam from Iran outward to the rest of the Middle East and beyond. Its acts of terrorism can be regarded as acts of Iranian state-sponsored terrorism.

Hezbollah first coalesced as an organization in 1982 – not in Iran, but in Lebanon, where a band of young Shi'ites were drawn to a charismatic cleric, Muhammad Hussayn Fadlallah. They were a disaffected group who felt oppressed by Sunni and Christian elites in Lebanon and by Israel's 1982 invasion of their country. They found solace and inspiration in the story of the Iranian Revolution, which replaced repressive anti-Islamic powers with what they regarded as pure Islamic leaders (Goldberg, 2002a; Ranstorp, 1997).

By 1985, Iran's support of this band of young men became more than merely inspirational. Iran came to see in this fledgling group the makings of a pro-Iranian stronghold in the region. With Iran's active support, Hezbollah became a major innovator in using tactics of surprise in waging acts of terrorism, a model that al Qaeda would emulate. According to *New Yorker* essayist Jeffrey Goldberg,

> Al Qaeda learned the value of choreographed violence from Hezbollah. The organization virtually invented the multipronged terror attack when, early on the morning of October 23, 1983, it synchronized the suicide bombings, in Beirut, of the United States Marine barracks and an apartment building housing a contingent of French peacekeepers. Those attacks occurred just twenty seconds apart; a third part of the plan, to destroy the compound of the Italian peacekeeping contingent, is said to have been jettisoned when the planners learned that the Italians were sleeping in tents, not in a high-rise building (2002a).

The two suicide truck bomb explosions caused unprecedented destruction. They leveled the four-story barracks that held the American military personnel, killing 242 Americans, mostly Marines. The other bomb killed fifty-eight French paratroopers and six Lebanese civilians. The entire multinational force was removed within less than a year. Thus, Hezbollah showed in 1983 that innovative tactics of terror used on a grand scale could force powerful Western governments to withdraw their military presence from Muslim lands.

Hezbollah also induced other groups to join in the cause of militant jihad against alien forces, often distancing themselves from terrorist attacks to make it difficult to trace their involvement and that of Iran (Taheri, 1987). These operations included suicide attacks against enemies in Lebanon, assassinations of public officials, and kidnappings and killings of foreigners.

Several leaders emerged in the Hezbollah organization to complement Muhammad Hussayn Fadlallah's initial spiritual leadership. Abus Musawi – like Fadlallah, a Muslim cleric – emerged as the organization's leader in the late 1980s and early '90s. He was named Secretary General of Hezbollah in 1991. Musawi was known for his close ties to Iran's leadership. In November 1991, three months after Musawi declared that Hezbollah would wipe out every trace of Israel in Palestine and undermine the peace process, Israeli attack helicopters killed him, his wife, a son, and four others traveling in a motorcade in southern Lebanon.

Hassan Nasrallah replaced Musawi as Hezbollah's leader in 1992. Nasrallah was a natural heir to Musawi – he had distinguished himself as a fiery Shi'ite cleric, an early member of Hezbollah in 1982, and a Hezbollah militia leader in the 1980s. As Hezbollah's new leader, Nasrallah demonstrated

231

skill as a strategic-minded leader – organizing Shi'ite militia groups through-out Lebanon; building Hezbollah's arsenal of weapons; taking bolder, more effective action against Israeli military forces; strengthening ties with Syria; supporting Hamas, its Sunni counterpart in Palestine; expanding Hezbollah's international reach to Europe, Asia, and the Americas; and attempting to legitimize Hezbollah by involving it in Lebanon's political system. However, Nasrallah miscalculated how Israel would respond to Hezbollah's kidnap-ping of two Israeli soldiers in 2006. The Israeli military retaliated by killing hundreds of Hezbollah fighters and about 10,000 civilians, reducing much of southern Lebanon to rubble. Yet, Nasrallah managed to save face by launch-ing missile attacks into Israel throughout the month-long battle, a feat that had never before been accomplished in the relatively short history of Arab battles against Israel.

Today, Hezbollah is a legitimate political party in Lebanon – albeit a small minority party – with members who have been elected to the parlia-ment largely on the strength of Nasrallah's leadership and Hezbollah's social service programs (Goldberg, 2002a). This has given the party some stand-ing, an antidote to its richly deserved terrorist label. Hezbollah also has a propaganda machine in the form of its al Manar satellite television station. At the same time, however, Hezbollah continues to commit terrorist acts throughout the world (Stephens, 2007). Moreover, its leaders continue to take uncompromising positions on Israel's right to survival (holding that it must be wiped out), on Lebanon's relations with Iran and Syria (they must be solidified), on whether accommodations can be made with Sunnis and Christians (they cannot), and on the promotion of suicide bombing as acts of martyrdom on its al Manar network – keeping the state of Lebanon in political gridlock (Goldberg, 2002a; Young, 2006).

3. Palestinian Terrorist Groups

Other extremist groups have engaged frequently in terrorist activities in the neighboring Palestine area and Israel, inflicting enormous damage on both places. In the twenty-first century, some of the most active are Hamas, the al Aqsa Martyrs Brigades, the Palestinian Islamic Jihad, and the Popular Front for the Liberation of Palestine. The ultimate goal of these groups is the eradi-cation of Israel – land that the groups believe rightfully belongs to Arabs. They see Israel as an artificial state imposed on them by Zionists in 1947 through the United Nations, at the behest of the United States and Great Britain, in the name of providing a sanctuary for Jews after the Holocaust. Palestini-ans argue that the Israelis have only added insult to injury by humiliating the Palestinian people through superior military power and economic and social oppression and by building settlements in Arab territories taken after the 1967 Six-Day War – on the West Bank, Gaza Strip, the Sinai Peninsula,

1990 Intifada poster by Ayman Bardaweel.

the Golan Heights, and in East Jerusalem. The extremist groups give expression to those frustrations, which reflect both political opposition to the state of Israel and hatred of the Jews, through protest and acts of terrorism.

In response, Israelis hold that the Jewish people have lived peacefully alongside Arabs in the region for thousands of years, often in close friendship, and that they would be perfectly happy to see this situation return in a two-state solution, with Israel and Palestine coexisting as separate independent nations, living side by side in harmony. They argue that the sanctions they have imposed – making Israel into a fortress physically, economically, and socially – have been invoked only in self-defense; they have been needed to stem the rising tide of suicide bombers and mortar attacks from adjacent Arab lands, including lands given up as defense buffers along Israel's borders in 2006. They see their defense as an "existential" struggle, with Israel's very survival in the balance.

The process of developing a peaceful two-state solution to the problem has been supported not only by Palestinian moderates but also by many, if not most, neighboring Arab states and by most other nations throughout the world. Yet, the process of creating a "road map" to such a solution has been undermined repeatedly by extremists both in Israel and Palestine, and expressions of moderation have virtually disappeared. Even if an accord were reached, it is difficult to imagine how the moderates on either side could prevent the extremists in their communities from violating them. Still, even though prospects for a two-state solution have faded, moderates on both sides continue to cling to hope. A few point with optimism to the example of Fatah, which transformed itself from a terrorist faction of the secular Palestine Liberation Organization (PLO) into a dominant political party that has expressed opposition to terrorism, hoping that others can follow suit.

The major Palestinian extremist groups that have engaged in acts of terrorism are profiled below.

Hamas. Hamas (an acronym for *Harakat al-Muqawama al-Islamiyya* or "Islamic Resistance Movement") was created at the start of the first Intifada (a mass Palestinian uprising against Israel) in 1987 by Sheikh Ahmed Yassin

233

of the Gaza wing of the fundamentalist Muslim Brotherhood. The group started in the Jabalia refugee camp and spread quickly through Gaza, the West Bank, and East Jerusalem, escalating its tactics from stone throwing and graffiti to the use of Molotov cocktails and grenades. Hamas's first suicide attack occurred in 1993. It then became an umbrella group that recruited and armed Palestinians to wage war against Israel. Individual cells that make up Hamas operate semi-autonomously. Over a three-and-a-half year period starting in November 2000, Hamas carried out an estimated 425 attacks against Israeli soldiers and citizens, killing 377 and injuring 2,076 (Israel Ministry of Foreign Affairs, 2004).

Hamas may be following the path of Fatah, as it attempts to legitimize its standing. In 2005, it suddenly stopped committing suicide bombings (King and Bekker, 2006). The organization has turned from an emphasis on violence to the provision of health, education, and social services to Palestinians through a network of charities. In 2006, Hamas achieved a stunning political victory over the more moderate Fatah Party in winning 76 of the 132 available parliamentary seats in the Palestine parliament. A few months later, they were criticized for failing to renounce a suicide attack by the Islamic Jihad, an attack that killed nine people in Tel Aviv (King and Bekker, 2006). Time will tell whether Hamas will continue to moderate its violent, extremist legacy.

Al Aqsa Martyrs Brigades. The al Aqsa Martyrs Brigades were formed in the refugee camps of the West Bank in around 2001, after the second Intifada.[10] Although the group is named after a mosque in East Jerusalem, it is more secular than religious. It is the militant arm of the Fatah Party, an offshoot of Yassir Arafat's Palestine Liberation Organization. The al Aqsa Martyrs have made extensive use of suicide bombings. In 2002, the U.S. State Department put al Aqsa on its list of foreign terrorist organizations following an attack in Jerusalem that killed eleven people. Less than a year later, an al Aqsa bomber killed twenty-two people at a bus station in Tel Aviv. They have targeted Israeli buses and places with large congregations of people and have assassinated prominent moderate Palestinians and journalists.

Palestinian Islamic Jihad. The Palestinian Islamic Jihad is a modest-sized group consisting of loosely associated factions. Like the other Palestinian terrorist groups, it is committed to the removal of Israel from Palestine. The group was created in the Gaza Strip in the 1970s by Fathi Shaqaqi, a Palestinian with close ties to the Egyptian Islamic Jihad. Shaqaqi was a pioneer in justifying the use of suicide as a technique of jihad, writing in the 1970s that it was acceptable as a form of sacrifice in battle against the enemy. The Palestinian Islamic Jihad has claimed responsibility for several suicide attacks and other strikes against Israel over the years. Shaqaqi was assassinated in Malta in 1995 and was replaced as leader soon after by Sheikh Abdullah Ramadan Shallah. In 2006 Shallah was placed on the FBI's list of most-wanted terrorists.

Popular Front for the Liberation of Palestine. One of the oldest Palestinian terrorist groups is the Popular Front for the Liberation of Palestine (PFLP). It differs from the other Palestinian terrorist groups in that it is secular – it is an Arab rather than a Muslim group. The PFLP is a small, Marxist-oriented terrorist organization created in 1967 by George Habash, a Palestinian Christian. Habash regarded his Palestinian Arab community as a downtrodden people who needed the infusion of an uplifting revolutionary spirit like that embodied by guerrilla Che Guevara to advance themselves (Cooley, 1973).

The PFLP is part of the Palestine Liberation Organization (PLO) network, second in size only to Fatah. It has traditionally taken a stronger, more militant stand than Fatah against the two-state solution and has for decades engaged in numerous terrorist attacks, including airplane hijackings, fatal bombings, and the taking of hostages. Its most devastating attack was carried out in 1970, when it planted a bomb on a Swissair flight from Zurich to Tel Aviv, killing forty-seven people. The group has claimed responsibility for several suicide bombing attacks in Israel since 2002.

4. Libya

Libya, an oil-rich nation of some six million people, became a pioneer in state-sponsored terrorism in the twentieth century under its mercurial leader, Colonel Moammar Gaddafi, who seized power in 1969 after heading a bloodless military overthrow of King Idris. Gaddafi then set up what he saw as a revolutionary system of "Islamic socialism" in the 1970s, with clear designs on following in the footsteps of the Egyptian leader, Abdul Nasser, who had blazed a trail toward becoming the pan-Arabic leader in the 1960s until he was assassinated in 1970. Elements of Gaddafi's model included Islamic restraint from excess (he banned alcohol and gambling), opposition to Western capitalism (he nationalized all large corporations), and the autocratic imposition of loyalty (he had dissidents assassinated, including five in 1980 who had escaped to Italy).

Central to Gaddafi's grand design was the rejection and removal of Western influences, by whatever means available. In 1979, the U.S. embassy in Tripoli was burned and closed permanently. In 1981, the Libyan government created the People's Committee for Students of Libyan Jamahariya, also known as the People's Committee for Libyan Students (PCLS) – a front for Libyan intelligence and terrorist activities in the United States. Afterward, Gaddafi actively promoted terrorism by building terrorist training camps and weapons stockpiles in selected countries throughout the world. In 1986, Gaddafi directed two bombings that killed U.S. citizens: first, a TransWorld Airlines jetliner in Greece killing four Americans, and then the La Belle Disco – a favorite Berlin nightclub for U.S. servicemen stationed in Germany – killing one GI and injuring seventy-nine other Americans. The following year, a merchant ship carrying about 150 tons of Libyan weapons was intercepted in the Bay of Biscay, off the north coast of Spain.

The most sensational of all Libyan-sponsored terrorist attacks was the 1988 bombing of Pan American Flight 103 over Lockerbie, Scotland, which killed 270 people, including 189 Americans. The jet, carrying 259 passengers from twenty-one countries (11 Scottish citizens were killed on the ground), was en route from London's Heathrow International Airport to New York's John F. Kennedy International Airport four days before Christmas. A three-year investigation resulted in the eventual conviction of two Libyans: an intelligence officer who headed security for Libyan Arab Airlines (LAA) and the LAA station manager in Malta, the jet's previous departure point.

An even greater threat of state-sponsored terrorism by Libya was averted in 2003, when it was revealed that the Libyan government had invested some $300 million in the development of a nuclear weapons program, with assistance from Pakistan's Abdul Qadeer Khan. The program was dismantled soon afterward (Miller, 2006).

Effective intelligence was key in the response to Gaddafi's state-sponsored terrorism. The interception by U.S. intelligence of a 1986 Telex communication from Tripoli to the Libyan embassy in East Germany exposed Libya's hand in the bombing of the La Belle Disco. The strength of the evidence against Libyans in the Lockerbie disaster and intervention by the United Nations led to Gaddafi's handing over the prime suspects to the Scottish police in 1999 and agreeing to pay $2.7 billion to the families of the victims – $10 million each – plus millions more to compensate families of earlier victims of Libya's terrorist attacks (Miller, 2006).

Gaddafi's ventures into the world of terrorism subsided throughout the 1990s after the collapse of the Soviet Union and the exposure of his role in the global spread of terrorism. He was among the first world leaders to publicly condemn the 9/11 attack. His conversion from exporter of terrorism to responsible international leader was almost complete in 2003 – Benjamin Barber (2007) calls it a transformation from "implacable despot" to "complex and adaptive thinker" – with two important developments: the U.S. removal from power of another dangerous despot, Iraq's Saddam Hussein, and U.S. intelligence that exposed Libya's nuclear weapons program through the interception and recording of telephone conversations between the head of the program and A. Q. Khan (Miller, 2006). Since then, Gaddafi has become friendly with the West. This shift to a more open and peaceful direction for his country's international affairs may be due partly to the man and partly to his people, but surely no less to the effective mix of hard power and diplomacy (see Box 8.3).

Policy Box 8.3. Libya – A Hard Power Success Story?

One of the apparent success stories in the use of hard power against terrorism is U.S. intervention against Libya over a period of two decades, starting in 1982. In that year, the United States banned the import of Libyan oil and the export of technology that could have helped Libya's burgeoning oil industry, following a series of belligerent acts by the country's leader, Moammar Gaddafi – including explicit threats to send hit men to the United States to assassinate then-President Ronald Reagan. Then, in 1986 the United States banned all private commerce with Libya, including all travel to or from the country.

Later that year – and just a few weeks after the 1986 Libyan bombing of a German disco that killed an American serviceman in Berlin – U.S. Air Force and Navy jets attacked Gaddafi's headquarters and other targets in Tripoli and Benghazi in "Operation El Dorado Canyon," killing about 100 Libyan military and government officials and destroying much valuable property. The attack also killed Gaddafi's adopted infant daughter and injured two of his sons.

In 2007 Gaddafi released the "Benghazi Six" – a Palestinian intern and five Bulgarian nurses – who had been falsely accused of conspiring to intentionally infect hundreds of Libyan children with HIV in 1998 and had received a death sentence and spent eight years in custody. Soon afterward, the United States removed Libya from its list of states that sponsor terrorism and restored full diplomatic relations with the country.

Gaddafi's conversion from terrorism to a member in good standing of the international community may have been stimulated by a variety of factors other than the use of U.S. sanctions, force, the threat of much greater force, and diplomacy – including negotiations to remove the sanctions and the promise not to overthrow him in return for an end to his involvement in terrorism. It may have been the product of his complex personality, the wisdom that comes with age and experience, the influence of his bright son, Saif al-Islam, a population that is more moderate than those in other Muslim nations, and other factors. He most certainly did not care to have it appear – especially among the international Arab-Muslim community he had once hoped to lead – that he was cowed into submission by the United States (Barber, 2007; Miller, 2006).

But the fact that he volunteered to abandon his nuclear weapons program and renounce terrorism soon after the United States removed Saddam Hussein from power and gave Gaddafi a CD with the recorded intelligence "goods" about his nuclear weapons program strongly suggests that hard power can be effective when applied with skill, under the right conditions, and in combination with diplomacy.

F. Prominent Contemporary Terrorist Leaders

Ideas are powerful, but perhaps even more persuasive are the charismatic spokesmen who deliver them. According to Fawaz Gerges, a scholar on violent Muslim extremists (whom he refers to as "jihadis"),

> In my conversations with former jihadis, one of the critical lessons I have learned is that personalities, not ideas or organizations, are the drivers behind the movement. . . . The most lethal and violent jihadist factions and cells were led by highly charismatic, aggressive, and daring personalities who captivated and inspired followers to unquestionably do their bidding.

In earlier chapters, we profiled men, and one woman, who created and led terrorist organizations. Let us continue this examination with a closer look at some of the more prominent leaders of terrorist organizations.

Osama bin Laden. Osama bin Laden is generally regarded as the person most responsible for moving the world out of the post-Cold War era and into the era of terrorism. Although not involved in the detailed planning and execution of the attack of September 11, 2001, as the leader of al Qaeda he was the inspiration behind the attacks, and he provided financial and logistical support for them and for several serious terrorist attacks that preceded the 9/11 attack: the 1993 attack on the World Trade Center; the 1998 U.S. embassy bombings in Dar es Salaam, Tanzania, and Nairobi; the 2000 *USS Cole* bombing; the Bali nightclub bombings; and bombings in the Jordanian capital of Amman and in Egypt's Sinai peninsula.

Lawrence Wright (2006a) sees bin Laden as the dominant figure in the sharp escalation of conflict between the West and the Arab Muslim world:

> One can ask, at this point, whether 9/11 or some similar tragedy might have happened without bin Laden to steer it. The answer is certainly not. Indeed, the tectonic plates of history were shifting, promoting a period of conflict between the West and the Arab Muslim world; however, the charisma and vision of a few individuals shaped the nature of this contest. . . . At a time when there were many Islamist movements, all of them concentrated on nationalist goals, it was bin Laden's vision to create an international jihad corps. It was his leadership that held together an organization that had been bankrupted and thrown into exile. It was bin Laden's tenacity that made him deaf to the moral quarrels that attended the murder of so many and indifferent to the repeated failures that would have destroyed most men's dreams. All of these were qualities that one can ascribe to a cult leader or a madman. But there was also artistry involved, not only to achieve the spectacular effect but also to enlist the imagination of the men whose lives bin Laden required (pp. 331–32).

Osama bin Laden.

Bin Laden was born in 1957 into a Saudi family that had become extremely wealthy in the construction industry. He earned degrees in civil engineering and public administration at King Abdulaziz University in Jeddah, but received his more significant extracurricular education from individual professors there – most notably Muhammad Qutb (younger brother of Sayyid Qutb) and Abdullah Yusuf Azzam, who introduced him to the Muslim Brotherhood and the anti-Western jihadist writings of Sayyid Qutb. In 1984 bin Laden worked with Azzam to help finance and organize the grassroots anti-Soviet insurgency in Afganistan (Wright, 2006a).

In the 1990s, bin Laden turned his energies to the overthrow of the Saudi monarchy, following his strong opposition to its alignment with the United States after Iraq invaded Kuwait in 1990. The Saudi government responded by expelling bin Laden to the Sudan in 1991, and in 1995 stripping him of his citizenship after he claimed responsibility for directing attacks on U.S. and Saudi military bases in Riyadh and Dahran. Stimulated by the transnational designs of his associate, Ayman Zawahiri (see below), bin Laden shifted focus from "near enemy" targets in the Middle East to "far enemy" targets from Africa to the United States (Gerges). In Sudan, and later in Afghanistan, bin Laden set up camps to train Islamist militants in the use of firearms and explosives. In 1996, he fled Sudan for Afghanistan, after the Saudi and U.S. governments pressured Sudan into expelling him from that country. In Afghanistan, bin Laden developed a close relationship with Mullah Mohammed Omar and leaders of the Taliban government. In return for financial and paramilitary support of the Taliban, bin Laden was granted sanctuary and a command post from which he could direct worldwide jihadist operations, including the 1997 Luxor massacre in Egypt and the 9/11 attack.

In inspiring others to commit themselves to his cause in an extremely public manner, bin Laden has left a long trail of evidence implicating him in terrorist attacks (see Box 8.4 showing some of his famous remarks made over several years). Videotapes of bin Laden reveling in the collapse of the World Trade Center towers and acknowledging that they were acts of al Qaeda provide

Box 8.4. Thoughts of Osama Bin Laden: 1995–2003

On fighting Russians and Americans:

To counter these atheist Russians, the Saudis chose me as their representative in Afghanistan. . . . I did not fight against the communist threat while forgetting the peril from the West. . . . For us, the idea was not to get involved more than necessary in the fight against the Russians, which was the business of the Americans, but rather to show our solidarity with our Islamist brothers. I discovered that it was not enough to fight in Afghanistan, but that we had to fight on all fronts against communist or Western oppression. The urgent thing was communism, but the next target was America. . . . This is an open war up to the end, until victory.

~ Interview with a French journalist, April 1995

Declaration of war against Americans occupying holy lands:

(Our) youths know that their rewards in fighting you, the USA, is double their rewards in fighting someone else not from the people of the Bible. They have no intention except to enter paradise by killing you. . . . Terrorizing you, while you carry arms on our land, is a legitimate and morally demanded duty. It is a legitimate right well known to all humans and other creatures. Your example and our example is like a snake which entered into a house of a man and got killed by him. The coward is the one who lets you walk, while carrying arms, freely on his land and provides you with peace and security. . . . Those youths are different from your soldiers. Your problem will be how to convince your troops to fight, while our problem will be how to restrain our youths to wait for their turn in fighting and in operations. These youths are worthy of commendation and praise. They stood up tall to defend the religion, at the time when the government misled the prominent scholars and tricked them into issuing Fatwas, which have no basis either in the book of Allah or in the Sunnah of the Prophet (Allah's Blessings and Salutations may be on him), for opening the land of the two Holy Places for the Christians armies and handing the Al-Aqsa Mosque to the Zionists. Twisting the meanings of the holy text will not change this fact.

~ Fatwa issued from the Hindukush Mountains, Afghanistan,
August 23, 1996

On why it was necessary to strike the United States and its allies:

The call to wage war against America was made because America has spearheaded the crusade against the Islamic nation, sending tens of thousands of its troops to the land of the two Holy Mosques over and above its meddling in its affairs and its politics, and its support of the oppressive, corrupt and tyrannical regime that is in control. These are the reasons behind the singling out of America as a target. And not exempt of responsibility are those Western regimes whose presence in the region offers support to the American troops there.

~ Interview with *Frontline*, May 1998

In response to a question about whether al Qaeda was responsible for the bombing of two embassies in Eastern Africa:

If the instigation for jihad against the Jews and the Americans in order to liberate al-Aksa Mosque and the Holy Kaaba (Islamic shrines in Jerusalem and Saudi Arabia) is considered a crime, then let history be a witness that I am a criminal. Our job is to instigate and, by the grace of God, we did that, and certain people responded to this instigation.

~ Interview with *Time* magazine, December 23, 1998

In response to the question, "What can the U.S. expect from you now?"

Any thief or criminal or robber who enters another country in order to steal should expect to be exposed to murder at any time. For the American forces to expect anything from me personally reflects a very narrow perception. Thousands of millions of Muslims are angry. The Americans should expect reactions from the Muslim world that are proportionate to the injustice they inflict.

~ Interview with *Time* magazine, December 23, 1998

In response to a question about whether he is trying to acquire nuclear weapons:

Acquiring weapons for the defense of Muslims is a religious duty. If I have indeed acquired these weapons, then I thank God for enabling me to do so. And if I seek to acquire these weapons, I am carrying out a duty. It would be a sin for Muslims not to try to possess the weapons that would prevent the infidels from inflicting harm on Muslims.

~ Interview with *Time* magazine, December 23, 1998

Terrorism throughout the World

On a U.S. plan to divide the Iraq into three parts:

These days, there is also a plan to divide Iraq into three – one in the north for Muslim kurds, a state in the middle, and a third in the south. The same applies to the land of the two mosques (Saudi Arabia) where there is a plan to divide it into a state for the two mosques, another state for oil in the eastern region, and a state in the middle. This would make the people of the two mosques always busy trying to earn a living, and would leave a few people in the oil region who can be easily controlled. This is a world design and Muslims should not focus on side effects. They should unify their ranks to be able to resist this occupation.

> ~ Interview with ABC, January 2, 1999

On the invasion of Afghanistan as a continuation of the Crusades:

Let us investigate whether this war against Afghanistan that broke out a few days ago is a single and unique one or if it is a link to a long series of crusader wars against the Islamic world. Following World War I, which ended more than eighty-three years ago, the whole Islamic world fell under the crusader banner – under the British, French, and Italian governments. They divided the whole world, and Palestine was occupied by the British.

> ~ "Bin Laden Rails against Crusaders and UN," *BBC News*,
> November 3, 2001

On viewing a videotape of the collapse of the World Trade Towers:

We calculated in advance the number of casualties from the enemy, who would be killed based on the position of the tower. We calculated that the floors that would be hit would be three or four floors.... Due to my experience in this field, I was thinking that the fire from the fuel in the plane would melt the iron structure of the building and collapse the area where the plane hit and just the floors above it. This is all that we had hoped for.... The brothers who conducted the operation, all they knew was that they had a martyrdom operation and we asked each of them to go to America, but they didn't know anything about the operation, not even one letter. But they were trained, and we did not reveal the operation to them until just before they boarded the planes.

> ~ Transcript of videotape dated November 9, 2001,
> released by the Pentagon in December 2001

On the United Nations:

> Are not our tragedies but caused by the United Nations? Who issued the Partition Resolution on Palestine in 1947 and surrendered the land of Muslims to the Jews? It was the United Nations in its resolution in 1947.... This is the United Nations from which we have suffered greatly. Under no circumstances should any Muslim or sane person resort to the United Nations. The United Nations is nothing but a tool of crime. We are being massacred everyday, while the United Nations continues to sit idly by.
>
> $\sim$ "Bin Laden Rails against Crusaders and UN," *BBC News*,
> November 3, 2001

On the vulnerability of the United States:

> America is a great power possessed of tremendous military might and a wide-ranging economy, but all this is built on an unstable foundation which can be targeted, with special attention to its obvious weak spots. If America is hit in one hundredth of these weak spots, God willing, it will stumble, wither away and relinquish world leadership.
>
> $\sim$ Sermon, Middle East Media Research Institute (MEMRI)
> (March 5, 2003), quoted in Pape (2005), p. 123

His appeal to disgruntled Americans and encouragement for them to convert to Islam:

> Iraq and Afghanistan and their tragedies; and the reeling of many of you under the burden of interest-related debts, insane taxes and real estate mortgages; global warming and its woes; and the abject poverty and tragic hunger in Africa; all of this is but one side of the grim face of this global system.... To conclude, I invite you to embrace Islam, for the greatest mistake one can make in this world and one which is uncorrectable is to die ... outside of Islam.
>
> $\sim$ Transcript of videotape released for the sixth anniversary of 9/11
> (September 11, 2007)

compelling evidence of his role in supporting, if not being closely involved in planning, the attack on the United States. His exhortations to resist the new American "Crusaders" may sound like absurd rhetoric to Western ears, but such words resonate deeply with millions of pious Muslims around the world who feel besieged by Western culture and values (Ahmed, 2003).

The FBI put bin Laden on its most-wanted list in 1998, and after the 9/11 attack, the U.S. government offered a reward of $25 million for his capture.

Ayman al-Zawahiri

Speculation has swirled for years over the precise whereabouts of bin Laden, with many of the opinion that he lives somewhere in the vicinity of the long, rugged Afghanistan-Pakistan border. Others have questioned whether he is still alive.

Osama bin Laden's message has continually changed as his targets have shifted and expanded. His later messages point clearly to his intention to solidify his legacy as inspirational leader of the transformation of the world to his brand of Islam (Applebaum, 2007; Aslan, 2007).

Ayman Muhammad Rabaie al-Zawahiri. Ayman Zawahiri, Osama bin Laden's chief associate, was born in 1951 to a family of professionals in Egypt. He became fluent in Arabic, French, and English; studied medicine; and earned a certificate in surgery. Whereas bin Laden came to the Salafist ideology through his education in Wahhabi schools in Saudi Arabia, Zawahiri joined the Muslim Brotherhood in Egypt at age fourteen (Esposito, 2002, pp. 5, 18). In 1966, Zawahiri's radicalism was deepened by the execution of one of his heroes, Salafist leader Sayyib Qutb; it was accelerated fifteen years later by his imprisonment and torture in Egypt – much in the same manner in which Qutb had been imprisoned and tortured earlier – as a conspirator in the assassination of President Anwar Sadat. According to Lawrence Wright, "One line of thinking proposes that America's tragedy on September 11 was born in the prisons of Egypt" (2006a, p. 52).

Zawahiri was a near-perfect match with bin Laden as co-leader of the al Qaeda organization. They had common backgrounds and interests. Like bin Laden, Zawahiri was educated, Arab, and an Islamic extremist. Like bin

Laden, he had become radicalized by political powers who rejected him in his home country. And he had needs and skills that complemented bin Laden's well. Wright describes Zawahiri and bin Laden as near-perfect complements: "Zawahiri wanted money and contacts, which bin Laden had in abundance. Bin Laden, an idealist given to causes, sought direction; Zawahiri, a seasoned propagandist, supplied it" (2006a, p. 127). This was genuine symbiosis:

> The dynamic of the two men's relationship made Zawahiri and bin Laden into people they would never have been individually; moreover, the organization they would create, al-Qaeda, would be a vector of these two forces, one Egyptian and one Saudi. Each would have to compromise in order to accommodate the goals of the other; as a result, al-Qaeda would take a unique path, that of global jihad (Wright, 2006a, p. 127; a similar assessment is offered by Gerges).

Wright (2006b) elaborates on the complementary inside role that Zawahiri played alongside bin Laden's al Qaeda: he was the strategist, ideologue, and detail-oriented schemer to bin Laden's charismatic dreamer. Zawahiri outlined a four-part plan for al Qaeda in a 2005 letter to the organization's field marshal, Abu Musab al-Zarqawi (described below).

> The first stage: Expel the Americans from Iraq. The second stage: Establish an Islamic authority or emirate, then develop it and support it until it achieves the level of a caliphate. . . . The third stage: Extend the jihad wave to the secular countries neighboring Iraq. The fourth stage: It may coincide with what came before – the clash with Israel, because Israel was established only to challenge any new Islamic entity.

One of Zawahiri's (2001) overarching themes has been the need for Muslim unity to achieve individual and collective goals:

> The struggle for the establishment of the Muslim state cannot be launched as a regional struggle. . . . The jihad movement must realize that half the road to victory is attained through its unity. . . . The movement must seek this unity as soon as possible if it is serious in its quest for victory.

Abu Musab al-Zarqawi. One of Osama bin Laden's most important associates was Abu Musab al-Zarqawi. If bin Laden was the spiritual leader of al Qaeda, Zarqawi was its field general in Iraq, al Qaeda's main battlefront after the fall of the Taliban in Afghanistan. Born in Jordan in 1966, Zarqawi was a tough high-school dropout who migrated to Afghanistan to fight the Soviets in 1989. In 1992 he was imprisoned for five years in Jordan for conspiracy to replace the Jordanian monarchy with an Islamic caliphate. After his release from prison, he traveled to Pakistan, Afghanistan, Iran, and Iraq. Following the U.S. invasion of Iraq, Zarqawi led a substantial force of insurrectionists from neighboring Middle Eastern countries to wage jihad against the U.S. military forces in Iraq and against all others who supported attempts

Abu Musab al-Zarqawi.

to bring stability and democracy to the country. His aim was to divide the Iraqis and move them away from sectarian order. Most of his victims were Iraqi Shi'a. As documented in video and audiotapes, Zarqawi took personal responsibility and pride in executing kidnapped hostages, selecting targets for suicide bombings, and killing thousands of civilians, soldiers, and police officers in Iraq. He personally decapitated three Americans: Eugene "Jack" Armstrong, Nicholas Berg, and Jack Hensley (Whitlock, 2004). In 2005, the prominent Muslim newspaper *al Jazeera* reported that Zarqawi declared "all-out war" on Shia Muslims in Iraq. He is widely held responsible for enraging Iraqi Shi'a by directing the bombing of the sacred Askariya mosque in Samarra in 2006 and for losing support for the jihadist cause following the 2005 bombing of a wedding party at a hotel in Amman, Jordan (see Chapter 2).

Essayist and author George Will characterizes Zarqawi as a "pornographer of violence." Will elaborates as follows:

> He was a primitive who understood the wired world and used an emblem of modernity, the Internet, to luxuriate in gore. But although he may have had an almost erotic enjoyment of the gore, it was also in the service of an audacious plan. And he executed it with such brutal efficiency that he became, arguably, the most effective terrorist in history.

Nassar

Although Zarqawi shared many jihadist goals with bin Laden and received financial support from him, Zarqawi was reported to be at sharp odds with bin Laden (Whitlock, 2004) and Ayman Zawahiri over methods used to achieve the goals of jihad. Zawahiri characterized these techniques as "unpalatable" at a time when "we are in a media battle in a race for the hearts and minds of our *ummah*" (Ignatius, 2005b). An official alliance between Zarqawi's group and al Qaeda was announced in 2004 in an audiotape in which bin Laden called Zarqawi "the emir (prince or commander) of al Qaeda in Iraq" and praised him for "his good deeds." As with bin Laden, the U.S. government offered a $25 million reward for information leading to Zarqawi's death or capture. Zarqawi was killed in a U.S. airstrike on June 7, 2006, near the Iraq city of Baquba.

Mustafa Setmariam Nasar. Mustafa Setmariam Nasar, who also goes by the name of Abu Musab al-Asuri and is widely referred to simply as "Setmariam," is a leading jihadi strategist. He is often singled out as the mastermind of the terrorist attacks on public transportation systems in Madrid in 2004 and London in 2005. Born in Syria in 1958, he fought the Soviet Union in Afghanistan during the 1980s, where he became an associate of Osama bin Laden. Setmariam later lived in Spain, where he married, became a citizen, and fathered two children. In 1995 he moved to London, and in 1998 to Afghanistan, where he collaborated with Abu Musab al-Zarqawi and led a terrorist training camp (Cruickshank and Ali, 2006; Whitlock, 2004).

247

Perhaps Setmariam's greatest impact on terrorism is his manifesto, *The Call for a Global Islamic Resistance*, issued on the Internet in December 2004. This document called for global conflict on as many fronts as possible – waged by small cells or individuals acting autonomously, rather than through traditional guerrilla warfare tactics based on cells coordinated closely with larger organizations. Setmariam's manifesto also emphasizes the use of the most deadly weapons possible to produce maximum destruction of the enemy.

In November 2005 Setmariam was captured in Quetta, Pakistan, by Pakistani police and turned over to U.S. authorities (Whitlock, 2006).

Shoko Asahara. Shoko Asahara was the founder and leader of the Japanese cult, Aum Shinrikyo, and the mastermind of the Tokyo subway attack in 1995 that killed twelve people and injured thousands of others. Born Chizuo Matsumoto in 1955, Asahara had a history of delinquency and criminality, starting as a bully at a boarding school for the blind (he was blind in one eye due to glaucoma) and advancing later to crimes of fraud and theft. In 1987 he formed Aum Shinrikyo, a quasi-religious cult that combined elements of conventional Eastern religions, including Hinduism and Buddhism, with apocalyptic notions of Christianity. Asahara wrote several books, including *Beyond Life and Death* in 1993. Inspired by his visions of violence, he learned about chemical, biological, and nuclear weapons and gathered large quantities of sarin and other deadly chemicals for planned attacks in Japan and the United States (Cameron, 1999; Kaplan and Marshall, 1996; Kristof, 1997; Lifton, 2000; Rosenau, 2001). He planned and carried out a sarin attack on an apartment complex in the central Japanese city of Matsumoto in 1994, killing eight people and injuring over two hundred others (Kaplan and Marshall, 1996). Asahara was convicted on thirteen counts of murder and sentenced to death by hanging in 2004.

G. Commonalities and Differences

Terrorism manifests differently from place to place, and where successive acts of terrorism have occurred in a particular place, they tend to vary over time in both severity and nature. Each terrorist group has its own unique history and characteristics. Each arises out of a unique cultural heritage, with a specific set of political, religious, ethnic, or tribal grievances against others. Terrorist groups typically are formed by charismatic leaders who are effective in enlisting others in their causes, usually persuading their followers that the mission is unique and of paramount importance. These are usually fascinating stories, often too bizarre to pass as plausible fiction. But the stories are real, and they have imposed incalculable harm and grief on their immediate targets and on others.

Most of the stories have factors in common. The followers are usually impressionable young men who have no strong stake in conforming to norms of civility or to peaceful virtues. Except for the lone wolves, they typically develop strong ties of camaraderie with others committed to the cause. The most committed followers are typically obsessed with hatred of the group targeted. Their leaders appear to be committed largely to the expansion of power and influence.

Interventions against terrorist groups, if they are to succeed, must account for both the commonalities and the uniqueness of each group. Some groups are more likely than others to collapse if the leader is taken out. Some are more inclined to simply disappear, self-destruct, or be destroyed privately when ignored by government. Some are more likely than others to be susceptible to inducements to replace their hostile intentions with prospects for a positive future. In the next chapter we focus on responses that have been found to work – or not to work – against various types of terrorist groups.

Discussion Questions

1. Has terrorism in the United States been fundamentally different from terrorism in other places? In what way(s)? In what ways has it been like terrorism in other countries?
2. How has the mix of home-grown and cross-national terrorist events differed from country to country? How do you explain the differences? The similarities?
3. What traits appear to be fairly commonly shared among leaders of terrorist organizations? What traits appear to make some leaders more effective than others?
4. What are the primary differences between the U.S. war on terror during the years 2001 through 2008 and al Qaeda's Management of Savagery doctrine? Are the two programs comparable? Which do you think was more effective over this period? Explain your answers to the last two questions.
5. What changes in terrorism before and after 9/11 strike you as the most significant? Might some of these changes have occurred in the absence of 9/11? Which ones? Might some not have occurred? Which ones? Explain your answers.
6. What strikes you as the most important lessons for policymakers from the terrorist events of the past thirty years? How has the public debate on terrorism dealt with these matters? What is needed to improve the quality of this ongoing debate?

Responses to Terrorism

This chapter addresses principles for and alternative approaches to responding to terrorism. We begin with the most basic questions of how to use diplomacy and when to rely on force to intervene against terrorism, using the "just war" theory as a basis for addressing these fundamental issues. We then turn to the question of collective or unilateral responses. Specific interventions are then discussed, including the tactic of torture to extract information, covert and other special operations, use of bounty programs and extradition treaties to facilitate the capture of terrorists, and international courts and tribunals to decide in such cases.

A. Investigative, Diplomatic, and Military Responses

After the initial shock, serious terrorist attacks are usually countered quickly by a mix of investigative and diplomatic activities and, in some cases, a military response. The first objective is to establish the source or sources of the attack and then to mobilize power against the terrorists both to deal with immediate threats and deter future attacks. To achieve this first objective, standard crime scene forensic analysis is used to establish the "signature" of the attacker or attackers. Investigative methods include the following:

- Thorough search and photographic documentation of the scene
- Deliberate recovery of evidence
- Chemical analysis of explosives
- Ballistics tests to establish the precise location and impact of the explosion
- Methods to determine the identity of the bomber

- Analysis of earlier intelligence reports of suspected individuals and groups involved
- Analysis of prerecorded confession tapes of suicide bombers
- Interrogation of suspected collaborators
- Interviews of witnesses
- Analyses of telephone records, bank and credit card data, receipts, and computer files

The aim of the investigation should be to identify the offenders and their collaborators and to learn more about the methods used to plan and execute the attack. Accounts of the investigations following the bombings of Pan Am Flight 103 over Lockerbie, Scotland, in 1988; the World Trade Center in 1993; the Murrah Federal Building in Oklahoma City, Oklahoma, in 1995; the *USS Cole* in 2000; and the commuter train bombings in Madrid in 2004 and London in 2005 show how these basic components of criminal investigation have been effectively applied – and sometimes misapplied – to the problem of determining who committed the terrorist events (Bolz, Dudonis and Schulz, 2005; De Koster, 2004; G. Lee, 2004; Trento and Trento, 2006).

Once the investigation provides a clear sense of the source of the attack and identity of the attackers, the diplomatic and military responses must be planned and executed. Let us consider each of these in turn.

1. Diplomatic Responses

Joseph Nye, Jr., former dean of Harvard University's Kennedy School of Government, once wrote, "Security is like oxygen – you tend not to notice it until you begin to lose it, but once that occurs there is nothing else that you will think about" (1995, p. 91). The 2001 terrorist attack on United States soil caused Americans to notice the need for security against terrorism as they never had before, and to think seriously about little else for some time. In times of calm, a diplomatic approach to the prevention of terrorism seems more viable than a military response. Could it also be viable even when under the frantic spell of insecurity? Let us consider the prospects.

To begin with, formal diplomatic contacts with terrorists are generally incompatible with both diplomacy and terrorism, as terrorists operate typically outside of formal state authority and often make themselves inaccessible. Moreover, states threatened or attacked by terrorists are loathe to legitimize or honor their assailants by establishing diplomatic relationships with them. One can imagine diplomats meeting informally with terrorists to obtain information that might be useful as intelligence, but such information may not be reliable and may be designed to misrepresent the facts and mislead rather than inform. The prospect of meeting with terrorists for purposes of negotiation is generally dubious in any case, as terrorists rarely can be trusted to keep agreements that could compromise their own schemes and designs.

Diplomacy plays a more important role when conducted among sovereign nations that have either been attacked by terrorists or that see themselves as likely candidates for future such attacks. The primary goal of diplomacy in these cases is to organize actions against terrorists so that they can be brought to justice and so that subsequent acts of terrorism can be prevented. Diplomatic coalitions can provide a unified front that serves to de-legitimize the terrorists and make counterterrorist efforts more effective and efficient.

2. Military Power

When diplomacy fails, military force must be considered. As noted in Chapter 1, Clausewitz referred to such reliance on military power to resolve what diplomacy cannot as policy by other means (Howard, 1983). Military force can be an effective and legitimate response to aggression, or it can be used to prevent a devastating impending aggression by one nation against another (Walzer, 1992) The use of military force against terrorism can also achieve both tactical and strategic gains – by removing immediate terrorist threats in the short term and deterring future attacks over the long term. Military intervention could conceivably succeed in reducing the long-term prospects of terrorism if the removal of dictators or regimes whose acts have clearly worsened the conditions that feed terrorism were to give rise to governments that create conditions less hospitable to terrorism, or if the intervention deterred autocrats in other nations from contributing to terrorism, or both.

Immediate Costs, Consequences, and Risks of Military Force. The immediate costs of a military operation can be substantial – even when it succeeds in ousting a government that harbors terrorists or supports terrorism, and even when the overthrow is followed eventually by order, legitimate local authority, and the preservation of vital resources in the lands previously under dictatorship. Innocent lives are often lost, and the resources expended and destroyed in the operation can be substantial. Additional problems arise from abrupt political change and the destruction of stable, if seriously flawed, public institutions. Public and private institutions and services are typically disrupted, and refugees are created both in the land targeted and often in neighboring states.

Moreover, for the invading power or powers, political capital may be spent in the effort both at home and abroad, as the gains are often difficult to establish and military intervention can be hard to sell politically to others. The coalitions useful for attaining international legitimacy must also overcome the free-rider problem: countries may derive benefits from united support while not paying for the effort, and they may even voice opposition to the cause to justify the free ride.

Long-Term Consequences and Risks. Military force applied directly against terrorists raises other prospects that can have more serious long-term consequences. One such problem is strategic: even when military force succeeds in producing short-term security gains, it can produce lasting set-backs by creating sympathy for the terrorists and their cause and unifying disparate adversaries, thus feeding the clash of civilizations monster. Two recent examples are the U.S. invasion of Iraq in 2003, initiated and conducted in the name of its war on terror, and Israel's invasion of Lebanon in 2006 following a Hezbollah attack on Israeli soil, in an attempt to destroy Hezbollah's capacity to wage further such attacks. Both were sold to the citizens of the invading nations on the grounds that their security overrode all other considerations. In both cases, the articulated objectives of victory over the terrorists were not achieved. In both cases, worldwide support for the more powerful nation plummeted following vivid videotaped footage of carnage to women, children and elderly populations in the weaker nation and perceptions that the invading armies did not exercise sufficient concern about casualties to innocents caught in the crossfire. In both cases, the general conclusion of several respected military analysts was that the actions were carried out hastily, with insufficient planning, flawed intelligence, and unattainable goals (Carr, 2006). Both operations ended up strengthening the foothold and influence of an Iranian theocracy over the Middle East (Nasr, 2005; Slackman, 2006). We examine each of these operations in more detail later.

Training Terrorists in Asymmetric Warfare. Another problem relates to the adaptive capacity of terrorists. Terrorists do not have the resources to wage conventional warfare against a technologically sophisticated opponent, so they wage asymmetric warfare, fighting without uniforms, situating themselves in populated civilian areas, and violating other rules of warfare to which sovereign nations are bound. Both the Iraq and Lebanon invasions provided extensive and invaluable on-the-ground training for terrorists and insurgents to perfect techniques that would level the playing field; the insurgents in both cases also found ways to achieve major victories in the larger war for the hearts and minds of people both in the region and elsewhere worldwide through the media. Both invasions revealed that air power and highly sophisticated weaponry, guidance and communications systems, and other resources developed to achieve Cold War superiority were of limited value for attacking a modest force of a few thousand insurgents operating in small, highly mobile teams. The terrorists' use of human shields in densely populated areas, urban guerrilla warfare techniques, and kidnapping and assassination of soldiers and dissidents allowed them to neutralize the strengths of better equipped foot soldiers by drawing them into deadly ambushes and using improvised explosive devices and suicide bombing attacks (Wilkinson and Chu, 2006).

Responses to Terrorism

Conventional armies may find their institutional, bureaucratic approach to war to be particularly ineffective in fighting terrorism. Terrorists have nothing to gain from trying to engage with such a war machine. Designed for battlefields and Cold War encounters, conventional military power has proven to be especially limited in urban areas plagued by terrorism and insurgency, as Max Boot (2006) argues:

> Urban areas present a particularly difficult challenge: There are far more things to track (individuals) and far more obstructions (buildings, vehicles, trees, signs) than at sea or in the sky. Figuring out whether a person is a civilian or an insurgent is a lot harder than figuring out whether an unidentified aircraft is a civilian airliner or an enemy fighter. It is harder still to figure out how many enemy soldiers will resist or what stratagems they will employ. No machine has yet been invented that can penetrate human thought processes. Even with the best equipment in the world, U.S. forces frequently have been surprised by their adversaries.

The effective use of military hard power, in short, requires that several questions be thoughtfully addressed: How is homeland security served – and how is it hindered – by military operations abroad? When should military force be deployed against terrorists generally? When should it be applied against sovereign nations in an effort to reduce terrorism? Under what circumstances does the application of such force actually tend to reduce terrorism over the long term? Let us consider these questions by looking at three case studies, beginning with an early, successful post-9/11 episode involving the use of military power against terrorism: the invasion and overthrow of the Taliban government in Afghanistan. We then examine in more detail the cases of the much larger U.S. invasion of Iraq in 2003 and the Israeli invasion of Lebanon in 2006.

Case Study #1: The War in Afghanistan. Two of the great empires of the twentieth century – Great Britain and the Soviet Union – came to regard Afghanistan as an exceedingly inhospitable, indomitable, and ruinous hellhole. Both the British and the Soviets wasted vast resources and reputations in attempting to control the poor, but proud and tough inhabitants of a land of rugged terrain at high altitude, people who lived as they had for centuries in ancient tribal cultures and conditions of unfathomable poverty, illiteracy, and poor health.

From 1996 to 2001, the horrible conditions of the Afghan people were exacerbated by the severe autocratic regime of the Taliban government, under the rule of its Commander of the Faithful, Mullah Mohammed Omar. While Afghanis had not fared much better under the traditional rule of warlords, the Taliban managed to oppress the Afghan people with fanaticism institutionalized as government policy, as illustrated by the banning of kite flying and singing and dancing at weddings (Rashid, 2001). The Taliban also

254

engaged in extreme acts of religious intolerance, including the destruction of the 1,500-year-old statues of Buddha at Bamiyan in March 2001.

But the policy that doomed the Taliban in 2001 was its earlier agreement with Osama bin Laden that permitted al Qaeda to operate its international terrorist planning headquarters and training camps in Afghanistan. In the weeks after the 9/11 attack in 2001, a coalition of Western forces found a way to accomplish what the British and Soviets had been unable to do: use hard power effectively in Afghanistan, this time primarily to destroy terrorist havens and training camps and overthrow the Taliban government. The United States launched its war on terror on the ground in October 2001 with "Operation Enduring Freedom." During the first few months of the campaign, the effort was successful by all conventional standards. It was the product, first, of a clear consensus on the need for military intervention and the strong support of a broad coalition of NATO nations – including Australia, Canada, France, Germany, Great Britain, Italy, New Zealand, Pakistan, Portugal, and Spain. It was also the product of a thoughtfully developed and well-executed plan of coordinated military attack by ground and air forces.

In overthrowing the government that harbored the world's most prominent and dangerous terrorist organization, and in creating conditions for the legitimate popular election of a new government, the coalition forces achieved the strategic goal of creating a model for transformation in a land that had known only dictatorships and brutal authoritarian regimes. The operation sent two clear messages: first, that the West will not tolerate governments that support terrorism and terrorist groups, and second, that democratic governance is a viable alternative to authoritarian rule.

In the years that followed the immediate successes of military collaboration and political reform, the campaign to continue moving Afghanistan to a more stable and secure status – one less conducive to terrorism both there and elsewhere – proceeded less successfully. Kabul, the capital and urban heart of Afghanistan, was secured and returned to a condition of economic vibrancy for a time after 2001; however, the vast countryside soon returned to the long-prevailing rule of warlords and drug lords, its economy based once again on the harvesting of poppies for international opium trade – nearly 90 percent of the world's total supply. Kandahar, the major city in the south of Afghanistan, was beset by insecurity and violence. As Afghan citizens became increasingly disenchanted with the performance of President Hamid Karzai, the Taliban eventually re-emerged by 2006 in significant numbers as insurgents, supported largely by opium profits and operating out of sanctuaries in Pakistan. At that time, twenty-seven NATO nations were still officially part of the operation, but only five – the United States, Canada, Britain, the Netherlands, and Romania – had troops in Afghanistan's southern provinces where nearly all of the fighting with insurgents took place

(Kaplan, 2006). The NATO forces worked principally to root out the Taliban and help Afghan farmers replace the vast poppy fields with legitimate crops.

The initial military operation had been successful, but it became clear that much more than conventional military power is needed to realize the goals of building a secure, legitimate democratic government based on the rule of law and a reliable system of justice, especially in a land where these are hollow foreign abstractions. The legitimacy of the Afghan government was undermined in short order by corrupt and inept police, judges, and other government officials (Kaplan, 2006; "Losing Afghanistan," 2006). The development of infrastructure – both hard (roadways, sewage systems, public works programs, and so on) and soft (education, health, welfare and other social support services, banking, nongovernmental organizations, and so on) – was needed to create an economy based on trade in legitimate goods and services. However, that development was corroded by disorder, corruption, and fear and largely overlooked by the United States because of its preoccupation with the war in Iraq in the years following 2002.

Case Study #2: The War in Iraq. Eighteen months after its initial military successes against terrorism in Afghanistan, the United States led an invasion of Iraq – a campaign named "Operation Iraqi Freedom" – to overthrow Saddam Hussein and the ruling Ba'ath party. Although it received considerably less international support than the invasion of Afghanistan, the campaign in Iraq was nonetheless supported politically and publicly in the United States. The White House justified the operation on four primary grounds, all stimulated by the 9/11 attack on the United States: first, to find and remove weapons of mass destruction from Iraq; second, to transform Iraq from a brutal dictatorship that represented a peril to the Middle East and the world into a free and democratic state; third, to send a message to rogue states both in the region (particularly Iran and Syria) and elsewhere (North Korea, for one) that their threats to global economic interests generally – especially the disruption of oil supplies – and the dangers they posed to the well-being of the United States, in particular, would not be tolerated; and fourth, to win the war on terror.

The Iraqi army was defeated after just three weeks of intense air strikes and a highly mobile ground attack waged by a predominantly U.S.-British force, with modest help from a few other nations. Subsequent military operations did not go as well as they had in Afghanistan, however, revealing limits to the use of hard power invoked in the name of counterterrorism. At first, many Iraqis perceived the ground troops to be a force of liberators; this was especially true of the Kurdish and Shi'a populations, those most victimized by Hussein and his Sunni associates during the preceding thirty years. After a few months and then years, however, the invading troops became viewed less as rescuers and increasingly as an alien occupying power, especially among the Sunni minority but eventually among the Shi'a as well, as Iraqis grew increasingly impatient with the limited ability of the forces to restore either order or such basic services as electricity and clean water.

This perception of the Western military forces as alien occupiers rather than liberators deepened as hostile opponents – mostly Iraqi Sunni insurgents and terrorists recruited from neighboring Middle Eastern states, but many Shi'a as well – mobilized and became increasingly effective in driving the American forces into a more defensive posture. These strongly factionalized resistance forces succeeded also in destabilizing Iraqi attempts to build a local security infrastructure. A wedge was thus driven between the locals and the soldiers, who had difficulties at the outset in understanding the extraordinarily complex culture into which they waded, however noble their intentions. The Westerners were not only unfamiliar with Iraqi language, social customs, and taboos but they also did not fully understand important long-standing conflicts between and within the Sunni and Shi'ite sects, between tribal and ethnic factions, between and within militias and political groups, as well as other critical historical realities that shaped the thinking of the resistance movements (Galbraith, 2006; Ricks, 2006; Stewart, 2006).

It did not take long for impatient Iraqi citizens to grow hostile toward the Western forces, and then for U.S. citizens to grow impatient with the progress made by the Iraqis to "step up so that the U.S. could step down," in the words of the White House. What started as gestures of U.S. goodwill – sweets for the local children and promises of stability and freedom to the adults – eventually developed into a collapse of security and order and a siege mentality on both sides. Soldiers and marines showed increasingly less sensitivity to local social mores and values as threats to their own safety mounted. At the same time, terrorists in Iraq developed on-the-ground experience in finding and exploiting vulnerabilities in the occupying forces and developing more lethal weapons and means of deploying them. Especially devastating was the use of suicide car bombings and roadside improvised explosive devices (IEDs) – bombs built with directional blast features and explosive boosters that enable them to penetrate the armor of tanks and personnel carriers and that could be set off by mobile phones or radio signals sent by other readily accessible electronic equipment. IEDs accounted for about one-third of all fatalities to U.S. troops in Iraq[1] (Capaccio, 2005). As the Americans stepped down, they were taken less and less seriously by the Iraqi government and people, and Iraq descended into a civil war fought among local militia factions, especially in Baghdad and other fault lines between and within Sunni and Shi'a populations. A "surge" of additional troops and a new counterinsurgency strategy in 2007 reduced the violence toward the end of that year, but the deaths of more than 900 U.S. military forces in Iraq in 2007 were higher than in any preceding year.

Responses to Terrorism

Mark Danner (2006) summarizes the primary causes of the failure of the U.S. military effort in Iraq as follows:

> By dismissing and humiliating the soldiers and officers of the Iraqi army our leaders, in effect, did much to recruit the insurgency. By bringing far too few troops to secure Saddam's enormous arms depots they armed it. By bringing too few to keep order they presided over the looting and overwhelming violence and social disintegration that provided the insurgency such fertile soil. By blithely purging tens of thousands of the country's Baathist elite, whatever their deeds, and by establishing a muscle-bound and inept American occupation without an "Iraqi face," they created an increasing resentment among Iraqis that fostered the insurgency and encouraged people to shelter it. And by providing too few troops to secure Iraq's borders they helped supply its forces with an unending number of Sunni Islamic extremists from neighboring states. It was the foreign Islamists' strategy above all to promote their jihadist cause by provoking a sectarian civil war in Iraq; by failing to prevent their attacks and to protect the Shia who became their targets, the US leaders have allowed them to succeed.

There were a few silver linings in these dark clouds, most notably the capture and trial of Saddam Hussein, the liberation of the Iraqi Kurdish and Shi'a populations from oppressive and often brutal Sunni control, and an historic election in January 2005 to create a body that would form a legitimate constitutional authority for Iraq. But these gains were largely offset by a rise in the power of well-armed Shi'ite militias, financed largely by Iran, with logistical support for Sunni insurgents from al Qaeda, general support from Syria as a haven and passageway for armaments and supplies, and a flight of the middle class from Baghdad to Jordan and other Middle Eastern sanctuaries. While the surge of U.S. troops in 2007 and new counterinsurgency strategy helped to stabilize conditions, the elusive goal remains: a self-sustainable democracy perceived as legitimate throughout the Shi'ite, Kurdish, and Sunni populations and capable of defending itself both against insurgents from within and against terrorists supported by hostile neighbors, particularly Iran (against whom Iraq had waged a major war from 1980 to 1988, at a cost of one million men).

The Iraq War also inflicted damage on the capacity of the United States to use hard power against terrorism in places where the need may have been much greater, such as Afghanistan and Pakistan. The war turned out to be exorbitantly expensive, with costs for just the first five years in the neighborhood of $500 billion, 4,000 American lives lost, and more than 30,000 other serious U.S. casualties (Belasco, 2007; Congressional Budget Office, 2007; Reuters, 2007; Stiglitz and Bilmes, 2008). Enlistments and re-enlistments for the U.S. military services became strained by lagging support for the war and existing forces became stretched to levels that had not been seen for decades, while terrorist activity in Afghanistan and Pakistan worsened. The support of the U.S. public for the effort was weakened further as the political justifications for the effort shifted, benchmarks for success remained ambiguous, with an ever present danger of violence both in Iraq and in neighboring countries (Byman and Pollack, 2006).

With regard to the four initial goals of the war in Iraq, the first, finding and removing weapons of mass destruction, turned out to be a nonissue, as no significant stores of such weapons turned up there. The second, transforming Iraq into a free and democratic state, remained a distant goal, as the country descended into sectarian strife and a virtual partitioning into three regions: Shia, Sunni, and Kurd. Instead of a free and vibrant country, Iraq became a strife-torn place that produced millions of refugees throughout the region (Packer, 2007; Tyson, 2007).

As to the third goal, sending a message to rogue states, the effort had mixed effects. It appears to have had some desirable effects on regimes in Libya and Saudi Arabia, but served clearly to harden the positions of Korea, Syria, and other dangerous authoritarian states. Of even greater significance, it radicalized Islam and strengthened the influence of Iran in the Middle East immeasurably (Galbraith, 2007; Packer, 2007).

Attaining the fourth goal, winning the war on terror, appears to have been one of the most serious failures of the war in Iraq. The 2006 National Intelligence Estimate – a consensus based on the assessments of sixteen U.S. intelligence agencies – concluded, "Although we cannot measure the extent of the spread with precision, a large body of all-source reporting indicates that activists identifying themselves as jihadists, although a small percentage of Muslims, are increasing in both number and geographic dispersion." The report attributed the increase largely to the war in Iraq: "The Iraq conflict has become the 'cause celebre' for jihadists, breeding a deep resentment of U.S. involvement in the Muslim world and cultivating supporters for the global jihadist movement" (White House, 2006).[2] According to counterterrorism officials in Pakistan, the United States, and Europe, al Qaeda's core leadership, referred to as "al Qaeda Central" by intelligence analysts, grew stronger following the invasion of Iraq, rebuilding the organizational framework that had been severely damaged after the U.S.-led invasion of Afghanistan in 2001 (Whitlock, 2007b).

Some of the sharpest critics of the invasion of Iraq have been members of the military. Many had long raised the criticisms noted earlier by Danner (2006), pointing out serious flaws in the manner in which the campaign was conducted. They argued that there were too few troops on the ground in the early stages to establish security. In addition, the decisions to disband the Iraqi army and Ba'athist government were disastrous, resulting not only in the loss of their services in the effort to restore order but also alienating them and converting many of them to adversaries in the process (W. Clark, 2004; Galbraith, 2006; Ricks, 2006).

Others questioned the heavy reliance on military power to fight terrorism generally and the tendency for proponents of the invasion to deny the reality of a strong insurgency movement (Packer, 2006a). Several argued that the misapplication of U.S. military power in Iraq, invoked in the name of defeating terrorism but lacking a coherent counterinsurgency strategy warranted by the dominant reality of the conflict – sectarian strife that escalated to civil war among rival militia forces – served instead as a recruitment tool for terrorist and insurgency forces, breeding further resentment throughout Islam and elsewhere, and increasing deadly reprisals. The result was to empower terrorists and insurgents in the name of counterterrorism, weaken worldwide support for the United States, and reduce the security of the American public and the rest of the world in the process (Bacevich, 2005; Boyer, 2006; W. Clark, 2004; Gordon and Trainor, 2006; Murtha and Plashal, 2004; Shanker, 2006; Solaro, 2006; Zinni, 2006).

The Iraq experience provided a rich laboratory for insurgent operations in Afghanistan and elsewhere on how to defeat sophisticated military technology through stealth, cunning, and the use of inexpensive yet sophisticated weaponry of their own. This laboratory operation in Iraq received considerable support from outsiders with strong sectarian and political interests in the region and equally strong religious and ideological opposition to Western influence in Islamic cultures. The development of new battlefield tactics came to neutralize technological superiority, rendering much of the sophisticated weaponry and Cold-War-era training of Western ground and air operations obsolete and radically transforming the conduct of warfare itself for the twenty-first century.

A goal of the U.S. operation in Iraq was to produce stability through democracy there and throughout the region, and the use of military power in Iraq was in fact followed by a taste of democracy and popular elections. But the long-term prospects for freedom and democracy are less clear. The use of hard power in Iraq may instead have contributed more to instability and hostility toward the United States and the spread of sectarian violence in the region and elsewhere for years to come. In any event, even democracy provides no guarantee against terrorism, especially if it takes the form of a democratic theocracy, which could embolden terrorists and reduce the long-term prospects for reducing terrorism.

Political scientist Eliot Cohen (2006) observes, "It will be important in future years to settle whether the Iraq war was the right idea badly executed, an enterprise doomed to disappoint, or simply folly." Some argue the former, that the size of the military force used to establish democracy was too small to control the forces of insurgency on the ground (e.g., Gordon and Trainor, 2006; Ricks, 2006). Others argue that the United States engaged in a hopeless undertaking to begin with, as with prior Western attempts to hold together the former Yugoslavia. Iraq's history suggests that strong dictatorial rule is the only way to quell the deep divisions among sects, ethnic groups, and tribes that make up what we call a country (e.g., Stansfield, 2007; Wong, 2007). Moreover, the United States lacked the legitimacy and consent, the political will, and resources needed to hold Iraq together and create secure conditions in which a democracy could thrive there (e.g., Stewart, 2006).

One fact is clear: the unilateral use of military power and rhetoric by the United States to justify the invasion of Iraq caused people throughout the world who had been sympathetic to the United States in the immediate aftermath of the 2001 attacks on New York and Washington to turn their sympathies elsewhere. Public opinion polls abroad revealed plummeting support for U.S. policies – largely because of the war in Iraq – in every country for which data have been available, and especially in the Middle East, where the need for support has been particularly great (Cillizza and Goldfarb, 2006; Kohut and Stokes, 2006; Pew Global Attitudes Project, 2004). Much of the negative assessment may be a product of hindsight bias – the tendency for people to claim that they were always opposed to a policy only after events changed for the worse (Vedantam, 2006). The escalation of negative assessments was real nonetheless. In addition, while the United States could have been devoting resources and energy toward the job-producing benefits of globalization throughout the world, it was "too busy settling disputes between Sunnis and Shiites in downtown Baghdad" (Zakaria, 2006).

It remains to be seen what lessons will ultimately be learned about the application of hard power in Iraq in the name of a war against terrorism. For Mark Danner (2006), the lesson of the war was simple: it clearly and decisively disproved "the proposition ... that bold action must always make us safer."

Case study #3: Hezbollah and Israel. For more than fifty years, since its establishment as a sovereign nation in 1948, Israel had become accustomed to winning wars against Arab adversaries very quickly, usually within a week. The 2006 war with Hezbollah in Lebanon once again saw Israel impose substantial losses on a hostile adversary. Israel again killed hundreds of enemy fighters and destroyed much of its weaponry, but this time the fighting was much more intense than ever before, and it lasted for a month. Also for the first time, Israel did not wipe out the enemy forces or its leaders, nor did it disable the enemy's capacity to rain hundreds of deadly rockets daily for several weeks on cities in northern Israel. Israel had underestimated both the quantity and quality of Hezbollah's accumulated weaponry and the extent of logistical and training support it had received from Iran, as well as logistical support from Syria. Many of the Israeli battlefield deaths were the result of unexpectedly powerful armor-piercing antitank missiles.

Israel also underestimated Hezbollah's capacity to win the media war. The 2006 campaign was initiated by the kidnapping by Hezbollah of two Israeli soldiers and the killing of three other Israeli soldiers just inside the Israeli border. Israel responded with an attack on Hezbollah mobile rocket-launching positions in southern Lebanon that killed some 10,000 innocent Lebanese civilian bystanders and all but wiped out a growing physical infrastructure and vibrant young Lebanese economy. The Israeli response also substantially undermined the country's fragile new, moderate government. The result was to shift sympathy and political support to Hezbollah. Many Lebanese were angry at Hezbollah for its aggressive acts, but the vast destruction of much of Lebanon was inflicted by Israel, not Hezbollah. The fighting stopped after a month, and the United Nations sent a peace-keeping force to help the Lebanese army restore order in southern Lebanon. When the dust had settled, the losses that Israel had inflicted on Hezbollah forces were overshadowed by the severe losses incurred by Lebanese innocents, and Israel was unable to accomplish what it had set out to do and had succeeded in doing over the years in previous campaigns against Arabs in Palestine and Lebanon. Hezbollah cultivated further goodwill after the hostilities ended by distributing money from Iran to Lebanese citizens who had lost their homes: $12,000 in U.S. currency to each family. As a result, Hezbollah leader Hassan Nasrallah rose to iconic status throughout the region, both as a military hero and caring soul.

Israel's inability to destroy Hezbollah's capacity to fire rockets into Haifa and other sites in northern Israel was attributed to a variety of factors: flawed intelligence, poorly trained and inadequately equipped reservists, terrain that is virtually impassable for heavy tanks, rusty fighting tactics, and weak support from Israeli politicians at the highest levels (Wilkinson and Chu, 2006). These miscalculations resulted in an emboldened Hezbollah, a delegitimized independent democracy in Lebanon, a more frustrated and less secure Israeli people, and a Middle East even more solidly unified against Israel than before. They also induced a shift in the locus of power from Sunni Arabism to Shi'ite Islamism centered in Tehran, which had created Hezbollah in the first place and then provided strong encouragement and support to it, along the way deflecting attention from international concerns about Iran's rapidly expanding nuclear capacity.

Former Secretary of State Henry Kissinger (2006b) argues that the implications of Hezbollah's success go well beyond Lebanon's borders. Its success represents the emergence of a network of military power rooted in Iran that threatens the very stability of the nation-state system in the Middle East and possibly beyond:

> We are witnessing a carefully conceived assault, not isolated terrorist attacks, on the international system of respect for sovereignty and territorial integrity. The creation of organizations like Hezbollah and al-Qaida symbolizes that transnational loyalties are replacing national ones. The driving force behind

this challenge is the jihadist conviction that it is the existing order that is illegitimate, not the Hezbollah and jihad method of fighting it. For the jihad's adherents, the battlefield cannot be defined by frontiers based on principles of world order they reject; what we call terror is, to the jihadists, an act of war to undermine illegitimate regimes.

Let us turn now to a more thorough consideration of this question of legitimacy and the moral use of military force against terrorism, the conditions under which it is justified, and considerations that shape its application.

B. Just War Theory and Terrorism

Military hard power is widely accepted on both moral and utilitarian grounds as necessary to counter aggression, especially aggression against innocents. Terrorism clearly qualifies for the application of such power, as long as that force is applied according to basic rules of ethics. Moral philosophers and military historians have sought and proposed such rules for centuries. The ethical principles set forth by philosopher Michael Walzer (1992), rooted in social contract theory, provide a body of moral doctrine on war that came to be widely accepted by scholars and military practitioners alike in the twentieth century. Walzer observes that nonviolence as practiced along the lines of Gandhi is the noblest of prospects, but without civilian participation on an unprecedentedly large scale, it cannot be counted on to end warfare. Instead, we are left to adhere to a basic set of rules of military engagement, to deal effectively with the moral dilemmas of such engagements as they arise, and to work effectively to prevent the occurrence and reoccurrence of moral lapses.

What should be the basic shape of such rules? What constitutes a moral lapse in war? The key condition for a war to be just, according to Walzer, is that both the ends and the means of the war must be just. *Jus ad bellum* refers to the condition that the cause or ends of the war are just, and *jus in bello* refers to the condition that the manner or means of waging the war is just.

The first criterion for *jus ad bellum* – that the cause is just – holds that military force is justified only as a defensive action, when an act of aggression has occurred against a sovereign nation, violating both its political sovereignty and its territorial integrity, which Walzer asserts are to nations essentially what life and liberty are to individuals. Walzer argues further that preventive wars are justifiable against a prospective aggressor only when an act of aggression is about to occur with virtual certainty and when the preventive action is essential to survival. He also distinguishes preventive wars – campaigns that can last for years – from preemptive strikes, which are justified only when three factors are present: the manifest intent to injure, a degree

Policy Box 9.1. Use of the Military to Confront Terrorism

In this chapter, we considered three recent case studies of the use of military power for dealing with terrorism. From these and other examples over the past 150 years – several are discussed elsewhere in this book – a mixed picture emerges. Military force has occasionally been an effective tool in countering terrorism, as in the cases of Afghanistan, Bosnia, and Libya. However, it is most effective against terrorism only when used with extreme care and humility and as a last resort, with full awareness of the consequences to intended targets and innocents alike. If the force is widely perceived to have been misused, the costs and consequences can be severe and persistent. Essayist Jim Hoagland (2006) argues that the improper use of military power is wrong on other grounds as well:

> Military intervention can be justified when it changes things for the better. It does not have to be perfect. But conducting a military occupation that has lost the ability to change the situation for the better for those being occupied is unwise and ultimately untenable. It is also immoral.

General Wesley K. Clark, who led a successful alliance of military forces in the Kosovo war in 1999, draws from the experiences of Kosovo, Afghanistan, and Iraq to elaborate on Hoagland's assessment. He argues that before launching an invasion against the forces of terrorism it is necessary to define what it means to change the situation for the better and then ensure that the means are available to make the change: he warns, "Don't ever, ever go to war unless you can describe and create a more desirable end state" (W. Clark, 2007).

How can the military create a more desirable end state? According to the Department of Defense (2007) *Army/Marine Corps Counterinsurgency Field Manual*, designed and written principally by Army General David Petraeus, the key is to deprive the terrorists of legitimacy while establishing and enhancing your own. "To establish legitimacy," the manual says, "commanders transition security activities from combat operations to law enforcement as quickly as feasible. When insurgents are seen as criminals, they lose public support." To discourage the production of more terrorists requires a shift from conventional "enemy-centric" thinking about how to destroy terrorists to a larger "population-centric" strategy of winning over the population from which the terrorists emerge (Hoffman, 2007).

In confronting terrorism in years to come, the military will continue to be seriously tested by changes in the nature of its adversaries, by ethical questions pertaining to particular methods of operation and accountability for the acts of individuals, and by changes in the sophistication of the technologies available to terrorists. The military will have to adapt its strategies and tactics for engaging with terrorists in the process. In doing so, however, the question of legitimacy, raised so prominently in the *Counterinsurgency Field Manual,* will remain of paramount importance. It will be essential that the military neither suspend nor relax its core values or those of the society it serves – even as its members occasionally pay the ultimate price in the process.

of active preparation, and when failure to strike preemptively would greatly magnify the risk to territorial integrity or political independence. These principles are applicable to a nation's defense against terrorism, even when the aggressor is not a sovereign nation.

In the case of the U.S. invasion of Iraq, the White House made what appeared in early 2003 to be a compelling case that the cause was just, that Saddam Hussein was a menace to the United States and the rest of the world, and that failure to remove the immediate threat presented by his weapons of mass destruction threatened the United States, the Middle East, and the entire world. As events unfolded, however, it became clear that the evidence used to support this case was not assembled and presented in a manner that many would consider legitimate. Evidence to the contrary collected by the CIA and by the United Nations Monitoring, Verification and Inspection Commission (UNMOVIC) was ignored or dismissed, and not presented to the public (Isikoff and Corn, 2006). It is possible, of course, that events might have turned out even more badly than they did for Iraq, the Middle East and the United States had the invasion not taken place, although few have attempted seriously to make this argument. In any event, the United States lost considerable moral authority and prestige in the world because of its failure to make an honest, balanced, and therefore legitimate *jus ad bellum* case for its decision to invade Iraq in 2003.

Two essential aspects of *jus in bello* are especially pertinent to the problem of terrorism: *discrimination* and *proportionality*. The participants in war must discriminate between combatants and noncombatants and should prevent harm to noncombatants to the extent possible. Thus the principle of discrimination requires that the combatants be sensitive to the goal of minimizing collateral damage, which is clearly violated when either side uses civilian populations as "human shields" to protect themselves against attack.

Responses to Terrorism

Proportionality refers to the extent of force used: military action should be calibrated so that it is sufficient to achieve the primary objectives of a war, but not substantially stronger than that. Thus the principle of proportionality contradicts the idea often emphasized in counterterrorist campaigns that terrorists must be completely destroyed to ensure the safety of civilization. The commonsense rationale for this principle is that civilization is lost when counterterrorist activities use unjust terrorist tactics in the name of protecting civilization. This rationale has practical ramifications: the failure of a counterterrorism effort to honor either the principle of proportionality or that of discrimination can be exposed and exploited by the other side, thereby undermining the moral authority of a counterterrorist campaign. The abuses of detainees at the Abu Ghraib prison in Iraq, revealed in 2004, stands as a clear example of the devastating impact that such violations of *jus in bello* principles can have on the success of a military counterterrorist effort.

A fundamental problem with the just war theory is that it applies primarily to wars or threats of war between sovereign nations – real wars, not rhetorical ones, such as wars against international drug trafficking or terrorism. As originally conceived, the just war theory does not apply to matters that are between sovereign nations and groups of individuals operating outside of legitimate sovereign authority. Walzer updated his just war theory in 2005 to accommodate some of the contemporary issues raised by terrorism, but his update is more a statement against the invasion of Iraq than a revision of his earlier principles of how a sovereign nation should deal with terrorists. In his updated version he adds to the principles of *jus ad bellum* and *jus in bello* the principle of *jus post bellum*, which holds that a nation using military power to deal with terrorism in another country has a responsibility to take reasonable measures to restore the invaded country to an acceptable condition after the terrorist threat has been dispatched. As Walzer (2005) explains, "Surely occupying powers are morally bound to think seriously about what they are going to do in someone else's country." With regard to the aftermath of the invasion of Iraq, Walzer adds, "That moral test we have obviously failed to meet."

Attempting to apply just war theory to the problem of terrorism raises another problem, which is related to the principles of discrimination and proportionality: the theory fails to distinguish fully between strategic (long-term goal-related) and tactical (related to the objectives of specific battles) aspects of conflicts. Military historian Caleb Carr (2006) observes that military failures in the Middle East are often the product of failures to exercise tactical restraint, especially in subjecting civilians to large-scale suffering, intended or otherwise, to achieve a strategic advantage. Carr notes that, to achieve such advantage, it may be necessary to absorb smaller blows in the short term in order to maintain the support needed for the delivery of decisive strikes later, a central tenet of the great ancient Chinese military thinker, Sun

Tzu (2002). Walzer addresses the notion of sacrificing lives in the short term to spare many more lives in the long term, but the ability to achieve a lasting peace in the presence of terrorists operating with long-term apocalyptic designs outside of sovereign nations clearly calls for something more than Walzer's theory provides.

U.S. General Wesley K. Clark (2007) summarizes and simplifies the case against the use of military force to fight terrorism by considering the lessons of successes and failures over the previous decade. He concludes:

> The big lesson is simply this: War is the last, last, last resort. It always brings tragedy and rarely brings glory. Take it from a general who won: The best war is the one that doesn't have to be fought, and the best military is the one capable and versatile enough to deter the next war in the first place.

A more definitive, comprehensive theory of the just response to terrorism, along lines that parallel Walzer's earlier work and accounting for significant features of recent wars in the Middle East, has yet to be established.[3] The barriers to developing such a theory are considerable, especially because the distinctions among terrorism, insurgency, civil war, and wars of liberation remain blurred on the ground. These barriers are particularly formidable when fledgling democracies are called on to resolve them in an even-handed manner and in the presence of larger forces operating beyond the state. In Lebanon, for example, members of Hezbollah serve in the parliament, operating as a state within a state, and the Lebanese army and government were too weak to disarm Hezbollah when it launched its attack on Israel in 2006. Hezbollah achieved some legitimacy by providing both security and social services to Lebanon's Shi'ite population, thanks largely to substantial support from Iran, but Hezbollah's attacks on Israel were more than the Lebanese government could handle.

In Iraq, meanwhile, sectarian militias conducted systematic attacks against civilians regarded as enemies in the community, as in the case of the Mahdi army of Muqtada al Sadr defending the Shi'a community in the Baghdad area against devastating attacks by disgruntled Sunni insurgents and al Qaeda terrorists. The newly formed Iraqi government was not prepared to resolve the problem any more than the Lebanese government could control Hezbollah. When people have little experience of governments operating ethically and effectively to protect and serve such local interests, they become inclined to take matters into their own hands.

We have yet to establish how external powers can adapt just war principles to deal with such problems. The just response to terrorism is not always effective in achieving peace and order, and the effective response is often unjust. It is essential that policymakers remain clear about the importance of the moral side of the ledger, at the very least in the interest of maintaining legitimacy.

C. Unilateral vs. Collective Responses

The tension between a response to terrorism that is just and one that is effective can be worked out collectively through a consensus of sovereign nations, which enhances the response by lending legitimacy to it, often under the authority of international law. Put bluntly, if terrorism brings misery, and misery loves company, then nations subject to terrorism from the same source should be inclined to collaborate against that source. And as the number of nations involved in such an alliance of power grows, there should be greater power in numbers, as well as greater opportunities for shared information, more opportunities to realize economies of specialization, and increased moral authority for the enterprise.

The alternative is to operate unilaterally, which can have strong negative effects: doing so relinquishes the advantages of collective action in deterring and defeating terrorism and, in the process, may alienate others who have similar interests in preventing terrorism and responding to it when prevention fails.

Of course, collective action against terrorism is not always necessary, especially when the scale of a terrorist act or group is small or its nature unique, of little concern to others. Moreover, multilateral responses can complicate matters, creating the need to coordinate activities carefully, providing greater opportunities for leaks of sensitive information, and allowing terrorists to play one or more members of the alliance against others. Nations can agree amicably not to collaborate in certain counterterrorist operations.

The United States has a long legacy of unilateralism. George Washington's farewell address in 1796 included a strong warning against foreign entanglements:

> As avenues to foreign influence in innumerable ways, such attachments are particularly alarming to the truly enlightened and independent Patriot. How many opportunities do they afford to tamper with domestic factions, to practise the arts of seduction, to mislead public opinion, to influence or awe the Public Councils! Such an attachment of a small or weak, towards a great and powerful nation, dooms the former to be the satellite of the latter.... The great rule of conduct for us, in regard to foreign nations, is, in extending our commercial relations, to have with them as little political connexion as possible.[4]

President Washington's skepticism was echoed even more strongly by John Quincy Adams, who wrote an influential essay in 1793 asserting that real independence required that the United States sever itself "from all European interests and European politics" (Gaddis, 2004). Adams argued that America should neither accept binding obligations nor align its interests with those of other nations, nor should it pledge mutual support when its interests were challenged. He put these principles in action in dealing with Great Britain and with Spanish authorities in Latin America.

U.S. unilateralism reached a peak under the Monroe Doctrine of 1823, which held that European nations should end their colonization of the Americas and their interference in the affairs of sovereign nations in the Americas, including the United States, Mexico, and the nations of Central and South America and the Caribbean. In return, the United States would remain neutral in wars among European nations and in wars between European nations and their colonies. Presidents McKinley, Theodore Roosevelt, Taft, and Wilson practiced versions of unilateralism with interventions in the Caribbean, Central America, and Mexico. Unilateralism has remained a staple of U.S. foreign policy up to the present.

At the same time, the United States proved to be an effective multilateral collaborator in military operations throughout most of the twentieth century: in the two world wars, in the creation and operation of NATO, and in a variety of peace-keeping actions sponsored by the United Nations. It moved in a decidedly multilateral direction under the presidency of Franklin D. Roosevelt, who entered into a variety of international agreements in a strategy of cooperation with allies to defeat Nazism, fascism, and other forms of authoritarian rule. Presidents Truman, Eisenhower, Kennedy, Nixon, Ford, and Carter carried forward FDR's spirit of collaboration with Western European and other free world nations throughout the Cold War era, toward the goal of prevailing against communism.

A fairly recent multilateral operation that was by most accounts quite successful was the UN Protection Force (UNPROFOR) deployed in Bosnia in the 1990s. The United States was one of forty nations that contributed troops to help bring an end to hostilities that had cost more than 100,000 lives among various factions of the former Yugoslav republic. The UNPROFOR contingent of nearly 40,000 personnel operated security zones in Sarajevo, Srebrenica, Tuzla, and elsewhere; protected the Sarajevo airport; and coordinated with NATO to manage the interdiction of military aircraft in the Bosnia and Herzegovina skies. The three-year operation cost about five billion dollars and resulted in 320 deaths. The operation ended with the Dayton Peace Accord in 1995, which delineated the geographic boundaries and structural and political divisions of Bosnia and Herzegovina.

A parallel international effort, under the United Nations, was the 1993 creation of an international tribunal to prosecute crimes of state terrorism committed in Bosnia: the International Criminal Tribunal for the former Yugoslavia (ICTY). Located at The Hague, in Holland, the ICTY has interviewed thousands of victims and witnesses of the crimes and associated activities. Slobodan Milošević was the first sitting head of state indicted for war crimes under the ICTY. He was convicted for crimes against humanity at the tribunal in 2001. More than fifty others were sentenced under the jurisdiction of this tribunal in its first fourteen years of operation.

We noted earlier that the 2001 invasion of Afghanistan was another example of effective collaboration among nations with similar interests in reducing the menace of violence against innocent people. After the operation in Afghanistan, however, international support for the U.S. war on terror diminished rapidly, beginning with Operation Iraqi Freedom. One of the frequently made accusations was that the United States was operating much in the manner of an empire: unilaterally and arrogantly, without regard to the legitimate interests of other nations (Brzezinski, 2005; Nye, 2002). Others have countered that it is perfectly in order for the United States to step up and do the right thing – to promote liberty and democracy throughout the world and use its vast military power to defeat authoritarianism and terrorism – when other nations refuse to do so (Ferguson, 2004; Gaddis, 2004). They assert that in emphasizing freedom and democracy, the United States shifts the notion of "empire" to a more honorable calling than empires of old, which were interested primarily in the exercise of power and the accumulation of wealth at the expense of the colonized nations. Others have observed that freedom and democracy are little more than lofty platitudes in the absence of the provision of basic security, a precondition for any stable form of government (Kissinger, 2007).

D. The Tactic of Torture

Suppose your government has captured a terrorist suspect who may have important knowledge about terrorist plans, activities, leaders, and collaborators. How should your government establish that the suspect really does have such information? How should it then extract the information from the suspect? Are coercive techniques justifiable? Under what circumstances? What frameworks are available to guide the exercise of discretion in managing the extraction of such information? These questions raise both ethical and instrumental issues, and reasonable, intelligent people do not agree fully on how to resolve them.

1. What Is Torture?

Guidelines against torture have been set forth by several international bodies, including the 1949 Geneva Conventions, Amnesty International, and the United Nations. Under its 1984 convention against torture and other cruelty, the UN defined torture as follows:

> any act by which severe pain or suffering, whether physical or mental, is
> intentionally inflicted on a person for such purposes as obtaining from him

or a third person information or a confession, punishing him for an act he or a third person has committed or is suspected of having committed, or intimidating or coercing him or a third person, or for any reason based on discrimination of any kind, when such pain or suffering is inflicted by or at the instigation of or with the consent or acquiescence of a public official or other person acting in an official capacity (Part I, Article 1, Number 1).

Torture, in short, involves the use of techniques that impose grave physical or emotional harm on subjects under interrogation or coerced confinement, or that threaten life or impose severe physical or psychological suffering.

Notice that this definition involves the treatment of subjects being interrogated or held involuntarily. Coercive techniques are also used against trainees in military boot camps and police academies, but these do not qualify as torture because the trainees chose to be there, understood generally what they were getting into, and signed statements indicating their awareness of the conditions of emotional and physical duress as instruments for developing conditioning for difficult situations, including that of being hostages subject to torture. The same coercive techniques used in boot camp that do not qualify as torture against volunteers could qualify as torture if used against detainees.

Specific techniques that fit clearly within the definition of torture we use here include the infliction of severe pain, mock executions, the simulation of suffocation or drowning (e.g., "waterboarding"), and severe deprivations of sleep or nutrition. Such methods are in violation of 18 USC Section 2340 (the federal torture statute) and Army Field Manual 34–52 ("Intelligence Interrogation"). More ambiguous are various forms of humiliation and the imposition of mild elements of physical discomfort, such as forced standing, shackling, the use of stress positions, extreme heat or cold, and moderate sleep deprivation.

2. Is Torture Ever Justifiable?

The argument in favor of the use of torture in the era of terrorism is that desperate times call for desperate security measures. Proponents argue that the problem of terrorism was neither envisioned nor appreciated when the rules about torture were drawn up in Geneva or at the United Nations. This position was advanced in a memorandum from then-White House Counsel Alberto Gonzales to President George W. Bush in 2002 on the question of whether the Geneva Conventions apply to al Qaeda and Taliban detainees:

> The war on terror is a new kind of war . . . in my judgment this new paradigm renders obsolete Geneva's strict limitations on questioning of enemy prisoners and renders quaint some of its provisions requiring that captured enemy be

271

afforded such things as commissary privileges, scrip (i.e., advances of monthly pay) athletic uniforms and scientific instruments.

The Ticking Time Bomb. A staple argument to support the use of torture is the hypothetical case of an apprehended terrorist who knows about a nuclear device that will detonate soon unless drastic action is taken. It is clearly preferable to save many thousands of innocent lives than to satisfy what strike many as fussy legal constraints about mistreatment of the terrorist. A standard response to this argument has three parts: first, such a case has not in fact happened and is not likely to present itself, despite its common portrayal in public entertainments; second, the hypothetical, based on a person known to have the information, may provide the basis for routinely torturing people who are only suspected of having such information but who in fact do not; and third, in the event that a person should show up who fits the hypothetical, who is known in fact to possess such information, then an interrogator who uses whatever means necessary to extract the information is likely to be exonerated from any law against torture (Ignatius, 2005c).

The second of these three points provides the basis for a strong argument against any use of torture: there is a slippery slope from the ticking-time-bomb hypothetical to the widespread use of torture (Ignatieff, 2004). Acceptance of the idea that torture may be morally legitimate can turn decent people into bad apples, causing them to blur distinctions between the hypothetical case of terrorists known to have critical information and real-world suspects who do not. People who consider themselves to be patriots may not be inclined to compromise their country's security for a moral abstraction that applies to an enemy alien, especially after they've lost buddies in warfare. According to national security authority Phillip Carter (2004), a former Army officer,

> There are few slopes more slippery than the one from small war crimes to large ones, as evidenced by the incremental movement of U.S. interrogation tactics from "a little bit of smacky face," as one intelligence officer described the officially sanctioned tactics at Gitmo to the *Wall Street Journal*, to the abuses depicted in the Abu Ghraib photographs ... once discipline is lost, it is nearly impossible to restore.

The debate over the use of torture became particularly heated after September 11, 2001, especially in light of the widespread public fear of weapons of mass destruction and the nasty "fog of war" conditions of Afghanistan and Iraq. The essay by Geoffrey Nunberg in Box 9.2 sets forth essential elements of this debate.

Nunberg suggests that certain conditions might justify the use of torture, that torture might in some cases be the lesser of two evils. We take here a less equivocal position, on the grounds of both ethics and effectiveness:

Torture is neither legal nor ethically acceptable.

Satar Jabar, one of the prisoners tortured at Abu Ghraib. Jabar was apprehended for vehicle theft; he had no known connections to terrorist activities.

Torture is inhumane and immoral, a violation of human rights, and a violation of the law. It is not the lesser of two evils, because there are effective alternatives to torture that are not evil. Torture has been found also to be *in*effective or even counterproductive: people under torture will say anything to end their suffering, regardless of the reliability of what they say (Applebaum, 2005). Moreover, a government that allows torture encourages its adversaries to inflict torture when the tables are turned. Such a government also loses legitimacy, even when the act of torture remains out of public view. Thus, the use of torture can be extremely counterproductive.

Box 9.2. Conversations about Torture

– Geoffrey Nunberg

In 1978, the philosopher Henry Shue wrote an influential essay about torture that began with the sentence, "Whatever one may have to say about torture, there appear to be moral reasons for not saying it." Once we bring the subject up, he asked, mightn't we risk loosening the inhibitions against the whole terrible business? It was easy to have that feeling over the last month or so, as you listened to the country debate just how much cruelty and degradation we were going to allow in interrogating terror suspects. I mean, were we really having this conversation?

In the end, Shue himself wound up saying that torture had to be talked about – as he put it, "Pandora's Box is already open." But then the topic is irresistible to philosophy professors, since it seems ideally suited to getting students to question their most cherished moral certainties. On the face of things, you'd figure the prohibition of torture would be a top candidate for a categorical moral rule; as the UN convention on torture puts it, there are no exceptional circumstances that justify torture. But what about the scenario of a captured terrorist who has hidden a nuclear bomb that's set to go off in a couple of hours. Would torture be justified then?

Some people try to dodge the dilemma by saying that torture never works anyway. But that "never" is a leap of faith – how can you be sure? And anyway, that response leaves the deeper moral question open: would it be okay for you to torture the terrorist if you were convinced it would get him to tell you where the bomb is? Say no and you're risking a million lives; say yes and you've suddenly become a situational relativist, balancing the moral cost of inflicting pain and humiliation against the potential saving of lives.

Most of us find these hypothetical scenarios troubling, as we damn well should. But if we're honest we'll admit that the idea that torture might some-times be justified can also kindle a prurient thrill. That explains the appeal of the last two seasons of "24," where episode after episode presents agent Jack Bauer with another opportunity for shooting someone in the kneecap or shocking him with electric wires, always in the interest of getting him to reveal some bit of life-saving information. Whatever your intellectual position on torture, you don't change the channel.

This may be a morbid fascination, but it has deep roots in the folklore of childhood. Who doesn't recall all the ordeals and torture games that children visit on each other? Depending on where or when you grew up, you called them pink belly, the Indian or Chinese rope burn, the noogie, or the Russian haircut (the names often evoked alien archetypes of cruelty and inhumanity, since even then we knew that Americans didn't do this stuff).* But the rituals were compelling even so – a setting for acting out our forbidden fantasies and proving our toughness.

Not surprisingly, the administration was at pains to keep any of that atavistic fascination with torture from bubbling to the surface. We're not suggesting permitting actual torture, they insisted – if a terrorist doesn't break under waterboarding or sleep deprivation, we're not going to go all Jack Bauer on him, ticking bomb or no. The challenge was to find language that made the appropriate distinctions: carving the grave breaches of the Geneva Convention from the lesser ones, the inhuman from the merely regrettable, the stuff that shocks the conscience from the stuff that merely rocks it back on its heels a bit.

"Alternative sets of procedures," "enhanced interrogation techniques," "vigorous questioning" – the phrases had a comforting sound of professional routine. In his September 15 speech, in fact, President Bush used the word "professionals" 26 times, by way of reassuring Americans that the people administering the procedures would not only know what they were doing, but would presumably take no pleasure in doing it.

Still, some of the administration's supporters were clearly enjoying the discussion, particularly when it came to making light of the procedures under consideration. We're not talking about maiming or killing, they said, and these people have it coming. And anyway, what's the big deal? When the subject of sleep deprivation came up at a House Judiciary Committee hearing last week, Republican Tom Feeney of Florida observed that "there is not an American mom that is guaranteed eight hours of sleep every night." And if playing loud music is inhumane treatment, he added, "virtually every teenager I know is torturing mom and dad." Bill O'Reilly reported that one terrorism suspect had broken when subjected to Red Hot Chili Peppers music, then added, "Well, wouldn't you?" And The *American Spectator*'s Emmett Tyrell argued that waterboarding was infinitely less dangerous than skateboarding, which causes sprained ankles and broken bones.

People have often said that state-approved torture coarsens a society, yet even so it's remarkable how eager some people are to embrace their inner schoolyard bully. But then we knew that in fifth grade.

---

* I distinguish these from the purely opportunistic assaults like the wedgie and the Hertz Donut.
 [This essay is an excerpt from Nunberg's "One for Flinching" (2006)]

Responses to Terrorism

Waterboarding. One particularly controversial procedure that amounts to torture under most conventional definitions is waterboarding, or simulated drowning, noted in the essay by Geoffrey Nunberg in Box 9.2. The procedure creates the sensation of drowning either by temporarily immersing the head in water, by covering the mouth and nose with a water-saturated cloth, or by pouring water into the nose or mouth. The person administering the procedure aims usually to extract information from a captured suspect by repeating the procedure over and over until the subject "breaks" and provides the information desired. Some question whether waterboarding qualifies as torture, as it only simulates drowning and, even when it produces unconsciousness, it does not result in permanent physical harm. This position is untenable, however, because it ignores its psychological damage, which is immoral and erodes the legitimacy of the larger effort of engagement with an adversary, producing a loss of goodwill and moral standing. It also violates international law under the Geneva Conventions and other international treaties, noted earlier in this chapter.

A more defensible argument is that waterboarding should be regarded as torture and simply not be permitted (Wallach, 2007). Advocates of waterboarding argue that real conditions akin to the ticking-time-bomb scenario might conceivably justify using waterboarding, if the prospects of obtaining vital information are truly likely. Alan Dershowitz (2007), for example, argues that a president would be foolish not to permit waterboarding "if he believed that this was the only way of securing information necessary to prevent an imminent mass casualty attack. . . . (G)overnment officials must strike an appropriate balance between the security of America and the rights of our enemies." He argues that a special court should be empowered to issue warrants that permit the use of extreme methods to extract information in exceptionally dangerous circumstances.

The problem with this argument is that the allowance of torture under the law could easily open the door to officials routinely erring on the side of seeing cases as "exceptional." What judge would like it publicized that he or she had rejected a request to extract information using waterboarding and that a calamity occurred afterward, linked to an associate of the suspect under question? However, to allow torture under certain exceptional circumstances is to travel a slippery slope toward the routine use of torture, by stretching the meaning of "exceptional." It might be more prudent – and more effective in restoring international legitimacy, support, and security – simply to outlaw torture. A responsible agent confronted with a genuine ticking-time-bomb case with reliable information that the suspect has vital information that could save many lives could be expected to take appropriate measures and be held accountable for his or her actions if he elects to violate the law. An agent exercising sound judgment in such a situation is not likely to be punished for taking extreme measures under truly extreme circumstances.

3. If Not Torture, What?

For the reasons discussed above, torture is not generally acceptable, either as a matter of policy or practice. Suspects can be persuaded to provide information without the use of torture. Legal inducements, from positive persuasion to coercive methods short of torture, are available as more than suitable alternatives to torture. Suspects can be persuaded to provide useful information, first, by establishing rapport and mutual understanding between the interviewer and the suspect. A variety of techniques are available to determine whether a person under suspicion has important information and, if so, to induce the person to provide the information. If those methods are unsuccessful, coercion might be considered as an alternative.

Two questions must be resolved with regard to the use of coercive techniques. First, where does one draw the line between coercion and torture? Then, having drawn that line, under what circumstances is it justifiable to move from positive inducements to coercion? As to the first question, the line between coercion and torture should be based on the laws of the land, international laws and treaties, and commonsense notions of decency. All techniques that are ruled as beyond that boundary should be regarded as torture.

Once the boundary between acceptable coercive techniques and torture is established, we can then justify using coercive methods to extract information when the methods are known to be effective, when the information sought is critical to the preservation of lives and property, and when the threat is immediate.[5] These principles can be summarized in three maxims governing the acceptability of using a technique of coercion to extract information:

1. The technique falls clearly within the law, within the bounds of international treaty, and within the bounds of fundamental principles of decency.
2. The technique is known to be effective.
3. The technique is justified given the extent to which lives and property are at stake and in light of the immediacy of the threat.

Damage Done by Torture: The Case of Abu Ghraib. The Abu Ghraib affair attests to the serious consequences that can follow a failure to honor these principles (Carter, 2004). The torture that was vividly documented – in photographs of savaged corpses, dogs snarling at cowering men, chemical and cigarette burns, naked prisoners in human pyramids and on a leash being taunted by a woman in uniform, and forced homoerotic and other sexual humiliations – was sadistic, illegal, and immoral. These were more than sufficient reasons not to have done it, but it was also counterproductive in the extreme. The abuses not only failed to produce useful intelligence but they also eroded much of the legitimacy and moral high ground the United

States had claimed in Iraq. More profoundly still, they undermined the noble efforts of all the individuals who risked their lives in the service of the people of Iraq, the United States, and the world. The officials at Abu Ghraib who engaged in or permitted the use of torture, in short, inflicted severe damage not only on the prisoners at Abu Ghraib but also on the larger causes of security, justice, and legitimacy (Carter, 2004; Taguba, 2004).[6] The torture of prisoners by Americans was reported also at Bagram in Afghanistan and Guantanamo in Cuba (Danner, 2004).

The use of torture at Abu Graib against suspected terrorists also inflicted damage on those who engaged in it, even when justified by claims of trying to serve the larger war effort. Some of the torturers were punished, and they were revealed as bullies, thugs, and cowards as well. All of them are consigned to live the remainder of their lives with the public stigma of having committed extreme harm to the reputation of the military and the international standing of the United States by their actions. Other officials who supported, condoned, or turned a blind eye to the torture were demoted or otherwise sanctioned, and although some senior officials high up in the chain of responsibility were not sanctioned, their reputations were indelibly stained by the episode.

Earlier research by Stanley Milgram (1974) and Phillip Zimbardo (2007) has shown that this sordid matter is not just a case of a few "bad apples": ordinary people are indeed capable of inflicting suffering and lethal doses of harm on innocent people. Their studies have been validated more recently on the ground. Human Rights Watch (2005) has reported hundreds of officially documented cases of abuse in Iraq and Afghanistan. Milgram and Zimbardo reported also that the people who commit such acts often suffer psychological problems of their own afterward (see Box 9.3).

Rendition and Repatriation. What about *rendition* – sending suspected terrorists to interrogators in other countries to do the unpleasant business of extracting information – as an alternative to coercion or torture committed by citizens of a civilized land? Doesn't such a policy circumvent many of the most problematic aspects of torture? If torture is unacceptable and the prospect of either trying to prosecute these suspects or detain them indefinitely are both unlikely to succeed, why not "outsource" the aggressive methods of interrogation and punishment?

On the face of it, rendition has some appeal. Here is what Reuel Marc Gerecht (2005), a former CIA officer, says about rendition:

> Rendition appeals to the CIA because it is easy. Having others do your work for you is always bureaucratically commendable. And rendition leaves no counterterrorist debris. In foreign hands, terrorist suspects just disappear into the cells of Middle Eastern prisons or – for the lucky, with time – filter back to their homelands, where, *inshallah*, they will cause no further harm, at least

Box 9.3. An Iraq Interrogator's Nightmare

– Eric Fair

A man with no face stares at me from the corner of a room. He pleads for help, but I'm afraid to move. He begins to cry. It is a pitiful sound, and it sickens me. He screams, but as I awaken, I realize the screams are mine.

That dream, along with a host of other nightmares, has plagued me since my return from Iraq in the summer of 2004. Though the man in this particular nightmare has no face, I know who he is. I assisted in his interrogation at a detention facility in Fallujah. I was one of two civilian interrogators assigned to the division interrogation facility (DIF) of the 82nd Airborne Division. The man, whose name I've long since forgotten, was a suspected associate of Khamis Sirhan al-Muhammad, the Baath Party leader in Anbar province who had been captured two months earlier.

The lead interrogator at the DIF had given me specific instructions: I was to deprive the detainee of sleep during my 12-hour shift by opening his cell every hour, forcing him to stand in a corner and stripping him of his clothes. Three years later the tables have turned. It is rare that I sleep through the night without a visit from this man. His memory harasses me as I once harassed him.

Despite my best efforts, I cannot ignore the mistakes I made at the interrogation facility in Fallujah. I failed to disobey a meritless order, I failed to protect a prisoner in my custody, and I failed to uphold the standards of human decency. Instead, I intimidated, degraded, and humiliated a man who could not defend himself. I compromised my values. I will never forgive myself.

American authorities continue to insist that the abuse of Iraqi prisoners at Abu Ghraib was an isolated incident in an otherwise well-run detention system. That insistence, however, stands in sharp contrast to my own experiences as an interrogator in Iraq. I watched as detainees were forced to stand naked all night, shivering in their cold cells and pleading with their captors for help. Others were subjected to long periods of isolation in pitch-black rooms. Food and sleep deprivation were common, along with a variety of physical abuse, including punching and kicking. Aggressive, and in many ways abusive, techniques were used daily in Iraq, all in the name of acquiring the intelligence necessary to bring an end to the insurgency. The violence raging there today is evidence that those tactics never worked. My memories are evidence that those tactics were terribly wrong.

While I was appalled by the conduct of my friends and colleagues, I lacked the courage to challenge the status quo. That was a failure of character and in many ways made me complicit in what went on. I'm ashamed of that failure, but as time passes, and as the memories of what I saw in Iraq continue to infect my every thought, I'm becoming more ashamed of my silence.

Some may suggest there is no reason to revive the story of abuse in Iraq. Rehashing such mistakes will only harm our country, they will say. But history suggests we should examine such missteps carefully. Oppressive prison environments have created some of the most determined opponents. The British learned that lesson from Napoleon, the French from Ho Chi Minh, Europe from Hitler. The world is learning that lesson again from Ayman al-Zawahiri. What will be the legacy of abusive prisons in Iraq?

We have failed to properly address the abuse of Iraqi detainees. Men like me have refused to tell our stories, and our leaders have refused to own up to the myriad mistakes that have been made. But if we fail to address this problem, there can be no hope of success in Iraq. Regardless of how many young Americans we send to war, or how many militia members we kill, or how many Iraqis we train, or how much money we spend on reconstruction, we will not escape the damage we have done to the people of Iraq in our prisons.

I am desperate to get on with my life and erase my memories of my experiences in Iraq. But those memories and experiences do not belong to me. They belong to history. If we're doomed to repeat the history we forget, what will be the consequences of the history we never knew? The citizens and the leadership of this country have an obligation to revisit what took place in the interrogation booths of Iraq, unpleasant as it may be. The story of Abu Ghraib isn't over. In many ways, we have yet to open the book.

The writer served in the Army from 1995 to 2000 as an Arabic linguist and worked in Iraq as a contract interrogator in early 2004.

[*Source:* Fair (2007)]

to the foreign country that incarcerated and tortured them at America's request. Rendition gives the CIA power and clout in Washington. It has become an integral part of America's counterterrorist modus operandi – a thing nobody really wants to talk about but most probably view as valuable.

The rendition of detainees has in fact been used on occasion by the United States under both the Clinton and Bush administrations. But these instances were fairly rare and extremely controversial. When subject to public scrutiny, they were often discontinued, for several reasons. First, rendition is an abdication of the responsibility for intelligence gathering and therefore an abdication of professionalism. In outsourcing interrogation, the nation that exports prisoners loses control over the information obtained (Gerecht, 2005). Second, rendition is ineffective: it is torture, and as noted earlier, torture diminishes the reliability of the information obtained. There is little reason to expect that torture abroad produces more reliable information than torture at home. Third, and perhaps most important, it is unethical: if you believe that torture is immoral, then you cannot remove yourself from responsibility for the practice of torture by outsourcing it. Rendition has political consequences too: in sending detainees abroad to be tortured, a nation loses legitimacy and moral standing in the eyes of civilized people everywhere.

An alternative to rendition – when the goal is punishment rather than the extraction of intelligence – is punitive repatriation. Yet, prisoners who are returned to their homelands after periods of incarceration are sometimes tortured or killed. Because it is a form of punishment, the practice is particularly unjust for the innocent: suspicions raised by their foreign incarceration can condemn them to the presumption of collaboration with the enemy (Gerecht, 2005). Non-punitive repatriation, on the other hand, can be a perfectly appropriate alternative for detainees who are judged to be not dangerous, including religious zealots, although they too may risk suspicion and punishment on returning home.

E. Covert and Other Special Operations

Covert operations can be an indispensable tool for countering terrorism by eliminating terrorists and disrupting terrorist operations at their source. The success of terrorist acts depends on the element of surprise – and the point of covert operations is to counter surprise with surprise, to prevent terrorism by obtaining knowledge of who the terrorists are and what they are up to, and then acting on that knowledge, in some cases eliminating the terrorists as efficiently as possible wherever they are and doing so without revealing who was behind the operation. Efficiency in covert operations results in a minimum of collateral damage and no exposure, with little or no incriminating trail left behind to identify the sponsor. Covert operations may involve the use of force, as in the case of operations using assassinations, kidnappings, or secretly conducted preemptive strikes, or they may use nonviolent means, such as infiltration, the dissemination of disinformation, the use of subversion to upset terrorist organizations, and cyberwarfare. All of these operations share the characteristic of being conducted outside the range of public scrutiny with the aim of either eliminating terrorists and terrorist cells or severely disrupting their ability to carry out acts of terrorism.

Covert operations are not just secret operations. They are designed and executed in a way that often conceals the operation, but always attempts to conceal the identity of the sponsor or sponsors as well. The U.S. Department

Policy Box 9.4. Torture and Police Brutality

Given the strong inducements to engage in torture – unrealistic hypotheticals about ticking time bombs, misguided loyalty, retribution for fallen comrades, and so on – how can we avoid the slippery slope to torture?

The problem of torture is not the same as the problem of police brutality (the willful use of illegal violence by police), but it is sufficiently similar to warrant a consideration of policies used to reduce the likelihood of police officers engaging in brutality. Five basic solutions to the problem of police brutality emerge, and these can be applied to torture as well: careful screening, rigorous training, thoughtful assignment, effective accountability systems, and strong leadership (Skolnick and Fyfe, 1993).

1. Careful *screening* can ensure that people with histories of violent behavior, who are ill suited for positions that require the responsible use of force, are excluded from service. Army Specialist Charles Graner was one of the chief culprits of the Abu Ghraib scandal and the most severely punished by court-martial (sentenced to ten years in prison). He had a history of serious abusive behavior and a record of infractions as a prison guard in Pennsylvania in the 1990s. It is questionable whether the Army should have found him fit for service and more questionable still whether he should been sent to Iraq.

2. Rigorous *training* can ensure that, once properly screened, those placed in control of captured persons will know how to handle them. According to Human Rights Watch (2005), "US troops on the battlefield were given no clear guidance on how to treat detainees." Training should include instruction in the full range of the techniques of persuasion, from friendly, positive inducements to the legal use of strong coercive methods, and should clarify which technique is most appropriate for each circumstance that presents itself. Evidence suggests that a similar approach to training has been effective for preventing police brutality (Skolnick and Fyfe, 1993). The training should also include instruction on when military personnel should disobey orders "to kill innocent civilians, for example, or torture detainees – that are unlawful, and they cannot invoke 'superior orders' as a defense when those orders are illegal" (Carter, 2004; Taguba, 2004).

3. Thoughtful *assignment* can ensure that people properly screened and trained will be assessed as to their strengths and weaknesses and then assigned to positions that make the best use of their skills.

In Iraq, the abuse of prisoners has been attributed to the failure of frontline soldiers to move detainees to a rear area where they could be properly guarded, looked after, and prepared for interrogation by trained military police (Human Rights Watch, 2005).

4. Effective *accountability systems* will ensure that acts of torture are severely sanctioned and that any supervisors who allow torture to occur under their command will be sanctioned for dereliction of duty. Sound accountability systems establish structural reforms and overlapping checks on integrity and abuse throughout the command structure (Skolnick and Fyfe, 1993). An important element in accountability is the development of measures to ensure that soldiers who make credible allegations of detainee abuse are not punished for their actions (Human Rights Watch, 2005).

5. Strong *leadership* is needed to send a clear message to the entire force, and to the rest of the world, that torture will not be tolerated and that it will be subject to severe sanctions and discharge from military service. Police departments wracked with brutality and other abuses have been reformed most effectively by leaders who change the culture of the department with forceful actions to prevent such abuse, sweeping out all who do not share their intolerance for abusive behavior (Skolnick and Fyfe, 1993). In Iraq, by contrast, cases of abuse have been attributed to commanders who, according to Human Rights Watch (2005), demanded that their subordinates "extract intelligence from detainees without telling them what was allowed and what was forbidden. Yet when abuses inevitably followed, the administration blamed only low-ranking soldiers instead of taking responsibility" (see also the Taguba report, 2004). The leadership problem begins with the Commander in Chief, and the White House has been charged with giving strongly mixed signals about the need to take all measures to protect the public against terrorism while complying with the laws against torture (Hiatt, 2006; Packer, 2006b).

Each of these five measures can contribute to the prevention of torture. Collectively, they can create conditions that ensure that torture will be neither tolerated nor used. As with the problem of police brutality and its prevention, strong inducements to torture prisoners must be countered by practices, policies, and people in command that provide stronger inducements to prevent the use of torture.

of Defense, in its *Dictionary of Military and Associated Terms*, defines a "covert operation" as follows:

> An operation that is so planned and executed as to conceal the identity of or permit plausible denial by the sponsor. A covert operation differs from a clandestine operation in that emphasis is placed on concealment of identity of sponsor rather than on concealment of the operation.

Covert operations have been used frequently over the past century. The United States used them in North Vietnam in the 1960s to counter the Viet Cong's use of guerrillas in South Vietnam (Shultz, 1999). They have been used extensively by Israel against terrorists in Palestine and Lebanon, typically planned and executed by its covert operations agency, Mossad. They have been used more frequently by the United States since the 9/11 attack, in operations carried out by carefully screened and thoroughly trained forces, including commando strike teams, such as Delta Force, the Green Berets, and Sea-Air-Land (SEAL) forces.

Covert operations are controversial, a two-edged sword both morally and legally. The secrecy needed to succeed in covert operations runs counter to the idea of transparency, which is a foundation of a free and democratic society. The operations themselves often go well beyond what is permitted by law enforcement officers domestically under the Constitution, but they may be permitted under the war-making authority of the Commander-in-Chief as approved by Congress. However, they may lie outside the boundary of congressinal authority. Covert operations are controversial when used against terrorists largely because the war on terror does not fit neatly within the nation's conventional war authority as it applies to hostile nations. Covert operations conducted in foreign lands ordinarily require the consent of the nation in which the operations take place.

Assassinations are particularly controversial. They were expressly prohibited by President Gerald Ford in 1976, under Executive Order 11905, following revelations that the CIA had staged several attempts to assassinate Cuban President Fidel Castro. This prohibition was reaffirmed by Ronald Reagan in 1981, under Executive Order 12333. It was relaxed about a month after the 9/11 attack, however, when President George W. Bush signed an intelligence order (called a "finding"), instructing the CIA to engage in lethal covert operations to destroy Osama bin Laden and his al Qaeda organization. The tactic of assassination was used perhaps most famously in 2006 to kill Abu Musab al-Zarqawi in Iraq.

In addition to the dubious moral and legal implications of covert operations, they can also be counterproductive. When discovered, they can make martyrs of the persons targeted and raise questions about the transparency of the sponsoring nation, thus undermining the legitimacy of the cause of counterterrorism and giving a strategic advantage to the terrorist leaders and their organizations.

F. Dealing with Hostage-Taking

One of the most difficult types of counterterrorist operations is dealing with hostage crises. Hostage-taking is an ancient practice, dating back to the Middle Ages, and before that to the Roman Empire. Under the U.S. criminal code, the act is classified as a kidnapping. When done for a political purpose, usually on foreign soil, it is a terrorist act, which can escalate to a hostage crisis, in which the hostages may be barricaded in a building with the abductors or – in the case of an airline hijacking – an airplane. Alternatively, the hostages may be taken to an unknown location while the terrorists press for their demands. The demands typically involve an exchange of hostages for one or more political ends: a release of prisoners, promises to reduce or end counterterrorist operations, attention to a cause, or a ransom payment to help fund terrorist operations.

There is often considerable pressure on the governments of the countries from which the hostages came to comply with the demands made by the hostage-takers – which is often intensified by pressure from family members and the media. However, governments rarely comply with the demands, on the grounds that to give in to them would serve to feed the hostage beast and encourage an endless series of further such acts, thus increasing the costs of hostage crises over the long term. The 1986 Iran-Contra scandal, in which White House officials agreed to the sale of arms to Iran in exchange for help in securing the release of American hostages in Lebanon – with proceeds of the sale used to support Contra rebels in their fight to overthrow the Sandinista government in Nicaragua – serves as an embarrassing reminder of the severe costs that can accompany even secret deal-making to secure the release of hostages.

The pressure to submit to unreasonable demands and the immediate threats to life and property inherent in hostage crises make them extremely dangerous and difficult to resolve. Hostages are often tortured, killed, or both, for any of several reasons. The hostage-takers may feel compelled to punish the hostages and have no genuine intention to release them. They may kill the hostages for fear that, once released, the hostages could provide information that endangers the abductors. Or they may kill the hostages out of frustration or anger at not getting what they want, or because the operation simply spirals out of control, as in several notorious cases. The 1972 Munich Olympics hostage crisis that came to be known as "Black September" resulted in the deaths of nine Israeli athletes. In the 1974 Maalot crisis, twenty-one Israeli schoolchildren died in a commando raid. Many more lives were lost in similar botched rescue attempts in two separate Chechen hostage crises: one in

2002, when terrorists took over a theater, resulting in about 150 deaths, and another in 2004, when forty-two heavily armed terrorists took over a school in Beslan, killing some 350 hostages.

Other hostage episodes have had better outcomes. One of the most famous was the 1975 Entebbe incident, in which an Israeli elite special forces unit known as Sayeret Matkal carried out a carefully planned operation to rescue hostages after the hijacking of an airplane that was being held at the Entebbe Airport in Uganda. The hijackers were supported by Ugandan leader Idi Amin. When the dust settled, one Israeli soldier and three hostages were killed, along with all six of the hostage-takers and forty-five Ugandan soldiers. One hundred hostages were saved in the operation. Successes also followed operations in Egypt in 1976. Another successful operation followed the 1985 hijacking of TWA Flight 847, en route from Athens to Rome, by a terrorist group linked to Hezbollah. The plane, its crew, and passengers experienced a two-week ordeal during which one passenger was killed. However, more than 140 passengers were spared, thanks largely to the extraordinary skill of flight attendant Uli Derickson, who communicated in German in a calm and effective manner with the hijackers.

What lessons can be learned from these failures and successes? Two basic approaches are available: *dialogue* with the terrorists or an attempt to *rescue* the hostages, often involving the use of deadly force. In some cases, a rescue operation may follow the failure of dialogue to produce desirable results. Either approach is more likely to be successful when the counterterrorist team is skilled and well trained in role-playing exercises, when the team has reliable intelligence on the hostage-takers and on the physical layout of the place where the hostages are held, and when they engage with the terrorists in such a way as to avoid provoking them while resisting compliance with unreasonable demands. One person should speak for the counterterrorist team, and the message should be clear and positive, open to the prospect of a decent outcome.

When the location of the hostages is known, the counterterrorism team should begin developing and refining plans for a rescue operation, even while negotiations are taking place. Rescue plans should be developed based on information about the number of people guarding the hostages, the weaponry they possess, the physical layout of the place where the operation will occur, the prospect of booby traps, and the condition of the hostages. Rescue operations are extremely dangerous, as exemplified not only by the Munich Olympics, Maalot, and Chechen cases noted above, but more generally by the low percentages of fully successful rescue operations (Bolz et al., 2005). Hostages are often used as human shields or are immediately killed by the hostage-takers in response to a rescue attempt. One important element of the planning process is to determine whether to exploit the advantages of surprise or to encourage the hostage-takers to surrender before launching the operation. When it is clear that dialogue has gone as far as it can go and when the location of the hostages is known and the time has come to attempt a rescue operation, the option most likely to save hostage lives should be implemented. When attacked, the guards will engage in one or more of the following responses: fight back, try to escape, surrender, kill the hostages, or commit suicide. The plans should accommodate each of these prospects and combinations thereof, and the rescue operation should be prepared to deal with each contingency.

G. Reward (Bounty) Programs

The United States has successfully used bounties to capture or kill terrorists. A bounty is a reward, usually money, offered to provide an incentive for anyone who knows the whereabouts of a particular individual to come forward. The advantage of the bounty is that it leverages the intelligence about particular terrorists by engaging countless people on the ground to help bring about the capture of an individual.

The U.S. Department of State's Rewards for Justice Program offers amounts of up to $25 million to bring international terrorists to justice and thus prevent acts of terrorism, or for information that "prevents or favorably resolves acts of international terrorism against U.S. persons or property worldwide" (Department of State, 2006). It pays rewards also for information leading to the arrest or conviction of terrorists attempting, committing, or conspiring to commit or aid in the commission of terrorist acts. Created under the 1984 Act to Combat International Terrorism (Public Law 98–533), the program had awarded more than $62 million to more than forty informants from the time of its creation through 2006. It launched a Web site in December 2001 with photographs and names of most-wanted terrorists and information about how people could participate in the program. The amount of the award in any particular case is set by an interagency committee that includes representatives of the State Department, Department of Justice, CIA, and FBI. The largest single payment was in the amount of $30 million for the informant who provided information that led the military to the location of Saddam Hussein's sons, Uday and Qusay, in Mosul, where they were killed in 2003. The United States also offered $25 million rewards for information leading to the death or capture of Abu Musab al-Zarqawi and Saddam Hussein.

The State Department clarifies that this is a "reward" program, not a bounty program, noting that bounty hunters are discouraged from participating. Given the danger that would face anyone widely known to have received such a reward, it has not been revealed whether rewards were paid for the

House of Uday and Qusay Hussein in Mosul, Iraq, destroyed by U.S. air strikes, July 31, 2003.

information that led to capture of Saddam Hussein in 2003 and the killing of Abu Musab al-Zarqawi in 2006. The State Department does provide protection and will relocate a source and his or her family if it is judged necessary to protect the informant.

H. International Collaboration in the Investigation and Prosecution of Terrorism

Terrorism is an international problem, and terrorists may be more effectively dealt with through collaborations among nations than by individual nations trying to solve the problem unilaterally. A variety of cooperative arrangements have been created to facilitate international collaboration in the campaign against terrorism. Such efforts aim to provide greater legitimacy to the effort, but they offer instrumental advantages as well, by distributing the considerable costs and human toll, sharing critical information, avoiding redundant effort, and realizing the comparative advantages and complementary strengths of the participants. Important elements of this collaboration include the detection and prosecution of the crimes of terrorists through international policing, extradition treaties, and international courts and tribunals.

International Policing. The International Criminal Police Organization (INTERPOL) is the most expansive international policing organization in the world, with more than 180 member nations that contribute funding and share information and other resources. It was created in Vienna in 1923 to enhance policing worldwide through the sharing of information and cooperation in the investigation of crimes and the apprehension of major criminals. Its central office moved to Berlin in 1942, then to Saint Cloud outside of Paris, in 1945, and finally to its current headquarters in Lyon, France, in 1989.

Much of INTERPOL's focus today is on terrorism, attacks on civil aviation, maritime piracy, and drug trafficking. It works to detect such crimes by tracking the whereabouts of dangerous individuals, suspicious financial transactions, trafficking in weapons and drugs, money laundering, and seizures of nuclear, chemical, and biological materials. It also maintains data on terrorist organizations and hosts conferences on the detection of terrorists and terrorist activities.

INTERPOL also contributes to the detection and apprehension of prospective terrorists at border crossings. Since 2002 it has maintained a database of lost and stolen identification and travel documents, which can be used by terrorists to travel illegally across international borders. This database, which contained more than ten million records in 2006, is especially useful for detecting passport fraud, in which passports are stolen, altered, and then presented to immigration officers at international borders (see the Web site of the International Criminal Police Organization, http://www.interpol.int/Public/Terrorism/default.asp).

Another large multinational policing organization – with even more funding than INTERPOL – is the European Police Office (EUROPOL), the collaborative criminal investigation arm of the European Union. Established under the Maastricht Treaty of 1992, EUROPOL became fully operational in 1999, with headquarters in The Hague. It operates much like INTERPOL, but has a smaller membership of about thirty nations and a more intense focus on organized crime. EUROPOL provides information and training support to its member nations through information exchange, intelligence analysis, and training resources. It also coordinates with INTERPOL and its member nations on the movement of terrorists and activities of terrorist groups.

Extradition Treaties. The United States has entered into extradition treaties with most other nations of the world. (Exceptions include China, Iran, North Korea, Syria, and approximately fifty other countries.) These are bilateral treaties that require one nation in the treaty to send a person in custody who is suspected of committing a serious crime to the other country if the receiving nation requests extradition and the evidence suggests that the person committed an offense that is subject to imprisonment in both countries.

Extradition treaties can be effective tools to prevent the spread of terrorism, as long as they are used in a way that does not lead to the abuses discussed earlier, in which prisoners are tortured in the country to which they are sent under a rendition policy. However, these treaties are difficult to enforce when one nation refuses to cooperate with another to extradite a particular prisoner, for example, when it is anticipated that the person extradited will not receive a fair trial or a reasonable sentence in the other country, as in the case of a political crime. Countries that have abolished the death penalty – including Canada, Mexico, and most European nations – have ruled not to extradite prisoners to the United States when a capital offense is involved.

International Courts and Tribunals. An effective way to ensure the legitimacy of counterterrorism policies and actions is through the use of international courts and tribunals. The nations of the world have often been sharply divided on how to deal with terrorism, but it remains the case nonetheless that international courts sanctioned by a large corps of nations lend legitimacy to the enforcement of international law generally and to matters related to terrorism as well. We noted earlier in this chapter the effective use of an international tribunal to prosecute and convict Slobodan Milosevic for his grave violations of the Geneva Conventions in Bosnia.

The United Nations has played a central role in this process as perhaps the most widely recognized source of legitimacy internationally in the struggle against terrorism. Under Security Council Resolution 1444, passed in 2002, the UN officially supported actions taken by many of its members to root out terrorism in Afghanistan, and after the fall of the Taliban government, it recognized under Resolution 1453 (also passed in 2002) the transitional government of Karzai as "the sole legitimate Government of Afghanistan." As was noted in Chapter 1, the UN also has broadened the official definition of terrorism so that the organization could have a stronger mandate to intercede where needed. There have been strong precedents for such UN action, including the establishment of International Criminal Tribunals for the former Yugoslavia in 1993 and for Rwanda in 1994 to prosecute war crimes committed in those places and try the persons charged with the crimes.

International courts and tribunals have been established outside the authority of the United Nations as well, where they are formed under treaties among the participating nations.

I. Economic Sanctions

To counter state-sponsored terrorism, a type of aggressive intervention that falls short of military force is the use of *economic sanctions*. These include trade embargoes and government-enforced boycotts, tariffs, trade restrictions, import duties, and import or export quotas. Economic sanctions have been used to punish targeted nations or to induce them to reform, to forestall war, free prisoners, return captured land, respect human rights, encourage environmental responsibility, and discourage nuclear proliferation (Davis and Engerman, 2003).

Joseph S. Nye, Jr. (2004) characterizes economic sanctions as "hard" rather than "soft power" because they use the stick of coercion rather than the carrot of persuasion. They are coercive in that they are imposed unilaterally, usually by a large economic power, to inflict hardship on a usually weaker nation.[7] Economic sanctions have been used by the United States since the 9/11 attacks as part of the arsenal in the war on terror to deter state-sponsored terrorism by Iraq, Iran, and Syria. They have been used as well against Cuba, North Korea, and other nations over the past several decades. Elliott and Hufbauer (1999) report that trade sanctions were used in 117 cases between 1970 and 1998, with the United States primarily responsible for over two-thirds of these cases.

Are economic sanctions effective? Here is how Nye (2004) describes economic sanctions and their effectiveness:

> Governments can freeze foreign bank accounts overnight, and can distribute bribes or aid promptly (although economic sanctions often take a long time, if ever, to produce desired outcomes). . . . (E)conomic sanctions have historically produced their intended outcomes in only about a third of the cases where they were tried (p. 99).

In addition, the effects of economic sanctions appear frequently to have been much worse than mere failure to achieve their intended outcomes: they have often done considerable harm to the people living in places already under the thumb of dictatorship, while having done little to either influence or harm the dictators; thus, they can be both ineffective and unfair. If the goal of foreign policy is to isolate bad governments from the people governed while winning the support of the innocent victims, economic sanctions appear to have been mostly counterproductive (Davis and Engerman, 2003; Haass, 1998; Hufbauer, Schott and Elliott, 1990; Kristof, 2003; Pape, 1997; Powell, 1990).

Consider, for example, the case of Cuba. Americans have not been allowed to trade with, invest in, or travel to Cuba. Designed to encourage the ouster of Fidel Castro, economic sanctions have not only failed to achieve this objective but also have contributed to Cuba's status as one of the poorest nations in the Western Hemisphere. According to economist Daniel Griswold (2005),

> If the goal of U.S. policy toward Cuba is to help its people achieve freedom and a better life, the economic embargo has completely failed. Its economic effect is to make the people of Cuba worse off by depriving them of lower-cost

food and other goods that could be bought from the United States. It means less independence for Cuban workers and entrepreneurs, who could be earning dollars from American tourists and fueling private-sector growth. Meanwhile, Castro and his ruling elite enjoy a comfortable, insulated lifestyle by extracting any meager surplus produced by their captive subjects. . . . Cuban families are not the only victims of the embargo. Many of the dollars Cubans could earn from U.S. tourists would come back to the United States to buy American products, especially farm goods.

Griswold elaborates that the embargo hurts millions of innocent bystanders: Cubans and Americans, consumers and producers. He notes that a study by the U.S. International Trade Commission estimated that the embargo costs American firms between $700 million and $1.2 billion per year. The Cuban Liberty and Democratic Solidarity (Helms-Burton) Act, passed in 1996, spread the pain even further by extending the embargo to foreign companies trading with Cuba, thus straining relations with nations that opted not to join the United States in its economic sanctions against Cuba and imposing costs on producers in those countries as well.

Economic sanctions imposed on Iran following the overthrow of the Shah in 1979 appear to have had similarly harmful effects on the people of Iran, and – as with Cuba's Castro – the rule of the Islamic Republic has remained in force despite the imposition of the sanctions. Some argue that the sanctions on Iran have undermined the authority of Iran's rulers, but they may have also made them more desperate to develop nuclear power. The sanctions appear to have had other harmful consequences. A report sponsored by the International Civil Aviation Organization attributed the deaths of civilians in plane crashes in Iran to the U.S. embargo of planes, spare plane parts, and repair services to Iran (D. Phillips, 2005).

Two distinct trends have been noted regarding economic sanctions in recent decades: they have grown more prevalent, and they have become less effective. They have become more attractive at home politically as tools for "sending a message" to state sponsors of terrorism, giving the appearance that the government is "doing something" about hostile powers without waging war with them (Davis and Engerman, 2003). They appear to have become less effective largely because the forces of globalization have made it increasingly difficult for any nation to shut off the export of goods and services to any other nation. However, sanctions still do damage to the extent that they raise the prices of the goods under embargo.

By most reliable accounts, satisfying political demands through economic sanctions is a blunt and largely counterproductive instrument. It tends to isolate targeted countries from the global economy, puts their citizens deeper in poverty, and does little or nothing to facilitate the ouster of dictators and supporters of terrorism.

J. The 9/11 Commission: Findings and Recommendations

The attack of September 11 was preventable; it was a calamitous failure of security and intelligence. After the immediate task of minimizing the loss of life and property from the attack, the next order of business was to examine the facts to establish how future such attacks could be prevented. In November 2002, the President and Congress of the United States created an independent, bipartisan commission of five Democrats and five Republicans – formally, the National Commission on Terrorist Attacks Upon the United States – to examine the evidence, identify the problems and lessons learned, and make recommendations to prevent and minimize harm from future acts of terrorism. The recommendations provide insights for intelligence and law enforcement agencies on the role of diplomacy, immigration issues and border control, the flow of assets to terrorist organizations, commercial aviation, the role of congressional oversight, and resource allocation. The Commission reviewed more than 2.5 million pages of documents and interviewed some 1,200 people in ten countries, including nearly every senior official from the current and previous administrations who had relevant areas of responsibility. To establish the modus operandi of the attackers the Commission also reviewed many types of evidence, including airport security tapes, cockpit voice recordings, and audiotapes of direct eyewitness testimony of passengers as they described their fatal final moments to family members and authorities on air phones and cell phones from the cabins of the doomed airliners.

The Commission focused on two primary questions: What went wrong? How can future attacks be prevented? The next two sections present their answers.

1. What Went Wrong?

The Commission learned, first, that the nation was unprepared for the 9/11 attack, largely because it underestimated the threat posed by an enemy that was "sophisticated, patient, disciplined, and lethal":

> We learned that the institutions charged with protecting our borders, civil aviation, and national security did not understand how grave this threat could be, and did not adjust their policies, plans, and practices to deter or defeat it. We learned of fault lines within our government–between foreign and domestic intelligence, and between and within agencies. We learned of the pervasive problems of managing and sharing information across a large and unwieldy government that had been built in a different era to confront different dangers.

293

Responses to Terrorism

The Commission observed that we should not have been so surprised by the attack. Consider these events that occurred in the decade preceding the attack:

- In 1993 Islamic extremists tried to blow up the World Trade Center (WTC) with a truck bomb, killing six and injuring one thousand others.
- In the same year, Somali tribesmen supported by al Qaeda shot down U.S. helicopters in the Black Hawk Down incident, killing eighteen and wounding seventy-three.
- In 1995, police in Manila uncovered a plot by Ramzi Yousef, leader of the 1993 WTC episode, to blow up a dozen U.S. airliners as they were flying over the Pacific.
- In the same year, a car bomb exploded outside the office of the U.S. program manager for the Saudi National Guard in Riyadh, killing five Americans and two others.
- In 1996, a truck bomb demolished the Khobar Towers apartment complex in Saudi Arabia, killing nineteen U.S. servicemen and injuring hundreds of others.
- In 1998, al Qaeda carried out simultaneous truck bomb attacks on the U.S. embassies in Kenya and Tanzania, killing 224, including 12 Americans, and injuring thousands of others.
- In 1999, Jordanian police halted a plot to bomb hotels and other sites frequented by American tourists, and a U.S. Customs agent arrested Ahmed Ressam, an Algerian living in Canada, at the U.S.-Canadian border as he was smuggling explosives intended for an attack on the Los Angeles International Airport.
- In 2000, an al Qaeda team killed seventeen American sailors in Yemen and nearly sank the destroyer *USS Cole*, using a motorboat filled with explosives.

These events and discoveries point clearly to the existence of a strong, willful, and capable force bent on inflicting grave damage on the United States. In retrospect, the surprise is that the 9/11 attack came as a surprise, that a nation that spends so much on defense and domestic security allowed itself to become as complacent as it did about a known and serious threat in the face of so many tangible warnings. The Commission recognized that its assessment of this chain of events had "the benefit and handicap of hindsight." It was, nonetheless, all too clear that the United States had seriously underestimated al Qaeda's will and capacity to sustain and perfect its attacks on the United States.

Yet, the United States was not totally blind to these events; it had previously responded to terrorist acts. The Clinton administration retaliated in three ways against al Qaeda after the deadly bombings of U.S. embassies in Kenya and Tanzania. First, it launched cruise missile strikes against al Qaeda targets in Afghanistan and Sudan. Second, it applied diplomatic pressure in attempts to persuade the Taliban regime to expel bin Laden from Afghanistan. Third, it set up covert operations to use CIA-paid foreign agents to capture or kill bin Laden and his chief lieutenants. About a year later, in late 1999 and in anticipation of millennium attacks, intelligence experts uncovered information that led to the breakup of some al Qaeda cells. However, none of these actions worked either to deter bin Laden or remove him from his sanctuary in Afghanistan. Serious deficiencies remained.

The Commission worked to identify and catalogue these deficiencies and recommended ways of fixing them. It classified the failures of government in four distinct areas: failures of imagination, policy, capabilities, and management. The Commissioners asserted further, "The most important failure was one of imagination. We do not believe leaders understood the gravity of the threat. The terrorist danger from bin Laden and al Qaeda was not a major topic for policy debate among the public, the media, or in the Congress. Indeed, it barely came up during the 2000 presidential campaign (2004, p. 9)."[8]

The report elaborated on this criticism by citing particular failures: unsuccessful diplomatic efforts with the Taliban government in Afghanistan, lack of military options due largely to poor intelligence capabilities, problems within the U.S. intelligence community, problems within the FBI (it was excessively case-specific, decentralized, and geared toward prosecution), permeable borders and weak immigration controls, permeable aviation security, failure to track al Qaeda's financing of the 9/11 operation, an improvised approach to homeland defense, and a Congress that failed to respond adequately to the real threat of transnational terrorism.

The report of the 9/11 Commission concluded, in effect, that what went wrong was a failure of both capacity and will: "Al Qaeda's new brand of terrorism presented challenges to US governmental institutions that they were not well-designed to meet. . . . Terrorism was not the overriding national security concern for the US government under either the Clinton or the pre-9/11 Bush administration."

2. How Can Future Attacks Be Prevented?

The 9/11 Commission Report made a variety of recommendations in several areas to improve the nation's ability to respond to the threat of terrorism. The recommendations revolved around two questions: What to do? and How to do it?

Much of the commission report centered on ways to improve intelligence gathering about terrorist networks and plans, which is dealt with in Chapter 11 of this book. The report dealt as well with other approaches to minimize the threat of major acts of terrorism in the future. Chief among these was the development of a global strategy for dismantling the al Qaeda network and, over the longer term, prevailing over the ideology that contributes to Islamist terrorism. The accomplishment of this strategy would require the implementation of a balanced mix of tools, including formal and informal diplomacy, intelligence, covert action, law enforcement, economic policy, foreign aid, and homeland defense. The Commission recommended that such a balance could be achieved through the development of realistic objectives, clear guidance, and effective organization. Dismantling the network would require not only the effective use of the U.S. military to root out terrorist sanctuaries but also the nurturance of well-functioning alliances with other nations, particularly in the Middle East, to leverage U.S. resources, better coordinate international efforts against terrorism, and provide greater legitimacy to efforts to prevent terrorism.

The Commission also identified the need for greater coordination between and within the two major institutions of security: the Departments of Defense and Homeland Security. It argued specifically for a clearer delineation of roles, missions, and authority between and among the myriad components of these networks.

K. Ending the War on Terror

Perhaps the most effective response to terrorism is to avoid overreacting to it. A widely cited essay by James Fallows (2006) opens with this introductory overview: *"The United States is succeeding in its struggle against terrorism. The time has come to declare the war on terror over, so that an even more effective military and diplomatic campaign can begin"* (italics in the original).

Fallows goes on to argue that the United States committed a serious blunder in declaring a war on terror in the first place, that it played into the hands of the terrorists by using terrorism as a justification for invading Iraq and then staying there too long, and that it wasted billions of dollars worth of scarce resources on a host of dubious homeland security programs, yielding a million-to-one payoff ratio to al Qaeda for an operation that cost it only about $500,000 (2006, p. 70).

He is careful to observe that much of what the United States did was effective, especially the dismantling of al Qaeda on the ground, which undoubtedly contributed to the absence of subsequent attacks for several years and a reduction of attacks elsewhere. But the extreme U.S. overreaction, together with sensational revelations of brutal acts against detainees and the killings of countless innocent civilians in Iraq, caused international support for U.S. foreign policy to plummet and raised serious questions about the moral authority of the United States in conducting its war on terror. Citing the work of Saad al-Faqih and Ian Lustick, Fallows likens the U.S. reaction to that of a clueless giant attacked by a jujitsu expert:

> The United States is immeasurably stronger than al-Qaeda, but against jujitsu forms of attack its strength has been its disadvantage. The predictability of the U.S. response has allowed opponents to turn our bulk and momentum against

us. Al-Qaeda can do more harm to the United States than to, say, Italy because the self-damaging potential of an uncontrolled American reaction is so vast (2006, p. 71).

The solution, says Fallows, is to announce an end to the global war on terror and to justify this announcement by saying that the central objectives of the war – destroying the bulk of al Qaeda's operations and substantially reducing its opportunities for subsequent acts of terrorism – had been largely achieved. He argues that future terrorist attacks against the United States were virtually inevitable, some of which might be inspired by the al Qaeda model, but that they would be dealt with much more effectively if the responses were proportionate and were conducted outside of rhetorical, self-defeating wars on terrorism.

The most effective responses to acts of terror, in short, are thoughtful, measured ones, not reactions driven by fear and emotion, the topic of the next chapter. Proportionate responses to future acts of terrorism might not only restore the lost moral authority of the United States but they might also lessen the prospect of future such attacks.

Discussion Questions

1. *Responsibility for security.* How are the public and private sectors, separately and collectively, responsible for security against terrorism? How are federal and local authorities responsible? What sort of interventions are available to each of these entities?

2. *Diplomacy and terrorism.* How has diplomacy been used effectively to deal with the problem of terrorism? How has it been misused? How has it been underused? Can it be overused?

3. *Military force against terrorism.* Under what circumstances should military force be used to respond to terrorism? Under what circumstances should it be used to prevent terrorism? What sort of measures are needed to ensure that military force is used legitimately? What sort of measures are needed to ensure that it is used effectively in the short term? How can we ensure that the short-term effects last over the long term?

4. *Just war theory and terrorism.* Which of Michael Walzer's just war principles apply to the problem of terrorism? Which do not? How do you think his *jus ad bellum* and *jus in bello* principles should be adapted to deal properly with terrorism? What barriers stand in the way of such an adaptation? How do you think they should be dealt with? How do your adapted *jus ad bellum* and *jus in bello* principles apply to the 2001 invasion of Afghanistan, the 2003 invasion of Iraq, or Israel's 2006 invasion of Lebanon?

5. *Moral justification for asymmetric warfare.* Does inferior military power justify the bending of just war principles? Suppose a militia has no way to

protect a local population against an alien occupying force other than to violate those principles. Does the end of victory justify such means to accomplish it? Why, or why not? Do you see any instances for which exceptions might be made? What should be the basis for international court rulings in prosecuting cases involving these moral decisions?

6. *Coercion and torture.* Is torture ever justifiable to prevent terrorism? What about coercion? Under what circumstances? How should we establish what level of coercion is most effective for obtaining useful information about terrorist plans and activities from detained persons who are suspected of having such information? Suppose that research had established a valid correspondence between various levels of coercion and the extraction of reliable intelligence. What use should be made of such knowledge?

7. *Conclusions of the 9/11 Commission Report.* Can the major conclusions of the 9/11 Commission be recast under the framework of routine activities theory, described in Chapter 2? How?

8. *Ending the war on terror.* Do you think the war on terror should be declared officially over? If so, how might this be done in a way that overcomes charges of being soft on terrorism? If not, how do you counter the arguments made by Fallows and others that the war has been a disaster and should be ended as quickly as possible?

Fear of Terrorism

This chapter describes the role of fear in matters of terrorism and security, starting with the truism that acts of terrorism serve the purposes of terrorists by exploiting the public's fear. It presents an anatomy of fear – its relationship to actual risks, perceived risks, and internal and external stimuli that contribute to perceived risk and fear – and a model of fear management. It considers the roles of the media and politics as both stimuli of fear and tools for managing it.

A. Fear of Terrorism: Basics

Until 2001, people in the United States had relatively little fear of terrorism. Two vast oceans had insulated the United States from serious acts of violence from foreign sources, and its citizens were further protected against hostile alien forces by the strongest military on earth. Fear was reserved largely for street crime and cancer, airplane crashes and shark attacks, judging from the attention paid to stories on these subjects in media news programming. The suicide attacks on New York and Washington marked the opening of a new chapter in the history of fear in the United States. In the days that followed September 11, people throughout the United States bought many millions of dollars worth of duct tape and gas masks, puzzled over how to act when the terror alert color code was orange, and became extremely suspicious of men in turbans and women in head scarves. Four days after the attack, a Sikh gas station owner, Balbir Singh Sodhi, was shot and killed in Phoenix by an Arizonan who assumed that Sodhi was a Muslim.

Fear of Terrorism

The Homeland Security Advisory System, a color-coded terrorism threat advisory scale.

What is the nature of the fears that drive such behaviors? To what extent are these fears useful and reasonable, and to what extent are they harmful and irrational? What, if anything, should public officials do about fear? What can ordinary citizens do about it? These are the issues we take up in this chapter.

1. The Significance of Fear

Terror is very much a matter of fear: "terror" means fear in the extreme. (The word derives from the Latin verb *terrere*, to cause trembling.) Terrorism is fueled by the public's fear; its power lies "almost exclusively in the fear it creates" (Martin and Walcott, 1988). Terrorists commit acts of violence against noncombatant populations typically because they anticipate that doing so will strike fear into the hearts of the population. They might, of course, have other motives for attacking innocents, such as sheer hatred, a desire to exterminate another group, and so on. In those cases, too, fear is a critical factor: fear generated by acts of terrorism creates new problems and imposes further harms, above and beyond those caused by the acts themselves, and in both the near and long term.

From the perspective of the terrorist, acts of violence are successful when they cause mass hysteria, inducing target populations to impose vastly greater harms on themselves as a consequence of their own fear than from the immediate damage associated with the initial acts. As we have seen in Iraq and elsewhere, this can produce a cycle that defines defeat in a war against terrorism. To borrow Michael Ignatieff's (2004) words about what defeat in

300

such a war looks like: "We would survive, but we would no longer recognize ourselves or our instiutions. We would exist but lose our identity as free peoples" (p. 154). Thus, the yield to the terrorist of a considerably larger payoff than from the initial attack may in turn be an incentive for further acts of terrorism. This cycle can be broken either when the public sees that the acts have subsided or when prospective terrorists understand that their acts, even substantial ones, draw limited attention and have little subsequent impact on the target population. The self-perpetuating nature of the problem is captured in the words of the twentieth-century cartoon character, Pogo: "We have met the enemy, and it is us."[1]

Because fear is an essential aspect of terrorism, our ability to understand terrorism and deal with it effectively depends critically on our understanding the nature and sources of fear and the harms it imposes on society. Strategies for dealing with offenders and protecting targets against street crimes have been effectively complemented with strategies for managing the public's fear of crime. Such fear-management strategies could be even more effective for dealing with terrorism, because fear is more central to terrorism than it is to crime. Our efforts to deal more directly with terrorists and to protect targets of terrorism may also be more effective if coupled with effective strategies for managing the public's fear of terrorism.

2. Short- and Long-Term Consequences of Excessive Fear

Fear is not all bad. Doctors distinguish between short-term *acute pain* and long-lasting *chronic pain*, and a similar distinction has been made between *acute fear* – the natural and immediate response to danger that tends to subside quickly – and *chronic fear*, the sort that persists after an immediate danger has passed (Hollander, 2004; Mahl, 1952). Reasonable levels of fear can generate the sort of concerns that help us develop coherent responses to various dangers – acting to prevent them in the first place and then dealing with them effectively when they do occur.

There are many compelling reasons to conclude, however, that the public's fears of terrorism are inflated, and inflated fears tend to harm us in both the short term and long term. In the short term, an extreme level of fear tends to divert people from productive activities, it induces them to consume resources that may do little to protect them against harm, and it can produce severe stresses and reduce social capital and the quality of life. In extreme cases, fear can produce public panics, severe social and financial disruptions, and sharp spikes in accidental deaths, injuries, and suicides. The stresses and reductions in social capital can persist beyond the short term, bringing about detachment and distrust – harming emotional and physical health and economic well-being. These larger effects can spread in a costly social contagion: fear of violence is deeply ingrained, with a strong potential to spread to

301

others. In their landmark essay, "Broken Windows," James Q. Wilson and George Kelling (1982) observe, "In cases where behavior that is tolerable to one person is intolerable to many others, the reactions of the others – fear, withdrawal, flight – may ultimately make matters worse for everyone, including the individual who first professed his indifference."

Over the longer term, fear can induce politicians to pander to and thus aggravate the public's chronic fears, reducing freedoms and invoking responses at home and abroad that may serve to alienate prospective allies rather than to reduce the sources of the threats and thus enhance security. In the case of terrorism, excessive fear makes all targets more attractive. *New Yorker* essayist Adam Gopnik (2006) puts it succinctly: "Terror makes fear, and fear stops thinking." *New York Times* essayist Thomas Friedman (2007) says it even more succinctly: "9/11 has made us stupid." He elaborates sarcastically, "Since 9/11, we've become 'The United States of Fighting Terrorism.'"

There can be good reason to fear fear itself, as President Franklin D. Roosevelt warned in his 1933 inaugural address. Today the public's fear of the fear of terrorism appears to be too *small*, and the consequences of this lack of concern for the hazards of excessive fear could be great.

3. Fear of Crime, Fear of International Violence

Terror means fear in the extreme largely because terrorism is crime in the extreme. Criminologists have found that fear of crime can impose costs on society that exceed those of crime itself, manifesting as reduced quality of life, wasteful expenditures on resources and measures that do little to prevent crime, stress-related illnesses and health costs, and related social costs (M. Cohen, 2000; President's Commission, 1967; Warr, 2000). Because the damage associated with a typical act of terrorism is considerably greater than for a typical street crime, the level of fear and the associated social costs are generally much greater for terrorism than for ordinary crime. Raising fear levels is, after all, a primary goal of terrorism. It is no coincidence that the subject of terrorism has dominated the news since September 11, 2001 – and it may well continue to do so for years to come – while crime has been moved from the front page to the metropolitan section of most major newspapers, despite the fact that the level of crime did not decline appreciably in the years following 9/11 and in fact began to increase around 2005.

In one important respect, the public's fear of international violence is very much like its fear of crime: fear of terrorism has remained high even after several years without a serious terrorist incident on U.S. soil. This is not a new phenomenon. Fear of crime remained high throughout the 1990s even as crime rates plummeted: the homicide rate, a bellwether of crime generally in the United States, dropped from 9 homicides per 100,000 residents in 1990 to about 5 per 100,000 in 2000 (Federal Bureau of Investigation, *Uniform Crime Reports*).

Just as crime rates have declined, so have other forms of international violence over the past few decades. The ending of the Cold War brought with it a huge decline in the amount of international violence. There were 40 percent fewer conflicts throughout the world in 2003 than in 1992; 80 percent fewer deadly conflicts involving 1,000 or more battle deaths; and an 80 percent decline in the number of genocides and other mass slaughters of civilians. International terrorism did increase during the period, but terrorists killed just a fraction of the number killed in wars during the same period (Mack, 2005).

4. Community-Oriented Interventions to Reduce Excessive Fear

In the 1980s, police departments introduced fear reduction programs as an essential part of a community policing movement. A centerpiece of these programs was putting police in closer contact to the public – largely through the use of foot patrols and bike patrols, the establishment of mini-precincts in local neighborhoods, and new incentive systems to induce police officers to become less authoritarian and more service-oriented (Cordner, 1986; Skogan, 1990). These programs spread to the courts and correctional sectors and to the community at large – in the form of neighborhood watch networks – thus making the control of fear a central element of community-oriented criminal justice systems and a complement to conventional strategies for preventing street crime. Such practices and policies may be applicable to the problem of terrorism, as is discussed further in the section, "Fear and Public Policy: Managing Fear."

Some fear reduction interventions for street crimes will be more relevant and practical than others for the prevention of terrorism. We would do well, in any case, to consider the full range of strategies and interventions to ensure that policies and practices that are applicable to the public's fear of terrorism are not overlooked. At the federal level, homeland security officials are authorized and responsible as well to consider approaches that will effectively manage the public's level of fear to ensure that it is neither excessively high nor too low relative to objective threat levels.

B. The Anatomy of Fear and Its Relationship to Risk

We can begin to understand the fear of crime in general and the fear of terrorism in particular by asking the following questions: What is the nature of fear? What are its sources? And, how is fear related to real risks and to factors that are independent of those risks?

Fear of Terrorism

1. The Nature and Sources of Fear

Thomas Hobbes (1651/1996) documented the significance of fear in the seventeenth century, regarding it as a natural passion that shapes human behavior. Psychologists validated this claim over the next three centuries, starting with the definition of fear as the sensation of alarm caused by the anticipation of a threat; they then elaborated on the definition with evidence that the sensation is typically accompanied by physiological changes such as increased pulse, perspiration, rapid breathing, and galvanic skin response (Mayes, 1979). People may fear for their own safety, for the safety of loved ones, or both. Fear is not all bad: it keeps us out of harm's way. Some of it is innate – fear associated with abrupt change is clearly evident in newborn babies – but it is mostly learned, either through the recurrence of a previously experienced harm or the anticipation of a harm about which one person has been warned by another. In the case of crime, fear may be induced by an actual victimization, an immediate threat such as a menacing person behaving strangely in a high-crime area at night, by news of a series of violent stranger attacks in an area, or by other signals of danger ahead.

Fear is a matter of *biology*: the emotion we refer to as "fear" is stimulated by physical phenomena. Neuroscientist Joseph LeDoux (1998) describes the mechanics of fear as centered in the amygdala, an almond-shaped mass of gray matter in the anterior portion of the temporal lobe, the "hub in the brain's wheel of fear." Stimulation of the amygdala generates an outpouring of stress hormones, including adrenaline, which produces a state of extreme alertness, followed by the secretion of a natural steroid, cortisol. Research physician Marc Siegel (2005) describes the result as follows: "The heart speeds up and pumps harder, the nerves fire more quickly, the skin cools and gets goose bumps, the eyes dilate to see better and the brain receives a message that it is time to act." Although the triggers of fear vary from one species to the next, all animals with this brain architecture experience fear through this basic mechanism.

Fear is in the genes. Cognitive barriers that cloud one's ability to recognize legitimate threats can be inherited. Creatures with too little fear of genuine threats are more inclined to be killed by the threatening entities, and the genetic lines of those victims tend to diminish or vanish altogether as a result. Age and gender are obvious biological factors that influence one's level of fear. Younger people tend to be less fearful than older people; hence they more often engage in behaviors that bring greater risks to their own safety and the safety of others – due in part to lower levels of experience, but due largely as well to inherent differences in tastes for risk between the young and old. The young are more likely to succumb to accidental deaths than the old, and they are more likely as well to be victims of crime. And because males

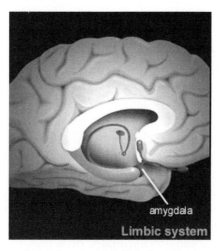

Diagram of the brain, highlighting the amygdala.

tend to be more aggressive and less fearful, they tend to experience higher rates of accidents and violent victimizations than females.

Fear is also *environmentally determined*. First-born children tend to be more cautious than second-born children. And it is *learned*: we tend to fear the most what we understand the least, often through lack of experience or awareness. Most of us are inclined not to repeat behaviors when, through direct experience, we know that those behaviors threaten our safety or the safety of others. Fears are shaped as well by others: parents, neighbors, teachers, the media, and peers. What is learned from each of these sources may produce misperceptions of actual risks, but it is learned nonetheless, and it in turn alters fear levels, for better or worse.

2. The Universality of Fear

The misperceptions that give rise to inflated fears and the extreme social costs that typically accompany these distortions and fears are by no means unique to the United States. Europeans have expressed concerns about terrorist attacks in Spain, Holland, and elsewhere on the continent; they are considerably more exposed to threats of terrorist attacks than are citizens of the United States. Akbar Ahmed (2003) observes that with the 9/11 attack came 24-hour television coverage under the large letters – "America Under Siege" – which tended to overlook the effects the attack had on the Muslim world. Traditional societies the world over had feared the corruption of their youth following years of invasive Western pop culture broadcast through new communication and information technologies, and the 9/11 attack left Muslims everywhere feeling even more under siege than before and fearing reprisal.

305

Phobias are ubiquitous, and they are as old as humankind. We have discovered that they are common in isolated and connected societies alike, that modern technology not only fails to inoculate people against fear but can actually contribute to the rapid spread of fear.

3. Fear and Risk

Fears often do not correspond closely to the actual risk levels of the threats perceived. Each person's unique combination of inherent inclinations and personal experiences shapes both her or his sense of the risks associated with various threats and the fear attached to those perceptions. The lack of correspondence between fear and actual threat is caused by a myriad of factors, including the widespread tendencies to ignore certain types of pertinent information and, under the *precautionary principle*, to give excessive weight to the worst possible outcome (Sunstein, 2005). It is also fed by *emotional contagion* based on misinformation obtained from parents, peers, media, and other sources, which can be significantly heightened through tipping point mechanisms, such as social cascades (i.e., the rapid spread of ideas through social networks) and group polarization. Furedi (2004) notes, "If vulnerability is the defining feature of the human condition, we are quite entitled to fear everything." The influence of others serves to validate and deepen such individual inclinations toward vulnerability.

We can identify two distinct facets of an individual's tendency to overreact, or occasionally to underreact, to threats: (1) making subjective assessments of risks that are high or low relative to the objective risk levels and (2) having fear levels that are high or low relative to those subjective assessments. Rare but extreme threats tend to activate both aspects of distortion. For example, only a dozen or so shark attacks occur annually worldwide. Yet, thanks in no small measure to the horrendous nature of an individual attack, which affects our sense of vulnerability, and sensational media accounts that exaggerate people's perceptions of the risks of shark attacks, the fear of such attacks is considerably higher than the fear of fatal threats that are *thousands* of times more likely to occur. More than 100,000 deaths in the United States are caused each year by car crashes and gunshot wounds; 75,000 people die each year due to alcohol abuse alone (Simao, 2004).

Much the same can be said of fears of serial murders as of shark attacks (and, even more so, of threats of asteroid collisions and cell phone radiation). They are presented by media as legitimate threats, and people tend to fear them at levels that are vastly out of proportion to any reasonable assessment of their incidence (the frequency of occurrence per year, or per century in the case of fatal asteroid collisions) or prevalence (how many people have been victimized cumulatively to date).

Curiously, fear levels are often highest among the very groups that face the least risk, as in the case of the elderly and crime. At the other extreme, people who are frequently exposed to real threats often learn to live with the dangers and exhibit fear levels that would seem appropriate for groups that are in fact much safer. In the case of natural hazards, such as floods, earthquakes, and volcano eruptions, groups with little economic or political power tend to be more at risk than others (St. Cyr, 2005). Because the poor and powerless often live in places where terrorism is more common and do not have the resources to defend themselves against natural disasters, they may be too preoccupied with day-to-day survival to get caught up in frenzies of fright that safer, yet more fear-obsessed populations often experience.

4. Subjective vs. Objective Assessments of Risk

Our sense of danger is so often out of line with reality largely for two reasons: (1) it is based on unsystematic evidence and (2) our perceptions are often distorted – even when our fear level is parallel with our perception of the risk of various threats. Unsystematic evidence, whether experienced first hand or learned indirectly, can be highly unrepresentative of reality due to a variety of causes: the nature of the event experienced directly may itself be unrepresentative of the class of events with which we associate the experience; the occurrence of the event may be more or less rare than we realize; our perception of the event may be distorted by physical interference or emotion; recollections of events change over time; and our filtering of information about events not directly experienced may distort our perceptions of the risk and actual nature of the thing feared.

The accumulation of mixed messages from others can add to this individually imposed confusion. Parents often condition children to err on the side of caution and to overestimate threats; peers often counter parental messages, encouraging their friends to engage in thrill-seeking behaviors. Social scientists have discovered that this interaction of our unique innate predispositions with the vast jumble of mixed information from the environment can cause our *subjective assessments of risk* of a particular threat to be at considerable variance with the actual *objective risk* of the threat. We tend to blow some threats well out of proportion and underestimate others.

Our understanding of the discrepancy between subjective assessments of risk and actual objective risks was informed substantially by research conducted in the 1970s by experimental psychologists Daniel Kahneman,[2] Amos Tversky, Paul Slovic, and others, following the path-breaking research of psychologist and decision theorist Ward Edwards in the 1950s and '60s. They found that people use a variety of *heuristics* – simple rules of thumb that are easier to use than more rigorous methods involving complex computations – to draw inferences and make decisions. They found further that people use heuristics to assess and respond both to ordinary situations and to extraordinary hazards. The various heuristics used, however, often contradict fundamental laws of probability and tend to distort people's perceptions of risk.

Kahneman and Tversky (2000) refer to the tendency of people to distort probabilities as the *psychophysics of chance*. One of the most common distortions is the tendency for most people to give excessive weight to improbable events (pp. 1, 7–9, 209). They have difficulty distinguishing between small probabilities, like 1 in 100, and extreme rarities, like 1 in 1,000,000. The former is, in fact, 10,000 times more likely than the latter. These distortions tend to produce excessively risk-averse behaviors in most situations involving rare but sensational threats, incoherent behaviors in situations involving uncertainty in which facts are presented in convoluted terms, and excessively risk-taking behaviors in situations involving large but uncertain benefits, as in lotteries in which odds are stacked against the bettor.

Tversky and Kahneman (1982) refer to another such distortion as the *availability heuristic* (or simply *availability*): people tend to think that events are more probable when they have occurred recently. The events loom large because they are fresh in the memory. For example, people are inclined to fear earthquakes more when they have occurred in the past year than when they have not occurred recently, even though the risk may in fact be lower a few months after an earthquake than years later, at the start of the next earthquake cycle. Cass Sunstein (2002) observes that the availability heuristic was readily evident in the aftermath of the 9/11 attacks, when "many Americans were afraid to travel in airplanes and even to appear in public places" (p. 50).

Similarly, Gary Kleck et al. (2005) find that perceptions of punishment are unrelated to actual levels of punishment. They speculate that these misperceptions are a product of the weak relationship between the number of highly publicized punishment events and the actual rate of routine, largely unpublicized punitive activities of the criminal justice system (p. 654). The challenge of maintaining public order by discouraging people from overreacting to prospective acts of terrorism thus has parallels to the challenge of maintaining public order by discouraging prospective offenders from believing they can get away with committing crimes.

A variety of factors can distort perceptions of threats by influencing one's immediate emotional state, much like a pang of hunger or whiff of fresh donuts can overwhelm the prudent shopper's sense of good health (Kahneman and Thaler, 2006). Vivid media images of the victims of rare disasters, in particular, serve to inflate the public's perceptions of threats and thus create levels of fear that can harm the public welfare. When people see the photograph of a victim of a one in a million event on the evening news – a person killed by lightning or a shark attack, or by a suicide bomber in Madrid or London – typically, their first reaction is *not* that it is virtually impossible for them also to be victimized by such an event. Even when they are told that the risk is less than one in a million, they tend to distort the risk when confronted with the incontrovertible image of a real victim of disaster. The photograph of a death scene accompanied by a photo of the previously live victim offers more palpable information about a threat and thus is more compelling than the information that such episodes actually occur at an extremely small rate. Finucane et al. (2000) refer to this as the *affect heuristic* – the tendency for perception and behavior to be excessively influenced by images that trigger emotional responses.

Cass Sunstein (2002) refers to the tendency for people to suspend rational inference in the face of the affect heuristic as "probability neglect." He notes that the tendency for people to ignore probabilities and behave less rationally is particularly great in the case of terrorism[3]:

> When probability neglect is at work, people's attention is focussed on the bad outcome itself, and they are inattentive to the fact that it is unlikely to occur. Almost by definition, an act of terrorism will trigger intense fear, and hence people will focus on the awfulness of the potential outcomes, not on their probabilities (p. 51).

Sunstein (2002) observes that people's judgments of uncertain threats tend to be distorted in the following conditions: when the threat is unfamiliar or misunderstood, when people have less personal control over the situation, when the media give more attention to the threat, when the situation is irreversible, when the threat originates with another person rather than from a natural phenomenon (p. 59), and when people are influenced by the fears of others, a process known as *group polarization* (p. 88). Sunstein (2003b) speculates that the millions of Americans who devoted time and energy to purchasing duct tape and emergency supplies would have been far safer had they spent that same time and energy losing weight, staying out of the sun, driving carefully, and ending their smoking habits.

Frank Furedi (2002a) amplifies many of these points in his book, *Culture of Fear*, arguing that perceptions of risk, ideas about safety, and controversies over health, the environment, and technology have little to do with science or empirical evidence. They are shaped more profoundly by deeply rooted cultural assumptions about human vulnerability. These forces have worsened in the post-9/11 era: "'The end is nigh' is no longer a warning issued by religious fanatics; rather, scaremongering is represented as the act of a concerned and responsible citizen. . . . The culture of fear is underpinned by a profound sense of powerlessness, a diminished sense of agency that leads people to turn themselves into passive subjects who can only complain that 'we are frightened'" (Furedi, 2004; see also Brzezinski, 2007).

The consequences of the public's excessive fear of sensational events such as terrorist acts appear to be considerably greater than is widely understood. According to Marc Siegel (2005),

> We feel the stress and become more prone to irritability, disagreement, worry, insomnia, anxiety and depression. We are more likely to experience chest pain, shortness of breath, dizziness and headache. We become more prone to heart disease, cancer and stroke, our greatest killers.... Worry about the wrong things puts us at greater risk of the diseases that should be concerning us in the first place.

It remains to be determined precisely how much stress-related illness and injuries and other social harms have been stimulated by gross exaggerations of danger in media and political messages. In the meantime, existing evidence suggests that the social costs of fear are high. For example, during the three months following the 9/11 attack, about 1,000 more people died in traffic fatalities than in the same period the previous year, due to a combination of factors that almost surely included a fear-induced spike in the demand for driving rather than flying distances of more than 100 miles (see Box 10.1 by David Ropeik).

Virtually every day, someone somewhere becomes the widely publicized victim of a tragic but rare event. Yet for each such person who is harmed, the quality of many thousands of other lives may be diminished substantially when they live their lives, taking unreasonable precautions, in fear that they too might succumb to the unlikely tragic prospects that have befallen the few – about whom we may know more than is good for our own safety and well-being.

C. Media and Fear

We learn about serious acts of violence in general, and about terrorism in particular, through the media: television, radio, newspapers, magazines, and, increasingly, the Internet. In our free and open democratic society, the public is served with such information under the First Amendment to the Constitution: "Congress shall make no law... abridging the freedom of speech, or of the press." Restrictions on such information would make it more difficult for the public to hold their elected officials accountable for failures to provide protection for which they are responsible. The public obtains useful information about terrorism principally through the media.

At the same time, however, the media serve as an essential instrument of terror: without media, terrorists would have no stage on which to perform

Box 10.1. We're Being Scared to Death

– David Ropeik

I wonder whether the politicians who are using fear to get themselves elected would stop if they knew the harm they may be doing to people's health. Real physical harm. Making people sick. Perhaps even killing them. Not intentionally, of course, or knowingly. But this kind of "be afraid" message does more than encourage people to think that you are the candidate who will make them safe. It creates stress and may be at least as much of a threat to public health as terrorism itself.

The University of Michigan's Transportation Research Institute found that, in the period of October through December 2001, about 1,000 more Americans died in motor vehicle crashes than during the same period the year before. Why? Fear of flying certainly played a big role. Though that fear wasn't something created by the government, it demonstrates that when people are afraid, they make choices like driving instead of flying that make them feel safer, even though such choices raise their risk.

Here's another example. Around the 2002 July Fourth holiday – the first post-9/11 national birthday celebration – government warnings suggested an increased likelihood of terrorism. FBI records indicate that requests for handgun purchases in the latter part of June were one-third higher than average. Own a gun if you choose, but let's be honest. The likelihood that a gun will protect you from a terrorist attack is pretty low. But having a gun around does increase the chance of an accident.

Remember when anthrax was in the mail? Tens of thousands of us took antibiotics prophylactically. That made us feel safer, but taking such drugs in advance doesn't do much good – it just helps drug-resistant strains of bacteria proliferate.

And then there are the insidious effects of persistently elevated stress. Chronically elevated stress weakens our immune system. It is associated with long-term damage to our cardiovascular and gastrointestinal systems. It impairs formation of new bone cells, reduces fertility and contributes to clinical depression.

Making people afraid threatens their health. Are we stressed more than normal? A poll by the National Mental Health Association about the psychological effects of 9/11 (released in January of 2004) found that 49% of Americans described themselves as worried, 41% described themselves as afraid, 8% said they were more often emotionally upset for no apparent reason, and 7% were having trouble sleeping. In New York City, evidence suggests increased drug and alcohol abuse and smoking in the three years since the Sept. 11 attacks.

It is hard to estimate how much harm has been caused by all this anxiety. The increased death toll on the roads in late 2001 alone is more than a third of the total number of victims on 9/11. It is entirely plausible to suggest that, because of our fears, as many people have been harmed, and maybe even died prematurely, as died on that awful day.

It's simplistic and overly cynical to say that every government communication about terrorism, such as raising the alert level or announcing an arrest, is political. There are thousands of government workers earnestly trying to protect us. But politicians of both parties who use fear to manipulate our votes contribute to the very harm from which they say they are trying to protect us.

Public health is at stake. And not just mental health. Our physical well-being is on the line here. People are being harmed as politicians frighten us to curry our votes. It is fair to demand that they stop, and we should hold them accountable at the polls if they don't.

[*Source: Los Angeles Times* (September 22, 2004)]

their acts of flagrant violence against noncombatants (Frey, 2006; Nacos, 1994; Norris, 2003). The fear that defines terrorism requires media broadcasting; the wider the audience reached, the greater the fear and more effective the act.[4]

1. Do the Media Exploit Our Sense of Powerlessness?

The public is especially fearful of extreme predatory acts of violence, acts against which they are powerless to defend or protect themselves. This sense of powerlessness surely contributes to the public's exaggerated fears of terrorism, violent crime, and shark attacks. Accidents in cars and homes, in contrast, are more likely to be a product of one's own behavior than that of a predator, as in the case of terrorism and street crime. Media accounts of surprise attacks by predators against innocent victims seize the public's attention more indelibly than do depictions of readily preventable fatal falls down staircases or from ladders, or of heart attacks that result from overeating and lack of exercise. The sense of powerlessness that lies beneath the public's exaggerated fears of predatory attacks offers vicarious thrills for the many who are not affected, who can sit safely in their homes and witness the aftermath of such attacks on hapless victims. In the weeks preceding the 9/11 attack, two of the most prominent items in the news were the disappearance of Washington intern Chandra Levy and shark attacks. Although

Box 10.2. Calvin & Hobbes: Calvin's Dad Gets the News (January 13, 1995)

– Bill Watterson

sheer curiosity often draws attention to such events presented as news, some also derive pleasure, secretly or otherwise, in beholding from a distance sensational stories of predatory tragedies befalling others (see Box 10.2).

For the media, these curiosities and vicarious thrills stimulate enhanced audience shares and, in turn, more extensive media airing of such events (Schaffert, 1992). The disproportionate attention these events receive is often justified on the grounds that the media are simply satisfying the public's demand. The "if-it-bleeds-it-leads" approach to media programming, however, brings with it a moral hazard: the disproportionate media attention given to extreme acts of predatory violence can further distort the public's already inflated fears of terrorism and other predatory events. Disproportionate publicity given to such events leads people to perceive that the risks are greater than they actually are. Sunstein (2005, pp. 78–98) points to several examples of the phenomenon of "this month's risk," including the Love Canal scare in the late 1970s, the Alar apple pesticide scare around 1990, and the summer of the shark in 2001. Robinson (2006) notes, in a similar vein, the disproportionate attention given by media to the occasional disappearance of a photogenic young white woman, clearly aimed at improving ratings rather than at informing the public about legitimate interests of public safety. Most Americans would probably be surprised to discover, as Anne Applebaum observes in Box 10.3, that their lives are actually far safer and that they live much longer than just about any group in human history, even in the era of terrorism (see also Spencer and Crossen, 2003).

Fear of Terrorism

The public's gross misperceptions of risk derive largely from the tendency of mass audiences to unconsciously take information provided over the airwaves and cables unskeptically as gospel. The late Marshall McLuhan (1996), celebrated authority on the power of media, likened the public's difficulty in distinguishing between media presentations and the real world to a fish that has no experience of life outside the pond: "We don't know who discovered water but we're pretty sure it wasn't the fish."[5]

Box 10.3. Finding Things to Fear

– Anne Applebaum

Is life today more dangerous than it used to be? It certainly seems that way. Between Alar in apples (remember that one?), acrylamide in crackers and trans fats in just about everything, our food has become inedible. What with the radiation emitted by our houses, the arsenic in the water and the toxic rays coming out of cell phones, it isn't really safe to sleep, drink, or talk, either.

Last week the entire Metro system in Washington, the capital of the free world, had to close down for a whole day because someone might be blown onto the tracks during a hurricane that began after dinner. This week children in Washington were not allowed to go to school for a whole day because streets were blocked by fallen trees and power lines, and because traffic lights at some intersections weren't working. A previous generation might have walked around the fallen trees and looked both ways before crossing the street, but the children of this generation clearly live in a much more dangerous world than did its parents, and we need to protect them.

Or maybe a previous generation was simply better at calculating risks than this one is. Consider this: In 1996 British scientists claimed, on fairly flimsy evidence, to have established links between mad cow disease in cattle, the human consumption of hamburgers, and a fatal brain disease called CJD in humans. "We could virtually lose a whole generation of people," one scientist infamously intoned, predicting a CJD epidemic of "biblical proportions."

In response, the British government slaughtered millions of innocent cattle. The costs were astronomical; the economy of the countryside was devastated; British agriculture has never recovered. Yet there were only 20 cases of CJD in Britain in 2000, 17 in 2002. So far, this year there are 12. At the same time, more than 1,000 people in Britain will die this year from falling down stairs. More lives would probably have been saved, in other words, if the British government had simply banned the construction of two-story houses.

It's pretty easy to laugh at British hysteria, especially when it concerns something called mad cow disease. But are we any better? After Sept. 11, 2001, thousands of people in this country swore off airplanes and began driving cars, apparently believing that cars are safer. In fact, the number of deaths on U.S. highways in a typical year – more than 40,000 – is more than double the number of people who have died in all commercial airplane accidents in the past 40 years. To put it differently, the odds of being killed in a terrorist incident in 2002 were one in 9 million. In that same year, the odds of dying in a traffic accident were about one in 7,000. By taking the precaution of not flying, many people died.

There are, I concede, some clear psychological explanations for some of this. It is a fact, for example, that people fear man-made disasters (terrorism, pesticides) far more than they fear natural disasters (hurricanes, snowstorms), even when the latter are more dangerous. It is also a fact that people fear unfamiliar things, such as SARS, far more than they fear familiar things, such as pneumonia, even though the latter kills a lot more people than the former. Indeed, thousands refused to fly to Asia for fear of catching SARS, but people didn't quit smoking in similarly large numbers, even though the chances of dying from smoking-related diseases were, and remain, a lot higher.

Although it is equally illogical, people are also more afraid of things they do not control, which is why driving a car does feel safer than flying in an airplane. When I am driving, I am behind the wheel. When I am in an airplane, someone else is driving, and for all I know he might be ill, or drunk, or incompetent, or flirting with the stewardess, or absent altogether.

Finally – although I have no proof – I'll also hazard a guess that people are disproportionately frightened by things they read about in the newspaper. By contrast, they are disproportionately willing to discount the evidence of their own experience. If you look around your neighborhood, you'll notice that the water is clean – which it wouldn't necessarily have been 100 years ago – and that the food isn't rotten or stale. Most children aren't dying young. Most adults aren't dying in middle age.

Life is far safer and lasts much longer for the average American than it ever has for just about anybody at any other time in human history – and maybe that explains the ludicrous precautions that city officials and federal bureaucrats and teachers and doctors and everyone else feels obligated to take nowadays to satisfy the public's demands. Now that we've eliminated most of the things that the human race once feared, we've just invented new ones to replace them.

Fear of Terrorism

McLuhan's sentiments were echoed by George Gerbner (Oliver, 2005) two decades later. In testimony before a Congressional subcommittee on communications in 1981, Gerbner said the following[6]:

> The most general and prevalent association with television viewing is a heightened sense of living in a "mean world" of violence and danger. Fearful people are more dependent, more easily manipulated and controlled, more susceptible to deceptively simple, strong, tough measures and hard-line postures.... They may accept and even welcome repression if it promises to relieve their insecurities. That is the deeper problem of violence-laden television.

In their news coverage of terrorism, the media have not passed up opportunities to exploit the public's innate fear of sensational tragedy. Former Vice President Al Gore (2007) highlights another form of media exploitation: thirty-second spot commercials that run during each election cycle and facilitate political pandering. As philosopher Ray Tallis (2007) puts it, "Apocalypse sells product, and one should not regard the epidemiology of panic as a guide to social or any other kind of reality."

Let us consider first how news coverage exploits public fears (the use of media for political ends is addressed later in this chapter). In late 2006, after more than five years without a serious episode of terrorism on U.S. soil, Wolf Blitzer and his colleagues at CNN continued to conclude television stories about violence in the Middle East and stories related to homeland security with this statement: "Stay tuned to CNN day and night for the most reliable news affecting your security."[7] CNN was not exceptional in this regard; it is in the mainstream of TV news reporting in the United States. Some networks, such as Fox News, have been even more exploitive. What are the consequences of this fear-feeding frenzy?

Perhaps the most serious consequence of media preoccupations with terrorism is that they may contribute significantly to self-fulfilling cycles of fear and violence. Some of this is self-evident: terrorists use the media as a tool for terror, taping videos of the beheadings of noncombatants and broadcasting warnings of further attacks by jihadist leaders. Western media outlets ordinarily edit and often censor the more gruesome of these media images, but there can be little doubt that the widespread airings of these events and threats in news reports feed the fires of fear and overreaction. Media coverage shapes public opinion, and public opinion, in turn, shapes public policy.

Even in the domain of crime, where the perpetrators typically have little or no interest in making the public more fearful, evidence indicates a statistical association between fear of crime and media. Wesley Skogan and Michael Maxfield (1981), for example, found a systematic positive correlation between the fear of crime and the number of hours spent watching television, after controlling for crime rates and other factors. Linda Heath (1984) found similar correlations between fear of crime and reading newspapers

316

that emphasize the reporting of crime. Although such systematic evidence has not yet been reported for the case of terrorism, largely because frequent acts of terrorism are a relatively recent phenomenon, the impact of 9/11 gives reason to expect an even stronger association between media presentations and fear for terrorism than for crime.

2. Reliable Media Accounts, Invalid Risks

The reporting of information about terrorism, crime, and other threats to public safety (including natural disasters, accidents, and illnesses) appears on the whole to be relatively *reliable* in all major media sources. The way that it is reported, however, provides an exceedingly *invalid* sense of the likelihood that an individual will be a victim of any of these threats. The media have more incentive to provide public information that is accurate – a growing corps of media ombudsmen has helped in this effort – than to ensure that the information is representative of ordinary life. Ordinary life is, by definition, not newsworthy. Rare, extreme events are more newsworthy than commonplace trivial ones, but the problem with even accurately reported extreme events is that they tend to overwhelm the senses.

Mark Warr (2000) notes that the reporting of such events typically provides insufficient historical or geographical context. Information that focuses on the extreme rarity of the most severe events is considered less interesting, hence less newsworthy. The problem is likely to be worse with respect to terrorism. We have learned much more about the rates and causes of crime based on valid information in the United States and elsewhere; we have very little comparable evidence about terrorist events and their causes. Scary stories supplant such evidence, and however reliable those stories may be, they are no substitute for valid evidence of the prevalence of the threats described.

The scary stories are particularly toxic with regard to relations between Islam and the West. We are confronted repeatedly by apocalyptic images of suicide bombers acting in the name of Allah. Muslims have been assaulted no less by grotesque images of Abu Ghraib and of women and children killed by U.S. military, the collateral damage inflicted in the name of freedom and democracy. These images have become etched in the minds of the general public on each side, yet extensive interviews with ordinary people reveal that neither set bears any resemblance whatever to the lifestyles, morals, and aspirations of the mainstream of either side (Ahmed, 2007; Burke, 2007; see also Esposito, 2002; Gerges, 2006).

The problem has been exacerbated by several profound changes in the very nature of media. Throughout most of the twentieth century, major news networks controlled the broadcast reporting of news. Toward the end of the century we witnessed a proliferation of channels of electronic communication – the Internet, blogs, e-mail, chat groups, online journals, and the thousands of cable and satellite television channels. Jonathan Sacks (2002) refers to this change as the replacement of broadcasting with "narrowcasting." People throughout the world have thus been given the means to listen only to those who agree with them and to screen out voices of dissent. Vivid television images, especially, evoke emotion rather than generate understanding (Gore, 2007). The result: the most visually compelling protests, the angriest voices, and the most extreme slogans dominate, contributing to the replacement of a culture of conciliation with a culture of conflict. With these developments comes a loss of conversation, which Sacks (2002) regards as the heartbeat of democratic politics, and in turn a reduction in the prospects for civic and global peace and an expansion of the breeding grounds for terrorism.

3. Media Objectivity

The reliability of media accounts of terrorism and other events that stimulate public fear grows out of the media's responsibility for objective reporting. Reporters who fail to satisfy high standards of accuracy, and their employers, can become stories themselves, as occurred in the cases of Jason Blair and the *New York Times*, Dan Rather and CBS, and Eason Jordan and CNN. Checks against biased, inaccurate, or otherwise irresponsible reporting are further enhanced by ombudsmen, noted earlier, and by a growing industry of media-on-media reporting, such as WNYC's weekly "On the Media" program, Slate Magazine's "Press Box" column, and numerous Internet media watch "bloggers."

Media Rights and Responsibilities. Terrorism raises unique and extremely vexing questions about media objectivity:

- How do reporters balance their responsibilities to their employers to provide exciting stories with high standards of professionalism and decency?
- How do reporters balance both of those with their sense of patriotic duty when conflicts emerge?
- How can they report about terrorism responsibly when such reports call attention to and thus legitimize the agendas of the terrorists?
- How should a hostage event be reported when the reporting can itself worsen the outcome of the event and increase incentives for further hostage-taking?
- How much detail should a reporter provide about the vulnerability of domestic targets if doing so might give new ideas to potential terrorists?
- Should reporters protect their sources of information when doing so can endanger innocent others?
- Why do terrorist events in the Middle East receive so much more attention than equally, if not more, serious events in Africa or Southeast Asia?
- Does "balanced" reporting require that every point of view, however unrepresentative or extreme, be included in the story?

- What circumstances and rules should govern whether an attacker is called a "terrorist" or "mass murderer" or "Islamo-fascist"[8] rather than an "insurgent" or "freedom fighter" or "revolutionary"?
- How should conflicts between freedom of the press and the sensitivities of others be resolved?
- How, in short, does a reporter honor the right of the public to have accurate information when doing so feeds fear and terrorism?

Several commentators have drawn conclusions about where reporters come down on these questions. Some argue that the reporting tends to favor the terrorists excessively (Alexander, 1984; Bassiouni, 1982; Y. Cohen, 1983; Podhoretz, 1981), whereas others argue that the reporters allow their sense of patriotism to overwhelm the objectivity of their reporting (Ewers, 2003). Still others assert that the reporting reveals the incivility of the terrorists and thus hurts the causes they intend to advance (L. Martin, 1985; Paletz, Fozzard and Ayanian, 1982).

A major difficulty in assessing objectivity is that such assessments are largely in the eyes of the beholder. Those who think Fox News's reporting of terrorist events is objective will rarely be inclined to see Al Jazeera's reporting of the same events as objective, and vice versa. Many regard both to be biased, with Fox News giving a distinctly pro-American perspective and Al Jazeera reporting from a strong pro-Arab perspective. The facts reported by both may in fact be accurate, but the selection of events reported, people interviewed, and segments shown may not be at all representative of the respective populations from which each of these selections is made. The selection may, instead, be designed to feed the point of view of a particular audience.

The Danish Cartoon Episode. Tension between freedom of the press and the need for media to exercise self-control and refrain against inflaming passions reached a boiling point in early 2006. The ordeal began in September 2005, when the Danish newspaper *Jyllands-Posten* published twelve cartoon depictions of the prophet Muhammad, one showing a bomb in his turban. Many Muslims regard any picture of their revered founder as blasphemous, and the cartoons were considered especially insulting. The initial response was in the form of restrained protests by Danish Muslims; this was followed by sharp criticisms throughout most of the Muslim world. Other European newspapers expressed solidarity with the principle of freedom of the press by reprinting the cartoons. By late January 2006 the reaction had became incendiary, resulting in boycotts of Danish products, demands that Denmark's prime minister apologize, burning of the Danish flags, bomb threats, the issuance of fatwas against offending cartoonists, the destruction of European embassies and consulates, rioting, and the deaths of dozens of people in Afghanistan, Pakistan, Nigeria, and elsewhere.

The affair was portrayed initially in much of the Western media as a clash of civilizations, a conflict between the hallowed principle of freedom of press and quaint "premodernistic" notions of blasphemy ("Clash of Civilization," *Wall Street Journal*, 2006). The editor of *Jyllands-Posten* argued that, in inviting and publishing the cartoons, he was just following Karl Popper's adage of avoiding tolerance of the intolerant: "Our goal was simply to push back self-imposed limits on expression that seemed to be closing in tighter" (Rose, 2006).

Arguing on the side of moderation, op-ed essays and editorials elsewhere expressed the idea that with the right of freedom of the press comes the responsibility to exercise restraint and show respect for ideas that some hold as sacred (Hiatt, 2006). Urging Western media to lead by example, Reza Aslan (2006) argued that the cartoons "fly in the face of the tireless efforts of so many civic and religious leaders – both Muslim and non-Muslim – to promote unity and assimilation rather than hatred and discord; because they play into the hands of those who preach extremism; because they are fodder for the clash-of-civilizations mentality."

Along a similar line, Robert Wright (2006) observed that the error of the Danish newspaper "was to conflate censorship and self-censorship." He argued for asymmetric standards, asserting that the need to exercise restraint in publishing material offensive to Muslims was greater than for followers of other religions because contemporary grievances of Muslims run deeper. Wright reasoned that, in much the same way that the Kerner Commission recommended in 1967 a greater show of respect for the dignity of poor urban minorities and the need to recognize the difference between what *triggers* a riot (how police handle a traffic stop in Watts) and what *fuels* it (discrimination, poverty, and so on), so is it essential to support peaceful coexistence with Muslims by avoiding offensive acts, to "let each group decide what it finds most offensive."

Guidelines for Finding a Balance. What compass should journalists and producers use, in both the print and broadcast media, to guide them through this thicket of difficulties, balancing the public's right to know with its right to be protected from harm? Several treatises have been written on the role of journalists and the standards of professional journalism. Most lists of such standards include the commitment to reporting that is truthful and unbiased, responsible and in good conscience, engaged and relevant, comprehensive and proportional, honest yet respectful of things held sacred. One such list of journalistic standards, based on a survey of some 300 journalists conducted by Bill Kovach and Tom Rosenstiel (2001) and sponsored by the Pew Research Center, is shown in Box 10.4.

Kovach and Rosenstiel explain that it had been common, but is no longer acceptable, to reduce journalism to simple platitudes like "We let our work speak for itself." Instead, they write, "The primary purpose of journalism is to

Box 10.4. Kovach and Rosenstiel's Elements of Journalism

1. Journalism's first obligation is to the truth.
2. Its first loyalty is to citizens.
3. Its essence is a discipline of verification.
4. Its practitioners must maintain an independence from those they cover.
5. It must serve as an independent monitor of power.
6. It must provide a forum for public criticism and compromise.
7. It must strive to make the significant interesting and relevant.
8. It must keep the news comprehensive and proportional.
9. Its practitioners must be allowed to exercise their personal conscience.

[*Source:* Bill Kovach and Tom Rosenstiel, *The Elements of Journalism: What Newspeople Should Know and The Public Should Expect* (Three Rivers Press, 2001)]

provide citizens with the information they need to be free and self-governing (2001, p. 17)." This is particularly essential, they observe, in emerging nations. In advanced nations, and particularly the United States, they see another danger – namely, that "independent journalism may be dissolved in the solvent of commercial communication and synergistic self-promotion (p. 18)." They see the ideal of a free and independent press threatened for the first time not just by intrusive governments, but no less by commercial interests that may conflict with high goals of public service.

Journalism professor Philip Meyer (2004) puts it starkly: "Our once noble calling is increasingly difficult to distinguish from things that look like journalism but are primarily advertising, press agentry, or entertainment. The pure news audience is drifting away as old readers die and are replaced by young people hooked on popular culture and amusement." Comedy Central's Stephen Colbert spoofs this tendency: "Anyone can read the news to you. I promise to *feel* the news *at* you" (quoted in Peyser, 2006, p. 53). Programming is driven by ratings and profits, and news that merely informs cannot compete for large audiences with news that grabs the attention, shocks, and entertains (Altheide, 2006). Meyer sees the source of the problem in a shift in media ownership. Outlets previously owned by people with stakes in local communities are now run by faceless investor-owned corporations.

Columnist Jim Hoagland (2005a) sees the commercialization of media as having dire consequences both for the responsible coverage of terrorism and the larger conversation on national security matters. He sees this as more disturbing even than the decline of civility in society:

> It is not so disturbing that the national political discourse has become detached from civility. That has been true, and not fatal, at other periods in American history. . . . What is disturbing is that the national political discourse is increasingly detached from reality. The emotionalism and character assassination practiced by both sides . . . is mistaken for "politics."

> Instead of turning out more engineers or scientists, American society seems at times more geared to forming consumers, producers and critics of a particularly bombastic kind of political theater, which comes in entertainment and information flows that are increasingly hard to distinguish.

Can the media find a way of controlling itself more responsibly and effectively in the face of these pressures? If it fails, what recourse can the public take? Philip Meyer argues that the only way to save journalism is to develop a new business model that rewards community service, one "that finds profit in truth, vigilance, and social responsibility." He observes that the nonprofit sector may be more amenable to responsible public service journalism and that support from foundations can be a more than suitable complement to conventional commercially supported media. Meyer regards National Public Radio (NPR) as a suitable model for nonprofit journalism[9]:

> While subscriber support is an important source of its revenue, more than 40 percent comes from foundation and corporate sponsors. NPR keeps a policy manual that spells out the limits of permissible relationships with funders. It does not allow grants that are narrowly restricted to coincide with a donor's economic or advocacy interest.

There are other prominent nonprofit broadcast media outlets, including C-SPAN and the Corporation for Public Broadcasting, created by Congress in 1967. C-SPAN is significant for its distinctly noncommercial format and educational mission. It presents unedited broadcasts of lectures, congressional hearings, academic panel discussions, and book reviews on matters of public interest, policy, international affairs, science, politics, economics, literature, health, the environment, and ethics.

One of the distinctive features of the nonprofit broadcasting media is that they present more thoughtful, less sensational coverage of critical issues. Thus, nonprofit broadcasting offers an answer to William Raspberry's (2005) lament of the "death of nuance" in contemporary media:

> Some of the blame for the death of nuance must be laid to the mindless divisiveness of those cable news outlets that treat politics as a blood sport. It's hard to acknowledge that the other guy maybe has a point when he is

determined to prove to the world that you have no point whatsoever. Nuance starts to sound wimpy.

Clearly, there are many ways to strengthen the ability of media to serve the public more effectively in the era of terrorism. Paul Wilkinson (1997), director of the St. Andrews University Centre for the Study of Terrorism and Political Violence, reminds us that the stakes are high and that journalism standards need not be sacrificed as the media strive to avoid serving the interests of terrorism. He recalls Margaret Thatcher's metaphor: "Democratic nations must try to find ways to starve the terrorist and the hijacker of the oxygen of publicity on which they depend." In Box 10.5, Wilkinson offers several suggestions for improving the media's ability to help in the fight against terrorism without compromising in any fundamental way professional journalistic standards.

The problem that Wilkinson does not address is that some media outlets are more responsible and show more self-restraint than others, and members of the audience – responsible and irresponsible alike – can choose to go wherever they want. Although the solutions to this problem are elusive in a free and open society, the problem itself is clear and extremely dangerous: irresponsible media feed the terrorists and create bad policy (Frey, 2006). *Wall Street Journal* columnist Daniel Henninger (2006), commenting on gruesome television images from the 2006 war between Hezbollah and Israel, puts the matter as follows:

> Whatever the purpose, a world in which people get fed streams of awful images to drive political conclusions produces a familiar effect: They eventually become inured to the images. Human wells of moral outrage are deep, but not bottomless. If emotional outrage is the basis on which they are expected to make judgments about politically complicated events like Lebanon, many will turn away, rather than subject themselves to a gratuitous, confusing numbing of their sensibilities. This is not progress.

D. Exploitation of Fear by Politicians

The media are not alone in feeding and inflating our fears. Politicians often take it a step further and convert the inflated fear into bad policy (Altheide, 2006; Mueller, 2006). Why should they wish to do so? Because they know that voters are often influenced more by emotion than by reason (Westen, 2007). Politicians have learned – through direct experience or from their advisors or both – that the voters' fear of crime and terrorism can be used to advantage in campaigning for public office, whereas the failure to do so can end political careers. In a televised debate with George H. W. Bush, in the presidential election of 1988, Michael Dukakis was asked about his opposition to capital punishment: Would he not support the death penalty

Box 10.5. The Media and Terror: Managing the Symbiosis

– Paul Wilkinson

The relationship between terrorists and the mass media is inherently symbiotic. For mass media organizations the coverage of terrorism, especially prolonged incidents such as hijackings and hostage situations, provides an endless source of sensational and visually compelling news stories capable of boosting audience or readership figures. For the terrorists, modern media technology, communications satellites and the rapid spread of television have had a marked effect in increasing the publicity potential of terrorism. As long as the mass media exist, terrorists will hunger for what former British Prime Minister, Margaret Thatcher, called 'the oxygen of publicity.'

The free media clearly do not represent terrorist values. Generally they tend to reflect the underlying values of the democratic society. But the media in an open society are in a fiercely competitive market for their audiences, constantly under pressure to be first with the news and to provide more information, excitement, and entertainment than their rivals. Hence they respond to terrorist propaganda of the deed because it is dramatic bad news. This does not mean that the mass media are controlled by the terrorists. It does mean that terrorists attempt to manipulate and exploit the free media for their own ends. It also means that responsible media professionals and the public need to be constantly on their guard against terrorist attempts to manipulate them.

Terrorists view the mass media in a free society in cynical and opportunistic terms. They have nothing but contempt for the values and attitudes of the democratic mass media. For example, they view the media's expressed concern for the protecting of human life as mere hypocrisy and sentimentality. However, many terrorist leaders are well aware that their cause can be damaged by unfavorable publicity. Hence the more established and sophisticated terrorist movements invest considerable time and effort in waging propaganda warfare directed both at domestic and international audiences.

The free media in an open society are particularly vulnerable to exploitation and manipulation by ruthless terrorist organizations. In using TV, radio, and the print media the terrorists generally have four main objectives:

1. To convey the propaganda of the deed and to create extreme fear among their target group

2. To mobilize wider support for their cause among the general population, and international opinion by emphasizing such themes as righteousness of their cause and the inevitability of their victory
3. To frustrate and disrupt the response of the government and security forces, for example, by suggesting that all their practical anti-terrorist measures are inherently tyrannical and counterproductive
4. To mobilize, incite, and boost their constituency of actual and potential supporters and in so doing to increase recruitment, raise more funds, and inspire further attacks

Police face considerable obstacles in dealing with this. In an open society with free media it is impossible to guarantee that police anti-terrorist operations will be safeguarded against being compromised or disrupted by irresponsible media activity. However, a great deal can be achieved by ensuring that expert press liaison and news management are an intrinsic part of both the police response to any terrorist campaign and the contingency planning and crisis management processes. Indeed, in a democratic society a sound and effective public information policy, harnessing the great power of the mass media in so far as this is possible, is a vital element in a successful strategy against terrorism. This power of the media and the political leadership to mobilize democratic public opinion, so contemptuously ignored by the terrorist movements, reveals a crucial flaw in terrorist strategy.

There are a number of other important ways in which responsible media in a democracy serve to frustrate the aims of terrorists. Terrorists like to present themselves as noble Robin Hoods, champions of the oppressed and downtrodden. By showing the savage cruelty of terrorists' violence and the way in which they violate the rights of the innocent, the media can help to shatter this myth. It is quite easy to show, by plain photographic evidence, how terrorists have failed to observe any laws or rules of war, how they have murdered women and children, the old and the sick, without compunction.

What else can the media do in a positive way to aid in the struggle against terrorism? There are numerous practical forms of help they can provide. Responsible and accurate reporting of incidents can create heightened vigilance among the public to observe, for example, unusual packages, suspicious persons or behavior. At the practical level the media can carry warnings to the public from the police, and instructions as to how they should react to an emergency. Media with international coverage can provide valuable leads concerning foreign movements and links between personalities and terrorist organizations.

Finally, the media also provide an indispensable forum for informed discussion concerning the social and political implications of terrorism and the development of adequate policies and counter-measures. And media which place a high value on democratic freedoms will, rightly and necessarily, continually remind the authorities of their broader responsibilities to ensure that the response to terrorism is consistent with the rule of law, respect for basic rights, and the demands of social justice.

These contributions by the media to the war against terrorism are so valuable that they outweigh the disadvantages and risks and the undoubted damage caused by a small minority of irresponsible journalists and broadcasters. The positive work of the media has been either gravely underestimated or ignored. The media in western liberal states are a weapon that can be used as a major tool in the defeat of terrorism. The media need not become the instrument of the terrorist. In the end, voluntary self-restraint aimed at avoiding the dangers of manipulation and exploitation by terrorist groups is likely to be the most effective and responsible approach available to mass media organizations.

[Adapted from Paul Wilkinson's "Media and Terrorism: A Reassessment," *Terrorism and Political Violence*, Volume 9, Number 2 (Summer 1997), pp. 51–64.]

for a hypothetical offender who had raped his wife? His deliberate, bland defense of his position against capital punishment, together with his having been held accountable for a heinous crime committed by convicted felon Willie Horton following a furlough release while Dukakis was governor of Massachusetts, all but sealed Mr. Bush's victory. Few presidential candidates of either political party have expressed opposition to the death penalty for twenty years after the Bush-Dukakis election, and it became common practice for a political candidate to seek political advantage by "Willie Hortonizing" the opponent, attempting to persuade the electorate that the opponent was weak on crime.

A similar political strategy of exploiting public fear has developed on the issue of terrorism. In the 2004 Presidential campaign, Democratic candidate John Kerry accused the Bush administration of waging a thoughtless, insensitive response to terrorism, resulting in a less secure United States. Vice President Cheney responded with this retort: "America has been in too many wars for any of our wishes, but not a one of them was won by being sensitive" (Milbank and Hsu, 2004). Senator Kerry responded in kind, approving a televised commercial of a woman saying, "I want to look into my daughter's eyes and know that she is safe, and that is why I am voting for John Kerry." Although many saw the Bush team as the leading fearmongers, sociologist Frank Furedi (2004) wrote that the "politics of fear" transcends the political divide: "In fact, Kerry is a far more sophisticated practitioner of the politics of fear than his Republican opponents." Politicians who avoid fueling the fires of fear can be found in both major political parties, but many other politicians across the political spectrum have shown little reluctance to exploit public fears about threats to domestic and foreign security in order to win votes, and they appear to be able to do so with impunity.

Parents often aim to overcome their children's lack of awareness of real dangers such as street traffic, and mythical ones such as razor blades in Halloween apples, by magnifying the risks, hoping to replace their children's inexperience with protective information, however distorted. They often take the opposite approach to deal with imaginary threats such as monsters under the bed by reading calming bedtime stories. Paternalistic governments may be inclined to treat their citizens in much the same way, blowing some risks out of proportion and enacting overly protective laws – Furedi (2002b) and Sunstein (2005) refer to this as the "precautionary principle"[10] – and underplaying others, especially when special interest groups (the tobacco lobby is a prominent example) make such distortions attractive. One of the characteristic strengths of an established free society is a bond of mutual trust and responsibility between the elected and the governed: government ensures that the information the public has about domestic and foreign threats is accurate and balanced, and it trusts them to handle the information responsibly. Terrorism can erode this cohesion, and politicians who use terrorism for political ends may accelerate the erosion.

Brzezinski (2007) argues that, by obscuring the public's ability to reason, fear "makes it easier for demagogic politicians to mobilize the public on behalf of the policies they want to pursue." Furedi (2006) goes on to observe that politicians and governments find it easier to exploit the idea that the public is vulnerable than to lead the public to higher ground:

> The politics of fear can flourish because it resonates so powerfully with today's cultural climate. Politicians cannot simply create fear from thin air. Nor do they monopolize the deployment of fear; panics about health or security can just as easily begin on the Internet or through the efforts of an advocacy group as from the efforts of government spin doctors. Paradoxically, governments spend as much time trying to contain the effects of spontaneously generated scare stories as they do pursuing their own fear campaigns. The reason why the politics of fear has such a powerful resonance is because of the way that personhood has been recast as the vulnerable subject.

This sort of exploitation of public fear by the White House following 9/11 has been asserted perhaps most forcefully by Pulitzer Prize-winning journalist Ron Suskind (2006), based on extensive interviews with former CIA Director George Tenet and his intelligence associates. Suskind writes that a guiding principle behind the invasion of Iraq and other policies associated with a questionable war on terror was Vice President Dick Cheney's "one percent doctrine": the best way to think about a low-probability, high-impact event is to treat it as though it were a certainty. (Recall the Furedi and Sunstein's precautionary principle, described earlier.) Suskind reports that intelligence experts accustomed to providing the executive branch with systematic evidence and objective conclusions about security threats found their analyses ignored under this doctrine – except when their findings or conclusions supported preferred policies – so that predetermined initiatives could be sold to the American public.

The problem with the logic of the one percent doctrine is that it may actually produce conditions that raise a small probability of catastrophe to a much larger likelihood. A safer and saner approach may be to recognize that fear is precisely what terrorism is designed to exploit and to deprive the terrorists of opportunities to exploit our fear. Political leaders are in positions to follow this approach. Political scientist Audrey Cronin (2006) argues that al Qaeda is dangerous, but that we can inoculate ourselves against its dangers by depriving it of its ability to manipulate us psychologically. Terrorism ends with us, not with al Qaeda.

Political pandering in the presence of serious threats to security is neither inevitable nor inescapable. Effective political leadership does occasionally emerge, especially in times of grave threats to national security. One has only to consider Prime Minister Winston Churchill's effective exhortations to the people of England, Londoners in particular, to be courageous in the face of brutal and incessant blitzkrieg bombings by the Germans in World War II. He led both by word and example, holding cabinet meetings at 10 Downing Street rather than in bunkers, often well into the dangerous nighttime as bombs exploded nearby. The people followed Churchill's lead, and the courage of the British helped first to enable them to survive the attacks and carry on, and eventually to contribute in significant ways to the defeat of Germany. (On the occasion of his eightieth birthday, in 1955, Churchill remarked that it was Britain that "had the lion's heart," that he merely "had the luck to be called upon to give the roar.")

A memorable display of fear reduction leadership echoing Churchill's was shown by New York Mayor Rudy Giuliani in the hours and days following the 2001 attack on the World Trade Towers. Of particular significance is the fact the Giuliani became a serious presidential contender in 2007 based principally on his display of extraordinary leadership in that time of duress. Although his reputation for calming the public's fears were diminished by what many regarded as a shameless, nonstop exploitation of his 2001 accomplishment for political gain in the presidential campaign of 2008 (see, e.g., Friedman, 2007), Giuliani had revealed in 2001, nonetheless, that showing courage can be a considerably more successful political strategy than stoking the coals of fear.

328

E. Fear and Public Policy

1. Managing Fear

Given the central role that fear plays in terrorism, public policymakers would do well to combine their focus on interventions against terrorists and the protection of targets with attention to managing the public's fear of terrorism. Fear is not an immutable given, a phenomenon over which we have no control. It is manageable, both for individuals and groups, and by both public and private agents. How can public officials work with private citizens to do this?

First and foremost in any campaign to reduce unwarranted fear is a credible system of security against terrorism. The general public is sophisticated enough to recognize that nothing is as credible as the passing of several years without a serious incident of terrorism. It is almost inevitable that serious terrorists will slip through even strong security defenses from time to time, but over the long haul, political rhetoric is no match for the reality of security on the ground.

Second, in the post-9/11 era the fear of terrorism, by most reasonable accounts, has been excessive. A basic element in a strategy of fear management is to treat excessive fear as a public health problem and have the U.S. Department of Health and Human Services develop a coherent and comprehensive set of programs for preventing and responding to the problem (Butler, Panzer, and Goldfrank). To deal with inflated fears of terrorism, authorities can also consider applying fear reduction programs that have proven successful in managing the fear of crime to the fear of terrorism. Fear reduction strategies for conventional crime instituted as part of the 1980s community policing movement, described earlier, have elements that are applicable to the problem of terrorism, where the stakes may be much higher. Local authorities can legitimately regard acts of terrorism as extreme violent crimes under state law. From their perspective, fear management interventions should be both highly relevant and useful.

These interventions are likely not to be uniform over time and place. Some fear reduction interventions for street crimes are likely to be more relevant and practical than others for the prevention of terrorism. Effective outreach programs to mosques in neighborhoods with Muslim populations, for example, are likely to be more useful in dealing with fear within both the Muslim and non-Muslim communities than programs aimed at removing ordinary graffiti. Introducing guardianship at airports after 9/11 was a great expense and inconvenience, but the public was quite willing to endure both the costs and the intrusions in order to reduce their fear level. Fear reduction programs that induce effective adaptive behaviors – such as avoidance, seeking professional help and pertinent information, getting insurance, planning, and finding suitable coping and protective actions – appear to be among the more effective programs (Kirschenbaum, 2006).

As noted earlier, federal officials are also responsible for ensuring that public fear levels are neither excessively high nor too low relative to objective threat levels. As Gregg Easterbrook observes in Box 10.6, the federal government plays a critical role in managing the public's fear of terrorism.

Box 10.6. The Smart Way to be Scared

– Gregg Easterbrook

WASHINGTON. Thursday, I walked into a hardware store in suburban Maryland to buy de-icing crystals in advance of a predicted weekend snowstorm. Lines of customers waiting to pay snaked through the aisles, dozens of men and women with shopping carts full of duct tape and plastic rolls. Needless to say, I left without de-icing compound. I also left thinking, What's the point of this?

Flashing "threat level" warning boxes on newscasts. Police officers with shotguns wandering Times Square, antiaircraft missiles near the Washington Mall. Federal instructions to stockpile water and batteries and obtain plastic and tape for a "safe room." Yet it's far from clear that this security rush will help anyone.

Government cannot, of course, know what will happen or when. During the 1960s, when the menace was missile attack by the Soviet Union, citizens were urged to do both the useful (stock fallout shelters) and the useless (crouch under the desk at school). Officials suggested such things because it was what they were able to think of.

Today, with no sure defense against terrorism in a free society, officials concerned about chemical or biological attack are suggesting the things they are able to think of. But this may only distract attention from the more likely threat of conventional bombs – and the ultimate threat of the atom.

Consider the mania for duct tape. As Kenneth Chang and Judith Miller reported in *The New York Times* last week, experts view the taped-up room as mainly a psychological benefit. Moreover, many now rushing to buy duct tape may have exaggerated, media-pumped fears of chemical or biological weapons.

If terrorists use chemical weapons, they will probably affect a tiny area at worst, because terrorists would have chemical agents in relatively small amounts. Though any amount of chemical agent might seem ghastly, in actual use chemicals have proved no more deadly, pound for pound, than conventional bombs.

The British and Germans used one ton of chemical weapons per fatality caused during World War I. The 1995 release of the nerve gas sarin in the Tokyo subways by the Aum Shinrikyo sect killed 12 people, fewer than a small, standard bomb might have killed in that crowded, enclosed area. An estimated 5,000 Kurds died in Saddam Hussein's chemical attack on Halabja, Iraq, in 1988, but this involved dozens of fighter-bombers making repeated low passes over the town. It's hard to imagine that terrorists could pull off such a coordinated heavy military maneuver.

A terrorist release of chemical weapons in an American city would probably have effects confined to a few blocks, making any one person's odds of harm far less than a million to one.

Your risk of dying in a car accident while driving to buy duct tape likely exceeds your risk of dying because you lacked duct tape.

Last week, a Washington talk radio host discussed what listeners should do if "a huge cloud of poison gas is drifting over the city." No nation's military has the technical ability to create a huge, lingering gas cloud: in outdoor use, chemical agents are lethal only for a few moments, because the wind quickly dilutes them. Chemical agents are deadly mainly in enclosed circumstances – subways, for example, or in building ventilation systems. The duct-taped room in a home is of little use in such a scenario.

A 1993 study by the Office of Technology Assessment found that one ton of perfectly delivered sarin, used against an unprotected city, could kill as many as 8,000. But the possession by terrorists of a ton of the most deadly gas seems reasonably unlikely, while perfect conditions for a gas attack – no wind, no sun (sunlight breaks down nerve agents), a low-flying plane that no one is shooting at – almost never happen. Even light winds, the 1993 study projected, would drop the death toll to about 700.

Seven hundred dead would be horrible, but similar to the harm that might be inflicted in a crowded area by one ton of conventional explosives. Because these explosives are about as deadly as chemicals pound for pound, but far easier to obtain and use, terrorists may be more likely to try to blow things up. Almost all recent terrorist attacks around the world have involved conventional explosives.

The image of millions cowering behind plastic sheets as clouds of biological weapons envelop a city owes more to science fiction than reality. The Japanese use of fleas infected with bubonic plague against Chinese cities in World War II was the only successful instance of bioattacks in contemporary warfare. In 1971, "weaponized" smallpox was accidentally released from a Soviet plant; three people died. In 1979, an explosion at another Soviet site released a large quantity of weapons-grade anthrax; 68 people died.

Fear of Terrorism

In 1989, workers at an American government laboratory near Washington were accidentally exposed to Ebola, and it was several days before the mistake was discovered; no one died. A coordinated anthrax attack in the fall of 2001 killed five people, a tiny fraction of the number who died of influenza during the time the nation was terrified by the anthrax letters.

None of this means bioweapons are not dangerous. But in actual use, biological agents often harm less than expected, partly for the simple evolutionary reason that people have immune systems that fight pathogens. Also, as overall public health keeps improving, resistance to bioagents continues to increase.

Conceivably, being in a duct-taped room could protect you if a plane dropping anthrax spores were flying over. Smallpox, on the other hand, must be communicated person to person. Those in the immediate area of an outbreak might be harmed, but as soon as word got out, health authorities would isolate the vicinity and stop the spread. By the time you knew to rush to your sealed room, you would either already be infected or the emergency would be over.

Another point skipped in the public debate: smallpox is awful and highly contagious, but with modern treatment usually not fatal. Anthrax doesn't necessarily kill, either, as the nation learned in 2001. Only in movies can mists of mysterious bioagents cause people to drop like stones. In reality, pathogens make people ill; medical workers rush in and save most of the exposed.

If germs merely leave sick people whom doctors may heal, terrorists may favor conventional explosives that are certain to kill.

While government officials now emphasize improbable events involving chemical or biological arms, less is being said about how to be ready for two macabre threats the public is unprepared for: atomic explosion, and the radiological, or "dirty," bomb.

The chance that a crude atomic device will someday detonate on American soil is, by a large margin, the worst terror threat the nation faces. Yet the new Department of Homeland Security has said little about atomic preparedness.

To think the unthinkable, if an atomic device bearing about the yield of the Hiroshima weapon went off outside the White House, people for roughly a mile in each direction might die. But most people in the District of Columbia would survive, while the main effect on Washington's suburbs would be power failures and broken windows. So the majority of people in Washington and its suburbs who would not die would need to know what to do. But do they? Generally not, because there has been scant discussion.

(Here's what to do: Remain indoors at least 24 hours to avoid fallout; remain on ground floors or in the basements of buildings; if you are upwind of the explosion stay put; if downwind, flee by car only if roads are clear since buildings provide better fallout protection than cars.)

Perhaps more likely than an atomic detonation would be a "dirty bomb," in which conventional explosives spread radioactive material. Since this has never been used, effects are hard to project. Most likely, even an extremely large dirty bomb (say, an entire truck converted to one) might kill only those within a city block. Fallout would probably threaten only those a few hundred or thousands of yards downwind.

Yet if people heard on the radio that a dirty bomb had exploded – if they so much as heard the word radiation – panic might set in. In Manhattan or Washington, mass chaos to escape might result in more deaths than the bomb itself.

But is the government explaining to the public how to react if a dirty bomb goes off? (Stay indoors; if upwind do nothing; if downwind, drive away only if roads are clear; take potassium iodide pills to prevent some effects of fallout.) The Department of Homeland Security Web site, for one, has loads of information about anthrax, but offers essentially zero on what to do in the event of radiological explosions.

Increased presence of police and military units in cities may help deter terrorists, and by being more visible and waving bigger weapons, law enforcement is doing what it can think of. But government officials who are advising people to buy plastic sheets create unnecessary anxiety while achieving little beyond helping hardware stores. The advice people need to hear concerns the atomic threat – and why potassium iodide matters more than duct tape.

We have not exhausted the prospects for reducing fear at either the local or federal level, in large part because we have put so many more resources and so much more energy into the war on terror in general and operations in the Middle East in particular. In turning people throughout the world against the United States, these efforts appear to have given the U.S. public reason to be more fearful of terrorism rather than less fearful. As we work to reverse this trend, we would do well to find new ways to adapt effective fear reduction programs used in other domains – for individuals and institutions, public and private – to the problem of fear of terrorism.

2. Finding a Balance

The total elimination of fear is neither an attainable nor a desirable goal. Just as it would not be healthy to eliminate pain altogether, so would it be unsafe to seek a way to eliminate fear altogether. Some level of fear is necessary for us to feel compelled first to take ourselves out of the path of immediate danger and then to take measures to counter the sources of the danger (de Becker, 1997). The 9/11 Commission concluded that there was too little concern about terrorism before the 2001 attack, and by many accounts inflated fear of terrorism afterward has imposed vast unnecessary costs on people throughout the world (Applebaum, 2003; Furedi, 2006; Ropeik, 2004).

In the case of both crime and terrorism, the goal should be twofold: first, to make accurate objective assessments of the risks of threats and then realign subjective assessments of the risks so that they correspond to the objective assessments, and second, to remove elements of fear that serve no useful purpose. In much the same way that we can consider frameworks helpful for finding the proper balance of security and liberty and assessing criminal sanctions in terms of the total social costs of crimes and sanctions (Forst, 2004), so should we consider policies that aim for optimal levels of fear for various threats. See page 335 for a depiction of an optimal level of fear, the level that balances the cost of fear with the cost of victimization averted by fear. Such frameworks cannot determine public policies, but they can help identify the key factors for consideration and determine how to organize them coherently to provide a basis for assessing those policies.

F. An Agenda for Reducing the Social Costs of Fear

We have noted that Mayor Rudolph Giuliani showed exemplary leadership skills in the days after the 2001 terrorist attack on New York City. Two years later he remarked, "Courage is not the absence of fear; rather it is the management of fear" (quoted in Gambrell, 2003). Then, in the presidential campaign of 2008, he became widely criticized for excessively exploiting his status as a 9/11 hero. In 2007, the satiric newspaper, *The Onion*, ran the spoof headline: "Giuliani To Run for President of 9/11" (author anonymous). Although presidential candidate Giuliani clearly had lost his way by exploiting public fear for political gain, his message as Mayor Giuliani on the importance of managing fear still has resonance.

How might policymakers and public officials begin to think about the management of the public's fear? At the local level, fear reduction strategies that have been a key aspect of successful community policing programs can be tailored to deal with fear of terrorism, as noted earlier. At the federal level, just as effective energy policy cannot ignore the public's insatiable demand for and often wasteful consumption of scarce energy resources, so must an effective terrorism policy recognize the importance of interventions that deal effectively with a parallel problem on the "demand side" of terrorism: dysfunctional fear. Excessive fear makes all targets more attractive, as noted earlier, but they also produce misallocations among targets. Strategies for

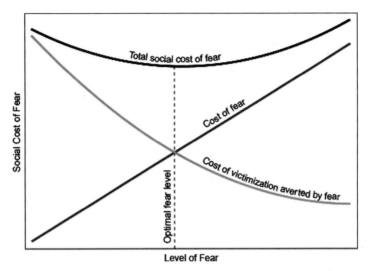

Optimal level of fear.

managing the public's fear of terrorism might be developed in such a way that deals with both problems, satisfying liberals and conservatives alike. No side of the political spectrum can take comfort in the prospect that we may have actually contributed to our insecurity and misallocated resources along the way by placating exaggerated public fears – for example, by overemphasizing airport security at the expense of vulnerability at ports, nuclear and chemical facilities, and other critical, more vulnerable targets. Several authorities argue persuasively that such misallocations have been induced by misplaced fears (Applebaum, 2003; Fallows, 2005). Systems of accountability used by the Office of Homeland Security and associated agencies can be reshaped to support fear management as a legitimate goal of those agencies.

Sunstein proposes that deliberative democracies should be strengthened to help manage fear generally (2005). He proposes, in particular, that a federal risk assessment agency should be established to collect data and conduct research aimed at reducing actual risks and better aligning objective and subjective risk levels (2002). He notes that a significant barrier to the adoption of such reform is that public-minded administrators who dismiss the public's irrationality are often overruled by populist politicians who respond to parochial agendas and short-term concerns, however irresponsible for the nation as a whole, and to public concerns of the moment, however irrational and short-sighted (Sunstein, 2002, 2005). He adds that education and public information can help restore rational deliberation to the process. Tharoor (2005) suggests along a similar line that the media, for too long a source of fearmongering, is capable of serving no less as an instrument of education and tolerance.

335

Fear of Terrorism

Protection of the public is the first responsibility of government, and misplaced fears undermine public safety. The effective public management of fear is central to this responsibility of government. In cases of extreme abuse of the media's responsibility to not harm the public, the courts may be able to step in to provide protections. Justice Oliver Wendell Holmes observed in the landmark 1917 case of *Schenck* v. *United States*, "The most stringent protection of free speech would not protect a man in falsely shouting fire in a theater, and causing a panic." This could apply as well to needlessly incendiary media accounts of violence or threats of violence.

Effective, credible leadership is extremely important. Good leaders educate the public, providing useful information that reduces the fears born of ignorance. They can counter what Zbigniew Brzezinski (2007) refers to as "the terror entrepreneurs . . . usually described as experts on terrorism . . . engaged in competition to justify their existence." They can promote and fund public education programs that reduce excessive fear levels (Altheide, 2006). By doing so, they help build bonds of trust between the government and the governed, a social contract in which the people will follow loyally and manage their fear responsibly when they have sufficient reason to believe that the government is leveling with them without divulging information that helps terrorists needlessly, when the government attains a proper balance between liberty and security. On February 23, 1942, Franklin D. Roosevelt, spoke words that echoed Churchill's effective leadership across the Atlantic Ocean in the same war effort: "Your government has unmistakable confidence in your ability to hear the worst, without flinching or losing heart. You must, in turn, have complete confidence that your government is keeping nothing from you except information that will help the enemy in his attempt to destroy us."

When leadership of this sort fails to emerge, or when exceptional leaders get assassinated – an all-too-frequent occurrence in places most desperately in need of effective leaders – nongovernmental organizations and responsible citizens are left to find ways to fill the void. In such cases ordinary citizens must become extraordinary; they must step up and become leaders. Citizens of India, Iraq, and Israel have shown extraordinary courage in the face of extreme terror in recent years even in the absence of a Churchill-like figure. The day after a series of bombings on commuter trains in Mumbai (formerly Bombay) killed more than 200 people, Mumbai's tracks were cleared, trains resumed their routes, and the Bombay Stock Exchange's stock index rose by 3 percent[11] (Wonacott and Bellman, 2006).

Some portion of fear is, of course, unmanageable. Fear is, after all, in our genes; it is a natural survival instinct. Yet when such biological instincts get out of hand and worsen the dangers we confront, it is precisely the capacity of humans to reason – to find ways to control our instincts under stress – that has contributed immeasurably to the resilience of our species.

336

We have reason to fear terrorism, surely more so today than before September 11, 2001, but we would do well to keep in perspective the risks that terrorism poses to our national security and the security of our allies. Cataclysmic risks were more immediate in the United States in World War II and during the 1962 Cuban Missile Crisis than today, and people in most other countries have for decades been considerably more exposed to terrorism than have people in the United States. There is no cause for alarm if we take reasonable and effective measures to neutralize persons who have demonstrated a clear intent to commit acts of terrorism, if we protect the primary targets of terrorism, *and* if we can manage to manage our fear. The 9/11 attack revealed that concerns of the U.S. government and its citizens about terrorism had been inadequate, that the risks exceeded our fear (Clarke, 2004).

Today fear is the greater problem, and it is dangerous because of the strong tendency for it to feed on itself, to make us behave badly, to allow our instincts to overrule our ability to think, and to make us more attractive targets of terrorism as a consequence. Perhaps our greatest challenge is to master our capacity to "get a grip" when confronted with real danger, to find ways of strengthening our capacity to reason, to overcome our natural tendency to be more easily frightened than unfrightened[12] – and to groom leaders who will reduce the demand for terrorism by dousing the flames of our inflated fears. Doing so will help not only reduce the attractiveness of targets in the West to prospective terrorists but also improve the quality of life throughout the world, regardless of the effects on terrorism.

Discussion Questions

1. *Media and fear of terrorism and crime.* How do the media distort terrorism and crime? Explain why you think these distortions either worsen matters or do not. What feasible interventions are available to countervail against these distortions and the associated harms?

2. *Private citizens and fear of terrorism.* How do private citizens and institutions outside of the media distort terrorism and crime? Explain why you think these distortions either worsen matters or do not. What can be done to counteract these distortions and the associated harms? What can you do? What stands in the way of your acting to reduce excessive fear?

3. *State and local management of fear of crime.* What have elected and appointed state and local officials done to manage the fear of crime appropriately? What have they done that is inappropriate? What makes these actions appropriate or inappropriate? What incentives or disincentives might state and local authorities invoke to induce individuals, the media, and other institutions to reduce excessive fear?

4. *Federal management of fear of terrorism.* What have elected and appointed federal officials done to manage fear of terror appropriately? What have

they done that is inappropriate? What makes these actions appropriate or inappropriate? What incentives or disincentives might federal officials use to induce individuals, the media, and other institutions to reduce excessive fear of terrorism? Does a free society have a special responsibility to avoid manipulating the public's sense of fear by demonizing aliens and exaggerating the threats they pose? Explain. Do you agree that even in a free society – in Washington as in Hollywood – when the chips of fear are on the table, toughness trumps sensitivity and restraint? What should be done about this?

5. *Fear as an attractor of terrorism.* Is the suggestion that our fear attracts terrorism akin to the suggestion that a woman's provocative attire attracts rape? Do both suggestions have the effect of shifting the culpability for violence from the attacker to the victim? If so, does this imply that we should refrain from attempting to place restraints on victim behaviors that may provoke violence?

Preventing Terrorism: Short-Term Approaches

Clearly, it is preferable to prevent acts of terrorism in the first place than to have to respond to them after they occur. In this chapter and the next we consider ways of preventing individual acts of terrorism, first as a set of tactics and policies for the short term to deal with immediate threats, and then as a long-term strategy to address the deeper sources of terrorism. In this chapter we consider approaches that appear to have merit for the near term, focusing on obtaining and analyzing intelligence information about terrorist plans, the removal of opportunities for terrorists to carry out their acts and, where dialogue and understanding are either impractical or impossible for warding off immediate threats, exploring alternatives such as the use of hard power and homeland security protections.

A. Introduction

We noted in Chapter 2 that the key to preventing aggression is to understand its sources and that an array of crime prevention strategies have been developed following extensive and systematic inquiry into the nature of crime. This inquiry has been systematic in that it has been based on the accumulation of reliable data and use of research methods that provide a more thorough and unbiased understanding of crime's causes than had ever been available before. Like crime, terrorism is a manifestation of aggression. If we are to prevent terrorism through the design of effective intervention strategies and policies, it will be essential first to better understand its causes too. And as with the design of strategies that aim to prevent crime, it is important to distinguish between long-term ("root") causes – especially, the causes of deep alienation and hatreds that can form the foundation for individual acts of terrorism – and short-term causes, which serve to ignite such acts once the alienation has become deeply rooted. These distinctions are useful both for a coherent understanding of terrorism generally and for the development of sound policies and programs, both public and private.

If we are to make use of effective crime prevention models to develop policies that prevent terrorism, we must first understand how terrorism is *not* like street crime and what these differences imply for the kind of policies and strategies that aim to prevent terrorism. Even to the extent that terrorism is similar to conventional crime, the development of effective antiterrorism strategies faces substantial barriers: measurement difficulties, obstacles to the accurate analytical portrayal of real-world complexities, situational nuances that fit no known pattern and hence defy prediction, and so on. The reporting and counting of terrorist incidents are even less reliable, the explanatory variables more elusive, the frequency of incidents fewer, the rise of new unanticipated developments more unpredictable, and the consequences more severe and less readily measurable. We end up having to rely much more on judgment and draw what are, at best, indirect inferences from what we know about the success of crime prevention strategies.

Let us now consider some of the major differences between crime and terrorism and their implications for the development of terrorism prevention strategies.

B. Dealing with a Thinking Adversary

Terrorism is more difficult to predict than ordinary street crime largely because those who commit acts of terrorism tend to be more scrupulous about avoiding patterns that would make their acts discoverable than are ordinary criminals. Crime has been found to cluster both in time and space (Eck et al., 2005; Sherman, Gartin and Buerger, 1989). Pin maps in urban police precincts have reflected such patterns for many decades, and the patterns have been analyzed more systematically in recent years using computerized crime mapping systems, analyses of "hot spots," and geographic crime profiling (Harries, 1999; Rossmo, 1999). Yet the most elusive and successful criminals stake out their targets, learn about guardians – including human guards, automated surveillance and alarm systems, locks, and other protective devices – and they avoid patterns of behavior that make their detection and capture more likely. So, too, do the most elusive and effective terrorists.

The most devastating terrorist attacks, employing particularly potent destructive weaponry aimed at the most attractive targets, require especially large investments in planning, training, and financial support if they are to successfully evade and penetrate the victim's defenses. Terrorists have incentives to protect these investments by operating well outside the web of surveillance and counterterrorism and doing so in ways that defy prediction. They think and adapt in order to maximize their prospects for success in striking their targets. Accordingly, the most effective strategies for preventing terrorism are likely to derive from approaches that treat terrorists as people who anticipate counterterrorism strategies and then plan and operate accordingly. Because the stakes are so much higher with terrorism than with crime, it is more important to make use of the most powerful analytic tools available to inform the deployment of scarce preventive resources.

The assessment of strategies for dealing effectively with thinking adversaries falls within a field of applied mathematics known as the *theory of games* (Davis, 1997; Luce and Raiffa, 1989; Myerson, 1997; Schelling, 2006). One of the fundamental principles of game theory is that an optimal strategy against a thinking opponent is to maximize the effectiveness of scarce resources by applying what is known as a *mixed strategy*: roughly speaking, from the guardian's perspective, the terrorist will have the most difficulty anticipating the likelihood of detection and capture if scarce mobile protective resources are randomly allocated across the array of vulnerable targets in proportion to the net value that the terrorist attaches to each prospective target, taking into account the cost to the terrorist of attacking each target. This randomized strategy will apply to personnel and other movable resources, rather than to fixed protective resources, such as barricades and other target-hardening capital resources, which should also be allocated in proportion to the value of the target, but in a fixed rather than random manner.

Randomized and other strategies for preventing terrorist attacks in the short term can be assessed under a variety of scenarios by applying simulation gaming models. This analytic approach has proven useful in developing military strategies for dealing with both conventional combat operations and with insurgency and other forms of unconventional warfare (Myerson, 1997). They could prove equally useful for assessing alternative preventive approaches to protecting any prospective target against threats posed by terrorism.

C. The Role of Intelligence

Given the impossibility of preventing terrorism by protecting every potential target against a very large number of thinking, hostile adversaries, the most potent element in any arsenal of defense against terrorism is likely to be an effective system of intelligence. *Intelligence* is information about the plans or operations of a suspicious organization or individual that can be used to prevent hostile acts either at their source or at a targeted site. Intelligence on terrorism permits officials to learn about the activities and intentions of those planning to engage in acts of terrorism and intercede before the intentions and plans manifest as successful incidents.

Intelligence is essential to security. It permits an understanding of an adversary's thinking and motives, a fundamental aspect of defense against any form of aggression. According to military strategist Sun Tzu, "If you know your enemy and know yourself, you will not be imperiled in a hundred battles." On the ground, intelligence can enable the penetration of an adversary's cells and creation of discord in the adversary's ranks, thus weakening him from within; it also provides an understanding of how he thinks, so that one can anticipate how he is likely to act in various situations and be able to conduct effective counterterrorist interventions to prevent terrorist attacks. It can help discover what is needed to win the support of a population to help dismantle the insurgent's infrastructure.

Intelligence typically combines *passive* information, which provides relevant background descriptions of the suspect group or individual and modes of operation and goals, with *active* information about current plans, specific activities, whereabouts, and assignments. The passive information may be obtained through both closed espionage sources and open public sources such as newspaper and magazine articles or Internet postings. Active information is usually obtained through spies, wiretaps, dead letter drops (to pass secrets, instructions, or money in exchange for information), and other closed, classified sources.

Background information can be an essential complement to active intelligence. Some background information is basic, related to geography and sociodemographic factors such as wealth, education, and ethnicity, as well as information about origins and local histories. Other background information is *strategic*, related to stated missions, political and religious agendas, financial support, availability of weapons, technical capabilities, and ties with governments and like-minded groups and influential people.

1. Integrating Intelligence Activities

The organization and incentives of intelligence agencies are critical to the ability of the intelligence community to coordinate activities effectively to prevent terrorist attacks. Political scientist Amy Zegart (2007a) observes, based on government documents in the public domain, that two crucial components of the U.S. intelligence establishment – the Central Intelligence Agency (CIA) and the Federal Bureau of Investigation (FBI) – missed at least twenty opportunities to prevent the 9/11 attacks. One of the primary causes of this failure was an intense and often counterproductive rivalry between the two organizations (L. Wright, 2006a). Another was structural weaknesses in both the CIA and FBI, which as Zegart (2007a, p. B1) notes, "prevented all 15 U.S. intelligence agencies from working as a unified team."

Two other factors, she noted, were agency cultures that led officials to resist new ideas, technologies, and missions and a system of promotion incentives that rewarded the wrong things (see also R. Posner, 2007; Weiner, 2007). Zegart goes on to report that the serious organizational deficiencies had been well documented before 9/11:

> Between 1991 and 2001, a dozen reports examining U.S. intelligence and counterterrorism capabilities found serious organizational problems and urged immediate action. The consensus was stunning. Of 340 recommendations, 84 percent focused on the same four deficiencies: poor coordination across intelligence agencies, terrible information sharing, inadequate human intelligence and insufficient attention to setting priorities.... If you think these problems have been solved, think again. Despite the recent creation of a director of national intelligence, the U.S. intelligence community remains a dysfunctional family with no one firmly in charge.

Zegart observes elsewhere (1999, 2007b) that these problems emerged largely because of the absence of design in the intelligence agencies' structure and organization. The intelligence establishment evolved haphazardly, as a product of random historical events, quirky political processes, explicit and vaguely perceived threats, the interests of self-interested bureaucrats, and the fragmented nature of federalism in the United States. With the end of the Cold War in 1991, the CIA and FBI failed to adapt to the rapidly emerging problem of terrorism.

Before 9/11, virtually all intelligence information was separated between foreign and domestic intelligence. Responsibility for foreign intelligence had been shared traditionally between the CIA, responsible for information from international sources; the Defense Intelligence Agency (DIA), which collects and analyzes intelligence to support all military operations; and the National Security Agency (NSA), which collects and analyzes signal intelligence information using advanced satellite and computer technologies. Domestic intelligence on terrorism had been the primary responsibility of the FBI. In 2005 most of these functions were consolidated into a single agency, the National Security Service, within the Federal Bureau of Investigation.

This consolidation followed the findings of several commissions, most notably the 9/11 Commission, which identified gaps; tensions among the CIA, the FBI, and other competing intelligence agencies; refusals to share important information with other agencies that had a need to know; and other forms of waste. The poor performance of this incoherent assortment of intelligence agencies, working largely at cross-purposes with one another, contributed mightily to the 9/11 intelligence failure (9/11 Commission Report, 2004; Pillar, 2006). Poor intelligence was found also to have contributed to numerous fiascos associated with the invasion of Iraq in 2003, including the failure to find weapons of mass destruction there (Robb and Silberman,

2005). The commissions outlined the principal ways in which the "dots" of information about various aspects of terrorism could be collected and connected more efficiently across the various intelligence agencies so that the intentions of terrorists could be thwarted as quickly and fully as possible and practicable.

The 2005 agency consolidation came three years after the creation of the Department of Homeland Security (DHS) as a cabinet-level department, reporting directly to the president under the Homeland Security Act of 2002. The DHS is responsible for coordinating with foreign intelligence services such as Great Britain's counterparts to the FBI and CIA – MI-5 and MI-6, respectively – and with counterpart agencies in Germany, France, and elsewhere. When information is obtained that suggests terrorist planning, intentions, or activity, governments can freeze bank accounts and other sources of financing, make arrests, file charges in court, and work with agents internationally to stop the activities before they cause damage.

One of the chief concerns with the consolidation of intelligence operations is the prospect of "groupthink," the risk that independent analysis – and possibly accuracy – will be lost in the process (Bennett, 2006; Kringen, 2006; Whyte, 1952). Decision makers often dislike uncertainty and dissent, and the integration of agencies with different sources of intelligence into a single entity can force a consensus that is incorrect, as in the case of the widespread misunderstanding that Saddam Hussein had vast inventories of weapons of mass destruction prior to the U.S. invasion of Iraq in March 2003. Some agencies raised serious doubts about the evidence of such inventories, but were discouraged from advancing their conclusions once the decision had been made to invade Iraq. The agency consolidation has been criticized for being bureaucratically inefficient and politically unwise (Lehman, 2005; Posner, 2006b; Weisberg, 2005).

The problem of groupthink is countered in part through cooperation between federal intelligence agencies and intelligence agencies of other countries. Federal agencies obtain much information through collaborations with intelligence agencies of friendly nations, especially those in Great Britain and Europe, and occasionally with agencies in countries with weaker historical ties to the United States. Even countries with long-standing mutual hostilities, such as Pakistan and India, work together occasionally to share intelligence when their interests coincide (United Press International, 2006).

2. Collection, Processing and Analysis, and Dissemination of Intelligence

Both background and active intelligence must be collected and processed. The full intelligence process encompasses three basic phases: *collection, processing and analysis*, and *dissemination*. Let us look at each of these in turn.

Collection. Intelligence data must first be gathered. The data come from sources of one or more of the following types: human intelligence (HUMINT), signal intelligence (SIGINT), and imagery intelligence (IMINT).

Human intelligence is the oldest type of intelligence, involving information obtained from people operating in any of several capacities: disgruntled member, paid insider, observer, agent paid to provide information obtained through deception (the conventional spy), embassy officials and staff, and so on. In his memoir, *The Craft of Intelligence*, former CIA director Allen Dulles (2006) notes that Chinese military strategist Sun Tzu was aware of the importance of human intelligence some 2,400 years ago: "What is called 'foreknowledge' cannot be elicited from spirits, nor from gods, nor by analogy with past events, nor from calculations. It must be obtained from men who know the enemy situation."

Popular novels and motion pictures typically portray agents from the Central Intelligence Agency (CIA) or the British Secret Intelligence Service, MI-6, working under cover as the most pervasive type of human intelligence. In the real world, spies from the West who insinuate themselves covertly into enemy networks and provide useful information were rare even during the Cold War and are virtually nonexistent today. Terrorist cells today are smaller, more decentralized, and more impenetrable to outsiders than Soviet networks of the twentieth century. Loyalties among the members of these smaller cells tend to be intense and more deeply ideological. Members of terrorist cells do occasionally "flip" and become valuable sources of information, but such instances are rare and the information they provide is often obsolete.

The CIA and Defense Intelligence Agency (DIA) are the two primary centers of human intelligence in the United States. These agencies coordinate the collection of information from a variety of sources, much of it obtained from human sources on the ground overseas. Defense intelligence is obtained largely through military police or patrols in their contacts with various sources – prisoners of war, refugees, or civilians – some of whom are more reliable than others.

Human intelligence can be an indispensable source of information about terrorists. Media sources or nongovernmental organization (NGO) agents often develop effective and close working relationships with people on the ground, and these can be rich sources of intelligence. Or it may be obtained from "walk-ins" who volunteer to side with counterterrorist forces. One of the most common and effective sources of human intelligence is the use of friendly diplomats and journalists to collect information about key individuals and activities in an area, often with the assistance of paid local interpreters with whom trust is often built over weeks or even years of collaboration. People who provide covert information because of a loyalty to the targets of the terrorists or a deeply rooted commitment to the rule of law, or both, often provide the most valuable human intelligence (Wallace-Wells, 2006).

345

Preventing Terrorism: Short-Term Approaches

Human intelligence can be more effective and reliable also when it comes from sources who know the language and culture intimately; such people are less likely to be viewed with suspicion by terrorists. Locals generally make the most reliable sources of human intelligence, as they understand often critical nuances in the meanings of words, phrases, and behaviors. However, such information is not always available, even when the terrorists are unpopular; human sources often put themselves at considerable risk in providing such information, so measures are usually taken to protect these sources from harm, sometimes requiring their removal from the area and change of identities.

The assurance that information provided by informants will be kept secret thus accomplishes several ends: it keeps information about our knowledge of terrorist plans and activities out of the terrorists' reach, thus protecting targets of terrorism; it protects the sources of the intelligence against reprisal; and it enhances the prospects for continued inflow of such information over the longer term.

One increasingly important form of human intelligence is the use of people raised in cultures that breed terrorism to monitor Web sites of terrorists and terrorist supporters. Their understanding of local dialects and social conventions gives them advantages in interpreting important nuances in the information. The people who monitor these sites may do so with the support of a patron, such as the CIA or NSA. However, in rare instances, they may do so without pay so that they can provide the information to an array of interested government officials who have a legitimate need for the information and can be trusted to use it responsibly, but who would otherwise have difficulty obtaining it; for example, federal attorneys who use the information to prosecute cases and officers in foreign theaters who need information about the characteristics of new explosive devices (Wallace-Wells, 2006).

Other measures to gain covert access to reliable human intelligence can be effective, but often at a price. Local police and federal agents often develop ties with local mosques and other Muslim enclaves to encourage a healthy blend of good citizenship with respect for diversity. Pressuring people to spy on associates, however, can be a toxic approach to human intelligence. One especially corrosive approach is to threaten people seeking residence in the United States with deportation if they refuse to spy on associates. These and other inducements to develop confidential sources to provide covert information about other Muslims typically generate resentment, are likely to be harmful in the long run, and produce information of dubious value in the short term. Muslims with loyalties to both Islam and the United States report that their affection for the United States is likely to be the strongest incentive to report terrorist activity and that additional inducements, positive or negative, tend to undermine their natural inclination to live in and love a land of peace and security (Waldman, 2006). When informants do come forth voluntarily, it can be helpful if officials provide letters of support, which can not only build and maintain their morale but also help them when they are questioned by suspicious public officials (Wallace-Wells, 2006).

A common problem with local human intelligence is its unreliability. Such information is often a result of locals aiming to settle scores with warring tribes or factions in an unsettled area. In other cases, sources make up stories in exchange for pay or special privileges. Both types of deceit can bring tragic consequences, not only for local innocents victimized in the name of counterterrorism but also for the larger campaign to win the support of local populations and build goodwill and legitimacy.

Human intelligence may be particularly critical in preventing acts of nuclear terrorism. Satellites and other sophisticated detection technologies cannot detect the development or exchanges of atomic weapons that have been brought indoors and out of view. Imagery intelligence can help detect the movement of large munitions and launching devices, but in the age of terrorism, nuclear devices can be developed under cover and moved with stealth by people skilled in evading sophisticated detection devices. Agents on the ground can be indispensable in overcoming these limitations in the technology of detection (Bernstein, 2006).

Electronic *signal intelligence* is a common source of intelligence today, designed to provide information about the plans, sources of financing, means, and activities of terrorists as they are transacted by telephone, computer, radio, or electromagnetic pulse. The resulting data present a special challenge: the success of signal intelligence depends heavily on the ability of intelligence agents to accurately interpret various Arabic or other dialects reflected in the data obtained through signal intelligence. Much potentially useful information remains collected but not analyzed because it has not yet been translated reliably from different forms of Arabic into English. American universities teach modern standard Arabic, but the messages intercepted are often in Arabic dialects that many translators are not able to translate. Capable translators are often not allowed to help break this logjam, as they are often viewed with suspicion by intelligence agencies (Ephron, 2006).

Imagery intelligence consists of detailed photographs taken at high altitudes. Collected principally by the National Geospatial-Intelligence Agency, IMINT provides photographic information about geographic details (topography, vegetation, cleared areas, and so on) and the placement and movement of people, munitions, and other resources of aggression. This information can be particularly useful in updating maps, correcting misinformation in maps provided by governments that aim to mislead, and providing focus for military operations.

Processing and Analysis. Once collected, intelligence data must be processed and analyzed to provide information about the strengths and weaknesses of adversaries, so that conclusions can be drawn about their current operations and plans. Foreign affairs columnist David Ignatius (2006c) refers to intelligence analysis as "the least sexy but arguably most important part of the spy world." Some intelligence information is derived from the processing of evidence collected by military personnel, agents, and others. Much of this work falls within the domain of *measurement and signature intelligence* (MASINT), a miscellany of intelligence techniques that include the use of acoustics, electro-optics, infrared, laser, or spectroscopic instruments or sensors of effluents and debris that may point to weapons of mass destruction: radiation, biological, or chemical weapons.

In can be extremely difficult to ferret out and make sense even of reliable, useful intelligence data. Political scientist James Q. Wilson (2002) offers a simple explanation: "intelligence agencies are often playing catch-up because it is so hard to separate signals from noise." The job of intelligence analysis is to make precisely that separation.

All intelligence – HUMINT, SIGINT, IMINT, and MASINT – must be analyzed and integrated to ensure that all pertinent "dots" are connected. Combining disparate data sources – records of telephone calls, credit card statements, bank transactions, and so on – can provide opportunities to find connections to terrorists not available through a single database analyzed in isolation (Harris and Naftali, 2006; Ignatius, 2005). The analysis of collected intelligence follows basic methods of science, based in part on a systematic approach developed by Sherman Kent during World War II. Considered the father of intelligence analysis, Kent was a professor at Yale University who pioneered methods of intelligence analysis that form the basis of much of contemporary intelligence analysis.

The analysis of signal intelligence data includes more than just investigation into individual telephone calls made by and to suspects, It also involves the analysis of large data sets about telephonic and other signal message transmissions to provide a basis for analyzing patterns of communications. The mining of these data sets can unearth suspicious patterns of communications by individual sender or receiver, place and time, duration of communication, frequency of calls, and so on (Harris and Naftali, 2006). General Michael Hayden, former head of the National Security Agency, explains the basic idea of signal intelligence analysis by using the analogy of Super Bowl Sunday: if you could monitor the timing and pattern of telephone calls on that day, you would be able to establish which teams were playing, quite possibly how the game progressed, and perhaps even who won the game, and you could do all this without monitoring a single individual call (Ignatius, 2006b).

An essential goal of all analysis of intelligence data is that it be "actionable" – valuable for people who need the information on the ground – so that they can adjust their operations effectively in light of the information. Analysis of intelligence pertaining to the asymmetric threats of terrorism and the emergence of nonstate adversaries calls for adjustments to conventional intelligence analysis. One such adjustment is the replacement of hierarchies and "stovepiped" analyses with flatter, more collaborative, and flexible networked approaches (R. M. Clark, 2006).

As with science generally, the validity of the results of intelligence analysis can be seriously undermined when the inquiry is compromised by political pressure or ideology. Congressional confirmation and hearings involving interrogations of intelligence agency directors and executives provide one check against such distortion of intelligence analysis through pressure from the executive branch.

Unfortunately, intelligence analysis is not widely regarded as a high-status position in all the agencies in which intelligence is collected and analyzed. The former chairman and vice chairman of the 9/11 Commission, Thomas Kean and Lee Hamilton, wrote in 2007 that six years after the 9/11 attacks the United States was not safer than at the time of the attack, and much of this decline in safety was due to the low status of domestic intelligence analysis: "The number of bureau intelligence analysts has more than doubled since 9/11 (to about 2,100), but they are still second-class citizens in the FBI's law-enforcement culture" (see also Byman, 2007).

Packaging and Dissemination. Essential intelligence is not worth much if it is not made readily available to the people who need it. Once analyzed, intelligence must be "packaged" – organized in a way that serves the development of effective strategy, the protection of vital resources, and tactical counterterrorist operations. Intelligence officers can serve these users by understanding their unique needs and making the information readily accessible yet secure, indexed, and in a clear format. This has been done traditionally in the form of secure briefing books for policymakers and counterterrorist forces on the ground. It is commonly done today through secure computers.

One prevalent type of intelligence to be packaged and disseminated focuses on the terrorist. In any theater of operation, the following information must be made available: who are the known terrorists, where are they, and what are they up to? In the case of extremely dangerous terrorists and imminent acts of terrorism, the information may be used to support both overt and covert counterterrorist operations by informing military or police authorities so that they can intervene by destabilizing, damaging, capturing, or destroying terrorist cells, individual terrorists, their leaders, and their resources. Special operations forces and other counterterrorist operatives are particularly important users of such intelligence. These highly trained, specialized forces include reconnaissance and surveillance operations, hostage negotiation and rescue teams, commando strike forces who carry out raids (e.g., Delta Force and Sea-Air-Land [SEAL] forces), and covert counterterrorism agents engaged in infiltration, disinformation, and cyberwar operations aimed at disrupting and corrupting computer operations. Effective military intelligence officers generally anticipate and respond to the needs of these forces in a timely manner through close, responsive communication, answering questions as they arise. Doing so enables them to identify and prioritize prospective targets of operations in a way that minimizes the risk of errors – both of failing to prevent a terrorist strike and of harming innocent people or alienating prospective allies.

Another type of intelligence focuses on the targets of terrorists; it provides a basis for allocating resources to harden and otherwise protect targets through improved guardianship. Intelligence on terrorists' plans to strike specific targets may be used either to intercept the terrorist, protect the target, or both.

Special care must be taken to protect the sources of information by ensuring that the intelligence is disseminated in a way that makes it impossible to trace the information readily back to its source, especially when the source is a person associated either directly or indirectly with the terrorist organization. Failure to provide such protection not only puts the sources in harm's way but also can shut down critical sources of intelligence. This is a legitimate justification for the tight secrecy of much intelligence, but it can also be used as a political ruse for keeping embarrassing information about botched practices and failed policies out of public view.

D. Public Prevention: Homeland Security

While long-term strategies for the prevention of terrorism are being developed and implemented (discussed in Chapter 12), it is necessary to provide short-term preventive solutions. In Chapter 2 it was noted that *routine activities theory* provides a framework for designing preventive solutions, especially for the short term, based on the idea that acts of aggression are the product of three essential components: motivated offenders, suitable targets, and the absence of capable guardians to protect the targets. Effective intelligence capabilities are essential for enabling the government to identify prospective terrorists, as are target hardening and guardianship to protect potentially attractive targets of terrorism. Guardianship is provided largely by public safety authorities at the federal, state, and local levels.

1. Department of Homeland Security

Much of the public responsibility for the prevention of terrorism in the United States, in both the short and long term, resides within the Department of Homeland Security (DHS). The DHS is a cabinet-level department of the executive branch of the federal government, responsible for protecting the United States from terrorist attacks and responding to natural disasters. The department was created by integrating twenty-two pre-existing federal agencies on November 25, 2002, under the Homeland Security Act of 2002, some fourteen months after the creation of its precursor, the Office of Homeland Security, which had been established days after the 9/11 attacks. The DHS is the third largest cabinet-level department in the executive branch, with nearly 200,000 employees, surpassed in size only by the Department of Defense and the Department of Veterans Affairs.

The DHS has become both the center and umbrella of activities associated with the prevention of terrorism. Its twenty-two component agencies include Immigration, Customs, Border Patrol, Transportation Security, Coast Guard, and the Federal Emergency Management Agency, among others. These agencies operated with a budget of about $40 billion in 2008, the bulk of which was used to secure U.S. borders, ports, and transportation facilities. The DHS coordinates with state and local law enforcement authorities, which constitute another 700,000 sworn officers. To bring a logical order to this assortment of functions and resources, the DHS has identified the following as its primary strategic goals: awareness, prevention, protection, response, recovery, service, and organizational excellence. The DHS has identified six objectives for achieving the first and perhaps most important of these strategic goals, the prevention of acts of terrorism:

1. Secure the borders against terrorists, means of terrorism, illegal drugs, and other illegal activity.
2. Enforce trade and immigration laws.
3. Provide operational end users with the technology and capabilities to detect and prevent terrorist acts and the means of carrying out such acts and other illegal activities.
4. Ensure that national and international policy, law enforcement, and other actions to prepare for and prevent terrorism are coordinated.
5. Strengthen the security of the country's transportation systems.
6. Ensure the security and integrity of the immigration system.

Agents of the DHS thus not only provide guardianship, one of the three components of routine activities theory (see Chapter 2), but also target prospective terrorists, largely by arresting illegal immigrants, some of whom may have terrorist intentions. The DHS made about 80,000 arrests of illegal immigrants in 2004. Although the vast majority of these arrests are not likely to involve viable terrorist threats, the arrests are legitimate under the law for other purposes and may have prevented a few serious terrorist acts in the process.

Another approach focuses on the third side of the routine activities theory triad: attractive targets. The DHS works with other agencies – federal, state, and local – to harden potentially attractive targets throughout the United States, including airports, federal buildings, urban skyscrapers, bridges, and monuments. It has done so by installing barriers and changing traffic patterns to reduce the exposure of structures to threats of vehicular bombings,

U.S. Border Patrol of U.S.-Mexico border.

installing cameras and other sophisticated surveillance systems, imposing entry restrictions, and strengthening security staffs. Similar protections have been deployed in buildings, airports, bridges, and monuments throughout the world.

The Department of Homeland Security has not received many high marks from authorities on domestic security. Its sharpest critics have described it as pork-laden, incompetent, and largely symbolic (Clarke, 2005; Glasser and Grunwald, 2005). Perhaps the most common criticisms are leveled at its sprawling, incoherent structure and bewilderingly broad mandate. A 2005 *Washington Post* editorial entitled "Saga of Incompetence" refers to it as the product of a "haphazard, irrational and unabashedly political" process. The result is an agency with extremely low morale, not a characteristic most citizens would prefer for an agency with such an important mandate (Noah, 2005).

Systems of coordination and accountability have been put in place in response to these charges. The DHS created the National Incident Management System (NIMS) and the National Response Plan (NRP) in 2004, with the aim of better aligning federal homeland security resources. Then in 2006, Secretary of Homeland Security Michael Chertoff introduced a risk management system to provide a coherent method for ordering priorities and allocating scarce resources toward the greatest risks and needs. He described the program as follows: "For our department, risk management starts with weighing threats, vulnerabilities and consequences of a potential terrorist attack or catastrophic event, then conducting a rigorous, information-driven analysis both to set priorities for resources and to give focus and strategic direction to our policies and programs" (Chertoff, 2006).

The fact that the United States has been spared a terrorist event of any consequence on its soil for several years following 9/11 reflects in no small measure the success of government preventive efforts at home. Many people here and abroad regard the restrictions to freedom and privacy, the decline in international support for the U.S. war on terror, and the threat to long-term security of this strategy to be too high a price to pay, but the short-term security success of these activities should not be ignored and cannot be reasonably denied.

2. Terrorism and Natural Disasters: Lessons from Hurricane Katrina

While a long period of calm following 9/11 may reflect successes of the DHS, the government response to Hurricane Katrina, which struck New Orleans, Louisiana, and Biloxi, Mississippi on August 29, 2005, four years after the 9/11 attack, revealed severe shortcomings in the ability of federal and local authorities to prevent and respond effectively to epic disasters. If 9/11 was a failure of intelligence, the response to Katrina was a failure of preparedness and planning. Earth scientists had predicted for years that the area was extremely vulnerable to a hurricane of this magnitude, that such a strike was an eventual inevitability, and, more recently, that the 2005 hurricane season would be more serious than average. Residents had been warned for several days in advance of the hurricane that it posed a serious threat to human life and property as it churned slowly and developed into a massive Category 5 hurricane over the warm waters of the Gulf of Mexico. Few events with dire consequences have been more accurately predicted than this one.

Yet, despite the grim warnings of a clear and present danger of extraordinary proportion, hundreds of lives and hundreds of billions of dollars worth of property were lost in the tragedy: first by the blast of the hurricane; then by the devastation caused by floods following a breach of the levees that had protected New Orleans from the water that surrounded the city on three sides; then by looting and a breakdown in law and order; then by the deaths and severe illness due to dehydration following several days without clean water, food, electricity, emergency power, or plumbing; and finally the national impacts on fuel prices, the blow to the local and national economy, and subsequent rebuilding costs. People in the New Orleans area and in southern Mississippi sat helplessly on rooftops and huddled by the thousands in the New Orleans Superdome and Convention Center – from the Monday the hurricane struck until Friday, when National Guard trucks finally arrived with water, food, and relief supplies (Roig-Franzia and Hsu, 2005). Afterward, problems emerged in the distribution of emergency relief funds to households and rebuilding loans to businesses, in educational services to displaced children, and funding for child care, Head Start, and

353

Superdome, post-Katrina.

welfare programs. Texas and other neighboring states found their educational and social service systems suddenly overwhelmed with displaced persons from Louisiana and Mississippi (Gaouette, Miller and Alonso-Zaldivar, 2005).

Much of the damage was beyond prevention, especially in southern Mississippi – the consequence of a natural disaster of extraordinary proportion. But in New Orleans much more of the chaos and loss was preventable, the consequence of grave weaknesses in the levee protection system built by the U.S.

Army Corps of Engineers and the social infrastructure of the area, the colossal lack of preparedness for the event, the slowness of rescue and relief operations of state and local governments and the Federal Emergency Management Agency (FEMA) arm of the Department of Homeland Security, and poor coordination among the various responders.

There were a few success stories, which have implications for terrorism disasters. Most of the residents of the region left the area in private vehicles for higher ground inland, on the weekend before the hurricane struck on Monday morning. Under the contraflow evacuation plan, which required the cooperation of the governor of Mississippi, traffic exited the city in both the ingoing and outgoing lanes on every major highway. The U.S. Coast Guard, the American Red Cross, and a few other large organizations mobilized quickly and effectively to provide relief services to those in need. As in the case of 9/11, a few public leaders distinguished themselves throughout the crisis, including Mississippi Governor Hayley Barbour and Vice Admiral Thad Allen. Barbour provided stern warnings of the impending disaster and gave the residents of his state clear and reassuring instructions in advance of the storm. In helping organize an orderly recovery process, Allen mobilized the Coast Guard to save the lives of hundreds of people stranded in flooded areas after the hurricane struck. And as in 9/11, private citizens also rose to the occasion, using private motorboats to rescue stranded residents and then graciously offering hospitality to displaced residents. They also gave generously to the Red Cross and other relief agencies to help people harmed by the hurricane and subsequent flood damage. Americans gave more than a billion dollars to the American Red Cross. Doctors and emergency responders from California to New England came to the area to provide help; thousands of volunteers gutted and rebuilt homes in the days after Katrina.

The poor government response emboldened the national press corps to ask more incisive questions of the president and his homeland security policies than they did prior to Hurricane Katrina.[1] A 2005 editorial in *The New York Times* entitled "Revising 9/11" on the fourth anniversary of 9/11 offered an assessment of the failed governmental response to Hurricane Katrina and the implications of the failure for homeland security:

> Given the area it affected and its potential death toll, Katrina perfectly simulated a much larger terrorist attack than the one that hit New York. It was nearly nuclear in scale. Everyone did not behave well. Local first responders went missing, or failed to rise to the occasion, or were simply overwhelmed. Leaders did not lead, and on many counts the federal government was less prepared to respond than it had been when the World Trade Center towers still stood.

The Federal Emergency Management Agency (FEMA) was created by President Jimmy Carter in 1979 to provide federal assistance to victims of disasters; it was assembled from components of smaller agencies. Prior to its creation, no single federal agency had been responsible for dealing exclusively with disasters. Over the course of its first two decades of operations, FEMA received mixed marks for its responses to Hurricane Hugo in 1989 and Andrew in 1992, and generally high marks for its response to the 1995 Oklahoma City bombing.

Even well after the government failures in prevention and immediate response, FEMA continued to be understaffed and undertrained in processing requests for aid and in working effectively with other federal, state, and local authorities in coordinated relief activities (Gaouette et al., 2005). In one example, evacuees were trapped in the Superdome and Convention Center for nearly two days as the Transportation Security Administration (TSA) delayed an airlift, insisting that all passengers and luggage be screened. The TSA also requested special flights to bring in generators to operate x-ray equipment and undercover air marshals to fly on the outbound planes (Cooper and Block, 2006).

In an attempt to identify the sources of the failures revealed in the DHS response to Hurricane Katrina, reporters Susan Glasser and Josh White (2005) interviewed more than a dozen senior officials and experts in the week after Katrina struck. They identified several problems: failure to heed warnings of the seriousness of the storm as it developed and to react quickly with the highest level of governmental response; delays and rejections of offers of aid from the military, states, and cities; incomplete and insufficient planning for disaster response; lack of competent leadership; insufficient funding for FEMA and the demotion of the agency from cabinet-level status to its incorporation within the DHS as just another one of twenty-two component agencies; and a shift in emphasis from emergency response to natural disasters to emergency response to acts of terrorism. When Katrina struck, the federal government was spending $20 billion annually against terrorism and less than 1 percent as much, $180 million annually, for natural disasters. The budget for core FEMA functions had been reduced by one-third for fiscal year 2005 (Glasser and White, 2005). FEMA had conducted an exercise in 2004 to prepare for a major hurricane in New Orleans and prepared a 448-page report describing problems and needs identified by the exercise, but the report was not disseminated and the recommendations were not implemented (Block, 2005a). The morale at FEMA and the DHS reflected these problems: in 2005 the Partnership for Public Service, a nonpartisan nonprofit organization that monitors the federal workforce, ranked the DHS twenty-ninth out of thirty large federal agencies in morale level (C. Lee 2005).

Political commentator Fred Kaplan (2005b) raises this question about the longer term implications of the lack of DHS preparedness revealed by the Hurricane Katrina episode:

How ready is DHS for the disaster that its officials *have* been focused on the last two and a half years? If New Orleans' levees had been broken not by a hurricane but by terrorists' bombs, the nightmares we see now – the lack of planning and therefore of food, water, transportation, shelter, and public order – would be no different. And yet the Department of Homeland Security had scant little to deal with it, either on hand or ready for quick mobilization, and nothing in the 2006 budget suggests it will be any readier next year, whether for a hurricane or another 9/11.

Much soul-searching and recrimination followed the disaster. Michael Brown, director of FEMA, resigned less than two weeks after Katrina struck the Gulf Coast. He was replaced by R. David Paulison, an experienced firefighter and emergency responder from Miami. FEMA's mission was narrowed to emergency response, and its budget was increased. But questions remain about how the public can be better protected by federal and local authorities against future such disasters, whether caused by terrorists or by forces of nature. Which current vulnerabilities are most prone to future calamity? What can be done over the long term to protect the public exposed to such problems, and at what cost? When an impending threat materializes, what can be done immediately to minimize the damage? After the disaster strikes, how can resources be mobilized more effectively, more efficiently, and more quickly to save lives and minimize residual damage? What scripts should public officials and leaders of private organizations follow for various types of disasters: natural calamities such as massive hurricanes and earthquakes and terrorist disasters following nuclear, chemical, or biological attacks? Hurricane Katrina made it all too clear that some catastrophes are unavoidable, but that much of the catastrophic harm may be self-imposed and preventable. It revealed that the harms that come in the aftermath of the initial disaster can be much greater than the initial damage and that much more can be done to minimize both the initial harms and the harms that follow.

One of the most serious lapses revealed by the Katrina episode was failure in communication. Baruch Fischhoff (2005) identifies the critical importance of responsible government agents giving affected populations clear instructions about what to do and what not to do in the face of impending disaster; he also identifies the barriers that often keep responsible agents from communicating effectively (see Box 11.1).

The 9/11 Commission Report anticipated many of the failures in homeland security that were later revealed by the Hurricane Katrina episode. The four kinds of failures in preventing the 9/11 attacks noted in Chapter 9 – failures in imagination, policy, capabilities, and management – are relevant as well to the prevention of and response to natural disaster, and these were

Box 11.1. Finding the Right Words to Weather the Storm

– Baruch Fischhoff

In an emergency, our future may hang on a few words, provided by someone in authority, as we face a fateful decision. The clock might be ticking quickly, as when a severe storm approaches, or slowly, as when we ponder treatment for a severe illness.

Good information doesn't make the world better, but it does tell us what we're up against. The back-to-back calamities on the Gulf Coast have shown what can happen when people have bad or incomplete information to act upon. Sadly, many of the problems there were predictable, given how official communications were managed and how rampant rumors became. Preparations could have been a lot better had state, local, and federal authorities spoken with a single voice and made sure that their words were being understood.

There are lots of things that might be said in advance about any looming risk, whether immediate or long-term. Far from the action, it's interesting to think about how oceanic loop currents may (or may not) affect hurricane intensity or how tighter airport security does (or does not) reduce the odds of a terrorist attack or how dietary fat may (or may not) affect cancer risk. But when we need to make a quick decision, what we really need are the most critical facts, such as:

- Will there be enough gas available on the evacuation route?
- Is the third rail still active when the lights are out in the Metro?
- Is vaccination at all effective *after* exposure to smallpox?
- How dangerous is the fallout from a dirty bomb?
- Can I trust the schools to protect my children, while I ride out the crisis at work?
- Just how bad are the side effects of those painkillers?

It's not that hard to understand the answers to these questions. It's not even hard to understand a well-prepared explanation of the research that allows us to say that the answers are true and accurate. But if people who need to know these facts don't get them in a timely and understandable way, then those responsible for communicating the facts have failed.

Without a scientific analysis of what happened after Hurricanes Katrina and Rita, we won't know exactly what officials said and what citizens heard. A preliminary assessment suggests that the messages worked much better for some people than for others. In both hurricanes, many people got out of harm's way. In Katrina, many others remained behind and suffered. Some stayed behind willfully; some didn't understand their predicament; some had no options. With Rita, many people left who could have stayed home had they only understood – and believed – official communications. Instead, many fled, creating a massive traffic jam in which a bus overheated and exploded, killing 23 passengers.

This confusion has unnerved people far from Hurricane Alley, who are left wondering whether they can rely on what the authorities are saying. That uncertainty raises new questions. Will they be forced to choose among competing experts? Will they feel duped into actions that leave their families vulnerable?

Communicators fail for known reasons. Here are some possibilities that a Katrina Commission should examine looking backward, and that every citizen should consider looking forward, in assessing the communicators in a crisis:

They don't understand how to talk to their public. People tend to exaggerate how well they can put themselves in others' shoes. That happens sometimes among friends. It is even more likely when experts address nonexperts. As a result, the experts say things that people already know, in terms that the public doesn't understand, while omitting important information. When talking to patients, physicians have some chance of recognizing that they're missing the mark. Experts making official announcements, over the radio and television, have no chance at all.

Nor is there any substitute for asking people in the intended audience how they interpret a message, before releasing it to the world. Seemingly simple terms, such as "shelter in place," "climate," "rare side effect," and even "safe sex" mean different things to different people. No one would put a drug on the market without testing it. Yet we rely on labels that leave users guessing at the extent of the risks and benefits. We issue emergency instructions without running them by anyone.

They don't trust their public. Sadly, once we misunderstand other people's predicaments, we often judge them harshly if their actions don't make sense to us. We don't guess that a woman might have stayed behind in a hurricane because she didn't know that her ex-husband had already taken their child to safety, or that a man on probation might decide he couldn't leave because he hadn't been able to reach his probation officer.

Unless they know their public well, officials are not immune to these biases. One often hears "experts" predict mass panic in an emergency. Yet studies since the London blitz during World War II have shown that people behave responsibly, even bravely, in crises.

In surveys, Americans say that they want to be leveled with, even if things are bad. Both Israel and the United Kingdom have communication policies that embody such a fundamentally respectful stance. Living in Jerusalem during the 1973 Yom Kippur War, my wife and I were not happy to hear the Israeli authorities say "Our troops are still in the process of slowing down the enemy." However, we were grateful to know where things stood.

They don't care solely about their public. Risk communication is a public health function, helping people make the best choices for themselves and their loved ones. Yet the communications job is often given to public affairs, or public relations, or even marketing people. These professionals have valuable skills. Any organization without them can get eaten alive. However, they naturally focus on their employers' welfare, and not just that of their audience. When people feel that their lives are on the line, they just want unspun facts.

Only the most cynical and shortsighted public affairs person would emphasize spin over substance in a crisis. However, research finds that changing hats is not that easy. Conventional concerns so permeate people's thinking that they cannot set aside their habitual ways of communicating, however hard they try.

My wife and I were in London during the third week of July. On the 21st, the day of the second bombing that month, we heard a public health-focused response, soberly revealing the facts as they became known. On the 22nd, we heard the same agencies provide what turned out to an inaccurate account of the police killing of an innocent Brazilian immigrant, creating a crisis of confidence that is still reverberating.

They have nothing to tell their public. Without the proper research in advance, an agency cannot assess the risks that its public faces. In that case, it's better to plead ignorance than to offer confident guesswork. Of course, no one wants to be told, "Beats me. You're on your own." But that's a more useful message than an unsupportable "Trust me." Still, there's always the temptation to pretend to know what should have been known, and to blame the victims for not doing the impossible.

Communication is part of any relationship. After Katrina and Rita, after the anthrax mailings, the D.C. sniper attacks and the abortive smallpox vaccination campaign – indeed, after any public crisis – citizens will ask, "Did you listen to us, so that you could tell us what we needed to know?" When the answer is yes, the authorities increase their standing as information providers. When the answer is no, the authorities undermine our resilience as a society.

[*Source: Washington Post* (October 2, 2005), p. B5.]

evident in the case of the Katrina disaster. FEMA revealed itself as lacking in preparedness, and this was a product of the four lapses noted above, perhaps especially imagination. One of the more incisive remarks of the report was this: "Imagination is not a gift usually associated with bureaucracies" (2004, p. 344).

Many New Orlineans decided not to return to their former homes. Yet neither the U.S. Congress nor the White House seemed willing to address this question seriously: What is the appropriate federal role in discouraging people from putting themselves in harm's way by moving to an area prone to disaster? Because the risks are well known, the lowest lying areas tend to be the most affordable, leaving the poor especially vulnerable to subsequent disasters. Economist Edmund Phelps (2005) puts it as follows: "A hard truth . . . is that most of New Orleans is so vulnerable to hurricanes that it is not rational for governments to recreate its infrastructure on the former scale. Parts of the city are 10 feet under sea level and cannot be reliably guarded against storms in category four or five. These parts are best made non-residential."

A related strategic question was also left largely unaddressed. What sort of federal expenditures are legitimate to secure the region and the national economy? Politicians called widely for rebuilding a "better" New Orleans, without specifying what that meant.[2] A popular sentiment – locally, nationally, and internationally – was to restore New Orleans approximately to its prior state of charm. Even if it were built differently to better withstand the forces of nature, how much should people from Hawaii to Maine be obliged to pay to induce people to move to a place that cannot fully defend itself against those irresistible forces?

An answer to these questions lies in the fact that the government has a legitimate role in protecting the public's access to goods and services in the presence of market failures. People in Hawaii and Maine benefit from repairs to a great port's capacity to ship grain from farmers upriver to markets everywhere. They benefit also from the restoration and preservation of essential aspects of a unique open-air museum that competes with Venice, Amsterdam, and a handful of other international cultural treasures. They benefit even from federal subsidies that restore the ability of the working poor to participate in the labor market. Leaving aside the international embarrassment of the world's wealthiest nation appearing helpless and incompetent in the face of thousands of poor people huddled in the Superdome, the simple fact is that impaired schools, drug use, and crime impose external costs on all of our society (Phelps, 2005).

Regardless of how these matters are eventually resolved, a simple fact remains: the Department of Homeland Security can neither anticipate nor prepare for every conceivable future disaster that might strike. Hurricane

Katrina was a well-anticipated threat for which the City of New Orleans and the DHS were clearly unprepared. Terrorist acts are fundamentally different from acts of nature in one important respect: nature finds weaknesses randomly and over long periods of time, whereas terrorists seek them consciously and exploit them intentionally, and can do so more quickly. The two forces are nonetheless similar in that eventually both expose weaknesses, and the result is harm to life and property. The cat-and-mouse complexities in defending against terrorism and the dynamics of asymmetric warfare make it likely that over time the terrorists will occasionally succeed, especially given a virtually limitless array of suitable targets and the large number of people willing and eager to strike those targets. Any program of homeland security must work to minimize the prospects for committing such acts. When those efforts fail, public officials, private organizations, and citizens must be prepared to respond quickly and effectively to disasters regardless of their source.

E. Financial Interventions

Sources and Terrorist Uses of Financing. A basic and essential short-term strategy for preventing terrorism is to cut off terrorists' sources of financial support. Terrorist operations are considerably less expensive than conventional warfare, but funding is required nonetheless, especially to finance the more sophisticated and deadly schemes. The 9/11 terrorists needed money to finance their flying lessons and living expenses in the United States, both while learning to fly and then afterward, to support them as they rehearsed, planned, and waited for the right moment to deploy their attack. Estimates of the costs of financing the operation range from $400,000 to $500,000 (9/11 Commission Report, 2004; Rice-Oxley, 2006). Estimates of the costs of the transit system attacks on Madrid and London are considerably lower: the Madrid bombings of 2004 have been estimated to cost $15,000; the 2005 London attacks –involving four bombs, detonators, and backpacks; train tickets; some gasoline; and a few phone calls – are estimated at around $2,000 (Rice-Oxley, 2006). Gus Martin (2006) estimates the costs of most solo suicide bombings at around $2,000 each. Yet, expenses must be covered even in fairly inexpensive solo suicide bombings, including those in which aging vehicles are used and destroyed in the attack. Banks and other institutions of financial transfer become less essential to the terrorists in such cases; hence, they become less useful as sources for detecting low-cost terrorism. For operations involving more lethal weaponry or more distant targets, requiring travel and living costs, the financial requirements are greater, as are opportunities to trace the movement of money associated with the acts. Ramzi Yousef, convicted mastermind behind the 1993 truck bombing of the

World Trade Center, admitted after his capture in 1995 that the terrorists were unable to purchase enough material to build as large a bomb as they had intended and the operation had to be carried out earlier than originally planned because the cell had run out of money. The attempt of one of Yousef's associates to reclaim the deposit fee on the rental truck used to transport the bomb provided a key break in the case (Freeh, 1999; Levitt, 2003). Financial analysis also revealed evidence that led to the arrest and conviction of Zacarias Moussaoui, an al Qaeda operative involved in the 9/11 plot (Lormel, 2002).

The financial support for terrorist operations both large and small typically comes from a combination of external sources and illicit activities conducted locally (Adams, 1986; Ehrenfeld, 2005; Levitt, 2003; Napoleoni, 2005). The illicit activities range from drug trafficking; smuggling of weapons, stolen property, and other contraband; to kidnapping-ransom and extortion schemes; to document fraud or various combinations thereof. External sources of funding include wealthy individuals, like Osama bin Laden, and private charities and foundations. The foundations and charities are sometimes terrorist fronts, but often are organizations set up primarily to serve legitimate charitable interests, such as providing food and shelter for the poor, but that manage also, either intentionally or inadvertently through weak controls, to serve as conduits for funding of terrorist indoctrination programs and terrorist operations (A. Cohen, 2001).

A distinct advantage for the terrorist organization of having internal financial support is that it can have a degree of autonomy that may not be as easily achieved when it is heavily reliant on external sources of funding (Napoleoni, 2005). The need for internal funding obtained through illicit activities may be especially great in countries that are disconnected from the global economy – what Thomas Barnett (2005) refers to as "gap nations." A nation's distance from the forces of globalization may thus deepen the vicious cycle of terrorism and illegal activities needed to support it, each feeding the other and breaking down formal and informal social control systems along the way. The greater the distance, the greater the inclination for terrorists to disrupt the forces of order and finance their operations autonomously through illegal activities – as exemplified by the poppy fields of Afghanistan and the coca plantations of Colombia.

Role of Banking and Quasi-Banking Systems. A key to the disruption of terrorist operations is the disruption of the organization's ready access to funds used to support its activities, regardless of their source. Terrorism operations of any significance typically require that money be available from banks through the electronic transfers of money. The nineteen 9/11 hijackers made extensive use of the U.S. banking system. According to the Executive Summary to the 9/11 Commission Report (2004), "The hijackers opened accounts in their own names, using passports and other identification documents. Their transactions were unremarkable and essentially invisible amid the billions of dollars flowing around the world every day." Analysis of financial transactions provided by banks produced key early evidence identifying the 9/11 attacks as an al Qaeda operation and linking the perpetrators to the Hamburg cell in Germany (Lormel, 2002).

One of the most basic counterterrorist strategies is to use the banking system to identify money laundering and other schemes for financing terrorist operations before the attack and to obtain information about known terrorists or suspects. These interventions become increasingly problematic as they encroach on basic rights to privacy, and especially so when investigative nets widen from known terrorists to terrorist suspects. Counterterrorist activities often encounter barriers when suspects use banks in countries that protect the clients' anonymity, such as Switzerland and the Caribbean.

Banks traditionally have resisted investigations seeking information on money laundering and illegal activity on the grounds of their customers' rights to privacy. This resistance weakened substantially after the attacks of September 11, 2001; few bank executives anywhere wanted to be regarded as terrorist accomplices or enablers. Terrorists responded by moving their assets out of banks and into valuable commodities such as gold and diamonds, which can be readily moved, hidden, and exchanged for cash or for goods and services (DeYoung and Farah, 2002).

Terrorists responded also by reverting to an ancient system of financing known as *hawala*. Hawala is an informal IOU system traceable at least to the centuries-old Silk Road trade that moved goods from China through the Middle East to Europe and back.[3] Under the hawala system, money is transfered through a network of brokers, usually for a fee, at black market exchange rates for the local currency. The hawala honor system avoids the use of promissory notes common to modern business. The absence of a paper trail and its operation outside of formal legal processes make hawala an attractive option for terrorists interested in moving money needed to support operations without detection.

The hawala system has been a particularly important source of al Qaeda's ability to finance and carry out acts of terrorism. Hawala transactions are fast and cost effective, particularly for people who prefer to transfer funds anonymously and operate outside the reach of the conventional financial sector (Department of Treasury, 2002, p. 15). Tracing hawala transactions presents an especially challenging obstacle for counterterrorism efforts (9/11 Commission Report, p. 171). Al Qaeda turned to more exclusive reliance on the hawala system after the 1998 East Africa bombings, due to increased worldwide scrutiny of its financial fund flows through the formal financial system (Roth, Greenburg and Wille, 2004, p. 25). After passage of the USA Patriot Act, financial supporters of terrorism are known to have relied more on slower, low-profile couriers to move money (Roth et al., 2004. p. 26).

Terrorism investigators today confront not only the burdens of finding and disrupting financial support of terrorist activities but also doing so in such a way that distinguishes these flows from donations of money to legitimate charities, so as not to interfere with those legitimate flows of financial support. Much of the burden of truth has fallen on religious and secular nongovernmental agencies involved in humanitarian projects around the world, which now find themselves having to cooperate with counterterrorist efforts and monitoring these flows more carefully than before to ensure that their legitimate charitable activities remain viable.

Formal Interventions. Authorities have long argued that terrorism may be deterred most effectively by attacking the sources of funding of terrorist activities (Adams, 1986). The fundamental importance of this approach to the deterrence of terrorism is reflected in the USA Patriot Act, passed by Congress just one month after the 9/11 attack. This act includes several provisions that provide legal tools to counter the financing of terrorism, including criminal sanctions against people who knowingly give material support to terrorists. Several elements of the act are aimed at reducing the financial support of terrorism by requiring the following:

- Brokers and dealers as well as commodity merchants, advisors and pool operators to file suspicious activity reports (SARs)
- Financial institutions and law enforcement agencies to share information concerning suspected money laundering and terrorist activities
- Financial institutions to maintain anti-money laundering programs that include one or more compliance officers, an employee training program, the development of internal policies, procedures and controls, and an independent audit
- Penalties to be imposed against money laundering in support of terrorism

International efforts have also been initiated against the financing of terrorism. One such initiative is the Financial Action Task Force (FATF), a multinational organization aimed at developing and promoting domestic and international policies to combat money laundering and terrorist financing. Established in 1989 by the G-7 Summit held in Paris, FATF and its more than three dozen member nations work to build cooperation and lobby for legislative and regulatory reforms aimed at discovering and deterring the laundering of money used to support terrorist activities. The FATF issued a set of special recommendations on terrorist financing following the 9/11 attacks, focusing on wire transfers, the financing of black market operations, cash couriers, and nonprofit organizations.

F. The 9/11 Commission and the Intelligence Gap: Findings and Recommendations

Aspects of the 9/11 Commission Report pertaining to responses to terrorism were discussed in Chapter 9. We turn now to those parts of the report that pertain to the goal of preventing terrorism through improved intelligence and action.

1. Intelligence Shortcomings and Goals

The report noted that during the spring and summer of 2001 U.S. intelligence agents received a series of warnings that al Qaeda was planning "something very, very, very big." Director of Central Intelligence George Tenet told the Commission, "The system was blinking red." The Commission identified a series of specific shortcomings in homeland security in the months leading up to September 11:

- Operational failures and opportunities that were not or could not be exploited by the organizations and systems of that time: not watchlisting future hijackers Hazmi and Mihdhar, not trailing them after they traveled to Bangkok, and not informing the FBI about one future hijacker's U.S. visa or his companion's travel to the United States
- Not sharing information linking individuals in the *USS Cole* attack to Mihdhar
- Not taking adequate steps in time to find Mihdhar or Hazmi in the United States
- Not linking the arrest of Zacarias Moussaoui, described as interested in flight training for the purpose of using an airplane in a terrorist act, to the heightened indications of attack
- Not discovering false statements on visa applications; not recognizing passports manipulated in a fraudulent manner; not expanding no-fly lists to include names from terrorist watchlists; not searching airline passengers identified by the computer-based CAPPS screening system; and not making aircraft cockpit doors more secure or taking other measures to prepare for the possibility of suicide hijackings

To overcome such shortcomings in the future, the 9/11 Commission identified three goals to provide the basis for preventing terrorism:

> Root out terrorists and terrorist sanctuaries, especially in Pakistan and Afghanistan, and confront problems with Saudi Arabia to build a relationship beyond oil

Prevent the growth of Islamic terrorism through a broad, integrated plan that emphasizes the expansion of educational and economic capacities, coalition-building, and the countering of the proliferation of weapons of mass destruction

Protect the borders of the United States against terrorist attacks through better screening procedures at points of entry, including greater use of biometric technology and improved document validation

2. Need for Coordination

The 9/11 Commission emphasized throughout its report that the overarching means of achieving these goals was improved coordination – both among the organizations that gather and analyze foreign and domestic intelligence information and among those that use it to create and adjust policies and determine an efficient allocation of security resources. The most significant recommendation was a reorganization and overhaul of the U.S. intelligence system. Five specific recommendations were advanced to achieve such coordination:

The unification across the foreign-domestic divide of strategic intelligence and operational planning against Islamic terrorists through the creation of a National Counterterrorism Center, borrowing from the joint, unified command concept adopted in the 1980s by the American military

The integration of foreign and domestic intelligence through the creation of a new National Intelligence Director, with oversight over the CIA, Defense Department intelligence agencies, the FBI, and national intelligence centers focusing on the proliferation of weapons of mass destruction, international crime, and narcotics, by geographic region

The creation of a network-based information sharing system to unify the key participants in the counterterrorism effort and their knowledge, transcending traditional boundaries

The creation of a single, principal point of congressional oversight and review for homeland security, to unify and strengthen oversight to improve accountability

The strengthening of the FBI and other homeland defenders, with greater emphasis on agents with special skills in linguistics, analysis, and surveillance technologies

The Commission also recommended changes in immigration policy and the tightening of procedures to secure the nation's borders and stem the influx of prospective terrorists.

The Value of Coordination and the Questions It Raises. The benefits of coordinating intelligence and security activities can be substantial. Coordination can reduce waste and enhance the ability of security agents to ensure comprehensive intelligence coverage, producing more useful "dots" to connect and opportunities for more thoughtful consideration of conflicting intelligence information. Lack of coordination between the FBI in its domestic operations and the CIA and Defense Intelligence Agency in their foreign and military operations stems from a long-standing wall separating the operations of the two agencies, created because of the FBI's need to respect constitutional protections to which foreign and defense intelligence operations are not bound. The problem of terrorism generally, and of the 9/11 attacks in particular, poked substantial holes in the wall separating domestic security from traditional military and international security responsibilities, and the Commission recognized that coordination not previously needed was clearly in order. In the deployment of security resources, greater coordination is particularly important to minimize risk of harm and waste.

Lapses in coordination are often related to territorial and intramural rivalries among agencies, and they can be understood but not easily justified. One example of such as lapse is that between the FBI and U.S. Attorneys who prosecute violations of federal laws. Both the FBI and the ninety-four U.S. Attorneys report to the Attorney General, and documented failures of the FBI to cooperate with federal prosecutors have defied suitable explanation (Roth et al., 2004, p. 33).

In the collection of intelligence, however, coordination is neither costless nor risk free. It can actually reduce the effectiveness of intelligence operations. The process of coordination itself usually consumes resources, and it can reduce the extent to which valuable information is obtained from different sources operating independently of one another, which are immune to the problem of "groupthink." The respective roles and responsibilities of the FBI for domestic intelligence, the CIA for foreign intelligence, and the DIA for military intelligence are largely complementary, and coordination done improperly could undermine this strength.

Greater coordination among domestic, international, and military intelligence can also threaten the balance between the protection of constitutionally grounded rights to liberty and privacy on the one hand and to the preservation of domestic tranquility on the other. We consider the problem of improving coordination while maintaining a proper balance between the goals of security and liberty in greater detail in Chapter 13.

3. Criticism of the 9/11 Commission Report

The 9/11 Commission Report was widely praised following its release in July 2004, particularly for its clarity, not often found in governmental reports, and its nonpartisan character. It spread responsibility equally across the Clinton and Bush administrations and across the executive and legislative branches of the federal government. It became an instant best seller and won widespread acclaim for the quality of its prose, lucidity, and incisiveness (Kennicott, 2004; Yagoda, 2004). Author, essayist, and federal appeals court judge Richard A. Posner (2004) called it an "improbable literary triumph."

However, Judge Posner and others (e.g., W. Cohen, 2004; Devine, 2004; Ignatius, 2004) also found much to criticize in the report's recommendations. Posner was particularly critical of the recommendation that U.S. intelligence operations should be unified within a single directorate: "Insistence on unanimity, like central planning, deprives decision makers of a full range of alternatives." He pointed out that even before the September 11 attack Condoleezza Rice had effectively demoted Richard Clarke, the government's leading bin Laden hawk and foremost expert on al Qaeda, excluding him from meetings of the cabinet-level "principals committee" of the National Security Council; this action was a product of what Posner referred to as the administration's "bin Laden fatigue." Posner also found the Commission's focus on a repeat of a 9/11-type attack by Islamist terrorism to be excessively short-sighted:

> The report states that the focus of our antiterrorist strategy should not be "just 'terrorism,' some generic evil.... The catastrophic threat at this moment in history is more specific. It is the threat posed by Islamist terrorism." Is it? Who knows? The menace of bin Laden was not widely recognized until just a few years before the 9/11 attacks. For all anyone knows, a terrorist threat unrelated to Islam is brewing somewhere (maybe right here at home – remember the Oklahoma City bombers and the Unabomber and the anthrax attack of October 2001) that, given the breathtakingly rapid advances in the technology of destruction, will a few years hence pose a greater danger than Islamic extremism. But if we listen to the 9/11 commission, we won't be looking out for it because we've been told that Islamist terrorism is the thing to concentrate on.

Two related criticisms of the 9/11 Commission Report are noteworthy. One is that, in its "rush to reorganize," the report had the effect of closing out real debate on the nature of the problem and the options available (Ignatius, 2004). Commission Co-Chairmen Hamilton and Kean responded to this criticism in a 2006 book that explained the difficulty of balancing the goal of making the report comprehensive with that of getting it out without delay and moving forward the process of reorganizing the intelligence community as quickly as possible. Another such criticism is that the report failed to deal sufficiently with the danger of stifling open analytic inquiry posed by keeping the nation's intelligence operations embedded squarely within the executive branch, thus subjecting them to excessive political pressure (W. Cohen, 2004;

Devine, 2004). The report did emphasize the need for strong congressional oversight, but critics of excessive power concentrated in the executive branch of government regard such oversight as insufficient.

G. State and Local Initiatives

Questions raised by critics of the 9/11 Commission Report about the concentration of homeland security authority are not restricted to the central government in Washington. Under the federal system of U.S. governance, changes in the lines of authority at the federal level inevitably affect the nature and quality of coordination between federal and state or local agents and activities. Federalism means that each constituent member retains jurisdiction over its own internal affairs while ceding authority to a central government that holds the federation or confederacy together. Does the centralization of power under the Department of Homeland Security improve or hinder operations at the state and local level?

This question can be addressed by starting with basics. Many state and local officials prefer not to rely heavily on federal support for the prevention of terrorist attacks and interventions to secure the homeland against terrorism and other disasters. They often find the strings attached too onerous, and they generally find it more effective to complement federal involvements with participation in intelligence and information-sharing networks with state and local officials at home and abroad. For example, police in several jurisdictions have engaged in exchange programs, sending their officers to work with police overseas, creating liaisons with foreign agents, setting up independent intelligence operations, and creating secure communication networks for information sharing (see Box 11.2).

The development of nonfederal government initiatives is consistent with fundamental notions of federalism set forth by the founders. As Box 11.2 indicates, these initiatives can produce a healthy competition in the market for intelligence and security against terrorism. It would be unreasonable to expect that a single vast agency in Washington would be fully responsive to unique local settings and needs, regardless of how much more effective it might be after centralization.

The creation of complementary networks does, however, have a downside: it could contribute to an undermining of the quality of federal information. Local authorities might, after all, find themselves unwilling to produce redundant information to their own networks and to the DHS, especially when DHS reporting requirements impose additional costs on state and local operations. Moreover, while local officials might prefer to have autonomy over terrorism in their jurisdictions, the citizens in these places could become confused by mixed signals from local and federal authorities, as became all too clear in the Hurricane Katrina experience.

Box 11.2. Local Police Develop Antiterror Plans Independent of Washington

– Robert Block

As tensions simmer between big-city police chiefs and federal officials over the quality of information on terrorist threats and natural disasters, local law-enforcement officials are developing their own systems to share information and fight terrorism. Their goal: to decrease dependence on intelligence and advice from Washington.

Police in Los Angeles, Washington, D.C., Miami, Las Vegas, Seattle, and Houston are sending their officers to work with overseas police agencies, accepting liaisons from foreign forces, setting up their own intelligence shops, and creating their own secure communication networks to share information among themselves. The aim is to better enable big cities to develop response plans to threats in their jurisdictions.

At the heart of the effort is a pilot project to develop a communications system so police chiefs around the country can share real-time information independent of the federal government.

The developments take on new significance in the wake of jostling last week between the Department of Homeland Security and New York City after the city announced a possible terrorist threat against the subway system and beefed-up security. No sooner had Mayor Michael Bloomberg announced the threat alongside a senior Federal Bureau of Investigation agent than Homeland Security officials accused him of overreacting to a threat that they said wasn't credible.

The willingness of New York City to disregard Homeland Security advice underscores the frustrations that many local law-enforcement agencies have with the nearly three-year-old department's stumbling over its handling of everything from threat advisories to the response to Hurricane Katrina. It also underlines continuing confusion over who is in charge of sounding the nation's terrorist warning bell and disseminating intelligence.

Homeland Security is playing down the police departments' moves, saying that it has already started to improve its communications with local authorities, reducing the urgency for independent networks. "We give local authorities intel (intelligence) data and they do what they think is right," says Homeland Security spokesman Russ Knocke. "They need to have the right information to do what they deem appropriate to protect their communities."

But some experts like former Homeland Security adviser Richard Falkenrath worry that a city's failure to follow federal advice could undermine intelligence-gathering efforts overseas and compromise sources. It also risks unsettling a public left perplexed by contradictory statements about threats from different levels of government.

The split between federal and local law-enforcement authorities illustrates the difficult balancing act officials face in a post-Sept. 11, 2001, world in determining when information should be made public and how to respond, and who is responsible for making that decision. Indeed, federal officials have been criticized for raising the terror alert on what turned out to be questionable grounds.

Many police chiefs say local forces need independent means to verify intelligence and share advice about threat responses. The aim, according to Los Angeles Police Chief William Bratton, is not to sever or supplant information from Homeland Security and the Department of Justice but to have a "multiplicity of channels of information that will allow chiefs of police to make decisions," he said.

Mr. Bratton is in many ways following in the footsteps of his old friend and colleague, Raymond Kelly, the New York City police commissioner who believes the city was betrayed by a lack of information from the federal government before the Sept. 11 attacks. Mr. Kelly and other top officials have established the NYPD almost as a rival to federal law-enforcement agencies.

New York City police officers are stationed in London with Scotland Yard; in Lyons, France, at the headquarters of Interpol; and in Singapore, Tel Aviv, and Toronto. Two officers are on assignment at FBI headquarters in Washington, and New York detectives have traveled to Afghanistan, Egypt, Yemen, Pakistan, and the military's prison at Guantanamo Bay in Cuba to conduct interrogations.

Frustrations with federal officials have been building for years, even before Sept. 11. But the push for independence has gained new momentum after a wave of terrorist bomb attacks on London's mass-transit system last summer (2005) and the disputes between Washington and local officials after Hurricane Katrina hit the Gulf Coast on Aug. 29.

Homeland Security Secretary Michael Chertoff acknowledged the problem last month in Miami Beach, Fla., at the International Association of Chiefs of Police Conference, where he announced that his department, in response to police pressure, would soon start to send email "alerts" to some police chiefs at the same time that federal officials receive them. "I want to assure you that as a department we will continue to listen, continue to work with you," he said.

But police chiefs still see a need for their own network. At the time of the second wave of London bombings July 21, Mr. Bratton already had an LAPD official in London to learn about the previous attacks. The official was able to provide first-hand information to Mr. Bratton and police in other U.S. cities hours before they had information from Homeland Security, Mr. Bratton said.

He said he recently signed an agreement for an Australian police intelligence officer to work alongside the LAPD. During the recent terrorist bombings in Bali, he received information from police in Sydney, Australia, who had officers on the ground in Bali – before he got it from Homeland Security or the FBI.

Mr. Bratton said the London bombings – apparently the work of local groups – also demonstrated that the terrorist threats of the future were likely to be homegrown, a problem that was more likely to be first spotted by local police. A suspected homegrown terrorist threat was recently uncovered in Los Angeles following a wave of gas-station robberies.

The proper mix of federal and local responsibility for specific types of terrorist threats may not, in any case, be easily preordained. It is a matter that will unfold depending on a variety of factors, including the personalities of key players and the unique local needs of the state, county and municipal jurisdictions.

Discussion Questions

1. *Models for preventing acts by terrorists.* Gaming models are much more widely relied on by the military than by local police departments. Why do you suppose this is the case? Do you see any value in using such models to assess counterterrorist policies and determine the allocation of homeland security resources? If so, how should the models differ from those designed to support military operations?

2. *The Department of Homeland Security.* What do you see as the greatest strengths and weaknesses of the Department of Homeland Security? If you were Secretary of Homeland Security, would you try to change the department in terms of its priorities, policies, or the allocation of resources? If so, how?

3. *Financing of terrorism.* What are the primary sources of terrorist funding? What are the primary uses of the funding? How has the financing of terrorism changed over the past few years, and what are the policy implications of this change? What strikes you as the most effective way or ways to disrupt the terrorist's access to financial support? What more should be done? Do

you think civil libertarians would see your proposed solutions as a threat to legitimate rights to privacy? If so, how would you respond to their concerns?

4. *The 9/11 Commission Report.* The 9/11 Commission Report asks what caused the 9/11 attacks and what can be done to prevent future such attacks. Do you agree with its assessment? What do you see as the greatest strengths of the report? What do you see as its greatest shortcomings? Do you think that national intelligence should be more centralized or more decentralized? Why?

TWELVE

Preventing Terrorism: Long-Term Strategies

In this chapter we continue to consider approaches for preventing terrorism, shifting focus from preventing individual acts of terror in the short term to removing terrorism's sources as a long-term strategy. A central purpose is to examine possibilities for moving the train of civilization from the track of clash and conflict to that of dialogue, mutual understanding, and cooperation among nations and cultures. The chapter concludes with a discussion of the prospect of building an international community that can be more effective in preventing terrorism by removing its deeper causes.

A. Introduction

Prudent planning calls for preparing for both short- and long-term contingencies. Just as we may be able to prevent crime in both the short term and the long term, it may be no less possible to remove opportunities for terrorists to carry out attacks in the short term while altering the conditions that induce people to want to commit acts of terror in the first place.

How do we establish what works over the long term in preventing terrorism? It is difficult enough to know about long-term preventive strategies even in the area of crime, due to difficulties in sorting out relationships of bewildering complexity, in measuring factors of central importance accurately, in anticipating new developments and adaptations, and so on. It is considerably more difficult in the area of terrorism, because the reporting and measurement of terrorist incidents are even less reliable than in the area of crime, the explanatory factors more elusive, the frequency of incidents lower, and the consequences more severe and less readily measurable. We end up having to rely much more on common sense, drawing indirect inferences from what we know about the success of crime prevention strategies, and making use of educated guesses and producing a range of predictions. Despite the considerable institutional flaws of the CIA noted in Chapter 11, CIA analysts have done this pretty well over the years, and the eclectic approach used in this sort of analysis should be useful for dealing with the problem of terrorism too.

In preceding chapters we have considered what appear to be the primary sources of alienation: bad governments, absence of the rule of law, extremism, illiteracy and poverty, technology, misinformation and fear accentuated by sensationalist media and pandering politicians, and the spread and deepening of hatred by charismatic demagogues. We turn now to the consideration of interventions, public and private, that may serve to neutralize these influences.

B. From Clash of Civilizations to Dialogue

We may agree that hostility harms our health and well-being, that it is wrong morally, and, at the level of civilizations, that the prospect of clash in the age of nuclear and biological weapons seriously threatens everyone's survival. Yet however much we may abhor and resist it, some degree of hostility and clash appear to be inevitable – a historical fact and fundamental condition of humankind and life itself. The question is not how to eliminate clash, but how to minimize the depth and breadth of the hostilities we confront. And when clash does emerge, how can we deal with it most effectively and move as many people as possible forward to a better place? Our challenge is to find ways both to defend ourselves against hostile others and to remove the conditions and incentives that induce them to continue to commit acts of aggression and enlist others to join with them; in other words, to accomplish the goal of defense in ways that do not interfere with the goal of removing the root sources of terrorism. We can justify attempts to meet this challenge both on practical grounds of security and health and on ethical grounds as well.

1. Why Dialogue?

The two conventional approaches to dissuading others from hostility are the (1) sticks of force, sanctions, removal, and deterrence and the (2) carrot of security through mutual understanding and cooperation, exchange, mutual respect, and friendship. As we debate how best to defend ourselves, we must also explore and expand prospects for engaging in *dialogue*, for it has been demonstrated time and again that there can be little hope of achieving long-lasting security through mutual understanding and collaboration without dialogue and exchange.

2. What Is Dialogue?

Dialogue includes face-to-face discussion and other forms of communication, the exchange of factual information and opinions, and sometimes mere chit-chat. But dialogue has a defining characteristic that makes it much more than just discussion. *Dialogue aims to transform relationships among the participants.* It does so by attempting to expose, deal with, and resolve their problems – often ones that have deep historical roots that predate the lives of those engaged in dialogue.

Dialogue has its origins in Sicily in the 5th century BCE, when it was created as a form for transmitting ideas. It developed not long afterward into the philosophical dialectic perfected by Plato around 400 BCE. It has evolved today into a forum within which each participant consciously listens to the thoughts of the other participants – a process of committed thinking together, toward the goal of reaching a mutual understanding (Isaacs, 1999). Dialogue does not require agreement, although in genuine dialogue, points of agreement are bound to show up along the way.

David Bohm (1996) describes dialogue as a process with a meditative quality in which "streams of meaning flow among and through us"; it is a forum that is also considerate, in which "everybody wins if anybody wins." He emphasizes the seriousness and openness of dialogue and that it calls for a willingness to engage in matters that are often otherwise regarded as non-negotiable or untouchable; it is a process that calls for commitment among the participants. Thus, dialogue goes well beneath and beyond ordinary discussion.

Box 12.1 gives life to these abstract principles. It is an excerpt from a public dialogue between two scholars from quite different cultural and religious backgrounds and academic orientations: Pakistani anthropologist Akbar Ahmed and Israeli American artificial intelligence researcher Judea Pearl. A series of dialogues began two years earlier when Professor Pearl invited Professor Ahmed to engage in a public conversation to help Pearl understand the brutal murder of his son, Daniel, a *Wall Street Journal* reporter, in Karachi, Pakistan, in February 2002. (Ahmed, an internationally recognized authority on Islam, was Pakistan's ambassador to England in the late 1990s.)

3. Dialogue and Social Capital

One of the most useful and attractive features of dialogue is its capacity for building *social capital*, a basic and intangible asset of a society or smaller

Judea Pearl and Akbar Ahmed in dialogue at the Purpose Prize Innovation Summit, Stanford, California, September 8, 2006.

Box 12.1. Dialogue: Why Doesn't Islam Excommunicate Bin Laden?

Judea Pearl and Akbar Ahmed

Judea Pearl: My friend Akbar knows that my mantra for the past three years has been that all the condemnations that we have heard from Muslim leaders [against terrorism and violence in the name of Islam] have been cast in secular vocabulary. And it's very clear that they mean nothing to the perpetrators or to the people who sent them. They do not understand the logic of secular language or the logic of rational reasoning. They are motivated, by their own admission, by religious metaphors. And therefore, condemnations need to be cast in religious terminology.

So for the past three years, in various outlets, I have been calling on Muslim leaders to condemn terrorist acts in Muslim-certified vocabulary. And they do have these instruments: fatwa, takfir [denying the basic principles of the faith], fasad [corruption, permitting that which is forbidden or forbidding that which is required by God], heresy, apostasy – and we haven't heard that.

With one exception. It happened on March 13, 2005, when the Muslim council of Spain issued a fatwa against Bin Laden. And it generated some vibrations in the grand mosques of Egypt and the Middle East, but not what one would expect.

It was, I believe, an unprecedented and very meaningful step. Seventy-five percent of all Spanish mosques got together and said enough is enough. We ought to excommunicate Bin Laden, who is the arch symbol of the ideology of terrorism, from our midst, and we ought to do it in the language he understands, the language that his followers understand, the language of Islam. And they issued that fatwah, and declared him an apostate.

On Sunday, in the *Times* of London, I have an op-ed, which calls for the Muslim community in England to issue a fatwa against Bin Laden, with the idea that the perpetrators of the bombings in London will understand that they are hereby excommunicated religiously.

Akbar Ahmed: Judea has raised an important issue about legitimacy. The problem is that we are translating from one culture into another. In Muslim culture, there is no such thing as [universal] excommunication. So a fatwa, or no fatwa, does not mean anything to anyone outside that particular sectarian boundary. A Shi'a fatwa means nothing to the Sunnis. A second problem is this: the condemnation of Osama bin Laden has been issued. All the important sheikhs did condemn him as they condemned what happened on 9/11. It wasn't heard here [in the U.S. media]; people said it wasn't reported. But there was no question, it was completely unequivocal; there was condemnation. As far as the London bombings are concerned, I've been following the media, all the major organizations – including the Muslim Council of Britain – have loudly, unequivocally condemned what happened.

The business of all the imams issuing fatwas, again has some limited value. I think, Judea, you are simply giving them far more importance than they have in real life.

Judea Pearl: Here is the quote from our friend Sir Iqbal Sacranie [Secretary-General of the Muslim Council of Britain]. He said that nothing in Islam can ever justify the evil actions of the bombers. Further, he added, that the criminals needed to be distanced from the Islamic faith. And now is the turn of the Muslim clerics in Britain to issue a religiously formulated excommunication or condemnation. They can call him *fasad* or a heretic, but there are formal methods within Islam that are available for such condemnation.

Why do I insist on the religious formulation? Not so much for the perpetrator, because he has already made his decision and chosen his mission in life. But for the thousands of potential recruits, who are currently on the verge of joining or not joining that culture [of terrorism]. It's very important for them to know that here are the leaders of their religion, at least in Britain, who condemn it in the language in which they have been educated, that this is a sin against God. Not only against man, or against a political institution, but against God. And God is going to be punishing them, and Osama bin Laden will be going to hell and not to paradise. This difference is very important, I believe, to the people who are on the verge of that decision.

Akbar Ahmed: Judea, the Muslim Council of Britain represents all the major Islamic organizations of Britain, all the major Islamic centers – that is exactly what you need. Not some obscure imam in Britain issuing a fatwa, because the Muslim community, the young men, are going to be looking to the major organizations like the Muslim Council of Britain. That is why I am pleased that the Muslim Council of Britain has taken a very clear, unambiguous reaction to this [London subway bombing on 7/7].

Judea Pearl: Indeed, very clear, and empowering, especially to us, who are concerned about possible backlash. Absolutely.

[Excerpt from "Pushing Past Terror to Dialogue," *Beliefnet* (September 2005)]

collection of beings. Social capital comprises the networks of association and cohesion among people, networks that foster trust and commerce and create a sense of community. The term "social capital" was coined by the urbanist scholar Jane Jacobs in 1961. Sociologist James Coleman (1990) subsequently developed the concept to include norms of reciprocity and civic engagement.

Others have further extended these notions. Robert Putnam characterizes social capital as the elusive vibrancy of civil society, "most powerful when embedded in a network of reciprocal social relations." He goes on to describe the erosion of social capital throughout the latter half of the twentieth century as reflected in the decline of civic engagement generally and, in particular, the reduced participation in such community associations as bowling leagues, parent-teacher associations, and Sunday picnics with friends (2001). He notes specifically that television and other technologies have isolated people, making them less likely to engage in conversation and other forms of active social exchange (Putnam and Feldstein, 2003). Robert Reich (2002) echoes Putnam's lament in describing the obsolescence of loyalty, with people increasingly "bound to one another by little more than temporary convenience." In a similar vein, Jonathan Sacks (2002) sees the loss of human contact as a problem that erodes social cohesion, as children spend less and less time with their parents and more and more with television and the computer.

The importance of social capital had been recognized for several centuries before the term was coined. North African scholar Ibn Khaldun wrote of *asabiyya*, an Arabic term for the spirit of kinship or social bonding, in fourteenth-century Islam (Ahmed, 2003). British statesman and social philosopher Edmund Burke (1790/1993) wrote of the power of the thick bonds of public affection and association in civil society in eighteenth-century France, as did French social philosopher Alexis de Tocqueville of nineteenth-century America (1835/2003). Toward the end of the nineteenth century, French sociologist Emile Durkeim (1895/1951) attributed social problems such as suicide to *anomie*, a condition of normlessness, which he considered to be a product of the absence of social bonding (see Chapter 2).

The building of social capital became a central characteristic of community-oriented criminal justice policies in the late twentieth century, which were aimed at encouraging both individual and collective acts of guardianship as a way of discouraging criminal activity (Skogan, 1990; Wilson and Kelling, 1982). A key aspect of many of these programs was the organization of community meetings to discuss the progress of neighborhood efforts to build protective alliances.

In discussing the importance of social capital as an insulator against terrorism, Jonathan Sacks (2002) describes a deep social cohesion that reflects Bohm's emphasis on commitment in dialogue and is embodied in the idea of covenant. For Sacks, covenant is a biblical concept that suggests love, loyalty, responsibility, and compassion among those who join in covenantal relationships. Covenant is a bond of belonging; it is open ended and enduring, characteristic of marriage and friendship. Entering into a covenant is likely to seem hopelessly unrealistic for people who are strongly alienated from others, considerably beyond what may be attainable over the near term. Sacks's conceptualization does serve, however, as a direction toward which dialogue may head even when it is not an immediately achievable objective. For Rabbi Sacks, the process of dialogue that leads purposefully away from clash begins with conversation:

> The greatest single antidote to violence is *conversation*, speaking our fears, listening to the fears of others, and in that sharing of vulnerabilities discovering a genesis of hope. I have tried to bring a Jewish voice to what must surely become a global conversation, for we all have a stake in the future, and our futures have become inexorably intertwined (2002, p. 2).

The goals of honest conversation about our fears and committed listening to the fears of others are surely elusive, as is Sacks's more recent aphorism: "Who is a hero? One who turns an enemy into a friend" (2005). Sacks sees dialogue as a "hard but sacred" step-by-step process that begins with forgiveness. He regards the enormous social payoffs that are available to those who are willing to engage in this process as more than sufficient compensation for the elusiveness of its goals. The act of one enemy forgiving another in a moment of truth opens the door to mutual reconciliation. The process requires courage, a moral courage that is as strong as the physical courage

381

needed on the battlefield. It is worth considering because the outcome of security through reconciliation is infinitely better for all than the alternatives.

These are lofty standards. Bohm's emphasis on openness and commitment and Sacks's notions of honest conversation and committed listening are often beyond the immediate reach of the participants in a dialogue. There is, in fact, no guarantee that dialogue will build social capital – it may even diminish it. Dialogue engaged in for the purpose of building social capital generally calls for a set of rules, at least informal ones. Roberts' Rules of Order is a commonly used set of rules for engaging in productive discussion, but formal rules may stifle honest discussion. The creation of an environment for the building of social capital generally requires at least a tacit agreement that the participants in dialogue will engage in honest discussion and a willingness to listen and be open.

4. Barriers to Dialogue

Basic Communication Barriers. Perhaps the most fundamental barrier to effective dialogue – dialogue that leads to mutual understanding – is the absence of requisite skill in speaking with and comprehending the person with whom dialogue is undertaken. Basic skill is needed in understanding both the language and culture of the other. Interpreters can help in overcoming problems in language, but skilled interpreters who can accurately translate both the words and their deeper meanings are generally in short supply.

Understanding the culture of another can be even more critical, as effective dialogue generally calls for a basic understanding of the mores and taboos of the people involved. Many a breakdown in dialogue is the product of a perceived rudeness that stems from a lack of awareness of the rules and customs of another. Diplomats of state are usually schooled in both the language and culture of the foreign states to which they are assigned, and this knowledge is generally essential to effective negotiations. Serious attempts to engage in dialogue outside of these official channels, if they are to be effective, require the learning of basic skills in the language and culture of those with whom the dialogue is planned.

Barriers among Individuals. If the path of dialogue can lead us to mutual understanding, reconciliation, and the building of social capital and security, why would anyone be so foolish as to choose the dark path of alienation that so often leads to hostility? One has only to look to one's own personal experience to find answers. Why have *you* sometimes been unable to turn enemies into friends? Possibly because it never occurred to you to try or even care. Perhaps you just don't like the other person, for any number of reasons: the person may compete with or otherwise threaten you in some domain, or may seem not to like you. Possibly the dislike is based on unfamiliarity: you don't understand him or her and have more important things to do than

382

invest scarce time and effort on such a project. Or perhaps you thought that reaching out to the person would alienate a friend who has a problem with that person, or might be viewed as an act of disloyalty to a group of which you are a member, as in Shakespeare's story of Romeo and Juliet and their clans, the Montagues and Capulets. Possibly also because you see too little benefit in it, you do not try to build a relationship or even make contact, as the person could be successfully ignored without any further repercussion. Or maybe you did in fact reach out on an earlier occasion and then regretted it, having felt rejected or insulted or otherwise unhappy with the response of the other person, and the result was further psychic distance or hostility. Attempts at dialogue can in fact *worsen* relationships, especially if poorly timed or presented in a manner that is misinterpreted.

Overcoming such barriers can begin with an understanding of the consequences of alienation, which can be especially dire when many people are involved. A basic way to overcome barriers to dialogue is to seek areas of common ground from which shared interests can be identified. When people who know each other but bring the baggage of a history of conflict to an arena of dialogue, it often works for them to acknowledge this history and then move forward by finding and expanding on areas about which they care and agree. Strangers without such baggage can move more directly to identify areas of common interest. In both cases – with strangers and with prior adversaries – it works generally for each side to listen carefully to the other and then think about what each cares about most and identify common priorities. World-renowned cellist Yo-Yo Ma puts it as follows: "If I know what music you love and you know what music I love, we start out having a better conversation" (quoted in Covington, 2002). Areas of common ground can serve as opportunities for the parties to join in the mutual protection of common interests and use that as a foundation for the search for other such opportunities. When the parties involved become aware that the protection of their common interests is more important than the issues that divide them, the dialogue will have served a major purpose.

Barriers among Groups. Barriers among individuals have parallels in relationships at higher levels, between groups of people and, in the aggregate, between sovereign nations and between civilizations. Groups bound by friendship, culture, and language often feel no particular need to reach out to others; they typically prefer the company of like-minded people. Some groups follow Samuel P. Huntington's (1996) maxim that cultural identity requires the creation of enemies. They define themselves in terms that mark them as distinctly different from others – as typically superior in at least some ways – and having distinguished themselves in this way, they will be disinclined to dirty themselves in dialogue with inferiors. Some groups have deep hatred for one another, dating back for decades or even centuries, and these enmities often re-emerge over issues that other groups might be inclined to ignore or easily resolve, such as squabbles over property rights, territorial boundaries, laws governing displays of culture, or local rule.

Attempts by individuals, either insiders or outsiders, to resolve any of these issues without the consent of a critical mass of the members of the respective groups can be met with resistance or hostility. And as with individuals, dialogue among groups can lead to further alienation and hostility – especially when attempts at dialogue result in a spiral of miscommunication, humiliation, negative information, and subsequent embarrassment and anger. When circumstances are ripe for such negative outcomes, attempts at dialogue must be entered into more thoughtfully than otherwise or put off until openings for positive dialogue present themselves.

At the same time, creativity and leadership can prevail against barriers that seem otherwise too difficult to overcome. Box 12.2 offers an example of an enterprising librarian who found a "living library" solution to cross-cultural education in Malmo, Sweden.

Barriers among Nations. Barriers to dialogue among nations are revealed in the collapse of the League of Nations in 1939 and in subsequent difficulties experienced by nations in resolving their differences through the United Nations. The League of Nations was founded in 1919 in the wake of World War I, based largely on terms set forth at the Paris Peace Conference and the Treaty of Versailles. Its charter reflected the explicit aim of creating a covenant among nations, with these opening words:

> The high contracting parties, in order to promote international co-operation and to achieve international peace and security by the acceptance of obligations not to resort to war, by the prescription of open, just and honourable relations between nations, by the firm establishment of the understandings of international law as the actual rule of conduct among Governments, and by the maintenance of justice and a scrupulous respect for all treaty obligations in the dealings of organised peoples with one another, agree to this Covenant of the League of Nations.

Dialogue at the League of Nations in fact worked quite effectively in the early years of the organization. In its first six years, the organization settled a dispute between Sweden and Finland over the Åland Islands, guaranteed the security of Albania, rescued Austria from economic collapse, settled a dispute between Poland and the Czech Republic over the division of Upper Silesia, and prevented a war in the Balkans between Greece and Bulgaria. The League also helped restrict trafficking in white slaves and opium, extended considerable aid to refugees and to poor countries, launched ground-breaking health surveys, and stimulated international cooperation on matters of labor, health, and education. For a time the League of Nations was the very model of successful dialogue among nations at the highest political level.

Box 12.2. Not a Swedish Joke

– Editors of the Wall Street Journal

If you find yourself in Malmo, Sweden, and happen to see a homosexual, an imam, and a gypsy walk into a bar, it's not a joke. These are just some of the people who can be borrowed – yes, borrowed – from the local library for a 45-minute chat in a nearby pub as part of an effort to fight discrimination.

Ullah Brohed pioneered the "Living Library" project earlier this month. "You sometimes hear people's prejudices and you realize that they are just uninformed," she says. And since a library exists to educate, she decided to give Swedish bigots the opportunity to come face to face with the prejudice of their choice. The Malmo library also offers a Danish man (since some Swedes and Danes don't get along too well) and, to our great embarrassment, even a journalist. "Maybe not all journalists are know-it-all and sensationalist," Ms. Brohed says.

Inspired by this example, a library in the Dutch city of Almelo plans to start its own human lending program next month. "The customers can rent a veiled Muslim woman and finally ask her all the questions they would never dare to ask if they met her on the street," says the director, Jan Krol. Of course, Mr. Krol must adopt his offerings to local tastes. So apart from the usual suspects – a gay man, a Muslim, and a gypsy – there will also be a politician, a hard-drug user, a gay woman, and a German (that World War II episode).

Given the daily reports of widespread anti-Americanism in Europe, we are surprised that neither Mr. Krol nor Ms. Brohed has a Yank in stock. Should Americans ever become available in libraries in, say, Paris or Berlin, even Jacques Chirac and Gerhard Schröder could check them out.

Eventually, however, tensions emerged over economic difficulties associated with the worldwide depression in the 1930s and over failures to intercede effectively in several serious acts of aggression, including the Japanese invasion of Manchuria in 1931, the Chaco War between Bolivia and Paraguay in 1932–35, and Italy's attack on Ethiopia in 1935. International dialogue through the League of Nations ended in the late 1930s, as the League collapsed under the weight of the Spanish Civil War, the resumption of Japan's war against China, and sharp differences among nations over how to deal with Adolf Hitler, especially after Nazi Germany's seizure of Austria in 1938.

Preventing Terrorism: Long-Term Strategies

The Preamble to the Charter of the United Nations, officially created in 1945, reflects the same essential idea of international cooperation as that of its predecessor: "to unite our strength to maintain international peace and security and to ensure, by the acceptance of principles and the institution of methods, that armed force shall not be used, save in the common interest... have resolved to combine our efforts to accomplish these aims." The success of the UN has tended to rise and fall with the ebbs and flows of world tensions. During most of the Cold War, it served as a useful forum for dialogue and action on a host of issues from health and education to labor and human rights. It has served as an effective system of international governance, providing public services that would not otherwise have been delivered because of the "free rider" problem: in the absence of an overarching authority like the UN, individual nations would have too little incentive to bear their fair share of the costs of providing such services if some nations could derive the benefits without having to pay for them. Determining each nation's fair share is no small task, but nations usually find ways to resolve this problem when the collective benefits are sufficiently great.

Failings of the League of Nations and the United Nations in matters of international security have been due in part to limitations in the charters of those organizations, as well as to the preferences of individual nations, and especially the major powers, to handle the most serious matters they confront either unilaterally or bilaterally rather than submit to collective authority. James Traub (2005) proposes a complementary framework consisting of nations committed to a set of core principles of rule of law (see Box 12.3).

Controversy will be inevitable in any attempt to form the sort of organization proposed by Traub, as the charter nations must attempt first to determine precisely the boundaries establishing qualification for membership and then whether particular candidates meet those standards. Weaknesses of the United Nations may, in any case, suggest the need for another formal organization, such as the North Atlantic Treaty Organization (NATO), to deal more effectively with terrorism.

Organizations such as the United Nations, NATO, and the World Trade Organization provide legitimate frameworks and settings for formal transactions among collectives of nations, and each of these organizations has its strengths and weaknesses. Although UN failures have been widely publicized and much maligned – failures to stop genocide in Darfur, Rwanda, and Srebrenica were conspicuous – the majority of UN peace-keeping and peace-building operations have been fairly effective. In fact, a 2005 study by the RAND Corporation found a two-thirds success rate and a high level of efficiency (Dobbins et al., 2005). The UN was quietly successful in East Timor, Eastern Slovenia, El Salvador, Mozambique, and Namibia. During the entire year of 2005, the UN spent less money running seventeen peace operations around the world than the United States spent in Iraq in a single

386

Box 12.3. The UN–U.N.

– James Traub

Two years ago, Kofi Annan, the secretary-general of the United Nations, gravely informed the UN General Assembly that the organization had reached "a moment no less decisive than 1945 itself, when the United Nations was founded." The world was no longer chiefly menaced by hostility among nations, as it had been then; the UN had to adapt to a world threatened by failed states, ethnic hatred, crippling poverty, and nonstate actors like Al Qaeda. Annan convened a "high-level panel" to recommend "radical" changes in the UN's structure and culture. Later this week, more than 170 heads of state, gathered in New York for the UN's 60th anniversary, will respond to Annan's challenge. It appears, at the moment, that their answer will be "We're O.K. where we are, thanks."

But perhaps rather than reconciling ourselves to the UN's inherent limits, we should ask whether we can imagine a different kind of institution – one, for example, that looks more like NATO, which consists only of members with a (more or less) shared understanding of the world order and thus a shared willingness to confront threats to that order. This new body, which I will call the Peace and Security Union (PSU) until someone comes up with a more resonant name, would require members to accept, in advance, a set of core principles, including: Terrorism must be unambiguously defined and confronted both through police and, where necessary, military means; states have a responsibility to protect their own citizens, which in turn confers an obligation on the membership to intervene, at times through armed force, in the case of atrocities; extreme poverty and disease, which threaten the integrity of states, require a collective response.

Who should be eligible to join? There has been some discussion, mostly in conservative circles, of a new organization of democracies. But many Third-World democracies resist almost any encroachment on other countries' sovereignty, whether in the case of "humanitarian intervention" or the singling out of human rights abusers; to grant them automatic admission would be to jeopardize the PSU's commitment to core principles. And it would be just as dangerous to automatically exclude China, since large parts of Asia – and not only Asia – would be reluctant to cross a Chinese picket line.

A better solution is to stipulate that any state that formally accepts the core principles and pledges to put them into effect will be permitted to join the PSU. Very few nondemocratic states would be willing to meet this threshold, especially if they could be ejected should they renege on their commitments. But no state could reasonably claim that it had been unfairly excluded.

Anyone, of course, can swear to anything; the key issue would be the commitments entailed by that pledge. In order to prevent the shameful passivity that the UN showed in Rwanda and Darfur, a unit in the PSU would make findings in the case of alleged atrocities; an affirmative finding, whether or not the state in question was a member of the organization, would automatically trigger a graduated series of measures, culminating in armed intervention, which members would have to support. And in order to distribute the peacekeeping burden fairly, states (including the U.S.) would have to designate military units for enforcement activities, as well as the kind of muscular peacekeeping that involves howitzers and helicopter gunships. They would have to make specific pledges to increase foreign aid and debt relief and to lower trade barriers to benefit impoverished countries.

The major Western states would be inclined to join the PSU because they fear that the UN as currently constituted is not up to the challenge of halting atrocities, confronting terrorism and stopping the spread of nuclear weapons. But if the PSU is seen as an alliance of Western states, it will have very little legitimacy in the Third World, where most of its forceful actions would inevitably occur. Developing nations must be given a powerful motive to join. This is one reason that the PSU would take seriously the "soft" threats of poverty and disease, which are of consuming interest to the developing world. The PSU will also find room on its Security Council equivalent for countries like India, Brazil, and South Africa - as long as they embrace the organization's objectives, of course.

The PSU would function as a more coherent and effective version of today's Security Council, but it would not be able to ignore the political realities that so often hamstring the council. No such organization, no matter how constituted, could prevent the United States from pursuing what it deemed a matter of vital national interest, as the U.S. did in the case of Iraq. What it could do, however, is offer a forum sympathetic enough to American views and interests to coax the U.S. back into the admittedly vexing world of multilateral diplomacy. That, in fact, would be a major selling point for other states, who fear that absent an effective UN, the U.S. will settle the world's hash on its own or with ad hoc coalitions of the willing.

It took World War I to create the League of Nations and World War II to make the case for the UN. The failure of Kofi Annan's reform package would not exactly be World War III. But does that mean that we have to wait for another cataclysm to get things right? In early 1945, F.D.R., thinking of the failed League of Nations, said, "This time we are not making the mistake of waiting until the end of the war to set up the machinery of peace." Perhaps this time we should not wait for the war to begin.

[Excerpted from the *New York Times Magazine* (September 11, 2005)]

month. Use of diplomacy by the UN (what it refers to as "peacemaking") was even more successful: about half of all the peace agreements negotiated between 1946 and 2003 were signed since 1992 (Mack, 2005).

Where weaknesses in organizations like the United Nations are evident, *informal* multilateral relationships can fill gaps and build alliances that can be invaluable in contributing to dialogue and building social capital among nations. Much has been made, for example, of the collapse of both formal and informal goodwill between the United States and major European nations such as France and Germany in the years immediately following the attacks of 9/11. The breach has been attributed to the arrogance of both "Old Europe" elitism and U.S. "go-it-alone" Jacksonian unilateralism. It has been attributed as well to an imbalance of military power and to disagreement over a variety of issues from global warming and the environment to strategies for resolving tensions in the Middle East and for countering nuclear proliferation. Political scientist Tod Lindberg (2004) observes, however, that accounts of these differences often overlook a more profound, fundamental, and shared cultural heritage and common interests that link the United States with Europe. These strong bonds create an enduring network of informal multilateral engagements between the United States and Europe that encourage cooperation in matters that seriously threaten either side, including terrorism and the sharing of counterterrorist information.

When multilateral relations through formal organizations such as the United Nations break down, an important alternative is bilateral relationships, both formal and informal. In a relatively harmonious world, each nation would coordinate its dialogues and actions in the multilateral collective of nations alongside its bilateral dialogues and actions with each and every other individual member nation. Such multiple pathways to dialogue have contributed to healthier relations and prospects for sustained peace and goodwill in much of the world.

The dynamic of bilateral dialogue between pairs of countries and dialogue among collectives involving three or more nations parallels the dynamic at the level of the individual: one's social standing in a group tends to be higher when one is on good terms with each of the members of the group. At both the individual and international levels, the success of dialogue in the group depends largely on the goodwill developed through bilateral dialogues and relations, and for individuals and nations alike the dialogue tends to become more complicated as more participants enter the mix and form competing coalitions. At both levels, the success of dialogue depends on the willingness of each participant to engage in committed listening, to operate as an equal rather than as a superior. The barriers to dialogue grow increasingly insurmountable as the participants reveal a preference to advance their individual agendas and retain or gain advantage over others, often in the interest of maintaining popularity and support among constituents at home.

What about the case of the incorrigible adversary, such as the megalomaniac with hostile designs or the deranged leader of a rogue state? Germany under Adolph Hitler and Iran under the Grand Ayatollahs Ruhollah Khomeini from 1979 through 1989 and Ali Khamenei afterward may qualify as countries ruled by the former type of adversary, and Iraq under Saddam Hussein and North Korea under Kim Jung Il might qualify as cases ruled by the latter (Barnett, 2004; Hoagland, 2005b). Some argue that dialogue is counterproductive in such cases, as it lulls us into a false sense of security and gives the adversary time and opportunity to develop bigger and more deadly weapons to be used with more devastating effect later (Gingrich, 2006). Should dialogue be rejected in such cases?

There are two good reasons not to reject dialogue even in such cases. One is that it can produce useful intelligence that is not otherwise available. The information thus obtained may be unreliable – designed to obfuscate rather than inform – but this prospect should be taken into account in interpreting the information. A more basic reason not to reject dialogue is that it may worsen the problem by way of the self-fulfilling prophecy: rejecting the adversary can make the threat more likely. By convincing the adversary that we regard him as the enemy, we solidify our position as his enemy. The best strategy for dealing with the incorrigible adversary may be one similar to the approach recommended for negotiating with the deranged kidnapper: don't ignore, don't upset, don't encourage, don't vilify, be patient. In such cases, the prospects for meaningful dialogue are likely to be severely constrained, but they should not be abandoned.

5. Understanding What Works in Dialogue: A Research Agenda

Our knowledge of what works in dialogue is based primarily on a wealth of experience rather than systematic evidence. The experience tells us much that is useful, yet we have much still to learn about the specifics of dialogue. We stand to learn more through the use of valid research designs and the analysis of reliable data on dialogue than through a continuing reliance on episodic evidence and anecdote. The strongest data are derived from experimental or quasi-experimental research, collected from a variety of dialogues in different settings, with different purposes, different numbers and types of participants, and so on. Here are some questions for which empirically validated answers would be extremely valuable:

a. *Under what circumstances does dialogue work best?* What sort of outcomes are desirable, both in the short and long term, and how might they be measured? Based on these measures, how much more successful is dialogue among people who already know each other than among strangers? What sorts of settings for dialogue appear to contribute most effectively to successful dialogue, and what sorts should be avoided? What sort of planning contributes most to successful dialogue? What conditions are most critical for success in interfaith dialogue?

b. *Whom and how many to include?* What sort of people should be included in or excluded from dialogue in order to advance specific objectives? What mix of types of people and how many of each appear to work best? Are certain mixes likely to produce more harm than good, to set relations back and create further alienation? How many participants are too many, and how many too few to accomplish specific objectives?

c. *How much structure?* How specific should the agenda for dialogue be for various purposes, settings, and types and numbers of participants? How should a facilitator be chosen to guide the dialogue? What sorts of rules (e.g., Roberts' Rules of Order) work best? When should open-ended brainstorming be used to complement or substitute for structured dialogue? What works best to get dialogue back on track when it shows signs of turning negative or destructive? How should the dialogue be concluded?

d. *How to overcome language and culture barriers?* What language barriers stand in the way of effective dialogue – dialogue that leads to mutual understanding among people who are culturally diverse? What rules and patterns of interpersonal communication and behavior that are unique to particular cultures must also be understood? How can these barriers be most effectively overcome?

e. *How much preparation and follow-up?* What elements of planning are most essential to the success of each major type of dialogue? What information should be provided to each of the participants in advance? What sort of feedback and commitments work best to ensure that good results have permanence and unresolved issues can get resolved satisfactorily? How can dialogue be made into an ongoing process without growing stale?

We have much to learn about dialogue. The United States spends some $500 billion annually on defense, and $10 billion for the State Department to conduct diplomacy. We spend vastly more on defense research than for research on how to build bridges of social connection that might be capable of making war unthinkable. Thomas Barnett (2004) and others have written about the need for a fundamental reshaping of the military to make it more responsive to the growing demand for peace-keeping forces – maintaining an effective capability to wage war while expanding the capacity of the military to secure peace by strengthening local security and building and maintaining other critical infrastructure needed for civil society in places where hostilities have been pervasive. Learning to engage in effective dialogue may be essential to preventing war in the first place and to securing peace when preventive interventions fail.

Effective dialogue is not a sufficient condition for avoiding a clash of civilizations, but it is almost surely essential. The opportunities to improve the quality of dialogue everywhere are substantial. They should be seized at home and abroad and the sooner the better. In the process, we can discover both the thoughts we have in common – what makes us human – and the differences that make us interesting.

C. Government Initiatives: Soft Power

Joseph Nye (2004) defines *soft power* as "the ability to get what you want through attraction rather than coercion." He observes that a key to exercising soft power is to get others to want what you want, and this power can be attained through a process that begins with careful listening (Nye, 2005). For the long term, the primary tools of soft power – thoughtful diplomacy, inducements to political and social reform, economic assistance, and policies that stimulate participation in the global economy (Barnett, 2004; Friedman, 2000, 2005) – may be the most effective ways for governments to remove the underlying sources of terrorism. Soft power is based on the essential understanding that attempts to avenge terrorism through the use of military force tend to worsen the problem by feeding the alienation that breeds terrorism.

1. Ambassadors, Consulates, and Embassy Staffs

Official systems of diplomacy, operating principally through networks of embassies the world over, provide rich opportunities for each nation to exercise soft power by maintaining open channels of communication with other nations. These channels of communication occur both bilaterally and through collectives such as the United Nations and the World Trade Organization. Networks of ambassadors, consulates, and embassy staffs provide a structure for bilateral relations through readily available contacts, both formal and informal; from these contacts can develop personal relationships between representatives of each country with every other country. These networks are complex not only because of the large number of players involved in cross-national diplomacy but also because effective relationships developed by these players can be disrupted by other branches of government, including heads of state, who may act through other channels to violate arrangements worked out through the official diplomatic mission, often without warning.

Civility and congeniality are the lubricants that facilitate effective diplomatic relations, but congeniality is not sufficient. The goals of each party engaged in diplomacy should be the overarching concern. Finding common ground between any two nations typically requires that the diplomatic goals of each nation be clearly articulated and honestly pursued. Henry Kissinger (2006a), one of the most influential Secretaries of State in the past century, puts it this way:

> Diplomacy never operates in a vacuum. It persuades not by the eloquence of its practitioners but by assembling a balance of incentives and risks. Clausewitz's famous dictum that war is a continuation of diplomacy by other means defines both the challenge and the limits of diplomacy. War can impose submission; diplomacy needs to evoke consensus. Military success enables the victor in war to prescribe, at least for an interim period. Diplomatic success occurs when the principal parties are substantially satisfied; it creates – or should strive to create – common purposes, at least regarding the subject matter of the negotiation; otherwise no agreement lasts very long. The risk of war lies in exceeding objective limits; the bane of diplomacy is to substitute process for purpose. Diplomacy should not be confused with glibness. It is not an oratorical but a conceptual exercise. When it postures for domestic audiences, radical challenges are encouraged rather than overcome.

Some nations, such as North Korea, Syria, and Myanmar (formerly Burma), have extremely limited formal and informal contacts with other nations, making the sort of consensus Kissinger refers to difficult to achieve. The use of diplomacy to shape relationships with isolated nations is often restricted to the use of diplomats from other nations as third-party agents, other covert channels of communication, and political speeches, which tend to be more assertive and confrontational than conciliatory and consensus-building. Such speeches are designed typically to provide a sense of security to domestic constituents and send a message to other nations that toughness will prevail against external threats.

For these nations, and for others as well, the improvement of diplomatic results requires a deeper understanding of the culture, if not the language, of others. Throughout the West, deficiencies have become especially apparent in understanding the cultures of the Middle East and their languages, particularly Arabic and Farsi, the language of Iran. Misunderstandings due to culture and language have become the critical barrier to the effective use of soft power since the 9/11 attack. Jennifer Bremer (2005), professor of business at the University of North Carolina, observes that three years after the attack the U.S. State Department could call on a pool of only twenty-seven

Arabic language specialists certified at Level 4 or 5 (highly skilled interpreters as rated by the Foreign Service arm of the State Department, with "5" ratings reserved for natives of a country), and just eight at the highest levels of 4+ or 5.[1] Such a small pool of experts cannot reasonably be expected to serve adequately some 300 million Arabic-speaking people in the Middle East through twenty-one embassies and consulates. Bremer notes that this deficiency works to solidify the view that the United States does not take the Arab world seriously. She calls for a substantial expansion of language skills.

2. Peace Processes

A specialized tool of soft power is the *peace process*, which aims to mediate and resolve long-standing hostilities that breed terrorism. Two prime examples are the peace processes aimed at easing tensions between Israelis and Palestinians and between the Irish Republic and Northern Ireland. The success of the Northern Ireland process, which included the disarmament of paramilitary groups, may offer a model for resolving tensions in other places. A substantial margin of voters in the Irish Republic and Northern Ireland approved the Good Friday Agreement of April 10, 1998. This accord has remained firmly in place even in the face of attempts by insurgents to derail the peace process. Although the prospects for such a solution in the Middle East seem far away, they seemed similarly elusive in Northern Ireland throughout the 1980s and '90s.

The Israeli-Palestinian dispute has thus far proven more difficult than that in Northern Ireland and has substantially greater implications for tensions elsewhere in the Middle East and other regions that are especially vulnerable to jihadist terrorism. The perception that American foreign policy is heavily tilted in favor of Israel and against Palestine has become one of the major rallying cries of protest against U.S. policy in the Middle East – not only for Muslims, but for many others throughout the world as well; some of this protest is based on legitimate concerns about the imbalance of military and economic power and some is based on ancient hatreds. The United States and most other nations have advocated a two-state solution to the continuing crisis and have attempted to move Israeli authorities to a more moderate position, but have been thwarted by the Israeli conservative wing and by some conservatives in the United States. The death of Yassir Arafat in 2004 opened a window of opportunity for the resolution of the peace process in this sensitive area, but the election of Hamas in 2006 has chilled those prospects and created a new set of problems for Palestinians and Israelis. The Palestinian government must find ways to provide services to its people and agree to a solution that preserves the state of Israel. A significant easing of tensions between Islam and the West may be unattainable as long as this grave problem goes unresolved.

3. Public Diplomacy

Traditional diplomacy – dialogue among official state diplomats of different nations – has been effective especially when combined with open public diplomacy, the dissemination of the country's positive values and culture. This has been achieved by the United States over the years through academic and cultural exchange programs, such as the Fulbright Scholarships and the Peace Corps. It has been accomplished as well through public affairs programming via the United States Information Agency (USIA) and the Voice of America, as well as through private organizations supported by public and private funding, such as Radio Free World and Radio Free Europe/Radio Liberty.

A decline in academic and cultural exchange programs started before 9/11, however, perhaps attributable largely to the decline in public-spiritedness of the sort that characterized John F. Kennedy's New Frontier idealism of the 1960s and the associated drying up of federal support for such programs (Putnam, 2001). Although the need for such programs has become more apparent since 9/11, severe constraints and burdens related to international travel in today's post-9/11 security world and the perception, if not the reality, of increased dangers in many parts of the world where Peace Corps volunteers are most needed have reduced the numbers of Peace Corps missions and volunteers in many poor countries.

The decline of public diplomacy through broadcast media is another story. Public diplomacy is least effective when it is regarded as government propaganda – as a distortion of the truth – by the audiences exposed to it. During the Cold War, the Voice of America (VOA) and Radio Free Europe (RFE) were highly effective media for communicating about the fruits of freedom and democracy, human and property rights, educational opportunity, and other positive aspects of American culture. The information provided in these radio broadcasts gave hope to people oppressed by Soviet-era dictators during the Cold War and may well have expedited the fall of the Berlin Wall in 1989. The information was propaganda and was often perceived as such, but it carried enough credibility among citizens throughout the world to have been widely perceived as more plausible than most of the information broadcast over communist state-controlled airwaves.

VOA and RFE became less prominent, however, after the fall of the Berlin Wall, despite the worldwide explosion of satellite broadcasting, the Internet, and other communication technology breakthroughs. The United States Information Agency (USIA), created in 1948, was abolished in 1999 and its functions absorbed into the State Department, whereas the VOA was absorbed into the Broadcasting Board of Governors. The de-emphasis and decline of these conduits of public diplomacy have been driven largely by budgetary and safety concerns and a perception that these agencies and functions had outlived their usefulness with the coming of the new millennium. This decline may be a product as well of the inclination for elected officials to give more emphasis to interventions that yield short-term gains than to those that provide benefits primarily after the time of their next re-election.

Growing suspicion about American foreign policy since 9/11 is perhaps a more fundamental reason for the decline of public diplomacy. The VOA and RFE had been transmitted to much of the communist world over short-wave radio networks. Today many homes throughout the Middle East receive television through satellite dishes. Through the visual medium of TV, audiences see more clearly than was previously possible the differences between lofty rhetoric and policy on the ground. The U.S. war on terror has become a particularly tough sell in the face of images of the abuse of detainees at the Abu Ghraib prison and stories of abuses of prisoners and of the Qur'an in Guantanamo. Advertising of the sort that appears often to work in U.S. political campaigns is almost certain to be now more negatively received by audiences abroad, who tend to be more skeptical, if not more sophisticated, than is widely understood in the United States. For example, Harold Pachios, chairman of the Advisory Commission for Public Diplomacy, observed in 2003 that Middle Easterners often know much more about the discrepancies between American ideals and its policies than do citizens of the United States:

> Understand how Israel came about and why it was created. We can explain that it is another democracy and the United States has this common interest with democracies in the world – common Judeo-Christian values. We can explain that. What we can't explain is why the Congress of the United States makes it a law that the United States Government cannot publish a document that identifies the Capitol of Israel as Tel Aviv. It must identify, according to United States Law, Jerusalem. Of course, this is one of the unresolved points of contention between the Israelis and Palestinians.... Very few people in the United States know that this is the law in the United States. Everybody at every level of society in the Middle East knows that is the law in the United States and knows that that law was passed last year.

Pachios goes on to note that this suspicion of Americans is fairly recent: Germans and Japanese citizens came to think of American GIs as liberators rather than as occupiers after World War II, as did Bosnians in the 1990s when American soldiers came to save the lives of Muslims during Serbian "ethnic cleansing." Public diplomacy provides useful channels for the dissemination of information about such noble principles and practices as well.

While Al Jazeera (founded in 1996), Al Arabiya (founded in 2003), and other foreign media networks have become widely watched in the Middle

396

East, once-effective instruments of positive American values and culture have all but disappeared. As U.S. foreign policy has become increasingly unpopular abroad, the selling of positive aspects of American culture and values – an antidote to images that are often perceived as decadent and negative, transmitted through the motion picture and music industries – has become especially difficult. Republican Senator Charles Hagel of Nebraska noted in 2003, "Madison Avenue-style packaging cannot market a contradictory or confusing message."

That Osama bin Laden is more popular than George W. Bush among millions of people throughout the world may attest in part to a failure of public policy – a combination of our having neglected Islamic people and their values prior to 9/11 and then engaging in unpopular actions to deal with terrorism since. It has been attributed as well to our failure to offer more compelling justifications to support those actions. The message from the United States, both public and private, has emphasized freedom over justice. Bin Laden's message has, by contrast, been sharply at odds with that of the Voice of America and Radio Free Europe during the Cold War by emphasizing justice for Muslims. It has been attractive throughout much of the Islamic world, also because of his disparaging references to the West.

Clearly, there is a need to ask how a more credible message of hope can be sent to the oppressed people of our time, especially in the Muslim world, as was done elsewhere through much of the last century. The fundamental values of freedom, democracy, and the spirit of entrepreneurship and creativity that are in many ways uniquely American are still popular throughout much of the world, and they may be made more attractive to Muslims if presented in a way that is more respectful of their core cultural values and sensitivities. Poor people in many parts of the world today are in fact pulling themselves up, and they are doing so largely by following essential aspects of our culture – practicing entrepreneurship and assuming personal responsibility.

A serious obstacle to presenting these positive values is the negative impression that the world receives nonstop from American media sources that depict a violent and debased popular culture (see, for example, Box 12.4 by Martha Bayles). Attempts have been made to send more positive media messages through new media outlets such as Alhurra, founded in 2004 by the U.S. government and based in Northern Virginia. It remains to be seen how successful such efforts will be in disseminating information that can balance the many negative messages about the United States received by people throughout the world over the past several years.

These barriers notwithstanding, one fact is beyond serious dispute: For the United States to use soft power more effectively to counter the sources of jihadist terrorism, it will have to expand substantially its understanding of the languages and cultures of Islam and show greater respect for both. However

Box 12.4. Exporting the Wrong Picture

– Martha Bayles

A striking pattern has emerged since the end of the Cold War. On the one hand, funding for public diplomacy has been cut by more than 30 percent since 1989, the National Science Board reported last year. On the other hand, while Washington was shrinking its funding for cultural diplomacy, Hollywood was aggressively expanding its exports. The Yale Center for the Study of Globalization reports that between 1986 and 2000 the fees generated by the export of filmed and taped entertainment went from $1.68 billion to $8.85 billion – an increase of 427 percent. Foreign box-office revenue has grown faster than domestic, and now approaches a 2-to-1 ratio. The pattern is similar for music, TV, and video games.

This massive export of popular culture has been accompanied by domestic worries about its increasingly coarse and violent tone – worries that now go beyond the polarized debates of the pre-9/11 culture war. For example, a number of prominent African Americans, such as Bill Stephney, co-founder of the rap group Public Enemy, have raised concerns about the normalization of crime and prostitution in gangsta and "crunk" rap. And in April 2005, the Pew Research Center reported that "roughly six-in-ten [Americans] say they are very concerned over what children see or hear on TV (61%), in music lyrics (61%), video games (60%), and movies (56%)."

These worries now have a global dimension. The 2003 report of the U.S. House of Representatives Advisory Group on Public Diplomacy for the Arab and Muslim World stated that "Arabs and Muslims are . . . bombarded with American sitcoms, violent films, and other entertainment, much of which distorts the perceptions of viewers." The report made clear that what seems innocuous to Americans can cause problems abroad: "A Syrian teacher of English asked us plaintively for help in explaining American family life to her students. She asked, 'Does "Friends" show a typical family?'"

One of the few efforts to measure the impact of popular culture abroad was made by Louisiana State University researchers Melvin and Margaret DeFleur, who in 2003 polled teenagers in twelve countries: Saudi Arabia, Bahrain, South Korea, Mexico, China, Spain, Taiwan, Lebanon, Pakistan, Nigeria, Italy, and Argentina. Their conclusion, while tentative, is nonetheless suggestive: "The depiction of Americans in media content as violent, of American women as sexually immoral, and of many Americans engaging in criminal acts has brought many of these 1,313 youthful subjects to hold generally negative attitudes toward people who live in the United States."

Popular culture is not a monolith, of course. Along with a lot of junk, the entertainment industry still produces films, musical recordings, even television shows that rise to the level of genuine art. The good (and bad) news is that censorship is a thing of the past, on both the producing and the consuming end of popular culture. Despite attempts by radical clerics in Iraq to clamp down on Western influences, pirated copies of American movies still make it onto the market there. If we go by box office figures, the most popular films in the world are blockbusters like "Harry Potter." But America is also exporting more than enough depictions of profanity, nudity, violence and criminal activity to violate norms of propriety still honored in much of the world.

But instead of questioning whether Americans should be super-sizing to others the same cultural diet that is giving us indigestion at home, we still seem to congratulate ourselves that our popular culture now pervades just about every society on Earth, including many that would rather keep it out. Why this disconnect? Partly it is due to an ingrained belief that what's good for show business is good for America's image. During both world wars, the movie studios produced propaganda for the government, in exchange for government aid in opening resistant foreign markets. Beginning in 1939, the recording industry cooperated with the Armed Forces Network to beam jazz to American soldiers overseas, and during the Cold War it helped the Voice of America (VOA) do the same for thirty million listeners behind the Iron Curtain.

American popular culture is no longer a beacon of freedom to huddled masses in closed societies. Instead, it's a glut on the market and, absent any countervailing cultural diplomacy, our de facto ambassador to the world. The solution to this problem is far from clear. Censorship is not the answer, because even if it were technologically possible to censor our cultural exports, it would not be politic. The United States must affirm the crucial importance of free speech in a world that has serious doubts about it, and the best way to do this is to show that freedom is self-correcting – that Americans have not only liberty but also a civilization worthy of liberty.

From Franklin's days, U.S. cultural diplomacy has had both an elite and a popular dimension. Needless to say, it has rarely been easy to achieve a perfect balance between the two. What we could do is try harder to convey what the USIA mandate used to call "a full and fair picture of the United States." But to succeed even a little, our new efforts must counter the negative self-portrait we are now exporting. Along with worrying about what popular culture is teaching our children about life, we need also to worry about what it is teaching the world about America.

[Adapted from *The Washington Post* (August 28, 2005), pp. B1-2.]

natural and understandable, centuries of U.S. focus on its own problems and its European roots have isolated the United States from Muslim people and alienated them, especially as globalism has caused our culture to intrude itself on theirs. It will be necessary first for U.S. citizens to understand how deeply most Islamic societies perceive themselves as under siege and as victims of grave injustice (Ahmed, 2003, 2007). Creating both a broad understanding of Islam through public education and a corps of specialists who understand the cultures and languages (especially modern standard Arabic, Farsi, and Urdu, the language of Pakistan) would enhance U.S. capabilities in the critical area of human intelligence. But it will achieve something of more fundamental importance: it will allow us to build bridges of mutual understanding across a deep chasm of alienation and hostility between two historically great cultures with common roots that have for centuries coexisted mostly in peace and mutual compatibility, and often with mutual respect.

4. Creative Public Initiatives

Biographer Walter Isaacson (2005) observes that there are distinct prospects for the success of public policy against terrorism, just as there were distinct prospects for success against the great menace of the Cold War. He identifies creative policies and leadership as the key ingredients and argues that the same sort of opportunities exist today for a creative approach to succeed as those that existed, despite appearances to the contrary, at the end of World War II:

> Our leaders reacted with a burst of creativity. Working across party lines, they created a military alliance, NATO, to counter Soviet aggression. To win the economic struggle, they formed institutions such as the World Bank and the International Monetary Fund and programs such as the Marshall Plan. To win hearts and minds, they created Radio Free Europe and revamped Voice of America. They defined the struggle clearly and articulated it publicly with the Truman Doctrine. Then, in such documents as NSC-68, they worked to agree on the balance of commitments and resources necessary to sustain this struggle for as long as it would take to prevail.

Isaacson offers a portfolio of hard and soft power interventions that could serve as parallels to the mix of programs introduced to deal with the Soviet nuclear threat in the 1940s and '50s:

- A defense alliance to supplement NATO, focusing on radical Islamic extremism and terrorism in the Middle East, to support moderate nations such as Jordan and Egypt
- A plan that would correspond to the Marshall Plan, to provide loans to small businesses and promote a stable middle class across the Middle East

400

- An organization to bring public diplomacy to Muslims and others through digital technologies, featuring credible personalities via virtual social networks: blogs, digital streaming, and satellite broadcasts, and so on
- A corps of professionals – doctors, engineers, teachers, administrators, municipal workers, and so on – young and old (including retirees), deployed to countries in need of such services, to help build hospitals, schools, governments, utility and information infrastructures, and so on, operating as a neo-Peace Corps hybrid with nongovernmental agencies such as Doctors without Borders
- An energy policy that reduces both U.S. dependence on foreign oil and environmental problems caused by the emission of greenhouse gases
- A national commitment along the lines of the Truman Doctrine, designed to induce long-term bipartisan support – stating clearly our national interests and values, the nature of the new global challenge of terrorism, and a strategy for dealing with it

Richard Armitage and Joseph Nye, Jr. (2007) have produced a similar agenda, which they call "smart power": the effective blending of hard power inducements through military and economic sticks with soft power persuasion through diplomatic carrots. Their program calls for alliances and partnerships, global development, effective public diplomacy, economic integration, and technological innovation. Both the Isaacson and the Armitage-Nye programs begin with leadership and a shift from fear-based politics to forward-looking statecraft, as was noted in Chapter 9. A country of more than 300 million people – many well educated, accomplished, and enlightened in the ways of the world – possesses a large pool of people from whom such leadership can emerge.

D. Private Initiatives

As our government and others work to remove the sources of terrorism, private citizens need not sit back and wring their hands in despair. Those who feel helpless about the prospects for humankind under the threat of terrorism stand to learn a useful lesson from the outpouring of billions of dollars of private support and assistance to victims of the Indian Ocean tsunami disaster of December 2004. The response revealed not only the generosity of rich and poor alike but it also showed how modern communication and information technologies can be used effectively in the service of worthy aims and how private citizens can take the lead when their governments appear to be doing too little. These acts of generosity made a significant crack in the wall of misunderstanding between people of different cultures, including the stimulation of more positive Muslim views about Americans (Pew Global Attitudes Project, 2004). In revealing the willingness and ability of private citizens to confront a disaster of epic proportion – the tsunami

Supplies meant for tsunami refugees in Sumatra, Indonesia. These initiatives saved lives and built goodwill for the West in much of the Muslim world.

took some 200,000 lives and caused billions of dollars in property damage – this response may embolden others to find ways to challenge the tsunami of terror that struck on September 11, 2001, and the clash of civilizations that is presumed to have spawned it.

Tsunamis are, of course, quite different from acts of terrorists. They are acts of nature, not acts of aggression. Is it naive to think that private citizens might be able to help in matters of terrorism and aggression, as they do in matters involving natural disaster?

It would have been naïve twenty years ago to think that private citizens would take the lead in responding to a man-made disaster related to war, that of land mines. Yet Jody Williams was a teacher of Spanish and English as a second language in Vermont – a modestly paid, largely public-minded endeavor – when she saw an even higher calling and decided to take a stand. Before long she was leading an international movement of citizens and non-governmental organizations against the use of land mines; she founded the International Campaign to Ban Landmines (ICBL), took the lead in drafting an international treaty banning antipersonnel land mines during the diplomatic conference held in Oslo in September 1997, and then won the Nobel

Peace Prize the same year for this courageous and creative work. The ICBL today includes more than 1,400 nongovernmental organizations active in more than ninety countries.

There are other precedents for the prospect of ordinary citizens contributing to the prevention of human tragedy. The participation of millions of Americans in neighborhood watch programs and community associations (Warr, 2000) is one such example of our considerable capacity to take collective action against violence. The Internet today provides rich opportunities to build virtual bridges connecting a much larger community, a world restricted by 9/11 travel barriers. As technology has extended the reach of terrorists, so has it expanded opportunities for ordinary people to take extraordinary measures against the sources of terrorism.

E. Building Trust and Community

We noted in Chapter 2 that terrorism is a product of alienation, and alienation tends to be greatest when and where social capital – networks of association, cohesion, and cooperation among people – is weakest. In this chapter we have considered how thoughtful dialogue is an essential, although not sufficient, condition for the building of social capital and trust. If dialogue is not sufficient, what else is needed to build social capital and reduce alienation? We consider, briefly below, four important complements to dialogue: awareness of cultural variation and the need to be sensitive to cultural traditions and social mores, tolerance and the need to resolve the paradox of confronting intolerance, good government and rule of law, and the use of effective voluntary organizations to build a sense of community and an awareness of others.

It will be useful, first to sort out basic relationships among social capital, trust, and community. Social scientists have long observed that people have a *natural moral sense*, a desire to experience and sustain connections with others (A. Smith, 1759/1976; J. Wilson, 1993). Such connections build trust, whereas the absence of connections to a larger community breeds alienation. When the conditions in larger social settings – neighborhoods, communities, and entire societies – allow for these connections to extend beyond individuals and families, the result is the building of social capital and an increased willingness of individuals to trust strangers within the larger social aggregates. Trust among strangers, in turn, is generally associated with social and economic well-being (Fukuyama, 1995). And economic well-being provides job opportunities that can divert young people from the directionless existence that feeds alienation to useful participation in the production of goods and services needed by others in the immediate community and elsewhere. There is, in short, much to be gained by the building of social capital and trust, and much to be lost when these are eroded.

Preventing Terrorism: Long-Term Strategies

1. The Importance of Culture

Culture matters. A precondition to successful dialogue is an awareness of cultural differences among the participants and a sensitivity to the social mores to which each participant subscribes. Fukuyama (1995) sees cultural variation, more broadly, as the primary determinant of international differences in the levels of trust and stock of social capital. Any interventions aimed at the prevention of terrorism, if they are to be effective over either the long or short term, must be sensitive to the unique cultural traditions and values of the people the interventions are intended to serve.

In the West, the sense of trust among strangers in larger social settings is nurtured by a culture that relies heavily on the rule of law. In the United States, trust among strangers has been further enhanced through the shift from a sharply segregated society in the mid-twentieth century to one that celebrates cultural diversity to a degree that is uncommon throughout most of the world. Other elements commonly associated with American culture that have contributed to social capital and trust include a spirit of voluntarism, a work ethic that encourages commitment to a larger purpose, and an entrepreneurial tradition that aims to create a loyal base of satisfied customers. Although these traditions appear to have experienced substantial erosion in the latter half of the twentieth century – as reflected, for example, by the decline of voluntary associations (Putnam, 2001), the emergence of an emphasis on rights over responsibilities (Etzioni, 1993; Fukuyama, 1995), and the decline of character (J. Wilson, 1993) – elements of these traditions still remain.[2]

In Asia, trust derives less from the formal rule of law and participation in informal community associations than from a sense of duty to others in the community and to the homeland. In Japan, China, and other Eastern nations and cultures, trust is largely a matter of informal relations and reciprocity; social ostracism is a serious deterrent to misbehavior (Fukuyama, 1995; J. Wilson, 1993). Citing the research of anthropologist Grace Goodell, Wilson attributes this Eastern norm to a unique sense of obligation to the maintenance of social harmony.

2. Tolerance and Trust

The level of trust in a community, society, or culture tends to be greatest when the level of tolerance – the capacity to exercise restraint in the presence of a negative assessment of another – is high. The relationship between tolerance and trust is reciprocal: mistrust and alienation breed intolerance, and intolerance breeds mistrust and alienation. Intolerance can be the product of religious, cultural, ethnic, or political differences between people or groups of people. Any of these conditions can lead to hostility and aggression, and most wars and acts of terrorism are attributable to one or more of these sources of intolerance.

Tolerance represents a weaker level of one group's affiliation with another than does acceptance or respect – one individual or group can tolerate another without accepting or respecting them. Tolerance is nonetheless important not only because it provides an atmosphere that is conducive to the building of trust and cooperation but also because it may lead to acceptance and, eventually, to respect for another. Both of these qualities – the presence of trust and the prospect of mutual respect – tend to lessen the levels of social instability and hostility between groups of people who are aware of their fundamental difference or differences. Aristotle's conception of morality includes the qualities of temperance, gentleness, and justice, all associated with contemporary notions of tolerance.

Religious philosopher Martin Marty (2005) sees tolerance as a gate that opens a pathway to respect and the prospect of friendship. Rabbi Jonathan Sacks (2002) regards tolerance as akin to biodiversity: just as the natural environment depends on biodiversity to thrive, so does the human environment depend on cultural diversity, as no single civilization encompasses all the spiritual, ethical, and artistic expressions of mankind. Quoting the sages – "Who is wise? One who learns from all men" – Sacks reminds us that tolerance is very much about humility and openness. The wise person is one who is willing to learn from others, one who understands that "none of us knows all the truth and each of us know some of it."

The United Nations Declaration on Tolerance. In 1995, the United Nations Educational, Scientific and Cultural Organization (UNESCO) issued a Declaration of Principles on Tolerance, defining tolerance as "harmony in difference." The Declaration asserts that tolerance is not only a moral duty, but should be regarded as a political and legal requirement: "Tolerance, the virtue that makes peace possible, contributes to the replacement of the culture of war by a culture of peace." The United Nations also acknowledges the profound importance of tolerance explicitly in its charter:

> We, the peoples of the United Nations determined to save succeeding generations from the scourge of war . . . to reaffirm faith in fundamental human rights, in the dignity and worth of the human person . . . and for these ends to practice tolerance and live together in peace with one another as good neighbors.

Pope Benedict XVI's talk on "Faith and Reason." The limits of tolerance were pushed sensationally on September 12, 2006, when Pope Benedict XVI went beyond the usual boundaries of calm papal rhetoric in a talk entitled "Faith, Reason and the University," given at the University of Regensburg in Germany. The Pope called for a civilized "dialogue of cultures" and, as a precondition for such dialogue, the explicit rejection of violence in the name of religion: "Not to act reasonably . . . is contrary to the nature of God." The Pope's pointed reference to a fourteenth-century Byzantine emperor's disparaging remarks about the Prophet Mohammed drew attention to an urgent request for dialogue by the Pope that might otherwise have gone unnoticed.[3] The Pope's speech provoked a furious reaction by Muslims throughout the world, who saw the message as insulting to their faith; their protests led to the killing of a nun at a children's hospital in Mogadishu, calls for attacks on the Vatican by Muslim terrorist groups, and sharp condemnation of the Pope by many Muslim leaders.

The Pope may have underestimated the immediate damage his words produced – he quickly expressed deep regret for the way his reference to an obscure criticism of the Prophet had been interpreted. Many in the West joined Muslims in criticizing the Pope for insensitivity, arguing that he should never have made such inflammatory remarks (Fisher, 2006). Others praised him for stimulating more honest dialogue, even if he had done so in a highly provocative manner. Middle East scholar Reuel Marc Gerecht (2006) put it bluntly: "We need to stop treating Muslims like children, and viewing our public diplomacy with Islamic countries as popularity contests. Given what's happened since 9/11, a dialogue of civilizations is certainly in order. . . . Westerners are doing Muslims an enormous disservice – a lethal bigotry of low expectations – by telling the pontiff to be more diplomatic." One week after the talk, the Pope offered few regrets about what he had said: "I trust that after the initial reaction, my words at the University of Regensburg can constitute an impulse and encouragement toward positive, even self-critical dialogue both among religions and between modern reason and Christian faith."

Learning Tolerance. Robert Wright observes that it is often much easier to preach tolerance than to practice it, using a familiar example to which most drivers can relate (see Box 12.4).

As Wright observes, intolerance is a part of the human condition. Some people's deep intolerance may be a pathology so extreme as to render them as incorrigibles. People who act out such hatreds in displays of terrorism are suitable targets of the criminal justice system and counterterrorist interventions. For most people, however, a sense of tolerance can be learned and developed. While much of the decline in aggression that occurs with age can be attributed to biology, much of the process of maturation to adulthood involves the natural accumulation of experience that reinforces one's ability to control both fear and the intolerance that arises from fear. Aristotle (1998) observed that this learning process is most effective when it is done consciously and purposefully, ingrained as habit, and perfected through practice: "We become just by doing just acts, temperate by doing temperate acts, brave by doing brave acts." (Book II, Chapter 4).

Box 12.5. Robert Wright on the Difficulty of Being Tolerant

Large numbers of people all around the world truly, deeply understand that if they were in the shoes of people who are geographically distant and seem culturally alien to them, they would probably see the world the way those people see the world. It sounds like a completely elementary point. But very few people are good at practicing it, and I don't claim that I am. It's hard to do. I mean, on an everyday basis, we all go through life with moments where we deem other people as really bad, just on the basis of trivial evidence. For example, take road rage. We've all felt at least incipient road rage. And I would submit that usually we're mad at somebody who's doing something that we ourselves have done at least once.

So when you put it in terms of precepts, it almost sounds trivial. And yet, in a geopolitical context, the failure of large numbers to practice it leads to large-scale trouble. The Middle East is an example. You may realize that if you were on the Israeli side, yes, you'd probably be as outraged as most Israelis are. And if you were on the Palestinian side, yes, you would probably be as outraged as most Palestinians are. Now, if you could get the Israelis and Palestinians to appreciate that about each other, you would be very close to a solution to the problem. Yet we haven't been able to do that.

Intellectually, it's almost easy to do.... Actually *living* the philosophy is very, very hard.

[Excerpted from *What Is Enlightenment?* (August-October, 2004), p. 35.]

3. Good Government and the Rule of Law

The process of learning tolerance can be supported by effective government and the rule of law. The local culture and conditions on the street largely shape the level of tolerance in a community or society. But whether that level is high or low, the quality of government often weighs heavily in creating and sustaining conditions for tolerance. Authoritarian systems of government tend to be associated with intolerance. The most extreme manifestation of intolerance is genocide, which has been associated historically with authoritarian rulers such as Adolph Hitler and Slobodan Milosevic.

High levels of trust are most common in stable democracies that rely on the rule of law and are least common in countries ruled by autocrats. Every sovereign nation has a constitution, a charter that sets forth a set of basic rules

407

of governance. When those rules are unclear – subject to wide interpretation – unenforced, or subject to change at the whim of an autocrat, informal rules and controls tend to fill the void. Systems of government that have any or all of these deficiencies generally do not provide healthy environments for the maintenance of trust and the building of social and economic capital. The specific rules of law vary from country to country, principally so that these rules can be responsive to the culture, but they often vary because of unique historical precedents and quirks. Thus, the laws of a land are both the product of culture and the formal system that contributes to the subsequent shaping of culture and maintenance of cultural traditions.

Good government – under democracy, government that is of the people, by the people, and for the people – is the vehicle through which the laws can be tailored to serve the needs of the people governed. Although not a popular idea in the West, democracy is not necessarily the form of government that provides the governed with a desired mix of security, freedom, and justice. Some people prefer a paternalistic system that frees them from the responsibility to think about matters of governance. They may complain, but – as in the case of Russia in the early part of the twentieth century, after the breakup of the Soviet Union – they often reveal a preference for a government that provides security over one that emphasizes freedom and encourages entrepreneurship.

The key to good government, democratic or otherwise, is the *rule of law*. Under both democratic and nondemocratic authority (as in the case of a benevolent dictator, for example), the rule of law provides a framework that supports the development of trust among strangers. In drafting the constitution for the Commonwealth of Massachusetts, in 1780, John Adams famously wrote that the state shall be "a government of laws and not of men." Two essential premises of Adams's framework of governance are that (1) those who make the law and enforce it are themselves bound to adhere to the law and (2) to provide a system of accountability, a system of checks and balances is needed, with separation of powers between the executive, legislative, and judicial branches of government. These basic principles have been endorsed by the U.S. Supreme Court and every state supreme court in the United States.[4]

If good government with the rule of law is at one end of the political spectrum, the failed state is at the other end. Walter Russell Mead puts it as follows:

> Governments that cannot police their territory – where government authority does not penetrate into the backcountry or where swollen urban slums create large and unpoliced zones under the authority of criminal gangs – pose serious security risks in a world where terrorists are looking for safe havens and bases (2004, p. 167).

Francis Fukuyama (2004) shares these sentiments, adding that intervention is needed to deal with the problem:

> The end of the Cold War led to the emergence of a band of failed and troubled states from Europe to South Asia. These weak states have posed threats to international order because they are the source of conflict and grave abuses of human rights and because they have become potential breeding grounds for a new kind of terrorism that can reach into the developed world. Strengthening these states through various forms of nation-building is a task that has become vital to international security but is one that few developed countries have mastered. Learning to do state-building better is thus central to the future of world order (p. 120).

The idea that the failed state is a primary source of breakdown of order generally and of terrorism in particular has considerable empirical support. According to Pauline Baker, president of the Fund for Peace, failed states are those with high levels of migration and other indicators of social turbulence, weak economies, and high levels of crime and factional strife. Four nations with extremely serious terrorism problems – Afghanistan, Iraq, Pakistan, and Sudan – all ranked in the top ten in 2006 among the 146 nations rated using the twelve-point failed states index (Fund for Peace, 2006).

Baker recommends a variety of interventions to prevent further decline in failed states:

1. Reduce carnage by taking arms out of circulation through the gathering of intelligence on arms pipelines, advocacy of an arms brokering convention, promotion of criminal prosecutions, and support for multilateral organizations engaged in the destruction of surplus arms
2. Work together to promote the rule of law, protect human rights, and engage in dialogue in conflict zones, using business and human rights groups and foreign policy constituencies
3. Intervene militarily only as a last resort to protect civilian populations

Should the United States engage more aggressively to intervene in failed states? The United States has the largest military force in the world – Josef Joffe (2006) refers to it as an "überpower" that is not just stronger than its largest potential enemy but stronger than all potential enemies combined – and it certainly could intervene aggressively in failed states if it desired. However, the sobering experience of the U.S. overthrow of Saddam Hussein and his Ba'athist government in Iraq serves to reinforce Baker's third point above, that there are limits even to the effectiveness of the immense military power of the United States.

But this does not mean that the United States should not work more actively toward the improvement of governments in failed states. It may suggest, instead, that there are more effective ways to do so than it has done in Iraq. It can start with a return to the skillful use of diplomacy of the sort employed in the 1940s and '50s, when the United States relied more extensively on collaborations with allies, working to create and build bilateral cooperation and multilateral alliances through such organizations as the United Nations and NATO. A consensus has formed among a large number of authorities that the art of state-building is likely to be more effective than the use of military power to reduce terrorism over the coming years, and the United States should be taking a lead role in this critical work (see, e.g, Brzezinski, 2005a; Fukuyama 2004; Nye, 2004).

In a televised 2007 conversation among three major architects of U.S. foreign policy during the latter half of the twentieth century – Henry Kissinger (Richard Nixon's Secretary of State), Zbigniew Brzezinski (President Jimmy Carter's national security adviser), and Brent Scowcroft (National Security Adviser for Presidents Gerald Ford and George H. W. Bush) – a clear consensus emerged on the need to recognize, first, that the world was changing radically, with the decline of power of the nation-state, and second, that this change calls for a more collaborative, less arrogant approach to foreign policy, with a greater need than ever for dialogue, with an emphasis on listening (Ignatius, 2007).

4. Strengthening of Civil Associations

We noted earlier in this chapter that social capital and trust tend to rise and fall with the extent of public participation in voluntary community associations, such as parent-teacher associations and picnics with friends. Participation in such organizations – quite apart from private initiatives directed specifically at the immediate sources of terrorism, discussed earlier in this chapter – tends to build a sense of community, an awareness of others, and a greater sensitivity to their needs. Several authorities see the strengthening of such associations as a primary path to the building of trust (Fukuyama, 1995; Putnam and Feldstein, 2003).

How can civil associations be strengthened, especially in an era when many people isolate themselves through engagements with cable television "narrowcasts," computer games, and other high technology entertainments? Putnam and Feldstein report that civil participation can be expanded, although not generally in the same forms as when bowling leagues and Girl Scouts were more common. They give numerous examples of "virtual" communities that draw people together through Internet chatrooms and online bulletin boards, bringing about networking among artists and patrons of the arts, educators, public advocates, and religious associations, including interfaith dialogue networking. Some of these receive support from federal, state, and local governments, but most are initiated and operated outside of government.

410

F. Reducing Dependence on Foreign Oil

There are still other ways to remove the long-term sources of terrorism. One strategy that has been promoted by several prominent public figures is a reduced dependence on oil, the revenues of which have been identified as a major contributor to the supply of terrorists from the Middle East. *New York Times* essayist Thomas Friedman (2005) argues that America's appetite for oil feeds the profits on which terrorism thrives:

> If President Bush made energy independence his moon shot, in one fell swoop he would dry up revenue for terrorism, force Iran, Russia, Venezuela, and Saudi Arabia on the path of reform – which they will never do with $50-a-barrel oil – strengthen the dollar, and improve his own standing in Europe by doing something huge to reduce global warming.

There are a few leaps of faith in Friedman's conjecture, but some are beyond dispute. For one, the United States consumes about one-fourth of the world's demand for oil – about twenty million barrels daily (Energy Information Administration, 2005). Of course, the United States is not the only culprit in demanding so much oil. The growth of the economies of China, India, and other rapidly developing nations is another driver of higher oil prices and profits. For another, Friedman is in good company in making a connection between oil and terrorism. Former CIA Director James Woolsey (2002) and former Secretary of State (and former Dean of the University of Chicago Business School) George Schultz (Schultz and Woolsey, 2005) have also argued that our appetite for oil feeds terrorism.[5] Political scientist John Duffield (2007) adds that there are immeasurable but substantial social costs associated with the world's coddling of authoritarian regimes in oil-rich countries at the expense of promoting democracy, human rights, and other factors that are retardants to terrorism. Any serious attempt to reduce the long-term sources of terrorism is likely to have reduced dependence on foreign energy as a centerpiece of its strategy.

G. Further Perspectives

There is no shortage of ideas for removing the seeds of alienation that underlie terrorism. A 2005 survey of some prominent thinkers – including Kofi Annan, Zbigniew Brzezinski, Jean Bethke Elshtain, Amitai Etzioni, President Khatami of Iran, Bernard Lewis, Queen Noor of Jordan, Joseph Nye, Judea Pearl, Sir Ravi Shankar, Archbishop Desmond Tutu, E.O. Wilson, and fifteen distinguished others – produced a rich array of prospects for dealing with the sources of terrorism (Ahmed and Forst, 2005). Each contributor wrote an essay describing his or her view of the primary sources of alienation and terrorism and ideas about how to deal with them. Although they disagreed on a few issues, such as the net effect of religion on terrorism and war, there was a general consensus on the need for the expansion of dialogue and the promotion of constitutional democratic initiatives that emphasize the rule of law and basic human rights to stimulate initiatives that can strengthen the voices of moderation and civility in all nations and avoid a clash of civilizations. They added that the support of such programs can lead to more effective public education systems, equal rights for women, the creation and reinforcement of positive social networks that build trust, self-restraint on the export of entertainments that glamorize violence, and the creation of inducements to cross-cultural collaboration and research on dialogue.

Several (Annan, Brzezinski, Khatami, Noor, Nye) emphasized that all such initiatives should be launched with humility, and with eyes wide open to the need to respect the traditions of others and their institutions, subject to the protection of basic human rights, even in the face of resistance. Such an approach is likely to be essential not only to counter the alienation that breeds terrorism but also to achieve a more enduring peace and build a more secure international order, one that permits people to live without fear. The long-term prevention of terrorism requires an understanding that we can secure our own safety and prosperity most effectively by showing more interest in the welfare of others.

Discussion Questions

1. *Dialogue at the United Nations.* The United Nations has been sharply criticized for a variety of failures to deal effectively with terrorism. To what extent do those failures appear to be related to matters of dialogue? To what extent do they appear to be related to other factors? Might those other issues be addressed effectively through dialogue? If so, who should participate in it? What should be the agenda of such dialogue? What else is needed to make the dialogue more effective?

2. *Alternatives to UN dialogue.* What sort (or sorts) of dialogue should the United States consider as complement(s) or substitute(s) for United Nations dialogue on terrorism, in order to overcome the deficiencies of UN dialogue? Who should initiate and implement those alternative dialogues? Who should participate in them?

3. *Refusals to engage in dialogue.* The United States has been criticized for its unwillingness to engage in dialogue with North Korea and Iran, both of which are developing nuclear capabilities. What are the dangers in engaging in dialogue with those countries? What are the dangers in not engaging in dialogue with them? If we were to engage in dialogue with them, what sorts of ground rules would be appropriate? Might it be useful to have informal

secret dialogues aimed simply at getting to know each other better? Explain why or why not.

4. *Nongovernmental dialogue initiatives.* Do you see prospects for nongovernmental organizations and private citizens to complement governmental dialogue on the prevention of terrorism? Explain. How should such dialogues be initiated and implemented? Who should participate in them? Will the answers to these questions vary by cultural setting, from the United States to Europe to the Middle East? How so?

5. *Complements to dialogue.* We have considered complements to dialogue in considering long-term solutions to terrorism: tolerance, good government with the rule of law, and greater voluntary participation in civil associations. In which of these areas do you see the greatest opportunity for removing the seeds of terrorism? Why? What other prospects do you see? What should others do to make these ideas effective on the ground? What can you do?

Balancing Security and Rights to Liberty and Privacy

Protecting a nation or community against acts of terrorism can come at the expense of rights to liberty and privacy. This chapter identifies the range of security interventions that intrude on these rights, from relatively benign passive screening systems at one end to torture on the other. It describes the historical foundations of the problem and offers examples of interventions that involve a tradeoff between security and liberty, those that enhance security without an adverse effect on liberty, and those that reduce both security and liberty. It then deals with two specific interventions: profiling to detect terrorists and the USA Patriot Act. It concludes by considering frameworks for identifying and organizing key variables to assist in weighing the effectiveness of alternative interventions and their costs as invasions of the public's rights to privacy and freedom.

A. The Problem and Its Historical Precedents

Perhaps the most fundamental problem raised by the threat of terrorism is this: How can liberal democratic society and all its fruits be protected against terrorism without intruding on the very properties of liberal democracy that make it worth protecting? The basic problem was raised in the eighteenth century in a frequently quoted statement widely attributed to Benjamin Franklin, emphasizing the liberty side of the coin: "Those who would give up essential liberty to purchase a little temporary safety, deserve

414

neither liberty nor safety."[1] The security side of the coin was emphasized prominently by Abraham Lincoln, and later by Justice Robert H. Jackson, in stating that the Constitution is not a "suicide pact"[2] – in other words, guaranteeing rights to very dangerous people could result in our own demise. The problem has been put more simply and neutrally by many commentators as one of finding a balance between the public's need for security and its basic rights to liberty and privacy (e.g., Posner and Vermeule, 2007; Waldron, 2003).[3]

The problem of security – the provision of defense against aggression – is as old as our species. The problem of protecting rights is much more recent on the anthropological time scale, and is fairly recent on the scale of recorded history. But it too has deep historical and political roots. The United States was founded on inalienable rights – to life, liberty, and the pursuit of happiness. The founders saw that democracy was the pathway to creating and preserving these basic rights, written into the Bill of Rights under the Fifth Amendment, directed at the federal government, and subsequently broadened to state governments under the Fourteenth Amendment to the Constitution. Both amendments specify explicitly that no person shall be deprived of life, liberty, or property without due process of law. These protections are grounded on essential moral principles, and they have contributed as well to an open, vibrant, creative society and a productive economy in the United States and throughout the free world.

These fundamental constitutional notions did not originate with the founders of the world's oldest surviving democracy. The origins of the protection of basic rights under the rule of law preceded the Constitution by more than five centuries, with the signing of the Magna Carta in 1215. Article 39 of the Magna Carta is explicit on these matters:

> No free man shall be seized or imprisoned, or stripped of his rights or possessions, or outlawed or exiled, or deprived of his standing in any other way, nor will we proceed with force against him, or send others to do so, except by the lawful judgment of his equals or by the law of the land.

B. How Terrorism Alters the Balancing Act

Balancing the need to protect life and property with the need to protect rights to liberty and privacy has been a problem for centuries, and in times of war the balance has tended to shift temporarily in favor of security over liberty. Abraham Lincoln suspended the writ of habeas corpus without congressional approval during the Civil War; Congress passed the Espionage and Sedition Acts to restrict speech during World War I; and Japanese Americans were foolishly, and tragically, sent to internment camps during World War II. Each of these restrictions were relaxed at the conclusion of each war.

Balancing Security and Rights to Liberty and Privacy

Even in peacetime, however, citizens have generally received favored treatment over foreigners in the protection of civil liberties. Citizens have entitlements that derive from their paying taxes, voting, serving in the military, and fulfilling other obligations of citizenship. It might seem strange, indeed, to give people who try to destroy constitutional democracy the same full protections afforded to the citizens of the country. Accordingly, "firewalls" have been built between domestic and foreign intelligence agencies to provide greater protections for citizens against external threats. In 1978, Congress passed the Foreign Intelligence Surveillance Act (FISA) to create a special federal court to rule in secret on requests by counterintelligence officers to exchange information about espionage and terrorist suspects and to obtain warrants to put them under surveillance, including the use of wiretaps without probable cause. The FISA court can grant a surveillance warrant to an FBI agent only if the primary purpose of their surveillance is foreign intelligence, not criminal prosecution.

This set of arrangements served well enough until 2001, but the 9/11 attack altered the already delicate balance. Because the war on terror presents a more open-ended and lengthy struggle than conventional wars, it suggests the prospect of a longer term set of restrictions to the rights of individuals to liberty and privacy. The dangers revealed by 9/11 and the emergence of new and more deadly forms of terrorism since 2001 pose new and potentially grave threats to liberal democracy. What is it about terrorism in the post-9/11 era that uniquely threatens the security not only of our lives and property but also of our system of liberal democracy and the protection of our unalienable rights stipulated under the law? Walter Enders and Todd Sandler put it clearly:

> Terrorism poses a real dilemma for a liberal democracy. If it responds too passively and appears unable to protect life and property, then the government loses its legitimacy and may be voted from office. If, however, the government reacts too harshly, then it also sacrifices popular support and may even increase popular support for the terrorists (2006, p. 27).

Enders and Sandler proceed to illuminate the dilemma with prominent examples of administrations brought down after widespread public perceptions that they committed one or the other of the two basic types of error. They offer the following as examples of the political consequences of too-passive responses to terrorism: President Carter's losing the 1980 election after his failure to resolve the Iranian takeover of the U.S. embassy in Tehran, the 1985 collapse of the Craxi administration in Italy five days after the release of terrorist Abu Abbas (mastermind of the *Achille Lauro* cruise ship hijacking), and the sudden reversal of Prime Minister Aznar's near-certain re-election as prime minister of Spain after his mishandling of the Madrid train bombing of 2004. As examples of too-aggressive responses to terrorism that tended to enhance the ability of terrorists to recruit new members and thus weaken administrations, they cite the French overreaction to the Front de Libération Nationale in Algeria in the late 1950s and early '60s, Israel's assassination of several Hamas leaders in 2004, and the United States' handling of detainees at Guantanamo following the 9/11 attack.

One can find in each of these examples, and in numerous others, unique mixes of defective policy and poor public relations. In some cases, the ruling authority may have been brought down no less by failure to offer satisfactory explanations that their actions or inactions were justified than by the policies and actions themselves. It is impossible to know, in each case, how events would have played out had things either been done or justified differently. A common link in all these cases is that the problem for the ruling authority arises largely because the power to act decisively to protect the public against terrorism resides primarily in the executive rather than the legislative or judicial branches. As Michael Ignatieff (2004) and others point out, this is why there is a strong tendency to strengthen the power of the executive branch in the face of terror, at the expense of the other branches, and to increase the government's dependency on secrecy. This tendency can be especially troublesome when the executive branch uses such powers to control opponents and people it regards as undesirable, people who have no association to terrorism, real or apparent.

It is clear, in any case, that terrorism presents a new set of complications to the already difficult problem of protecting lives and property without intruding excessively on the rights that enhance the quality of life. Unlike crime or war, terrorism creates new challenges by operating in the ambiguous areas that are neither exclusively foreign nor domestic and in presenting threats that are "existential," ones that threaten the very survival of liberal democracy.[4]

C. The Tradeoff: What Is Given Up? What Is Gained?

Tensions between security and freedom could be substantially reduced. The bounties of freedom are enhanced by security, and the desire to remain free enhances a society's interest in staying secure. At the same time, threats to the security of life and property can produce interventions that intrude on rights to liberty and privacy. Some interventions raise few objections from civil libertarians, such as surveillance systems at U.S. ports and other infrastructure and the screening of all persons at points of entry into the country and at or near targets that may be particularly attractive to terrorists, including national monuments, major tunnels and bridges, chemical and nuclear energy facilities, federal buildings, skyscrapers, and so on. Somewhat more intrusive and controversial are interventions that require institutional permissions to conduct electronic searches of databases or court warrants to tap telephone lines or other communication devices. The most serious and invasive intrusions include aggressive interrogation methods that border on or amount to torture.

The least controversial intrusions are ones that clearly enhance our ability to detect and prevent acts of terrorism and that do so at a minimum of invasion to the rights of individuals. The vulnerability of commercial air travel to the threat of terrorism was clearly revealed by the 9/11 attack, and although compelling objections have been expressed to some of the policies and practices used to screen travelers and their luggage, most people are quite willing to comply with the intrusions to enhance their personal safety in the skies and the safety of others. Similarly, few people object seriously to tamper-proof driver's licenses and passports and noninvasive methods of scanning cargo entering the United States. Even procedures that slow down and add to the costs of importing goods to the United States are often easy to justify, given the potentially incalculable costs associated with the prospect of weapons of mass destruction entering the country through ports and border crossings along the U.S.-Canada and U.S.-Mexico boundaries.

Other interventions are more questionable. Some may serve political interests that pander to fear without actually enhancing security. Politicians are rarely voted out of office either for protecting the public too vigorously or for elevating the interests of the safety of the majority of the public above the interests of the liberties of a minority – thereby creating a bias for excessive security at the expense of rights to liberty. Some are problems of execution rather than principle, as in the case of the flawed exercise of judgment by agents assigned to carrying out security and screening operations (McGovern, 2002; Morrison, 2002; Zakaria, 2002). Those problems could be minimized with well-designed interventions and systems of accountability that induce agents to act properly, recognizing that errors can occur even under well-designed systems.

And even for interventions that do enhance the general security, the benefits may not be sufficient to justify the social costs associated with intrusions on the public's rights to liberty and privacy. Some policies may buy short-term security at the expense of the long term. Examples include ethnic profiling – the singling out of Muslims and Arabs for more intensive scrutiny or interrogation at points of entry to the United States or in the vicinity of potential targets of terrorism (discussed more fully in the next section) – and aggressive interrogation methods used to extract information from credible terrorist suspects, methods that fall short of torture. A few interventions have been lampooned as "annoyingly stupid," "flagrantly intrusive," or worse (see Box 13.1.)

Box 13.1. The Security Follies

Restrictions to liberty imposed in the name of preventing terrorism often do nothing at all to reduce the risk of terrorism. They may even increase it occasionally by displacing security resources from productive activities and alienating people in the process. Fareed Zakaria (2002), a prominent foreign policy essayist and commentator, speculates that the greatest obstacle to fighting terror is government inefficiency. In an article written a few weeks after Zakaria's essay just cited, former Senator George McGovern offers support for Zakaria's observation by noting the wasteful "grip of bureaucratic devotion" that causes too many people to miss flights needlessly, disrupts operations at airports, and frustrates many others.

Tests of airport screening procedures show that the screening conducted by the Transportation Security Administration (TSA) is not only intrusive but often ineffective as well. In these tests, agents were instructed not to conceal simulated bombs and other weapons as terrorists might, but rather to pack their bags in ways that would test simply whether screeners could spot basic items they had been trained to recognize. In spite of this lower, less useful standard, 58 percent of the screeners failed to pass such a test at the international airport in Cincinnati, 50 percent failed in Las Vegas, 50 percent in Jacksonville, and 41 percent in Los Angeles. Overall, TSA personnel failed to detect any hazards in 25 percent of the screening tests conducted at thirty-two airports (Morrison, 2002).

Incompetent screening procedures were all too evident in the case of attempted suicide airplane bomber Richard Reid in late 2001, less than three months after the 9/11 attack. Although his name and ethnicity did not suggest a clear link to terrorism – his father was British and his mother Jamaican – his record of ten prior convictions, together with his strange behavior and unruly appearance, ought to have raised more than a few red flags and induced a more thorough search to uncover the potentially lethal explosives in his shoes. He was nonetheless given a seat on the jet, and it took off for Miami. Were it not for the prompt action of a perceptive flight attendant who thwarted Reid's intention to blow up the airplane, more than 300 lives might well have been lost over the Atlantic.

The problem is not restricted to airports. Six months *after* the 9/11 attack, the Immigration and Naturalization Service approved student visas for two of the nineteen men responsible for the 9/11 attack to attend flight school in Florida.

These problems have given rise to dark humor, spawning the Privacy International Stupid Security Contest. In 2003, the winners included the following:

- *Most Inexplicably Stupid Award* went to the Philadelphia International Airport for its overreacting to a bottle of cologne
- *Most Flagrantly Intrusive Award* to the Delta Terminal at JFK International Airport for forcing a nursing mother to drink three bottles of her own breast milk before being allowed to board an airplane.

Awards were also given to the Australian government (Most Egregiously Stupid Award), to T-Mobile of the United Kingdom (Most Annoyingly Stupid Award), and to the San Francisco General Hospital (Most Stupidly Counter-Productive Award).

One unfortunate aspect of such stories is that they may create alarm and misinformation. These cases were selected as extremes – they are atypical. The work of screening is important and largely thankless. Although the evidence from systematic screening tests is not reassuring, the vast majority of screening activities may well be both efficient and effective. The very presence of these screening systems may deter countless attempts to inflict damage on innocent people, although it is difficult to prove such successes either through systematic or anecdotal evidence.

Still other intrusions are beyond serious consideration: they reduce both our security and, because they are so extremely invasive and harmful, our quality of life. They are typically instituted through misguided policy or politically opportunistic scare tactics. Examples include the use of torture (see Chapter 9), the use of deadly force against suspected terrorists when nondeadly alternatives are available (see Box 13.2), and failures to justify intrusions against anyone who is cleared of suspicion following the intrusion.

How do we establish whether the benefits of a particular intervention justify its costs to personal liberty and privacy? Several commentators note that these are not matters that can be weighed on a scale, that the idea of "balancing" the security benefits against the costs to liberty is a flawed metaphor (e.g., Benn, 2004; Kleinig, in press; Waldron, 2003). For one thing, the central components to be weighed – the value of security versus the cost of intrusions to liberty – defy precise measurement. For another, the benefits and costs may fall unevenly on different members of the population and such distributional questions are not easily resolved. And for yet another, some interventions are costly not because of their immediate or inherent impact, but because they are too easily abused; they are used arbitrarily against

Box 13.2. Case Study: The Police Killing of a Terrorist Suspect – An Innocent Brazilian

On July 25, 2005, just fifteen days after a sensational suicide bombing attack had killed fifty-two morning rush-hour commuters on London's transit system, members of the London Metropolitan Police Department (MPD) shot and killed an unarmed man they thought was a terrorist. How could such a serious error occur?

The episode had the characteristics of a "perfect storm," a tragic confluence of coincidental events. The police were on high alert not only from the July 7 commuter bombing attack, but also because a second – this time unsuccessful – bombing attempt occurred the previous day, causing the closing of all stations and connecting transit lines. (The second attack failed because only the detonator caps exploded, not the bombs.) The bombers in the second attack were recorded on surveillance cameras, but they escaped capture. The police made arrests the day of the bombing, but the arrestees were found to have no connection to the attempted attack. The following morning, the police, determined to find the culprits, were staking out a block where three suspects were believed to reside, and at about 9:30 a dark-skinned young man emerged wearing a backpack. An officer called in information about the sighting to headquarters and was instructed to follow and closely watch the suspect and prevent him from entering the underground system.

Plainclothes officers followed the suspect as he boarded a bus, exited it a few miles later at the Stockwell Tube station, and made a phone call to a colleague (telling him that he would be late to work due to transit delays). The police phoned headquarters saying that they were sure they had the right guy, as he "had Mongolian eyes" and matched the description of one of the previous day's suspects. This information led the authorizing commander to use "code red" tactics, which meant that the suspect should be presumed to be armed and dangerous, should be detained, and could be shot with intent to kill. The suspect then entered the subway station, stopped to get a free newspaper, paid his fare to board the train, and proceeded through the barriers, down the escalator, and then ran to catch the arriving train. He boarded the train and took an available seat. Three surveillance officers took seats nearby, followed by a team of firearms officers, who challenged the now-standing suspect, grabbed him, pushed him back onto the seat, and then fired eleven hollow-point bullets at him, seven to the head, killing him in seconds. The MPD then issued false reports to the media, claiming that the suspect had been wearing bulky clothing, had vaulted the ticket barriers, and had run from police.

The dead suspect was soon identified as Jean Charles de Menezes, a Brazilian electrician working in London to support his family in South America. He came to Britain on a tourist visa and then remained on a student visa, which had expired two years before his shooting. The MPD issued an apology, stating that de Menezes had been mistaken for a suspect in the previous day's failed bombings, that he was carrying no explosives, and that he had no connection to the bombing attempts.

A thorough investigation of the incident revealed that police had been granted shoot-to-kill authority for suspected suicide bombers, with targeting to the head recommended to avoid either detonating a bomb that might be concealed at the chest or allowing the bomber to do so himself. Documents revealed, further, that mistakes in police surveillance procedures led to the improper identification of Menezes as a viable suspect – the error that set in motion the events that led to the killing. The misinformation given to the media served only to further undermine the credibility of the police in the matter and, more generally, their legitimacy as enforcers of the rule of law.

Is a shoot-to-kill policy justifiable in the case of a suspected suicide bomber? Well, that depends on the likelihood that the suspect is a real terrorist rather than an innocent bystander like Mr. Menezes. Terrorists can be expected to inflict far more harm on the public than ordinary street criminals, so different standards may be in order. The keys to minimizing errors in dealing with suspected terrorists are clear guidelines and effective training. Here is one thoughtful view of the problem:

> The head-shot order has its origins in Israeli practice. But the lessons of the Israeli experience with suicide bombings are not exclusively about the best way to kill would-be bombers. Israeli police are reported to have behaved with great restraint when confronted by explosives-laden Palestinians. In numerous instances, they have isolated potential bombers and disarmed them, sometimes at great peril to officers. And officials say they have shot a potential bomber dead only when an officer was unable, in a physical struggle, to disable him – and in no circumstance in which the supposed bomber turned out to be a bystander. The key lesson here is that with rigorous training, authorities can learn to identify suicide bombers with greater accuracy, and to disarm them in most instances without killing. Shooting to the head may be a necessary last resort, but if through rash actions and poor judgment innocent people end up as the victims, the main battle has already been lost ("Shoot to Kill," 2005).

Shoot-don't-shoot simulation training has proven effective in improving officers' instinctive responses to dangerous criminals (Skolnick and Fyfe, 1993), and similar training may be equally effective for officers who confront terrorist suspects. In the end, a thoughtful use of the rule of law by properly screened and effectively trained law enforcement officers is likely to be the best way to minimize the risks of costly errors in protecting the public against terrorism.

people viewed as undesirable, in the name of security, thus undermining the legitimacy of government.

Solutions to the problem are elusive, especially with regard to the fundamental right to due process, broadly described in the Constitution. Due process is the principle that the government must respect *all* of a person's legal rights, except under extraordinary circumstances. Questions of due process are, fundamentally, questions about the legitimacy of the government and its authority to enforce the laws. They deal, specifically, with the authority of the state to conduct surveillance and searches, access personal records, wiretap phones and other communication devices, monitor people, and interrogate them. The war on terror has caused the courts to lower the burden of proof to make it easier for law enforcement officials to intrude on individual civil liberties. As Michael Ignatieff (2004) observes, this can spiral to a problem with incalculable damage: "A war on terror is not just a challenge to democracy; it is an interrogation of the vitality of its capacity for adversarial review" (p. 12).[5]

In those instances in which the interventions increase security without restricting rights to liberty and privacy, no complex social calculus is needed. For other interventions, difficult decisions must be made, and analytical tools that can help measure the social benefits and costs are worth considering. In the end, of course, the rules will be determined through political processes. The problem here parallels that of crafting laws regulating moral hazards such as smoking and irresponsible driving; it is not uncommon to use the best available estimates of social costs and benefits to inform the shaping of those policies (Forst, 2004). If the restrictions of liberty are clearly excessive relative to the plausible gains in security that follow, the result will be not only to impose needless burdens on people at a considerable social cost but also to undermine what may be the greatest strength of liberal democracy in its long-term struggle to control terrorism: its moral standing (Dworkin, 2003; Powers, 2003).

D. Profiling of Terrorists

There is considerable appeal to the idea of preventing terrorism by catching terrorists before they commit intended acts of terror. One of the indelible images of the 9/11 terrorists is that all nineteen were Middle Eastern men,

Mohammed Atta walking through airport security.

a fact made all the more vivid by frequent postings of their pictures in print and broadcast media and the iconic photograph of Mohammed Atta and a fellow terrorist walking through airport security at Boston's Logan Airport. The clear message was that airport security had been too lax, and young Middle Eastern men should have been screened more carefully. Two of the nineteen – Mohammed Atta and Hani Hanjour – had prior immigration visa violations. Several were known to have taken flying lessons at a flight school in Florida. The event could have been prevented, and profiling might have been a critical aspect of this process of prevention.

There are both truths and half-truths in this assessment. Clearly, the event could have been prevented had we known then what we know now. Airport security policy then included routine checks for bombs in luggage, but it did not take seriously the prospect of suicide hijackings on such a large scale. The terrorists had carefully studied airport security procedures, found the vulnerabilities that could be exploited, rehearsed their plan, and then carried it out, using box cutters to overpower the airplane crews and subdue the passengers on all four planes, although passengers on one of the four managed to thwart an attack on the intended target. Airport security has been overhauled in response to these lapses. But one of the largely unresolved questions in this massive overhaul of security procedures centers on profiling: should airport screeners today screen all passengers with equal scrutiny, as

People getting carefully checked post-9/11.

though an 80-year old Japanese woman warrants the same degree of attention as a 20-year old Egyptian man?

This question implies that ethnicity is an important factor in screening for suspected terrorists. However, other factors, taken together with ethnicity, tend to be substantially more useful. The question also overlooks the longer term consequences of a policy of ethnic profiling. Let us examine each of these in turn.

First, it is unclear how powerful ethnicity is as a predictor of terrorism. Even if certain ethnic groups do in fact tend to engage in terrorist activities at a higher rate than others, other factors are generally more salient for a policy of selective screening: nervousness or other suspicious behavior, dress that is inappropriate for the weather conditions or the occasion, specific intelligence about a person, irregular paperwork or documentation, the response of a drug-sniffing dog, and so on (Gladwell, 2006, p. 42). But ethnic profiling is a limited predictor of terrorism also because of adaptive behaviors taken by terrorists. Because of ethnic profiling, women, for example, are used in the place of men as suicide bombers in the Middle East and Europe, Jamaicans are used in lieu of Middle Easterners on airplanes and trains in Europe, and people with white skins and baptized as Christians who have become radicalized as Muslims are used in terrorist plots in Europe and elsewhere (Whitlock, 2007a).

Therefore, ethnicity may be effectively used in screening only when combined with other factors that tend to have greater predictive power, factors that often call for mature, trained screeners to exercise good judgment and common sense. Airline screeners, for example, may profile passengers based on whether the passenger purchased a one-way or round-trip ticket, whether cash was used, how recently the ticket was purchased, and whether the passenger displays behavior suggesting any of three categories of hijacking candidates: crazies, crusaders, or criminals (Gladwell, 2002).

The second problem with ethnic profiling is that it can have harmful consequences, especially over the long term. Statisticians and clinicians refer to the error of falsely attributing a trait (in this case, "terrorist") to a particular individual (for example, a person named "Mohammed") as the problem of "false positives." But this is no mere statistical error; it is an error of due process (Forst, 2004). To subject a person to closer scrutiny *solely* because of his or her ethnicity violates fundamental notions of justice (Kennedy, 1999). As such errors accumulate, they tend to alienate the people so selected. The vast majority of any particular ethnic group, after all, are not terrorists. People of Middle Eastern descent, or with Arabic names, or dressed in modest clothing common to Muslim cultures have suffered indignities in public places and have been picked out for thorough screening at points of entry in a manner that resembles decades of racial profiling of blacks by the police. The detentions and humiliations associated with "driving while black" have thus been replaced by those associated with "traveling while Arabic." Many of those detained are tolerant and understanding of the grave threat of terrorism committed by people of similar ethnicity, but – especially as the false positive errors accumulate – the practice of ethnic profiling tends to work against the goal of building goodwill with mainstream Muslims; it places stumbling blocks in the struggle to win over the hearts and minds of moderates, those best positioned to discourage extremism in their populations.

This is not to suggest that we should ignore factors over which a person has no control, such as ethnicity, but rather that it is more effective to consider ethnicity with other information that may provide, collectively, a more accurate assessment of dangerousness. One such factor is demeanor (see Box 13.3).

Clearly, the profiling of suspected terrorists is an essential tool in the public's arsenal of protections against terrorists. When the factors on which profiling is based are known to be systematically related to the characteristics of terrorists, they can provide a useful basis for identifying terrorists and preventing them from carrying out attacks, especially when the stakes are very high. As Yale law professor Peter Schuck (2002) observes, profiling is more justifiable when it prevents a "social calamity of incalculable proportions."

Box 13.3. How to Spot a Terrorist on the Fly

– Paul Ekman

The man in the cheap brown jacket stood slumped in line, staring at the ground. His hands were fidgety, reaching repeatedly into his inside jacket pocket, or patting it from the outside. A momentary look of anguish, just 1/15th of a second or so, occasionally flashed across his face – the inner corners of his eyebrows would go up, so that his brows sloped down from the center of his forehead, his cheeks would rise, and the corners of his lips would pull down slightly. He was exhibiting what I call a micro-expression, a sign of an emotion being concealed.

The question was: What was he concealing? And why?

To the behavior-detection officers I was with at Boston's Logan International Airport, his combination of mannerisms – the micro-expression, the slumped posture, the pocket-patting – was unusual enough to raise a red flag. They called a uniformed state police officer, who asked the man the purpose of his travel. It turned out that he was on the way to the funeral of his brother, who had died unexpectedly. That was the reason for the bowed head. The frequent chest-patting was to reassure himself that he had his boarding pass. The micro-expression was an attempt to conceal his grief.

The man was not a terrorist, nor a malefactor of any kind, but just an innocent traveler carrying some extra emotional baggage that day. So why single him out for questioning because of a fleeting expression and a sad-sack posture?

Critics of the controversial new security program I was taking stock of – known as SPOT, for Screening Passengers by Observational Techniques – have said that it is an unnecessary invasion of privacy, based on an untested method of observation, that is unlikely to yield much in the way of red-handed terrorists set on blowing up a plane or flying it into a building, but would violate fliers' civil rights.

I disagree. I've participated in four decades' worth of research into deception and demeanor, and I know that researchers have amassed enough knowledge about how someone who is lying looks and behaves that it would be negligent not to use it in the search for terrorists. Along with luggage checks, radar screening, bomb-sniffing dogs, and the rest of our security arsenal, observational techniques can help reduce risks – and potentially prevent another deadly assault like the attacks of Sept. 11, 2001.

A lot has been said about the 9/11 hijackers' unusual behavior in the days before they boarded their ill-fated flights. Several of them were repeatedly questioned, but no one recognized their lies. An airport screener later said he had been suspicious of one because of his strange demeanor on the day of the attacks. But the screener had no training that would have given him the confidence to act on his suspicions.

The hijackers' lies – to visa interviewers and airport check-in workers – succeeded largely because airport personnel weren't taught how to spot liars. They had to rely on their hunches. The people who might have saved the lives of many Americans were needlessly handicapped.

Imagine if that screener had been taught to discern the signs of deception in a person's facial expressions, voice, body language, and gestures. With such training, he could have been confident enough to report the hijacker's behavior. SPOT, which the Transportation Security Administration introduced in 2006 at 14 U.S. airports, is the first attempt at using observational techniques as part of our security approach, and it is promising. Preliminary findings show that the overwhelming number of those who are taken out of line and detained for further investigation were intending to commit or had committed some kind of wrongdoing: They were wanted criminals, drug smugglers, money smugglers, illegal immigrants – and, yes, a few were suspected terrorists.

SPOT's officers, working in pairs, stand off to the side, scanning passengers at a security checkpoint for signs of any behaviors on the officers' checklist, such as repeated patting of the chest – which might mean that a bomb is strapped too tightly under a person's jacket – or a micro-expression.

The items on the SPOT checklist are culled from law enforcement experience and research on deception and demeanor. What about your face, voice, and body betrays the fact that you're lying? I've been studying this question for nearly 40 years, ever since I began researching it in the 1970s with Maureen O'Sullivan of the University of San Francisco and, several years later, with Mark Frank of the State University of New York at Buffalo.

In our studies, we recorded interviews set up in such a way that we knew when a person was lying. Afterward, we replayed the videotapes over and over in slow motion to identify the expressions and behaviors that distinguish lying from truth-telling. We spent hours identifying the precise moment-to-moment movements of the facial muscles based on my Facial Action Coding System (FACS) – a catalogue of every conceivable facial expression that I created and published in 1978 – to get comprehensive evidence of the kinds of facial looks that accompany spoken lies. Once such expressions are identified, people can be quickly trained to recognize them as they occur.

We also looked at the behavioral signs that accompany the act of thinking up an answer on the spot (e.g., an increase in pauses) and signs of emotion in the face, voice, or gesture that contradict the words being spoken ("The answer is definitely no" accompanied by just a slight nod of the head).

The facial expressions we identified allowed us to correctly determine who was lying 70 percent of the time; when the rest of demeanor is added, it pushes accuracy close to 100 percent.

Tools like this are indispensable to the future of airport security, and more are coming. Within the next year or two, maybe sooner, it will be possible to program surveillance cameras hooked to computers that spit out FACS data to identify anyone whose facial expressions are different from the previous two dozen people in line.

Someday, remote surveillance devices may identify anyone whose blood pressure and heart rate are much higher than those of the previous two dozen people. While this will provide an important new way of knowing that something is amiss, it does open a Pandora's box. Legislation to protect privacy and prevent misuse of such a technique should be enacted now.

Civil libertarians have raised the expected concerns about using observational techniques at airports: that SPOT spots more than just terrorists; that minorities, who fear discrimination and might act more nervous than others, may be unfairly singled out; that most of the people identified are innocent.

But the day I spent at Logan confirmed for me that SPOT violates no one's civil rights. Few people were identified. Nearly always, the answers to initial questions made further investigation unnecessary. No record was made, and the passenger lost no time.

Observational techniques are not a substitute for all the other techniques we now use to catch would-be terrorists. But they add another layer to transportation security. They are now being used at fewer than one in 10 major U.S. airports. We need to use them everywhere.

[*Source:* Excerpted from an op-ed article by Paul Ekman, professor emeritus of psychology at the University of California at San Francisco and pro bono adviser to the Transportation Security Administration's SPOT program. *Washington Post* – Outlook (October 29, 2006), p. B3]

More generally, profiling systems should aim for both efficiency and justice. They can be *effective* when they increase the prospects of identifying terrorists while reducing the intrusions on innocent people, and they can be *just* when they minimize intrusions on ethnic minorities.

At the same time, however, the institution of more profiling raises the incentives for terrorists to recruit people who do not fit the standard profile. Medical doctors, for example, might ordinarily be regarded as candidates for lower scrutiny in a security check, but car bombing attacks in London and Glasgow in 2007 were organized by a team of physicians, and three were arrested following the attack. One would expect terrorists to rely on people who do not fit the profile especially in attempting the most damaging terrorist attacks at places where people are screened. The more transparent and systematic the procedures for profiling, the greater will be the inclination for terrorists to use individuals who do not fit the terrorist profile. Profiling may, in short, provide a false sense of security against a threat that relies on asymmetric tactics to achieve its ends. The practice of random screening rather than systematic profiling may be both more just and, more effective in preventing the most devastating attacks.

In the interests of transparency and common courtesy, the officials who profile should be prepared to explain clearly to the people affected why it is needed, so that all persons inconvenienced by the practice can be helped to understand the policy. When the factors used to profile suspects are employed injudiciously, arbitrarily, or impolitely, profiling may have the unintended effects of undermining the legitimacy of the screening authorities and alienating the very people who are essential to maintaining and building the goodwill needed to eliminate the underlying attitudes that tend to breed terrorism in the first place.

E. The USA Patriot Act

The U.S. Congress acted quickly to respond to the 9/11 terrorist attack by enacting legislation designed to bolster the nation's security, at least temporarily. On October 24, 2001, the Senate passed H.R. 3162, the "Uniting and Strengthening America by Providing Appropriate Tools Required to Intercept and Obstruct Terrorism (USA PATRIOT ACT) Act of 2001." The act passed by a vote of 98 to 1 in the Senate and 357 to 66 in the House, and it was signed into law by the president on October 26, 2001. The law was renewed in March 2006, although by a smaller margin: 89 to 11 in the Senate and 280 to 138 in the House.

The act is organized in ten major sections or "titles" with these purposes:

I. Increase funding for homeland security
II. Enhance the detection of terrorist plans and activities not only through telephone and Internet surveillance but also by examining records of third parties such as employers, schools, and libraries
III. Counter money laundering and the financing of terrorism
IV. Protect the borders
V. Remove obstacles to investigating terrorism
VI. Provide for victims of terrorism, public safety officers, and their families
VII. Increase information sharing for the protection of the nation's critical infrastructure, most notably between the FBI and CIA
VIII. Strengthen criminal laws against terrorism
IX. Improve intelligence capabilities
X. Enact miscellaneous provisions such as funding for first responders and restrictions on licensing for the delivery of hazardous materials

The act also included provisions to protect the civil rights of American Arabs and Muslims and condemn discrimination against these and other minority groups who fall under a shadow of suspicion as terrorists. And it created the new crime category of "domestic terrorism," making acts of terrorism on U.S. soil a federal crime.

Two aspects of the Patriot Act have received more attention than the others: Titles II and III. Title II, and in particular Section 215 of that title, has been particularly controversial. It covers the examination of private records: financial, medical, telephone, and travel records of individuals, as well as the records of mosques, churches, and synagogues, libraries, physicians, and video rental outlets. What has particularly troubled many observers is that these searches can be conducted in secrecy, without the knowledge of those whose records are searched. More than two dozen safeguards were introduced in the 2006 reauthorization of the act requiring, for example, that such searches could be conducted only if approved by one of three persons (the FBI Director, Deputy Director, or Official-in-Charge of Intelligence); that applications for searches include statements of facts showing the relevance of the records to an authorized investigation to obtain terrorism intelligence information; and that the searches were subject to expanded provisions for judicial review.

Title III of the Patriot Act has been less controversial, as it aims largely to cripple the money-moving system used by al Qaeda to finance the 9/11 attacks. Al Qaeda had relied largely on hawalas, discussed in Chapter 4, to move money with impunity, leaving no trails that would permit investigators or analysts to trace the sources and uses of the funding. Title III requires all hawalas in the United States to register with the federal government as money service businesses. More than 100,000 were registered with the federal government within a year of the passage of the Patriot Act.

Most authorities see the Patriot Act as critically important in closing security gaps by tearing down the wall that previously prevented the transmission of essential information between domestic law enforcement officials and national intelligence officials. In Box 13.4, sociologist Amitai Etzioni observes that much of the criticism of the act has been misguided, blinded by anger about other executive branch weapons in the war on terror.

As Etzioni indicates, sharp criticism has been directed against the Patriot Act. Some claim that it intrudes excessively on civil liberties, civil rights, and the rights of immigrants. Others assert that it represents a triumph of form over substance, that some of the provisions may actually induce terrorist acts in the name of preventing them.

A fundamental problem with the Patriot Act is the potential for, if not the likelihood of, abuse. A 126-page report issued in March 2007 by the Inspector General of the Department of Justice revealed in fact that the expanded law enforcement powers contained in the Patriot Act were neither

Box 13.4. Politics and the Patriot Act

– Amitai Etzioni

A steady stream of revelations, and the ensuing news media reports, have portrayed a president hungry for power, doing whatever is necessary – legal or not – to protect this country. In the wake of such news, some lawmakers in Congress see weakness and an opportunity to gut one of President Bush's vital weapons in the war on terror: the USA Patriot Act.

Congress should not hold up extending vital sections of the Patriot Act in reaction to these recently revealed power grabs. The president's authorization of spying on Americans by the National Security Agency has nothing to do with the Patriot Act; nor do secret prisons, nor memos allowing torture. Questions over how much power the commander in chief can exercise must be sorted out by Congress and the courts, but the Patriot Act shouldn't be held for ransom.

Many of the 161 measures included in the law aren't contested by any major figure on the right, left or center. Even a representative of the American Civil Liberties Union said the group seeks to fix the act, not to kill it. An examination of some of the contested sections demonstrates that the measures involved are hardly out of line:

- **Phones**: Before the Patriot Act was passed, soon after 9/11, authorities had to obtain a court's permission to tap a phone, but the warrant had to be "particularized" to a given instrument, reflecting the days when people had one phone. Cell phones made this narrow rule obsolete. The Patriot Act changed this requirement to a suspect rather than to one of his instruments. What is wrong with that?
- **Libraries**: Critics have been outraged by the right of the government to search the computers of public libraries. Actually, the term "library" is not mentioned in the act. The bill authorizes searches of "books, records, papers, documents and other items . . . to protect against international terrorism or clandestine intelligence activities." Critics have singled out libraries because such searches evoke more public outrage than if one would refer to the actual wording of the bill.
- **Homes**: The "sneak and peek" clause has been particularly vilified. The act grants authorities the right to search a home without notifying the owner for a period of days. But how long is enough? Sen. Russ Feingold, D-Wis., favors seven days; Republicans in the House of Representatives want 180 days. But there has been little discussion of the grubby details in such a search. How long does it take to de-encrypt a PC? To translate messages?

And to find any collaborators? Once these matters are examined, it should not be difficult to come up with a compromise on notification.

- **Money**: The clause that penalizes giving "material support" to terrorists applies only if the donor knew where the funds were headed. If clearer wording is needed to protect those who thought they were giving to a charity, so be it.

We tend to swing wildly in one direction and then in the opposite one. The Senate Church Committee, responding to the abuses such as spying on civil rights groups and public leaders by the FBI under J. Edgar Hoover, tied the agency in knots.

The initial responses to the 9/11 attacks might well have been excessive. As time has passed – without a new attack on the USA – many security measures are being questioned, as they should be. Even so, when it comes to critical components of the act, such as those listed above, minor tweaks – not massive overhauls – would make the Patriot Act work for all Americans.

The same can't be said for the other security measures that the public has recently learned about. Those fully deserve the kind of extensive hearings to which the Patriot Act is being subjected.

Amitai Etzioni is the author of *How Patriotic Is the Patriot Act? Freedom vs. Security in the Age of Terrorism* and a member of the Markel task force on national security and information. This essay is excerpted from a 2006 op-ed article: "The Patriot Act is a Convenient Target," *USA Today* (January 12, 2006), p. 11A.

exercised carefully nor monitored closely. The audit on which the report was based found that the FBI improperly obtained telephone logs, banking records, and other personal information on thousands of Americans. From 2002 through 2005, information in more than 50,000 cases had been made available to some 12,000 agents without establishing that the information matched the FBI's needs or requests, without correctly tallying and reporting its efforts to Congress, and without checking systematically for abuses in the collection of the information and then reporting them to an intelligence oversight board. A specific abuse was the FBI's issuance of national security letters – used to obtain information such as credit and financial data and telephone or e-mail subscriber records (but not the content of messages) without having to secure a court order – without adequate oversight or justification. A thorough review of a sample of investigative case files at four FBI field offices found serious irregularities in 22 percent of those cases (Jordan, 2007; "Abuse of Authority," 2007).

The Patriot Act may indeed have contributed substantially to the nation's security in the years following 9/11. However, it surely could have done so with greater sensitivity to constitutional protections and greater use of effective controls to ensure that those entrusted to keep the country secure do so without undermining fundamental rights of the people.

F. Toward a More Informed Balance of Security and Liberty

Several obstacles stand in the way of achieving the goal of balancing the public's need for security with its rights to liberty and privacy. Security and rights are intangibles that do not lend themselves readily to measurement; they are disparate "goods" that are difficult to weigh against one another and broad concerns that are difficult to pin down. They involve distributional problems, with the costs of reduced liberty falling much more heavily on some groups than others, and the benefits being bestowed unevenly as well. They involve sacrifices in the near term in exchange for uncertain benefits – and often unintended reductions in security – over an unspecifiable future period.

To simplify the assessment of whether particular rules and procedures are in balance, a broad solution is to make use of rules of thumb, such as Ignatieff's (2004) "lesser evils" guidelines: "Sticking too firmly to the rule of law simply allows terrorists too much leeway to exploit our freedoms. Abandoning the rule of law altogether betrays our most valued institutions." A more exacting solution is to hold all agents accountable both for lapses in security and violations of rights to liberty and privacy. If the U.S. courts do not do so, other courts throughout the world may fill the void, holding U.S. agents accountable for actions carried out in the line of duty.[6]

But the solution to this problem goes beyond finding a better set of rules. Central to the proper balancing of security and liberty is the effective exercise of discretion by security and screening agents. Once the rules that govern the operations of these frontline officers are established as effective and fair, it falls on these officers not only to follow the rules but also to make the difficult calls at the margins, to accurately identify individuals and situations as worthy of closer scrutiny. Will we have a sufficient supply of qualified security officers, adequately trained and supervised, and assigned to positions and tasks that ensure that they will exercise discretion effectively and fairly, when and where they are most needed? Who will screen the screeners? Will those who exercise discretion in restricting the liberties of others be held accountable in ways that do not encourage conservative bureaucratic behaviors that interfere with the goals of both security and liberty? Difficult times call not only for thoughtful polices and procedures, but perhaps most importantly, they call for thoughtful people.

The question raised early in this chapter remains unresolved. How can we secure the bounties of liberal democracy without destroying them in the process? We may be willing to endure temporary reductions in the quality of our lives to enhance our own survival and that of future generations, but if they are seriously intrusive and not temporary, then the terrorists will have won the "war." In the end, the greatest gains to our security may derive not from restrictions on liberty, but from our ability to find ways to remove the causes that make others interested in threatening our security in the first place.

Discussion Questions

1. Do you think the greater problem today generally is too little security or too little liberty and privacy? Explain your answer.
2. Outline and describe the consequences of too little security. Outline and describe the consequences of too little liberty and privacy. What are the primary social costs associated with each of these consequences? Which of these costs can be estimated to provide a basis for assessing policies that intrude on individual rights?
3. Are the interests of security, liberty, and privacy always in conflict? Give examples of tensions among these goals. Can you give examples of solutions that have reduced all three? Examples of solutions that can expand all three?
4. Do you think the Patriot Act does more good than harm? More harm than good? Do you think it should be revised? If so, how?

FOURTEEN

Toward a Safer and Saner Twenty-First Century

We conclude with a brief discussion of the value of remaining open to multiple perspectives on terrorism, the danger of fixed thinking and certainty on any aspect of the subject, the power of education, and the need to remain vigilant against terrorist acts while building bridges between people of goodwill throughout the world. How can we protect ourselves from grave harm while removing the causes of terrorism, nurturing civility, and building international community against intolerance?

We noted in Chapter 9 that the 9/11 Commission attributed the attacks on New York and Washington to various kinds of failures, the first and foremost of which was the failure of imagination. At the end of the twentieth century, Americans were known for their creativity, competency, and entrepreneurship, their courage and spirit of community. Less than a decade later, symbols of U.S. integrity and competency, such as the Statue of Liberty and images of the 1969 moon landing, were replaced by images of Abu Ghraib and the aftermath of Hurricane Katrina.

A major challenge that lies ahead is to restore the reality of American competence and integrity. This can begin by mobilizing and channeling the considerable intellectual and social skills of the United States, through both public and private means, to the noblest of callings: to convert hundreds of millions of people widely perceived as aliens, if not enemies, into friends, to borrow from an idea of Jonathan Sacks (2005). Assisted by the tools of modern information and communication technology, can we commit ourselves imaginatively to the goal of empowering others – particularly, Islam's

436

moderates and liberals – to marginalize its most extreme factions who are real terrorist threats?

The approach used by the United States to confront terrorism following the 9/11 attack – declaring a war on terror and fighting the fire of terrorists with technology and vastly more firepower – has revealed itself to be not only ineffective but also counterproductive. The al Qaeda terrorists succeeded beyond their wildest expectations in inducing the United States to respond to the attack in such a way that caused the world to turn sharply against the United States. Essayist James Fallows (2006) puts it succinctly: "In the modern brand of terrorist warfare, what an enemy can do directly is limited. The most dangerous thing it can do is to provoke you into hurting yourself" (p. 69). He argues that the sensible alternative is to use just enough force to deal effectively with the terrorist. Too much force, or its inappropriate application, can more than offset the benefits.

Fallows goes on to describe how al Qaeda had been defeated on the ground: its training camps in Afghanistan had been dismantled, thousands of its operatives had been killed or otherwise incapacitated, and its leadership and organization had been largely destroyed or otherwise had virtually disappeared. In addition, the Taliban had been dispersed in Afghanistan, and communications, travel, and the flow of finances to support further jihadist operations had all been severely disrupted. In short, much of the immediate response to the 9/11 attack had been largely effective.

But the downside of the response may indeed have more than offset the benefits, not only in terms of the cost of the resources involved but also in terms of the loss of international goodwill and the prospect that it may have created many more terrorists bent on destroying the United States than it did to eliminate them. Fallows argues that this cycle of costly overresponses to acts of terrorism, which tends to breed further, more serious acts of terrorism, can be ended: "The United States can declare victory by saying that what is controllable has been controlled: Al-Qaeda Central has been broken up. Then the country can move to its real work" (2006, p. 72).

This real work, according to Fallows, will occur on three levels: domestic protection, worldwide harassment and pursuit of al Qaeda, and an all-fronts diplomatic campaign. Domestic protection can be improved by shifting from a "panicky" color-coded security alert warning system to a more practical and productive triage-minded system, in which various types and degrees of threat are dealt with at each stage by the appropriate level of response. Neutralizing al Qaeda can continue in the reasonably successful manner that it did in the years immediately following 9/11 by emphasizing close surveillance, keeping the leaders off balance, and disrupting its operations. An all-fronts diplomatic campaign can induce international cooperation in these and related efforts and can help restore the luster of democracy and respect for human rights that once served as the U.S.'s core resource for confronting adversaries and undermining their appeal. He argues that these pieces will fall in place only when we are guided effectively by leaders who are realistic, courageous, and optimistic even in the face of substantial obstacles.

Improved knowledge of foreign cultures and languages – through formal and informal education processes – will help immeasurably in these pursuits. This knowledge is needed not only in the military and in formal diplomatic missions. It is also essential for initiatives by nongovernmental organizations and private individuals operating both professionally in other domains and purely on their own behalf as tourists and members of an international community interested in the pursuit of knowledge and engagement with others. It will be necessary to create a shift in awareness and education, to open people's minds to the vital importance of connecting people so that our experience of common humanity can provide a deterrent against aggressive thought and action. At the end of the Cold War, the United States led the world in education, especially in math and the sciences. Today we have fallen behind in math and science literacy, are woefully unprepared to communicate with others throughout the world in languages other than English, and largely uninformed about the cultures that have become breeding grounds for terrorists.

A primary barrier to the success of efforts to shift to a more exemplary and compelling vision of America is politics. Politics fostered the spirit that won the Cold War, but it also created the war on terror – color-coded security alert system and all – and politics contributed to the failure of this newer "war." Politics contributed to the elevation of rhetoric that exploited fear at the expense of attention to effective diplomacy and the thoughtful allocation of foreign aid to the sources of alienation that breed terrorism. The emotional language of politics mobilized radical Islam and created vastly more terrorists than the war on terror eliminated.

Politics, according to George Packer (2006b), "turned 'freedom' into a dirty word, and it needs to be rehabilitated before it can be made a rallying cry" (p. 95). He goes on to say that the United States has been waging its war on terror through a Cold War lens that has greatly oversimplified the nuanced world that lies behind terrorism:

> Ultimately, the Cold War analogy is unhelpful, because it allows Americans to make a virtue of our ignorance.... Islamism is far stranger to us than Communism. It requires a deeper, subtler knowledge of local realities around the Muslim world, in all their variety, than most American writers and politicians have shown. The policymakers of the Kennedy era overlooked the essentially nationalist nature of Vietnamese Communism because they were swept up in the binary thinking of Kennedy's call to "pay any price, bear any burden." How much less do today's policymakers know about the Egyptian Muslim Brotherhood, the factions vying within the Arab Gulf states, the Muslim

438

minorities in Europe, the configuration of power in Iran, the causes of the Taliban resurgence in Afghanistan, the Islamist takeover in Mogadishu, or the rising terrorist threat in Bangladesh?

Packer argues that this limited thinking has created a variety of troubles in a chaotic world and that it has substituted will for understanding, which contributed to the costly failure of the Iraq war, among other harmful consequences. The challenge that lies ahead is to develop more thoughtful policies to rescue democracy, human rights, and national security.

One element of the Cold War experience is significant and relevant to the long-term struggle against terrorism. In his book, *Cold War: A New History*, historian John Lewis Gaddis (2006) observes that the United States defeated the Soviet Union not because of military or technological superiority, but because of a more persuasive ideology and a way of life that were vastly more open, healthier, and more prosperous than communism's utopian promise, which grew increasingly remote from reality. The United States won the Cold War on the battlefield of ideas. The specifics of the clash in which we are now engaged over the ideologies that breed terrorism are quite different from America's clash with the Soviet Union, to be sure, but an ideology that respects human rights and promotes justice and liberty is likely to be vastly more effective over the long term than military and technological superiority.

Of particular importance is the need to be more aware of the obligations that come with power. Technological, military, and economic superiority took centuries of diligence and creativity to develop. These great strengths do not automatically command legitimacy, respect, or international goodwill. They can be lost if not accompanied by sincere humility, a deep sense of responsibility, and fundamental respect for the humanity of others. They may be most seriously undermined by an impulse to succumb to deeply rooted fear instincts and a compulsion to overreact to terrorism.

Perhaps the most urgent need – the most viable long-term prospect for ending the scourge of terrorism – is to find ways to activate the world's most effective force against violence: women. The potential for using this vast resource has been stifled through the repression of women in many places throughout the world. Middle East scholar Bernard Lewis (2006) puts it clearly: "Women are our best hope in dealing with the Muslim world, because they have so much to gain from modernization." Women constitute the majority of the planet's population. They have been the dominant force for peace in virtually every culture. For eons they have been the primary nurturers of children, every next generation of leaders and followers. When given the opportunity, they have proven themselves to be extremely effective in leading people through difficult times. Gradually, in one culture after the next, women have made enormous gains in education, employment, and social status. The places in which women have made the most advances have

439

tended to become more civil, more productive, and less inclined to produce wars and terrorists. Women's gains, it turns out, are men's gains too. One of the great tragedies is that their opportunities have been most severely limited in poor, failed states, the places most in need of effective leaders and followers. It will be difficult to change the deeply held prejudices that keep cultures stuck in this condition, but it may facilitate reform to regard the prejudices primarily as cultural rather than religious.

As we continue working to expand human dignity at home and abroad, we can continue also to find ways to overcome the large lapse in imagination that permitted the September 11 attack and to understand that the vast majority of the world prefers security and liberty to clash and repression. It may be difficult for people of goodwill and civility, here and elsewhere, to find ways to control their fringe elements, but we should be able to find ways to help everyone become more aware of their hatreds and fears and rechannel their energies to positive pursuits. Former terrorists have, after all, reformed themselves and gone on to win the Nobel Peace Prize, as noted in the opening chapter of this book. The alternative to such imaginings could be to make our worst fears self-fulfilling. The choice is ours to make.

Discussion Questions

1. *Assessment of public policy to prevent terrorism.* What strikes you as the most important lessons learned over the past ten years in protecting the public against terrorism?

2. *Advancing from clash to mutual understanding and beyond.* What more can be done to get ordinary citizens to engage actively in building bridges across cultural divides, to act where their governments are slow to act, and to change the course of the world, moving from positions of intolerance and hopelessness to risking hospitality? What can you do?

3. *The most critical domain of terrorism prevention.* Which of the major prospects for preventing terrorism considered in this book – hard power, fear management, government soft power, dialogue, and other private initiatives – do you consider to be the most critical? Why? How, specifically, should we act to improve in that area? If we were to shift emphasis away from another domain to help finance this modification, which area would you recommend? Why?

Notes

Chapter One

1. We note in Chapter 5 that "jihad" is the term generally given to one's personal struggle to live virtuously in accordance with God's commands.
2. Prostitution, drug use, gambling, fraud, and embezzlement are examples of crimes that are not themselves acts of aggression, although they may be motivated by aggressive sentiments.

Chapter Two

1. An earlier version of alienation theory is traceable to Karl Marx, arguing that alienation ("*Entfremdung*") results from capitalism's fundamental opposition to human nature, particularly in its tendency to deprive workers of control over their livelihoods. (*Capital*, Volume 1, "The Process of Capital Production," Chapters 1 and 21) This idea provided a central basis for the alienation theory of crime as developed by the critical social school of criminology.
2. Ayman Zawahiri, Osama bin Laden's leading associate, is described in Chapter 8 of this text.

Chapter Three

1. Estimates by the General Progress Report and Supplementary Report of the United Nations Conciliation Commission for Palestine.
2. Slate commentator Michelle Tsai has asked, "If male martyrs can expect to find 72 virgin maidens in paradise when they die, what rewards can female suicide bombers expect?" The answer she finds in the Islamic literature is this: their husbands. She finds also religious commentaries arguing that "paradise will make them beautiful, happy, and without jealousy."

3. Psychologists Neuburger and Valentini, for example, see the study of the participation of women in terrorism conflicted by a tragic mixing of "the meaning of creating life with that of dispensing death." They go on to remark how strange it is that such important aspects of the life experience of the female half of the human species are shrouded in mystery, interpreted on the basis of suppositions, hypotheses, and personal feelings. The lack of interest, especially at the scientific level, in certain unexpected responses of women to certain social problems is proof of this.

4. Here is the passage introducing the concept from President Bush's speech: "States like these, and their terrorist allies, constitute an axis of evil, arming to threaten the peace of the world. By seeking weapons of mass destruction, these regimes pose a grave and growing danger. They could provide these arms to terrorists, giving them the means to match their hatred. They could attack our allies or attempt to blackmail the United States. In any of these cases, the price of indifference would be catastrophic."

5. There could be a grain or two of truth in the narratives of both the political left and right, but somewhere in between, more useful explanations might be available – ones that could help the United States deal more effectively with its own home-grown terrorists, like the Unabomber and Timothy McVeigh, while finding more discreet and effective ways to empower Islamic nations to deal more decisively with their Osama bin Ladens and suicide bombers.

Chapter Four

1. The term "Silk Road" is generally attributed to the nineteenth-century German scholar, Baron Ferdinand von Richthofen, to describe the network of caravan routes that linked China with the Mediterranean. For Europeans, the term widely conveyed a sense of mystical explorations to distant and dangerous lands in Asia.

2. Comments made on May 13, 2002, at the Commonwealth Club in answer to a question following the speech, "Regulating Biotechnology to Save Democracy."

3. Fukuyama: "The clash consists of a series of rearguard actions from societies whose traditional existence is indeed threatened by modernization. The strength of the backlash reflects the severity of this threat. But time and resources are on the side of modernity, and I see no lack of a will to prevail in the West today" (2001).

4. Fukuyama: "The single area in which my thinking has changed the most dramatically from 1989 to the present concerns the likelihood and speed with which modernization and democratization will occur – what one might call the 'timetable' question" (2006).

5. Sen elaborates further: "The same person can be, without any contradiction, an American citizen, of Caribbean origin, with African ancestry, a Christian, a liberal, a woman, a vegetarian, a long-distance runner, a historian, a schoolteacher, a novelist, a feminist, a heterosexual, a believer in gay and lesbian rights, a theater lover, an environmental activist, a tennis fan, a jazz musician, and someone who is deeply committed to the view that there are intelligent beings in outer space with whom it is extremely urgent to talk (preferably in English)."

6. With his tongue in his cheek, Robert Wright (1996) offers a remedy: "All Huntington needs to do is narrow his focus to the real pitfalls, the genuinely stubborn intercultural barriers, thus cutting the book's first 300 pages to, say, 50. Then he can expand the book's closing tribute to one-worldism to, say, 200 pages. And finally, he can delete the first half of the book's title. Thus: *The Remaking of World Order*."

Chapter Five

1. Huntington and others refer to "Islamist" rather than "Islamic" terrorism. This seems preferable at least to the extent that it dissociates mainstream Islam from terrorism, characterizing terrorism as a by-product of the dogma of Islamists rather than as a natural outgrowth of the Islamic religion.
2. Harris attributes moderation in religion to economics: "societies appear to become considerably less productive whenever large numbers of people stop making widgets and begin killing their customers and creditors for heresy" (p. 17).
3. Stern used a standard form of qualitative research: nonparticipant observer field research with convenience sampling. As with Juergensmeyer's case study approach, the nonprobability sampling and absence of a control group precluded the testing of hypotheses as to how the people or groups studied differed from others.
4. Norris and Inglehart (2004) report a strong correlation between religious values and fertility rates (with a correlation coefficient of $R = .77$).
5. Wilson elaborates that, although swift indoctrination in dogma gave the Darwinian edge to myth in Paleolithic times, rationalism and proved knowledge give the edge today.
6. Dennett (2006a, p. 330) attributes the metaphor of the rapid spread of religious intolerance to modern technology.
7. Intolerance is not unique to the religious faithful. The late Richard Rorty, once an avowed atheist, observed that even those who do not "hear the music of religion" will do well to choose a more nuanced and charitable approach to matters about which they do not see eye-to-eye with others (Vattimo and Rorty, 2006).
8. Dennett (2006b) takes strong exception to Dyson's assertion: "Traditional reverence is a large part of the problem: the risk of hurting somebody's feelings encourages critics to let apologists get away with inexcusable lapses in both rationality and evenhandedness. Why shouldn't we treat religions with the same respect – no more, no less – that we accord to, say, the pharmaceutical industry, or the world of music, or banking? If religions deserve more respect than that, let those who think so demonstrate it on a level playing field. That is all that I ask, but it is too much for Dyson, who confesses that he sees no way to 'draw up a balance sheet' and hence must stick to his 'prejudice' and declare in favor of religion. I think we can do better."
9. Berger (1999) notes that religion has become more popular on most continents, except for Europe and particularly among highly educated elites there and elsewhere. Although the numbers of these elites are not great, their influence is substantial (p. 10).

Chapter Six

1. Pape has estimated that about 95% of all suicide terror attacks are based on a secular rather than a religious goal – to rid a territory of an occupying military force: "Religion is rarely the root cause" (p. 4). Hewitt has counted terrorist incidents and fatalities in the United States from 1954 through 2000 and estimated that among the 3,228 incidents counted for the period, in 31.2% the responsible persons were white racists or rightists, 21.2% were revolutionary leftists, 14.7% were black militants, 6.2% were anti-abortionists, 3.6% were Jewish, 1.1% were Muslims, and the rest were members of an assorted mix of fringe groups. Among the 661 deaths during the same period, 51.6% were attributed to white racists or rightists, 25.0% to black militants, 2.0% to revolutionary leftists, 1.7% to Muslim offenders, 0.8% to Jewish groups, and the rest to various other fringe groups.

Many terrorist events are marked by elements of both political and religious extremism, so one should interpret such precise numbers with a grain of salt.

2. More politically provocative was the famous line uttered by presidential candidate Barry Goldwater at the 1964 Republican Convention: "Extremism in the defense of liberty is no vice." The statement was clearly unrelated to terrorism, but it did spark great controversy in condoning extremism and encouraging the Republican Party to take polarizing positions on certain issues. Goldwater was soundly defeated by Lyndon B. Johnson in the general election.

3. Judaism is an ancient a religion (see Chapter 5), and the Jewish people are generally regarded both as members of a particular religion and as an ethnic group. Distinct Jewish ethnic subgroups are also identifiable, starting with the Ashkenazim (European) and Sephardic (Iberian and Middle Eastern) Jews. Ethnic Jews are often not religious, and converts to the Jewish faith are generally of non-Jewish ethnicity.

4. Because hate crimes are not politically motivated, they are not universally regarded as terrorist events (Martin, 2006). We regard them as situated within the definition of terrorism given in Chapter 1: the premeditated and unlawful use or threat of violence against a noncombatant population with either a political agenda or the aim of destroying or intimidating a population identified as an enemy. In the United States, hate crimes are defined precisely under various state laws, as is murder and other crimes, but the term "hate crime" also has generic meaning for social scientists and others. The use of a definition that restricts terrorism to political motivation could eliminate not only hate-motivated violence against innocents, but religiously motivated acts of violence as well. Such restrictive definitions are at considerable variance with common usage.

5. In Germany the group went by the name "Rote Armee Fraktion." It was called a "terrorist group" and a "gang" by the German government, whereas it referred to itself as a group of urban guerrillas and revolutionaries engaged in resistance. As to the fact that the founding members grew out of a university environment, Kellen warns that the association is easily overdrawn, that they should not be confused with scholars: "To be sure, many of them have been students, in particular social science students. But...they were not very successful students."

6. Acts of terror were not new to individual members of the RAF. Baader and three associates had been convicted of arson in 1968 for setting fires in several department stores in protest to the Vietnam War. Baader served about a year of a three-year sentence, was released on parole, and then went underground and formed the RAF as a fugitive of justice.

7. This is the original version, in German: "Vor fast 28 Jahren, am 14. Mai 1970, entstand in einer Befreiungsaktion die RAF. Heute beenden wir dieses Projekt. Die Stadtguerilla in Form der RAF ist nun Geschichte."

8. The name literally means "circle clan." The Greek word for circle is kuklos (in Greek letters: κύκλος).

9. A third person, Michael Fortier, played a supporting role in the crime. He was a key witness who helped convict the pair, and he received a twelve-year sentence following a guilty plea for failure to report the crime.

Chapter Seven

1. Two separate mailings were postmarked from Trenton, New Jersey, the first on September 18, and the second on October 9, 2001. Of some 600 mailboxes that could have taken mail resulting in a Trenton postmark, only one in Princeton, New Jersey, tested positive for anthrax spores.

2. Another prospect – a commando raid on a nuclear power or military facility to steal nuclear material or weapons by force – has been discounted as too difficult to accomplish successfully to be taken seriously (Langewiesche).

3. The estimate from the Internet Usage and World Population Statistics for June 2007 was 1.1 billion. The estimate is based on data compiled by AMD, Inc. from Nielsen-NetRatings, the International Telecommunications Union, local network information centers, and other sources.

Chapter Eight

1. A few cases qualify as both domestic and international, such as the bombings of the London transit system in 2005 by second-generation Pakistanis, born in London, radicalized by clerics, and trained in Pakistan. Cases with both domestic and international roots have been extremely rare in the United States to date. A prominent exception is the case of the "Buffalo Six" (or the "Lackawanna Six"), a group of six Yemeni-Americans born in the United States who were convicted in 2003 of providing material support to al Qaeda after planning a bombing attack in the United States.

2. The origins of the SDS can be traced back to 1959, when a precursor student group arose out of the remnants of the Socialist League for Industrial Democracy. The organization crystallized formally out of a manifesto written by Hayden at a gathering in Port Huron, Michigan, in 1962 (Janke, 1983, pp. 405–07). Hayden's "Port Huron Statement" was written largely in rebuttal to the "Sharon Statement," which launched the Young Americans for Freedom at the Sharon, Connecticut, estate of William F. Buckley, Jr., in 1960.

3. For those interested in trivia, Assata Shakur is the godmother of the late hip-hop artist, Tupak Shakur (Williams, 2005).

4. It is noteworthy that the U.S. atomic bombings of Hiroshima and Nagasaki in 1945 were more devastating attacks on civilians than the 9/11 attack – the two bombs produced perhaps fifty times more civilian fatalities than the 9/11 attack. The 1945 bombings have been characterized as genocide (R. Frey, 2004), and they meet two of the criteria of terrorism: both cities were primarily civilian rather than military targets, and the purpose was to terrorize the Japanese into submission. The 1945 attacks were fundamentally different from 9/11, however, in that they were part of a declared war between sovereign nations, and they were followed soon afterward by the official surrender of the Japanese, ending World War II and possibly saving more civilian lives than they destroyed. Michael Walzer has argued that President Truman's decision to target civilian populations with nuclear bombs was, nonetheless, immoral: it violated the *jus in bello* (just means) principle of just warfare. Walzer explains that the United States was already close to victory, having killed more than 80,000 people in the fire bombings of Tokyo, and it could have saved many more lives without dropping the nuclear bombs: "In the summer of 1945 the victorious Americans owed the Japanese people an experiment in negotiation" (1992, p. 268).

5. Pape identifies seven Muslim countries with American military bases: Afghanistan, Kuwait, Oman, Saudi Arabia, Turkey, the United Arab Emirates, and Uzbekistan. He identifies fourteen Sunni Muslim countries with large fundamentalist Salafi populations: Afghanistan, Algeria, Bangladesh, Egypt, Indonesia, Jordan, Nigeria, Oman, Pakistan, Saudi Arabia, Somalia, Sudan, Tunisia, and Yemen. The three countries that are on both lists – Afghanistan, Saudi Arabia, and Oman – produced a disproportionate number of suicide bombers. Of course, there could well be factors other than an American military presence and large fundamentalist populations that make the suicide bombers from these

countries more prone to committing suicide attacks; Pape implicitly assumes them to be randomly distributed across individuals and countries.

6. Abu Bakr (which means "father of the virgin" in Arabic) was also the name of the Prophet Muhammad's closest friend and the first Muslim caliph, from the year 632 to the time of his death, due to natural causes, in 634.

7. Jessica Stern (2003), for one, suggests that the U.S. invasion of Iraq played "certainly" into Naji's strategy of "provoking America into direct military intervention in the Islamic world" (her words). Robert Pape observes, along the same line, that "the United States can only bolster al-Qaeda's appeal if it pursues military policies that actually confirm the group's portrayal of American intentions" (2005, p. 104).

8. Reporter David Adams cites a speech made in March 2003 by Gen. James T. Hill, the military commander of the U.S. Southern Command, in Miami.

9. Under UN Security Council Resolution 1267, October 25, 2002.

10. The second Intifada ("uprising" in Arabic) occurred in 2000, following concessions made by Yassir Arafat at the Oslo Accords. The first Intifada started in late 1967, in response to Israel's occupation of the West Bank and Gaza Strip following the Six-Day War.

Chapter Nine

1. See the Iraq Coalition Casualty Count for IED fatalities by month, http://icasualties.org/oif/IED.aspx.

2. A minority has argued that such assessments are never definitive, as we can never be certain that things might have worked out even worse had the United States not overthrown Saddam Hussein (Kagan, 2006).

3. A rough counterpart to Walzer's work from the Islamic perspective is Brigadier General S. K. Malik's *Quranic Concept of War*, written in Lahore, Pakistan in 1979. It is fundamentally different in that it is premised on the notion that "in Islam, a war is fought for the cause of Allah" (p. 50). It does, nonetheless, recognize limits in warfare. Malik explains,

> The Quranic philosophy of war is, for the better part, a philosophy of checks and restraints on the use of "force" in inter-state relations. The very Quranic command that directed the Muslims to go to war with the Pagans also bade them not to exceed limits. "Fight in the cause of Allah those who fight you," it said, "but do not transgress limits; for Allah loveth not transgressors" (p. 46).

4. Washington was especially skeptical of alliances with European nations. Later in his Farewell Address, he wrote (the address was never delivered orally) the following:

> Europe has a set of primary interests, which to us have none, or a very remote relation. Hence she must be engaged in frequent controversies, the causes of which are essentially foreign to our concerns. Hence, therefore, it must be unwise in us to implicate ourselves, by artificial ties, in the ordinary vicissitudes of her politics, or the ordinary combinations and collisions of her friendships or enmities.

5. Acccording to Bentham (1830), the extent of the coercion should be no more than is sufficient to yield the needed information.

6. According to Carter, "Being seen as the good guys – and more importantly, actually being the good guys – helps to win battles on the ground, too. Those tens of thousands of Iraqis who surrendered during the two Gulf Wars did so because they believed they would be treated better as prisoners by the United States than as soldiers by the Hussein government. But in the wake of Abu Ghraib, more future battles fought by America will have to be fought to the death."

7. Hufbauer, Schott and Elliott (1990) report that in the majority of the 115 cases of economic sanctions imposed from 1914 through 1990, the gross national product of the nation imposing the sanctions was at least fifty times larger than that of the nation on which the sanctions were imposed (p. 63).
8. The full report elaborated on failures of imagination at pp. 339–48.

Chapter Ten

1. "Pogo" was a popular comic strip created by Walt Kelly in 1951, depicting life in a fanciful Southern swamp and how the creatures there dealt with issues that parallel the human condition. A favorite theme was political satire. The strip ran in hundreds of newspapers throughout the United States in the latter half of the twentieth century.
2. Kahneman was awarded the Nobel Prize in economics in 2002 for his research on the departures of individual behavior from standard neoclassical economic assumptions of rationality.
3. It must be noted that the risks of some threats defy objective assessment. It is one thing to observe precise miscalibrations between actual and subjective rates of mortality associated with shark attacks, tornadoes, commercial jet crashes, and lung cancer – about which we have a wealth of empirical information – and quite another to talk about excessive weight that a person gives to the risk of a nuclear terrorist attack, given the absence of any such event to date. Still, there are enough terrorist events of many sorts about which ample evidence does exist to make such assessments. For example, the Rand Corporation and the U.S. State Department have collected data on terrorist attacks, and such data have been analyzed by Bruce Hoffman, Brian Jenkins, Robert Pape, and others.
4. For a thoughtful discussion of the media's awkward symbiotic relationship with terrorism see Wilkinson (1997).
5. Although we do not know when McLuhan first uttered these words, they have been widely attributed to him by several colleagues, including anthropologist Edmund Carpenter and media authority John Culkin.
6. As reported by Myrna Oliver in a *Los Angeles Times* obituary, December 29, 2005.
7. Source: Several transcripts of CNN's "Situation Room" from broadcasts during 2005 and 2006. See, for example, transcript for program of August 18, 2006, at http://transcripts.cnn.com/TRANSCRIPTS/0608/18/sitroom.02.html
8. Many observers, Muslims and non-Muslims alike, find the term "Islamo-fascist" or "Islamic fascist" particularly troublesome, polarizing, and confusing (Ignatius, 2006d).
9. Some commentators see NPR and public television as biased (see, e.g., Farhi, 2005; R. Novak, 2005). These criticisms may be valid to the extent that foundation support comes disproportionately from either the left or the right and with strings attached, explicitly or otherwise. Meyer's argument for the nonprofit model recognizes this problem; it aims primarily to deal with the problem of commercial pressure for sensational reporting.
10. Frank Furedi (2002b): "The aftermath of 11 September has given legitimacy to the principle of precaution, with risk increasingly seen as something you suffer from, rather than something you manage." Cass Sunstein's 2005 book, *Laws of Fear: Beyond the Precautionary Principle*, addresses the consequences of the problem.
11. Prime Minister Manmohan Singh offered helpful words of inspiration to his people, but Wonacott and Bellman attribute India's strength in the face of terror to the indominatable spirit of ordinary people, a deep understanding that life must go on.
12. As psychologist Paul Slovic observes, "It's much easier to scare than unscare" (Spencer and Crossen, 2003).

Chapter Eleven

1. This point was emphasized by Marvin Kalb in a guest lecture on media objectivity and responsibility, delivered to a class on terrorism at American University, March 22, 2006.
2. President Bush: "Across the Gulf Coast, among people who have lost much and suffered much and given to the limit of their power, we are seeing that same spirit: a core of strength that survives all hurt, a faith in God no storm can take away, and a powerful American determination to clear the ruins and build better than before" (*Washington Post*, September 15, 2005).
3. References to hawala can be found in texts of Islamic jurisprudence as early as the eighth century.

Chapter Twelve

1. According to Bremer (2005), "No responsible person would ask a 3 to speak before an unfriendly crowd at the local university (or at the embassy gates), much less put a 3 in front of a television camera and expect a clear, engaging and cogent discussion of U.S. Middle East policy in Arabic. For that you need a 4, and preferably a 4+ or a 5."
2. Etzioni (1993) argues for the restoration of a sense of responsibility through a renewed commitment to social engagement (pp. 226–67). Wilson (1993) sees the revival of the development of character as critical to a restoration of a vibrant society, a noble goal that can be achieved only by habit, in small steps, day-in and day-out (pp. 240–47).
3. The Pope gave an account of the Byzantine Emperor Manuel II's dialectic with an educated Persian on the truth of both Christianity and Islam, which included the following: "Show me just what Mohammed brought that was new, and there you will find things only evil and inhuman, such as his command to spread by the sword the faith he preached."
4. A similar concept is found in Thomas Paine's *Common Sense* (1776): "The world may know, that so far as we approve of monarchy, that in America THE LAW IS KING. For as in absolute governments the King is law, so in free countries the law OUGHT to be King; and there ought to be no other."
5. Schultz: "How many times will we be hit in the head with a two-by-four before we make a really determined effort to use less oil?" (Bernardoni, 2005). And this from Woolsey: "We must act, for the consequences of not acting are dire indeed. . . . If we do not forge a strategy and act now, we will leave major aspects of our national fate in the hands of a regime that was once our ally but has fallen increasingly under the sway of fanatics who have chosen to spread hatred of us, indeed of freedom itself. This hatred fires and sustains those who make war on us with the intention of destroying our way of life. Their power derives from their oil, and it is time to break their sword" (2002, p. 33).

Chapter Thirteen

1. The quote is from early papers of the Pennsylvania government in which Franklin participated. In 1738, he wrote a similar proverb in his *Poor Richard's Almanack*: "Sell not virtue to purchase wealth, nor Liberty to purchase power." Even more well known is Patrick Henry's "Give me liberty or give me death!" – really more a call to arms than a matter of balancing liberty and security when he gave the famous speech with these words in 1775.
2. Lincoln is said to have made the comment in response to charges that he was violating the U.S. Constitution by suspending habeas corpus during the Civil War. Justice Jackson used

the phrase in his dissenting opinion in *Terminiello v. Chicago*, a 1949 Supreme Court case involving free speech. See also Posner (2006a).

3. Eric Posner and Adrian Vermeule do indicate a clear preference for more security in the post-9/11 era: "No nation preserves liberty atop a stack of its own citizens' corpses, but if one did, it would not be worth defending."

4. Here is how National Security Director Condoleezza Rice characterized the unique threat of terrorism in 2002: "Perhaps most fundamentally, 9/11 crystallized our vulnerability. It also threw into sharp relief the nature of the threats we face today. Today's threats come less from massing armies than from small, shadowy bands of terrorists – less from strong states than from weak or failed states. And after 9/11, there is no longer any doubt that today America faces an existential threat to our security – a threat as great as any we faced during the Civil War, the so-called 'Good War', or the Cold War" ("Dr. Condoleezza Rice," 2002).

5. He elaborates on the slippery slope nature of the war on terror – that coercive means can cease to serve agreed-upon political ends and become ends in themselves: "Terrorists and counterterrorists alike end up trapped in a downward spiral of mutually reinforceing brutality. This is the most serious ethical trap lying in wait in the long war on terror that stretches before us" (Ignatieff, 2004, p. 115).

6. In one case, involving the "extraordinary rendition" by CIA operatives of Khaled Masri – a German citizen of Lebanese descent from Macedonia to Afghanistan – a German prosecutor charged thirteen U.S. intelligence operatives with the kidnapping, beating, and secret detention of Masri. The CIA suspected Masri of having links to terrorist networks, based largely on his having attended a radical mosque in Macedonia and sharing the name of a member of al Qaeda. The operatives conducted themselves much in the manner of characters in Ian Fleming's novels about James Bond. Two of the operatives checked into a Majorca hotel using the aliases "Kirk James Bird" and "James Fairing." The team's charges there included a food bill of $1,625 and $81 for a massage. Masri had filed a suit against the CIA in a U.S. district court in 2005, but a federal judge dismissed the case the following year, on grounds that a trial would "present a grave risk of injury to national security." While the case was under appeal in the United States, the German government stepped in to resolve the matter. (Fleishman and Goetz, 2007). See Chapter 9 for more on torture by proxy under the policy of "extraordinary rendition."

References

9/11 Commission Report (New York: W. W. Norton, 2004); also available at http://www. gpoaccess.gov/911/pdf/fullreport.pdf

Abadie, Albert, "Poverty, Political Freedom, and the Roots of Terrorism," NBER Working Paper No. W10859 (October 2004); also available at http://ksghome.harvard.edu/ ~aabadie/povterr.pdf

Abramowitz, Alan and Kyle Saunders, "Why Can't We All Just Get Along? The Reality of a Polarized America," *The Forum*, Vol. 3, No. 2 (2005); also available at http://www. bepress.com/forum/vol3 /iss2/art1

"Abuse of Authority: The FBI's Gross Misuse of a Counterterrorism Device," *Washington Post* (March 11, 2007), p. B6

Abuza, Zachary, *Militant Islam in Southeast Asia: Crucible of Terror* (Boulder, CO: Lynne Rienner, 2003)

Adams, James, *The Financing of Terror* (New York: Simon & Schuster, 1986)

Agnew, Robert, "Foundation for a General Strain Theory of Crime and Delinquency," *Criminology*, Vol. 30, No. 1 (February 1992), pp. 47–87

Agnew, Robert, *Why Do Criminals Offend? A General Theory of Crime and Delinquency* (Los Angeles: Roxbury, 2005)

Ahmed, Akbar S., *Jinnah, Pakistan and Islamic Identity* (London: Routledge, 1997)

Ahmed, Akbar S., *Islam under Siege* (Cambridge: Polity Press, 2003)

Ahmed, Akbar S., *Journey into Islam: The Crisis of Globalization* (Washington, DC: Brookings Institution Press, 2007)

Ahmed, Akbar S. and Brian Forst, editors, *After Terror: Promoting Dialogue among Civilizations* (Cambridge: Polity Press, 2005)

Aho, James, *The Politics of Righteousness: Idaho Christian Patriotism* (Seattle: University of Washington Press, 1995)

Ajami, Fouad, "The Summoning," *Foreign Affairs* (September/October 1993)

Ajami, Fouad, *The Foreigner's Gift: The Americans, the Arabs, and the Iraqis in Iraq* (New York: Free Press, 2006)

Akerlof, George and Janet Yellin, "Gang Behavior, Law Enforcement, and Community Values," in *Values and Public Policy*, Henry J. Aaron, Thomas E. Mann, and Timothy Taylor, editors (Washington, DC: Brookings, 1994)

References

Alexander, Yonah, "Terrorism, the Media, and the Police," in *Terrorism, Political Violence and World Order*, Henry Han, editor (Lanham, MD: University of America Press, 1984)

Alexander, Yonah and Dennis A. Pluchinsky, *Europe's Red Terrorists: The Fighting Communist Organizations.* (London: Routledge, 1992)

Ali, Ayaan Hirsi, *The Caged Virgin: An Emancipation Proclamation for Women and Islam* (New York: Free Press, 2006)

Alibek, Ken, *Biohazard: The Chilling True Story of the Largest Covert Biological Weapons Program in the World* (New York: Random House, 1999)

Altheide, David L., *Terrorism and the Politics of Fear* (Lanham, MD: AltaMira Press, 2006)

"Al-Zarqawi Declares War on Iraqi Shia," *Al Jazeera* (September 14, 2005)

Anderson Economic Group, *Northeast Blackout Likely to Reduce US Earnings by $6.4 Billion*, Working Paper 2003–2 (August 19, 2003)

Applebaum, Anne, "Finding Things to Fear," *Washington Post* (September 24, 2003), p. A29

Applebaum, Anne, "The Torture Myth," *Washington Post* (January 12, 2005), p. A21

Applebaum, Anne, "Bin Laden's Mortgage Calculation," *Washington Post* (September 11, 2007), p. A17

Arena, Michael P. and Bruce A. Arrigo, *The Terrorist Identity: Explaining the Terrorist Threat* (New York: New York University Press, 2006)

Aristotle, *Politics* (New York: Penguin, 1981 revised edition)

Aristotle, *Nicomachean Ethics* (New York: Oxford University Press, 1998)

Armitage, Richard L. and Joseph S. Nye, Jr., *Report of the CSIS Commission on Smart Power* (Washington, DC: Center for Strategic and International Studies, 2007)

Armstrong, Karen, *A History of God* (New York: Ballentine, 1994)

Armstrong, Karen, *The Battle for God* (New York: Ballentine, 2001)

Armstrong, Karen, *Islam: A Short History* (New York: Modern Library, 2002)

Aseltine, Jr., Robert H., Susan Gore and Jennifer Gordon, "Life Stress, Anger and Anxiety, and Delinquency: An Empirical Test of General Strain Theory," *Journal of Health and Social Behavior*, Vol. 41 (2000), pp. 256–75

Aslan, Reza, *No god but God: The Origins, Evolution and Future of Islam* (New York: Random House, 2004)

Aslan, Reza, "Depicting Mohammed: Why I'm Offended by the Danish Cartoons of the Prophet," *Slate* (February 8, 2006)

Aslan, Reza, "Why Do They Hate Us?" *Slate* (August 6, 2007)

Avrich, Paul, *The Haymarket Tragedy* (Princeton, NJ: Princeton University Press, 1986)

Ayton, Mel, "The Black Panthers: Their Dangerous Bermudian Legacy," *George Mason University History News Network* (October 9, 2006)

Bacevich, Andrew F., *The New American Militarism: How Americans Are Seduced by War* (New York: Oxford University Press, 2005)

Ballard, James David and Kristine Mullendore, "Weapons of Mass Victimization, Radioactive Waste Shipments, and Environmental Laws: Policy Making and First Responders." *American Behavioral Scientist*, Volume 46, Number 6 (February 2003)

Barabasi, Albert-Laszlo, *Linked: How Everything Is Connected to Everything Else and What It Means for Business, Science, and Everyday Life* (New York: Plume, 2003)

Barber, Benjamin R., "Jihad vs. McWorld," *The Atlantic* (March 1992)

Barber, Benjamin R., *Jihad vs. McWorld: How Globalism and Tribalism Are Reshaping the World* (New York: Ballentine, 1996)

Barber, Benjamin R., "Gaddafi's Libya: An Ally for America?" *Washington Post* (August 15, 2007), p. A11

Barnett, Thomas, *The Pentagon's New Map: War and Peace in the Twenty-First Century* (New York: Putnam, 2004)

Barnett, Thomas, "Dear Mr. President, Here's How to . . . Make Sense of Your Second Term, Secure Your Legacy, and, oh yeah, Create a Future Worth Living," *Esquire* (February 2005)

Barro, Robert, "The Myth that Poverty Breeds Terrorism," *Business Week* (June 10, 2002); also available at http://www.businessweek.com/magazine/content/02_23/b3786027.htm

Barton, Greg, *Indonesia's Struggle: Jemaah Islamiyah and the Soul of Islam* (Sydney: University of New South Wales Press, 2003)

Bassiouni, M. Cherif, "Media Coverage of Terrorism," *Journal of Communication*, Vol. 32 (1982), pp. 128–43

Bawer, Bruce, *While Europe Slept: How Radical Islam is Destroying the West from Within* (New York: Doubleday, 2005)

Bayles, Martha, "Exporting the Wrong Picture," *Washington Post* (August 28, 2005), pp. B1–2.

Beinart, Peter, "The War of the Words," *Washington Post* (April 1, 2007), p. B7

Belasco, Amy, *The Cost of Iraq, Afghanistan, and Other Global War on Terror Operations since 9/11* (Washington, DC: Congressional Research Service, November 9, 2007)

Pope Benedict XVI, "Address at the University of Regensburg: Faith, Reason and the University," *Catholic World News* (September 20, 2006)

Ben-Itto, Hadassa, *The Lie That Wouldn't Die: The Protocols of the Elders of Zion,* (Portland, OR: Vallentine Mitchell, 2005)

Benjamin, Daniel and Steven Simon, *The Next Attack* (Times Books, 2005)

Benmelech, Efraim and Claude Berrebi, "Human Capital and the Productivity of Suicide Bombers," *Journal of Economic Perspectives*, Vol. 21, No. 3 (Summer 2007), pp. 223–38

Benn, Stanley I., *A Theory of Freedom* (New York: Cambridge University Press, 2004)

Bennett, Drake, "Soldier, Spy," *Boston Globe* (May 14, 2006)

Bentham, Jeremy, *The Rationale of Punishment* (1830), *Book I, General Principles*, Chapter 6, "Measure of Punishment"

Bergen, Peter and Paul Cruickshank, "Meet the New Face of Terror," *Washington Post* (August 12, 2007), p. B4

Berger, Peter L., *The Desecularization of the World: Resurgent Religion and World Politics* (Grand Rapids, MI: William B. Eerdmans, 1999)

Berger, Peter L., "The Cultural Dynamics of Globalization," in *Many Globalizations: Cultural Diversity in the Contemporary World*, Peter L. Berger and Samuel P. Huntington, editors (New York: Oxford University Press, 2003)

Bernardoni, Melissa M., "Shultz, Faculty Discuss Oil Dependence at GSB London Center," *University of Chicago Chronicle*, Vol. 25, No. 1 (September 22, 2005)

Bernstein, Jeremy, "The Secrets of the Bomb," *New York Review of Books*, Vol. 53, No. 9 (May 25, 2006)

Bhagwati, Jagdish, *In Defense of Globalization* (Oxford: Oxford University Press, 2004)

Black, Chris, "First Lady Opposes Presidential Clemency for Puerto Rican Nationalists," *Cable News Network* (September 5, 1999)

Blair, Tony, "Not a Clash between Civilizations, but a Clash about Civilization," March 21, 2006 speech delivered in London; available at http://www.pm.gov.uk/output/Page9224.asp

Block, Robert, "U.S. Had Plan for Crisis Like Katrina," *Wall Street Journal* (September 19, 2005), pp. A3–4

Block, Robert, "Miffed at Washington, Police Develop Own Antiterror Plans," *Wall Street Journal* (October 10, 2005), pp. B1,6

Block, Steven M., "Living Nightmares: Biological Threats Enabled by Molecular Biology," in *The New Terror: Facing the Threat of Biological and Chemical Weapons*, Sidney D. Drell, Abraham D. Sofaer, and George D. Wilson, editors (Stanford, CA: Hoover Institution Press, 1999)

References

Bloom, Mia, *Dying to Kill: The Allure of Suicide Terror* (New York: Columbia University Press, 2005)

Blustein, Paul and Walter Pincus, "Port Problems Said To Dwarf New Fears," *Washington Post* (February 24, 2006), p. A6

Bohm, David, *On Dialogue*, Lee Nichol, editor (London: Routledge, 1996)

Bolz, Jr., Frank, Kenneth J. Dudonis and David P. Schulz, *The Couterterrorism Handbook: Tactics, Procedures, and Techniques* (Boca Raton, FL: CRC Press, 2005)

Boot, Max, "The Paradox of Military Technology," *New Atlantis*, No. 14 (Fall 2006), pp. 13–31, adapted from *War Made New: Technology, Warfare, and the Course of Modern History, 1500 to Today* (New York: Gotham Books, October 2006)

Boyarin, Daniel, *A Radical Jew: Paul and the Politics of Identity* (Berkeley, CA: University of California Press, 1994)

Boyer, Peter J., "Downfall: How Donald Rumsfeld Reformed the Army and Lost Iraq," *New Yorker* (November 20, 2006), pp. 56–65

Braithwaite, John, *Crime, Shame, and Reintegration* (New York: Cambridge University Press, 1989)

Bremer, Jennifer, "Our Diplomats' Arabic Handicap," *Washington Post* (October 16, 2005), p. B1

Brooks, David, "The Grand Delusion," *New York Times* (September 28, 2006)

Low, Cassell Bryan with Robert A. Guth, "Chasing Internet Villains Privately in Eastern Europe," *Wall Street Journal* (September 1, 2005)

Brzezinski, Zbigniew, *The Choice: Global Domination or Global Leadership* (New York: Basic Books, 2005)

Brzezinski, Zbigniew, "The Simple Power of Weakness, the Complex Vulnerability of Power," in *After Terror: Promoting Dialogue among Civilizations*, Akbar Ahmed and Brian Forst, editors (Cambridge: Polity Press, 2005)

Brzezinski, Zbigniew, "Terrorized by 'War on Terror,'" *Washington Post* (March 25, 2007), p. B1

Burke, Edmund, *Reflections on the Revolution in France* (New York: Oxford University Press, 1993)

Burke, Jason, *On the Road to Kandahar: Travels through Conflict in the Islamic World* (New York: St. Martin's Press, 2006)

Bursik, Jr., Robert J., "Social Disorganization and Theories of Crime and Delinquency: Problems and Prospects," *Criminology*, Vol. 26 (November 1988), pp. 519–51

Bush, George W., "President Bush Delivers Remarks on Hurricane Katrina Recovery," *Washington Post* (September 15, 2005)

Bushart, Howard L., John R. Craig, and Myra Barnes, *Soldiers Of God: White Supremacists and Their Holy War for America* (New York: Kensington, 2000)

Byman, Daniel, "The Logic of Ethnic Terrorism," *Studies in Conflict and Terrorism*, Vol. 21 (Spring 1998), pp. 149–70

Byman, Daniel, "Homeland Insecurities," *Slate* (September 11, 2007)

Byman, Daniel and Kenneth M. Pollack, "What Next?" *Washington Post* (August 20, 2006), p. B1

Cameron, Gavin, "Multi-Track Microproliferation: Lessons from Aum Shinrikyo and al Qaida," *Studies in Conflict and Terrorism*, Vol. 22 (1999), pp. 277–309

"Can Anyone Fix the U.N.? Annan Has a Useful Idea" *USA Today* (March 29, 2005), p. 10A

Capaccio, Tony, "More U.S. Troops Die in Iraq Bombings Even as Armoring Improves," *Bloomberg News Service* (October 13, 2005)

Carr, Caleb, "A War of Escalating Errors," *Los Angeles Times* (August 12, 2006), p. B15

Carter, Phillip, "The Road to Abu Ghraib," *Washington Monthly* (November 2004)

454

Casteel, Steven W., "Narco-Terrorism: International Drug Trafficking and Terrorism – A Dangerous Mix," Statement before the U.S. Senate Judiciary Committee (May 20, 2003); available at http://www.usdoj.gov/dea/pubs/cngrtest/ct052003.html

Castells, Manuel, *End of Millennium* (London: Blackwell, 2000)

Centers for Disease Control and Prevention

Chalmers, David M., *Hooded Americanism: The First Century of the Ku Klux Klan, 1865–1965* (Durham, NC: Duke University Press, 1987)

Chertoff, Michael, "There Is No Perfect Security," *Wall Street Journal* (February 14, 2006), p. A22

Church, George J., "Proliferation Soviet Nukes On the Loose," *Time* (December 16, 1991)

Cillizza, Chris and Zachary A. Goldfarb, "Bush's Approval Ratings Slumping Further in Europe," *Washington Post* (September 10, 2006), p. A5

Clark, Robert M., *Intelligence Analysis: A Target-Centric Approach* (Washington, DC: CQ Press, 2006)

Clark, Robert M., "Patterns in the Lives of ETA Members," *Terrorism*, Vol. 7, No. 3 (1983), pp. 423–54

Clark, Terry Nichols and Seymour Lipset, editors, *The Breakdown of Class Politics: A Debate on Post-Industrial Stratification* (Baltimore, MD: Johns Hopkins Press, 2001)

Clark, Wesley K., *Winning Modern Wars: Iraq, Terrorism, and the American Empire* (New York: Public Affairs, 2004)

Clark, Wesley K., "The Next War," *Washington Post* (September 16, 2007), pp. B1, 5

Clarke, Richard, *Against All Enemies: Inside America's War on Terror* (New York: Free Press, 2004)

Clarke, Richard, "Things Left Undone," *Atlantic Monthly* (November 2005), pp. 37–8

"Clash of Civilization," *Wall Street Journal* (February 11, 2006), p. A8

Cleaver, Eldridge, *Soul on Ice* (New York: McGraw-Hill, 1967)

Cleaver, Kathleen, "The Fugitive," *Essence* (August 2005)

Cloward, Richard and Lloyd Ohlin, *Delinquency and Opportunity: A Theory of Delinquent Gangs* (New York: Free Press, 1960)

Coady, C.A.J. (Tony), "Defining Terrorism," in *Terrorism: The Philosophical Issues*, Igor Primoratz, editor (London: Palgrave, 2004)

Cogan, Jeanine C., "Hate Crime as a Crime Category Worthy of Policy Attention," *American Behavioral Scientist*, Volume 46, Number 1, (2002), pp. 173–85

Cohen, Adam, "Following the Money," *Time* (October 8, 2001)

Cohen, Albert K., *Delinquent Boys: The Culture of the Gang* (New York: Free Press, 1955)

Cohen, Eliot A., "Plan B," *Wall Street Journal* (October 20, 2006), p. A12

Cohen, Lawrence E. and Marcus Felson, "Social Change and Crime Rate Trends: A Routine Activity Approach," *American Sociological Review*, Vol. 44 (1979), pp. 588–608

Cohen, Mark A., "Measuring the Costs and Benefits of Crime and Justice," *Criminal Justice 2000*, Vol. 4 (Washington, DC: U.S. Department of Justice, 2000), pp. 263–315

Cohen, William S., "Learning from 9/11," *Washington Post* (August 1, 2004), p. B4

Cohen, Yoel, "The PLO: Guardian Angels of the Media," *Midstream* (February 1983), pp. 7–10

Coleman, James S., *Foundations of Social Theory* (Cambridge, MA: Belknap, 1990)

Collina, Tom Z. and Jon B. Wolfsthal, "Nuclear Terrorism and Warhead Control in Russia," *Arms Control Today*, Volume 32, Number 3 (April 2002), p. 15

Collins, Paul, "Hot Stuff: The Quest for Radioactive Items on eBay," *Slate* – culturebox (June 14, 2007)

References

Congressional Budget Office testimony, *Estimated Costs of U.S. Operations in Iraq and Afghanistan and of Other Activities Related to the War on Terrorism*, testimony of Robert A. Sunshine before the Committee on the Budget of the U.S. House of Representatives, July 31, 2007

Cook, Robin, "The Struggle against Terrorism Cannot Be Won by Military Means," *The Guardian* (July 8, 2005)

Cooley, John K., *Green March, Black September: The Story of the Palestinian Arabs* (London: Frank Cass & Co., 1973)

Cooper, Christopher and Robert Block, *Disaster: Hurricane Katrina and the Failure of Homeland Security* (New York: Times Books, 2006)

Cooperman, Alan, "Is Terrorism Tied To Christian Sect? Religion May Have Motivated Bombing Suspect," *Washington Post* (June 2, 2003), p. A3

Cooperman, Alan, "Survey: U.S. Muslims Assimilated, Opposed to Extremism," *Washington Post* (May 23, 2007), p. A3

Cordner, W. Gary, "Fear of Crime and the Police, An Evaluation of a Fear-Reduction Strategy," *Journal of Police Administration*, Vol. 14, No. 3 (September 1986) pp. 223–33

Corn, Tony, "World War IV as Fourth-Generation Warfare," *Policy Review* (January 2006); also available at http://www.policyreview.org/000/corn.html

Covington, Richard, "Yo-Yo Ma's Other Passion," *Smithsonian*, Vol. 34 (June 2002)

Crenshaw, Martha, *Terrorism, Legitimacy, and Power* (Middletown, CT: Wesleyan University Press, 1983)

Crenshaw, Martha, editor, *Terrorism in Context* (University Park, PA: Pennsylvania State University Press, 1994)

Crenshaw, Martha, "The Logic of Terrorism: Terrorist Behavior as a Product of Strategic Choice," in *Origins of Terrorism: Psychologies, Ideologies, Theologies, States of Mind*, Walter Reich, editor (Washington, DC: Woodrow Wilson Center Press, 1998)

Crenshaw, Martha, "The Causes of Terrorism," in *Violence: A Reader*, edited by Catherine Besteman (New York: New York University Press, 2002)

Cronin, Audrey Kurth, "How al-Qaida Ends: The Decline and Demise of Terrorist Groups," *International Security*, Vol. 31, No. 1 (Summer 2006), pp. 7–48

Cronin, Isaac, editor, *Confronting Fear: A History of Terrorism* (New York: Thunder's Mouth Press, 2002)

Cruickshank, Paul and Mohannad Hage Ali, "Jihadist of Mass Destruction," *Washington Post* (June 11, 2006), p. B2

Danner, Mark, "Torture and Truth," *New York Review of Books*, Vol. 51, No. 10 (June 10, 2004)

Danner, Mark, "Iraq: The War of the Imagination," *New York Review of Books*, Vol. 53, No. 20 (December 21, 2006)

Darwin, Charles, *The Descent of Man* (Amherst, NY: Prometheus Books, 1997)

Davis, Lance and Stanley Engerman, "Sanctions: Neither War nor Piece," *Journal of Economic Perspectives*, Vol. 17, No. 2 (Spring 2003), pp. 187–97

Davis, Morton D., *Game Theory: A Nontechnical Introduction* (Mineola, NY: Dover, 1997)

Dawkins, Richard, *The God Delusion* (New York: Houghton Mifflin, 2006)

de Becker, Gavin, *The Gift of Fear: Survival Signals That Protect Us from Violence* (New York: Dell, 1997)

DeFreeze, Donald, *Symbionese Liberation Army Declaration of Revolutionary War and the Symbionese Program* (unpublished manifesto, 1973)

De Koster, Philippe, *Terrorism: Special Investigation Techniques* (Strasbourg, France: Council of Europe Publishing, 2004)

De Lange, Sarah L., "Political Extremism in Europe," *European Political Science*, Vol. 4, No. 4 (December 2005), pp. 476–488

Dennett, Daniel, *Breaking the Spell: Religion as a Natural Phenomenon* (New York: Viking, 2006a)

Dennett, Daniel, "Response to Freeman Dyson's June 22, 2006 Review of Dennett's Book, *Breaking the Spell*, *New York Review of Books*, Vol. 53, No. 13 (August 10, 2006b)

Dershowitz, Alan, "Democrats and Waterboarding," *Wall Street Journal* (November 7, 2007), p. A23

de Tocqueville, Alexis, *Democracy in America* (New York: Penguin, 2003; originally published in 1835)

Devine, John J., "Learning from 9/11," *Washington Post* (August 1, 2004), p. B5

DeYoung, Karen, "Terrorist Attacks Rose Sharply in 2005, State Dept. Says," *Washington Post* (April 29, 2006), p. A1

DeYoung, Karen and Douglas Farah, "Al Qaeda Shifts Assets to Gold," *Washington Post* (June 18, 2002), p. A1

Dickey, Christopher, "Women of Al Qaeda," *Newsweek* (December 12, 2005)

Dobbins, James, Seth G. Jones, Keith Crane, Andrew Rathmell, Brett Steele, Richard Teltschik and Anga R. Timilsina, *The UN's Role in Nation-Building: From the Congo to Iraq* (Santa Monica, CA: RAND, 2005)

"Dr. Condoleezza Rice Discusses President's National Security Strategy" (White House press release, October 1, 2002)

Duffield, John, *Over a Barrel: The Costs of U.S. Foreign Oil Dependence* (Palo Alto, CA: Stanford Law and Politics, 2007)

Dulles, Allen W., *The Craft of Intelligence: America's Legendary Spy Master on the Fundamentals of Intelligence Gathering for a Free World* (Guilford, CT: Lyons Press, 2006)

Durkheim, Emile, *Suicide: A Study in Sociology* (Glencoe, IL: Free Press, 1951; originally published in 1895)

Dworkin, Ronald, "Terror and the Attack on Civil Liberties," *New York Review of Books*, Vol. 50, No. 17 (November 6, 2003)

Dyson, Freeman J., "Religion from the Outside," *New York Review of Books*, Vol. 53, No. 11 (June 22, 2006)

Easterbrook, Gregg, "The Smart Way to Be Scared," *New York Times* (February 16, 2003)

Ebadi, Shirin, *Iran Awakening: A Memoir of Revolution and Hope* (New York: Random House, 2006)

Eck, John, Spencer Chainey, James Cameron, Michael Leitner and Ronald E. Wilson, *Mapping Crime: Understanding Hot Spots*, Report NCJ 209393 (Washington, DC: National Institute of Justice, 2005)

Ehrenfeld, Rachel, *Narco-Terrorism* (New York: Basic Books, 1992)

Ehrenfeld, Rachel, *Funding Evil: How Terrorism is Financed – and How to Stop It* (New York: Bonus Books, 2005)

Ekman, Paul, "How to Spot a Terrorist on the Fly," *Washington Post* (October 29, 2006), p. B3

Elliott, Kimberly Ann and Gary Clyde Hufbauer, "Same Song, Same Refrain? Economic Sanctions in the 1990s," *American Economic Review*, Vol. 89 (May 1999), pp. 404–05

Elliott, Michael, "When Cultures Collide," *Washington Post Book World* (December 1, 1996)

Ellul, Jacques, *The Technological Society* (New York: Vintage, 1967)

Enders, Walter and Todd Sandler, *The Political Economy of Terrorism* (New York: Cambridge University Press, 2006)

References

Energy Information Administration, *Official Energy Statistics from the United States Government* (Washington, DC: Department of Energy, 2005); available at http://www.eia.doe.gov/emeu/cabs/Usa/Oil.html

Ephron, Dan, "Smart, Skilled, Shut Out," *Newsweek* (June 26, 2006)

Ervin, Clark Kent, "Strangers at the Door," *New York Times* (February 23, 2006)

Esbensen, Finn-Aage, "Preventing Adolescent Gang Involvement," *Juvenile Justice Bulletin* (September 2000), pp. 1–11

Esposito, John L., *Unholy War: Terror in the Name of Islam* (New York: Oxford University Press, 2002)

Esposito, John L., "Want to Understand Islam? Start Here." *Washington Post* (July 22, 2007), p. B4

Etter, Lauren, "Dubai: Business Partner or Terrorist Hotbed?" *Wall Street Journal* (February 25, 2006), p. A9

Etzioni, Amitai, *Spirit of Community* (New York: Crown, 1993)

Etzioni, Amitai, "The Patriot Act is a Convenient Target," *USA Today* (January 12, 2006), p. 11A

Ewers, Justin, "Is the New News Good News?" *U.S. News & World Report* (April 7, 2003)

Fair, Eric, "An Iraq Interrogator's Nightmare," *Washington Post* (February 9, 2007), p. A19

Fallows, James, "Success without Victory: A 'Containment' Strategy for the Age of Terror," *Atlantic Monthly* (January/February 2005); also available at http://www.theatlantic.com/doc/200501/fallows

Fallows, James, "Declaring Victory," *Atlantic Monthly* (September 2006), pp. 60–73

al-Faqih, Saad, "The Essence of Al Qaeda," *Jamestown Foundation Global Terrorism Analysis*, Vol. 2, Issue 2 (February 05, 2004), interview by Mahan Abedin

Farhi, Paul, "Public Broadcasting Targeted by House," *Washington Post* (June 10, 2005), p. A1

Farrell, William, *Blood and Rage: The Story of the Japanese Red Army* (Lexington, MA: Lexington Books, 1990)

Federal Bureau of Investigation, *Terrorism 2000/2001* (Washington, DC: U.S. Department of Justice, 2004)

Federal Bureau of Investigation, *Uniform Crime Reports* (Washington, DC: FBI, selected years)

Feldman, Noah, "Choices of Law, Choices of War," *Harvard Journal of Law and Public Policy*, Vol. 25, No. 2 (Spring 2002), pp. 457–86

Ferguson, Niall, *Colossus: The Price of America's Empire* (New York: Penguin Press, 2004)

Ferracuti, Franco, "Ideology and Repentance: Terrorism in Italy," in *Origins of Terrorism: Psychologies, Ideologies, Theologies, States of Mind*, Walter Reich, editor (Washington, DC: Woodrow Wilson Center, 1998)

Fidler, Stephen, "From Alienation to Annihilation," *Financial Times* (July 6, 2007)

Filkins, Dexter, "The Plot against America," *New York Times* (August 6, 2006)

Finucane, Melissa L., Ali Alhakami, Paul Slovic and Stephen M. Johnson, "The Affect Heuristic in Judgments of Risks and Benefits," in *The Perception of Risk*, Paul Slovic, editor (London: Earthscan, 2000), reprinted from the *Journal of Behavioral Decision Making*, Vol. 13 (2000), pp. 1–17

Fischhoff, Baruch, "We Need the Right Words to Weather the Storm," *Washington Post* (October 2, 2005), p. B5

Fisher, Ian, "Pope Calls West Divorced from Faith, Adding a Blunt Footnote on Jihad," *New York Times* (September 13, 2006)

Fleishman, Jeffrey and John Goetz, "Germany May Indict US Agents in 2004 Abduction," *Los Angeles Times* (January 31, 2007)

458

Forst, Brian, *Errors of Justice: Nature, Sources and Remedies* (New York: Cambridge University Press, 2004)

Frank, Thomas, "U.S. Is Building Database on Iraqis: Biometrics Key Part of Tracking Suspects," *USA Today* (July 13, 2007), pp. 1A, 7A

Franklin, Karen, "Good Intentions: The Enforcement of Hate Crime Penalty-Enhancement Statutes," *American Behavioral Scientist*, Volume 46, Number 1 (2002), pp. 154–72

Franklin, John Hope, "Propaganda as History," in *Race and History: Selected Essays 1938–1988* (Baton Rouge, LA: Louisiana State University Press: 1989), pp. 10–23

Freeh, Louis, Statement of the Director of the Federal Bureau of Investigation for the Record of Congress on the President's Fiscal Year 2000 Budget (February 4, 1999); available at http://www.fbi.gov/congress/congress99/freehct2.htm

Frey, Bruno S., "How to Deal with Terrorism," *Economists' Voice*, Vol. 3, No. 7 (June 2006)

Frey, Robert S., *The Genocidal Temptation: Auschwitz, Hiroshima, Rwanda and Beyond* (Lanham, MD: University Press of America, 2004)

Friedman, Thomas L., *The Lexus and the Olive Tree: Understanding Globalization* (New York: Farrar, Straus and Giroux, 2000)

Friedman, Thomas L., *The World Is Flat: A Brief History of the Twenty-First Century* (New York: Farrar, Straus and Giroux, 2005)

Friedman, Thomas L., "9/11 is Over," *New York Times* (September 30, 2007)

Fukuyama, Francis, *The End of History and the Last Man* (New York: Free Press, 1992)

Fukuyama, Francis, *Trust* (New York: Free Press, 1995)

Fukuyama, Francis, "History is Still Going Our Way – Liberal Democracy Will Inevitably Prevail," *Wall Street Journal* (October 5, 2001)

Fukuyama, Francis, "Has History Started Again?" *Policy* (Winter 2002)

Fukuyama, Francis,, response to a question following the speech "Regulating Biotechnology to Save Democracy," delivered to the Commonwealth Club, San Francisco (May 13, 2002); available at http://secure.cwhost.com/archive/02/02–05fukuyama-qa.html

Fukuyama, Francis, *State-Building: Governance and World Order in the 21st Century* (Ithaca, NY: Cornell University Press, 2004)

Fukuyama, Francis, "The 'End of History' Symposium: A Response," *open Democracy* (August 25, 2006); available at http://www.opendemocracy.net/democracy-fukuyama/fukuyama_3852.jsp

Fukuyama, Francis, "Keeping Up with the Chavezes," *Wall Street Journal* (February 1, 2007), p. A17

Fund for Peace, "The Failed States Index," *Foreign Policy* (May–June 2006)

Furedi, Frank, *Culture of Fear: Risk-Taking and the Morality of Low Expectation* (New York: Continuum, 2002a)

Furedi, Frank, "Epidemic of Fear: We Were Scared to Death Long before 11 September," *Spiked* (March 15, 2002b); available at http://www.spiked-online.com/Printable/00000002D46C.htm

Furedi, Frank, "Politics of Fear," *Spiked* (October 28, 2004); available at http://www.frankfuredi.com/articles/politicsFear-20041028.shtml

Furedi, Frank, *Politics of Fear: Beyond Left and Right* (New York: Continuum, 2006)

Gaddis, John Lewis, *Surprise, Security, and the American Experience* (Cambridge, MA: Harvard University Press, 2004)

Gaddis, John Lewis, *Cold War: A New History* (New York: Penguin, 2006)

Galbraith, Peter W., *The End of Iraq: How American Incompetence Created a War without End* (New York: Simon & Schuster, 2006)

Galbraith, Peter W., "The Victor?" *New York Review of Books*, Vol. 54, No. 15 (October 11, 2007)

References

Gambrell, Jon, "Courage Is Managing Fear, Says Giuliani: Ex-NY Mayor Talks at Miami U," *Cincinnati Enquirer* (November 19, 2003)

Gaouette, Nicole, Alan Miller and Ricardo Alonso-Zaldivar, "FEMA's Woes Were Merely the Beginning," *Los Angeles Times* (September 18, 2005)

Gardela, Karen and Bruce Hoffman, *The RAND Chronology of International Terrorism for 1986* (Santa Monica, CA: RAND Corporation Report R-3890-RC, 1990)

Gartner, Lloyd P., *History of the Jews in Modern Times* (New York: Oxford University Press, 2001)

George, John and Laird Wilcox, *American Extremists: Militias, Supremacists, Klansmen, Communists & Others* (Amherst, NY: Prometheus Books, 1996)

Gerecht, Reuel Marc, "Against Rendition: Why the CIA Shouldn't Outsource Interrogations to Countries That Torture," *Weekly Standard*, Vol. 10, Issue 33 (May 16, 2005)

Gerecht, Reuel Marc, "The Pope's Divisions," *Wall Street Journal* (September 21, 2006), p. A16

Gerges, Fawaz A., *The Far Enemy: Why Jihad Went Global* (New York: Cambridge University Press, 2005)

Gerges, Fawaz A., *Journey of the Jihadist: Inside Muslim Militancy* (Orlando, FL: Harcourt, 2006)

Gertz, Bill, "North Korean Freighter Arrives in Iran with Scuds for Syria," *Washington Times* (March 11, 1992), p. A3

Gibbs, Jack P., "Conceptualization of Terrorism." *American Sociological Review*, Vol. 54 (June 1989), pp. 329–40

Giddens, Anthony, *The Consequences of Modernity* (Cambridge: Polity Press, 1990)

Giduck, John, *Terror at Beslan: A Russian Tragedy with Lessons for America's Schools* (Golden, CO: Archangel Group, 2005)

Gillham, Patrick F. and Gary T. Marx, "Complexity and Irony in Policing and Protesting: The WTO in Seattle," *Social Justice*, Vol. 27, No. 2 (2000), pp. 212–36

Gingrich, Newt, "The Only Option Is to Win," *Washington Post* (August 11, 2006), p. A19

Ginzburg, Ralph, *One Hundred Years of Lynching* (Baltimore: Black Classic Press, 1996)

"Giuliani to Run for President Of 9/11," *The Onion* (February 21, 2007)

Gladwell, Malcolm, "Checking Out the Checkpoints: The Curious Irrationality of Airport Security," *Slate* (April 11, 2002)

Gladwell, Malcolm, "What Pit Bulls Can Teach Us about Profiling," *New Yorker* (February 6, 2006), pp. 38–43

Glasser, Susan B., "U.S. Figures Show Sharp Global Rise In Terrorism: State Dept. Will Not Put Data in Report," *Washington Post* (April 27, 2005), p. A1

Glasser, Susan B. and Michael Grunwald, "Department's Mission Was Undermined from Start," *Washington Post* (December 22, 2005), pp. A1,14–15

Glasser, Susan B. and Josh White, "Storm Exposed Disarray at the Top," *Washington Post* (September 4, 2005), pp. A1, 31

Glenny, Misha, "The Lost War," *Washington Post* (August 19, 2007), pp. B1, 5

Goldberg, Jeffrey, "In the Party of God (Part I)," *New Yorker* (October 14, 2002a)

Goldberg, Jeffrey, "In the Party of God (Part II)," *New Yorker* (October 28, 2002b)

Gonzales, Alberto, "Decision Re Application of the Geneva Convention on Prisoners of War to the Conflict with al Qaeda and the Taliban" (memorandum to the President, January 25, 2002)

Gopnik, Adam, "Read It and Weep," *New Yorker* (August 28, 2006), pp. 21–22

Gordon, Michael R. and Bernard E. Trainor, *Cobra II: The Inside Story of the Invasion and Occupation of Iraq* (New York: Pantheon, 2006)

Gore, Al, *The Assault on Reason* (New York: Penguin, 2007)

References

Graves, Philip, "The Source of 'The Protocols of Zion': An Exposure," *London Times* (August 16, 17 & 18, 1921)

Green, James, *Death in the Haymarket: A Story of Chicago, the First Labor Movement and the Bombing That Divided Gilded Age America* (New York: Anchor Books, 2007)

Griswold, Daniel, "Four Decades of Failure: The U.S. Embargo against Cuba," Lecture at Cato's Center for Trade Policy Studies (October 12, 2005)

Gurr, Ted Robert, "Some Characteristics of Political Terrorism in the 1960s," in *The Politics of Terrorism*, Michael Stohl, editor (New York: Dekker, 1988)

Haass, Richard N., *Economic Sanctions and American Diplomacy* (Washington, DC: Council on Foreign Relations Press, 1998)

Habeck, Mary, *Knowing the Enemy* (New Haven, CT: Yale University Press, 2006)

Hagel, Charles, "Challenges of World Leadership," speech to the National Press Club (June 19, 2003)

Hanson, Victor Davis, *A War Like No Other: How the Athenians and Spartans Fought the Peloponnesian War* (New York: Random House, 2005a)

Hanson, Victor Davis, "Has Iraq Weakened Us?" *Commentary* (February 2005b), pp. 43–47

Harries, Keith, *Mapping Crime: Principle and Practice*, Report NCJ 178919 (Washington, DC: National Institute of Justice, 1999)

Harris, Sam, *The End of Faith: Religion, Terror, and the Future of Reason* (New York: W.W. Norton, 2005)

Harris, Shane, and Tim Naftali, "Tinker, Tailor, Miner, Spy," *Slate* (January 3, 2006)

Heath, Linda, "Impact of Newspaper Crime Reports on Fear of Crime: A Methodological Investigation," *Journal of Personality and Social Psychology*, Vol. 47 (1984), pp. 263–76

Heidegger, Martin, "The Question Concerning Technology" in William Lovitt, *The Question Concerning Technology and Other Essays* (New York: Harper Torchbooks, 1954), pp. 3–35

Heilbrunn, Jacob, "The Clash of the Samuel Huntingtons," *American Prospect*, Vol. 9, Issue 39 (July 1, 1998/August 1, 1998)

Henninger, Daniel, "Media War Images Drain the Wells of Moral Outrage," *Wall Street Journal* (August 4, 2006), p. A16

Hewitt, Christopher, *Understanding Terrorism in America* (London: Routledge, 2003)

Hiatt, Fred, "The Consequences of Torture," *Washington Post* (June 14, 2004), p. A17

Hiatt, Fred, "The Goal of These Pages," *Washington Post* (February 5, 2006), p. B7

Hirschi, Travis, *Causes of Delinquency* (Berkeley, CA: University of California Press, 1969)

Hitchens, Christopher, *God Is Not Great: How Religion Poisons Everything* (New York: Twelve-Warner, 2007a)

Hitchens, Christopher, "Defending Islamofascism," *Slate* (October 22, 2007b)

Hoagland, Jim, "Politics as Theater," *Washington Post* (August 18, 2005a), p. A21

Hoagland, Jim, "Two Perfect Storms for Iran and N. Korea," *Washington Post* (September 25, 2005b), p. B7

Hoagland, Jim, "Thinking Outside the Iran Box," *Washington Post* (May 14, 2006a), p. B7

Hoagland, Jim, "Morality in Iraq, Then and Now," *Washington Post* (August 27, 2006b), p. B7

Hobbes, Thomas, *Leviathan* (New York: Cambridge University Press, 1996; originally published in 1651)

Hoffman, Bruce, *Inside Terrorism* (New York: Columbia University Press, 1998, 2006)

Hoffman, Bruce, "Security for a New Century," Senate Foreign Affairs Committee briefing (September 23, 2005)

Hoffman, Bruce, "We Can't Win If We Don't Know the Enemy," *Washington Post* (March 25, 2007), p. B5

References

Hollander, John, "Fear Itself," *Social Research* (Winter 2004)

Holley, David, "China, Iran Missile Sales Confirmed," *Los Angeles Times* (March 19, 2005)

Howard, Michael, *Clausewitz* (Oxford: Oxford University Press, 1983)

Hufbauer, Gary, Jeffrey J. Schott and Kimberly Ann Elliott, *Economic Sanctions Reconsidered*, 2nd ed. (Washington, DC: Institute for International Economics, 1990)

Huff, C. Ronald, *Gangs in America* (Thousand Oaks, CA: Sage, 1996)

Human Rights Watch, "Torture in Iraq," *New York Review of Books*, Vol. 52, No. 17 (November 3, 2005)

Human Security Centre, *Human Security Report 2005: War and Peace in the 21st Century* (New York: Oxford University Press, 2006)

Huntington, Samuel P., "The Clash of Civilizations?" *Foreign Affairs* (July–August 1993a)

Huntington, Samuel P., "If Not Civilizations, What? Samuel Huntington Responds to His Critics," *Foreign Affairs* (November–December 1993b)

Huntington, Samuel P., *The Clash of Civilizations and the Remaking of World Order* (New York: Simon & Schuster, 1996)

Huntington, Samuel P., *Who Are We? The Challenges to America's National Identity* (New York: Simon & Schuster, 2004)

Iannaccone, Laurence R., "The Market for Martyrs," Global Prosperity Initiative Working Paper Number 35 (Fairfax, VA: George Mason University, 2006)

Ignatieff, Michael, *Blood and Belonging* (London: Viking, 1993)

Ignatieff, Michael, "Lesser Evils," *New York Times Magazine* (May 2, 2004)

Ignatius, David, "The Rush to Reorganize," *Washington Post* (July 30, 2004), p. A19

Ignatius, David, "Taking Back Islam: The U.S. Has Little to Contribute to the Theological Struggle," *Washington Post* (September 18, 2005a), p. B7

Ignatius, David, "Window into Al Qaeda," *Washington Post* (October 16, 2005b), p. B7

Ignatius, David, "Stepping Back from Torture," *Washington Post* (December 16, 2005c), p. A35

Ignatius, David, "Eavesdropping and Evading the Law," *Washington Post* (December 28, 2005d), p. A21

Ignatius, David, "From 'Connectedness' to Conflict," *Washington Post* (February 22, 2006a), p. A15

Ignatius, David, "Spy Tools in Need of a Law," *Washington Post* (May 17, 2006b), p. A23

Ignatius, David, "Avoiding Another 'Slam-Dunk,'" *Washington Post* (May 24, 2006c), p. A23

Ignatius, David, "Are We Fighting 'Islamic Fascists'?" *Washington Post* (August 18, 2006d), p. A21

Ignatius, David, "Young Anger Foments Jihad," *Washington Post* (September 13, 2006e), p. A17

Ignatius, David, "Wise Advice: Listen, and Engage," *Washington Post* (June 24, 2007), p. B7

Inter-American Commission on Human Rights, *Report on the Situation of Human Rights in the Republic of Nicaragua* (Washington, DC: IACHR, 1981)

Inter-American Commission on Human Rights, *Report on the Situation of Human Rights of a Segment of the Nicaraguan Population of Miskito Origin* (Washington, DC: IACHR, 1983)

Isaacs, William, *Dialogue and the Art of Thinking Together* (New York: Random House, 1999)

Isaacson, Walter, "Benjamin Franklin's Gift of Tolerance," in *After Terror: Promoting Dialogue among Civilizations*, Akbar Ahmed and Brian Forst, editors (Cambridge: Polity Press, 2005)

Isikoff, Michael and David Corn, *Hubris: The Inside Story of Spin, Scandal, and the Selling of the Iraq War* (New York: Crown Books, 2006)

Israel Ministry of Foreign Affairs, *Hamas Terrorist Attacks* (March 22, 2004); available at http://www.mfa.gov.il/MFA/Terrorism-+Obstacle+to+Peace/Terror+Groups/Hamas+terror+attacks+22-Mar-2004.htm

Jacobs, Jane, *The Death and Life of Great American Cities* (New York: Random House, 1961)

Jaffe, Greg, "A Loophole Emerges in Yemeni Campaign against Extremists: Islamic Law Allows Jihad," *Wall Street Journal* (August 14, 2006), p. A1,6

Jain, Anil K., "Biometric Recognition: How Do I Know Who You Are?" *Proceedings of the IEEE Twelfth Signal Processing and Communications Applications Conference* (April 28–30, 2004)

Janke, Peter, *Guerrilla and Terrorist Organizations: A World Directory and Bibliography* (New York: Macmillan, 1983)

Jarboe, James F., "The Threat of Eco-Terrorism," testimony of FBI Chief of Domestic Terrorism before the House of Representatives Resources Committee (February 12, 2002)

Jenkins, Brian M. and Janera Johnson, *International Terrorism: A Chronology, 1968–1974*, (Santa Monica, CA: RAND Corporation Report R-1597-DOS/ARPA, 1975)

Joffe, Josef, *Überpower: The Imperial Temptation of America* (New York: W. W. Norton, 2006)

Johnson, Ian, "Conflicting Advice: Islamic Justice Finds a Foothold in Heart of Europe," *Wall Street Journal* (August 4, 2005), pp. A1, A8

Jordan, Lara Jakes, "Gonzales, Mueller Admit FBI Broke Law," Associated Press Newswire (March 9, 2007)

Juergensmeyer, Mark, *Terror in the Mind of God: The Global Rise of Religious Violence* (Berkeley, CA: University of California Press, 2003)

Jusik, Julia, *Die Bräute Allahs. Selbstmordattentäterinnen aus Tschetschenien* (St. Pölten, Austria: Niederösterreichisches Pressehaus, 2005)

Kaczynski, Theodore, *The Unabomber Manifesto: Industrial Society And Its Future* (Filiquarian Publishing, 2005)

Kagan, Robert, "More Leaks, Please: Questioning the Iraq Intelligence Report," *Washington Post* (September 26, 2006), p. A21

Kahneman, Daniel, Paul Slovic and Amos Tversky, *Judgement under Uncertainty: Heuristics and Biases* (Cambridge: Cambridge University Press, 1982)

Kahneman, Daniel and Richard Thaler, "Utility Maximization and Expected Utility," *Journal of Economic Perspectives*, Vol. 20, No. 1 (Winter 2006), pp. 221–34

Kahneman, Daniel and Amos Tversky, *Choices, Values and Frames* (Cambridge: Cambridge University Press, 2000)

Kaplan, David E., and Andrew Marshall, *The Cult at the End of the World: The Terrifying Story of the Aum Doomsday Cult, from the Subways of Yokyo to the Nuclear Arsenals of Russia* (New York: Crown Books, 1996)

Kaplan, Fred, "It's Time to Talk to Pyongyang," *Slate* (February 11, 2005)

Kaplan, Fred, "$41 Billion, and Not a Penny of Foresight," *Slate* (September 2, 2005)

Kaplan, Fred, "Knitting Together an Afghan Strategy," *Slate* (June 20, 2006)

Karabell, Zachary, *Peace Be Upon You: Fourteen Centuries of Muslim, Christian, and Jewish Coexistence in the Middle East* (New York: Knopf, 2007)

Karp, Jonathan and Laura Meckler, "Which Travelers Have 'Hostile Intent'? Biometric Device May Have the Answer," *The Wall Street Journal* (August 14, 2006), p. B1

Karsh, Efraim, *Islamic Imperialism: A History* (New Haven, CT: Yale University Press, 2006)

Katz, Rita and Michael Kern, "Catching a Jihadi Cyberterrorist," *Washington Post* (March 26, 2006)

References

Kean, Thomas H. and Lee H. Hamilton, *Without Precedent* (New York: Knopf, 2006)

Kean, Thomas H. and Lee H. Hamilton, "Are We Safer Today?" *Washington Post* (September 9, 2007), p. B1

Keegan, John, *A History of Warfare* (New York: Vintage, 1994)

Kellen, Konrad, "Ideology and Rebellion: Terrorism in West Germany," in *Origins of Terrorism: Psychologies, Ideologies, Theologies, States of Mind*, Walter Reich, editor (Washington, DC: Woodrow Wilson Center, 1998)

Kennedy, Randall, "Racial Profiling May Be Justified, But It's Still Wrong," *New Republic* (September 13, 1999), pp. 30–35

Kennicott, Philip, "A Novel Approach," *Washington Post* (August 1, 2004), p. B1

Kent, Sherman, *Strategic Intelligence for American World Policy* (Princeton, NJ: Princeton University Press, 1949)

Kepel, Gilles, *The War for Muslim Minds: Islam and the West* (Cambridge, MA: Harvard University Press, 2005)

Khilnani, Sunil, "The Politics of Terrorism," *Political Quarterly*, Vol. 64, No. 3 (1993)

Khwaja, Maruf, "Terrorism, Islam, Reform: Thinking the Unthinkable," *OpenDemocracy* (July 28, 2005)

King, Laura and Vita Bekker, "Suicide Bombing Stokes Israel-Hamas Tensions," *Los Angeles Times* (April 18, 2006)

Kirkpatrick, Jeane J., "The Modernizing Imperative: Tradition and Change," *Foreign Affairs* (September–October 1993)

Kirschenbaum, Alan, "Terror, Adaptation and Preparedness: A Trilogy for Survival," *Journal of Homeland Security and Emergency Management*, Vol. 3, No. 1 (2006); available at http://www.bepress.com/jhsem/vol3/iss1/3

Kissinger, Henry A., "The Next Steps with Iran," *Washington Post* (July 31, 2006a), p. A15

Kissinger, Henry A., "After Lebanon," *Washington Post* (September 13, 2006b), p. A17

Kissinger, Henry A., "The Disaster of Hasty Withdrawal," *Washington Post* (September 16, 2007), p. B7

Kleck, Gary, Brion Sever, Spencer Li and Marc Gertz, "The Missing Link in General Deterrence Research," *Criminology*, Vol. 43, Issue 3 (August 2005), pp. 623–59

Klein, Aaron J., *Striking Back: The 1972 Munich Olympics Massacre and Israel's Deadly Response* (New York: Random House, 2005)

Kleinig, John, "Liberty and Security in an Era of Terrorism," in *Security and Justice in the Homeland: Criminologists on Terrorism*, Brian Forst, Jack R. Greene, and James P. Lynch, editors (New York: Cambridge University Press, forthcoming)

Kohut, Andrew and Bruce Stokes, *America against the World: How We Are Different and Why We Are Disliked* (New York: Times Books, 2006)

Kovach, Bill and Tom Rosenstiel, *The Elements of Journalism: What Newspeople Should Know and The Public Should Expect* (New York: Three Rivers Press, 2001)

Kringen, John A., "How We've Improved Intelligence: Minimizing the Risk of 'Groupthink,'" *Washington Post* (April 3, 2006), p. A19

Kristof, Nicholas, "Japanese Cult Said to Have Planned Nerve-Gas Attacks in U.S.," *New York Times* (March 23, 1997)

Kristof, Nicholas, "Sanctions Don't Work," *New York Times* (November 10, 2003)

Krueger, Alan, *What Makes a Terrorist?* (Princeton, NJ: Princeton University Press, 2007)

Krueger, Alan and Jitka Maleckova, "Education, Poverty, Political Violence and Terrorism: Is There a Causal Connection?" *Journal of Economic Perspectives*, Vol. 17, No. 4 (Fall 2003), pp. 119–44

bin Laden, Osama, *Messages to the World: The Statements of Osama bin Laden*, edited by Bruce Lawrence, translated by James Howarth (London: Verso, 2005)

LaFree, Gary, "Expanding Criminology's Domain: The American Society of Criminology 2006 Presidential Address," *Criminology*, Vol. 45, No. 1 (February 2007)

LaFree, Gary and Laura Dugan, "How Does Studying Terrorism Compare to Studying Crime?" in *Terrorism and Counter-Terrorism: Criminological Perspectives*, edited by Mathieu Deflem (Amsterdam: Elsevier, 2004)

Lalami, Laila, "The Missionary Position," *The Nation* (June 19, 2006)

Lansford, Lynn Milburn, *Beslan: Shattered Innocence* (Seattle, WA: BookSurge Publishing, 2007)

Laqueur, Walter, *The Age of Terrorism* (Boston: Little, Brown, 1987)

Laqueur, Walter, *The New Terrorism: Fanaticism and the Arms of Mass Destruction* (New York: Oxford University Press, 1999)

Laqueur, Walter, *A History of Terrorism* (New York: Transaction Publishers, 2001)

Laqueur, Walter, *No End to War: Terrorism in the Twenty-First Century* (New York: Continuum, 2003)

Laub, John H. and Robert J. Sampson, *Shared Beginnings, Divergent Lives: Delinquent Boys to Age 70* (Cambridge, MA: Harvard University Press, 2006)

LeDoux, Joseph, *The Emotional Brain: The Mysterious Underpinnings of Emotional Life* (New York: Simon & Schuster, 1998)

Lee, Christopher, "OMB Is Ranked No. 1 Federal Workplace; Small Agencies Rise to Top of List," *Washington Post* (September 14, 2005), p. A29

Lee, Gregory D., *Conspiracy Investigations: Terrorism, Drugs and Gangs* (Upper Saddle River, NJ: Prentice Hall, 2004)

Lehman, John. "Getting Spy Reform Wrong: September 11 Commission's Proposals Were Turned into Bureaucratic Bloat," *Washington Post* (November 16, 2005), p. A19

Leiken, Robert S., "Europe's Angry Muslims," *Foreign Affairs* (July–August 2005)

Lengel, Allan, "Little Progress in FBI Probe of Anthrax Attacks: Internal Report Compiled as Agents Hope for a Break," *Washington Post* (September 16, 2005), p. A1

Lesser, Ian O., Bruce Hoffman, John Arquilla, David Ronfelt and Michele Zanini, *Countering the New Terrorism* (Santa Monica, CA: RAND, 1999); available at http://www.rand.org/publications/MR/MR989/

Levitas, Daniel, *The Terrorist Next Door: The Militia Movement and the Radical Right* (Surrey, England: St. Martins Griffin, 2004)

Levitt, Matthew, "Stemming the Flow of Terrorist Financing: Practical and Conceptual Challenges," *Fletcher Forum of World Affairs*, Vol. 27 (Winter-Spring 2003), pp. 59–70

Lewis, Bernard, "The Roots of Muslim Rage," *Atlantic Monthly*, (September 1990), pp. 47–60

Lewis, Bernard, "I'm Right, You're Wrong, Go To Hell," *Atlantic Monthly* (May 2003), pp. 36–42

Lewis, Bernard, "Modernizing the Muslim World," *Toronto Star* (May 8, 2006)

Lewis, Bernard, *The Multiple Identities of the Middle East* 1998

Lifton, Robert Jay, *Destroying the World to Save It: Aum Shinrikyo, Apocalyptic Violence, and the New Global Terrorism* (New York: Henry Holt and Company, 2000)

Lilla, Mark, "Coping with Political Theology," *Cato Unbound* (October 8, 2007a); available at http://www.cato-unbound.org/2007/10/08/mark-lilla/coping-with-political-theology/

Lilla, Mark, *The Stillborn God: Religion, Politics and the Modern West* (New York: Knopf, 2007b)

Lindberg, Tod, "The Atlanticist Community," in *Beyond Paradise and Power: Europe, America, and the Future of a Troubled Partnership*, Tod Lindberg, editor (London: Routledge, 2004), pp. 215–36

Locke, John, *Letter Concerning Toleration* (New York: Prometheus Books, 1990; originally published 1689)

References

Lombroso, Cesare, *L'uomo delinquente (The Criminal Man)*, (Durham, NC: Duke University Press, 2006; originally published 1876)

Lormel, Dennis M., Statement of the Chief of the Financial Crimes Section of the Federal Bureau of Investigation for the Record of Congress (February 12, 2002); available at http://www.fbi.gov/congress/congress02/lormel021202.htm

"Losing Afghanistan," *New York Times* (August 24, 2006)

Lowe, Theodore J., editor, *The Pursuit of Justice* (New York: Harper and Row, 1964)

Luce, R. Duncan and Howard Raiffa, *Games and Decisions: Introduction and Critical Survey* (Mineola, NY: Dover, 1989)

Lustick, Ian S., *Trapped in the War on Terror* (Philadelphia: University of Pennsylvania Press, 2006)

Macfarlane, Alison, "The Limits of the Bioweapons Threat," *Technology Review* (March–April 2006)

Mack, Andrew, "Peace on Earth? Increasingly, Yes." *Washington Post* (December 28, 2005), p. A21

MacLean, Nancy K., *Behind the Mask of Chivalry: The Making of the Second Ku Klux Klan* (New York: Oxford University Press, 1995)

Mahbubani, Kishore, "The Dangers of Decadence: What the Rest Can Teach the West," *Foreign Affairs* (September–October 1993)

Mahl, George F., "Relationship between Acute and Chronic Fear and the Gastric Acidity and Blood Sugar Levels in *Macaca mulatta* Monkeys," *Psychosomatic Medicine*, Vol. 14 (1952), pp. 182–210

Malik, S. K., *Quranic Concept of War* (Kathmandu, Nepal: Himalayan Books, 1986)

Malinowski, Tom, "When Terrorists Become 'Warriors,'" *Washington Post* (March 18, 2007), p. B7

Manji, Irshad, *The Trouble with Islam: A Muslim's Call for Reform in Her Faith* (New York: St. Martin's Press, 2003)

Manwaring, Max G., *Street Gangs: The New Urban Insurgency* (Carlisle, PA: U.S. Army War College, 2005)

Marighella, Carlos, *Minimanual of the Urban Guerrilla* (Unpublished pamphlet, 1969); available at http://www.marxists.org/archive/marighella-carlos/1969/06/minimanual-urban-guerrilla/index.htm

Marks, Alexandra, "Radical Islam Finds US 'Sterile Ground,'" *Christian Science Monitor* (October 23, 2006)

Martin, David C. and John Walcott, *Best Laid Plans: The Inside Story of America's War Against Terrorism* (New York: HarperCollins, 1988)

Martin, Gus, *Understanding Terrorism: Challenges, Perspectives, and Issues*, 2nd edition (Thousand Oaks, CA: Sage, 2006)

Martin, L. John, "The Media's Role in International Terrorism," *Terrorism*, Vol. 8 (1985), pp. 44–58

Martin, Susan E., "Investigating Hate Crimes: Case Characteristics and Law Enforcement Responses," *Justice Quarterly*, Vol. 13, No. 3 (September 1996), pp. 455–80

Marty, Martin, "Risking Hospitality," in *After Terror: Promoting Dialogue among Civilizations*, Akbar Ahmed and Brian Forst, editors (Cambridge: Polity Press, 2005)

Marx, Karl, *Capital, Volume 1: A Critique of Political Economy*, translated by Ben Fowkes (New York: Penguin Classics, 1992; originally published in 1867)

Marx, Patricia, *Him Her Him Again: The End of Him* (New York: Scribner, 2007)

Mayes, Andrew, "The Physiology of Fear and Anxiety," in *Fear in Animals and Man*, W. Sluckin, editor (New York: Van Nostrand Reinhold, 1979)

466

Mazerolle, Paul and Alex Piquero, "Linking Exposure to Strain with Anger: An Investigation of Deviant Adaptations," *Journal of Criminal Justice*, Vol. 26 (1998), pp. 195–211

McCormick, Gordon H., *The Shining Path and the Future of Peru* (Santa Monica, CA: RAND, 1990)

McGirk, Tim, "Moms and Martyrs," *Time* (May 3, 2007), pp. 48–50

McGovern, George, Flying the Unfriendly Skies," *Wall Street Journal* (July 29, 2002), p. A14

McLain, Charles, *In Search of Equality: The Chinese Struggle against Discrimination in Nineteenth-Century America* (Berkeley: University of California Press, 1996)

McLuhan, Marshall, *Essential McLuhan*, edited by Eric McLuhan and Frank Zingrone (New York: Basic Books, 1996)

McNeill, William H., "Decline of the West?" *New York Review of Books*, Vol. 44, No. 1 (January 9, 1997)

McQuade III, Samuel C., *Understanding and Managing Cybercrime* (Boston: Pearson, 2006)

Mead, Walter Russell, *Power, Terror, Peace and War: America's Grand Strategy in a World at Risk* (New York: Alfred A. Knopf, 2004)

Media Awareness Network, "Deconstructing Hate Sites" http://www.media-awareness.ca/english/issues/online_hate/deconst_online_hate.cfm

Mednick, Sarnoff, Terrie E. Moffitt and Susan A. Stack, *The Causes of Crime : New Biological Approaches* (New York: Cambridge University Press, 1987)

Merton, Robert K., "Social Structure and Anomie," *American Sociological Review*, Vol. 3 (October 1938), pp. 672–82

Meyer, Philip. "Saving Journalism: How to Nurse the Good Stuff Until it Pays," *Columbia Journalism Review*, Issue 6 (November–December 2004)

Meyerson, Harold, "Globalization's Stir-Fry," *Washington Post* (June 28, 2007), p. A25

Mickolus, Edward F., *International Terrorism: Attributes of Terrorist Events, 1968–1977 (ITERATE 2)* (Ann Arbor, MI: Inter-University Consortium for Political and Social Research, 1982)

Milbank, Dana and Spencer S. Hsu, "Cheney: Kerry Victory Is Risky: Democrats Decry Talk as Scare Tactic," *Washington Post* (September 8, 2004), p. A1

Milgram, Stanley, *Obedience to Authority: An Experimental View* (New York: Harper-Collins, 1974)

Miller, Judith, "How Gadhafi Lost His Groove," *Wall Street Journal* (May 16, 2006), p. A14

Milton, John, *Areopagitica* (Chicago: Liberty Fund, 1999)

Minkenberg, Michael, "The Renewal of the Radical Right: Between Modernity and Anti-Modernity," *Government and Opposition*, Vol. 35, No. 2 (2000), 170–188

Moodie, Michael L., "The Chemical Weapons Threat," in *The New Terror: Facing the Threat of Biological and Chemical Weapons*, Sidney D. Drell, Abraham D. Sofaer, and George D. Wilson, editors (Stanford, CA: Hoover Institution Press, 1999)

Morrison, Blake, "Airport Security Failures Persist: Screeners Miss Even Obvious Items," *USA Today* (July 1, 2002), pp. 1A, 4A

Mueller, John, *Overblown: How Politicians and the Terrorism Industry Inflate National Security Threats, and Why We Believe Them* (New York: Free Press, 2006)

Muir, Diana, "Risks in a Muslim Reformation," *Washington Post* (August 19, 2007), p. B7

Mumford, Lewis, *Technics and Civilization* (Fort Washington, PA: Harvest Books, 1963)

Murphy, Caryle, "For Conservative Muslims, Goal of Isolation a Challenge," *Washington Post* (September 5, 2006), p. A1

Murtha, John P. and John Plashal, *From Vietnam to 9/11: On the Front Lines of National Security with a New Epilogue on the Iraq War* (University Park, PA: Pennsylvania State University, 2004)

References

Myerson, Roger B., *Game Theory: Analysis of Conflict* (Cambridge, MA: Harvard University Press, 1997)

Nacos, Brigitte, *Terrorism and the Media* (New York: Columbia University Press, 1994)

Naji, Abu Bakr, *Management of Savagery: The Most Critical Stage through Which the Umma Will Pass*, translated by William F. McCants (Cambridge, MA: Harvard University, 2006; original Arabic version published by the Center for Islamic Studies and Research, 2004)

Napoleoni, Loretta, *Terror Incorporated: Tracing the Dollars behind the Terror Networks* (New York: Seven Stories Press, 2005)

Nasr, Vali, *The Shia Revival: How Conflicts within Islam Will Shape the Future* (New York: W.W. Norton, 2005)

National Counterterrorism Center, *Report on Terrorist Incidents – 2006* (Washington, DC: NCTC, April 30, 2007)

Neuburger, Luisella de Cataldo and Tiziana Valentini, *Women in Terrorism* (New York: Palgrave Macmillan, 1996)

Noah, Timothy, "Homeland Security's Lousy Morale: Only the Small Business Administration Has Unhappier Employees," *Slate* (September 14, 2005)

Nordland, Rod and Babak Dehghanpisheh, "Surge of Suicide Bombers," *Newsweek* (August 13, 2007), pp. 30–32

Noriega, Roger F., "It's Our Drug War, Too: How America and Mexico Can Defeat the Cartels," *Washington Post* (August 16, 2007), p. A15

Norris, Pippa, *Framing Terrorism: The News Media, the Government and the Public* (London: Routledge, 2003)

Norris, Pippa and Ronald Inglehart, *Sacred and Secular: Religion and Politics Worldwide* (New York: Cambridge University Press, 2004)

"Not a Swedish Joke," *The Wall Street Journal* (August 25, 2005), p. A8

Novak, Michael, *The Universal Hunger for Liberty: Why the Clash of Civilizations Is Not Inevitable* (New York: Basic Books, 2004)

Novak, Robert, "Public Air Wars," *Chicago Sun-Times* (July 21, 2005)

Nunberg, Geoffrey, "'Terrorism': The History of a Very Frightening Word," *San Francisco Chronicle* (October 28, 2001), p. C-5

Nunberg, Geoffrey "One for Flinching," *Fresh Air* radio commentary, National Public Radio (October 10, 2006)

Nye, Jr., Joseph S., "East Asian Security: The Case for Deep Engagement," *Foreign Affairs*, Vol. 74, No. 4 (July/August 1995), pp. 90–102

Nye, Jr., Joseph S., *The Paradox of American Power: Why the World's Only Superpower Can't Go It Alone* (New York: Oxford University Press, 2002)

Nye, Jr., Joseph S., *Soft Power: The Means to Success in World Politics* (New York: Public Affairs 2004)

Nye, Jr., Joseph S., "Hard Power and Soft Power," in *After Terror: Promoting Dialogue among Civilizations*, Akbar Ahmed and Brian Forst, editors (Cambridge: Polity Press, 2005)

Oliver, Myrna, "George Gerbner, 86; Educator Researched the Influence of TV Viewing on Perceptions," *Los Angeles Times* obituary (December 29, 2005)

Ornstein, Norman, "Worst Case Scenario: The Decapitating Strike," *Washington Post* (July 12, 2007)

Pachios, Harold C., "Public Diplomacy and the War on Terror," remarks to Newhouse School of Communication, Syracuse University (January 28, 2003); available at http://www.state.gov/r/adcompd/rls/19104.htm

Packer, George, "Name Calling," *New Yorker* (August 8, 2005), pp. 33–34

Packer, George, "The Lesson of Tal Afar," *New Yorker* (April 10, 2006a), pp. 48–65

Packer, George, "Fighting Faiths," *New Yorker* (July 10, 2006b), pp. 93–97

Packer, George, "Prisoners," *New Yorker* (September 18, 2006c), pp. 25–26

Packer, George, "Betrayed: The Iraqis Who Trusted America the Most," *New Yorker* (March 26, 2007)

Page, Susan, "Tsunami Aid Pushes Up U.S. Image, While Iraq Pulls It Down, Poll Finds," *USA Today* (June 24, 2005), p. 10A

Paletz, David L., Peter A. Fozzard and John Z. Ayanian, "The IRA, the Red Brigades, and the FALN in the *New York Times*," *Journal of Communication*, Vol. 32 (1982), pp. 162–71

Palmer, David Scott, *The Shining Path of Peru* (New York: Palgrave Macmillan, 1994)

Pamuk, Orhan, "On Trial," *New Yorker* (December 19, 2005), pp. 33–34

Pape, Robert A., "Why Economic Sanctions Do Not Work," *International Security*, Vol. 22, No. 2 (Autumn, 1997), pp. 90–136

Pape, Robert A., *Dying to Win: The Strategic Logic of Suicide Terrorism* (New York: Random House, 2005)

Paternoster, Raymond and Paul Mazerolle, "General Strain Theory and Delinquency: A Replication and Extension," *Journal of Research in Crime and Delinquency*, Vol. 31 (1994), pp. 235–263

Pearlstein, Richard M., *Fatal Future? Transnational Terrorism and the New Global Disorder* (Austin, TX: University of Texas Press, 2004)

Perry, Barbara, "'Button-Down Terror': The Metamorphosis of the Hate Movement," *Sociological Focus*, Vol. 33, No. 2 (May 2000), pp. 113–31

Perry, Glenn E., "Huntington and His Critics: The West and Islam," *Arab Studies Quarterly* (Winter 2002)

Peters, Ralph, "Myths of Globalization," *USA Today* (May 23, 2005)

Peterson, Dale and Richard Wrangham, *Demonic Males: Apes and the Origins of Human Violence* (New York: Mariner Books, 1997)

Petrosino, Carolyn, "Connecting the Past to the Future: Hate Crime in America," in *Hate and Bias Crime: A Reader* (London: Routledge, 2003)

Pew Global Attitudes Project, *A Year after Iraq War Mistrust of America in Europe Ever Higher, Muslim Anger Persists* (Washington, DC: Pew Research Center, March 16, 2004)

Pew Global Attitudes Project, *Islamic Extremism: Common Concern for Muslim and Western Public's Support for Terror Wanes among Muslim Publics* (Washington, DC: Pew Research Center, 2005)

Pew Research Center, *Muslim Americans: Middle Class and Mostly Mainstream* (Washington, DC: Pew Forum on Religion and Public Life, May 22, 2007)

Peyser, Marc, "The Truthiness Teller," *Newsweek* (February 13, 2006), pp. 50–56

Phelps, Edmund S., "Remedies for New Orleans," *Wall Street Journal* (October 10, 2005), p. A12

Phillips, Don, "Iran Sanctions' Risk to Air Safety Is Cited in Report," *International Herald Tribune* (December 13, 2005)

Phillips, Timothy, *Beslan: The Tragedy of School Number One* (London: Granta Books, 2007)

Pillar, Paul R., "Intelligence, Policy, and the War in Iraq," *Foreign Affairs* (March–April 2006)

Pincus, Walter, "Intelligence Agencies 'Must Do Better': Panel Faults Quality of Information on Insurgency, Militias," *Washington Post* (December 8, 2006), p. A31

Pipes, Richard, "Book Review of Samuel P. Huntington's *The Clash of Civilizations and the Remaking of World Order, Commentary*, Vol. 103, No. 3 (March 1997)

Podhoretz, Norman, "The Subtle Collusion," *Political Communication and Persuasion*, Vol. 1 (1981), pp. 84–89

Popper, Karl, *The Open Society and Its Enemies* (Princeton, NJ: Princeton University Press, 1966)

References

Posner, Eric A. and Adrian Vermeule, "Judicial Cliches on Terrorism," *Washington Post* (August 8, 2005), p. A15

Posner, Eric A. and Adrian Vermeule, *Terror in the Balance: Security, Liberty, and the Courts* (New York: Oxford University Press, 2007)

Posner, Richard A., "The 9/11 Report: A Dissent," *New York Times* (August 29, 2004)

Posner, Richard A., *Not a Suicide Pact: The Constitution in a Time of National Emergency* (New York: Oxford University Press, 2006)

Posner, Richard A., *Uncertain Shield: The U.S. Intelligence System in the Throes of Reform* (Lanham, MD: Rowman & Littlefield, 2006)

Posner, Richard A., "Time to Rethink the FBI," *Wall Street Journal* (March 19, 2007), p. A13

Post, Jerrold M., "Terrorist Psycho-Logic: Terrorist Behavior as a Product of Psychological Forces," in *Origins of Terrorism: Psychologies, Ideologies, Theologies, States of Mind*, Walter Reich, editor (Washington, DC: Woodrow Wilson Center, 1998)

Powell, Jim, "Why Trade Retaliation Closes Markets and Impoverishes People," *Cato Policy Analysis* No. 143 (November 20, 1990)

Powers, Thomas F., "Can We Be Secure and Free?" *The Public Interest*, No. 151 (Spring 2003), pp. 3–24

Prahalad, C. K., *The Fortune at the Bottom of the Pyramid: Eradicating Poverty Through Profits* (Philadelphia: Wharton School Publishing, 2004)

President's Commission on Law Enforcement and Administration of Justice, *The Challenge of Crime in a Free Society* (Washington, DC: U.S. Government Printing Office, 1967)

Primoratz, Igor, "What is Terrorism?" in *Terrorism: The Philosophical Issues*, Igor Primoratz, editor (London: Palgrave, 2004)

Privacy International, "Stupid Security Contest Winners"; available at http://www.privacyinternational.org/activities/stupidsecurity/winners.html

Putnam, Robert, *Bowling Alone: The Collapse and Revival of American Community* (New York: Simon and Schuster, 2001)

Putnam, Robert and Lewis Feldstein, *Better Together: Restoring the American Community* (New York: Simon and Schuster, 2003)

Quinney, Richard, *The Problem of Crime* (New York: Dodd, Mead, 1970)

Raine, Adrian, "The Biological Basis of Crime," in James Q. Wilson and Joan Petersilia, editors, *Crime: Public Policies for Crime Control* (Oakland, CA: ICS Press, 2002)

Ranstorp, Magnus, *Hizb'allah in Lebanon: The Politics of the Western Hostage Crisis* (New York: Palgrave Macmillan, 1997)

Rashid, Ahmed, *Taliban: Militant Islam, Oil and Fundamentalism in Central Asia* (London: Pan Books, 2001)

Raspberry, William, "All the Nuance That's Fit to Print," *Washington Post* (March 21, 2005), p. A19

Reich, Robert, *The Future of Success: Working and Living in the New Economy* (New York: Vintage, 2002)

Reich, Walter, editor, *Origins of Terrorism: Psychologies, Ideologies, Theologies, States of Mind* (Washington, DC: Woodrow Wilson Center Press, 1998)

Ressa, Maria, *Seeds of Terror: An Eyewitness Account of Al-Qaeda's Newest Center of Operations in Southeast Asia* (New York: Free Press, 2003)

Reuters International, "U.S. CBO Estimates $2.4 Trillion Long-Term War Costs" (October 24, 2007)

"Revising 9/11," *New York Times* (September 11, 2005)

Reynolds, David S., *John Brown, Abolitionist: The Man Who Killed Slavery, Sparked the Civil War, and Seeded Civil Rights* (New York: Knopf, 2005)

Rice-Oxley, Mark, "Why Terror Financing Is So Tough to Track Down," *Christian Science Monitor* (March 8, 2006); available at http://www.csmonitor.com/2006/0308/p04s01-woeu.html

Ricks, Thomas E., *Fiasco: The American Military Adventure in Iraq* (New York: Penguin, 2006)

Robb, Charles S. and Laurence H. Silberman, *Report of the Commission on the Intelligence Capabilities of the United States Regarding Weapons of Mass Destruction* (Washington, DC: U.S. Government Printing Office, 2005) http://www.wmd.gov/report/index.html

Robb, John, *Brave New War: The Next Stage of Terrorism and the End of Globalization* (Hoboken, NJ: John Wiley and Sons, 2007)

Robinson, Eugene, "Top Ten Stories of 2006," *Washington Post* (January 3, 2006), p. A17

Roig-Franzia, Manuel and Spencer Hsu, "Many Evacuated, but Thousands Till Waiting," *Washington Post* (September 4, 2005), pp. A1, 24–25

Ronczkowski, Michael R., *Terrorism and Organized Hate Crime: Intelligence Gathering, Analysis and Investigations* (Boca Raton, FL: CRC Press, 200)

Ropeik, David, "We're Being Scared to Death," *Los Angeles Times* (September 22, 2004)

Roper, Roy E., and Catherine Goodzey, "Extreme Emergencies: Humanitarian Assistance to Civilian Populations following Chemical, Biological, Radiological, Nuclear and Explosive Incidents – A Sourcebook," *Journal of Homeland Security and Emergency Management*, Vol. 2, No. 2 (2005); available at http://www.bepress.com/jhsem/vol2/iss2/11

Rose, Flemming, "Why I Published Those Cartoons," *Washington Post* (February 19, 2006), pp. B1, 4

Rosenau, William, "Aum Shinrikyo's Biological Weapons Program," *Studies in Conflict and Terrorism*, Vol. 24 (2001), pp. 289–301

Rosenfeld, Rachel, Norman White and Carolyn Phillips, "The Effect of Network Ties on Criminal Victimization and Offending," paper presented at the 2003 annual meeting of the American Sociological Association, August 18, 2003

Rossmo, D. Kim, *Geographic Profiling* (Boca Raton, FL: CRC Press, 1999)

Roth, John, Douglas Greenburg and Serena Wille, *Monograph on Terrorist Financing: Staff Report to the Commission* (August 21, 2004); available at http://www.9-11commission.gov/staff_statements/911_TerrFin_Monograph.pdf

Roy, Olivier, *The Failure of Political Islam* (London: I.B. Tauris, 1994)

Roy, Olivier, *Globalized Islam: The Search for a New Ummah* (New York: Columbia University Press, 2004)

Rumi, Jalal al-Din, *Essential Rumi* (San Francisco, CA: Harper, 1997)

Russell, Charles and Bowman Miller, "Profile of a Terrorist," in Lawrence Freedman and Yonah Alexander, editors, *Perspectives on Terrorism*, (Lanham, MD: SR Books, 1983), pp. 45–60

Anna Sabasteanski, editor, *Patterns of Global Terrorism 1985–2004: U.S. Department of State Documents and Supplementary Material, with Updated 2004 Reports* (Great Barrington, MA: Berkshire Publishing, 2006)

Sachs, Jeffrey, *The End of Poverty: Economic Possibilities for Our Time* (New York: Penguin, 2005)

Sacks, Jonathan, *The Dignity of Difference* (London: Continuum, 2002)

Sacks, Jonathan, "Turning Enemies into Friends," in Akbar S. Ahmed and Brian Forst, editors, *After Terror: Promoting Dialogue among Civilizations* (Cambridge: Polity Press, 2005)

"Saga of Incompetence," *Washington Post* (December 26, 2005), p. A38

Sageman, Marc, *Understanding Terror Networks* (Philadelphia: University of Pennsylvania Press, 2004)

Said, Edward W., "The Clash of Ignorance," *The Nation* (October 22, 2001)

References

St. Cyr, Joseph F., "At Risk: Natural Hazards, People's Vulnerability, and Disasters," *Journal of Homeland Security and Emergency Management*, Vol. 2, No. 2 (2005); available at http://www.bepress.com/jhsem/vol2/iss2/4

Sampson, Robert J. and John H. Laub, *Crime in the Making: Pathways and Turning Points Through Life* (Cambridge, MA: Harvard University Press, 1993)

Sandall, Roger, "The Politics of Oxymoron," *The New Criterion* (Summer 2003); available at http://www.newcriterion.com/archive/21/sum03/sandall.htm

Saul, Ben, "The Legal Response of the League of Nations to Terrorism," *Journal of International Criminal Justice*, Vol. 4, No. 1 (2006), pp. 78–102

Saxton, Alexander, *The Indispensable Enemy: Labor and the Anti-Chinese Movement in California* (Berkeley: University of California Press, 1971)

Schafer, John R. and Joe Navarro, "The Seven-Stage Hate Model: The Psychopathology of Hate Groups," *FBI Law Enforcement Bulletin* (March 2003)

Schaffert, Richard W., *Media Coverage and Political Terrorists: A Quantitative Analysis* (New York: Praeger, 1992)

Schelling, Thomas C., *The Strategy of Conflict* (Cambridge, MA: Harvard University Press, 2006)

Schmid, Alex and E. J. Jongman, *Political Terrorism* (New Brunswick, NJ: Transaction Publishers, 1998)

Schuck, Peter, "Context Is Everything with Racial Profiling," *Los Angeles Times* (January 27, 2002), p. M6

Schultz, George and R. James Woolsey, "Oil and Security," *Committee on the Present Danger* (August 5, 2005); available at http://www.fightingterror.org/pdfs/O&S8-5-05.pdf

Scioline, Elaine and Eric Schmitt, "Algerian Reactor Came from China," *New York Times* (November 15, 1991), p. A1

Scruton, Roger, *A Dictionary of Political Thought* (New York: Hill and Wang, 1982)

Sen, Amartya, *Identity and Violence: The Illusion of Destiny* (New York: W.W. Norton, 2006)

Shanker, Thom, "Third Retired General Wants Rumsfeld Out," *New York Times* (April 10, 2006)

Sherman, Lawrence W., "Defiance, Deterrence, and Irrelevance: A Theory of the Criminal Sanction," *Journal of Research in Crime and Delinquency*, Vol. 30 (November 1993), pp. 445–73

Sherman, Lawrence, Patrick R. Gartin and Michael E. Buerger, "Hot Spots of Predatory Crime: Routine Activities and the Criminology of Place," *Criminology*, Vol. 27 (1989), pp. 27–55

"Shoot to Kill," *Washington Post* (August 10, 2005), p. A16

Shultz, Jr., Richard H., *The Secret War against Hanoi: Kennedy's and Johnson's Use of Spies, Saboteurs, and Covert Warriors in North Vietnam* (New York: HarperCollins, 1999)

Siegel, Marc, *False Alarm: The Truth about the Epidemic of Fear* (New York: John Wiley & Sons, 2005)

Siljak, Ana, *The Angel of Vengeance: The "Girl Assassin," the Governor of St. Petersburg, and Russia's Revolutionary World* (New York, St. Martin's Press, 2008)

Simao, Paul, "Alcohol Tied to 75,000 Deaths a Year in US," Reuters (September 23, 2004)

Sinclair, Andrew, *An Anatomy of Terror: A History of Terrorism* (New York: Palgrave Macmillan, 2004)

Skidmore, David, "Huntington's Clash Revisited," *Journal of World-Systems Research*, Vol. 4, No. 2 (Fall 1998), pp. 181–88

Skogan, Wesley G., *Disorder and Decline: Crime and the Spiral of Decay in American Neighborhoods* (New York: Free Press, 1990)

Skogan, Wesley G. and Michael G. Maxfield, *Coping with Crime: Individual and Neighborhood Reactions* (Beverly Hills, CA: Sage, 1981)

Skolnick, Jerome H. and James J. Fyfe, *Above the Law: Police and the Excessive Use of Force* (New York: Free Press, 1993)

Slabbert, Nicholas J., "The Future of Urbanization: How Teletechnology is Shaping a New Urban Order," *Harvard International Review* (June 2, 2006)

Slackman, Michael, "Shifting Sands: And Now, Islamism Trumps Arabism," *New York Times* (August 20, 2006)

Smith, Adam, *The Theory of Moral Sentiments*, D. D. Raphael and A. L. Macfie, editors (Oxford: Clarendon Press, 1976; originally published in 1759)

Smith, Brent, *Terrorism in America: Pipe Bombs and Pipe Dreams* (Albany, NY: State University of New York Press, 1994)

Solaro, Erin, "Retired Generals Rising Up Against Iraq War," *Seattle Post-Intelligencer* (April 16, 2006)

Solomon, Jay, "Jordan Emerges as a Vital U.S. Ally," *Wall Street Journal* (June 10–11, 2006), p. A4

Sorman, Guy, *Barefoot Capitalism* (Uttar Pradesh, India: Vikas Publishing House, 1989)

Spencer, Jane and Cynthia Crossen, "Why Do Americans Feel That Danger Lurks Everywhere?" *Wall Street Journal* (April 24, 2003), pp. A1, A12

Stansfield, Gareth, "Accepting Realities in Iraq," Chatham House briefing paper (May 21, 2007)

Steger, Manfred B., *Globalism: The New Market Ideology* (Lanham, MD: Rowman & Littlefield, 2001)

Steger, Manfred B., *Globalization: A Very Short Introduction* (New York: Oxford University Press, 2003)

Stephens, Bret, "Iran's al Qaeda," *Wall Street Journal* (October 16, 2007), p. A20

Stern, Jessica, *The Ultimate Terrorists* (Cambridge, MA: Harvard University Press, 1999)

Stern, Jessica, *Terror in the Name of God: Why Religious Militants Kill* (New York: HarperCollins, 2003)

Stern, Jessica, "Attacks In U.S. Aren't the Only Concern," *Foreign Affairs* (Round One response to article by John Mueller, September 7, 2006)

Stewart, Rory, *The Prince of the Marshes: And Other Occupational Hazards of a Year in Iraq* (Orlando, FL: Harcourt, 2006)

Stewart, Rory, "Iraq: The Question," *New York Review of Books*, Vol. 54, No. 9 (May 31, 2007)

Stiglitz, Joseph E., *Globalization and Its Discontents* (New York: W.W. Norton, 2003)

Joseph E. Stiglitz and Linda J. Bilmes, *The Three Trillion Dollar War: The True Cost of the Iraq Conflict* (New York: W.W. Norton, 2008)

Stohl, Michael, *Politics of Terrorism* (Boca Raton, FL: CRC Press, 1988)

Stone, Richard, "Down to the Wire on Bioweapons Talks," *Science*, Vol. 293, No. 5529 (July 20, 2001), pp. 414–16

Sullivan, John P., "Gangs, Hooligans, and Anarchists: The Vanguard of Netwar in the Streets," in *Networks and Netwars: The Future of Terror, Crime and Militancy*, John Arquilla and David Ronfeldt, editors (Santa Monica, CA: RAND, 2002), pp. 99–126

Sullivan, Kevin and Joshua Partlow, "Young Muslim Rage Takes Root in Britain" *Washington Post* (August 13, 2006), pp. A1, 14

Sunstein, Cass R., *Risk and Reason: Safety, Law and the Environment* (Cambridge: Cambridge University Press, 2002)

Sunstein, Cass R., "Fear Factor," *Los Angeles Times* (March 10, 2003a)

References

Sunstein, Cass R., *Why Societies Need Dissent* (Cambridge, MA: Harvard University Press, 2003b)

Sunstein, Cass R., *Laws of Fear: Beyond the Precautionary Principle* (Cambridge: Cambridge University Press, 2005)

Suskind, Ron, *The One Percent Doctrine: Deep inside America's Pursuit of Its Enemies since 9/11* (New York: Simon and Schuster, 2006)

Taguba, Antonio M., *Article 15-6 Investigation of the 800th Military Police Brigade*: The Taguba Report (New York: Cosimo Reports, 2004)

Taheri, Amir, *Holy Terror: Inside the World of Islamic Terrorism* (London: Sphere Books, 1987)

Tallis, Ray, "Enhancing Humanity," *Philosophy Today*, Issue 62 (July–August 2007)

Tannenbaum, Frank, *Crime and the Community* (New York: Columbia University Press, 1938)

Tennessee v. Garner, 105 S. Ct. 1694 (1985)

Tharoor, Shashi, "The Role of the Media in Promoting Tolerance," in *After Terror: Promoting Dialogue among Civilizations*, Akbar Ahmed and Brian Forst, editors (Cambridge: Polity Press, 2005)

Thornberry, Terence P., *Developmental Theories of Crime and Delinquency* (New Brunswick, NJ: Transaction, 1997)

Tiger, Lionel, *Men in Groups* (New York: Random House, 1969)

Tittle, Charles R., "Theoretical Developments in Criminology," in *The Nature of Crime: Continuity and Change*, Gary LaFree, editor (Washington: U.S. Department of Justice, 2000)

Tolson, Jay, "An Education In Muslim Integration: Could Islamic Schools Be Part of the Solution?" *U.S. News & World Report* (November 21, 2005), pp. 37–40

Townshend, Charles, *Terrorism: A Very Short Introduction* (New York: Oxford University Press, 2002)

Traub, James, "The Un–U.N.," *New York Times Magazine* (September 11, 2005)

"Trends in Global Terrorism: Implications for the United States," *New York Times* (September 27, 2006)

Trento, Susan B. and Joseph J. Trento, *Unsafe at any Altitude: Failed Terrorism Investigations, Scapegoating 9/11, and the Shocking Truth about Aviation Security Today* (Hanover, NH: Steerforth, 2006)

Tsai, Michelle, "Honey, I'm Dead! How God Rewards a Female Suicide Bomber," *Slate* (March 1, 2007)

Lao Tsu, *Tao Te Ching*, translation by Gia-fu Feng and Jane English (New York: Vintage, 1972)

Tversky, Amos and Daniel Kahneman, "Belief in the Law of Small Numbers," in *Judgment under Uncertainty: Heuristics and Biases* (Cambridge: Cambridge University Press, 1982), pp. 23–31

Tyson, Ann Scott, "Iraqi Refugee Crisis Seen Deepening," *Washington Post* (January 17, 2007), p. A4

Sun Tzu, *Art of War* (Mineola, NY: Dover, 2002)

UNESCO, *Declaration of Principles on Tolerance*, Declaration signed by the member states of UNESCO on November 16, 1995

United Nations Conciliation Commission, *General Progress Report and Supplementary Report of the United Nations Conciliation Commission for Palestine, Covering the Period from 11 December 1949 to 23 October 1950* (New York: United Nations Concilation Commission, October 23, 1950), Supplement No. 18, Document A/1367/Rev. 1 of the U.N. General Assembly, 5th Session

United Nations, *Convention against Torture and Other Cruel, Inhuman or Degrading Treatment or Punishment* (December 10, 1984); available at http://www.ohchr.org/english/law/cat.htm

United Press International, "Pakistan to Share Intelligence with India" (September 24, 2006)

U.S. Census Bureau, *Profile of General Demographic Characteristics*, 2000 Summary File, DP-1 (Washington, DC: U.S. Government Printing Office, 2000)

U.S. Department of Defense, *Army/Marine Corps Counterinsurgency Field Manual* (Chicago: University of Chicago, 2007)

U.S. Department of Defense, *Dictionary of Military and Associated Terms* (Washington, DC: U.S. Government Printing Office, 2007)

U.S. Department of Homeland Security, *Securing Our Homeland: U.S. Department of Homeland Security Strategic Plan* (Washington, DC: U.S. Department of Homeland Security, 2004); available at http://www.dhs.gov/interweb/assetlibrary/DHS_StratPlan_FINAL_spread.pdf

U.S. Department of State, *Patterns of Global Terrorism - 2003* (Washington, DC: U.S. State Department, April 2004)

U.S. Department of State, *U.S. Designated Terrorist Organizations* (Washington, DC: U.S. Department of State, Office of Counterterrorism, Center for Defense Information, Terrorism Project, 2006); available at http://www.infoplease.com/ipa/A0908746.html

U.S. Department of State, *Rewards for Justice Program*; available at http://www.rewardsforjustice.net/english/index.cfm?page=faq

U.S. Department of Treasury, *Contributions by the Department of the Treasury to the Financial War on Terrorism: Fact Sheet* (Washington, DC: US Department of Treasury, September 2002); available at http://www.treas.gov/press/releases/reports/2002910184556291211.pdf

Urban, Mark, *Big Boys' Rules: The Secret Struggle against the IRA* (London: Faber & Faber, 1992)

Vacca, John R., *Biometric Technologies and Verification Systems* (Burlington, MA: Butterworth-Heinemann, 2007)

Varon, Jeremy, *Bringing the War Home: The Weather Underground, the Red Army Faction, and Revolutionary Violence in the Sixties and Seventies* (Berkeley, CA: University of California Press, 2004)

Vattimo, Gianni and Richard Rorty, *The Future of Religion* (New York: Columbia University Press, 2006)

Vedantam, Shankar, "Iraq War Naysayers May Have Hindsight Bias," *Washington Post* (October 2, 2006), p. A2

Waldman, Peter, "A Muslim's Choice: Turn U.S. Informant or Risk Losing Visa," *Wall Street Journal* (July 11, 2006), pp. A1, 11

Waldron, Jeremy, "Security and Liberty: The Image of Balance," *Journal of Political Philosophy*, Vol. 11, No. 2 (2003)

Walker, Martin, "Europe's Mosque Hysteria," *Wilson Quarterly* (Spring 2006)

Wallace-Wells, Benjamin, "Private Jihad," *New Yorker* (May 29, 2006), pp. 28–41

Wallach, Evan, "Waterboarding Used to Be a Crime," *Washington Post* (November 4, 2007), p. B1

Walzer, Michael, *Just and Unjust Wars: A Moral Argument with Historical Illustrations* (New York: Basic Books, 1992)

Walzer, Michael, *Arguing about War* (New Haven, CT: Yale University Press, 2005)

Warr, Mark, "Fear of Crime in the United States: Avenues for Research and Policy," *Criminal Justice 2000*, Vol. 4 (Washington, DC: U.S. Department of Justice, 2000), pp. 451–89

References

Warrick, Joby, "Domestic Use of Spy Satellites to Widen: Law Enforcement Getting New Access to Secret Imagery," *Washington Post* (August 16, 2007), p. A1

Washington, George, "Farewell Address," *Independent Chronicle* (September 26, 1796)

Weeks, Albert L., "Do Civilizations Hold?" *Foreign Affairs* (September-October 1993)

Weiner, Tim, *Legacy of Ashes: The History of the CIA* (New York: Doubleday, 2007)

Weisberg, Jacob, "No Politics, Please – We're Spies," *Slate* (April 5, 2005)

Westen, Drew, *The Political Brain: The Role of Emotion in Deciding the Fate of the Nation* (New York: Basic Books, 2007)

White, Jonathan R., *Terrorism and Homeland Security*, 5th edition (Belmont, CA: Thompson-Wadsworth, 2006)

Whitlock, Craig, "Grisly Path to Power in Iraq's Insurgency," *Washington Post* (September 27, 2004), p. A1

Whitlock, Craig, "Architect of New War on the West," *Washington Post* (May 23, 2006), p. A1

Whitlock, Craig, "Terrorists Proving Harder to Profile: European Officials Say Traits of Suspected Islamic Extremists Are Constantly Shifting," *Washington Post* (March 12, 2007a), p. A1

Whitlock, Craig, "The New Al-Qaeda Central," *Washington Post* (September 9, 2007b), p. A1

Whyte, Jr., William H., "Groupthink," *Fortune*, Vol. 45 (March 1952), pp. 114–117

Wiktorowicz, Quintan, *Radical Islam Rising: Muslim Extremism in the West* (Lanham, MD: Rowman & Littlefield, 2005)

Wilcox, Laird, "What Is Extremism? Style and Tactics Matter More than Goals," in *American Extremists: Militias, Supremacists, Klansmen, Communists & Others*, John George and Laird Wilcox, editors (Amherst, NY: Prometheus Books, 1996)

Wilkinson, Paul, "Media and Terrorism: A Reassessment," *Terrorism and Political Violence*, Vol. 9, No. 2 (Summer 1997), pp. 51–64

Wilkinson, Tracy and Henry Chu, "Israel Encounters an Unexpectedly Different War," *Los Angeles Times* (August 13, 2006)

Will, George F., "Iraq's Atomization," *Washington Post* (June 15, 2006), p. A27

Williams, Houston, "U.S. Government Declares $1 Million Bounty for Assata Shakur, Tupac's Godmother," *All Hip Hop News* (May 2, 2005)

Wilson, Edward O., "All of Man's Troubles," in *After Terror: Promoting Dialogue among Civilizations*, Akbar Ahmed and Brian Forst, editors (Cambridge: Polity Press, 2005)

Wilson, James Q., *The Moral Sense* (New York: Free Press, 1993)

Wilson, James Q., "The Enemy Will Always Surprise Us," *Wall Street Journal* (June 3, 2002)

Wilson, James Q. and Richard J. Herrnstein, *Crime and Human Nature: The Definitive Study of the Causes of Crime* (New York: Free Press, 1998)

Wilson, James Q. and George L. Kelling, "Broken Windows," *Atlantic Monthly* (March 1982)

Wolf, Martin, *Why Globalization Works* (New Haven, CT: Yale University Press, 2004)

Wonacott, Peter and Eric Bellman, "India Is Resilient in Wake of Deadly Blasts," *Wall Street Journal* (July 13, 2006), p. A5

Wong, Edward, "Iraq's Curse: A Thirst for Final, Crushing Victory," *New York Times* (June 3, 2007)

Woolf, Amy, *Nuclear Weapons in Russia: Safety, Security, and Control Issues* (Washington, DC: Congressional Reference Service, 2003)

Woolsey, R. James, "Deafeating the Oil Weapon," *Commentary* (September 2002), pp. 29–33

Wright, Lawrence, *Looming Tower: Al-Qaeda and the Road to 9/11* (New York: Knopf, 2006a)

Wright, Lawrence, "The Master Plan," *New Yorker* (September 11, 2006b)

Wright, Robert, "Highbrow Tribalism: Is Harvard Geopolitical Theorist Sam Huntington the Next George Kennan, or Just the Thinking Man's Pat Buchanan?" *Slate* (November 2, 1996); available at http://slate.msn.com/id/2011/

Wright, Robert, *Nonzero: The Logic of Human Destiny* (New York: Vintage, 2001)

Wright, Robert, "The Globalization of Morality," *What Is Enlightenment?* (August–October 2004), pp. 32–36

Wright, Robert, "The Silent Treatment," *New York Times* (February 17, 2006)

Wright, Robin, "Since 2001, a Dramatic Increase in Suicide Bombings," *Washington Post* (April 18, 2008)

X, Malcolm, *By Any Means Necessary* (New York: Pathfinder Press, 1992)

Yagoda, Ben, "The 9/11 Commission Report: How a Government Committee Made a Piece of Literature," *Slate* (November 8, 2004)

Young, Michael, "Hezbollah's Other War," *New York Times Magazine* (August 4, 2006)

Zagorin, Perez, *How the Idea of Religious Toleration Came to the West* (Princeton, NJ: Princeton University Press, 2005)

Zakaria, Fareed, "Freedom vs. Security – Delicate Balance: The Case for 'Smart Profiling' as a Weapon in the War on Terror," *Newsweek*, Vol. 140 (July 8, 2002), pp. 26–31

Zakaria, Fareed, *The Future of Freedom: Illiberal Democracy at Home and Abroad* (New York: W.W. Norton & Co., 2003)

Zakaria, Fareed, "It's the Economy, Mr. President," *Washington Post* (November 20, 2006), p. A17

Zakaria, Fareed, *The Post-American World* (New York: W. W. Norton, 2008)

al-Zawahiri, Ayman, *Fursan Taht Rayah Al-Nabi* ("Knights Under the Prophet's Banner") (Casablanca, Morocco: Dar-al-Najaah Al-Jadeedah, 2001).

al-Zawahiri, Ayman, Letter to Abu Musab al-Zarqawi, July 9, 2005 (Office of the Director of National Intelligence); available at http://www.dni.gov/press_releases/20051011_release.htm

Zedalis, Debra D., *Female Suicide Bombers* (Carlisle Barracks, PA: Strategic Studies Institute, 2004)

Zegart, Amy, *Flawed by Design: The Evolution of the CIA, JCS, and NSC* (Palo Alto, CA: Stanford University Press, 1999)

Zegart, Amy, "Our Clueless Intelligence System," *Washington Post* (July 8, 2007), p. B1

Zegart, Amy, *Spying Blind: The CIA, the FBI, and the Origins of 9/11* (Princeton, NJ: Princeton University Press, 2007)

Zimbardo, Phillip, *The Lucifer Effect: Understanding How Good People Turn Evil* (New York: Random House, 2007)

Zinni, Tony, *The Battle for Peace: A Frontline Vision of America's Power and Purpose* (New York: Palgrave Macmillan, 2006)

Zuckerman, Mortimer, "Let's Use *All* the Tools," *U.S. News & World Report* (May 29, 2006), p. 60

Index

Index

Index

482

Index

Index

Index

Index

Index

Index